Unsustainable
South Africa

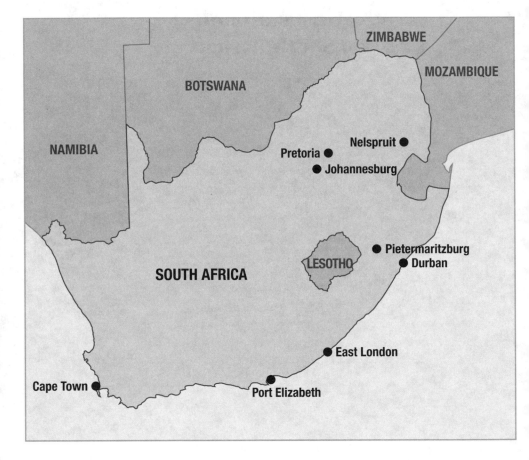

South Africa and its neighbours.

Unsustainable South Africa

Environment, development, and social protest

Patrick Bond

with George Dor, Michael Dorsey,
Maj Fiil-Flynn, Stephen Greenberg,
Thulani Guliwe, David Hallowes,
Becky Himlin, Stephen Hosking,
Greg Ruiters, and Robyn Stein

UNIVERSITY OF NATAL PRESS
PIETERMARITZBURG

THE MERLIN PRESS

Published by
University of Natal Press
Private Bag X01
Scottsville 3209
South Africa
E-mail: books@nu.ac.za
Website: www.unpress.co.za

Published in Europe by
The Merlin Press
P O Box 30705
London WC2E 8QD
Website: www.merlinpress.co.uk

ISBN 1-86914-018-4 (University of Natal Press)
ISBN 0-85036-522-8 (The Merlin Press)

Cover design by Ben Cashdan and Anthony Cuerden

Layout by Shahn Irwin and Olive Hendricks

Printed and bound by Intrepid Printers (Pty) Ltd

Contents

Introduction
A world in one country

PART ONE: AN UNSUSTAINABLE LEGACY

Chapter one
The environment of apartheid-capitalism: discourses and issues
with David Hallowes

PART TWO: UNSUSTAINABLE PROJECTS

Chapter two
The development of *under*development in Mandela Metropole: Coega's economic, social, and environmental subsidies
with Stephen Hosking

Chapter three
Lesotho's water, Johannesburg's thirst: communities, consumers, and mega-dams

PART THREE: UNSUSTAINABLE POLICIES

Chapter four
Eco-social *in*justice for working-class communities: the making and unmaking of neoliberal infrastructure policy
with George Dor, Becky Himlin, and Greg Ruiters

Chapter five
Droughts and floods: water prices and values in the time of cholera
with Greg Ruiters and Robyn Stein

Figures and tables

Abbreviations and acronyms

AEC   Atomic Energy Corporation
ANC   African National Congress
ANCYL   African National Congress Youth League
ARV   anti-retroviral
AU   African Union

CBD   Central Business District
CBD   Convention on Biological Diversity
CDC   Coega Development Corporation
CDM   Clean Development Mechanism
CFCs   chlorofluorocarbons
Codesria   Council for Development and Social Science Research in Africa
CSD-9   Commission on Sustainable Development

DA   Democratic Alliance
DCD   Department of Constitutional Development
DME   Department of Minerals and Energy
DPLG   Department of Provincial and Local Government
DRC   Democratic Republic of the Congo
DTI   Department of Trade and Industry
Dwaf   Department of Water Affairs and Forestry

ECB   Electricity Control Board
EDF   Environmental Defense Fund (US)
EE   Eskom Enterprises
EPZ   Export Processing Zone
Eskom   Electricity Supply Commission
EU   European Union

FAO   Food and Agriculture Organisation

G8   Group of Eight main industrial powers
GANP   Greater Algoa National Park
Gats   General Agreement on Trade in Services
GDP   Gross Domestic Product
Gear   Growth, Employment and Redistribution Strategy
GEM   Group for Environmental Monitoring
GMO   Genetically Modified Organism
GNP   Gross National Product

ABBREVIATIONS AND ACRONYMS

HCB	Cahora Bassa Dam Operating Company
HDI	Human Development Index
HIPC	Highly Indebted Poor Countries
HSRC	Human Sciences Research Council
ICC	International Criminal Court
IDA	International Development Association
IDC	Industrial Development Corporation
IDT	Independent Development Trust
IDZ	Industrial Development Zone
ILO	International Labour Organisation
IMF	International Monetary Fund
IRN	International Rivers Network
IUCN	International Union for Conservation of Nature
LDCs	Least Developed Countries
LDF	Lesotho Defence Force
LHDA	Lesotho Highlands Development Authority
LHWA	Lesotho Highlands Water Authority
LHWP	Lesotho Highlands Water Project
LPM	Landless People's Movement
Miif	Municipal Infrastructure Investment Framework
MSPs	Municipal Services Partnerships
Nedlac	National Economic Development and Labour Council
Nehawu	National Education, Health and Allied Workers Union
Nema	National Environmental Management Act
Nepad	New Partnership for Africa's Development
NER	National Electricity Regulator
NGO	Non-Governmental Organisation
NWA	National Water Act
OECD	Organisation for Economic Cooperation and Development
PBMR	Pebble Bed Modular Reactor
P&DM	Graduate School of Public and Development Management, University of the Witwatersrand
PPP	Public-private partnership
RDP	Reconstruction and Development Programme
REDs	Regional Electricity Distributors

RWB	Rand Water Board
RDSN	Rural Development Services Network
ROT	Rehabilitate, operate and transfer schemes
SAB	South African Breweries
SACC	South African Council of Churches
SACP	South African Communist Party
SADC	Southern African Development Community
Salga	South African Local Government Association
Samwu	South African Municipal Workers Union
Sanco	South African National Civic Organisation
SANDF	South African National Defence Force
Sangoco	South African Non-Governmental Organisation Coalition
Sappi	South African Pulp and Paper Industries
SARD	Sustainable Agriculture and Rural Development
SDI	Spatial Development Initiative
SEA	Strategic Environmental Assessment
SECC	Soweto Electricity Crisis Committee
SEEN	Sustainable Energy and Economy Network
SIDA	Swedish International Development Agency
SMMEs	Small, Medium and Micro Enterprises
SPD	Soweto People's Delegation
TAC	Treatment Action Campaign
TCTA	TransCaledon Tunnel Authority
TNC	Transnational corporation
TRC	Transformation Resource Centre
TRC	Truth and Reconciliation Commission
Trips	Trade Related Intellectual Property Rights
TWN-Africa	Third World Network-Africa
UNDP	United Nations Development Programme
UNHCR	United Nations High Commission for Refugees
US AID	US Agency for International Development
VIPs	Ventilated Improved Pit Latrines
WB	World Bank
WCD	World Commission on Dams
Wehab	water/sanitation, energy, health, agriculture and biodiversity
WHO	World Health Organisation
WSSA	Water and Sanitation South Africa

WSSD   World Summit on Sustainable Development
WTO   World Trade Organisation

Zesa   Zimbabwe Electricity Supply Authority

Contributors

George Dor is an independent analyst and activist in Johannesburg.

Michael Dorsey is Thurgood Marshall Fellow, Dartmouth College, USA.

Maj Fiil-Flynn, formerly with the Municipal Services Project, works on water issues with Public Citizen in Washington, DC.

Stephen Greenberg is a Johannesburg-based development researcher.

Thulani Guliwe is a doctoral student at Wits University Graduate School of Public and Development Management.

David Hallowes is an environmentalist associated with Critical Resource.

Becky Himlin is an urban planner based in Johannesburg.

Stephen Hosking is professor of economics, University of Port Elizabeth.

Greg Ruiters is senior lecturer in politics, University of the Witwatersrand.

Robyn Stein is visiting professor, University of the Witwatersrand School of Law.

Preface and acknowledgements

Antagonists and protagonists

We regularly need the opportunity to remind ourselves of those who fought and continue fighting the good fights, even if they/we are mainly losing – for now, at least. In many small ways, the backroom academic can support those who are at the coalface. One way is providing documentation of how a progressive line of activism and argument evolves, including the alliances which supported that line, and the contesting viewpoints.

Those who stood in the way of social and environmental progress, as I would subjectively judge it, also deserve personal mention, both in these endnotes and in the course of the following pages. Indeed, in a few cases where public debate has broken out in the press or in official correspondence, their argument deserves full recapitulation. Attention is warranted not because these are bad people, but because their *approach* to environment and development was consistent with the neoliberal project. History should have some record of that, since choices were possible and human agency was involved. As much as some might like to disguise this by marxologist talk of National Democratic Revolution or reconstruction and development or balance of forces or social democracy or merely efficiency, the new elites of Pretoria are implicated in the suffering and environmental destruction which litter post-apartheid South Africa.

So here arises an opportunity to identify specific antagonists who help set the agenda, and even sometimes pull the strings of those who are most explicitly repressive. Were it not for their effectiveness, stubbornness, disdain and occasional thuggishness, there would be no point in driving the argument forward through writing a provocative book.

But more systematically, many of us are periodically drawn to ask, how is it that so many African National Congress (ANC) government leaders and bureaucrats who once struggled relentlessly for racial justice, so quickly turned against low-income people and the environment? There are complex answers beyond the scope of this book. But the phenomenon of an 'exhausted nationalism' – our polite way of describing the sellout of the national liberation movement ideals – is captured by Frantz Fanon's work. In particular, Fanon forecast,

> A bourgeoisie that provides nationalism alone as food for the masses fails in its mission and gets caught up in a whole series of mishaps. But if nationalism is not made explicit, if it is not enriched and deepened by a very rapid transformation into a consciousness of social and political needs, in other words into humanism, it leads up a blind alley. The bourgeois leaders of underdeveloped countries imprison national consciousness in sterile formalism.[1]

And that's where we are now, after eight years of liberation. The sterile formalism which we will encounter at various points in projects, programmes and policies had evolved into a weak, ineffectual form of international reformism by the time ANC leaders attempted to impress global elites with projects like the New Partnership for Africa's Development (Nepad) and a 'deal' at the Johannesburg World Summit on Sustainable Development (WSSD). It was here that Fanon's warning of *compradorism* – i.e., acting in imperial not local interests – in its broadest sense appears, four decades later, so prescient:

> The national middle class discovers its historic mission: ... of being the transmission line between the nation and a capitalism, rampant though camouflaged, which today puts on the mask of neocolonialism. The national bourgeoisie will be quite content with the role of the Western bourgeoisie's business agent, and it will play its part without any complexes in a most dignified manner.[2]

One function of *Unsustainable South Africa* is to track how key figures within the emergent and often bureaucratic-based 'national patriotic' bourgeoisie – as distinct from the unpatriotic English-speaking capitalists who have fled to London – gave what they imagine is 'dignity' to names and concepts like Coega, Lesotho dams, public-private-partnerships, cost-reflective electricity pricing, lifeline as operating-and-maintenance-costs, Nepad and the WSSD. Yet this is not a book about *personal* errors, loyalties, values or dignified appearances.

The core of the problem, we must never forget, is *systemic*: global capitalism, augmented by patriarchy, racism/ethnicism, anthropocentrism, religious bigotry and many other easy vices. It is merely a necessary feature of the system's reproduction, that those at the helm repeatedly find able functionaries who promote neoliberal principles, projects and policies. I've run into a good few in the course of writing this book, some of whom are charismatic, charming and even politically progressive in certain respects.

In the case of Coega, these include men officially associated with the port and industrial zone as it finally got off the ground in 2002,[3] and those in support roles during earlier incarnations.[4] They impressed me not for venal self-interest,[5] but on the contrary for their selfless lavishing of vast taxpayer funds into their white elephant.

In comparison, in the construction of Lesotho dams, there was the small but telling matter of corruption. I suspect, given the lamentable trajectory of a certain dam-builder, ABB's Goran Lindahl,[6] that his man in Maseru, Masupha Sole, was drawn into a temporarily lucrative ($2 million) friendship with the 'dirty dozen' construction firms, rather than the other way around. But the racy bribery story aside, we must note the prevalence of mundane officials from Washington and Pretoria, with so much power over Lesotho's mountains, people and natural resources. As mere cogs in the wheel of an international financial-construction machine, they and many like them have steamrolled rivers across the world in the name of progress. Special attention must go to World Bank staff, the US executive director during the Clinton administration, and an Inspection Panel lapdog.[7] Their Pretoria cousins[8] were consistently negligent in considering the interests and needs of low-income people, whether in Lesotho or South Africa.

Likewise, when it came to policy-making, the top rank of South Africa's post-apartheid bureaucratic class learned sustainable-development talk, but many maintained a transparently neoliberal strategy throughout the first eight years of transition.[9] These officials would not have done so much damage were it not for a cadre of helpful consultants.[10] Important, too, was the South African state's growing tradition of 'captive regulators' who fold under pressure.[11] Allowing them the space were several ministers who either enthusiastically push unsustainable development themselves[12] or who let their staff push them into it.[13]

Without these characters, South Africa's post-apartheid environment and development crises could not have taken on the breathtaking, contradictory and supremely damaging character that they have, and without their arrogance and insensitivity to grievances, social protest would not have arisen as forcefully in some areas as it has. Hence without them, neither would this book have been necessary.

And yet as I insist, they are not their own masters, and merely play their role in a script written by forces far beyond their control. Luckily, though, there are activists who don't recognise such forces as legitimate.

The red, the green, and the brown

What kind of project is this fierce critique of the South African ruling class?, I am occasionally asked, once I reveal my distaste for existing political parties (as, forgive the contradiction in terms, an unorganised social-ist). To answer, a personal bibliography would locate my own crucial period of political radicalisation squarely within the Congress tradition during the 1980s, when the *Freedom Charter* was still the marker for South African liberation.

There are plenty of people who feel the same way and who have the courage to act on their beliefs at great cost. Some of their stories are told in the coming pages, but there are many thousands more who deserve book-length treatments of their contributions to social change. They are the main basis for hope in South Africa, and leave me humbled by an easier task: documenting neoliberalism and its implications for a small group of readers, occasional workshop participants and Wits University students. For you, *Unsustainable South Africa* is the penultimate effort in a collection of eight books on applied political economy drafted, often in a collective mode, over the past few years.

Here is a quick rundown, since most are obscure. Still, they follow a certain logic. The first publication – in collaboration with Meshack Khosa of the Human Sciences Research Council – was an empirical audit of vir-tually all the policies adopted by the ANC from 1994–99, using the Recon-struction and Development Programme (RDP) as a yardstick.[14] The next, *Elite Transition,* summarised the political lessons of the liberation process and its denouement.[15] In *Cities of Gold, Townships of Coal,* sev-eral comrades and I considered the specifically urban manifestations of South African neoliberalism, including social movement mobilisation and demobilisation.[16] The fourth, *Against Global Apartheid,* concentrated on Pretoria's international political-economic relationships, including the influence of the Bretton Woods Institutions and the inspiring Treatment Action Campaign fightback against pharmaceutical corporations which deny Africans inexpensive HIV/Aids medicines.[17] The fifth, *Zimbabwe's Plunge*, coauthored with Masimba John Manyanya, looked north and drew crucial lessons of exhausted nationalism and neoliberalism for South Africa.[18] The sixth, *Fanon's Warning*, gathered together critiques of Nepad and contemplated the prospects for South African-style neoliber-alism spreading up-continent in the form of sub-imperialism.[19]

After this, the last in the present series is being coauthored with John Saul, and will consolidate the most durable of the arguments into a holis-tic analysis. From John, especially, I've learned many extraordinary corre-lations between the eras of racial and class apartheid, and of the merits of marxian methods in a South African society whose intelligentsia has been, the past 15 years or so, mainly wont to turn away from class categories.[20]

My own persistence with critical analysis follows directly from two deeply invigorating experiences: theoretical and historical investigations of 'combined and uneven development' – using Zimbabwe as my doctoral research site – from 1985–90,[21] and township-based praxis-oriented activism from 1990–94.[22] To ground the arguments as soundly as possible entailed a base in academia: first Johns Hopkins School of Public Health, then the Wits University Graduate School of Public and Development Management (P&DM) and occasionally, too, the York University Department of Political Science.[23]

All these heartening projects and hospitable settings have combined with the opportunity to continue monitoring *global-scale* economy, geopolitics and environment. In spite of the waning of political-economic arguments during the 1980s–90s, there do exist several outstanding overarching studies of contemporary imperialism.[24] Somce cover issues such as, to retreat into shorthand jargon, the limits of commodification,[25] new processes of labour reproduction (and 'the articulations of modes of production'),[26] overaccumulated and overcompetitive capital,[27] rising/falling financial markets[28] and, especially, the spatio-temporal-ecological displacement of capitalist crisis. Here, the stimulating challenge is the application (and synthesis?) of arguments by, amongst others, Elmar Alvater, David Barkin, Paul Burkett, Peter Dorman, John Bellamy Foster, David Harvey, Istvan Meszaros, James O'Connor, and Neil Smith to the global economic situation.[29]

However, South Africans themselves are my main teachers: the many extremely talented people who are carrying forward social protest against and ruthless analysis of environmental and development crimes. Their passion for social justice (red) and environment (green) has generated a terrific 'brown' politics. There are practitioners in every corner of the land, too many to hail. A few, though, have helped me to coauthor the chapters below over the period 1998–2002: George Dor, Michael Dorsey, Maj Fiil-Flynn, Stephen Greenberg, Thulani Guliwe, David Hallowes, Becky Himlin, Stephen Hosking, Greg Ruiters and Robyn Stein. Their patience and tolerance was bountiful, and any blame for mistakes in redrafting must be directed to me.

We were, however, mainly just documenting what others were *doing*. Too many excellent campaigns for 'development', writ broad, have been waged since I moved to Johannesburg in 1990, for me to do justice in these brief acknowledgements. But in terms of the environment-development intersections that are the topic of this book, the Nelson Mandela Metropole Sustainability Coalition deserves a hand of applause for watchdogging Coega with virtually no resources and great determination for five years.[30] For taking an unpopular and at the time genuinely risky stand against the Lesotho dams, the three anonymous Alexandra residents are honoured, along with their local and international supporters.[31] Many good people cut their teeth on infrastructure policy and project fights, whether in Soweto,[32] the water/sanitation/anti-dam campaigns,[33] or struggles against dirty energy.[34] Others did rigorous international WSSD bullshit-detecting, which helped us enormously here at Ground Zero.[35]

Documentation by two sets of filmmakers has been invaluable to making these issues come alive, and giving them far greater exposure than would be possible otherwise. At Seipone Productions in Melville, Ben Cashdan and Vincent Moloi went from the mountains of Lesotho to the World Bank in 2000–01 by way of confirming our water horror stories, and *White Gold* is a worthy result. Ben also generously supplied photos. And at Hands-On in Orange Grove, Gillian Schutte and Sipho Singiswa did heroic work to record all sides of the electricity debate in 2001, producing *Sparks Fly!* as riots and a general strike unfolded around them. Excellent SABC-tv reporting from Coega by Marion Edwards on *50/50* and Jessica Pitchford on *Special Assignment* during 2001 confirmed that the 'ghost on the coast' should have an early exorcism and a proper funeral.

Yet other South Africans, who are not covered in this book simply due to my lack of time, space and competence, have fought good and sometimes winning fights during the last two decades. Because of them, we are aware of environmental issues like asbestos mining, biopiracy, genetic modification, hazardous incineration of waste, mercury poisoning, resources preservation, recycling, soil degradation, species protection, timber plantation damage, toxic dumping, water pollution, worker safety/health and many others.[36] Most of these labour and community campaigns have been supported by, or even gave rise to, environmental NGOs – exemplified by groundWork – that quickly transcended South Africa's classical tradition of white paternalist-conservationism.[37]

When not receiving guidance from these field activists, and stoking up anger at bureaucratic and political malfeasance, I've spent the last five years at Wits P&DM, an excellent site from which to learn from students and Municipal Services Project colleagues.[38] Publishers allowed earlier versions to see the lightof day and feel the heat of peer and public review.[39] A few institutions provided small doses of the necessary funds.[40] For getting the book into final form, the greatest admiration is due my favourite publishers, Glenn Cowley in Pietermaritzburg, Tony Zurbrugg in London, Kassahun Checole in Trenton, their overworked staff, and especially Darryl Accone, Riaan de Villiers and Shahn Irwin for heroically editing and laying out on an impossible deadline.

Mostly, gratitude goes to Odette and Jan, for mercy and love while my comrades and I took aim at the windmills. Closure is impossible, of course, but with this manuscript complete and some of the campaigns herein at least partially won, we may allow ourselves finally to enjoy the

South African environment and celebrate all those remarkable people who do try to look after it, and the society, against all odds.

Johannesburg
July 2002

Notes

1. Fanon, F. (1963)[1961], *The Wretched of the Earth*, New York, Grove Press, p. 204.

2. Ibid, p. 152. For more on the nature of the ascendant political class – 'imperialism's accomplice' – which Fanon criticises, see his biography: Macey, D. (2000), *Frantz Fanon: A Life*, London, Granta, pp. 485–87.

3. Pepe Silinga and Raymond Hartle of the Coega Development Corporation and Eastern Cape finance MEC Enoch Godongwana are most visible.

4. Presidential adviser Moss Ngoasheng, business representative Kevin Wakeford, Department of Trade and Industry project officer Paul Jourdan and Rick Wilson of the *Herald* newspaper.

5. When accused in the newspapers of corruption associated with Coega, Jourdan replied that the only benefits he received for his Coega work were some biscuits and tea. I have no reason to doubt that. (However, as noted in Chapter Two, Colm Allan has documented plenty of other suspicious relationships, which correspond to the mileu that we have come to know about the business ventures of ex-defence minister Joe Modise.)

6. In September 2001, Lindahl was chosen to replace Julian Ogilvie Thomson as chair at Anglo American Corporation, and without irony, *Business Day* celebrated the appointment: 'He has been recruited to ensure sound corporate governance'. ABB's role in the Lesotho bribery had been reported in the same paper two years earlier. By March 2002, the outgoing head of the giant Swedish/Swiss-based construction conglomerate had become Europe's answer to US corporate malgovernance scandals, as Lindahl apparently ripped off the company pension fund for tens of millions of dollars, which he was forced by the board to repay. Sole, the lead official in an $8 billion project that was highly profitable to ABB, received only a few tens of thousands of dollars in his Zurich UBS account from Lindahl's Swedish and German subsidiaries, at times when major decisions on contracts and extensions were made (at least, that's the amount discovered by prosecutors). Would Lindahl – who was also a leading member of the World Commission of Dams and an advisor to Kofi Annan on the UN's misguided Global Compact with the world's largest firms – have made a difference at Anglo, where by implication 'sound corporate governance' was not 'ensured'? Within hours of the pension-looting revelation, Thomson traveled to London to force Lindahl down from chair-designate, and then by mid-2002 the Swede was kicked off the board entirely.

    But it should not be forgotten that according to prosecutors, Anglo construction subsidiary LTA (subsequently sold) had deposited 50% more than ABB into the same Swiss account. Under the period of Thomson's rule, Anglo was also responsible for the Lesotho dam construction strike of 2,300 workers in September 1996 which led to the shooting deaths of five.

    Meanwhile, how many South African officials associated with the LHWP took contractor bribes? We don't know, but it would be amazing if none had their finger in the till, given the longstanding nature of Pretoria–Maseru power relations. The lead South African water official, Mike Muller, was 'reviewing the role of SA companies in the project' in May 2000, according to press reports, but he then proceeded with yet more contracts and paycheques to the corrupt firms, to build the unnecessary Mohale Dam. Two years later, Sole was convicted. To his credit, Muller quickly and publicly condemned the World Bank for not supporting the Lesotho government with prosecution finances as had been promised, and also for being slow to debar the companies implicated.

7. John Roome at the World Bank, former US Executive Director at the World Bank Jan Piercy and James MacNeill of the World Bank Inspection Panel all distinguished themselves.

8. Dwaf's Willie Croucamp was most effective, but the entire TransCaledon Tunnel Authority (TCTA) leadership should also be cited for their systematic misinformation in the South African media. Tellingly, George van der Merwe of TCTA put pressure on the MNet *Carte Blanche* television show once they began filming a critical expose of the dam, produced by Ben Cashdan, meant for airing in 2000 but then suspiciously canceled.

9. The most spectacular practitioners of talk left, act right maneuvres were probably Chippy Olver and Mike Muller. In the electricity debates, Nelisiwe Magubane and Jacob Maroga distinguished themselves for ruthless promotion of the cost-recovery philosophy. In the Department of Finance, the financial taps were quickly turned off by Andre Roux, Andrew Donaldson, Ismael Momomiat and Roland White.

10. The most important, in my own experience, were Ian Palmer, Michael Schur, Richard Tomlinson and Philip van Ryneveld.

11. Particularly useless, from the standpoint of low-income consumer and environmental interests, were Xolani Mkhwanazi in the electricity sector and Barbie Schreiner in water. The exception who proves the rule was Mandla Langa, whose heroic efforts to discipline telecommunications-sector corporations were defeated by weak, greedy politicians.

12. After President Mbeki himself, Alec Erwin and Trevor Manuel remain nearly unparalleled in their range of anti-social and anti-ecological activities.

13. There are too many cases to mention, but Kader Asmal, Valli Moosa and Sydney Mufamadi were the least self-empowered to carry out their eco-social mandates, even though they often carried off a kind of learned helplessness with elan.

14. Bond, P. and M. Khosa (Eds) (1999), *An RDP Policy Audit*, Pretoria, Human Sciences Research Council Press.

15. Bond, P. (2000), *Elite Transition: From Apartheid to Neoliberalism in South Africa*, London, Pluto Press, and Pietermaritzburg, University of Natal Press. The second edition is due in 2003.

16. Bond, P. (2000), *Cities of Gold, Townships of Coal: Essays on South Africa's New Urban Crisis*, Trenton NJ, Africa World Press.

17. Bond, P. (2001), *Against Global Apartheid: South Africa meets the World Bank, IMF and International Finance*, Cape Town, University of Cape Town Press. A second edition from Zed Press is forthcoming.

18. Bond, P. and M. Manyanya (2002), *Zimbabwe's Plunge: Exhausted Nationalism, Neoliberalism, and the Search for Social Justice*, Pietermaritzburg, University of Natal Press, London, Merlin Press, and Trenton, Africa World Press.

19. Bond, P. (Ed)(2002), *Fanon's Warning: A Civil Society Reader on the New Partnership for Africa's Development*, Cape Town, AIDC and Trenton, Africa World Press.

20. In the same way, I've also been intrigued by the contemporary writings, from often opposing marxian traditions, of Neville Alexander, Franco Barchiesi, Alex Callinicos, Jeremy Cronin, Ulrike Kistner, Ben Magubane, Hein Marais, Dale Mckinley, Darlene Miller, Joel Netshitenzhe, Blade Nzimande, Dan O'Meara, Greg

Ruiters, Vladimir Shubin and Raymond Suttner (amongst others). A bibliography of important Left analysis of contemporary South Africa can be found in *Elite Transition*.

21. My PhD at Johns Hopkins Department of Geography and Environmental Engineering was published as Bond, P. (1998), *Uneven Zimbabwe: A Study of Finance, Development and Underdevelopment*, Trenton, Africa World Press.

22. See *Cities of Gold, Townships of Coal* and Bond, P. (1991), *Commanding Heights and Community Control: New Economics for a New South Africa*, Johannesburg, Ravan Press; and I learned a great deal working with Mzwanele Mayekiso in Alexandra township and on his (1996) *Township Politics: Civic Struggles for a New South Africa*, New York, Monthly Review Press.

23. I am most grateful to the following scholar-activists for making my journey into academia at Hopkins, Wits P&DM and York trouble-free: Greg Albo, David Harvey, Guy Mhone, Alan Mabin, Anne McLennan, John Saul, Vicente Navarro, Leo Panitch, Sam Gindin and Mark Swilling. Mostly, I was taught best by all the excellent postgraduate students who tolerated and guided me along the way.

24. See, e.g., Biel, R. (2000), *The New Imperialism: Crises and Contradictions in North/South Relations*, London, Zed; Kagarlitsky, B. (2000), *The Twilight of Globalization: Property, State and Capitalism*, London, Pluto; and Petras, J. and H. Veltmayer (2001), *Globalization Unmasked: Imperialism in the Twenty-first Century*, London, Zed. Although its political conclusions are untenable, there are also many gems of insight into these issues in Hardt, M. and A. Negri (2000), Empire, Cambridge, Harvard University Press. I highly recommend the journals *Historical Materialism, Links, Capitalism Nature Socialism* and *Monthly Review*, and the annual *Socialist Register* as sites to track these debates.

25. The many books of Michael Perelman tackle issues of commodification as well as any author might. But the limits to commodification are just as crucial, at a time of such unprecedented income inequality, and evidence from settings such as even South Africa that privatised state services can only be attempted to a certain extent before the backlash becomes overwhelming.

26. This is the way that various theorists have described how women-dominated survival economies – some pre-capitalist, some marginalised by capitalism – contribute to the reproduction of labour power through migrancy relationships that cheapen workers. The South African Harold Wolpe was most forceful, though ultimately humble, in advancing and then retracting the marxian theory in its South African application. The time has come for a global analysis that tests the validity of the theory of 'articulations' as an explanation for systemic underdevelopment, particularly of rural areas dominated by women in the context of migrant labour relations.

27. Here, the challenge is to track how excessive competition and capital intensity in different sectors (and 'departments') of capitalism's productive circuits soon cause market gluts, excess capacity, idle labour and other manifestations of stagnation. Analyses by Simon Clarke and David Harvey remain most powerful, but not much has been done to track the process since their pathbreaking 1980s work. The most important recent books are Brenner, R. (2002), *The Boom and the Bubble*, London, Verso and Albritton, R., M. Itoh, R. Westra and A. Zuege (Eds) (2001), *Phases of Capitalist Development*, London, Palgrave.

28. This topic has fascinated political-economic theorists since the 1970s, and much contemporary debate recreates the famous and unresolved conceptual battle between Rudolf Hilferding's Finance Capital (1910) and Heinrich Grossmann's *The Law of Accumulation and Breakdown of the Capitalist System* (1929). See *Uneven Zimbabwe* for a review, and Doug Henwood's *Wall Street* (London, Verso, 1998) for one of the most important contemporary perspectives.

29. I thank them all for guiding me directly and indirectly, especially David Harvey whose (2001) *Spaces of Capital: Towards a Critical Geography* (New York, Routledge) sketches an intellectual trajectory of enormous importance.

30. The analysis in Chapter Two was supported, immensely, by Norton Tenille, Boyce Papu, Tom LeQuesne, and Ashwin Kumar of the SA Environment Project and Mandela Metropole Sustainability Coalition; Jason Bell of the International Fund for Animal Welfare; independent researchers George Niksic and Anton Cartwright. Its political grounding came from Papu, Moki Cekisani of Ubuntu Environmental Trust, and Mike Stofile and many other activists in the SA National Civic Organisation's Port Elizabeth branch. Additional thanks go to SDI/IDZ critics Liz Dodd, Lenny Gentle, Neil Newman, John Pape, and Leon Pretorius from the International Labour Resource and Information Group. All performed valiant work to demystify and protect the public interest at Coega, even if to no avail.

31. Thirty months after filing their World Bank Inspection Panel protest 'underground', the late David Letsie, Johny Mpho and Sam Moiloa did come forward at a World Commission on Dams hearing and the Pretoria launch to confront Kader Asmal. Liane Greef of the Environmental Monitoring Group has subsequently taken much of the work forward, along with the Lesotho community organisations noted in Chapter Three. Globally, Lori Pottinger, Ryan Hoover and Steve Rothert from the Berkeley-based International Rivers Network, Korinna Horta of the Environmental Defense Fund in Washington, Antonio Tricarico of the Italian group Committee for the Reform of the World Bank, and Dana Clark from the Center for International Environmental Law in Washington were among those trying hard, even if unsuccessfully, to keep the corporate and financial forces at bay.

32. Bongani Lubisi, Dudu Mphenyeke, Trevor Ngwane and Virginia Setshedi (to name just a few) inspired thousands of Sowetans, as well as their many local and international supporters.

33. The Rural Development Services Network (especially Eddie Cottle), International Labour Resource and Information Group (Hameeda Deedat, John Pape and Mthetho Xali) and the SA Municipal Workers Union (Victor Mhlongo, Rob Rees, Roger Ronnie, Jeff Rudin, Melanie Samson, Lance Veotte, Anna Weekes and many others) stand out as the most important advocacy groups on water access and opposition to privatisation; and the Group for Environmental Monitoring (Liane Greef) has done stellar anti-megadam education and advocacy.

34. Sowetans and I learned much from the Rising Tide youth movement that will soon sweep away uncritical proponents of Kyoto-style commodified air.

35. Progressive international organisations whose advocacy information on the WSSD is widely respected on the South African left include Aseed Europe, the Blue Planet Project, CarbonTradeWatch, Christian Aid, the Cornerhouse, Corporate Europe Observatory, Corporate Watch UK, Corpwatch, Friends of the Earth, Greenpeace, the Heinrich Boell Stiftung, the International Forum on Globalization, the International Rivers Network, the Rainforest Action Network and Rising Tide.

36. Some of their stories are told in an excellent book edited by the tireless David McDonald of Queens University: McDonald, D. (Ed) (2002), *Environmental Justice in South Africa*, Columbus, Ohio University Press and Cape Town, University of Cape Town Press.

37. To mention a few deserving our respect and support: Biowatch, Consumer Institute of South Africa, Earthlife Africa, the Environmental Justice Networking Forum, the Environmental Monitoring Group, the Group for Environmental Monitoring, Network for Advocacy of Water in Southern Africa, and the South African Climate Action Network. Amongst leading local environmentalists who inspired and taught me are Chris Albertyn, David Fig, Liane Greef, Philip Owen, Bobby Peek, Tebogo Phadu and Norman Reynolds.

38. In addition to our P&DM 'Advanced Topics in Political Economy' seminar in March 2002, Michael Dorsey of Dartmouth University helped co-facilitate two classes of 'Globalisation and the Environment' in May 2002 for the Open Society Initiative of Southern Africa and the Wits Professional Development Unit. Richard Tomlinson regularly co-teaches enjoyable 'Political Economy of Infrastructure' courses with me. Other Wits P&DM and Municipal Services Project-aligned researchers who advanced our understanding of the issues include Karen Cocq, Sean Flynn, Amanda Gillett, David Hemson, Grace Khunou, Rekopantswe Mate, Mandisa Mbali, Peter McGinnes, Theunis Roux and Thenjiwe Shimbira. For assistance during the preparation of this book, Thulani Guliwe, Khutso Madubanya and Horacio Zandamela are warmly thanked. Irene Kavallioratos was an amazing organiser for us all.

For inspiring the final write-up, I am also indebted to a group of exceptional international activist researchers who visited and encouraged us in May 2002 to take a firm, principled position on water, energy and the WSSD: Patrick Apoya, Citizens Against Privatisation, Ghana; Karen Bakker, Oxford University; Debi Barker, Int'l Forum on Globalization, SanFrancisco; David Barkin, Zapatista adviser, Metropolitan Autonomous University of Mexico; Maude Barlow, Council of Canadians, Ottawa; Kate Bayliss, Public Services International Research Unit, London; Nicola Bullard, Focus on the Global South, Bangkok; Marina Carman, Australia GreenLeft Weekly; Daniel Chavez, TransNational Institute, Amsterdam; Tony Clarke, Polaris Institute, Ottawa; Anis Daraghama, Palestine; Radha D'Souza, India; Sara Grusky, Public Citizen, Washington; Colin Leys, *Socialist Register*; Alex Loftus, Oxford University; Njoki Njehu, 50 Years is Enough; Tandeka Nkiwane, Smith College; Oscar Olivera, Defence of Water and Life, Cochabamba; Medha Patkar, National Alliance of People's Movements, India; Jane Stinson, Canadian Union of Public Employees; Yash Tandon, Seatini, Harare; Shiney Varghese, IATP, Minneapolis. Inspiring all of them, of course, were our opening conference speakers: Dennis Brutus, MP Giyosi, Mark Heywood and Fatima Meer.

39. In particular, thanks to James O'Connor and his team for excellent feedback on an article which contains the core arguments of *Unsustainable South Africa*: 'Economic Growth, Ecological Modernization, or Environmental Justice?: Conflicting Discourses in Post-Apartheid South Africa', *Capitalism Nature Socialism*, 11, 1, 2000. Other academic articles and book chapters from which I have drawn materials for substantial revision in the pages below include: 'The *New Partnership for Africa's Development*: Social, Economic and Environmental Contradictions', *Capitalism Nature Socialism*, 13, 2, June 2002; 'A Political Economy of Dam Building and Household Water Supply in Lesotho and South Africa', in McDonald, *Environmental Justice in South Africa*; 'African Dams: Did Large Dams Contribute to the Development of African Nations?', in C.Miller, M.Ciocc and K. Showers (Eds), *Water and the Environment Since 1945: Global Perspectives*, Detroit, St. James Press, 2001; 'Droughts and Floods: Water Shortages and Surpluses in Post-Apartheid South Africa' (with Greg Ruiters), in M.Khosa (Ed), *Empowerment through Economic Transformation*, Pretoria, Human Sciences Research Council, 2001; 'Transformation in Infrastructure Policy, from Apartheid to Democracy: Mandates for Change, Continuities in Ideology, Frictions in Delivery' (with George Dor and Greg Ruiters), in M.Khosa (Ed), *Infrastructure Mandates for Change, 1994-99*, Pretoria, Human Sciences Research Council, 2000; 'Infrastructure for Spatial Development Initiatives or for Basic Needs? Port Elizabeth's Prioritisation of the Coega Port/IDZ over Municipal Services' (with Stephen Hosking), in M.Khosa (Ed), *Empowerment through Service Delivery*, Pretoria, Human Sciences Research Council, 2000; 'Debating Supply and Demand Characteristics of Bulk Infrastructure: Lesotho-Johannesburg Water Transfer' (with David Letsie), in Khosa, Empowerment through Service Delivery; 'Regionalism, Environment and the Southern African Proletariat' (with Darlene Miller and Greg Ruiters), *Capitalism Nature Socialism*, 11, 3, September 2000; 'Infrastructure and Class Apartheid', *Indicator* SA, 17, 3, 2000; 'Contradictions in Municipal Transformation from Apartheid to Democracy: The Battle over Local Water Privatisation in South Africa' (with Greg Ruiters), *Working Papers*

in Local Governance and Democracy, 99, 1, 1999; 'Basic Infrastructure for Socio-Economic Development, Ecological Sustainability and Geographical Desegregation: South Africa's Unmet Challenge', *Geoforum*, 30, 1, 1999; and 'Competing Discourses of Environmental and Water Management in Post-Apartheid South Africa' (with Robyn Stein), in W. Wehrmeyer and Y. Mulugetta (Eds), *Growing Pains: Environmental Management in Developing Countries*, London, Greenleaf Publishing, 1999. Popular articles were published by *Business Day*, *City Press*, *Die Burger*, *Eastern Cape* NGO *Coalition Newsletter*, *Green Left Weekly*, *i'Afrika*, *Local Government Chronicle*, *Mail & Guardian*, *Multinational Monitor*, *New Internationalist*, *New Nation*, *South African Labour Bulletin*, *Sowetan*, *Sunday World* and *ZNet* Commentaries.

40.   The International Development Research Centre in Canada provided general research support to the Municipal Services Project, and Denise Deby and Jean-Marie Labatut were especially helpful (http://www.queensu.ca/msp). Minor research grants that assisted in materials preparation for this book came from the International Fund for Animal Welfare (Chapter Two), the University of Natal School of Development Studies Donor Funding project (Chapter Five), and the SA NGO Coalition and the globalisation project run by Omano Edigheji of Wits P&DM via the Ford Foundation (Chapter Seven). The original presentation of the *Capitalism, Nature, Socialism* article underpinning the book was made possible by the Wits travel fund. No funders are responsible for the conclusions reached or libelous commentary provided along the way.

Introduction

A world in one country

1. Introduction

It was a strange day: 25 June, 2002. Thabo Mbeki was on his way to the
G8 Summit at the Canadian Rocky Mountain protest hideaway of
Kananaskis, travelling in his controversial new R300 million refurbished
Boeing. A fortnight earlier, he made the cover of *Time* magazine above
the misleading title, 'Mbeki's mission: He has finally faced up to the Aids
crisis and is now leading the charge for a new African development plan.
But will he succeed?'[1]

Stopping en route in Rio de Janeiro, the South African president was
guest of honour at a UN Conference on Environment and Development
'torch handing over ceremony'. There, he told Brazilian president Hen-
rique Cardoso and Swedish prime minister Goran Persson that, in the
spirit of Stockholm '72 and Rio '92, South Africa's largest city would take
up the mantle of symbolic global leadership:

> The Johannesburg World Summit must take further our pledge at
> the Millennium Summit [of September 2000 in New York] to eradi-
> cate poverty. It must focus on implementation and action.
>
> Its outcome must make sense to she who has to walk for kilome-
> tres to fetch drinking water and to she who spends hours gathering
> firewood for energy. It must also speak to he who consumes more
> than the earth can give.
>
> When leaders of the world gathered here in 1992, my country
> was still under apartheid rule. I did not enjoy the right to vote.
> Uncertainty and conflict loomed.
>
> But the human spirit triumphed. South Africa is now a democracy
> in which we live in harmony as we struggle to eradicate the legacy
> of over 300 years of colonialism and apartheid. Since the victory of

democracy in 1994, seven million people have access to clean
water, over one million homes for poor people have been built,
over two million more homes now have electricity and every child
has a place in school.

And, South Africa is acting as host to the World Summit on Sustainable Development.[2]

And, as Mbeki spoke, evening fell in wintry South Africa. The majority of
rural women still walked to fetch water and gather firewood. The majority of bourgeois and petit-bourgeois urban men, your correspondent
included, still consumed far too much.

Black people had won the vote. But this did not, by any stretch of the
imagination, lead to harmony. As Mbeki addressed the world in mid-2002,
the struggle to eradicate the legacy of apartheid-capitalist misery was
intensifying in Johannesburg and across his country, because its replacement – the interchangeable local phrases 'neoliberalism' or 'class
apartheid' – was doing yet *worse* socio-economic and environmental
damage to poor and working-class South Africans.

Meanwhile, that same day saw the fruition of a bizarre financial deal
between Pretoria, Kinshasa and the International Monetary Fund (IMF) in
Washington, illustrative of the New Partnership for Africa's Development,
which Mbeki was on his way to Kananaskis to sell. According to the next
day's Cabinet announcement:

> The meeting noted the provision by South Africa of a bridge loan to
> the Democratic Republic of the Congo of Special Drawing Rights
> (SDR) 75 million (about R760 million). This will help clear the DRC's
> overdue obligations with the IMF and allow that country to draw
> resources under the IMF Poverty Reduction and Growth Facility.[3]

Crystallised economic oppression was accomplished in this act: the earlier generation of IMF loans made to Mobuto Sese Seko, riven with corruption and capital flight to European banks, would be codified by
Pretoria, whose citizenry would now hold a huge financial claim ($75
million) against the citizens of that most abused of all African countries.
The people of the DRC were previously victims of Pretoria's apartheid-era
allegiance with Mobuto, an arrangement that especially suited ecology-
destroying mineral extraction corporations headquartered in Johannesburg. The people's struggle against oppression had initially spawned
another ruler in 1996, Laurent Kabila, who unfortunately refused democracy and later fell to an assassin's bullet. The result on 25 June, thanks to
his unelected son Joseph's connections in Pretoria's Union Buildings and

finance ministry, was a triple backlash against the people of the DRC:

- the old odious Mobuto loans would not be repudiated but instead be honoured, and serviced thanks to new credits;
- repayment of the new credits would be backed up, if not by formal collateral, then probably one day by the $5 billion in high-tech arms that Pretoria was in the process of purchasing; and
- IMF staff would be allowed back into Kinshasa with their own new loans, and with neoliberal conditionalities again applied to the old victims of Mobuto's fierce rule.

The same day's Cabinet announcement from Pretoria also revealed that South Africans would generously fund the World Bank's main lending subsidiary for impoverished African countries, on behalf of a special constituency:

> Cabinet approved South Africa's contribution to the replenishment of the resources of the [Bank-subsidiary] International Development Association (IDA), to the tune of R83 million. This amount, which would be drawn down over a nine-year period, would benefit our private sector, which would be eligible to bid for contracts financed from these resources.[4]

Here we find underway the recapitalisation and legitimisation of perhaps the most hated, powerful institutions in Africa, the IMF and World Bank, with Pretoria politicians running cover for both Washington financial bureaucrats and Johannesburg capitalists. Similar IDA loans had recently gone to Lesotho, for example. At the precise moment Pretoria was seeking expanded IDA-based contracts for South African businesses across Africa, the courts in Maseru were preparing to prosecute a range of foreign firms, including several from Johannesburg, for bribing the head of the Lesotho Highlands Development Authority. The World Bank, whose loans had made the bribes possible, had declared itself uninterested in pursuing the bribers beyond a middleman or two. Pretoria had many opportunities to police its own firms and the multinationals by barring them from contracts, but made no moves to do so.

These elite linkages, the protective Washington gear and Mbeki's capacity for reproducing neoliberalism in such hostile conditions were, together, terribly impressive. The African masses would, as ever, pay the bills.

'Triumph of the human spirit' – or of neo-apartheid?

Since the time of Rio in June 1992 – when South African society nearly melted down in Beirut-style political conflagration – and especially since

Mbeki's African National Congress (ANC) took state power in May 1994, prospects for reconciling wealth and poverty here in Johannesburg, and across the African continent, had faded.

Vast sums of apartheid-era loot skipped South Africa since liberation, though sadly the most parasitic major business elite in the world (or perhaps second to Russia's) stayed behind to enjoy the sun and local standard of living, and to continue influencing politics and economics. The currency crashed periodically, setting average dollar-denominated GDP back to 1950s levels. Tens of billions of rands were spent by Pretoria's generals on sophisticated weaponry. Ten million people reported having had their water cut off, and another 10 million were victims of electricity disconnections, mainly due to affordability. Two million people were evicted from their homes or land. A million formal-sector jobs had evaporated. HIV/Aids was slowly, inexorably killing millions more South Africans, while Mbeki remained in denial, openly accused by Pretoria's leading state medical researcher of pursuing a 'genocidal' policy.

The contradictions associated with overconsumptive eco-destruction, and the trajectory of unsustainable non-development, as Noam Chomsky relabeled contemporary capitalism, had amplified massively since 1994, not least by the democratic South African government in its local, national, regional and even global enterprises. Mbeki's claims of dramatic delivery successes under ANC government deserve deep scepticism, as we will see throughout this book.

None of this is a secret at home. The day before Mbeki spoke in Rio, outsourced security firms acting for heartless municipal bureaucracies were forcibly evicting people who could not pay their bills in the country's main cities. In Johannesburg, *The Star* newspaper report was of a war zone not dissimilar to the 1970s–90s anti-apartheid uprisings:

> Men, women and children ran for cover as violence erupted in Lenasia on Tuesday morning after police opened fire with rubber bullets.
>
> A 15-year-old girl bled profusely after being hit in the eye by a bullet, while a man in his 20s lay doubled over after being hit in the abdomen.
>
> A few streets away, a man who had been hit in his legs and back sat crying loudly while others tried to help. An ambulance was called.
>
> The R554 highway to Lenasia, which had been closed off in protest by about 4,000 residents over the removal of Tembelihle informal settlement residents to Vlakfontein, was strewn with odd shoes, clothes and knobkerries after police started firing rubber bullets.
>
> The Johannesburg council wants to move the residents from the

area because they say there is dolomite in the area, but residents say that Vlakfontein, where they are supposed to be moved, lacks infrastructure such as schools and transport facilities.

Commuting in the area came to a standstill earlier when protesters prevented buses, taxis and cars going to work.

Tension mounted and residents refused to obey a police call for them to disperse.

'It was terrifying. We were all standing in front of the police, and next minute they started firing. We were running everywhere. I saw people fall to the ground. It is very bad', one distraught resident said.[5]

The next day, Mbeki flew from Rio to Calgary, while Cape Town became the site of state repression. A peaceful street protest of 300 Western Cape Anti-Eviction Campaign activists at the ANC provincial minister of housing's office was broken up. Police arrested 44 leaders and grassroots campaigners from the ironically named Mandela Park ghetto and Tafelsig. They were teargassed, assaulted by police and private security and charged with trespassing.

The minister, Nomatyala Hangana, had refused eight times over a period of weeks to meet the communities to discuss the housing crisis. Jailed Anti-Evictions Campaign leader Max Ntanyana complained, 'The communities only wanted a date from her today as to when she would meet them. Instead, she unleashed hundreds of police on the gathering of mainly women and pensioners'.

To Mbeki's local party officials, the demonstrators' slogan must have been irritating: 'ANC - NO HOUSES = NO VOTES!' Ntanyana continued, 'It is clear to the Anti-Eviction Campaign that the provincial government of the Western Cape is as rotten as ever. Whether the ANC or DA or NNP takes up portfolios, it makes no difference. The poor continue to be treated as if we are dogs who don't need houses but can sleep in the open in winter'.[6]

Across the world, meanwhile, Mbeki and his colleagues were also being treated as unworthy beggars. As *Business Day* reported, the Northern rulers' Africa Action Plan 'spurned a bid by African countries for a rethink on subsidies, which are seen as harming Africa's global competitiveness, saying any reduction would be done within the framework of the World Trade Organisation'. The *New York Times* confirmed, 'Little of what the United States committed to Africa today is new'. UN secretary general Kofi Annan lamented, 'By and large we know what needs doing. But we have been much too slow to act on that knowledge'.[7]

On the crucial issue of debt, despite talk of a new Marshall Plan, the G8 leaders' concessions amounted to only $1 billion: 'recycled peanuts'

5

according to the mainstream aid agency Oxfam UK. In Washington the same day, Africa's prospects continued to decline. According to the *Times*, 'While leaders endorsed a modest program for debt forgiveness, Treasury Secretary Paul H. O'Neill told Congress today that his tour of Africa had convinced him that eliminating debt burdens was not a solution to the continent's problems'.[8]

Back in Cape Town, local banks were tackling their borrowers' debt problems with similar sympathy. South Africa's largest financiers plus the semi-state agency (Servcon) that helps collectivise bank interests in negotiations with communities, suddenly interdicted the Mandela Park Anti-Eviction Committee from taking any steps to prevent further evictions. As the Committee explained,

> The Mandela Park houses are full of structural defects and are not worth anywhere near the high prices that the owners have already paid for them. The banks and Servcon say that government and the banking sector have made a 'constructive attempt' to address housing problems, yet they have all failed several times in the past months alone to show up at any meetings with the community. The banks are arguing that they should be allowed to 'rightsize' approximately 2000 housing bond defaulters living in Khayelitsha into tiny dog kennel-style RDP houses.[9]

In Kananaskis, a journalist from South Africa's largest-circulation paper reported that 'the leaders of the world's richest nations refused to play ball'. Said Mbeki, in contrast, 'I think they have addressed adequately all the matters that were put to them'. He termed the G8 Summit 'a defining moment in the process both of the evolution of Africa and the birth of a more equitable system of international relations. In historical terms, *it signifies the end of the epoch of colonialism and neo-colonialism*' (emphasis added).[10] But as the ridicule grew unbearable, rather more was revealed in the next day's front-page headline, reflecting a morning-after headache and transference of blame: 'Mbeki accuses NGOs of being ill-informed'.[11]

Such extreme contradictions abound, simply, because environment and development are experienced differentially by elites and masses. To observe merely the surface appearance of South Africa's unsustainability, visitors to the World Summit on Sustainable Development (WSSD) (Section 2), or anyone else coming to Johannesburg for the first time (Section 3), do not have to look far. One marker of early twenty-first century degradation is the rise of cholera (Section 4). Another is the way that environment and development debates are connected, and too often disconnected, from policy to project levels (Section 5). Our efforts here will focus on relinking empirical observations and daily ebbs and flows of social conflict, especially class struggle, back to underlying processes associated with the accumulation of power and capital.

2. The conquest of nature

For those of us fortunate to consume what should otherwise – in a just world – be our lifetime share of global warming gases via jet airplane transport, perhaps the initial warnings appear from the window seat of a 747 or Airbus. No doubt groggy as dawn breaks, we take our bird's-eye view of South Africa from an intercontinental flight bound for Johannesburg International Airport. As the sun rises, we might see the Kalahari Desert from the northwest on the South African Airways New York flight, or cross from Europe over the Zambezi and Limpopo Rivers and then the savannah prairie highveld, or perhaps fly westerly from Asia above Mozambique and the Kruger Park, or southeasterly on SAA from Atlanta or Latin America via a stop in Cape Town, after which craggy mountains give way to the semi-desert Karoo.

Arrival time approaches and the terrain below becomes recognisable, parcelled up in agricultural plots, cross-cut by roads and housing estates, stripped by mining enterprises and pocked by belts of industrial 'civilisation'. We quickly crack open a standard traveller's guide, in this case the *Lonely Planet*, quirky yet emblematic for its cliches of the land 10,000 metres below:

> The national parks are among the greatest in the world and there are few better places to see Africa's wildlife. The thrill of seeing animals like elephants and lions in the wild cannot be overestimated. The beaches are amongst the best and least crowded in the world, and the surf and fishing are as good as you can get. The countryside and particularly the mountains, are spectacular, and the walking and touring possibilities are endless. The climate is kind, and there is the added advantage that it is summer in southern Africa while the northern hemisphere is in the depths of winter ...
>
> In some eyes, southern Africa's most impressive endowment is its flora. There are more than 22,000 species, accounting for 10% of the world's total – that's more than in the USA, which is seven times larger. It is not just impressive numerically, it is both fascinating and spectacularly beautiful. South Africa is the only country with one of the world's six floral kingdoms within its borders.[12]

And on we read, a genuine excitement growing with each overhead glance at South Africa's geographic diversity and contradictory physical grandeur. Truly, 'A world in one country' – as tourist brochures insist – can be found amidst the other national, indeed regional, claim to fame: several centuries of ruinous social engineering, countered by an increasingly proud indigenous resistance and ultimately a victorious democratic spirit and strategy of national liberation. All along, ecologies and landscapes were managed, ruined, created, enhanced, and in many cases permanently changed.

'Commodification'

Is there a thread linking the country's outstanding physical features and the stressed human condition, where the intertwining of environment, development and social protest can be theorised? Colonial-era geographical thinking certainly located social outcomes in an allegedly foreordained relationship of people to their land, even though people struggled mightily against geographical determinism because their freedom and often their very survival depended upon it. Today most intellectuals, aside from outlyers like Jeffrey Sachs,[13] have also finally come to resist explanations of social processes by recourse mainly to inherited physical attributes such as land-lockedness or climatic conditions.

Yet fierce debates over utilisation of resources like energy and water do offer explicit linkages between human and environmental developments. What is different is that in the early twenty-first century, the interconnectedness appears strongest at the nexus of capital and state power, for the *commodification* of nature and society, together, has become the most profound experience of our time. But in the same historical-geographical-materialist spirit, can we also understand that eco-social thread as prone to snapping at different points? Or sometimes flexing thanks to innate social adaptability, even when entwined through such a tortured history? This country, after all, has featured periodic, profound transformations resulting from grandiose settler designs.

The conquest of nature dates to the arrival of Bantu people, but the most disastrous yet somehow unevenly productive moments were reserved for white traders, bureaucrats, farmers, bankers, miners, industrialists, tourist-industry moguls, road and dam-builders, even nuclear engineers. They twisted and buried the socio-environmental thread of mutual reliance all too often, to our present generation's loss. We owe the next generation far more forethought, and that responsibility includes unearthing the relationships between people and ecology, and addressing as much of the damage as possible.

How do we begin to make this case, when so many academics and intellectuals have gone before, and set the stage? The impact of humans on spatial form and ecology has been explored by historical-environmental scholars such as Sauer, Glacken, Wittfogel, Smith, Cronon, Beinart and others. Our own work in unveiling contemporary contradictions between capital accumulation and eco-social conditions today is, as any incoming visitor can attest, made easier by the very existence of Johannesburg. This city, whose contradictions embody life from Soweto shack settlements to the super-rich suburb of Sandton, requires an urgently politicised bird's-eye view of environment, development and social protest, foreshadowing some of the stories we will tell in later pages.

3. Unsustainable Johannesburg

Welcome to Johannesburg, whose retained name commemorates Johannes Rissik, the nineteenth century surveyor of the stolen land. When a genuine people's government comes to power, the name will surely be changed, just as will the inherited landscape of apartheid-era *and* post-apartheid urban, suburban and peri-urban capitalism.

In the struggle to remake the world in a humane and ecologically-sensitive image, names are trivial symbols, but 'Johannesburg' is also notable because it adorns yet another failed UN heads-of-state summit, known as the World Summit on Sustainable Development, or 'Rio+10'. When social progress advances more rapidly later in the century, then that conference's awful legacy – the commodification of nature and amplified underdevelopment of the Third World through heightened globalisation – will probably also be forgotten.

But in mid-2002, the contradictions in Johannesburg, and at the WSSD in ultra-bourgeois Sandton, are unmistakable. To return to our introductory journey, tens of thousands of conference delegates flying in to Africa's main commercial complex in late August will descend to the highveld by breaking through a thick brown cloud of particulates. Temperature inversions and the lack of rain for the past four months are the natural reasons Johannesburg's 1500 metre elevation and brisk winds still don't provide clean air in winter.

In this region, the settlers' conquest of nature, particularly since gold was discovered in 1886, is especially grotesque. Viewed from the air, filthy smudges of human fingerprints are everywhere to partake: concentrated industrial pollution over the east-west factory strip and the eight-chimneyed power plant astride the airport; gold-mine dumps to the south of the city which ceaselessly blow sand and dust into black neighbourhoods; periodic bush fires; and the ongoing use of coal and fuelwood for cooking and heating in impoverished townships like Soweto and Alexandra.

Township and suburban life

It would be wrong to blame the victims: low-income black people. Across the country, the drive towards electricity commercialisation and privatisation these past few years has meant supply cut offs for more than a million households who cannot afford price increases. From the air, be thankful that we do not experience the most dangerous results, such as the return to dirtier forms of energy and the re-emergence of tuberculosis and other rampant respiratory infections that threaten the lives of South Africa's five million HIV-positive people.

Just before landing, we are, however, close enough to notice the silvery glinting of thousands of tiny metal-roofed shacks in the bright sun, like cauterised wounds on the yellowish skin of Africa during the dry season. The township slums stretch to the horizon, and house the majority of Gauteng Province's ten million inhabitants. Because of a stingy government policy based on World Bank advice in mid-1994, shortly after Nelson Mandela was elected president, Johannesburg's post-apartheid squatter camps and meagre new formal residential areas for low-income black residents are actually further away from job opportunities and are worse served with community amenities, schools and clinics, than even apartheid-era ghettoes.

Looking down, our eyes are soon drawn away to the bright green of well-watered English-style gardens and thick alien trees that shade traditionally white – now slightly desegregated – suburbs, permeated by ubiquitous sky-blue swimming pools. To achieve the striking effect, the most hedonistic louts of Johannesburg abuse water. Waste occurs not only in the bourgeois and petit-bourgeois residential zones sprawling north and east of the city centre, but in the southern mining belt and the corporate-dominated farms on the city's outskirts.

Further scarce water is used for cooling coal-burning electricity generators. Jejune South African bureaucrats brag about supplying the world's cheapest energy for industrial use, because they fail to price in the damage to the environment, including one of the world's worst global greenhouse gas emissions, corrected for population size and income. The root cause is a phenomenon economists call 'Dutch Disease', to commemorate the rise of North Sea oil prices and hence the Dutch currency, which decapacitated Holland's manufacturing capacity. Likewise, South Africa's mineral wealth distorts and distends the local economy and annuls efforts at industrial balance. The implications for water supply are becoming critical.

Sucking the ground dry

When gold was discovered, thousands of fortune hunters and proletarians were drawn inland immediately. Johannesburg soon became the planet's largest metropolis with no substantial natural water source. Seventy-five kilometres to the south, the Vaal River is pumped uphill to Johannesburg, but by the 1980s it became apparent that the source would be insufficient for the next century's industries and suburbanites.

Apartheid-era engineers and World Bank project officers tried to solve the looming shortages with a dam and tunnel scheme that draws water several hundred kilometres from across a mountain range atop the small and perpetually impoverished nation of Lesotho. Africa's largest infrastructure project, costing an estimated $8 billion if all six dams are built, the project is now less than half finished but has already displaced tens of thousands of Basotho peasants, inundated sacred land, threatened endangered species and endangered the Orange River's downstream ecosystem.

Who pays the bills? Johannesburg water prices went up by 35% during the late 1990s, but township residents in the lowest consumption tier found themselves paying 55% more because of the cost of the Lesotho dams, for which the old Botha regime needed surreptitious funding during the mid-1980s due to apartheid-era financial sanctions. The World Bank set up a secret London account to facilitate matters, overriding objections from the liberation movement, including its then representative in Ireland, Kader Asmal.

As South Africa's water minister from 1994–99, Asmal was chosen to chair the 1998–2000 World Commission on Dams. Entangled in the massive contradictions and hypocrisies, he refused to let the Commission study the Lesotho dam and angrily rejected grassroots demands from Alexandra, Soweto and Lesotho that overconsumptive water users in the mines, factories and mansions be made more responsible for paying the dam's bills and for conserving water so as to prevent future dam construction. Such 'demand-side management' would also have included repair of ubiquitous leaks in the apartheid-era township infrastructure, where half of Soweto's water is lost.

Bankers were anxious to continue financing, and construction companies ready to keep building, the multi-billion dollar dams. The World Bank's Inspection Panel refused a full investigation of township residents' complaints in 1998. The Bank also went to great lengths to protect a corrupt senior official in the project, Masupha Sole, from being fired, in spite of documented bribes to his Swiss bank account by a dozen of the world's largest construction companies over the decade 1988–98.

11

Then, not only did the Bank refuse to bar the companies from further contracts, but it withdrew promised financial support for their 2001–02 public prosection in Lesotho by claiming that it was penalising only the three middlemen who abused the Bank's loan funds. The Bank's sleazy side was on such display that even Pretoria's director-general of water affairs was heard to comment on national radio that Washington should learn to 'walk the [anti-corruption] talk'.

Asmal's replacement as water minister, Ronnie Kasrils, finally announced a halt to further dam construction, once the second Lesotho mega-dam, Mohale, is complete in 2004. Yet no environmentalist or community activist trusts Kasrils' instincts, in the wake of his simultaneous rejection of the Dam Commission report's guidelines as binding, and his trip to China's ultra-destructive Three Gorges Dam on the Yangtze River, which he endorsed, inexplicably.

Kasrils has also failed to keep his own rivers clean, including the Vaal, less than an hour's drive south of Johannesburg. In what is quickly emerging as South Africa's most humiliating single environmental case of contemporary corporate heartlessness and government paralysis, the former mega-parastatal iron/steel firm Iscor is excreting cadmium-infected effluent waste from its main smelter at Vanderbijlpark. Uniting in opposition to the firm's lying management, black and white workers and other Vaal residents have discovered that beginning in 1961, the company has ruined the surrounding water table through toxic dumping into unlined dams.

Cancer has spread into the communities through what activists term 'vast lakes of toxic waste' stretching for 140 hectares. The seven kilometre plume of poisoned water will probably reach Boipatong township where tens of thousands of people are at risk. Repeatedly, and as recently as April 2002, government water officials granted exemptions from the Water Act. If withheld, the exemptions would have prevented further pollution – but that would have entailed Pretoria taking the environment seriously and tackling corporate power conclusively.

Behind the pollution

As is true across the world, Johannesburg's worsening environmental mess is mainly due to the logic of capital accumulation, at a time of rampant environmental deregulation associated with the 1992 United Nations Conference on Environment and Development in Rio. South Africa's traditionally racist and pollution-intensive companies have been embraced by a grateful black elite, including vulgar politicians and the neoliberal officials who control many arms of the government.

To be sure, the onset of free-market economic policies based on an export-orientation fetish preceded Mandela's ANC government by a few years. But a small clique of 'New Guard' ANC officials today work closely with the leftover 'Old Guard' bureaucrats whose commitment to racial apartheid is conveniently forgotten but who prosper just as nicely while building class apartheid.

Together, the ruling party and its new-found Afrikaner co-conspirators have:

- allowed vast sums of rich white people's loot to escape through relaxing already porous exchange controls;
- let the largest firms relocate their financial headquarters to London, hence sucking out profit and dividend flows forever;
- cut corporate tax rates from 48% in 1994 to 30% five years later in search of new investment that never materialised;
- watched aimlessly as business fired a fifth of all formal-sector workers;
- allowed industries like clothing, footwear and appliances to collapse under international competition;
- incessantly privatised once-formidable public assets;
- provided pollution permits to some of the world's most irresponsible companies; and now
- channel billions of taxpayer funds into bizarre projects like Blue IQ – to make smart Johannesburgers smarter and leave the rest behind – and the 'Gautrain' rail system linking the airport to Sandton, central Johannesburg and Pretoria for what are unselfconsciously termed 'elite' passengers.

The ANC's Igoli 2002 privatisation plan, drafted alongside World Bank consultants, was renamed by critics 'E.coli 2002' for a good reason: excrement from Johannesburg's slums – where water is still denied by the French water privatiser Suez, beneficiary of a huge commercialisation contract – regularly despoiled Sandton's borehole water supplies.

War on the poor

By then, cholera was devastating the countryside from which many Zulu-speaking migrant labourers emerge after their brief Christmas break. The disease spread, inevitably, to Alexandra township, Sandton's reserve army of labour which is home to an estimated 300,000 people crammed into just over two square miles of mainly squalid housing. The disease quickly killed four residents, and internationally televised apartheid-style forced removals were the bureaucrats' answer.

Likewise, when non-violent protesters from Soweto took a bus to Johannesburg mayor Amos Masondo's house in April 2002 to demonstrate against evictions and the cut offs of water and electricity due to unaffordability, his bodyguard responded by pumping eight rounds of live ammo into the crowd, wounding two. Emblematically for the South African 'justice' system, 87 Soweto Electricity Crisis Committee members (including elderly people and minors) were arrested and 50 were jailed for 11 days before getting a bail hearing, while the bodyguard remained at large. They were the highest-profile political prisoners of neoliberalism to date, and they wouldn't be the last.

The Johannesburg landscape is also being defaced by other greed-driven processes, including bank 'redlining' (denial of loan access) in many townships and inner-city sites of racial desegregation such as cosmopolitan but poverty stricken Hillbrow, Berea and Yeoville. Slum landlords from the kombi-taxi sector are running down huge inner-city blocks of flats while government officials yet again attempt the gentrification of the Newtown arts district which wealthy whites remain too fearful to patronise.

One reason is ongoing 'crime and grime' downtown, in spite of a new camera surveillance system that Foucault would have admired. The old Central Business District spent the 1990s being virtually emptied of whire professionals, with more than two-thirds of office space vacant at one point and Africa's largest prestige building, the Carlton Centre, sold in 2000 at 5% of its 1974 construction costs.

No escape from unsustainable development

Where, then, aside from London and 'EsCapeTown', did smart money flee? Fifteen kilometres northeast of the old CBD, the edge-city of Sandton attracted many billions of rands worth of 1990s commercial property investment, as well as world-class traffic jams, nouveau-riche conspicuous consumption and discordant postmodern architecture. Only the world's least socially conscious financial speculators would trash their ex-headquarters downtown to build a new city while draining South Africa of capital.

Sandton Square was quickly surrounded by skyscrapers, banks (including a brand new Citibank tower), boutiques for the ubiquitous nouveau-riche, 5-star hotels, a garish convention centre, Africa's biggest stock exchange and other architectural detritus showcasing brazen economic power. Only the most aesthetically barren of moneyed elites would build their little Tuscanies on Africa's beautiful highveld, behind three-metre high walls adorned with barbed wire to keep out the criminals. Jo'burg's cutting-edge high-tech surveillance systems are staffed by poverty-level black security-sector workers. Expensive car-tracking systems identify heart-of-darkness 'NoGo zones' like Alexandra, for which, if drivers dare venture inside, satellite alarm beams are activated and armed rescue teams are mobilised. In unison, these features of Sandton conjoin conspicuous consumption norms, the psychology of class insulation, phallic symbolism, and a profoundly distorted political economy.

The environmental destruction, malgovernance, political repression, social hypocrisy and parasitical financial activity together attract a backlash, of course. What was by all accounts the world's most impressive urban social movement, the South African 'civics', witnessed the ruling party's systematic demobilisation of their ranks during the mid-1990s. However, an independent network of community groups has arisen in several Johannesburg townships through the Anti-Privatisation Forum. Municipal workers and other public sector unions often demonstrate against grievances. Mass marches of workers and residents are increasingly common. Surgical Robin Hood theft of electricity and water by community activists is an everyday occurrence.

Yet virtue at the grassroots turns sour when NGO and trade union politics dominate. The 2001–02 fragmentation of the various hosting committees – the UN Civil Society Secretariat, the South African Civil Society Forum set up by pro-government trade union and church leaders, the Civil Society Indaba of groups tossed out of the function, and some resource-scarce independent-left social movements and intellectuals – symbolises why power relations remain so skewed. Still, elite Johannesburg's repeated attacks on both ecology and the poor will inevitably lead to a 'Social Forum' process, as the international meeting in Porto Alegre portends for many sites of anti-neoliberal struggle across the world.

Like the corporate-controlled WSSD itself, Johannesburg will continue to self-delegitimise the very idea of 'sustainable development' – until the grassroots, shopfloor, women, youth, church and environmental comrades get their acts together and take power away from those old and new rulers who have made such a mess of Africa's wealthiest city. But to do this, they will need to sharpen their ideology, and link local problems to global phenomena.

4. Learning from cholera

This book's birth came amidst heated policy debates in Pretoria over infrastructure in 1996. It hurriedly came of age during 1997–98 through red-green campaigning in which I was privileged to participate, first to halt further construction of Lesotho mega-dams and then against a white elephant industrial development in what is now called the Nelson Mandela Metropole, just north of Port Elizabeth. The arguments urgently matured in 2000 when cholera broke out in KwaZulu-Natal, and in 2001 as Soweto households suffered an upsurge of neoliberal electricity cut offs which at one stage numbered 20,000 families per month. Most of the pages below received their finishing touches between sessions of a dull academic conference in rainy Hamburg at the end of May 2002.

Keeping me company on the flight to Germany was what appeared at first glance to be a depressing tome, *Death in Hamburg* by historian Richard Evans, donated to me a few weeks earlier by a friend.[14] Torn between the conference, my editing duties and tours of the city offered by my cousin Caroline Flöel and her Uni.Hamburg Geography Department mates, I was stunned into an all-night reading of the Evans book, proving to myself again that a recurrent return to history rewards us with the most meaningful clues for interpreting the present and future.

Evans set out to explain how 10,000 people died of cholera over a six-week period in 1892 due to lethal ruling-class incompetence, a situation we return to in Chapter Five. Northern Germany was, at the time, undergoing epochal change, Caroline reminded me, as proletarianisation swept away old social relations. Not far from Hamburg, our great-grandfather, the sociologist Ferdinand Tönnies, captured the essence of that emerging urbanity, as the

> artificial construction of an aggregate of human beings which superficially resembles the *Gemeinschaft* (community) in so far as the individuals live and dwell together peacefully. However, in the *Gemeinschaft* they remain essentially united in spite of all separating factors, whereas in the *Gesellschaft* (society) they are essentially separated in spite of all the uniting factors ... Everybody is by himself and isolated and there exists a condition of tension against all others ... Nobody wants to grant and produce anything for another individual, nor will he be inclined to give ungrudgingly to another individual if it not be in exchange for a gift of labour equivalent that he considers at least equal to what he has given.[15]

What better place to seed an epidemic as profligate as cholera. Alienation, political apathy and self-survival fertilised the most barren of municipal social policies, in Hamburg especially. Due to the stingy character of the city's ruling business elite, municipal government aimed solely to assure the reproduction of labour power at the lowest possible cost, no matter the implications for public health and the environment.

The commodification of everything

Of course, the reduction of most urban citizens to mere workplace fodder and consuming units was not unique to Hamburg, but is indeed the hallmark of the capitalist city, as my doctoral supervisor David Harvey went on to explain:

> A city is an agglomeration of productive forces built by labour employed within a temporal process of circulation of capital. It is nourished out of the metabolism of capitalist production for exchange on the world market and supported out of a highly sophisticated system of production and distribution organised within its confines. It is populated by individuals who reproduce themselves using money incomes earned off the circulation of capital (wages and profits) or its derivative revenues (rents, taxes, interest, merchants' profits, payments for services). The city is ruled by a particular coalition of class forces, segmented into distinctive communities of social reproduction, and organised as a discontinuous but spatially contiguous labour market within which daily substitutions of job opportunities against labour power are possible and within which certain distinctive quantities and qualities of labour power may be found.[16]

For some, the idea of pure urban commodification is worth celebrating. In Chapter One, we revisit Larry Summers' eco-neoliberal ideas – codified in an infamous 1991 World Bank memo to fellow economists – about how 'the economic logic behind dumping a load of toxic waste in the lowest-wage country is impeccable'.[17]

In much the same spirit, one United Nations Habitat staffer enthusiastically explained urban neoliberalism in a house journal, during the run-up to the UN's 1995 Istanbul housing conference: 'The city is not a community, but a conglomerate of firms, institutions, organisations and individuals with contractual agreements among them'. Consequently, according to the same author, urban policy should focus on 'creating a level playing field for competition among cities, particularly across national borders; on understanding how cities get ahead in this competition; on global capital transfers, the new economic order and the weakening of the nation-state'.[18]

Whether in Hamburg, Washington, Istanbul or Johannesburg, these general features of capitalist urbanisation permit short-term decisions that may at surface level appear rational, within the context of impersonal, speculative flows of capital, an atomised labour market, and a myriad of consumer 'choices'. Occasionally a major state investment in the built environment such as a sewage or water treatment system is made when capital accumulation is anticipated to require infrastructure some decades into the future, or when the construction lobby scores a coup. But this is rare: such investments are far more common when the borrowing of capital is cheap, when the city settles into a predictable rhythm of production, residential settlement and transportation needs, and when ruling elites look up from their money-making to envisage future needs.

Unfortunately, neither South Africa at the turn of the twenty-first century nor Hamburg 110 years earlier qualified in most of these respects. As cholera broke out in both settings, the state's role was reduced to emergency after-the-fact interventions and moralising about hygiene. Chapters Five and Seven show how water policy in the time of cholera coincided closely with the mass death and destruction associated with state and capital's denialism around HIV/Aids.

From this incredibly depressing entry-point, what else does this book attempt to argue?

5. Environment and development?

Johannesburg was chosen to host the World Summit on Sustainable Development in August–September 2002. The world's largest-ever conference of its type, the WSSD was expected to attract 100 heads of state and tens of thousands of delegates, as well as thousands of demonstrators from the environmental, community, feminist and labour movements. *Unsustainable South Africa* attempts to analyse the largest and most revealing environmental and development projects and policies of the host country.

How do Coega, the Lesotho dams, water policy, energy practices and social protest relate to the major challenges that are under consideration at the WSSD? Have corporations already hijacked the agenda? And under the circumstances, is a South African-catalysed 'New Deal' between North and South, dealing with both poverty and environment, feasible?

This book argues that during the first period of democratic rule in South Africa, until the Johannesburg Summit, Pretoria's attempts to improve environment and development failed miserably. Certainly some delivery could be claimed. Yet profound contradictions emerged during the transition from the formal system of racial, class, gender and ecological exploitation known as apartheid, to informal systems based on neoliberal policies.

To unearth these, my coauthors and I highlight some central problems associated with state control, corporate power and social action in relation to ecological processes. Throughout, we confront three main 'discursive strategies': 'neoliberalism', 'sustainable development' and 'environmental justice'. These strategic arguments, used on behalf of differing interest groups, began to gel not only in South Africa but across the world by the beginning of the twenty-first century. The book's subject matter ranges across the government's ecological inheritance, illustrative large-scale development projects, the local and international economic circumstances, the most important political dynamics, and key policy/legislative debates.

What emerges from our review is that expedient decisions have been taken in all these spheres, with a distinct bias towards neoliberalism. We blame received conditions, mainly unaltered power relations and the ANC government's economic priorities. As a result, socio-ecological progress was generally set back from 1994–2002.

Still, if there is an overarching rhetoric associated with the post-apartheid state's environmental strategy, it parrots what has become known, in the wake of the 1987 Brundtland Commission, as sustainable development. This discourse is contrasted favourably with the neoliberal free-market approach and negatively with the environmental justice alternative.

The structure of the book

The contrasting interests are explored through studies of:
- the discourses and issues that are most common at the intersection of South Africa's environment and development debates (Chapter One);
- a vast, subsidy-dependent, pollution-ridden economic infrastructure project planned at the Coega Port and Industrial Development Zone (Chapter Two);
- a dramatic cross-catchment transfer of water from Lesotho to Johannesburg characterised by World Bank giganticism and dogmatism, mega-dam construction interests, corporate corruption, and a profound failure to redress existing resource inequalities (Chapter Three);
- the socio-ecological implications for urban and rural households of access to electricity and water/sanitation (Chapter Four);
- debates over the management and legislation of water at national and regional scales (Chapter Five);
- the contradictory facets of South Africa's energy crisis, by which too much goes to the dirtiest and too little to the poorest (Chapter Six); and

- a brief survey of eco-social movement activists and the arguments they are making about South African environment/development policies, Southern African and African socio-economic crises, and the WSSD (Chapter Seven).

The conclusion is simple. South Africa's inherited environmental challenges and the policies, projects and laws that emerged to address and in important ways, to compound these problems, together illustrate the elite's chosen macropolitical route: *neoliberalism disguised by sustainable-development rhetoric.*

It is an untenable combination. The ANC's bias towards foreign-corporate accumulation of capital can be only temporarily disguised by political centrism. For although on the surface, the ruling party's practices appear grounded in stakeholder ideology, in reality they cement apartheid-capitalism's social, economic, geographic and ecological legacy. If corrupted 'steakholders' in five-star Sandton hotels represent the ugly international face of sus-dev discourses and UN summits, then rising social protest is just one hopeful indicator of their negation. But all of this remains to be proven in the coming chapters.

Notes

1. *Time,* 10 June 2002. The misleading nature of the subtitle was revealed less than a month later when, after losing the Constitutional Court case brought by the Treatment Action Campaign, forcing the state to supply pregnant hiv-positive women with the antiretroviral medicine Nevirapine, Mbeki authorised an appeal of the judgement.

2. Mbeki, T. (2002), 'Address by the President of the Republic of South Africa, Thabo Mbeki, on the Occasion of the Torch Handing over Ceremony, From Rio to Johannesburg', Rio De Janeiro, 25 June.

3. South African Government Communications and Information Service (2002), 'Statement on Cabinet Meeting', Pretoria, 26 June.

4. South African Government Communications and Information Service, 'Statement on Cabinet Meeting'.

5. Johannesburg *TheStar*, 25 June 2002.

6. Western Cape Anti-Eviction Committee (2000), 'Jailed: Mandela Park and Tafelsig Anti-Eviction Campaign', Cape Town, 26 June.

7. *Business Day*, 28 June 2002; *New York Times*, 28 June 2002.

8. *New York Times*, 28 June 2002.

9. Western Cape Anti-Eviction Campaign (2002), 'Press Statement', Cape Town, 28 June. Similar anger was being expressed by activists against the same banks for evicting Aids orphans from houses where parents had died in default.

10. *Sunday Times*, 30 June 2002. The *Times*' political gossip columnist 'Hogarth' remarked, 'Just how many ends will this colonialism have?'

And across the page, the newspaper's editorialists were (unconsciously) just as brutal about Nepad's fate: 'The West's response to this initiative has been to play ridiculous games and make announcements that grab headlines but lack substance ... Little in the way of new money and nil in the way of opening markets was forthcoming. This is not only an act of dishonesty, but an extreme case of short-sightedness and foolishness on the part of the G8'. By replacing 'West' and 'G8' with 'Mbeki', and 'this initiative' with 'the G8 Summit' the reverse would also be true.

11. Business Day, 1 July 2002. Two days later, in Cape Town, Mbeki described criticism as 'easy, routine, uninformed and cynical' (Business Report, 4 July 2002).

12. Murray, J., R. Everist, and J. Williams (1996), Lonely Planet: South Africa, Lesotho and Swaziland, Hawthorn, Australia, Lonely Planet, p.11.

13. Sachs, J. and D. Bloom (1998), 'Geography, Demography, and Economic Growth in Africa', presented at the Brookings Panel on Economic Activity, Washington, September.

14. Evans, R. (1987), Death in Hamburg: Society and Politics in the Cholera Years, 1830-1910, Harmondsworth, Penguin, citations below from pp.567-68. Thanks, David Sogge.

15. Tönnies, F. (1955 ed), Community and Society, London, Routledge and Kegan Paul, pp. 64-65, 33-34.

16. Harvey, D. (1985), Consciousness and the Urban Experience, Oxford, Basil Blackwell, p. 250.

17. Summers, L. (1991), 'Memo', Office of the World Bank Chief Economist, Washington, December 12, http://www.whirledbank.org.

18. Angel, S. (1995), 'The Future Lies in a Global System of Competitive Cities', Countdown to Istanbul, 1, p. 4.

PART ONE

An unsustainable legacy

An example of 'class apartheid'. An advertisement by Matrix Vehicle Tracking in *Business Day*, 7 May 2002. The ad identifies the township of Alexandra as an example of a 'NoGo Zone', a 'dangerous area' its clients are 'not supposed to be' and which can be programmed to trigger off an automatic armed response should their vehicles enter it. The Sandton CBD, where clients are 'supposed to be', is in the background.

CHAPTER ONE

The environment of apartheid-capitalism:

Discourses and issues

With David Hallowes

1. Introduction

In South Africa, the past century's experience of industrialisation, urban-isation and rural dispossession did enormous damage to society's eco-logical inheritance. In some cases, core components of the eco-system, such as urban water and rural land in some overpopulated settings, were affected so badly that the limits to human habitation became evident. Not just a social construct, the problem of physical scarcity presented itself, for example, by way of fast-rising prices for Johannesburg water, which had to be pumped hundreds of kilometres across mountains.

Restoring the eco-socio-economic balance was one of the most chal-lenging of all the enormous responsibilities the first democratic South African government faced in 1994, just as the painful exercise of identi-fying capitalism's environmental self-destructiveness occupied global elites in Stockholm in 1972 and Rio de Janeiro in 1992. Locally and glob-ally, however, elites were not up to the challenge of adopting potential solutions. With the exception of cholorofluorocarbons (CFCs), virtually all the earth's environmental problems worsened.

In a concise summary of these problems, the German Green party's Heinrich Böll Stiftung issued *The Jo'burg-Memo*, edited by Wolfgang Sachs:

> Consider the environmental trends of the last fifty years: greenhouse
> gas concentrations have surpassed tolerable levels, one third of
> arable land has been degraded worldwide, just as one third of trop-

ical forests, one fourth of the available freshwater, and one fourth of the fish reserves have disappeared, not to mention the extinction of plant and animal species. Although it was just a minority of the world population, which fed off nature for just a couple of generations, the feast is quickly coming to an end ...

The Rio process has launched a number of successful institutional processes, without, however, producing tangible global results. In particular, economic globalisation has largely washed away gains made on the micro level, spreading an exploitative economy across the globe and exposing natural resources in the South and in Russia to the pull of the world market ...

In global aggregate terms, the only good news (at least for the environment, while not necessarily for people) is that the global surface area under environmental protection has increased, that CFC production has declined, and that the global carbon emissions have stagnated at 1998 levels. Apart from these cases, however, the excessive strain placed by human beings on nature's sources, sites, and sinks has continued to rise. The extinction of species and habitats has increased, the destruction of ancient forests continues unabated, the degradation of fertile soil has worsened, over-fishing of oceans has continued, and the new threat of genetically engineered disruption has emerged. Of course, global aggregate figures conceal successes in particular places, just as they hide breakdowns in others. As life is planetary in scale, what matters however in the end, is the integrity and resilience of those webs of life, which form the Biosphere. Even if the surgery at Rio was a success, the patient's overall health has definitely not improved.[1]

Wehab

By 2002, United Nations leader Kofi Annan had identified Johannesburg as a place to address five specific aspects of sustainable development: water, energy, health, agriculture and biodiversity, known by the acronym 'Wehab'. In the final chapter we consider reasons why the WSSD failed even to pose the problems correctly, much less come up with effective strategies.

We have also chosen five areas – water and sanitation, energy, waste, land use and pollution – that have foiled South African environmental management, social policy and economic transformation in the post-apartheid era. Health is mentioned periodically, agriculture is considered to overlap with waste and land use, and biodiversity remains an area that is still to be rigorously investigated and fought over in South Africa, although promising initiatives against the government's high-risk deregulation of corporate agriculture have begun.[2]

But a prior task exists in this chapter, namely pointing out the competing lines of argument most often deployed to explain, and prescribe about, these challenges (Section 2). The contrasts are particularly sharp when we see how sophisticated corporate greenwash has become, and how fragmented environmentalists remain (Section 3). However, South African issue areas still provide relatively manageable problems, around which progressive activists are demanding solutions: water (Section 4); energy (Section 5); waste (Section 6); land use (Section 7); and industrial and mining pollution (Section 8).

From these sectors, a case is made, and discussed throughout the book, for infinitely more powerful forms of workplace/community-based advocacy and state regulation than currently exist. Indeed, the environmental evidence is part of the broader case for a recommitment to a kind of socialism – having nothing in common with the old East Bloc bureaucracies – that treats people and ecology with the profound dignity that is lacking under capitalism.

2. Discourses of environment and development

There have emerged, over the past couple of decades, at least three distinctive environmental-developmental discourses that seem to apply equally well, though with different implications, in industrialised and Third World countries: neoliberalism, sustainable development and environmental justice.[3]

As a semi-industrialised country, South Africa's capital accumulation process originated in agriculture but came to be largely reliant upon diamonds and gold during the late nineteenth century and upon these and other minerals, energy and associated manufactures during the twentieth century.[4] Subsequently, South Africa has mainly suffered the *dis*accumulation of capital: its flight to London; its wastage through parasitical investments and conspicuous consumption; its false starts in overhyped 'Black Economic Empowerment' deals gone sour; its periodic devaluation during currency crashes; and its overaccumulation in sectors where profit rates remain low.[5]

Not unrelated, South Africa also suffers extremely high levels of poverty. Inequality is also worsening, as the proportion of black Africans under the poverty line rose dramatically during the period 1993-2001, from 50% to 62%.[6] It is therefore logical that the three discourses stand out particularly well against the socio-economic crises facing this middle-income country today.

Neoliberalism

The first discourse is a 'neoliberal' – free-market – concern with maximising Gross Domestic Product (GDP), showing only passing attention to associated environmental problems. The neoliberal approach is expressed well, if in caricature, in a 1991 memo signed by the World Bank's chief economist, Lawrence Summers: 'I think the economic logic behind dumping a load of toxic waste in the lowest-wage country is impeccable and we should face up to that'.[7] Rather than 'internalise the externalities' associated with pollution or ecological damage, the ready solution is attempting simply to displace these to somewhere political power is negligible and the immediate environmental implications are less visible, in the name of overall economic growth. After all, Summers continued, inhabitants of low-income countries typically die before the age at which they would begin suffering prostate cancer associated with toxic dumping. And in any event, using 'marginal productivity' as a measure, low-income Africans are not worth very much anyhow. Nor are African's aesthetic concerns with air pollution likely to be as substantive as they are for wealthy northerners.[8]

Neoliberal discourses emerged in South Africa just as they achieved hegemony in international environmental management. To illustrate, the United Nations Panel on Water declared in 1998 that 'water should be paid for as a commodity rather than be treated as an essential staple to be provided free of cost'.[9] The same principle was applied in South Africa in 1994, when the minimum price of water was set at 'marginal cost' – i.e., the operating and maintenance expenses associated with covering the next unit of water's production cost.

Providing water as an essential staple *free of cost* for at least a lifeline amount to all residents would have required a nation-wide water pricing policy with higher unit amounts for higher-volume water consumers, especially large firms, mines and (white) farmers. This was not an impossible task, but the first post-apartheid water minister, Kader Asmal, refused to grasp the nettle. His rejoinder to the demand that he respect the ANC's RDP promise of a 50 litre per day lifeline supply of water was telling:

> The positions I put forward are not positions of a sell-out, but of positions that uphold the policy of the South African government and the ANC ... The RDP makes no reference to free water to the citizens of South Africa. The provision of such free water has financial implications for local government that I as a national minister must be extremely careful enforcing on local government.[10]

It took a neoliberal leap of logic to redefine the word 'lifeline' to mean, not free, but instead the equivalent of the operating and maintenance costs (i.e., full marginal-cost recovery, namely the break-even cost of supplying an additional unit of the water to the customer). Under the influence of his own neoliberal bureaucrats and the World Bank, Asmal's slippery semantic solution was applied with increasing ruthlessness during the late 1990s.

The main neoliberal criticism of a free lifeline and rising block tariff offered by Bank water official John Roome, the taskmanager of the controversial Lesotho Highlands Water Project, was that municipal privatisation contracts 'would be much harder to establish' if poor consumers had the expectation of getting something for nothing. If consumers didn't pay, Roome continued, Asmal needed a 'credible threat of cutting service'.[11] As we will investigate further in Part Three, this was part of Roome's advice that the Bank's 1999 *Country Assistance Strategy* for South Africa termed 'instrumental'. Finally in 2000, when cholera exploded in KwaZulu-Natal and social protest rose to new heights, Asmal's replacement, Ronnie Kasrils, admitted that 'lifeline' should really mean 'free'. But a rapid neoliberal reaction by the Department of Trade and Industry prevented the government from paying for the cross-subsidy by charging corporations more, as we see in Part Three.

Neoliberal hostility to subsidies was a general phenomenon within the post-apartheid state. In 1996, Dr Chippy Olver, then deputy director-general of the Department of Constitutional Development and subsequently the Department of Environmental Affairs and Tourism director-general (and main manager of the WSSD) told the *Mail & Guardian* newspaper that low-income people should not receive lower-priced electricity than large firms. (They pay, on average, four times more.) He remarked offhandedly, 'If we increase the price of electricity to users like Alusaf [so as to cross-subsidise low-income consumers], their products will become uncompetitive and that will affect our balance of payments'.[12]

One of the most powerful critiques of the neoliberal version of 'environmental economics' is John Bellamy Foster's essay on 'The Ecological Tyranny of the Bottom Line'. Foster cites three fatal contradictions:

- the radical break with all previous human history necessitated by the reduction of the human relation to nature to a set of market-based utilities, rooted in the egoistic preferences of individuals;
- the radical displacement of the very idea of value or worth, resulting from the domination of market values over everything else ... it is this widespread humanistic sense of systems of intrinsic value that are not reducible to mere market values and cannot be

included within a cost-benefit analysis that so often frustrates the attempts of economists to carry out contingent value analyses among the general public;[13] and

- [market-based environmental economic] solutions, while sometimes attenuating the problems in the short term, only accentuate the contradictions overall, undermining both the conditions of life and the conditions of production. The reason for this is the sheer dynamism of the capitalist commodity economy, which by its very nature accepts no barriers outside of itself, and seeks constantly to increase its sphere of influence without regard to the effects of this on our biosphere.[14]

Sustainable development

A second discourse offers a longer-term, more comprehensive accounting of environmental processes within society, namely the argument on behalf of 'sustainable development' which, drawing from Brundtland Commission ideology and endorsed by high-profile politicians like Margaret Thatcher and Al Gore, has also been termed 'ecological modernisation'.

Occasionally, as we will see in the field of 'ecological economics', this strand of thinking does actually grapple with capitalism's ability to consume and accumulate beyond the limits of the biosphere. Yet the main point behind the sustainable development thesis is a technical and reformist one, namely that environmental externalities such as pollution should, in the classical example, be brought into the marketplace. By doing so through taxes or the trading of pollution rights, for example, regulators assure that these costs are adequately accounted for in 'polluter-pays' profit-loss calculations. However, many argue, prevention is preferable.

The idea of 'sustainability' was redefined in lowest-common-denominator intergenerational terms by Gro Harlem Brundtland's World Commission on Environment and Development in 1987: 'development that meets the needs of the present without compromising the ability of future generations to meet their own needs'. But other thinking about sustainability, especially by environmental economist Herman Daly, takes the argument further.[15] Daly's normative view was that 'We should strive for sufficient per capita wealth – efficiently maintained and allocated, and equitably distributed – for the maximum number of people that can be sustained over time under these conditions'.

Trying to make this philosophy operational, Daly grew frustrated and quit his backroom job at the World Bank in 1995, because 'Although the World Bank was on record as officially favouring sustainable develop-

ment, the near vacuity of the phrase made this a meaningless affirmation
... The party line [from Larry Summers] was that sustainable development was like pornography – we'll know it when we see it, but it's too
difficult to define'.

Daly offered a tougher definition than Brundtland in order to highlight
the difference between 'growth' and 'development' in a context in which
the earth's capacity to act as a 'sink' is a physical ecosystem limit to the
absolute size of the global economy. Daly's definition of sustainable development is 'development without growth beyond environmental carrying capacity, where development means qualitative improvement and
growth means quantitative increase'. Using this definition around the
World Bank, Daly found, 'just confirmed the orthodox economists' worst
fears about the subversive nature of the idea, and reinforced their resolve
to keep it vague'.

Daly proposed at least four operative policy recommendations for
both the Bank and governments:

- stop counting natural capital as income;
- tax labour and income less, and tax resource throughput more;
- maximise the productivity of natural capital in the short run, and
  invest in increasing its supply in the long run; and
- move away from the ideology of global economic integration by
  free trade, free capital mobility, and export-led growth – and
  toward a more nationalist orientation that seeks to develop
  domestic production for internal markets as the first option, having recourse to international trade only when clearly much more
  efficient.

The last recommendation is a radical break from the sustainability discourses of ecological modernisation, of course, and we will consider its
implications in Chapters Two and Six, since Coega is a prime example of
what's wrong with global economic integration. But all four are sufficiently radical that they have been rejected, in practice, not only by the
World Bank but also by the South African government. If, for example,
Pretoria's GDP figures were adjusted to exclude the non-renewable
resources that mining houses strip from the ground, South Africa would
have a long-standing net negative GDP. In turn, that might compel the ruling elites and bureaucrats to begin scrambling for a means of accumulat-
ing capital that is not so explicitly unsustainable.

Nevertheless, in myriad ways, the less radical sustainable development
arguments are used in official South African discourses. Some of these are
potentially progressive, for instance when the 1998 National Water Pric-

ing policy insists that water users be taxed first because of scarcity – often a social construct but in the case of water in Southern Africa, also a physical constraint – and second because their consumption patterns are terribly inefficient and wasteful. But as we will see, the crucial tests of whether development practices become genuinely sustainable are tests of power and need. In virtually all the highest-profile examples since 1994, expediency prevailed, corporations got their way because of power, and the needs of the environment and society were denigrated.

Environmental justice

The third discourse we can label 'environmental justice', for it sites ecological problems and possibilities within a socio-political context first and foremost, and poses firm moral and distributional questions about that context. Sometimes invoking the notion of justice requires resort to cultural defences and symbolic critique, which brings its own dangers. But mainly, the use of the rights-based arguments by social, labour, women's and environmental movements in post-apartheid South Africa has been rational, progressive and capable of the nuance required to transcend 'Not In My Back Yard', the 'Nimby' defence, with 'Not in Anyone's Back Yard!'

Indeed, the environmental justice discourse is grounded in values so well recognised that they were included in the South African Constitution's Bill of Rights in 1996: 'everyone has the right to an environment that is not harmful to their health or well-being ... everyone has the right to have access to healthcare services, including reproductive health care; sufficient food and water; and social security ...'[16]

Tellingly, however, that Constitution also provided a caveat in mandating 'reasonable legislative and other measures that prevent pollution and ecological degradation, promote conservation, and secure ecologically sustainable development and use of natural resources *while promoting justifiable economic and social development*' (emphasis added), quite consistent with international sustainable-development rhetoric.[17] And, underlining the central precept in neoliberal economics, it went on immediately to specify that 'No one may be deprived of property except in terms of law of general application, and no law may permit arbitrary deprivation of property'.[18]

Hence democratic South Africa is, even in its founding document, beset by conflicting discourses, the ramifications of which will be tested in the Constitutional Court for decades to come. Overall, the sense of liberal capitalist democracy prevails, augmented by 'second-generation' socio-economic rights beyond simply freedom of speech, association and the like. But if, in this discursive contest, even many environmental-justice advocates stop just short of questioning the roots of ecological damage within the capitalist mode of production, nevertheless this book attempts to do so.

The objective in outlining these discourses is to unveil what is extreme capitalist (in Summers' image), what is reformist (following Brundtland) and what is potentially revolutionary about environmental and developmental projects, policies and politics in South Africa. This requires that we understand neoliberal economic accounting, attempt to radicalise sustainable-development conceptions, draw upon the moral and political strengths of the environmental-justice movement, and posit an eco-socialist conception of environmental management appropriate to South African conditions.

3. Green business versus critical ecology

In the same spirit, one comradely critic of the green movement, Andrew Jamison, has recently devoted attention to unveiling the incoherence bound up in contemporary environmentalism.[19] For Jamison, there is a distinct division emerging. One mode of thinking and practice, 'green business', has co-opted environmentalism into the nexus of capital accumulation, using concepts of sustainable development. The interaction of academic and industrial research has generated a politics devoted to flexible or soft regulation regimes. The philosophical basis includes faith in science and technology, a methodology based upon instrumental rationality, and an ideological commitment to market democracy. This is the 'economising' of ecology.

In contrast, what Jamison calls 'critical ecology movements' have practised resistance to green business drawing upon concepts of environmental justice. Their repertoire includes critical research, demands for stronger legal enforcement, and active campaigns against corporate enemies of the environment. They remain sceptical of science and technology at a deeper philosophical level, they promote a communicative rationality, and they are committed to deliberative democracy. This 'politicising' of ecology runs counter to green business in virtually all issues and processes.

To dig deeper using Jamison's typology, green business relies upon arguments such as eco-efficiency, natural capitalism and ecological modernisation. The premier green business networks are the Business Council on Sustainable Development, Greening of Industry, Cleaner Production Roundtable, and Natural Step. New technology practices in this spirit include cleaner production, green products and environmental management systems. While diverse, the green business perspective *is* coherent and, to the extent that there is any genuine effort to address environmental issues by global elites, the green business strategy is dominant in settings like the WSSD.

Synthesising red-green politics?

In contrast, critical ecology movements have suffered a fragmentation of what Jamison terms 'cognitive praxis', resulting in four broad and often competing types of environmentalism, 'knowledge forms' and 'knowledge interests'.

First, 'civic' environmentalism includes local campaigns and social ecology. Its knowledge is based on both factual and traditional forms, and its core objective is empowerment. Second, 'professional' environmentalism flows from mainstream organisations and an ethos of green expertise, grounded in scientific and legal knowledge, aiming at enlightenment. Third, a 'militant' environmentalism is based upon radical splinters, especially direct action groups, whose knowledge is often rhetorical and symbolic, and which grounds and expands its knowledge through political protest. Fourth, a 'personal' environmentalism is growing, based upon new age practitioners and green consumers, fostering spiritual and emotive knowledge, and seeking authenticity.

In the final chapter, after considering evidence mainly from the first two of these four categories, we consider Jamison's ideas for a synthesis in the critical ecology movements and transcendence towards a durable eco-socialism. To do so with confidence requires that we first review praxis-oriented campaigning against the dominant green business logic in South Africa, and that we test local environmentalisms for fragmentation and incoherence. It means that we not shy away from the logical implications of red-green politics, even when these are disarmingly radical.

Ultimately, this is no mere academic exercise in discourse analysis. Our aim is to establish some of the ways in which these divergent arguments have competed to win public policy favour within South Africa's first democratic government, led by the ANC. We consider alliances and conflicts between different pressure groups in several distinct cases. Furthermore, we contextualise and set out an agenda for deepening the policy, legislative, enforcement and especially *political* character of future struggles over the environment and development.

To do so, it should be clear by now, requires consideration of debates that reach far beyond the scope of the present state, civil society and business. In South Africa, of all settings, it is crucial to avoid simplistic society-nature dualism, and to establish the material ways in which environment affects the socio-political landscape just as much as happens the other way around. One of the most important ecological determinants of South Africa's development, as argued in more detail below, is water and sanitation, and hence it is to these issues that we initially turn.

4. Water

Water management offers South African government and society possibly the most serious contemporary challenge. Amongst the main problems for environmental management are water scarcity; the maldistribution of water; pollution of water sources; other forms of structural damage to water ecosystems; and substandard or nonexistent sanitation. These are apartheid-era legacies, but in many respects they have been exacerbated by the application of neoliberal principles, policies, programmes and projects.

Access

Each of 42 million South Africans have access each year to, on average, only 1,200 kl of available water, of which half is already dammed. Ineffective and destructive uses of water are prevalent. Water scarcity is exacerbated by South Africa's erratic rainfall patterns, and the effect of periodic droughts on low-income people is particularly devastating, whereas wealthy white farmers traditionally gained access to state compensation during droughts.

Both domestic and regional geopolitical conflict over access to water has emerged repeatedly, with South Africa already draining Lesotho's water and with controversial plans underway to tap other regional sources from Swaziland to Zimbabwe, and with Mozambique and Namibia adversely affected by South Africa's questionable border and cross-border river management. Meanwhile, community protests against city councils which cut off water supplies to poor people have become a common feature of local politics.

Unequal distribution

The distribution of South Africa's water across its own population is even more unequal, measured in class, race and gender terms, than the distribution of income. More than half of the country's raw water is used for white-dominated commercial agriculture, of which half is considered to be wasted due to poor irrigation techniques and inappropriate crop choice. Another quarter is used in mining and industry. Around 12% of South Africa's water is consumed by households, but of that amount, more than half goes into (white people's) gardens and swimming pools, and less than a tenth is consumed by all black South African households.

Minimal water access is one reason for black South Africans suffering by far the highest infant mortality and water-related disease rates in all of Africa in relation to per capita GDP. Access by the majority is improving only marginally, notwithstanding massive cross-watershed pumping of water, for example, from Lesotho, done inexplicably (as shown in Chapter Three) in the name of development.

Moreover, in rural areas, the Departments of Agriculture and of Water Affairs and Forestry are making only minimal efforts to improve water access to black farmers, due to impending water shortages. In contrast to the main existing water supply systems – such as the Lesotho Highlands, the Tugela, Mkzomazi and Mzimvubu basins, the Orange River and Western Cape sources – only a tiny fraction of resources involved in irrigating white farmland in the recent past will now be spent on new schemes for 'emerging' (i.e., small-scale black) farmers.

Pollution

Water ultimately destined for human consumption is defiled by largely unregulated discharges from industry, from waste dump runoff, and from agricultural chemicals and mine tailings/slimes dams. Faecal pollution is a problem in many urban areas due to the inadequacy of most low-income households' sanitation. Acid rain is extremely prevalent in coal-burning regions of the country. All these features of pollution increase water treatment costs and raise public health risks to many low-income households dependent upon direct access to unpurified water.

Degradation

Water ecosystems suffer enormous water loss, soil loss and siltation through commercial agriculture, erosion caused by overcrowded rural areas, polluted aquifers from mining waste, the exhaustion of aquifers from excessive irrigation, and drainage of wetlands and regions with high levels of commercial forestry, especially invasive-alien eucalyptus and pine plantations.

There are also problems in declining natural flow-rates of rivers due to cross-watershed pumping, resulting in increased migration and hence urbanisation pressure. Siltation of dam storage capacity costs hundreds of millions of rands each year. Salination and waterlogging of land is also in evidence due to intensive irrigation.

Sanitation

Water-borne sanitation is available to only around one third of black South Africans, and excessive amounts of water – typically 13 litres per flush – are used in virtually all middle- and upper-class areas. Although a solid-waste sanitation system is desirable, so too would universal installation of low-flush and dual-flush toilets, as well as low-flow showerheads, save water and cut sewage treatment costs, while sanitation services could be extended to all households. That this would contradict current policy on household affordability grounds, regardless of the social and ecological consequences, is shown below. Dumping of untreated sewage into the sea remains an issue. Mass pit latrines in urban and peri-urban areas remain factors in the spread of faecal bacteria.

5. Energy

Similar problems apply to energy: a reliance on and oversupply of coal-generated electricity; lack of equitable access amongst households along class/race lines, with particularly severe gender implications; and related inefficiency in use associated with apartheid geographical segregation and urban sprawl. With the exception of equitable access, these apartheid-era problems are very much worse in 2002 than they were in 1994, and as we will see, access is being curtailed due to the drive to privatise electricity.

Dirty power

The strength of the coal mining industry fostered a reliance on electricity, with per capita consumption in South Africa as high as it is in England despite the fact that until recently only a quarter of South Africans had access to domestic sources. Most strikingly, emissions of greenhouse gasses are twice as high per capita as the rest of the world. In turn this reflects the importance of what has been termed the 'Minerals-Energy Complex' – South Africa's economic core, effectively run by a handful of mining-based conglomerates and friendly parastatal agencies – which has traditionally accounted for one quarter to one third of South Africa's GDP, and which even in the 1980s and 1990s, as the gold price declined, was the most important and dynamic sector.

As one example of the power still invested in these large firms, the parastatal electricity company Eskom justifies ignoring its own anti-pollution policies. It has, for example, refused to install scrubbers at coal-fired stations, earning the wrath of even its own accountants, and explains its actions by the need to generate cheap electricity for export-led minerals and metals growth. As a result, electricity generation has been associated with high levels of greenhouse gasses, very high levels of acid rain, enormous surface water pollution, badly regulated nuclear supplies, and ineffectual safety/health standards in coal mines. Poor planning two decades ago led to massive supply overcapacity – at peak in the early 1990s, 50% more than demanded – yet very little of the capacity has been used to provide low-income people with sufficiently cheap energy.

Access

The meagre electricity consumed by low-income households, i.e., about 3% of the total, comes at a high price in relation to the very low-cost supply of power to large corporate consumers, particularly the mines and minerals smelters. Corporations have enjoyed electricity at roughly one quarter of the price that low-income families in rural areas have paid. Hence even after more than a million households were added to the electricity grid during the 1990s, many could not afford to maintain consumption at levels sufficiently profitable for the state electricity company, relying instead for lighting, cooking and heating on paraffin, notwithstanding burn-related health risks; coal, in spite of high levels of domestic and township-wide air pollution; and wood, whose consequences for deforestation are severe.

Women are far more adversely affected by the unaffordability of electric power sources, as well as in expending time and energy to obtain alternative energy sources. The rationale for the higher prices low-income households pay is the far lower cost of supplying to large bulk consumers, yet these firms do not pay the full social and environmental costs of the electricity, including massive greenhouse gas emissions.

Wasted energy

There are numerous other examples of wasteful and polluting energy use. Due to the lack of effective public rail transport aside from primary commuter lines, South Africa relies excessively upon road transport and especially upon leaded petrol, although unleaded petrol was introduced in 1996. A major sanctions-era liquid fuel-from-coal conversion industry is universally condemned as inefficient. Alternative energy sources such as solar, wind and tidal, have barely begun to be explored. The few hydropower plants, especially in neighbouring Mozambique, are based on inappropriate large dams. Nuclear power, in the form of the pebble-bed reactor concept, continues to rear its head, as Eskom invested huge amounts alongside international partners which have subsequently dropped out.

6. Waste

South Africa still engages in extremely hazardous waste disposal practices. These occur in municipalities, hospitals and in the import of toxic waste. An excessive emphasis on pollution-intensive, export-oriented production systems has worsened.

Local solid waste

Municipal waste dumps do not, in the main, recycle or separate waste. They are poorly managed and often leach pollution into water sources. Hospitals rely on old-fashioned incineration. Dumps are located in sites close to low-income settlements, with a consequent propensity to encourage survivalist dump-picking by low-income residents.

More general disposal of hazardous waste is done on an ad hoc basis, with medical waste and toxic wastes often illegally dumped in residential areas. Dumping of energy-related waste is unsatisfactory, ranging from a poorly regulated nuclear waste dump that services Cape Town's power plant, to the more widespread dumping of ash from coal used for domestic purposes. Incineration of liquid toxic waste is practiced as an energy source without regulation. Regulatory bodies charged with monitoring pollution control lack capacity, and industry self-regulation of solid waste remains the norm.

Trade

There has been an important controversy over trade in toxic waste, as the first environment minister in the post-apartheid government, a National Party appointee, gained cabinet approval to import toxic waste. This led to a sustained public campaign against such import, but the democratic government has not signed the Organisation of African Unity's Bamako Convention to halt trade in toxic waste. More generally with regard to the environmental footprint of production, South Africa's emphasis on export-oriented beneficiation of raw materials pits the profits associated with economic growth – with very few spinoffs for workers in capital-intensive plants – for a cheapened valuation of the environment, as discussed in detail below in the case of Coega.

7. Land use

Aspects of inherited land use that require stronger environmental management and indeed radical state intervention include the inequitable use of rural land, and poorly planned urban and suburban sprawl. The post-apartheid government has generally allowed matters to deteriorate.

The apartheid countryside

The settler-colonial and apartheid divisions of South Africa's land, codified by the 1913 Land Act and numerous subsequent policies and laws, left 87% of the land under white ownership and control, with millions of African people displaced to overcrowded 'bantustans'. People were simultaneously impoverished and crowded together, such that the degradation of bantustan land was substantially caused by policies aimed at developing white commercial farms.

Given the private property protections afforded whites in the 1996 Constitution and a 'willing-seller, willing-buyer' land reform policy essentially designed by the World Bank, the scope for post-apartheid restitution and redistribution of land was severely limited. The first democratic government achieved only a handful of land restitutions, with fewer than 30 out of 40,000 cases were settled during the first government. Not even 1% of arable land was redistributed in a separate programme based on an individualised R16,000 grant, notwithstanding approximately 6% per annum turnover of land in the market and the mandate given the government in the RDP programme for a 30% land redistribution during 1994-99.

Partly as a result of politics, and partly as commercial agriculture became even more intensively overcapitalised, evictions of farmworkers increased dramatically at the time of the transition to democracy. Although tenant farmers and farmworkers ostensibly have won greater legal protection since 1994, this has not helped them in practice. The Departments of Land Affairs and Agriculture lack capacity to intervene on behalf of rural black people, and, argue emergent farmer organisations, the political will as well.

The overindebted commercial farms also typically overproduce for glutted domestic and global agricultural markets, with corporate agriculture becoming more dominant as many family farmers go bankrupt. Corporate plantations exacerbate the commercial farming sector's overuse of chemicals and fertilisers, contributing to environmental decay.

Degraded land

For those millions of residents – half the rural population – who reside in the ex-bantustans, overgrazing and inefficient farming methods on peripheral land have contributed to erosion, desertification and degradation of wetlands. Women are the majority of those adversely affected by environmental problems in the ex-bantustans. Dependence upon migrant labour remittances has only increased in the wake of more than a decade of political liberalisation.

Moreover, the expansion of traditional, oppressive conservation techniques to incorporate human considerations has been slow, and ecotourism controlled by communities is still extremely marginal.

Urban land

Apartheid-era urban planning was mainly attuned to the expansion of suburban land use associated with natural market forces in a context of severe income inequality. This left large garden plots, with consequent wastage of water, for white people and extremely densely-settled black townships often many kilometres from black workers' jobs and from legal commercial and recreational sites.

The transport and pollution implications are enormous, as are the infrastructural costs and hence wastage of water and energy. Arable lands have been another victim of encroaching suburban sprawl, and in Johannesburg and other mining areas the rational use of land is made difficult by mine dumps, slime dams, sink holes and undermined surfaces.

Land speculation and warehousing has been widespread, unhindered by taxation or zoning measures. Post-apartheid planning has offered rhetorical critiques of these problems, but no substantive interventions aimed at offsetting the abuse of land that follows from economic power and market processes.

8. Industrial and mining pollution

Since energy-related pollution was discussed above, there are several aspects of pollution associated with South Africa's skewed form of industrialisation to consider: the economy's dependence upon mining, smelting and the Witwatersrand industrial complex; mining-related pollution; manufacturing-related pollution; safety and health issues in mining and industry; and the environmental implications of macroeconomic policy.

To be sure, some minor improvements have been made with respect to mining safety and health since 1994, but emissions are still generally deplorable, especially the ongoing water table degradation which the Department of Water Affairs and Forestry allows through reckless granting of pollution permits.

Hooked on fossil fuels

The Minerals-Energy Complex has had to extract ever-deeper mineral deposits that are non-renewable in character, and whose prices have generally been falling, often in a severely fluctuating manner, on the world market for the past quarter-century. Since the development of deep-level mines in Johannesburg a century ago, following the 1886 discovery of extremely rich gold seams, the entire Witwatersrand complex grew up around a mining, mining-equipment, petro-chemicals and subsequently luxury-goods production nexus that is entirely illogical from the standpoint of economic geography and natural resources, especially water. The late apartheid and post-apartheid governments' macroeconomic orientation to export-led growth is exacerbating this intrinsic bias by rewarding export-platform developments near the Johannesburg airport, and an export-oriented corridor development to Maputo, including a toll road whose cost will be disproportionately born by migrant workers.

Mine pollution dumps

Pollution from mining and related activities – chemicals, explosives, mining equipment manufacturing – has not been mitigated by either falling international minerals/metals prices or state regulation, in view of the deeper levels from which minerals must be extracted. The state's capture of minerals resources ownership in 2002 is a positive development, but the problem of captive regulation appears to be debilitating.

In the absense of serious regulation, mining has, in recent decades, resulted in more thorough destruction of aquifers and consumption of water; more saline ground water being pumped to the surface causing salt concentrations in water systems; a greater dependence upon cheap energy; a greater reliance on deep-drilling technology, especially explosives; more intensive use of toxic chemicals to separate mineral ores; and a greater need for larger, surface-level slime dams which have high sulphuric-acid content, and mine dumps which in turn are liable to mud slides and severe dust-related pollution.

Mines also often release radiation, and coal dumps often release sulphur into the air from long-term smouldering. Asbestos is a widely-used mineral that is extremely harmful to miners and consumers, and mine tailings remain hazardous for many years.

Environmental regulation of mine pollution has been terribly weak, including in the post-apartheid era. The Department of Minerals and Energy allows highly-constrained, self-regulatory Environmental Management Programme Reports as a substitute for Environmental Impact Statements, downplays public participation, and in collaboration with the Chamber of Mines exempted mining from national radiation regulations. When issuing pollution permits, the Department of Water Affairs and Forestry made and still makes notorious, unnecessary compromises with the mining and steel industries.

Manufacturing pollution

Following in many cases directly from mining industry practices, South African manufacturing firms have extremely pollution-intensive production systems. As in the case of mining, a few large firms dominate virtually every production subsector, and the vertical linkage of producers to distributors and retailers means that even when production is shut down, the import of a competing product is still contained within the same conglomerate, with consequent lack of consumer benefits from international economic integration.

Moreover, the luxury-goods orientation of locally produced consumer products, heightened by an inordinate emphasis on packaging, raises the unnecessary pollution associated with South Africa's middle-income standard of living, while most South Africans are still denied most basic goods and services in sufficient supply. Regulation of industrial emissions is weak, as Integrated Environmental Management was traditionally voluntary. Fines are often far lower than the benefits of polluting and maintaining health and safety standards at low levels. Enforcement capacity is far less than is required to assure compliance with the current laws.

Polluting the workforce

Health and safety problems remain in mining and manufacturing. Cheap labour was a central motivating factor in the development of South Africa's mines, even where this had to be systematically established, in part at the expense of the environment, through apartheid-type labour recruitment and control mechanisms. Essentially based on women's role in the reproduction of labour, the system stretched more than 2,000 km into Malawi and elsewhere in Southern Africa. The artificial cheapness of labour also led to extremely low concern for worker safety and health, with the costs of illness – especially tuberculosis, in which South Africa has amongst the highest incidence in the world – often simply shunted to rural women as men were discharged.

A decade's worth of mining job retrenchments, reducing the mine labour force from more than 750,000 to fewer than 450,000, generated systematic poverty in rural areas that grew dependent upon remittances, and also heightened social tension. Unemployment is itself, of course, the source of high levels of violence, injury and death. Fatality rates have dropped only marginally on the mines since the 1980s, and are still at one death annually per 1,000 workers, although annual injury rates have fallen by about a third, to 15 per 1,000 employees, in part thanks to a long-overdue Mine Health and Safety Act. In other industries, typically between 8,000 and 10,000 major incidents causing injury are reported annually, with 5% of injuries fatal. About a fifth of injuries and half of deaths are in the iron and steel sector. The Department of Labour concedes it lacks investigative capacity, and sweatshop deaths are frequent.

Macroeconomic indifference

Post-apartheid macroeconomic policy, as spelt out in the Growth, Employment and Redistribution (Gear) strategy, contains just one token mention of 'environmental responsibility' in the attraction of new foreign investments, but no provisions to reverse any of the structural economic features associated with the legacy spelled out above. On the contrary, the emerging export strategy is based on expansion by minerals- and base-metals firms, partly thanks to massive state subsidies and consumer cross-subsidies. For example, because of discriminatory pricing that is possible due to concentration of the steel sector, local buyers have long paid a large premium so as to enhance export prices, and as a result US producers repeatedly file anti-dumping lawsuits.

Moreover, notwithstanding wildly overoptimistic claims about job creation, post-apartheid economic policies have generated job losses at an unprecedented level, which in turn are the basis for many urban ecological and health problems associated with lack of affordability of water, sanitation and electricity. Stagnation is the result of the country's highest-ever interest rates, fiscal spending cuts, and import liberalisation.

With an unemployment rate at approximately 30% in official terms and as high as 45% when those who are looking for work are also included, at least a million jobs – a fifth of the formal workforce by some measures – were lost during the late 1990s. The haemorrhaging appeared to only worsen as the world economy slowed, with one report of layoffs in the first quarter of 2002 alone counting 260,000 retrenchments.

South Africa's jobless problem is the worst of any industrial country, and is also an environmental hazard insofar as high unemployment threatens social stability, both in domestic (household) and political terms. Indeed, numerous municipal riots since 1994 have cost the lives of citizens as a result of rapidly-declining central-local government funding transfers, higher tariffs for water/sanitation and electricity. In a context of rapid job loss, cut offs of municipal services to individuals and indeed whole communities are common.

In one national survey in 2001, 10 million people reported that their water services were cut and a roughly equal number suffered electricity disconnections, as non-payments rose from apartheid-era levels of around 20% to more than 35% by the late 1990s.[20] In short, *status quo* economic policies only exacerbate the most damaging aspects of South Africa's environmental inheritance.

9. Conclusion

For the reasons sketched above, South Africa remains one of the world's most dangerous environments in which to live and work. It is difficult to know where to prioritise public policy debate and activism in this context, for each specific problem discussed above has any number of inter-relations within broader social, economic, political and ecological systems. Putting a regulatory thumb down on one problem typically generates unintended consequences and leads to a related problem bubbling up somewhere else.

This is particularly true given a century of highly mobile labour, which left very low investments in self-owned housing, rural infrastructure, livestock and crop investments by many rural and small-town residents. The countryside has also witnessed short-term ecological fixes in one area that generate social displacement via retrenchments, artificial urbanisation pressures and subsequent urban ecological problems somewhere else. These include switching untenable commercial agriculture to game farming, or removing subsidies that had gone to pollution-generating industries in decentralised locations. Women continue to bear the brunt of the suffering associated with these very durable eco-social oppressions.

The interrelations mean that individual case studies will always be incomplete in tracking the implications of environmental management or the lack thereof. The two subsequent chapters provide illustrative cases of environmental and related socio-economic conflict, covering debates over a mega-industrial project in the Nelson Mandela Metropole on the outskirts of the city of Port Elizabeth, and the transfer of water from the Lesotho Highlands Water Project to Johannesburg. Following these cases, we consider basic human environmental justice as well as macro-environmental challenges in the provision of water, sanitation and energy, so as to reflect upon the ways that change in the balance of forces has affected state strategies, capital accumulation, legislative language and social-movement politics.

Finally, the concluding chapter points to the simple lessons of social struggle. The ANC's failures to tackle environmental challenges more aggressively during the post-1994 window of opportunity suggest that activists, regulators and ordinary citizens in South Africa and across the world must become more serious about the underlying problem, which lies in the economic sphere, indeed in the capitalist mode of production itself. Debates over the WSSD are, hence, brought into sharp focus by the host country's environmental problems.

The aim of the following pages, simply, is to shed light on the existing neoliberal approach to environment and development, to unveil weaknesses in sustainable development rhetoric, and to show how environmental justice advocates are responding to the challenges. Not only are apartheid-era and post-apartheid socio-economic practices doing great damage to eco-social processes. This book insists that society must urgently address the ongoing *generation* of these outcomes, instead of just their symptoms. A fundamental change in power politics and the mode of production may well be required to do so.

Notes

1. Sachs, W. (Ed)(2002), *The Jo'burg Memorandum for the World Summit on Sustainable Development: Fairness in a Fragile World*, Berlin, http://www.boell.de

2. See, e.g., http://www.biowatch.org.za

3. Discussions of these discourses which I find persuasive can be found in Harvey, D. (1996), *Justice, Nature and the Geography of Difference*, Oxford, Basil Blackwell, Chapter 13; and Jamison, A. (2001), *The Making of Green Knowledge: Environmental Politics and Cultural Transformation*, Cambridge, Cambridge University Press.

4. Fine, B. and Z.Rustomjee (1996), *The Political Economy of South Africa: From Minerals-Energy Complex to Industrialisation*, London, Christopher Hirst and Johannesburg, Wits University Press.

5. Bond, P. (2000), *Elite Transition: From Apartheid to Neoliberalism in South Africa*, London, Pluto and Pietermaritzburg, University of Natal Press, Chapter One.

6. Similar trends were observed for the two other black race groups: from 26% of 'coloured' people living in households under the bread line (R755/month) in 1993, the ratio rose to 29% in 2001 (due to inflation, the bread line was R1270/month);

and Indian proportions were 8% in 1993 and 11% in 2001. Only 3% of white households were poor in 1993, and 4% in 2001 (*Focus* 26, Second quarter 2002).

In this book, apartheid-era race classifications are occasionally used, for the simple reason that durable residential and social segregation, and racism, remain serious barriers to progress.

7. Cited in *The Economist*, 8 February 1992; the memo is available at http://www.whirledbank.org.

8. Versions of the neoliberal economic discourse include the Wise Use movement and other arguments that place private property relations first and foremost in the ordering of society. Slight differences in the discourses mainly reflect debates over time periods and methods of valuation.

9. *New York Times*, 22 March 1998. An excellent discussion is provided in Ruiters, G. (2002), 'The Economics and Mechanics of Public Private Partnerships', forthcoming Municipal Services Project *Occasional Paper*; drawn from Ruiters' PhD thesis, Johns Hopkins University, Baltimore, 2002.

10. Asmal, K. (1998), 'Policy Directions of the Department of Water Affairs and Forestry', Letter to the author, Pretoria, 8 May, p. 1.

11 Roome, J. (1995), 'Water Pricing and Management: World Bank Presentation to the SA Water Conservation Conference', unpublished paper, South Africa, 2 October.

12 *Mail & Guardian*, 22 November 1996.

13 Such contingent valuation strategies often attempt to measure 'willingness to pay' in the absence of a functioning market. These studies, performed on human guinea pigs in South African during the late 1990s so as to determine how to price water, are exceptionally pernicious. They are one of the contributing factors to the callousness of the full cost-recovery ideology, especially the World Bank, that is explored in Chapters Three-Five.

14. Foster, J. (2002), *Ecology against Capitalism*, New York, Monthly Review Press, pp. 31-32.

15. Daly, author of the seminal *Steady State Economics* (1991, Washington, Island Press) worked with Robert Costanza to found the subdiscipline and journal Ecological Economics, and, with John Cobb coauthored, *For the Common Good* (1994, Boston, Beacon Press). The quotes below are drawn from Daly, H. (1996), *Beyond Growth: The Economics of Sustainable Development*, Boston, Beacon Press, pp. 220,9,88-93.

16. Republic of South Africa (1996), *The Constitution of the Republic of South Africa*, Act 108 of 1996, Cape Town, s.24.a, s.27.1).

17. RSA, *The Constitution*, s.24.b, emphasis added.

18. RSA, *The Constitution*, s.25.1.

19. Jamison, *The Making of Green Knowledge*, Chapter One.

20. See http://www.queensu.ca/msp, or *Sunday Independent*, 28 April 2002.

PART TWO

Unsustainable projects

Mohale Dam under construction.

Mohale Dam displacements.

The development of *under*development in Mandela Metropole:

Coega's economic, social, and environmental subsidies

With Stephen Hosking[1]

1. Introduction

'Two thousand years ago', South Africans learned during a ridiculous mid-2002 branding campaign more accurately described as brain-washing, 'a great port placed Africa at the centre of world trade. History is about to repeat itself'.

Full-colour newspaper inserts were decorated with the ancient Alexandria lighthouse shining across the African continent upon Port Elizabeth, which was flanked in the child-like drawings by a profusion of cargo ships and SAA 747s (Figure 1). Broadcast media advertisements intoned, through a deep, wise African voice without irony, the merits of a port, industrial facility and duty-free zone, 'to rival the merits of Hong Kong, Singapore and Dubai'.

Vast sums of money would be poured in. 'Coega is South Africa's single largest and most important long-term investment in economic infrastructure. In every dimension'.

The alleged benefits are unbelievable, and reflect the discourse of economic growth above all else: 'Ultimately, Coega will enable Africa to regain the economic might it enjoyed when Alexandria was the commercial and industrial capital of the world. The African renaissance is well and truly under way'.

Reality check

Should the deepwater Ngqura Port and Industrial Development Zone (IDZ) at Coega (Figure 2, p68) be constructed, at the cost of massive state subsidies, enormous opportunity costs of the resources involved (including water, air and electricity), and severe environmental degradation? A group of activists and researchers have been sceptically asking this question since the mid-1990s, recently under the banner of the Nelson Mandela Metropole Sustainability Coalition. Their answer, in the negative, draws upon two core discourses, sustainable development and socio-environmental justice, which are grounded in several areas of reasoning:

- Economically, there continue to be extremely high risks associated with fickle private-sector participation in the IDZ, and with shipping and container traffic associated with the deep-water port. With metals markets glutted and metal protectionism on the rise, a proposed new Pechiney Aluminium smelter would be expected to operate on very tight margins. As a result, Pechiney would logically attempt to reduce to a minimum their environmental and social responsibility compliance costs. Moreover, most of the income generated from the smelter can be expected to accrue outside of the Mandela Metropole. The little new employment anticipated at the port/IDZ would be the most expensive in terms of capital per job, of any major facility in Africa.

- Environmentally, the costs of the Coega projects in water consumption, air pollution, electricity usage and marine impacts are potentially immense. The scale of the pro-corporate infrastructure to be constructed by the state from scratch is nearly unprecedented in Africa. It crowds out the basic-needs development infrastructure required by deprived citizens of Mandela Metropole and across the Eastern Cape. Many other long-standing environmental concerns remain unaddressed. At a time global warming is under investigation, the proposed aluminium smelter would be a brutal attack on the world's environment.

- Politically, public law and participation processes associated with the port and IDZ development have been unsatisfactory. Reports of conflicts of interest for key decision-makers cloud the project's governance. Socially, there are significant costs as well, in the displacement of the existing residents and the future economic and environmental burdens on low-income people in the area.

- Most importantly, there are far better prospects for employment creation and socio-economic progress in an alternative economic development scenario proposed by community and environmental activists. The alternative strategy prioritises basic-needs infrastructure

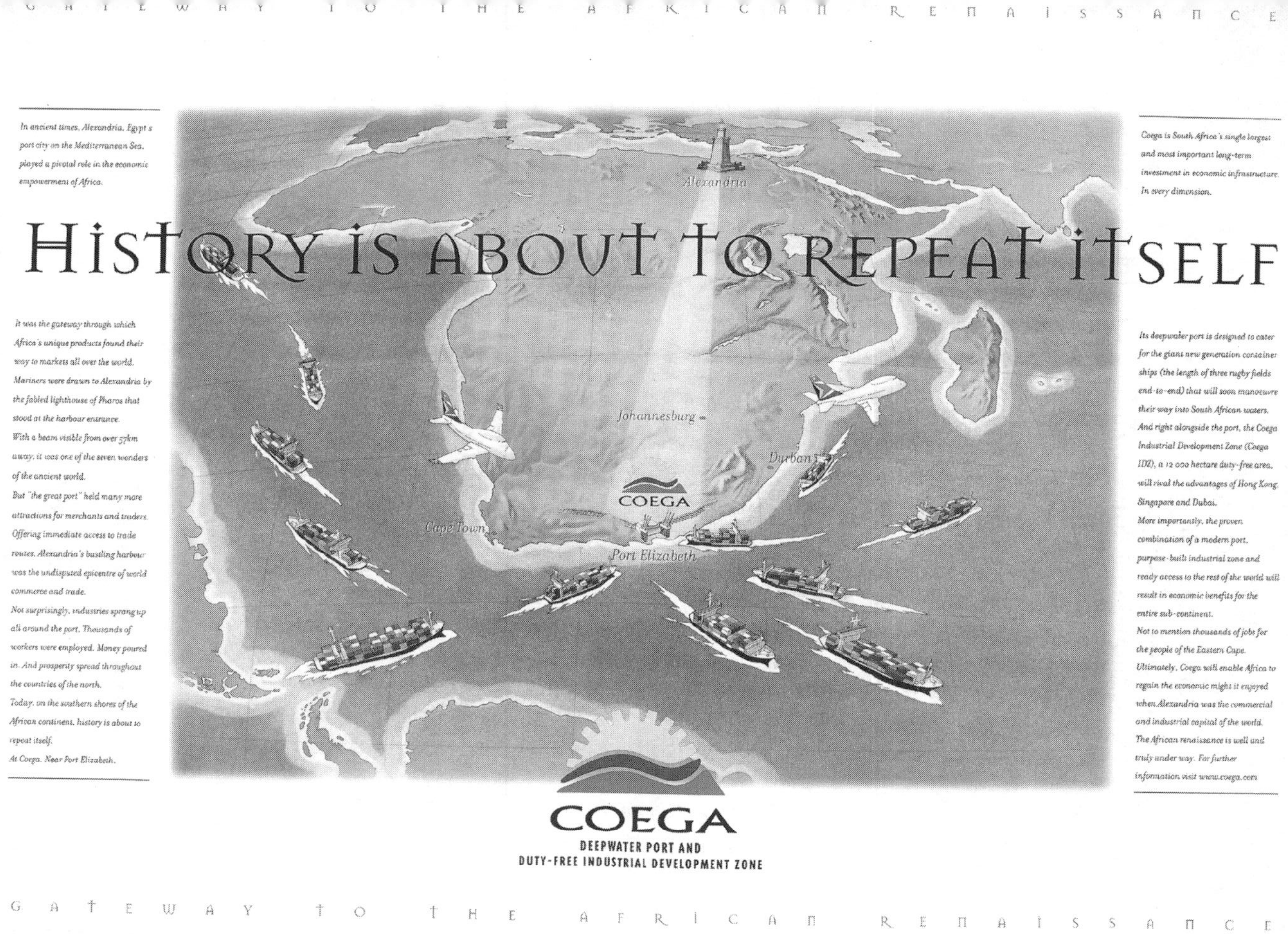
GATEWAY TO THE AFRICAN RENAISSANCE
In ancient times, Alexandria, Egypt's port city on the Mediterranean Sea, played a pivotal role in the economic empowerment of Africa.
HISTORY IS ABOUT TO REPEAT ITSELF
It was the gateway through which Africa's unique products found their way to markets all over the world.
Mariners were drawn to Alexandria by the fabled lighthouse of Pharos that stood at the harbour entrance.
With a beam visible from over 57km away, it was one of the seven wonders of the ancient world.
But "the great port" held many more attractions for merchants and traders. Offering immediate access to trade routes, Alexandria's bustling harbour was the undisputed epicentre of world commerce and trade.
Not surprisingly, industries sprang up all around the port. Thousands of workers were employed. Money poured in. And prosperity spread throughout the countries of the north.
Today, on the southern shores of the African continent, history is about to repeat itself.
At Coega. Near Port Elizabeth.
Alexandria
Johannesburg
Durban
Cape Town
Port Elizabeth
COEGA
Coega is South Africa's single largest and most important long-term investment in economic infrastructure. In every dimension.
Its deepwater port is designed to cater for the giant new generation container ships (the length of three rugby fields end-to-end) that will soon manoeuvre their way into South African waters.
And right alongside the port, the Coega Industrial Development Zone (Coega IDZ), a 12 000 hectare duty-free area, will rival the advantages of Hong Kong, Singapore and Dubai.
More importantly, the proven combination of a modern port, purpose-built industrial zone and ready access to the rest of the world will result in economic benefits for the entire sub-continent.
Not to mention thousands of jobs for the people of the Eastern Cape.
Ultimately, Coega will enable Africa to regain the economic might it enjoyed when Alexandria was the commercial and industrial capital of the world.
The African renaissance is well and truly under way. For further information visit www.coega.com
COEGA
DEEPWATER PORT AND
DUTY-FREE INDUSTRIAL DEVELOPMENT ZONE
GATEWAY TO THE AFRICAN RENAISSANCE

Figure 1: Coega advertisement, mid-2002.

investment throughout the Eastern Cape and, at Coega, the development of eco-tourism and small-scale agriculture and mariculture.

Port Elizabeth elites organised by then regional business leader Kevin Wakeford, and Pretoria and Bisho politicians led by trade and industry minister Alec Erwin disagreed with this reasoning. As of mid-2002, the project was stumbling ahead, being pushed through hyperbolic marketing, and pulled by massive taxpayer giveaways offered to some of the world's most eco-insensitive multinational corporations. There are, hence, numerous reasons to expect the resulting *under*development of the Mandela Metropole and the entire province. However, Coega's boosters must still distract the attention of the state and society from environmental challenges (including severe impacts at Coega), desperate rural poverty and the alternative, sound – but not grandiose – development strategies/initiatives so urgently required in the country's poorest province.

In spite of problems that would have sunk less committed entrepreneurs, men like Pepe Silinga and Raymond Hartle of the Coega Development Corporation (CDC) are coordinating the IDZ for the Department of Trade and Industry (DTI). Although beset by inefficiencies, underinvestment and controversies surrounding privatisation, the Portnet subsidiary of the parastatal Transnet is developing a deepwater harbour and container terminal (Ngqura Port) capable of accommodating the world's largest container ship carriers.

This chapter provides a critique of Coega as a development strategy, and provides the outline of an alternative strategy for the Coega area and for the Eastern Cape, South Africa's poorest province, according to most socio-economic indicators. Vast unmet needs in urban and rural areas could be resolved with the infrastructural resources that will be wasted at Coega. Instead, against advice from environmentalists, development economists, governance watchdogs and even the national *Business Day* newspaper, central government in Pretoria decided to feed the white elephant. We begin with the overall critique (Section 2), before focusing on core components: the economics of Coega (Section 3); the consumption of water, air and power (Section 4); and prospects for a more genuinely sustainable strategy for the Eastern Cape (Section 5) and Coega (Section 6).

2. The case against the Coega port/IDZ

In a September 2001 report for the Sustainability Coalition, *Sustainable Development at Coega?*, we advanced 10 main arguments.[2] Several are highlighted and updated in this chapter. The 10 points eventually attracted a weak rebuttal by Erwin in January 2002,[3] which was followed by a response from Hosking.[4] Erwin asserted that Coalition arguments were all incorrect, but generally did not deign to demonstrate why.

Still, it is worth considering Erwin's position at the outset, augmented by information from the CDC and their allies. Erwin's approach emblematises the economic growth discourse we reviewed in Chapter One. In contrast, our technicist efforts at marshalling sustainable development reasoning were ultimately rejected without being taken seriously. It may be that social progress must await a much more vigorous community and labour stance on behalf of eco-social justice, as the popular alternative to the Coega project.

1) Faulty analysis and false starts

First, there was the problem of the systematic failure of pro-Coega analysis, evident in the port/IDZ's several false starts. The initial idea of identifying an 'anchor tenant' – initially, a zinc refinery (Billiton-Mitsubishi) and then a steel plant (Ferrostaal) – was temporarily abandoned, and then revived in February 2002 when the French firm Pechiney publicly announced that it was investigating an aluminium smelter at the site.[5]

As Section 3 demonstrates, this strategy remains dubious even with an alleged $1.6 billion investment apparently on the verge of being announced. Vast problems remain in bringing such an enormous plant into operation: e.g., global markets remain glutted and considerable excess capacity has developed[6]; the offset programme motivating the investment is still vague and muddy; the new jobs created are few (less than 1000); greenhouse gas emissions have not been seriously considered; the required additional state investments are enormous (at least R4 billion but probably far more); and a local corporation willing to invest in at least 25% of the project must also be identified.

The international markets are simply not sustainable in sensitive sectors associated with environmentally destructive heavy metals exports. Prior to 2002, other metals companies had either withdrawn from Coega or, as with the Pechiney proposal, tried to increase Pretoria's subsidy stake in the project.

The plan to attract an anchor tenant was always based on the hope that the existence of a deep-water port could mitigate against Coega's unfavourable location, great distance from electricity-generation sources and lack of existing infrastructure. Yet CDC's main attempt at justifying the harbour, a 2001 report by Maritime Education and Research Information Technology (Merit, a Stellenbosch firm), was just as unconvincing. The consultancy group had to concede that none of the anchor tenant proposals 'contingent on investment in the port were based on their financial viability ... The notion that the port would serve as a generator of development in conjunction with the Coega IDZ and soon attract sufficient traffic to attain its financial viability, does not seem to have been really tenable'.[7]

Valid concerns are thus regularly expressed that Coega will ultimately be seen as another pie-in-the-sky project. Costs will be passed increasingly from unwilling private-sector investors to the taxpayer. Expectations of jobs and regional prosperity will falsely raise the hopes of millions of disempowered Eastern Cape residents, who desperately need sustainable development opportunities.

Indeed, because of the faulty analysis and false starts, Coega's evolution has generated growing cynicism on the part of the public at large, requiring the overkill marketing campaign noted at the outset. The project has wasted enormous time and funding which could have otherwise been utilised much more effectively, and urgently, for genuinely addressing the developmental needs of the Eastern Cape. Because we anticipate more such false starts, and because only a fraction of anticipated public spending has been committed so far, it is not too late to reverse course at the time of writing in mid-2002.

But we are not optimistic. Erwin has remained in denial on this crucial point, writing in his *Herald* rebuttal that 'Unlike the claims made, there have not been false starts ... The approach taken by Coega Development Corporation has been consistent'.[8] In reality, as the CDC's Silinga had publicly admitted nine months earlier, 'The philosophy that we needed an anchor tenant before work could begin was fatally flawed'.[9]

2) Faith in IDZ tenants is unconvincing

For want of a viable anchor tenant, the CDC changed focus entirely in late 2000, to promote a diversified export-oriented industrial park that combines traditional techniques associated with heavy industrial development, alongside a lighter industrial sector. The strategy amounts, simply, to faith that once the CDC builds the infrastructure, the investors will come. As Silinga put it in June 2002, 'We have to provide the infrastructure. Business would not invest otherwise. Face it, no one in his right mind would want to invest in the Eastern Cape if we don't make the infrastructure suitable'.[10]

Yet in spite of revived hopes due to the Pechiney negotiations, as of press time (July 2002), there was still no industrial group willing to make a firm commitment to the IDZ, either in the category of anchor tenant or any other cluster. As discussed below in Section 3, there are good reasons for Coega's failure, and blame should be in part placed upon the DTI's poor conceptualisation and implementation of industrial policy.

Writing in January 2002, before Pechiney had gone public with its expression of interest, Erwin insisted that 'the project is not dependent on an anchor tenant'.[11] This is debatable as a factual matter, as noted in the discussions of the port, container terminal and IDZ below. But his denial was also contrary to insider opinion. A few days after Erwin's rebuttal article was published, *Business Day*'s reliable company analyst Tim Cohen reported in his column, to the contrary, that 'The Coega project is desperately looking for an anchor tenant, and they are unlikely to forget that Billiton was originally supposed to fulfil this role'.[12]

3) The port and container terminal are probably not viable

Portnet's contribution to the project was fully approved in 2001. But tellingly, the port development project and container terminal are functionally separated from the IDZ, and other problems remained unresolved. Perhaps most significant, it remained unclear whether such an investment was advisable from a purely technical point of view.

The Merit consultancy report, allegedly demonstrating Coega's viability as a port and container terminal, actually raised major concerns, in part because of the study's substantial limitations and omissions. Still, the Merit study offered a damning indictment of the broader economics of container transport at Coega, when read carefully. This point is returned to below in Section 3, but developed much further in supporting documentation.[13]

Erwin's rebuttal is that 'a range of ways in which the port could be constructed ... are the subject of ongoing consultation with various interested parties'[14] – which actually suggests that *nothing* in relation to the port and container terminal was sufficiently certain as late as January 2002 to nail down publicly. Erwin continued, 'The Merit report confirms other studies'. Without citing these other studies, the public really only has the one hotly-contested report upon which to justify the huge Portnet investment. Only the Merit study is promoted in pro-Coega advertisements as justification.

4) Coega will create insufficient jobs

How many formal, full-time jobs will Coega create? The impact assessment for the harbour confirmed that only 80 permanent jobs would be created by the deep-water harbour, with projected temporary employment fluctuating between 100 and 800 jobs during construction. There were subsequent estimates of 350 jobs for the container terminal facility, of which only 20 would be 'unskilled' and 'drawn from the ranks of the unemployed'. If optimal conditions exist, as many as 2000 jobs might be generated by the port and container terminal by 2020.

Job estimates for the IDZ are harder to specify, since no tenants have yet committed to the CDC. CDC staff, however, claimed in early 2002 that 20,000 jobs will materialise, with a R3.5 billion contribution to the annual household income, of which R805 million would go to lower income groups.[15] The mid-2002 Alexandria-Coega advertisements claimed 22,000 jobs. But these are entirely speculative estimates, as we discuss below. The proposed smelters, for example, are some of the most capital-intensive projects underway anywhere in the world – in a society whose main urgent need is creation of employment.

Worse, hundreds of existing jobs are being destroyed in the closure of existing businesses at Coega, such as the salt works and abalone farm. As shown in Section 3, the net employment effect of the whole project is unremarkable and belies the ad man's claim of 'thousands of jobs for the people of the Eastern Cape'.

Erwin's rebuttal was twofold, namely that 'The statement made that hundreds of existing jobs will be destroyed is not accurate, as there is no reason to believe that the activities displaced will cease altogether'. In the same spirit, he continued, 'there is no incompatibility between the Coega development and both existing and new agricultural, marine harvesting, conservation developments, and eco-tourism'.[16]

Time will tell as to which position is correct. But Erwin only *asserts* his case, failing to provide any evidence to refute the documentation of Coega's anticipated damage to surrounding economic activities.

5) The port/IDZ is too expensive

Cost escalations have bedeviled Coega. The estimated cost of constructing the harbour rose during 2001 from R1.65 billion to R2 billion. In addition, Portnet's Port Authority Division estimates that an additional R3 billion is required for subsequent infrastructure investment.

These anticipated costs apparently do not yet include the need to upgrade the train line to Gauteng from single to dual carriage to provide a rudimentary justification for situating a container terminal at much greater distance from South Africa's main consumer market. Durban and Maputo are the main competition for shipping onwards to the main market in Gauteng. Durban's line is dual carriage. The distance, time and energy factors involved in utilising Coega as a container terminal for Southern African and South African imports will probably be prohibitive, as industry insiders such as *Freight and Trading Weekly* editorialists have pointed out.[17]

Moreover, installing even the minimal IDZ infrastructure will cost another R500 million, not including approximately R200 million for land purchase costs, hundreds of millions of rands for purchasing or relocation of saltworks and the abalone farm, and R150 million for 'marketing, management and development'.[18]

Erwin's rebuttal that 'The purpose of the IDZ programme is to add value and therefore increase the income generated in South Africa',[19] is banal, and avoids any reference to the vast state subsidies involved.

6) *The IDZ will force up regional water prices*

Water consumption in the Port Elizabeth municipality alone was projected to nearly triple from the late 1990s to 2025. The local catchment area will be unable to handle this level of increase unless the high-consumption practices of large corporations and wealthy people in the Mandela Metropole are curbed by conservation techniques. As for importing water, the inter-basin transfer from the Orange River at Garieb Dam is itself threatened by the Lesotho Highlands Water Project which also drains the Orange River for the sake of Gauteng industry and domestic consumption, as discussed in Chapter Three.

The Coega IDZ would dramatically exacerbate the overall trend towards water stress. Section 4 provides more details on this point. Yet Erwin accuses the Mandela Metropole Sustainability Coalition of 'a deliberate attempt to create the impression that this [increased demand for water] will reduce expenditure in other areas of infrastructure. This is wrong'. He also cites the 'increase of 47.7% in the capex budget in the next financial year', as announced in the 2002 national budget.[20]

In doing so, Erwin ducks the problem we raised of the *opportunity cost* of providing an environmental resource, water. He makes the elementary mistake of confusing our argument about the physical allocation of water – i.e., the costs and benefits of *recurrent* supply – with the issue of investing *capital* in water systems. He has not demonstrated that the effect of the IDZ will not be felt on water availability, and particularly on water prices, because he cannot.

In any case, as could have been predicted, the national Treasury's large paper commitment to spending increases was not followed through during the course of the first half of 2002, as Pretoria continued to squeeze funding to municipalities. Finally, when Erwin argues, further, that 'Modern industry has to be as conscious as anyone of the amount of water it uses', he again only provides an unsatisfying *claim* of corporate 'consciousness', without any further information.

7) *The IDZ will increase the costs of regional air pollution*

The limited safe waste assimilating capacity of the air is, similarly, a worrying constraint on the IDZ. Projected air emissions from what in 1998 was a proposed zinc refinery would, by themselves, have resulted in air pollution levels close to the limits set for the IDZ, thus precluding the development of any other polluting industries in the IDZ.

The development framework plan for the IDZ envisages the development of a substantial metallurgical cluster, two metal industry clusters, and two mineral and construction clusters in the IDZ. As Section 4 demonstrates, such development would be simply impossible due to air pollution constraints, particularly if a large-scale tenant (such as Pechiney) is eventually attracted to Coega.

Erwin's own environmental consciousness needs pricking, judging by his comment about our objections possibly being, 'merely [sic] opposition to the use of coal-based electricity'.[21] Opposition to extremely dirty coal-based electricity is quite logical and widespread, given the global warming issues discussed in Section 4 and Chapter Six.

8) *The IDZ will distort the Mandela Metropole's electricity tariffs*

Although it is impossible to predict electricity demand without a clear sense of whether the IDZ will contain anchor tenants, it is worrying that the original plans for at least two major anchor tenants entailed enormous amounts of electricity consumption: 968,000 million Watt hours per year. Section 4 provides a discussion of the implications of this upsurge in demand.

The amounts anticipated were 0.5% of Eskom's total supply capacity, 4% of its available surplus installed capacity, and 25% of Port Elizabeth's current demand. There is some likelihood, based on past experience such as Billiton's 'Megaflex' tariff structure deal with Eskom, that the Mandela Metropole will be called upon to subsidise the price of electricity to IDZ tenants so as to achieve comparable tariffs. The risk is that this would occur at the expense of supplying cheaper electricity to households and existing businesses. The risk is enhanced by the potential Pechiney aluminium smelter because, as *Business Day* phrased it, of the 'large increase in the capacity of the plant to chew electricity'.[22]

A few days earlier, Erwin had replied to us that 'It is difficult to follow the argument that the IDZ will use too much electricity'.[23] Erwin failed to address the opportunity costs of using power for Coega that could otherwise be allocated to residents. With excess existing capacity for households and smaller industries in the Mandela Metropole at present, Erwin resorts to *non sequitur* by insisting that new Coega supplies will provide 'access to a clean and reliable energy source for the community'.

9) *The IDZ has insufficient economic spin-offs*

Expectations of economic growth are being raised to absurd heights by Coega's marketing campaign, a point made above. But for the impoverished people of the Eastern Cape, this is an especially severe problem because there are so few spin-offs that would mop up the region's massive unemployment problem.

The excessively capital-intensive heavy industry targeted for the IDZ would, for example, allow little to no opportunity for the development of Small, Micro and Medium-Sized Enterprises (SMMEs), which are repeatedly identified as the crucial sector in meaningful poverty alleviation. In addition, the capital-intensive nature of the industries means that they will make no contribution to redressing the chasm in the Mandela Metropole's economy, between an affluent few and a vast, dispossessed majority.

The Coega project would do nothing to address structural needs and failings of the bulk of the economic activity in the Eastern Cape. Instead, it will simply incorporate a tiny group of people into the affluent sector, while leaving the prospects of the majority of people utterly unchanged.

For Erwin, 'The argument that the proposed IDZ will not have sufficient economic spin-offs and will not change structural barriers to development is not born out by the facts. Coega is not designed in itself to change the structure of the regional economy'.[24] The second sentence contradicts the first. As for spin-offs, Erwin alleges 'a positive effect' – but he provides no information that would allow his claim to be confirmed.

10) *Another Eastern Cape, another Coega are possible!*

For citizens of Mandela Metropole and the Province of the Eastern Cape, there are far better options than the Coega Port and IDZ. In Section 5, an argument is made to redirect billions of rands in state infrastructure funding to those who need it most, especially in rural areas of the province. There are numerous positive multipliers associated with even an increased lifeline supply of basic water and electricity: creation of more jobs and SMMEs, higher productivity and literacy, a cleaner local living environment, improved public health, less discrimination based on differential services, and greater gender equity.

Furthermore, in Section 6, we see how a Mandela Metropole job-creation strategy could combine eco-tourism with small-scale (black-owned) agriculture and mariculture. One eco-tourism initiative, for example, the Greater Addo Elephant Park, has the potential to create 4,800 net new jobs and R300 million in income.

Erwin sees neither opportunity cost issue, once again: 'The attempt to suggest that the Coega project will replace these activities is ill founded'.[25] His assertion that there are no serious tradeoffs in land, sea, air and water (river and subterranean) uses is not credible. It can only be interpreted as a deliberate attempt by government to mislead the public about the likely impacts of the Coega project.

The politics of Coega

In sum, Erwin's rebuttal is devoid of convincing content, which helps explain why he resorts to a coercive tone. By interpreting the Sustainability Coalition's critique of Coega as an 'obstructionist block' to 'all efforts to bring about economic development', Erwin's article demonstrates that he never read Part Two of the Coalition's report, which provides a two-pronged alternative economic development strategy, as summarised below in Sections 5 and 6. By noting the 'number of discussions with responsible environmental groups' with which Erwin will work 'very closely', he unveils the state's divide-and-conquer strategy.

Such political inputs are important to understand, as our conclusion (Section 7) points out. At the same time as Erwin drafted his rebuttal, in January 2002, National Intelligence Agency officials were visiting two Sustainability Coalition members, demanding information on what kind of 'embarrassment during the World Summit on Sustainable Development' – as Erwin feared – might be forthcoming.[26]

The Sustainability Coalition wilted under political pressure in 2002 and began to break up, largely as a result of its inability to make progress in technicist, research-based mode. The injustices associated with Coega would have to be addressed in other ways. And with Erwin's bloody-minded commitment to pursuing Coega at all costs, the rethinking process will have to occur in the wider society as a whole. Indeed, the chance to revisit Coega's economics also compels us to question the sustainability of Erwinomics more generally.

3. Rethinking Coeganomics

CDC's attempt to bring together a Pechiney aluminium smelter, a DTI IDZ, a Portnet deep-water harbour and a P&O Nedlloyd container terminal will cost taxpayers billions of rands. Even if profitable investments are

eventually generated, they will yield only meagre socio-economic benefits. Before considering ecological issues, how sensible is the strategy
from a socio-economic standpoint?

Comprising the fifth largest metropolis in South Africa, the Nelson
Mandela Metropole's component parts from the municipal restructuring
exercise of 2000 include the three large business centres of Port Elizabeth,
Uitenhage and Despatch and their black townships. The Coega promoters
had earlier attempted to stay out of the Port Elizabeth municipal area so as
to set up a deregulated site, but they were pulled in when demarcation
established wall-to-wall local government across South Africa.

Socio-economic conditions remain exceptionally distorted for most
of the area's 1.5 million residents, and unemployment is severe. The mid-
1990s Human Development Index (HDI) – measuring income, health (life
expectancy) and literacy – for Port Elizabeth was 0.67, equivalent to
South Africa as a whole. But the HDI for the city's African residents was
just 0.32, compared to 0.94 for white residents.[27]

At the centre of the Mandela Metropole, Port Elizabeth has a sordid
history, dating to the mid-nineteenth century, of intense inter-urban competition to attract transnational corporate investors. The giant international financial institution Standard Chartered Bank, for example, was
founded here in 1857, and spent the next three decades mired in controversies associated with its boom-bust financing of unsustainable and
uneven development across the Eastern and Northern Cape.[28] The city
subsequently promoted its position as an industrial and commercial centre, as a key entry and distribution point for goods and produce destined
for the regional and national hinterland, and as a processing, production
and export point for local industry and agriculture. An important aspect
of this was the municipal elites' strong sense of the need to compete
with alternative ports.[29]

For much of the twentieth century, Port Elizabeth's city fathers proved
relatively successful at promoting modernisation and industrial development. The local state was harnessed by the white elite in their efforts to
transform Port Elizabeth from a run-down, poorly serviced colonial town
into a suitable place for capitalist expansion. Merchants and traders
tended to dominate the city council. In the 1920s, their horizons shifted
from promoting their narrow local self-interest, to active encouragement
of industrial investment in the town.

But overall, the city's attempts to capture industry such as the motor
sector were dependent upon the dynamic and changing world market.
Substantial export-oriented infrastructural investment during the 1920s
was costly because the Great Depression followed. Later, Pretoria's strategy of inward-oriented investment led to much larger agglomerations of

industrial activity inland at Johannesburg, leaving Port Elizabeth to stagnate.

Moreover, the prioritising of industrial development meant that much of the best land in the city was set aside for industrial use, including areas which might have been more suitable for housing. Indeed, much of the land which came to be used for industry had previously been set aside or already occupied by poor people for residential purposes. Their periodic forced removals contributed to the current geographic skew of poorer communities in the town, including Motherwell township just to the west of Coega. Moreover, the subsidisation of industrial land sales and services diverted funds from other much needed housing and social facilities especially for the poor.

The potential for industrial development of the Coega area was first flagged in 1970 when local landowners and businessmen proposed the deep mouth of the river as a potential site for ship repairs. The proposal never got to the stage of being seriously considered by government as a project. Unfortunately, things would change during the late 1990s.

Revival of an old idea

In 1996, a combination of factors put the idea of building a port at the mouth of the Coega River back into the public eye: increased global trade volumes; trends towards building ships with greater capacity; high marginal costs of expanding capacity at Durban harbour; Pretoria's adoption of an export promotion strategy (Gear); a surge of interest in export processing zones; aggressive marketing by local business interests; and an expression of corporate interest by Gencor in building a major new zinc refinery in the Eastern Cape. At a personal level, Kevin Wakeford, a dynamic entrepreneur who headed up the Port Elizabeth Regional Chamber of Commerce and Industry through the late 1990s, was an effective Coega champion.[30]

The initial hope, from 1996–98, was that the proposed Billiton-Mitsubishi joint venture refinery would be the main industrial activity. This was dashed when a zinc glut emerged and the price crashed in the wake of the 1997–99 East Asian crisis. At the same time, concerns over environmental impacts became more serious.

Subsequently, in 1999–2000, Coega boosters hoped to attract a set of steel plants led by a major stainless production facility. The German firm Ferrostaal was the potential investor, as part of the controversial arms-deal offset package, and would be joined by Thyssen, Danielli and the IDC, which has major competing stakes in Iscor, Saldanha Steel and Highveld Steel. The integrated steel producing facilities would have potentially dovetailed with the region's automotive industry. The scope of the IDZ was expanded from 10,000 to 14,000 hectares.

However, during 2000 it became clear that the negotiation and ratification processes associated with offset deals were going to take much longer than initially thought. Troublesome questions were being raised over the wisdom of the deal, and over the integrity of some of the negotiators. Doubts arose over how a new facility would harmonise with South Africa's existing steel industry, which was already suffering from production far below capacity. The Coega project was abandoned when it became evident that either a standard stainless steel smelter would generate excess capacity and hence do damage in local markets, or that a steel mill to refine existing output would be better located closer to the source of steel, in Middleburg.

Fortunately, these issues delayed a deal. Had the project moved ahead more rapidly at Coega, billions of rands in sunk investments would be at stake. Coega would likely have simply repeated the debilitating experience of loss-making Saldanha steel production, which left Iscor beleaguered with R2 billion in unanticipated debt and cost taxpayers a large fortune through the Industrial Development Corporation's R3.7 billion investment. The more than 30% steel tariffs imposed on major steel competitors of the United States by George W. Bush in 2002, not to mention periodic dumping penalties applied by the US to South Africa, provide little confidence in the sector's near-term future.

Meanwhile, however, the key environmental issue, namely that heavy metals production contributes disproportionately to global warming both through energy generation and sulphur dioxide (SO_2) emissions, was downplayed. At the time, South Africa's decision to abide by the Kyoto Protocol did not seem to factor into the debates. Nor were Coega's Environmental Impact Assessments sufficiently thorough[31]

Government backing against all odds

No matter how disappointing the failures have been, Coega's backers soldiered on. Authorities from central, provincial and local government persistently maintained institutional, financial and personal support for a megaproject at Coega, notwithstanding growing cynicism and even ridicule in the national media, including the state-owned broadcaster.

In October 1996, central government set up the Coega Investment Initiative, to help push the process forward. In July 1997, despite that fact that there was no legislation or rules governing what an IDZ was or how it would be run, Cabinet gave the Coega IDZ the go-ahead in principle. A search began for private sector partners. Finally, in April 2000, CDC announced that Anglo-Dutch Consortium P&O Nedlloyd and TCI Infrastructure were granted the concession for developing a Container Terminal and Logistics Park.

But dramatic changes to the vision for Coega have been a regular feature of the development, with resulting confusion amongst even CDC analysts tasked with carrying out economic and environmental assessments. Pechiney's aluminium proposal was itself in question in mid-2002, because cheap sources of electricity were also being sought by the company in the East Timorese gas fields much closer to Australia's northern bauxite deposits. Thus Coega has become one of the world's most erratic sites of potential capital accumulation. Its political and business backers leave the impression that no matter *what* is proposed by the next passing transnational corporation, they will adopt it with open arms.

But the periodic shows of desperation became too much during the late 1990s. Even before Billiton cancelled plans for the zinc smelter, *Business Day* editorialists worried that costs would be passed increasingly from disappearing private-sector investors, to the taxpayer:

> The public and private financiers who will eventually decide the fate of the project need to be careful to separate sober projections from wild and wishful thinking. The world is littered with white elephants – from steel plants to airports – based on optimistic projections that within a few years turned out to be hopelessly wrong. Invariably, taxpayers are left carrying the can as governments are persuaded to rescue the project rather than leave workers and local communities in the lurch. Separating reliable projections from pie-in-the-sky predictions is never easy.[32]

The project

Prior to Pechiney's arrival on the scene in early 2002, the CDC's view of the project was based on four subprojects coming on line in the near future. The Stage 1 project components are as follows:

- subproject 1: setting up the IDZ, i.e., purchasing 4,000 hectares (ultimately towards a final 14,000 hectares) and building road and rail infrastructure on this land suitable to accommodate traffic related to a container facility and metallurgical heavy industry complex (CDC will be responsible);
- subproject 2: building the breakwater, quays and other port structures necessary to load and offload containers and bulk cargo (Portnet);
- subproject 3: building a container facility and logistics park (by P&O Nedlloyd and TCI Infrastructure);

- subproject 4: building of rail, road and other infrastructure necessary to link IDZ projects with inland markets (Transnet, Department of Transport, Eskom, Department of Water Affairs and Forestry, and others).

Mooted (or Stage 2) project components include three subprojects:

- subproject 1: Metallurgical industrial complex comprising an integrated set of factories producing stainless and specialist (cold) rolled steel. These projects are directly linked to South Africa's arms offset deals signed in 2000.33 The details of these projects are still subject to ongoing negotiation with the DTI and domestic partner firms. Ongoing changes and consolidation in the management, organisation and ownership structure of the domestic partner firms may well slow down this process. If it is approved by the foreign firm consortium, the domestic partners and the DTI, semi-processed material inputs will have to be brought to Port Elizabeth by rail or sea.[34]
- subproject 2: Downstream of the metallurgical industry and other industries will be automotive, textile and electronics. Investments in these areas are expected to flow from investments in the port and metallurgical ones. These projects are speculative.
- subproject 3: A ferrochrome refinery project is at the feasibility stage of investigation.

Derived from detailed discussions with CDC officials prior to the conjectured Pechiney smelter, the following table represents the main basis for judgement, but it remains incomplete due to partial data collection by Portnet and CDC. By 2012, the income/expenditure flows should balance, according to the CDC. Yet it is at the financial bottom line that so many prior incarnations of the Coega project have failed. Given that so little reliable information is available, the new phase may represent a case of blind faith.

Table 1: Estimated Coega port/IDZ investment flows[35]
(R million)

Year	IDZ	Port (1)	Containers
1996-7/2001 (2)	350	50	
7-12/2001	100	100	50
2002	150	600	300
2003	100	500	250
2004	100	400	200
2005	50		
TOTAL	**850**	**1,650**	**800**

NOTES: (1) Does not include road/rail and other infrastructural costs, which have been loosely estimated at an additional R3 billion.
(2) Feasibility study, land purchases and marketing from 1996-June 2001.

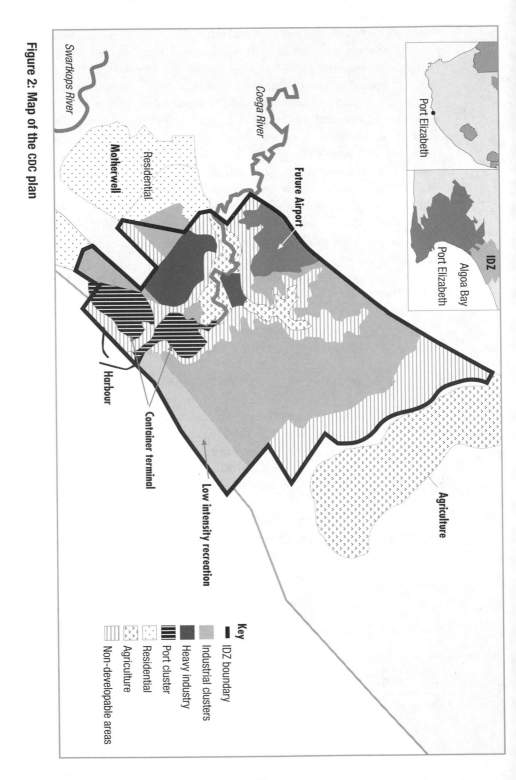

Figure 2: Map of the CDC plan

Is blind faith appropriate for the IDZ?

In 2001, *Leadership* magazine's Ed Richardson termed government's strategy for the Coega Port and IDZ a 'leap of faith'.[36] The CDC's attempt to locate 'leisure and agricultural areas' *adjacent* to mineral and construction industries (Figure 2), and its plan for an airport in the IDZ – while Port Elizabeth's existing airport proceeds with plans to become an international airport – suggests that *Leadership*'s (unintentionally insulting) characterisation was not an exaggeration.

The issue of the port and container terminal is not taken up fully in this chapter, as it has been the subject of extensive analysis and critique elsewhere.[37] But it is worth citing the report released in July 2001 by Merit, which conceded that 'none of the [earlier] proposals contingent on investment in the port were based on their financial viability *including that investment*' (original italics).[38]

In the wake of the withdrawal by Billiton and then Ferrostaal, the CDC changed its own focus in late 2000, to promote a port and container terminal accompanying a diversified export-oriented IDZ and industrial park combining traditional heavy industrial development techniques with a lighter industrial sector.[39] It is already evident that too much faith has been placed in the IDZ, given the lack of investor interest.

The CDC's own economic analysis, by the consultancy Merit, admitted that 'The lack of commitment so far by investors to establish industries at Coega obviously raises doubts about the rate at which it is likely to develop'.[40] Even given the onset of road construction, evictions of existing residents, and enormous hype about incentives for investors, no industrial group has made a firm public commitment to become a tenant. But hopes continue, in part because of Pretoria's national industrial strategy, which is partially pinned on trendy concepts in economic geography.

The SDI/IDZ gamble

There are a variety of general problems associated with South Africa's industrial policy that have a bearing upon the proposed Coega IDZ. Unfortunately, the policy hinges on the promise that the country can overcome its systematic lack of international competitiveness through Spatial Development Initiatives (SDIs)[41] and within these, IDZs.[42] The difficulty of overcoming this problem, inherited from apartheid, is reflected in the massive glut in unutilised international production capacity (worse than at any other time since the 1930s).[43]

Although during the late 1990s South Africa did manage to increase its trade/GDP ratio impressively, that was mainly due to the crashing value of the rand and increase in traditional exports such as minerals, base metals and cash crops. More durable inroads into US markets, for instance, are either marginal or entirely elusive. As the *Financial Times* reported in mid-2002, 'Less than two years after Congress enacted a big trade bill to open up US markets to Africa, the administration is considering for the first time removing some trade benefits under the act ... Pears, along with edible ice and windbreakers, have been the only real South African success stories so far under the Africa Growth and Opportunity Act' – and then pears rose high on a list of probable new protective agricultural tariffs.[44]

Uncompetitiveness in industrial production, meanwhile, is amplified by the net outflow of international direct investment from South Africa during the post-apartheid years. The uneven incoming foreign investments over the post-1994 period were largely of the merger/acquisition variety rather than greenfield projects. Most of the country's biggest companies – Anglo American, Old Mutual, Gencor/Billiton, South African Breweries, Didata – relisted in London to conduct their primary stock market trading, or in the case of DeBeers, delisted entirely in May 2001.

In the context of global economic turmoil, gluts of commodities and metals, and rampaging capital flight, does South Africa's recent reliance upon SDIs and future hope for IDZs make sense? If the Coega IDZ is based upon the existing DTI strategy, is that grounds for confidence or for concern about the project's success? Our perception of weaknesses in the SDI/IDZ strategy is based on several interrelated arguments.[45]

The Coega project fits into the envisaged Fish River SDI that would stretch along the Indian Ocean to East London. The SDI 'development corridors' were formulated in 1995 by the Departments of Transport and Trade and Industry, which aimed to reduce growth discrepancies between the regions of South Africa, as part of a process of economic rebalancing. However, the theory behind the SDI strategy has been criticised for being spatially-determinist (as if merely a corridor locational arrangement will solve durable problems of underdevelopment and uneven development), environmentally destructive, extraordinarily capital-intensive, and inappropriate for backward-forward linkages and for empowerment of previously oppressed people.[46]

IDZs are a variant of what are called Export Processing Zones (EPZs) in other parts of the world, particularly in low-income countries. They all have some common features:
- they are enclosed areas, often fenced off and protected;
- they are set aside for the production of goods for export, so are often located at a port or near an airport;
- they particularly aim to attract foreign investors;

- they have a special customs status, so goods coming in or going out do not have to pay customs duties;
- they offer companies special incentives to invest, such as tax holidays, cheap loans or discounted water or electricity; and
- some EPZs include exceptions to normal labour legislation, environmental standards or lower wages.

In similar international settings, such zones have often performed poorly. In many international EPZs, technology and skills transfers have been practically non-existent, with managerial and technical jobs mainly going to foreign nationals. Given that the import content of EPZ firms tends to be 60% or greater, foreign exchange earnings are often overstated as an advantage of EPZs. The main backward linkages tend to be packaging and simple engineering inputs. Diversification is difficult. And financial liabilities by governments to EPZ firms are often extremely high due to excessive bidding between competitive EPZ locations.

Recent thinking about IDZs has changed dramatically as a result of the experience with such installations in particularly the Organisation for Economic Cooperation and Development (OECD) countries. The large-scale traditional heavy-industry based approach generated slower growth and pollution externalities that hampered rather than helped promote competitiveness. The old, capital-intensive IDZ centred on a major industrial facility is being replaced by a more flexible, small-scale approach based on clusters that take advantage of the synergies created by investment in common sourcing, particularly for skill-intensive processes. Specific emphasis has been focused on research to ensure that there are complementarities in the use of local resources (backward linkages) and on the transformation of waste streams of one sector into productive inputs for another.

Throughout the OECD countries it has been observed that the traditional manufacturing centres and development zones, most especially around transportation hubs, had become 'brownfields', i.e., sites where chemical and other forms of toxicity were now requiring substantial investments to minimise the damages from the past. Because there appear to be important diseconomies of scale with regard to contamination, new IDZs will have to invest heavily in the infrastructure for environmental protection and remediation.[47]

Meeting the competition

What would a Coega IDZ face in the way of incentive competition and other concessions from other Third World EPZs? What kinds of labour law deregulation do competing EPZs engage in? How are women, in particular, affected? While it is certainly hoped that South African trade unions would not permit the relaxation of labour law, the question of whether a Coega IDZ will be competitive arises when considering the lengths to which EPZs in other countries go to lower production costs.

Table 2, prepared by regional labour organisations, provides a partial late-1990s glance at the race to the bottom in Third World EPZs. Enormous tax breaks, suspension of customs duties, government infrastructure and other concessions have been provided. Sometimes complete relaxation of labour law occurs in competing EPZs. In many cases, trade union organising has been brutally repressed, or sub-minimum (and sub-poverty) wages imposed.[48] During the mid-1990s, one study estimated that a third of all jobs in 230 EPZs in 70 Third World countries paid less than the host country's minimum wage.[49]

Invariably, women are most adversely affected by the declining standards. According to the ILO, 'EPZ jobs are primarily unskilled jobs in highly labour intensive industries, occupied for the most part by young women who are entering the salaried labour force for the first time, and who tend to leave their EPZ job a few years later when they get married'.[50] The predominance of young, unmarried women in EPZs is based on several cause-and-effect reflections of their vulnerability. Women constitute a cheaper labour force due to existing wage differentials. They are perceived as more docile than men and more willing to accept tough conditions, and monotonous, repetitive work.

Women are also perceived to possess nimble fingers which enhance their manual dexterity and adaptability to the textiles and electronics sectors that are predominant in EPZs. Their involvement in trade unions is minimal. Traditional ways of recruiting membership have not been effective, partly due to the male dominance of trade union leadership which often results in a neglect of issues that affect women. Finally, women are perceived as secondary wage earners. They are considered to be easily disposable, in a context where flexibility is essential, since the production strategy is so susceptible to frequent demand shifts.[51]

The international experiences of EPZs noted above are particularly important for the Mandela Metropole. Because of Cosatu's ability to maintain the balance of forces, there is, firstly, little chance of transnational corporations gaining the kinds of wide-ranging concessions – especially relaxation of labour standards and laws – required to outcompete low-wage country EPZs. At Coega, the CDC website argues that labour standards 'will be based on an accord involving organised labour and will take account of existing South African labour legislation as well as industry-specific agreements'.[53] Such an accord was still not in place in 2002.

Secondly, the Mandela Metropole will not fare well in competition

Table 2: Incentives in Third World EPZs[52]

Incentive or concession	Period and country applied
Exemption from corporate income tax (tax holiday)	Up to 15 years – Sri Lanka; Up to 10 years – Kenya; 1-5 years – China; Only for high tech industries – S.Korea; 5 years – Zimbabwe
Concessionary rate of income tax	Up to 15 years – Sri Lanka; Up to 15% tax – China, Mauritius
Tax exemption on share dividends to non-residents	During enterprise lifetime – Sri Lanka, Kenya
Imported goods duty / tax free	During enterprise lifetime – Kenya
Duty-free export of finished products	During enterprise lifetime – Sri Lanka, Malaysia, China
Exemption from Import/Export Control Act	During enterprise lifetime – Sri Lanka, Kenya
Exemption from Exchange Controls (or Foreign Currency Bank Accounts)	During enterprise lifetime – Sri Lanka, Kenya
Tax exempt share transfer to non-citizens	During enterprise lifetime – Sri Lanka
Exemption from income tax on capital gains arising from the transfer of shares	During enterprise lifetime – Sri Lanka, Kenya
Tax relief for investment in purchase of ordinary shares as deducted from purchaser's income (subject to limits)	During enterprise lifetime – Sri Lanka
Exemption from dividend tax on funds paid to resident shareholders from exempt profits	During tax holiday plus one year – Sri Lanka
Work permits for technical, managerial and training staff	During enterprise lifetime – Kenya, China
Repatriation of dividends by foreigners	During enterprise lifetime – Kenya, China
Exemption from labour standards	Factories Act and Industrial Regulation Act – Kenya; Labour Relations Act – Zimbabwe; Job security standards – China; Prohibition of unions and right to strike in electronics – Malaysia
High quality infrastructure in zone	During enterprise lifetime – Kenya, S.Korea; at concessional rates – Mauritius; subsidised factory space – Malaysia
Customs inspection at zone (not port)	During enterprise lifetime – Kenya
Income tax on royalties to non-residents	During tax holiday – Sri Lanka

with developed countries' higher-tech EPZs, due in part to the distinct lack of integration of local training facilities and higher education systems with the local productive development. At Coega, none of the international lessons associated with pollution externalities, complementarities and skills-training appear to have been built into the proposed IDZ. In particular, Mandela Metropole has not budgeted for sufficient public and social investments either to upgrade skills or meet basic needs of low-income residents in the vicinity.

Megaprojects

Not a genuinely *post*-apartheid phenomenon, SDIs with major anchor tenants date to the origin of a recent generation of late-apartheid 'megaprojects'. During 1992, several very large mineral beneficiation projects were given the go ahead by the then apartheid government, particularly Columbus Steel, Alusaf II and Namakwa Sands. Anglo's Middleburg Steel was to be reconstructed totally and opened as Highveld Steel & Vanadium. In 1995 Iscor set up Saldanha Steel and the Mozal aluminium smelter was opened in Mozambique in 2000 in part thanks to high-profile World Bank support.

These environmentally destructive, extractive and energy-intensive sites were termed megaprojects for many reasons, most notably:

- *Foreign Exchange*: The projects required enormous amounts of foreign exchange in proportion to the total capital expenditure to import plant and machinery (e.g. in 1992 it was estimated that Alusaf would need R2 billion in foreign exchange). This is why the projects needed state authorisation. But the owners argued that the projects would earn huge amounts of foreign exchange.
- *Capital*: Due to the enormous amounts of capital involved, critics argued that there would be a 'crowding out' of capital for other projects. Again the investors argued that the scale of the investment would serve as a confidence booster for the economy and so attract other investors.
- *Energy*: All the projects were to absorb enormous amounts of energy and there were fears that there would not be enough capacity left for national electrical programmes and that domestic consumers would end up subsidising these projects. The companies, however, argued that Eskom had a large capacity surplus and could therefore afford to provide the electrical energy required.
- *State support*: Given the scale of the investment required and the fact that world prices for these products were flat, some of the project owners argued for special concessions. Eskom, for example, linked

electricity charges to world prices. Also, transport costs were key to the profitability and the projects required location near ports or on special transport routes.

Who benefits from the mega-projects? Columbus Steel, Namakwa Sands and Highveld Steel & Vanadium are mainly owned by Anglo American Corporation (AAC), Alusaf by BHP Billiton, and Saldanha Steel by Iscor (which is mainly owned by BHP Billiton, and AAC). Mozal is mainly owned by BHP Billiton, a London-listed merger partner of Gencor, with the Mozambican government and the Japanese Mitsubishi Corporation taking minority shares.[54] All the projects also feature large share investments by the Industrial Development Corporation (IDC). Critics of these projects argue that the cost per job created has been extremely high (R1-3 million), with no guarantee of supplying downstream industries with employment potential. To illustrate one aspect of this bias, Mozal's wages for construction workers were just $50 per month, and Mozambican middle-managers are paid just a third of similarly qualified foreign managers.

Mozal is also important because it claims to be 'the most modern and lowest-cost smelter in the world'.[55] The World Bank's International Finance Corporation has also been a major investor, with $120 million in loans, its largest-ever African investment. Mozal's energy source, the Cahora Bassa dam, sends electricity to South Africa where Eskom sells it back at a good profit. But the power is still so cheap that Mozal's managers anticipate using 900 MW of electricity at peak output, which will be 75% of Mozambique's total consumption.

However, a critical study of Mozal, by the International Labour Resource and Information Group's Leon Pretorius, concluded: 'Far from being an example of the African Renaissance and regional cooperation, Mozal appears to be reinforcing historical inequalities, both in terms of control by South African capital and social relations at the workplace – especially crucial in the light of increasing xenophobia'.[56]

Mozal is also a profound threat to Maputo's environment, according to Ryan Hoover of the International Rivers Network:

> A year after the plant opened, a cooling tower in the treatment plant corroded and gave way, spewing sulphur dioxide and toxic fluoride into the air ... People living in villages nearby have already noticed strange smells, and strange tastes in fruit from their trees. Others complain of eye problems since the smelter began operating.
>
> According to the Mozal Environmental Impact Assessment, the plant emits 26 times more sulphur dioxide than other smelters, because it does not have a 'wet scrubber' installed, a standard component in many modern smelters. The absence of a wet scrubber

means less effluent from the plant, but impacts on water quality are still a concern. Fluoride-contaminated runoff is released into the nearby Matola River. Mozal has also not figured out a way to dispose of its hazardous solid waste. Currently, the toxic spent potliners are being stored on-site after officials decided it was not safe to allow a nearby cement plant to incinerate them.[57]

Such design and implementation flaws aside, what is the strategy of the more recent version of megaprojects, within SDIs/IDZs? According to the DTI's internet homepage, 'SDIs aim to unlock inherent economic potential in specific southern Africa locations by enhancing their attractiveness for investment. The SDIs aim to facilitate the creation of viable new jobs, as potential investment opportunities, identified through the process, are taken up by the private sector'. In the words of a key promoter who has been an active Coega port/IDZ proponent, Paul Jourdan, 'The SDIs are targeted, short-term and often extremely comprehensive initiatives driven by private capital, designed to facilitate global competitiveness, access to global capital and investment, infrastructure development and sustainable job creation in areas which have unrealized economic potential due to a range of historical and political reasons, primarily apartheid'. However, most potential IDZs aside from Johannesburg International Airport, City Deep and Mafikeng, are located at the coast so inland areas disadvantaged by apartheid economic geography will not benefit.

Clusters, incentives, linkages and jobs in question

Aside from IDZs, other local economic development projects are part of the SDI programme, including industry 'clusters' and local industrial parks. Massive state incentive programmes are typical. All these also feature in Coega's plans.

However, the potential for South African industrial clusters has been thrown into question by the DTI itself. After the Department commissioned detailed studies on thirty industrial clusters from 1994-96, the chief director responsible for the research testified to parliament in 1997 that the entire cluster strategy was 'in trouble'. *Business Day* reported a telling confession by the official: 'Many cluster studies had taken on the aspect of a religious reevaluation where participants bowed down to the God of globalisation, but few concrete and measurable targets had been laid down'.[58]

As for incentives, other countries' IDZ-type authorities have established special benefits to encourage investors to locate within the zones, over and above customs exemptions. In South Africa, investors in IDZs are only entitled to apply for the same package of government incentives as any other company operating within the country. But some of these incentives – such as help for new businesses, the critical infrastructure programme which provides support for companies investing in particular geographical areas, and the megaprojects programme which provides support for investments over R100 million – are more likely to suit companies investing in IDZs.

The generous incentive package announced in September 2000, at the same time as the IDZ programme was completed, appears geared specifically to encourage investment in IDZs. IDZ investors will not have to pay Value Added Tax (VAT) on inputs or supplies they buy from South Africa. According to the DTI, IDZ investors will benefit from high levels of service and investment support within the IDZ, including fast-tracking of planning applications through Provincial Government.

But it hasn't helped Coega's case that for several years, DTI's efforts to encourage manufacturing with a variety of such incentives, have fallen flat. In some years, more than R1 billion worth of industrial incentives was left unspent. Moreover, the benefits to the economy and society that should flow from such incentives, especially at Coega, remain questionable.

Another major concern with existing SDIs is that backward-forward linkages are either not happening, or are inappropriate. Given their orientation towards export promotion, most IDZs will not build in domestic forward linkages through supplying South African firms, and therefore no jobs will be created in this way. Moreover in the case of IDZs that involve steel companies, as was proposed for Coega by Ferrostaal, another problem is downstream pricing, whereby artificially high input prices do not encourage domestic companies to embark on job creation.[59]

Finally, how successful has the SDI/IDZ strategy been to date in creating jobs? Given that SDI projects are very capital-intensive, claims for sustainable new jobs appear highly exaggerated. For instance, Saldanha Steel employs only 700 people and Mozal only 400, whereas Columbus Steel was constructed over the shell of Middleburg Steel without creating a single new permanent job.

Overall, there is no doubt that the SDI programme has created some jobs. But in many cases the jobs have been exceptionally expensive given the capital-intensive nature of SDI-related production. Moreover, the number of net jobs may be even smaller given that existing jobs may be phased out. For example, Saldanha led to job losses at the Vanderbijlpark steel plant in Gauteng. The more incentives that are used to try to attract investment, the more that companies will relocate mainly to chase the incentives, thus replacing unemployment in one area with that in another.

Sometimes SDIs have only created temporary jobs, for example during the construction of the N4 toll road 2000 people were employed. A similar number are expected to be employed in construction work at Coega. But when the short-term jobs are finished, additional problems emerge with those who have migrated to the area.[60] Coega proponents claim that a huge registry of hundreds of thousands of names will exist of existing residents who will be chosen for jobs, but the scale of the raised expectations problem is vast, especially given the extraordinary marketing hype.

The type of jobs created in SDIs are also not optimal. Although the employment divisions of SDIs and IDZs typically promise to employ local residents, often they are only offered the lowest paid and lowest skilled jobs. Skilled and managerial positions still go to people from outside the area, sometimes even from outside the country.[61]

Who pays for Coeganomics?

The Coega project has been criticised from the outset as an expensive boondoggle, a white elephant. The review of South Africa's half-baked industrial policy, itself the regular target of criticism by even the ruling party's allies in the trade unions and Communist Party, provides good reason for doubt.

But the money still flows. Large government funding commitments have already been made for the first Coega project, namely support for feasibility studies and market research (much of which has not been available to the public); purchase of 12,000 hectares; and budget allocations for building water, road and rail infrastructure suitable to accommodate a container facility and metallurgical heavy industry complex. Anticipated expenses of R850 million in IDZ-related construction will occur until 2005. Tax holidays of six years, import/export duty exemptions, and large subsidies on water and electricity inputs have been offered to potential investors.

Moreover, given the shortage of investment capital in the Transnet parastatal, an even more pressing and questionable public subsidy associated with Fish River SDI and the Coega IDZ is the proposed Portnet investment in a controversial new deep-water harbour.

Is a new port viable?

At a time when Portnet has virtually no other capital for investment in badly needed projects across South Africa, a politically-inspired commitment appears to have been made to waste enormous sums on yet another port. Coega supporters have had to perform all manner of gymnastics to downplay the role of the existing harbour at Port Elizabeth, which is operating well below full-capacity, and instead gamble on building a new deep-water port and container terminal.

The cost to the taxpayer for construction of the port is already estimated at R2 billion. However, Siboyama Gama, CEO of Portnet's Port Authority Division, has stated that this figure is only the first instalment, and that an additional R3 billion will be required on related infrastructure.[62] Even without any major IDZ tenants established to date, and at a time that parent company Transnet's capacity for sound corporate governance is under severe question, Portnet's contribution has been approved and is now being delayed only by the land acquisition and consolidation process.

In mid-2001, the debate over the viability of the port was complicated by the Merit consultancy's incomplete study of the impact of the introduction of a container terminal. The study justified the construction of the harbour on the basis of additional container capacity. But it has errors and omissions that are yet to be corrected. It is important to note, however, that Portnet's commitment to the new harbour was made before this study was conducted.

Several other crucial issues associated with the port development project have not yet been satisfactorily addressed. Perhaps the most significant of these is whether such an investment is economically advisable from a purely technical point of view. There are several matters to consider here:

- the construction of a harbour and container terminal at Coega is being justified as a response to South Africa's requirements for an increase in container handling facilities, but while there is undoubtedly a need for an increase in container handling facilities in future, it is far from clear whether the construction of a new harbour at Coega is the best way to meet these needs;
- an ongoing concern remains the availability of alternative sites nearby for most shipping (Port Elizabeth, East London, Durban), and the inappropriateness of Coega's location from the standpoint of trans-shipment of containers to Gauteng;
- Coega is located at a considerable distance from the primary markets in Gauteng which the container terminal would be specifically designed to serve, and hence presents an on-going cost disadvantage to potential clients;
- there is a lack of immediately proximate accompanying infrastructure (road, rail, air) and appropriate Coega-Gauteng rail infrastructure to assure passage of trans-shipment goods from port to consumer market;

- the limited extent of Coega's economic hinterland has not been fully considered, from the standpoint of effective demand for products shipped in to Mandela Metropole;
- there is an ongoing debate in the shipping industry over the long-term viability of deep-water 'post-Panamax' ships that have few ports at which to dock;
- insufficient consideration has been paid to the availability of wide-structure designs for container ships that do not require the deep-water draught being discussed for Coega; and
- there appears to be an ongoing need for additional expensive public subsidies and financing guarantees so that the port can come to fruition.

All these problems have been raised in technical reports, and neither the DTI, CDC or Merit provided satisfactory answers.[63] The most important questions will ultimately be answered with respect to finances: can Portnet, which has been mooted for future privatisation, afford to subsidise the 'leap of faith' at Coega when building a deep-water harbour and container terminal is an enormous risk?

Those finances will have to cover vast new requirements that all international ports will face in coming years, in addition to depth: 3,300 m long berths; three to four cranes; 16-20 hectares of backlands per berth; on-terminal or contiguous rail links; feeder networks; dedicated terminals; flexible and reliable labour; competitive rail and trucking; equipment and customer support; and a medium to large local market. Inland from the port itself, requirements include efficient port-inland interface; multiple arterial roadways; immediate access to main rail lines; an inland depot network; transloading services; intermodal rail; high service frequency and fast transit times; and opportunities within the local market of balancing flows of trade.[64] Where these do not yet exist at Coega, they will be extremely expensive to construct, as noted above.

The main problem we foresee is overcoming further land-transport costs from Coega to other markets. P&O Nedlloyd wants what is widely considered an unreasonable guarantee from Portnet before it builds a shipping terminal: at least 1,000 containers a day to be shipped through Coega. Even if Spoornet continues to provide an illogical and often criticised new rail subsidy between Mandela Metropole and Johannesburg, there is little chance of attracting so many containers into the distribution system, given that Port Elizabeth's existing harbour operates at less than half capacity.[65]

One industry inside-source estimates the cost of the Transnet subsidy associated with a minimum 1,000 daily container shipment at R150 million a year.[66] Perhaps more worrisome still is that impoverished Eastern

Cape residents will pick up a large portion of the bill,[67] although the primary justification for the port and container terminal is to satisfy South Africa's *national* infrastructure requirements, in particular the needs of Gauteng industries. A significant element of the funding for the CDC is being provided by the Eastern Cape Provincial government.[68] The extent to which significant funding from the Eastern Cape government, either directly or through the CDC, is being used for elements of the preparation, enabling and construction of the harbour remains unclear.

But in sum, the use of provincial finance to subsidise a project whose benefits would be principally realised for industries in Gauteng, appears to reverse the objective of redressing geographical imbalances in the South African economy. The positive income effects of the port in the province are extremely limited, with Merit acknowledging that the operational phase of the development will make only '*a small contribution*' to the Gross Geographic Product of the area, while the impact of the construction 'is again *insignificant* in comparison with the gross regional product of the Port Elizabeth-Uitenhage area' (emphasis added).[69]

Can the port be privatised?

One of the main arguments, so far unsubstantiated in reality, for Coega's attractiveness to the private sector is that Portnet's future restructuring (a euphemism for privatisation) will draw in public-private partnership investment. As Kevin Wakeford argued in 2001, 'Coega should be a beachhead for port privatisation in South Africa'.[70] However, that prospect has been thrown into question by the many controversies and difficulties, including allegations of malgovernance and corruption, that have recently been associated with Transnet subsidiaries undergoing privatisation, not to mention increasingly vigorous protest by trade unions and other social movements.

Moreover, as was reported in 1997, 'The problem with finding private capital, as (then coordinator for special projects for DTI, Paul) Jourdan points out, is that the project will produce a real rate of return of only 2% in phase one'.[71] Likewise, according to cement company PPC official Mark Drewell: 'To expect a port's dead infrastructure to be financed by the private sector is totally devoid of economic reality. This kind of infrastructure requires a public sector commitment. Only once the infrastructure is in place can we realistically talk about a public-private sector partnership'.[72]

Given these kinds of uncertainties over rates of return, ownership, and Nedlloyd's unreasonable demands, full financing for the deep-water harbour and container terminal are by no means certain. Indeed, summing up the challenges, it would appear that prospects for the harbour and terminal at Coega are negative as a result of the CDC's failure to address the following:

- the huge, diverse public costs associated with construction of the port and related infrastructure, at a time Portnet is suffering a capital shortage (and faces potential stress if privatisation moves forward);
- the negative impact this port will have on the revenue of the existing ports in Port Elizabeth and East London;
- the merits of expanding deep water facilities at Richards Bay and Saldanha Bay instead of Coega;
- the need to attend to South Africa's container bottleneck where excess demand is already evident, i.e., at Durban;
- whether wide bodied or deep draught bigger ships are the way of the future; and
- the sufficiency of container volume growth potential at the Coega/Port Elizabeth location, and the financial implications for taxpayers, via Portnet and Spoornet, if such growth fails to materialise.

Jobs created, and jobs destroyed

Several rigorous independent analyses have been conducted of the employment generated (and destroyed) by the Coega harbour and IDZ, and alternative options.[73] Between 100 and 800 temporary jobs associated with harbour construction are anticipated, but the August 2000 impact assessment for the harbour estimated only 80 permanent jobs would be created by the harbour. Adding the container facility, according to consultants Merit, 'The initial operation of the terminal will create some 350 jobs if concessioned to a private undertaking, of which only a few will be open to unskilled workers'.[74]

Moreover, since no tenants have yet committed to Coega, there are no firm job creation estimates for the IDZ. But by way of illustration, the proposed Billiton refinery would have created only 600 permanent jobs and the proposed Pechiney smelter's employment would not exceed 1000. The types of employers targeted for the IDZ are also capital-intensive industries that by their very nature create few jobs.

There are several categories of employment that must be considered: permanent, construction, direct and indirect employment. The most important are permanent jobs that are directly created by the proposed Coega port and IDZ. The most optimistic job creation prospects emerged in the first round of assessments for the project, by two University of Port Elizabeth researchers.[75] The 'high road' scenario included not only the Billiton refinery, but the addition of several steel mills which would generate 1,350 jobs, and unspecified other tenants which would create a further 521.

Thus, with a series of major anchor tenants, around 2,500 permanent jobs would emerge. Even so, important caveats remained concerning the optimistic scenarios which should be borne carefully in mind when considering such projections. It is more likely that fewer than 1,000 permanent jobs would result from the IDZ in the near-term. And owing to the technical nature of the work, much of it would be for individuals from outside the area.

As for temporary construction work, including the 100-800 harbour construction jobs, the original economic assessment estimated that building the IDZ infrastructure would generate up to a peak of 1,700 jobs. It was unclear for how long a period this peak figure would be sustained. Had the zinc refinery been built, job creation estimates placed the peak of construction at 4,000 jobs. In the absence of any such major facility, construction jobs under the current proposals might reach a maximum of 2,500, with far lower figures for the bulk of the period. If any facilities are established, this will rise, although it is likely that facilities may be constructed after construction peaks, rather than concurrently.

In addition to permanent and construction jobs, there will be new indirect and induced jobs as a result of increased economic activity in the area. Estimating such job numbers is always difficult, and any results are at best speculative. Impact assessments conducted for the project so far have made the error of applying normal multiplier figures – used to estimate indirect job creation – to the construction phase of the project. Because of the temporary nature of construction jobs, downstream and induced jobs simply do not occur as reliably as do permanent jobs.

Caution is also needed when considering the indirect jobs that would result from the permanent phase of the project, in particular where heavy industrial facilities are concerned. Such heavy industries result in lower levels of consequent indirect employment creation than normal industries. This is in part due to the nature of the industries and the lack of local support services that are required for them, and in part to the repatriation of income by workers and companies based outside the area. Using speculative econometric techniques to estimate indirect job creation, and then presenting such indirect jobs as the direct employment consequences of the project, is highly misleading and dishonest. But this approach characterises the claims made by the CDC.

Meanwhile, much employment will be destroyed. As Table 3 suggests, several hundred existing jobs in the vicinity of Coega are already gone, with no immediate prospect of workers being re-employed. Thousands more will be threatened if the full industrial development proposed ever materialises. These include saltworks (136 workers),[76] mariculture (875),[77] commercial fishing (several thousand at risk)[78] agriculture (7,500) and eco-tourism (975). The last deserves more consideration, below.

Each sector is also responsible for a noticeable share of gross geographic product in the Mandela Metropole, with possibly an amount in the range of R700 million per year threatened by the Coega development. Obviously, because of multiple causalities and imponderable, subjective factors that will only be rigorously pinned down once Coega's construction begins in earnest, this is only a guesstimate. But the opportunity cost of Coega, and the numbers of jobs directly affected compared to those that will be created, together suggest once again that the current Coeganomics are ill conceived.

Table 3: Direct and opportunity costs of the IDZ and harbour

Sector	Income losses (R million/year)	Employment losses (# of jobs)
Salt production	20	136
Mariculture	116	875
Fisheries	not estimated	not estimated
Agriculture	510	7,500 (1)
Eco-tourism	60	975
Total	**706**	**9,486+**

NOTE: 1) Impacts on agricultural production are long term, and therefore of a different nature to the other job losses.

4. Should Coega consume so much water, air, and power?

Water scarcity – relative and absolute

A 1997 report by the Department of Water Affairs and Forestry (Dwaf) found that South Africa's water resources will be fully utilised before 2030, 'and that dramatic changes in water usage, with resultant large economic and social impacts, will then be forced upon the country over a relatively short period'.[79] Indeed, lack of fresh water is a key barrier to sustainable development in several communities along the Eastern Cape coast, and the Mandela Metropole is one of the worst affected areas.

Mostly the issue of water scarcity is 'relative': i.e., it is a social construct, reflecting choices made by the most powerful forces in a society, as to allocation of resources. But sometimes, in periods of severe drought, experienced as recently as 1992 in the Mandela Metropole, water scarcity can become absolute. As we will see, the contest between Coega and others in society over who gets water extends from the city's low-income townships out to the citrus growing areas in the vicinity of the project.

The metals processing and other heavy industries targeted for the Coega IDZ would consume considerable quantities of water, and a substantial water budget for the IDZ must be allocated by Mandela Metropole officials for this purpose.[80] The decision by the same municipal authorities to cut off the water supply to existing residents of Coega in September 2001, as part of their eviction drive, poignantly demonstrates what is at stake. Only a threat of legal – indeed constitutional – intervention prevailed in having the water supply reconnected prior to the displacement of the Coega-area residents.

How much extra water does Mandela Metropole have to share with potential IDZ industries? And by utilising water for the Coega IDZ, does this curtail the prospects for water consumption by ordinary Mandela Metropole residents? In 1996, water consumption in Port Elizabeth alone totalled 166 megalitres each day, with projections indicating an increase to 288–304 Ml/day by 2010, and 423–472 Ml/day by 2025.

The projected rise in water consumption poses considerable challenges for the sub-region. It is unclear the extent to which this challenge can be met by inter-basin water transfers, in particular from the Orange River scheme at Gariep Dam.[81] That scheme is already facing severe problems because upstream, at the Lesotho Highlands Water Project, water is being drained into the Katse and Mohale Dams, and in turn towards Gauteng. The effect of building all six dams, according to a 2000 Inflow Stream Requirement report, would be to turn the downstream Senqu/Orange River 'into something akin to waste water drains'.[82]

As current readily available bulk water supplies from local rivers are insufficient for Port Elizabeth, especially in times of drought, the city supplements its supplies from the Orange River system.[83] The city has no reason to look elsewhere for water at present because it is only using a fraction of what it is informed by the Department of Water Affairs and Forestry is available to it from this scheme. For this reason it sees no problem in providing water in the future for 'its' heavy industries.

Who gets water and at what cost?

Yet, as discussed in Chapters Two-Four, dramatic changes in water availability foreseen in the medium term by Dwaf will require hard choices between alternative water utilisation options. Under such constrained circumstances, water consumption by Coega IDZ industries can be considered a direct opportunity cost. Estimating this cost is hindered by the lack of information concerning the industries that will locate in the IDZ. Nonetheless, there are indications based on international experience. Water usage in industrial areas can be estimated on an area basis. Hence, light and service industries use on average 10-15 kilolitres per hectare per day, while the types of 'wet' industries that the IDZ is specifically targeting use 30-60 kl/ha/day.[84]

The actual price of the water to be used at Coega must still be negotiated. A three-tier tariff structure has been proposed for industry, but the way the tariffs are calculated – with normal or base consumption levels as the lowest-cost tier – will make it likely that only the lowest rate will apply to industrial users. The rate applied to Coega industries is the lowest rate (e.g., R2.49 per kl in 1998).[85]

The CDC's ultimate plan is the development of a 17,000 ha zone, although not all of this is to be targeted for industrial use. The first stage is envisaged as using 4000 ha. Were only half of this to be developed, and were water consumption to be 30 kl/ha/day – the lower end of the estimates for the envisaged industries – water consumption would total 60 Ml/day, roughly a third of Port Elizabeth's present consumption.

Who pays for IDZ water? While the Coega IDZ will likely use excessive amounts – in the event tenants are found – at least two other sets of users are systematically disadvantaged: low-income residents of Mandela Metropole and nearby commercial farms plus potential small-scale farmers. The first category includes hundreds of thousands of people whose household income does not permit them to enjoy a sufficient supply of water for hygiene and basic social requirements, and even leads to water cut offs. The second category includes citrus and vegetable farms that employ large numbers of people, and mariculture whose water supplies will be rendered useless or damaged through pollution.

Mandela Metropole households may be comforted by the South African Constitution's Bill of Rights guaranteeing sufficient water for all,[86] but their lack of water was evident on 1 July 2001, when the ANC was unable to fulfill its 2000 municipal election promise to supply a basic lifeline supply of 6 kilolitres per month to all households for free.

To make matters worse, each month prior to July 1, the Mandela Metropole's largest city, Port Elizabeth, cut off thousands of people, and maintained a list of more tens of thousands still to be cut. During April 2001, for example, 1,430 households had their water supplies cut due to non-payment. Officials had made provisions for only 33,000 families, a fraction of those who were genuinely poor, to get an indigence grant that would supply them water, where households had demonstrated through an onerous 'means-test' their inability to pay.[87]

In May 2001, City Engineer D.M. Michie reported to the unified Mandela Metropole Council that the poor who were cut off because of high arrears 'are likely to demand their Free Basic Services allocation each month. If granted, this will lead to an unsupportable loan on the disconnection/reconnection service as well as being impossible to know when to disconnect again after the consumption of the allocation'.[88] Already, more than half the R60 million funding Port Elizabeth has received of the 'equitable share' from Pretoria since 1998 has been spent on clearing arrears, rather than getting basic services to impoverished residents.[89] The combined Mandela Metropole municipalities saw their equitable share – the financial transfer from central to local governments mandated in the Constitution – rise to R60 million in 2001, which made water slightly easier to finance.

But the problem of competition for water resources remains. Early indications are that even where water will be supplied to low-income households for free, the 'basic' amount will be insufficient. A family of eight will receive just 25 litres per person free each day – enough for just two flushes of the loo. As for sewerage, the metro officials argued in a workshop, 'The sewerage service cannot afford to provide a free basic service to metered customers'. The one concession to the poor is that the hated bucket system, still in place in twenty-first century Mandela Metropole and costing R8 million in annual expenses, is free.[90]

As discussed in more detail in Chapters Four and Five, the solution for a large metropolitan area such as Mandela Metropole is not complicated. Policies should be reversed so that the larger users subsidise the low-income users, through a 'rising block tariff' system that gives everyone an amount consistent with their basic needs. Surpluses raised from large-volume users can be plowed rapidly into new capital investment in infrastructure. Social benefits would include job creation, improved public health, higher labour productivity, micro-enterprise spinoffs and gender equity.

Precisely such a plan for Port Elizabeth was proposed by Pretoria's Working for Water unit a few years ago. The response, by the assistant city engineer for hydraulics, was blunt: 'If a rising block water tariff were to implemented for industry, *Coega would not go ahead*' (emphasis added).[91] In other words, the perceived need to pump cheap water into South Africa's first IDZ prevents the ANC's objectives of social justice, public health, and economic growth from being achieved.

In addition to being able to supply residents' basic water needs, water that may be diverted to the proposed IDZ could also be used for agricultural development. The 60 Ml/day of water that we estimate Coega industries would consume will have, in the medium term, a large opportunity cost in the form of agricultural employment. This is especially true under conditions of water constraints envisaged by Dwaf. With access to the same amount of water, citrus farms in the area would generate 7,500 jobs and an annual income of R510 million. For the medium to long term, these job and income figures are direct opportunity costs of the IDZ. The lack of long-term water supply enhancements may mean that the long-term expansion plans of the IDZ would be impossible.

Farmers in the area, having experienced water restrictions of varying severity throughout the 1980s and 1990s, are suspicious about where the extra water will come from for heavy industry. It is suspected by citrus farmers that in droughts, the Sundays River farmer allocations will be cut first.[92] Their suspicions are based on the observation that they were threatened with a reduction in their allocations during the 1995 drought.

The apprehension of farmers about the availability of water is not shared by the Port Elizabeth municipality, nor by the water consultants commissioned by the Coega IDZ project team (Silva McGillivray), nor by the Department of Water Affairs and Forestry. The Silva McGillivray report argues first that supplying the extra water for the various phases of the Coega IDZ project not stretch existing distribution systems, and second that subject to a R250 million investment being made in water relaying structures, there is still sufficient water presently available from the Orange River Scheme at Gariep Dam also to supply the 200 Ml/day required for the mooted petrochemical industry.[93]

However, if these optimistic assumptions are not true, additional water will have to be diverted to the area through other means. Suggestions include: constructing new dams on south-flowing rivers in the Tsitsikamma mountain catchment; constructing an additional dam on the Kouga river; cutting back alien tree infestation in the Krom and Kouga catchments; treating sewerage water for reuse; and desalinating sea water. However, according to the CDC, the potential additional supply of water from the Orange River Scheme is currently thought to be about 207 million cubic metres per annum.

The recent experience with water allocations of citrus farmers in the Sundays River valley, on the other hand, casts doubt over just how much water is available from the Orange River Scheme in times of drought. It has not been possible to purchase new water rights in the Sundays River since August 1993. The problem posed by the Coega IDZ and Harbour Project is, therefore, not so much about whether there is sufficient water available for heavy industry, but *whether the case that heavy industry can make for using this water is stronger than that which can be made by other industries, for instance, agriculture*.

If water is available, farmers in the Eastern Cape - especially black farmers who were traditionally denied irrigation subsidies - would obviously also like to stake a claim to it. Water and forestry department officials may have erred in not weighing up the merits of the competing demands of agriculture and heavy industry for this water before confirming that there was sufficient water available from the Orange River Scheme and elsewhere for proposed heavy industries at Coega.

Despite massive differences in capital requirements it appears that many more jobs per million litres of water are created in agriculture than in the proposed heavy industry. For each million litres of water consumed, the original proposed zinc and phosphoric acid complex would have created approximately 56 permanent on-site jobs and an annual income of about R20 million from the complex's production. The same water applied to citrus farming in the lower Coega and Sundays river valleys would generate 188 permanent on-site jobs and an annual income of R4.4 million.

Although farm income is typically less than smelter income, there are three times as many farmworker jobs, albeit lower-paid, to be gained from redeploying the water. In comparison, the smelter income mainly leaves South Africa in the form of profit remittances to overseas headquarters. Local ongoing input purchases by the smelters are mainly limited to a few employees and extremely inexpensive electricity, for which the damage done to both South Africa's water and air is not yet accounted for in Eskom's pricing.

In sum, potential water usage by the Coega IDZ threatens to crowd out both Mandela Metropole's ability to meet basic human needs (and constitutional obligations), and the agricultural sector's ability to create jobs through expansion. Much the same set of problems emerge in relation to air.

How much will Coega contribute to air pollution?

Pollution that can reasonably be anticipated at the Coega IDZ poses substantial threats to existing agriculture and tourism in the region, and to the human health of nearby Motherwell residents. Environmentalists have long alleged that air pollution considerations make Coega highly unsuitable for a metallurgical complex or other heavy industrial development. The site is too close to major population centers, and an IDZ in the region will certainly compromise existing agriculture and eco-tourism activities that provide numerous jobs and generate income and foreign exchange.

Indeed, if air quality standards that are necessary to protect public health, promote agriculture, prevent deterioration of visibility and support tourism in the area were enforced, it would probably preclude establishment of a metallurgical complex at Coega. Even if these local air pollution problems were not considerations in the CDC's or Pretoria's thinking (as appears to be the case), South Africa's contribution to global warming through excessive emissions of greenhouse gases should be of concern to policy-makers.

What, first of all, is a valid way to measure Coega's air-pollution carrying capacity? Available data on existing conditions and typical emissions from metallurgical plants show the proposed Coega IDZ to be a 'no go zone' for the levels of pollution typical of a major metallurgical complex. There simply is not enough room, in air-quality terms, for the kind of industry being proposed.

Even if the relatively lenient existing South African guidelines were to be enforced, the emissions resulting from a metallurgical complex would exceed the assimilative capacity of the atmosphere around Coega. As early as 1997, the problem of SO_2 emissions was recognised by Coega consultants Arthur D. Little: 'SO_2 inputs from the zinc refinery, for example, may set a ceiling on capacity for future growth, and thus effectively foreclose on the possible range of IDZ options'.[94] The same problem can be anticipated from an SO_2-intensive aluminium smelter, if the Pechiney proposal becomes a reality.

The dangers of excessive pollution are real. Atmospheric pollution resulting from the Coega IDZ could have significant adverse effects on human health, the economy and the natural environment. Of major concern is the fact that the IDZ is being designed to attract and accommodate heavy industrial plants, i.e., 'dirty' industries, many of which would be clustered in a metallurgical complex. Such industries – including smelters, refineries, foundries, steel mills, and other minerals beneficiation plants – are major contributors to SO_2 and a range of other pollutants. In general, these electricity-intensive beneficiation industries are the reason that South Africa is amongst the world's dirtiest countries, when contribution to global warming is compared on a per-capita, income-corrected basis.

There is also a public health threat. The proximity of residential communities to the area designated for Coega's metallurgical complex makes Motherwell especially vulnerable to adverse health effects caused by air pollution. This is compounded by weather patterns: the relative stability of the air in the region at night prevents the effective dispersion of pollutants. Threats to existing economic activities are posed by fugitive emissions and dust. These could have devastating effects on established agricultural enterprises such as citrus and dairy farming and a successful and promising mariculture industry.

Further, the threat to visibility posed by emissions from the IDZ could significantly detract from the attractiveness of the Addo Elephant National

Park, which is slated for major expansion, and a growing number of private game reserves such as Shamwari that are attracting increasing numbers of visitors to the area. The damage to each aspect of sustainable development is considered in more detail below.

SO_2 *and the threat to public health*

SO_2, a major emission of minerals beneficiation plants, especially aluminium, is known to cause respiratory illnesses and abnormal lung function upon long-term exposure. Even at average annual exposure levels as low as 50 mg/m^3 (micrograms per cubic metre), there are significant effects on mortality levels and on hospital emergency admissions for respiratory causes and chronic obstructive pulmonary disease.[95] From data on mortality levels in Western European cities, researchers estimate that an increase of 50 mg/m^3 in SO_2 levels was associated with a 3% increase in daily mortality.

This concentration is close to one half of the *existing* South African guideline value, and nearly equal to more stringent standards recently recommended by the South African Department of Environmental Affairs and Tourism in the *Government Gazette*. Moreover, it does not incorporate the high danger to HIV-positive residents of Motherwell. People With Aids are much more likely to get opportunistic infections, such as tuberculosis (TB), with higher levels of dangerous particulates.

In other words, even ambient pollutant levels low enough to meet tough new standards based on World Health Organisation (WHO) guidelines pose a significant risk to neighboring populations. The sensitivity of individuals upon exposure to pollutants such as SO_2 and particulate matter is variable. In addition to those who are HIV-positive, people who suffer asthma are an extremely sensitive group. Recent data show that increased short-term exposure to pollutants such as SO_2 causes adverse health effects. One study found short term increases in ambient SO_2 levels, even by 200 mg/m^3, that caused acute effects requiring hospital admission. Instantaneous increases in ambient pollutant levels, which can be expected regularly if an IDZ is established, pose serious threats to human health in the region.[96]

In addition to SO_2, metallurgical industries emit particulates, heavy metals, and other toxic pollutants. Their impacts on human health must also be assessed in determining whether a project such as an IDZ at Coega should be allowed to continue. While such an assessment must be at the core of a proper environmental impact assessment, CDC has not yet released any data and analysis of the threats posed by an IDZ at Coega to human health, nor performed baseline surveys in Motherwell.

People living in Motherwell, where rates of respiratory diseases are already high, are particularly vulnerable to adverse health effects and conditions such as HIV/Aids opportunistic infections and asthma. Domestic coal combustion within these communities, particularly in residences that are not electrified, exposes residents, and especially women who do the bulk of cooking and heating, to hazardous pollutants such as fly-ash particles, carbon, sulphur and nitrogen oxides and smoke. These indoor pollutants are localised, and not likely to be measurable through ambient air quality monitoring (i.e., measuring the quality of the outside air).

Moreover, the proposed IDZ region already experiences significant background pollution,[97] and is subject to meteorological conditions such as local inversion layers that will exacerbate the impacts of emissions on nearby communities by preventing effective dispersion of pollutants. What is most striking is that because of the legacy of apartheid residential segregation, there are differential race/class impacts of pollution, given that Motherwell is populated nearly entirely by low-income black Africans.

This raises the spectre of environmental racism. No developed nation would allow a metallurgical complex to be situated as close as Coega to a growing population centre, composed largely of communities that are particularly vulnerable to air pollution-related health effects. Even in South Africa, such development would not be permitted as close to white residential areas as they are to Motherwell. Health-related injury to township residents will be one of the major 'costs' of the Coega industrial development, borne not by the industries that would profit from the Coega infrastructure but by the poorest and least powerful members of the surrounding communities.

The problems described above are potentially so serious that they are highlighted in one of the CDC's own draft Environmental Impact Assessments. The draft EIA for the proposed port of Ngqura states that 'the acceptability of a proposed development, in terms of its potential air quality impacts, depends on its ability to demonstrate compliance with both emission limits and ambient quality guidelines'. It estimates that the dust fallout levels due to all activities associated with the harbour development will be 'very heavy'.[98]

However, the EIA describes these high dust levels as merely 'temporary negative impacts'. What the EIA fails to acknowledge adequately is that pollutants such as SO_2 and other noxious gases which would be produced by an aluminium smelter act in conjunction with particulate matter to cause effects more adverse than when present alone.

Judging by the existing state of air pollution regulation by the South African government, it is unlikely that a strict and enforceable air quality regime will be established at Coega. Air pollution costs will be borne by local residents, in the form of increased respiratory disease, increased mortality levels and damage to highly productive local industries like citrus and abalone farming.

SO_2 and agriculture

In addition to Motherwell, damage can be expected to agricultural enterprises in the form of air pollution. SO_2 is widely regarded as the pollutant that causes the most harm to plants. It impairs photosynthesis, affects plant metabolism and inhibits pollen germination.[99] Plants are affected at much lower concentrations of SO_2 than humans. Consequently, agriculture is adversely affected by pollutant concentrations that are considered safe for humans.

The government cannot rely on WHO guidelines based on human health when seeking to protect agricultural enterprises from SO_2 emissions. More stringent standards may be required than those meant to protect humans. The citrus and dairy industries in the area from the Coega River valley to Alexandria have been especially anxious that emissions from the Coega IDZ, especially SO_2 and heavy metals, could cause severe damage to their enterprises.

The effect on citrus orchards of acid rain, which can result from SO_2 emissions especially in the presence of ozone, is a major concern.[100] Another worry is that small amounts of contamination from heavy metals or toxic chemicals on the surface of the fruits could render them unfit for export. Most Eastern Cape oranges and lemons are grown for the lucrative export market, which is highly competitive and demands exacting standards for chemical purity of fruits.

Similarly, with regard to mariculture, abalone grown near the Coega estuary are meant for an export market. It has been conceded that air emissions from an IDZ near Coega would require closure of the Marine Growers abalone farm and preclude the development of other abalone farms adjacent to it. This represents a loss of about 875 permanent jobs, in addition to many more foregone potential jobs, and a permanent direct annual income loss of around R120 million.[101]

Air pollution and eco-tourism

Tourism and eco-tourism are widely perceived as sectors with potential for major economic expansion in the wider Mandela Metropole area. The focus for this development is the expansion of the existing Addo National Park to form the Greater Addo National Park (GANP). The status of this plan, and its potential economic benefits, are discussed below. But the South African National Parks Board and others have expressed concern over the impact of industrial developments at Coega.[102]

Another area of concern is the impact of air pollution from heavy industrial facilities on the important bushveld vegetation of the southern section of the GANP. There are additional concerns about the impact of the harbour on the marine section of the proposed GANP, with threats having been identified to the bird, marine mammal, and fish populations of the bay.

Moreover, Coega's potential industrial development would adversely affect the attractiveness of GANP as a visitor destination. In the 1997 Strategic Environmental Assessment (SEA), the visual impacts of the back-of-port and industrial aspects of Coega were intended to be limited by the prohibition on development to the seaward side of the N2 national road.[103] However, the CDC's August 2000 Development Framework Plan provides for the establishment of four industrial clusters, a bulk storage area, two service centres and two business clusters on the seaward side of the N2.[104] And according to Portnet, the SEA constraints on the development on the seaward side of the N2 would threaten the viability of the port development.[105]

Together, according to experts from the Sustainability Coalition, the combined impact of the proposed Coega project on each of these sections of the park would result in a 15% reduction in the economic benefits, and could therefore result in a loss of 975 jobs and R60 million per year in income.[106]

Regulating air pollution?

Can the anticipated Coega air pollution be regulated to mitigate these problems? It is necessary to implement standards that will prevent significant deterioration of air quality in areas such as Coega where existing air quality complies with ambient standards. Stringent numerical limitations on permissable increases in ambient pollutant levels must be enforced to ensure that the assimilative capacity of the air is not consumed by industries locating to clean air areas. Limits on pollutant emissions by new establishments must also be enforced, along with standards requiring the use of the best available emissions control technologies. Such standards must be enforced at Coega to preserve and enhance air quality levels and maintain the aesthetic and tourism appeal of the region, in addition to preventing adverse effects on human health and existing enterprises such as agriculture.

To regulate more effectively than Pretoria has traditionally done, an air quality authority will have to be established with specific responsibilities for the Coega IDZ. Who would fund such an authority, and would it have the legal authority and the resources (human and technological) necessary to manage air quality in the area? Inadequate provisions for air pollution regulation in South Africa suggest that it is highly unlikely that an effective regulator will be established at Coega.

This pessimistic conclusion is even more logical in view of two other factors: the CDC's own insufficient guidelines and the disregard with which Pretoria and the CDC view the problem of greenhouse gas emission. The SEA, released in 1997, recommends guidelines for air pollutants, including particulate matter and SO_2.[107] These guidelines, particularly the 24-hour averages, are much more lenient than the WHO guidelines for SO_2, and are inadequate to protect public health. Indeed, air pollution guidelines originally recommended by the developers' own consultants as necessary to safeguard human health have been thrown out in favour of much higher levels of pollution, a change that has not been justified.

Does the political will exist to establish and enforce the necessary standards at Coega? The SEA estimated that the initially proposed zinc refinery/phosphoric acid plant combination would cause ambient SO_2 concentrations to the tune of 59 mg/m^3 (24-hour average), or 44% of the WHO standards. This would be in addition to existing 'background' levels of SO_2. A mini steel plant would emit five times as much sulphur oxides as the above combination, and an iron/steel plant about as much. Copper smelters emit two-and-a-half times as much SO_2 as a zinc refinery/phosphoric acid plant combination.[108]

If SEA estimates are accurate, either a copper smelter or a mini steel plant alone at Coega will render the background SO_2 levels unacceptable by WHO standards. At this point, aside from the Pechiney aluminium smelter proposal, it is not clear what, if any, metallurgical industries will be located at Coega. But air quality data show, simply, that there isn't the assimilating capacity for a metallurgical complex of the type proposed.

The role of Coega industry in global warming

Finally, in relation to air pollution, there is also the matter of South Africa's enormous responsibility for global warming. This issue is not one, obviously, that gets resolved at the level of a local project or of state regulation, and so is taken up again in Chapter Six as a national policy problem. But as for the proposed energy-intensive smelting at Coega, any assessment of the air pollution impacts must grapple with an issue that will be of central importance to the world for many years to come: greenhouse gas emissions.

Testifying in parliament to the National Assembly's minerals and energy and environmental affairs committees, University of Cape Town Energy and Development Research Centre analyst Harald Winkler observed,

> Compared to industrialised countries, South Africa puts out three times as much carbon dioxide to produce one US dollar of economic output. Other developing countries, such as China, India and Brazil, are much lower ...We cannot afford to wait until we are pressurised into a [greenhouse gas reduction] commitment ... We need to become proactive on climate change. If any commitment is required of developing countries in future, South Africa is in deep trouble.[109]

Four fifths of the worst greenhouse gases are related to energy use. As discussed next, the most disturbing aspect of the Pechiney aluminium smelter proposal is, as *Business Day* phrased it, the 'large increase in the capacity of the plant to chew electricity'.[110]

Will Coega use excessive electricity?

Given the failure of Coega to attract anchor tenants to date, estimates of electricity consumption are necessarily speculative. Instead, until Pecheney releases its own projections about smelter demand, estimates of potential usage must rely upon a proxy. Expectations were established by the two main firms associated with the zinc smelter in 1998, Billiton and Kynoch. They estimated peak consumption equivalent to about 0.5% of Eskom's total supply capacity and 4% of its available surplus installed capacity.[111] The amount is equivalent to a quarter of Port Elizabeth's consumption that year.

How much should this large volume cost? Thanks to economies of scale and purchasing power, mass amounts of electricity are on offer to any large consumer at an extremely cheap rate (often below R0.08 per kiloWatt hour), equivalent to the Alusaf concession which has been described by Eskom as the lowest-priced electricity in the world.[112]

There are major additional capital expenses associated with Coega's power supply. In May 2002, minister of public enterprises Jeff Radebe noted that Eskom would have to invest R1.2 billion in order to strengthen the transmission grid for Coega.[113] In the short run, Eskom budgeted R130 million for high-voltage electricity to the Coega IDZ. Pechiney requires huge power increases for its AP50 smelter, which is far more energy intensive than the systems in place at the Hillside and Mozal plants. Those plants are much closer to Eskom's main generation capacity in Mpumalanga province, raising yet more questions about the merits of Coega's location, given that the main ingredient Pechiney anticipates importing is alumina bauxite from Australia.[114]

At some point in the future, there may also be capital investments required for natural gas transmission from the Western Cape. A liquid petroleum gas facility has also been mentioned as an option.[115]

As we will explore in more detail in Chapter Six, the generous treatment for the smelters stands in stark contrast to electricity cut offs and to the municipal government's failure to connect low-income residents of the Mandela Metropole, as well as low-income people across the Eastern Cape province. The problem, in other words, remains identical to that argued by environmentalist Richard Fuggle in a 1997 review of the Coega project: 'No comparative studies or tables are presented to show that the inhabitants of Port Elizabeth will be better served by the Coega proposals than by the equivalent amount of money being spent to improve existing infrastructure in the region'.[116]

When it comes to cross-subsidising low-income users, for example, there are ominous implications of Coega's anticipated high-volume consumption of cheap electricity. In July 2001, Mandela Metropole residents anticipated getting access to the free municipal services that the ANC promised during the 2000 municipal election, but none of the area's municipalities honoured that undertaking. The two main contradictions are the tendency to privatisation, which mitigates against servicing the poor as a result of the cherry-picking incentive, and the related failure of the Mandela Metropole to apply a steep, rising block tariff.[117] These are discussed in relation to both water and electricity in subsequent chapters.

But next, we borrow the phrase 'Another world is possible!', used at the Porto Alegre World Social Forum, the annual international progressive gathering that rejects neoliberal development. It is useful to show the two prongs of the alternative strategy. The first is infrastructure resources for the Eastern Cape in general, and low-income areas in particular. The second is the alternative, environmentally appropriate use of space around Coega: for agriculture, mariculture and eco-tourism.

5. Another Eastern Cape is possible

There is no question that the Eastern Cape needs massive infrastructure investment, with the aim of generating employment, economic development and ecological sustainability. It is especially crucial to eradicate the enormous backlogs associated with roads, water, electricity, housing, education and health infrastructure.

Likewise, the Mandela Metropole also requires dramatic changes in consumption patterns so that low-income people in Motherwell and many other townships can access a fair share of water and electricity, and breath the local air safely. As we have seen, the bias towards subsidising the Coega port/IDZ makes the distribution of these basic infrastructural needs to Mandela Metropole residents far more difficult.

Recall the mandate offered by the 1994 Reconstruction and Development Programme for a *balanced* approach to infrastructure provision:

> The RDP integrates growth, development, reconstruction and redistribution into a unified programme. The key to this link is an infrastructural programme that will provide access to modern and effective services like electricity, water, telecommunications, transport, health, education and training for all our people. This programme will both meet basic needs and open up previously suppressed economic and human potential in urban and rural areas. In turn this will lead to an increased output in all sectors of the economy, and by modernising our infrastructure and human resource development, we will also enhance export capacity. Success in linking reconstruction and development is essential if we are to achieve peace and security for all.[118]

Infrastructure linkages

The desired linkages are obvious: 'major infrastructural programmes should stimulate the economy through increased demand for materials such as bricks and steel, appliances such as television sets and washing machines, and many other products'. In addition, the RDP continues, 'The key area where special measures to create jobs can link to building the economy and meeting basic needs is in redressing apartheid-created infrastructural disparities ... In particular, industrial expansion should follow from the extension of infrastructure to urban, peri-urban and rural constituencies'.[119]

Does the strong, progressive vision of infrastructure investment exist in Bisho? Or are many other opportunities for infrastructure extension to the province being overlooked because of the giganticism, wild claims and leaps of faith made by port/IDZ proponents? According to Rev. M.A. Stofile, premier of the Eastern Cape, in the struggle for 'a good balance between social stability and development on the one hand, and transformation to democracy and self-determination (as opposed to dependency on hand-outs) on the other hand ... we have simply not addressed the above challenges with adequate scale and impact'.[120]

This chapter has argued that 'balance' between economic development, social stability, environmental stewardship and political empowerment has not even been sought in the case of the proposed Coega project. It is a travesty to spend R5 billion or more in public infrastructure capital for a project whose new jobs for unskilled workers can be counted in the dozens, at best. If the Pechiney deal is consolidated, R4 billion or more in additional investment funds are expected from the IDC as a partner, yet only 1,000 new jobs will be created.

To make matters worse, the subsidised water, electricity and other resources that should be allocated to low-income people of the Eastern Cape will instead will flow to the well-connected companies that may eventually populate the Coega IDZ.

It is ironic that such public resources will be made available in the province's sole metropolitan area: a metro that is better equipped than any municipality in the province to provide its citizens with infrastructural resources.

Inequality in resource distribution was flagged in a 2001 infrastructure funding report for the provincial Ministry of Finance and Economic Affairs:

> The demographic and socio-economic structure of the Eastern Cape Province is characterised by severe spatial and racial discontinuities and inequalities that stem from the effects of decades of apartheid policies. Whilst these circumstances are deeply entrenched, and will continue to affect the nature and distribution of economic development for many years, it is imperative that they should be identified and addressed through constructive planning and reorganisation of the provincial space economy.[121]

If Eastern Cape leaders were serious about these problems, how would they go about designing an alternative infrastructure investment strategy? Ironically, such a strategy does exist in the document cited above. But the main deterrent is lack funding for capital investment.[122]

Less uneven development

There are three major aspects of the provincial economic-development vision that must be considered at the outset of any discussion of alternatives: geographical bias; urban or rural bias; and sectoral bias.

Firstly, there is the matter of *uneven development* within the province, which favours the Mandela Metropole and other sites in the white-dominated Western region. According to Stofile,

In our Province, historical imbalances between the Western and the Eastern parts must be taken into account. The Western region is better endowed (economic developmentally speaking). The gap can only be narrowed through the development of the productive forces. The Western region must be encouraged to accelerate its economic development. But policies must be developed to bolster the economy of the eastern part. Available natural resources must be utilised and non-available infrastructure provided.[123]

Secondly, provincial leaders have correctly focused on *rural underdevelopment* as their greatest shortcoming. Stofile highlighted the development of productive agricultural forces amongst the lowest-income residents:

To begin with, it is a well known fact that the Eastern Cape is a predominantly rural province characterised by extreme levels of poverty, landlessness, huge infrastructure backlogs, economic stagnation and unemployment ... Above all, the irregular agricultural production must be attended to. We must improve our capacity to feed ourselves and our neighbours. As productivity improves and the quality of the products becomes better, the income levels of the farmers and peasants will also improve. Cottage and village industries will develop. The lives of our people will improve.[124]

Thirdly, the most important backlogs identified in rural Eastern Cape relate to basic infrastructure and services. As analysed by the main development think-tank in Bisho, the Eastern Cape Socio-Economic Consultative Council,

Within the province, poverty is most concentrated in the rural areas, especially the former homeland areas which comprise a disproportionately high number of women and youth. The Eastern Cape is by far the poorest province in the country. The recently released 'Measuring Poverty' Report of Statistics South Africa found that the Wild Coast and the Kei District Council areas are the poorest in the country, and that we are home to 28 of the 30 poorest magisterial districts across all provinces. Apartheid underdevelopment has left the province with enormous infrastructure backlogs (roads, housing, health, education, telecommunications, water, sanitation, electricity, etc). The Eastern Cape has recently been ranked by Statistics South Africa as the province with the largest infrastructure and service backlog.[125]

Infrastructure investment needs in the Eastern Cape

An estimated R5 billion in public funds will be spent on the development of the Coega port and associated infrastructure.[126] Could those funds be better used for infrastructure elsewhere in the Eastern Cape?

The needs are enormous. The Eastern Cape is home to 6.3 million people, according to the last (1996) census. Of 1.34 million people counted in the Western district, 91% are urban residents. Of 1.09 million people in the Kei district, 91% are rural residents, and of 1.32 million in the Wild Coast district, 98% are rural. The Amatola, Stormberg and Drakensberg districts fall inbetween, with 40% of their total of 2.45 million people urbanised.

It was no exaggeration for Stofile to argue that 'The Western region is better endowed (economic developmentally speaking). The gap can only be narrowed through the development of the productive forces'. The R5 billion in public monies earmarked for the risky Coega project could instead make an enormous dent in the huge backlogs of both 'productive forces' and infrastructure across the province, generating impressive economic multipliers as well as alleviating – and in many cases eradicating – poverty.

The opportunity cost of investing in Coega, in relation to other infrastructure investments elsewhere in the province, deserves even brief investigation. The following considerations are only the first cut at understanding the urgent infrastructure needs that are not being met.

Increasing the productive forces in the Eastern Cape would involve massive state infrastructure investment in areas that generate human capital, offer better transport and assure that workers and communities are more productive as a result of getting access to electricity and water – the first time in the lives of many. Central to the strategy would be balancing the location of manufacturing within the region. According to a November 2000 infrastructure study for the provincial Ministry of Finance and Economic Affairs,

> The distribution of manufacturing is heavily skewed towards the urban centres of Port Elizabeth-Uitenhage and the Greater East London Area, where the Province's principal ports constitute a focus for industrial investment and development. In this regard, it has been indicated that some 90% of manufacturing Gross Geographic Product is generated in these two urban concentrations, which means that the benefits of manufacturing investment do not extend to the impoverished rural areas, specifically the previous bantustan areas, discussed above, and this contributes further to their marginalisation and exclusion from the Province's economic system.[127]

Basic infrastructure investments will make the Eastern Cape more productive. Such investments are desperately lacking, according to the infrastructure study, in

> housing and access to a wide range of basic services including water, sanitation, electricity/energy, telephones, education, health and safety/security. In all of these instances, the distributional characteristics reflect severe inequalities, which are to the disadvantage of rural areas, in general; and the previous bantustan areas, in particular. Thus, the imperative for addressing these entrenched spatial inequalities in the Provincial development planning and budgeting process cannot be overemphasised.[128]

What provincial policy guidance – even if merely rhetorical – is there? The main issue to be considered from the 1997 *Provincial Growth and Development Strategy* is how to determine 'crucial points of departure in deciding on the allocation of resources in the Provincial budgeting process'. The mandate from the Strategy's Provincial Priority Areas is, first and foremost, to promote integrated rural infrastructure.[129]

'Integrated rural development, with specific consideration accorded to infrastructure development' requires quantitative estimations. The provincial Ministry of Finance infrastructure document advocates increasing funding 'to address 50% of backlogs' over a five-year period in terms of capital investment. As noted below, in sector after sector, the amount required is far above the R1.73 billion allocated in 2001/2. One estimate of the shortfall is R5.27 billion.[130]

In order to make up the shortfall, the document calls for provincial officials to carry out various cost-saving measures, as well as 'approaching the national government with a view to obtaining higher levels of transfer payment to provincial and local government'.[131] Persuading Pretoria that R5 billion in infrastructure investment allocated to Coega would be better spent in integrated rural development requires concrete investment prioritisation. We take forward the preliminary investigation in relation to roads, water, electricity, housing and the two main modes of increasing human capital: education and health.

Roads

Beginning with roads, dramatic increases in capital spending are required. Estimated needs are R2.42 billion a year. Funds available in 2001/2 were just R860 million, leaving a shortfall of R1.56 billion.[132] Roads are the most vital transport infrastructure for low-income rural people. In 1995,

14% of surfaced roads in the Province were in 'poor or very poor condition', and 58% were in 'good or very good' condition. By 2000, 46% were in 'very poor condition', and 24% were in 'good or very good condition'.

As a result, according to the Ministry of Finance, 'most of surfaced roads have deteriorated to such a poor standard that the majority require replacement rather than rehabilitation or maintenance. In addition the situation in respect of gravel roads is even more serious', as 75% are in 'poor or very poor condition'. Worse, 'any delay in addressing the road maintenance backlog results, of course, in an exponential increase in costs in the future'. Yet the funding allocated in 2000/1 amounted to just R410 million, with a projected decline for 2001/2 to just R260 million – compared to the R1.85 billion required to maintain and provide rudimentary upgrading to the network.[133]

The distribution of transport infrastructure is biased towards the Western district, which has 21% of the Eastern Cape's residents.[134] Western residents and firms enjoy 38% of the province's surfaced roads, more than 27% of its gravel roads and only 1% of low-quality access roads. For maintenance, the Western District receives 27% of all road-related spending: R280 million. In contrast, the Wild Coast district has just 7% of the province's surfaced roads, 12% of its gravel roads and a disturbing 34% of low-quality access roads. But its share of total road-related spending is just 14%: R140 million.[135]

Investing R5 billion in infrastructure in the Western district, as proposed by Portnet, would contradict the province's need for a better distribution of potentially productive transport access.

Water/sanitation

The supply of water and sanitation in the impoverished rural areas of the Eastern Cape is even more disturbing. According to the Ministry of Finance,

> It has been estimated that 2.5 million people in the Province lack access to water services, but studies have indicated this could be as high as 5 million if sustainability problems with current schemes are taken into account. Up to 6.3 millon people do not have access to safe sanitation ...
>
> It is also imperative that the provision of water and sanitation not be looked at in isolation to other provincial programmes. For example, there are many instances where new schools, clinics, police stations, and similar community facilities have been established without consideration being paid to the provision of adequate water and sanitation services ...

> The primary water supply problem to be addressed in the
> Province is the reduction of backlogs in terms of water services
> (including sanitation) provision in rural areas.[136]

Yet despite the enormous backlog, only R250 million was budgeted for
capital expenditure on water and sanitation projects in 2000/1 – down
from R300 million in 1999/2000 – and only R360 million was budgeted
for 2001/2. Hence, according to the Ministry of Finance study, 'With a
current R4 billion water and sanitation infrastructure backlog, which
increases as the population grows, it will take 10 to 15 years at current
expenditure levels to work through the backlog'.[137]

Beyond spending on capital, additional funds are required for operating and maintenance expenses: 'In many of the completed projects, both
at Transitional Local Council and rural district level, the projects are experiencing major problems with respect to ongoing operation and maintenance'.[138]

Electricity

Enormous electricity backlogs continue to bedevil the province's former
homeland areas. In the Transkei, 75% of households have no electricity
connections. Of around 6,000 villages, 4,905 in the Transkei and Ciskei
remain off Eskom's grid.[139] The few high-priority projects that are considered feasible to start soon are estimated to cost R180 million. Even the
supply of off-grid electricity, which respondents often complain provides
insufficient ampage to run simple household appliances, is extremely
costly. In coming years, 25 pilots (Hybrid Remote Area Power System) are
budgeted at R50 million.[140]

No firm estimates are available for the cost of installing electricity in
rural areas off Eskom's grid. But the most important point is that the distribution would require no further electricity-generation capacity, unlike
the Coega IDZ, which will raise provincial consumption to such a great
degree as to require new capital expenditure.

Housing

It is possible to assess capital spending in this sector, although estimates
on the housing backlog are not available and in any case are highly subjective, given that traditional rural huts with impermanent materials are
sometimes counted in the housing backlog and sometimes not. Most
spending occurs through project-linked subsidies which favour urban,
not rural settings.

In 2000/1, for example, R302 million was spent in urban projects (71% of the budget), with only R11 million (3%) allocated to rural areas. Very conservatively estimated, at least R2.15 billion will be required to meet half the housing backlog over the next five years, implying a significant increase from R388 million in the housing budget to R430 million next year.[141]

Education

The number of classrooms required to meet Eastern Cape primary and secondary educational backlogs is 22,367. Based on trying to achieve a 40:1 pupil:classroom ratio, the low-income regions have extreme classroom backlogs: more than 7,000 in the Northern region and more than 5,000 in the Eastern and Northeastern regions.

Each school classroom costs R160,000. Shockingly, there are an additional 42,087 classrooms in need of repair and renovation (at R75,000 each). Eastern Cape schools are also short of 24,543 toilets (at R15,000), 3,004 water connections (at R30,000), 3,236 electricity connections (at R50,000), 3,819 telephone connections (at R1,500) and 1,985 fences (variable cost). In sum, the cost of building classrooms and associated facilities so as to meet only 50% of the backlog over five years (with normal maintenance) is R3.63 billion per year. Only R164 million is budgeted for 2000/1, however, including support from the European Union and Japan.[142]

Health

To eliminate only half its backlogs over the next five years, the Department of Health requires R275 million per year, roughly 10 times the amount spent this year. These are particularly urgent infrastructural needs, given the enormous health-sector backlogs in the rural areas.

For instance, while the WHO recommends no more than 10,000 persons per clinic within 5 km radius, the majority of rural Eastern Cape residents reside 18 km away from a clinic, with 81% being 10 km distant. As it stands, according to the Ministry of Finance, 'Currently no funds are available to refurbish or build new clinics'.

Merely to reach the 50% backlog stage within five years, the funds required for 120 new clinics would be R100 million (each small clinic with equipment costs R750,000, large clinics cost R1.7 million, and Community Health Centres cost R5 million). Refurbishing 57 existing clinics 'requiring urgent attention' will cost R40.9 million. To purchase 59 mobile health units for Primary Health Care services and 35 additional vehicles for supervision will cost R18.8 million. Rehabilitating hospitals to a satisfactory standard will cost R1.2 billion. In sum, R1.36 billion is needed to reach the halfway point of backlog eradication, with only R167 million available over the next five years to do so.[143]

A menu for infrastructure investment

As we have seen, the provincial Ministry of Finance embarked recently upon a somewhat conservative exercise of estimating 'needs' – socially constructed, and not necessarily at the levels that people really demand state services – of communities which are without roads, water and sanitation, electricity, housing, education and healthcare. The estimates, as described above, suggest that at least R7.32 billion in capital expenditure correlates to the 'priority requirements', so that just half the backlog would be eradicated within five years.

With only R1.73 billion allocated for capital spending in the 2001 budget, *the additional R5 billion that Portnet proposes spending on Coega infrastructure over the next few years would be greatly welcomed.* To redirect central state (and parastatal) resources from the speculative project at Coega into roads, water/sanitation, electricity, housing, education and health infrastructure would have enormous positive spinoffs.

While the development of South Africa's maritime resources, including port and container facility expansion will have to continue, we have asked in this chapter: why Coega? Why not invest state monies in infrastructure that cannot otherwise be funded in the Eastern Cape?

The point of having an overarching regulatory authority responsible for the restructuring of state assets – the mandate of the Department of Public Enterprises – is to assure that foolish decisions about public investment funds are not made. Coega surely qualifies as a case for the Department to investigate, especially given the many other problems that have come to light in the Transnet portfolio.

In addition, the second aspect of the alternative to the Coega port/IDZ is to take advantage of the Coega area's unique prospects for eco-tourism, agriculture and mariculture. The point of the second prong of the strategy is to achieve environmentally and economically sustainable development which will create lasting job prospects.

6. Another Coega is possible

The unique Coega setting and potential for job-creating economic development together represent the basis for an alternative to the port/IDZ, far more consistent with the provincial development mandate than the CDC's work. Agriculture, mariculture and eco-tourism offer the most important options for investment of public and private resources (Figure 3, Coega Alternative, below). Much smaller investment commitments are required from the public sector, thus allowing the massive resources anticipated to be available (via Portnet) for Coega to be redirected into the vast Eastern Cape infrastructure backlogs described above.

Agriculture and empowerment in the Sundays River Valley

While expansion of citrus in the Sundays River valley is occurring on an ongoing basis, it is crucial to redistribute land and farming opportunities. Precisely here, shortages of water and lack of funding for capital investment become a major barrier.

It is not utopian to project the deracialisation of South African agriculture. In one particular case for which full cost estimates have been established at Berkeley Bridge, black farmers in a joint-venture partnership would have access to scarce resources that are not available to existing commercial farmers:

- 3200 ha of land that have been targeted in the Lower Sundays River area for development;
- water supplies allocated by Dwaf for the scheme;
- capital (typically R20,000 per head) in the form of Land Redistribution for Agricultural Development Programme of the Department of Land Affairs;

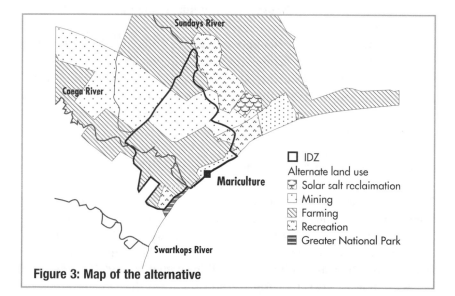

Figure 3: Map of the alternative

- preferential access to a deferred repayment loan, by which projects only start paying when their cash flow allows it;
- preferential access to export markets and assistance from the DTI;
- possible access, via a Water Users Association, to a long-term lease over the R300 million in water infrastructure proposed for construction; and
- access to grower groups, that provide exclusive access to plant material, markets and guaranteed prices for crops.

The model for joint-venture partnerships can take a number of forms, which fall broadly into two categories, equity sharing schemes and resource sharing schemes.[144] Expansion of existing land is feasible, if instead of the massive water consumption envisaged for the Coega IDZ, the Sundays River is used to irrigate the crops of small-scale black farmers.

Mariculture in Algoa Bay

The same principle of opportunity cost applies to mariculture. As discussed above, abalone farming could have a much greater job-creating and income-generating prospect than it does at present in 2002. Five plots yielding 80 tonnes per year (priced at R290/kg) were under consideration for investment and anticipated to create 175 permanent jobs. But these impressive additions to the local mariculture industry are impossible in the presence of the proposed Coega development.

The impact on sensitive market perceptions of the proximity of the Coega harbour and IDZ to the abalone operations is likely to eliminate demand for the products. Shellfish are bio-accumulators of heavy metals from both the air and the water. Even minimal contamination will render the output of mariculture farms worthless.

The conclusion that mariculture operations could not continue at the Hougham Park site was supported in an independent report commissioned by the CDC. Indeed, the proposals for Coega's industrial development have already curtailed the expansion of the existing operation, and have deterred Asian investors who had shown interest in developing an operation at the site.

Ecotourism in the Greater Addo National Park area

The Greater Addo National Park plan has been under consideration for some time, and South African National Parks (SANP) have been undertaking a piecemeal expansion of the park. Proposals for the acceleration of this expansion and consolidation into a 341,000 hectare terrestrial zone and a 57,000 hectare marine zone, were provided in 1997.[145]

According to SANP, the primary constraint on the expansion of the park will be the lack of capital for the purchase of land and the installation of required infrastructure, including fencing and roads. The total cost of the purchase of the remaining land has been estimated at R400 million.

What would the Coega area receive in return? Estimating returns from eco-tourist projects and national parks is complicated by the nature of the economic activities generated, the bulk of which occur not through direct SANP income and employment, but through edge-of-park developments and services. Nonetheless, reasonable estimates have been made by Mandela Metropole Sustainability Coalition researchers, that expansion of the Addo Park would generate approximately 4,800 net jobs and R300 million in income.[146]

The alternative to Coega measured by jobs/rand investment

Apart from the merits of an agriculture, mariculture and eco-tourism alternative, reason enough to replace the CDC proposal for Coega's development is the piddling number of jobs that the multibillion rand port/IDZ would contribute to the Eastern Cape economy. The massive potential for sustainable, environmentally friendly jobs proposed by the Mandela Metropole Sustainability Coalition is based upon a relatively small amount of public investment to assure the flows of water required. Ongoing benefits from the alternative strategy can be expected to the metropole, in additional jobs, contributions to regional income, tax revenue and the ability to utilise water, electricity and other resources for existing residents and businesses.

7. Conclusion

The weaknesses in the CDC's proposal for a new port, container terminal and IDZ follow directly from its failure to establish an argument for sustainable development. This chapter has documented how public funds, land, marine activities, water, and electricity would be utilised in enormous, irresponsible quantities at Coega.

In contrast, the combination of economic, social and environmental developments proposed by the Sustainability Coalition provides greater benefits, and more sensibly and sustainably utilises these resources. In short, for South Africa in general and its poorest province in particular, basic-needs infrastructure investment and a more balanced utilisation of resources such as water and electricity should be at the very foundation of any economic strategy.

If Coega continues along its current path, it will serve only as a model of unsustainability. While so much other basic infrastructure is not being delivered elsewhere in the Mandela Metropole and across the Eastern Cape, it is impossible to justify the vast sums to be invested in a major piece of transport infrastructure oriented to capital-intensive, export-oriented economic activity. The high risk that the proposed port and container terminal are not economically viable has been suggested by even the CDC's most recent consultancy report.

In all these respects, the Coega port and IDZ exacerbate the apartheid economic legacy of division, marginalisation, and grandiose, unworkable public-investment schemes. Such ventures were traditionally grounded not in a logic of development, but rather reflected the power of special interest groups. Here, the durability of the economically irrational Coega proposals has been explained, at least in part, by reference to malgovernance.

Explaining Coega

The rationale for Coega falls apart under scrutiny. Even the attempt in 2001 by shipping consultancy Merit to justify a R5 billion investment has profound flaws. As of mid-2002, the Pechiney aluminium smelter proposal has not seen the light of day, but first may not survive competition from inexpensive East Timorese and Australian competitors, and second would require vast public investments (R4 billion has been mentioned) for very low returns in job creation.

Why, then, does Coega continue to be promoted in its current form? There are various theories. The *perception* (not necessarily *reality*) has been lodged in the public consciousness, through several media and academic investigations, that systematic malgovernance within the South African state is the only explanation for the Coega project's otherwise inexplicable durability. This line of argument was documented by Colm Allan, Director of the Public Service Accountability Monitor at Rhodes University, in July 2001.

Allan's analysis includes allegations of procedural irregularities committed by several key Coega proponents[147] and also cites allegations of misconduct against the former Defence Minister, Joe Modise (who died in 2002):

> Joe Modise's irregular agreement with the German submarine consortium on 13 June 1999 to purchase three submarines at a cost of R4.5 billion in return for Ferrostaal's promise to construct a steel mill worth R6 billion at Coega, effectively resurrected the Coega

Project from the dead. Modise, after resigning as Minister of Defence, bought shares in and was appointed the chairperson of a company which has been awarded contracts to conduct work on the Coega project. Again, these contracts have been paid for out of tax-payer's money. Modise is the head of Harambee Investment Holdings, a black empowerment company, which bought a 30% shareholding in the BKS group in August 2000. BKS, one of South Africa's biggest firms of consulting engineers, established and partially owns a company called Khuthele Projects. In November 1999, the CDC announced that it had appointed Khuthele Projects as the engineering consultants responsible for conducting the integrated transportation study for the Coega IDZ. It also points out in its annual report that the contact to Khuthele would be extended for the 2000-2001 financial year. Modise effectively ends up benefiting financially as a businessman from a decision that he made whilst he was a Cabinet Minister. This constitutes a clear conflict of interests.[148]

If there remain question marks over the conduct of those with responsibilities for allocating vast sums of public monies to a project such as Coega, Allan is correct to warn that the entire project will be seen as illegitimate:

> What we would appear to be witnessing is a situation in which tax-payer's money is being used to fund infrastructure for companies and individuals, such as Modise, who have risked no capital at all, yet stand to reap financial benefits. If the Coega port and IDZ turns out to be an economic disaster, the private companies and individuals involved in the project will incur no losses.
>
> Yet, there is evidence to suggest that individuals associated with these companies have also participated in the policy process whereby public funds have been utilised in ways which might benefit them personally. This is not to suggest that there has been any necessary impropriety. But, it does indicate that a much tighter regulatory framework is required to prevent commercial conflicts of interest from influencing public decision makers ...
>
> The complexities of the private holdings and public positions relating to the individuals associated with Coega and the arms deal require further, official investigation. This would best be undertaken by a body with specialised forensic audit capabilities and a legal mandate to scrutinise contracts between public entities and private businesses. Government's decision to exclude the Special Investi-

gating Unit from the arms probe effectively prevents the issue of profiteering from commercial conflicts of interest from being examined. The Special Investigation Unit was the only public protection agency with the power to effectively investigate the awarding of sub-contracts. Uniquely, it was also empowered to have these contracts set aside by a Special Tribunal in the event of impropriety ...

If the Coega project is to meet its objectives, then the procedures used to establish the Port and IDZ and the grounds for its economic viability must be beyond reproach.[149]

Beyond the Minerals-Energy Complex

But potential cases of corruption or malgovernance are not the basis of our own primary research. The most important public policy argumentation against Coega has been made repeatedly throughout the pages above: neither 'sustainable development' nor 'economic development' will transpire as a result of massive public subsidies into construction, and into ongoing tax/rates/services subsidies, for a port and IDZ whose economic rationale is so faulty that no private investors have been attracted to anything aside from a potential container terminal (itself feasible only on the basis of yet other transport subsidies).

In relation to the IDZ, the establishment of a heavy-industrial complex reliant upon cheap water and electricity, with potential for fouling the air, is unsustainable for a variety of reasons. Indeed, it is the disconnection between South Africa's overinvested minerals/metals sectors, and the rest of the economy, that is most disturbing about the vision behind Coega.

One obvious casualty is the possibility of solving the unemployment crisis of the Mandela Metropole and the Eastern Cape, given that the huge investments create such little employment. Caution on jobs had, however, been thrown to the wind by Coega's promoters. In mid-2002, according to the *Herald*, the CDC

> delivered 600,000 registration forms to homes in the metropole, placed full-page advertisements in local newspapers and launched a radio campaign, inviting people interested in taking up job opportunities at Coega to register with the corporation. Another 81,000 forms were delivered for distribution via ward councillors, the municipality and libraries ...A day after the campaign launch, Port Elizabeth's main post office was so astounded by the volume of registration forms being submitted that it called the CDC. By late this week, some 8,000 forms had been submitted, and they were still flowing in fast.[150]

As we have seen, South Africa's depraved disconnection between the formal economy and the masses of unemployed people is not an accident. In the most detailed study conducted of the apartheid economy, Ben Fine and Zav Rustomjee conclude their 1996 book *The Political Economy of South Africa: From Minerals-Energy Complex to Industrialisation* with a devastating critique of 'the failure of this [Minerals-Energy Complex] to be vertically integrated forward into the rest of the economy'.

That critique continues to be relevant, applied to the Coega port/IDZ. In contrast, as Fine and Rustomjee remark, a relinking of the economy is possible, through meeting the needs of Eastern Cape residents for water, sanitation, electricity, housing, roads, schools and health facilities, to name a few:

> We place considerable emphasis upon a state programme of public expenditure to provide social and economic infrastructure. This forms part of a strategy to provide for basic needs. The problem of how to finance such a programme is less acute than the formation of the political, social and institutional capacity to carry it out.151

In this spirit, an alternative, sustainable-development strategy is required for Coega. We have sketched out the merits of expanded basic-needs infrastructure in Mandela Metropole townships and all over the Eastern Cape, and the development of agriculture, mariculture and eco-tourism at Coega.

What is lacking, however, is what Fine and Rustomjee refer to as 'the formation of the political, social and institutional capacity to carry [the alternative] out'. That capacity can only be built from a base of adequate information. While this chapter continues the process, perhaps, by identifying key problems and identifying new developments, far more work must be done on an optimal economic development strategy for the metro and the province. More importantly, the political balance of forces in the Mandela Metropole, the Eastern Cape Province and Pretoria itself, must change dramatically so that social, environmental and economic justice can be done.

To sum up, the chapter has levelled two core charges against Coega: that the proposed port/IDZ project is inappropriate, and that an alternative strategy would be far preferable. The public resources earmarked for the Coega port/IDZ deserve deployment elsewhere: to the alternative, combining basic-needs infrastructure for the entire province, and job-creating development of Coega's agricultural, maricultural and eco-tourist potentials. Only the alternative is truly a sustainable way forward for Mandela Metropole and the Eastern Cape.

The alternative was never given a hearing. Coega's promoters from the local corporate sector continued to insist upon massive public subsidies even though their project continued to show, in one executive's own words, 'fatal flaws'. Politicians and bureaucrats lined up behind the vision of a mega-project. Multinational corporations toyed with the project, taking out what they could get. Corruption appeared at the edges.

Meanwhile, the genuine development needs of low-income people were ignored. People in the way were displaced and many lost access to even their water because of poverty. Systematic underdevelopment continued in Mandela Metropole and across the Eastern Cape for the low-income majority, most of whom were formally unemployed and virtually all of whom had witnessed deterioration in their standards of living in recent years.

All of these problems characterise what *might* be post-apartheid South Africa's biggest single industrial project, a site which national advertisements regularly have us believe is 'vital to the future economic growth of South Africa and the whole Southern African region'. Much the same pattern can be found at a similar white elephant whose costs are borne by the poor and benefits nabbed by the wealthy: the Lesotho Highlands Water Project (LHWP).

Notes

1. The other researchers of the Mandela Metropole Sustainability Coalition and its allies, many of whom contributed original work edited for the chapter below, are warmly thanked: Norton Tenille, Boyce Papu, Tom LeQuesne, and Ashwin Kumar of the SA Environment Project, independent researchers George Niksic and Anton Cartwright, Mexican economist David Barkin, and Liz Dodd, Lenny Gentle, Neil Newman, John Pape, and Leon Pretorius from the International Labour Resource and Information Group.

2. Mandela Metropole Sustainability Coalition (2001), *Sustainable Development at Coega? Problems and an Alternative*, September, http://www.coega.org. The CDC's website is http://www.coega.com

3. 'Criminal not to develop Coega', by Alec Erwin, *Eastern Province Herald*, 1 February 2002:

    I have received a copy of the report *Sustainable Development at Coega? Problems and an Alternative*, submitted to me by hand. I have also asked my department to look at it and have consulted the considerable number of studies that have been done on this matter. It would not be possible to answer all the inaccuracies in the document. However, let me address briefly the arguments set out in the executive summary.
    1. Unlike the claims made, there have not been false starts. This development is being undertaken in a manner that has not been used in South Africa before. It involves different levels of government, different State organisations and a range of environmental studies. At all times the development of the project would have taken time. It should be borne in mind that during the preparation of the project the structure of both local government and Portnet has

changed. Portnet is now split into the National Ports Authority and Ports Operations.

2. The concept of an anchor tenant was used in the early stages of the proposal when conditions were different. However, the project is not dependent on an anchor tenant. The other points made here are not factual, but expressions of opinions.

    The approach taken by Coega Development Corporation (CDC) has been consistent as it fits with the intended purpose of the IDZ programme.

3. Government has consulted widely on the viability of the proposed port and the container terminal and received inputs from many potential developers. We remain of the view that the strategic and economic value of such a port is sufficient to warrant its construction. There is a range of ways in which the port could be constructed and these are the subject of ongoing consultation with various interested parties. The Merit report confirms other studies.

4. The final number of jobs that will be created in Coega will depend on the investments made. The statement made that hundreds of existing jobs will be destroyed is not accurate, as there is no reason to believe that the activities displaced will cease altogether. There is, however, an attempt to indicate that there are other ways of creating more jobs. This assumption is a basic inaccuracy. With suitable and legislatively imposed environmental precautions and actions there is no incompatibility between the Coega development and both existing and new agricultural, marine harvesting, conservation developments, and eco-tourism. As is well known this has been part of the strategy all along and other parts of the public sector are actively developing these economic activities.

5. The IDZ, as has been continually stated, brings in the possibility of internationally competitive and sustainable production to add value to our resources. The purpose of the IDZ programme is to add value and therefore increase the income generated in South Africa. The advantages of such investment in the Eastern Cape are obvious and desirable in order to bring about development throughout South Africa.

6. That the proposed port/IDZ is too expensive is merely an assertion. It is the responsibility of the State to provide infrastructure for development. There is a deliberate attempt to create the impression that this will reduce expenditure in other areas of infrastructure. This is wrong. The National Ports Authority builds ports and it finances these in the capital market. The DTI provides assistance to industry from its budget that is established within the total framework of the Medium Term Expenditure Framework. All other areas of infrastructure are still provided for and the amounts have been consistently increased. In fact, the Medium Term Budget Policy Statement provides for an increase of 47.7% in the capex budget in the next financial year.

7. The argument that the proposed IDZ will use too much water has no foundation in fact. Modern industry has to be as conscious as anyone of the amount of water it uses. Furthermore, the argument that the proposed IDZ will use too much clean air is merely an assertion that has already been tested and found wanting in the studies done.

8. It is difficult to follow the argument that the IDZ will use too much electricity unless it is merely opposition to the use of coal-based electricity. The project will in fact have the advantage of bringing more electricity to the area and thereby increasing its attractiveness to investors, and providing access to a clean and reliable energy source for the community.

9. The argument that the proposed IDZ will not have sufficient economic spin-offs and will not change structural barriers to development is not born out by the facts. Coega is not designed in itself to change the structure of the regional economy. It will have a positive effect and is an important complement designed to generate high value-adding investment to the many

other programmes in social and economic infrastructure. The statements on the auto industry are merely uninformed comment the meaning of which is hard to discern.

10. A job-creation strategy that combines tourism, agriculture and mariculture – an integrated strategy – is not an alternative. This is what is already happening with existing government policy and action. The attempt to suggest that the Coega project will replace these activities is ill founded.

In my view the presentation of the report does the fundamental cause of the environment more damage than it does good. If all efforts to bring about economic development are to be blocked by this sort of obstructionism and attempts to threaten government with embarrassment during the World Summit on Sustainable Development then you are merely discrediting this fundamental cause.

I regret to say that I can come to no other conclusion than that this report is a poorly prepared polemic designed to support your obvious opposition to this project. I would not make the above remarks if the document had any real merit. We have held a number of discussions with responsible environmental groups and will work with them very closely. As I have stated on many occasions on behalf of government, it is our policy to ensure that we adopt leading edge practice in balancing development and the environment.

As a trading nation that is developing a modern and sustainable economy our actions will have to be compatible with the sustainability of the environment. Consequently, the investments we are seeking can only remain competitive if we have world-class environmental standards. In any event our natural endowments are one of our greatest economic assets and will be crucial to our economic future. Accordingly, all projects will comply with South Africa's environmental legislation.

In the final analysis, and as indicated above, it is government's responsibility to unlock economic opportunity. The port and the Coega IDZ are prime investment opportunities. It would be an abdication of responsibility and downright irresponsible for a government of an industrialising economy like ours not to develop these opportunities.

– Alec Erwin, Minister of Trade and Industry

4. 'Coega, an investment in Ministerial ego?' by Stephen Hosking, *Eastern Province Herald*, 15 February 2002:

South Africa's Minister of Trade and Industry, Alec Erwin, is in a position of considerable power and influence. He oversees the rules for trading within South Africa, designs incentive structures that selectively promote industries and regions and influences the allocation of scarce public funding in other ministries. It is a very important job. If done well, it boosts investor confidence in South Africa and is good for growth. If done poorly, it does the opposite.

Recently his wisdom has been challenged on several issues. One of the most publicly known was the challenge that the premium (extra) paid for the arms to secure the offsets could have done more to promote investment, exports and growth if it had been used in more direct ways. Another is the challenge that his pet project, the Coega IDZ and harbour project, is inefficient. His responses to these challenges have been consistent: to dismiss them as poorly informed and inaccurate.

His dismissal of the challenge to the Coega project is his latest response, reported in the press under the heading 'Criminal not to develop Coega'. In it he stated that the government has consulted widely on the viability of the Coega project, and that the feedback has been overwhelmingly positive. It was positive not only because the expected benefits exceed the expected costs, but also because lots of jobs were to be created and poverty alleviated. The latest claims for the project are that up to R14.5 billion could be attracted in private investment and 20,000 jobs created.

Given this expectation it came as no surprise when the government announced it had decided to commit an additional R5.03 billion to construction work on the Coega project over the next few years, as well as funding future IDZ operations and purchases. All this adds to the substantial sums of money the government has already been persuaded to spend on the project.

I was one of the people who communicated my concerns about the project to Alec Erwin (as part of the Mandela Metropole Sustainable Coalition). We do not think that the Merit report he cites to back his support for the project is an adequate basis on which to make decisions about spending government money. Inter alia, it reached its recommendations on the basis of controversial projections of demand for container shipments through Port Elizabeth, dubious benefit pricing decisions, naive assumptions on the cost of building and maintaining the necessary linking infrastructure with Gauteng and without properly taking into account external environmental costs.

Our observation is that five years of expensive marketing and design revisions have attracted some private sector investor interest, but disappointingly little commitment. Our belief is that in order to lure tenants to the Coega IDZ the government will be forced to provide substantial incentives, but that this will make it difficult for the taxpayer to get a return on investment. Equally problematic is going to be resisting industries that are prepared to locate in the IDZ that will impose high environmental costs in the Algoa Bay area.

Erwin's view is that this is fine so long as they comply with environmental legislation. Ours is that it is not fine: the scale of environmental costs must be taken into account. This area supports enterprises in ecotourism, mariculture and agriculture and we believe it has the potential to support substantial further growth.

From the development perspective the project has also been unexciting. The lack of a deep water harbour is not a binding constraint on the current manufacturing industry of the Nelson Mandela Metropole. Most of the benefits of this project are likely to accrue outside of the Eastern Cape, certainly not to the poorest of the poor in the Eastern Cape.

Alec Erwin argues that by expressing our concerns we do the environmental cause (which he senses is very close to our hearts) more damage than good. He also clearly feels we need a lesson from Trevor Manuel on how the public finances work. We think that by spending more on the Coega project the government will reduce its capacity within the budget system to spend elsewhere (because there is opportunity cost). He rejects this!

We are not persuaded. What is clear is that the Minister is so deeply committed to this project that criticisms of it are interpreted as opposition rather than contributions.

– Stephen Hosking, Professor of Economics, University of Port Elizabeth.

5. Expectations are repeatedly raised about potential projects for Coega. For example, in April 2002, *Business Day* (17 April 2002) reported:

Two stainless steel beneficiation plants costing a total of R1.8bn were to be built at the Coega deepwater port and industrial development zone near Port Elizabeth, government officials said yesterday.

The trade and industry department has negotiated the investments, as part of the controversial arms for investment deal, with a consortium representing submarine suppliers and headed by German steel firm Ferrostaal. A department briefing document on the industrial offset programme, distributed yesterday, said engineering studies were in progress for the establishment of a R1bn ultrathin precision stainless steel strip facility, which would produce steel for products such as razor blades and automotive parts including catalytic converters.

This plant would employ about 200 people. The second investment of R800m would be in a plant employing 250 people to produce refrigerated stainless steel containers for use in transporting flowers, fruit and vegetables. The document said that equipment was installed and the project 'due to start'.

Another R2.5bn project, under negotiation between the department and

Ferrostaal would be to 'manufacture special steel for export' and might also be at Coega.

A Ferrostaal spokesman confirmed the accuracy of the department's project list, and said that 'Ferrostaal has always committed itself to Coega'.

Yet nothing further was publicised over the subsequent two months, notwithstanding the CDC's desperate attempts to promote Coega in May-June 2002.

6.   *Business Day*, 9 July 2002.

7.   Maritime Education and Research Information Technology (2001), *Report on the Economic Evaluation of the Proposed Port of Ngqura and Development of a Container Terminal*, Stellenbosch, p. 7. By mid-2002, Merit's name had been changed in the ubiquitous Coega advertisements to 'Maritime Education and Research Institute'.

8.   Erwin, 'Criminal not to develop Coega', p. 6. In the next paragraph, Erwin contradicts himself: 'The concept of an anchor tenant was used in the early stages of the proposal when conditions were different'.

9.   Richardson, E. (2001), 'Making the Leap', *Leadership*, April.

10.   *Herald*, 14 June 2002.

11.   Erwin, 'Criminal not to develop Coega', p. 6.

12.   *Business Day*, 15 February 2002.

13.   See the work of Tom Lequesne posted at http://www.coega.org

14.   Erwin, 'Criminal not to develop Coega', p. 6.

15.   *Business Day*, 1 February 2002.

16.   Erwin, 'Criminal not to develop Coega', p. 6.

17.   At the time the Merit report was circulating within the industry, the magazine conducted a survey of leading shipping executives. With the exception of P&O Nedlloyd, the preferred private partner for the project, opinion was unanimously against Coega (*Freight and Trading Weekly*, 22 June 2001).

18.   In 1997 estimates, the total cost of the harbour, IDZ infrastructure and associated expenditure was R1.6 billion, half of the sum envisaged in 2002. The land purchase costs were only R560,000, while the cost of the harbour construction was estimated at only R830 million. The closer the project gets to the stage of money actually flowing, the greater that cost escalation can be expected.

19.   Erwin, 'Criminal not to develop Coega', p. 6.

20.   Ibid.

21.   Ibid

22.   *Business Day*, 15 February 2002.

23.   Erwin, 'Criminal not to develop Coega', p. 6.

24.   Ibid

25.   Ibid

26.   This book is all there is. But see *Daily Dispatch*, 15 February 2002, for evidence of the pressure. Perhaps the fact that only two visits were made to Coega's environment and community opponents is explained by how busy the agents were, protecting national security interests in similarly constructive ways. According to the *Mail & Guardian* (12 July 2002), 'The head of the National Intelligence Agency in the Eastern Cape has been suspended following allegations that he solicited money from Cape-based mafioso Vito Palazzolo. The NIA this week confirmed the suspension last month of Dumisani Luphungela, the agency's Eastern Cape provincial manager, on allegations of corruption'.

27. Institute for Development Planning and Research (1997), 'The Port Elizabeth and Uitenhage Socio-Economic Development Monitor 1997', Port Elizabeth, p. 8.

28. Bond, P. (2001), *Against Global Apartheid: South Africa meets the World Bank, IMF and International Finance*, Cape Town, University of Cape Town Press, pp. 255-258.

29. See, e.g., Adler, G. (1993), 'From the 'Liverpool of the Cape' to 'The Detroit of South Africa': The Automobile Industry and Industrial Development in the Port Elizabeth-Uitenhage Region', *Kronos: Journal of Cape History*, 20, 17-43; Robinson, J. (1996), *The Power of Apartheid: State Power and Space in South African Cities*, Oxford, Butterworth-Heinemann.

30. Wakeford's fortunes declined when he took over the reins of the SA Chamber of Business (Sacob) in Johannesburg, for in 2001 he was accused of mismanaging a merger with black business, writing a hysterical and poorly considered letter to president Mbeki about a conspiracy behind the rand's crash, and even failing to stabilise Sacob's finances. However in June 2002, he was confirmed for another term as the organisation's director.

31. For example, in August 2000, the Coega IDZ Environmental Impact Assessment was finally conducted. But it did not seriously consider opportunity costs relating to the full utilisation of resources described in this chapter as part of the socio-economic and ecological survey of the project.

32. *Business Day*, 29 May 1998.

33. Government Communications and Information Services (1999), 'Defence Summary, September 1999', http://www.gov.za/projects/procurement/nip.htm.

34. At present the foreign consortium is led by Ferrostaal, with Thyssen and Danielli junior partners. The leading domestic firm is the IDC, which has major stakes in Iscor, Saldanha Steel and Highveld Steel. The latter three firms are undergoing a consolidation phase.

35. Source: Interview with CDC, May 2001.

36. Richardson, 'Making the Leap'.

37. See the full version of *Sustainable Development at Coega?* for citations, especially 'Appendix 1: Transport Container Economics' by Tom LeQuesne.

38. Maritime Education and Research Information Technology, *Report on the Economic Evaluation of the Proposed Port of Ngqura and Development of a Container Terminal*, p. 6.

39. The Coega IDZ metallurgical industrial complex still, however, aims to include an integrated set of factories producing stainless and specialist rolled steel, but prospects appear weak in the wake of Ferrostaal's refusal to commit to serving as anchor tenant. If the integrated steel complex and a ferrochrome refinery that is only in feasibility investigation stage do not materialise, prospects for downstream activity – automotive, textile and electronics – are also highly unlikely.

40. Maritime Education and Research Information Technology, *Report on the Economic Evaluation of the Proposed Port of Ngqura and Development of a Container Terminal*, p. 89.

41. Spatial Development Initiatives are specially identified areas of South Africa wherein the government is going to invest in infrastructure in a very focused way and hope to draw in private investment. According to government, the main aims of SDIs for South Africa are: to promote export orientation amongst South African firms; to earn foreign exchange; to ensure sustainable job creation; to ensure better utilisation of infrastructure and resources; and to broaden the ownership base of the economy. SDIs are to be managed and operated jointly by the state and the private sector and are sometimes designed to include a major road development.

Some of the SDIs also link, particularly the Witwatersrand/Johannesburg, to ports in neighbouring countries such as Namibia and Mozambique. See, e.g., Jourdan, P., K.Gordhan, D.Arkwright, and G.de Beer (1996), 'Spatial Development Initiatives (Development Corridors): Their Potential Contribution to Investment and Employment Creation', Working Paper, Development Bank of Southern Africa, Midrand, October.

42. South African IDZs will be controlled, fenced-off areas mostly around ports, which, for customs purposes, will be regarded as if they are not in South Africa. Firms that locate there do not pay customs and if they sell products in South Africa these are regarded as imports. The idea is that these firms should be geared towards exporting their goods and will not be hampered by regulations and paper work, and customs duty, which firms elsewhere in South Africa are faced with. Potential IDZs have been identified not only at Coega, but also in two other deep-water ports (Richard's Bay and Saldanha), as well as at other export-oriented production sites (East London and Johannesburg International Airport). As of mid-2002, only East London has been given approval to establish a formal IDZ.

43. *The Economist*, 22 February 1999.

44. *Financial Times*, 26 June 2002.

45. The discussion below is drawn in part from Bond, P., S.Hosking and J.Robinson (1998), 'Local Economic Development Choices in Port Elizabeth', paper presented to the Workshop on Local Economic Development, Department of Constitutional Development, Cape Town, April; from Jauch, H. and D.Keet (1996), *A SATUCC Study on Export Processing Zones in Southern Africa: Economic, Social and Political Implications*, Cape Town, International Labour Resource and Information Group; and from Pape, J. et al (2001), 'Spatial Development Initiatives and Industrial Development Zones: Part of the solution or part of the problem?', International Labour Information and Research Group, University of Cape Town.

46. Bond, P. (2002), 'Local Economic Development Debates in South Africa', *Occasional Paper*, Municipal Services Project, February, http://www.queensu.ca/msp.

47. This is no longer simply a matter of compliance with national standards, regulations or safeguards, but rather a matter of survival, since firms that are competing in global markets find that working up to international managerial and environmental standards (ISO 9000 and 14000) are increasingly prerequisites for successful market penetration and qualification in competitions for international contract tenders.

48. Jean-Paul, M. and M. Szymanski (1996), *Behind the Wire: Anti-Union Repression in the Economic Processing Zones*, International Confederation of Free Trade Unions, Brussels, April.

49. International Congress of Free Trade Unions (1995), *EPZs in Asia: Who Profits?*, Brussels.

50. Cited in Southern African Trade Union Coordinating Council (1996), 'Export Processing Zones in Southern Africa: Social, political and economic implications', International Labour Resource and Information Group, Centre for Southern African Studies, and Labour Law Unit, University of Cape Town, Cape Town, p. 12.

51. Nababsing V. (1997), 'Gender issues in EPZ industrialisation', in SATUCC/ILO, *Report of the Follow Up Regional Trade Union Workshop on Export Processing Zones, Environment and Sustainable Development*, Pretoria, 3-5 May.

52. Sources: Southern African Trade Union Coordinating Council (1996), 'Export Processing Zones in Southern Africa: Social, Political and Economic Implications', International Labour Resource and Information Group, Centre for Southern African Studies, and Labour Law Unit, University of Cape Town, Cape Town; Zimbabwe Congress of Trade Unions (1999), 'Industrial Relations and Sustainable Development in Export Processing Zones', Harare.

53. http://www.coega.com

54. In addition to Australians through the BHP merger, Billiton's leading shareholders include the Rupert family's Rembrandt Group and the state-owned Industrial Development Corporation.

55. *Business Report*, 22 March 2001.

56. Pretorius, L. (2001), 'Industrial Free Zones in Mozambique: A Case Study of Mozambique', International Labour Resource and Information Group, Cape Town, Occasional Paper #6, p. 29.

57. Hoover, R. (2002), 'Mozal Smelter Threatens Quality of Life in Mozambique', *groundWork*, 4, 2, June, p. 14.

58. *Business Day*, 10 March 1997.

59. To illustrate, Saldanha Steel charges export parity prices for foreign customers and has been accused of 'dumping' by the US government for doing so, resulting in restricted US imports. It charges import parity prices for South Africans. The import prices are much higher than export prices, leading to much higher than necessary input costs for South African manufacturing.

60. Many people moved to Saldanha to work on the construction of the Steel Mill, but when that was finished, they stayed, contributing to unemployment in the area. New squatter camps have been built and an extra burden was placed on local resources.

61. In the case of Saldanha, the contract to manage the construction of the mill went to a national company that had been involved in the Richard's Bay project. They brought in many of their own workers.

62. *Eastern Province Herald*, 20 February 2001.

63. Mandela Metropole Sustainability Coalition, *Sustainable Development at Coega?*, Appendix 1: Transport Container Economics.

64. Reid, R. (1998), 'Developments in the Structure and Ownership of Ports Worldwide', Presented to Intermodal Africa 98 Conference, Mercer Management Consulting, Inc, 11 March, pp. 11-12.

65. Increasing Port Elizabeth's draught and building a new breakwater is often claimed to be too expensive, but there are few details to provide points of comparison.

66. Noseweek, February 2001.

67. Not only do these include environmental costs and the indirect impacts on existing industries in the area, but also financial input from the Eastern Cape Provincial government. While the bulk of the finance for the construction of the port will be provided by Portnet, some of the land purchase and preparation costs for the port appear to be being provided by the provincially-owned CDC. By way of example, the July 2001 Environmental Impact Review for the harbour appears to have been commissioned by the CDC, as have a number of the further studies on the harbour and its impacts.

68. *Daily Dispatch*, 27 July 2001.

69. Maritime Education and Research Information Technology, *Report on the Economic Evaluation of the Proposed Port of Ngqura and Development of a Container Terminal*, pp. 87, 91.

70. Richardson, 'Making the Leap'.

71. Richardson, E. (1997), 'Who'll bankroll the R1,5bn harbour project?', *Financial Mail*, 10 July.

72. Richardson, Ed (1997), 'Coega: Now or never', Eastern Province Herald, 4 July.

73. See, e.g., Hosking, S. (1999), 'Comparing Heavy Industry and Agro-aquaculture

Options in the Coega River Mouth Area', *South African Journal of Agricultural Economics*, 38, 1.

74. Maritime Education and Research Information Technology, *Report on the Economic Evaluation of the Proposed Port of Ngqura and Development of a Container Terminal*, p. iv.

75. Pakes, T. and Nel, H. (1997), 'Proposed Coega Industrial Development Zone (IDZ): Preliminary Economic Assessment', Report commissioned by the Coega IDZ Section 21 Company, Port Elizabeth.

76. Tennille, N., and T. LeQuesne (1998), 'Coega IDZ and Harbour: The Issues', Cape Town, Southern Africa Environment Project.

77. Personal communication, Connie Muller, 25 May 2001.

78. Wooldridge, T., N.Klages, and M.Smale (1997), 'Proposed Harbour Development at Coega (Feasibility Phase): Specialist Report on the Near-shore Environment', Report commissioned by the Coega IDZ Section 21 Company, Port Elizabeth; Sauer, W. and A.Booth (1998), 'Impact Assessment of the Coega Harbour on the Fishing Activities, Estuaries and Phytoplankton Production in Algoa Bay', Port Elizabeth, January.

79. Department of Water Affairs and Forestry (1997), 'Overview of Water Resources Availability and Utilisation in South Africa', Pretoria.

80. Coastal Environmental Services, 'Environmental Impact Assessment'.

81. Grobicki, A. (1997), 'Proposed Coega IDZ Water Demands, and Constraints on Supply', Abbott Grobicki Consulting, Port Elizabeth, July.

82. Reported in Cashdan, B. (2001), *White Gold*, video, Johannesburg.

83. Algoa Bay Water Resources System Analysis, unpublished, 1993.

84. Grobicki, 'Proposed Coega IDZ water demands, and constraints on supply'. According to the Proposed Eastern Cape Zinc Refinery and Associated Phosphoric Acid Plant Final Environmental Impact Report the water requirement of the proposed zinc and phosphoric acid complex is 13,3 Ml/day (see African Environmental Solutions (1997), 'Proposed Eastern Cape Zinc Refinery and Associated Phosphoric Acid Plant: Final Environmental Impact Report', Report for the Coega Authority, Cape Town, pp. 4,11). The current average water demand for all existing industries in Port Elizabeth is calculated to be 14,6 Ml/day. See Silva McGillivray and Port Elizabeth Municipality (1997), 'Coega Industrial Development Zone Bulk water supply infrastructure requirements', Report commisioned by the Coega IDZ Section 21 Company, p. 32.

85. African Environmental Solutions, 'Proposed Eastern Cape Zinc Refinery and Associated Phosphoric Acid Plant: Final Environmental Impact Report', p. 14.

86. Republic of South Africa (1996), *Constitution of the Republic of South Africa*, Cape Town, Parliament, s.24.a, s.27.1.

87. Project Viability statistics for Port Elizabeth, April 2001. For more on the issue of indigence policy and subsidies, see Hosking, S. and P.Bond (2000), 'Infrastructure for Spatial Development Initiatives or for Basic Needs? Port Elizabeth's Prioritisation of the Coega Port/IDZ over Municipal Services,' in M.Khosa (Ed), *Empowerment through Service Delivery*, Pretoria, Human Sciences Research Council.

88. Nelson Mandela Metropolitan Municipality (2001), 'Workshop: Free Basic Services', 10 May.

89. Port Elizabeth (2001), Indigent Management Report, March.

90. Nelson Mandela Metropolitan Municipality, Workshop: Free Basic Services.

91. Port Elizabeth City Engineer's Department (1998), 'Memorandum', 22 January, p. 2.

92. Interview, Clyde Niven and Phillip Niven, 1998.

93. Silva McGillivray and Port Elizabeth Municipality, 'Coega Industrial Development Zone Bulk Water Supply Infrastructure Requirements', p. 72

94. Arthur D. Little (1997), 'Review of Environmental Impact and Strategic Environmental Assessment of Coega Harbour and Industrial Development Zone', July.

95. World Health Organisation (1999), 'Air Quality Guidelines', http://www.who.int/environmental_information/Air/Guidelines/Chapter3.htm

96. Henninen, O., H. Kruize, O. Breugelmans, E. Lebret, E. Samoli, L. Georgoulis, K. Katsouyanni, M. J. Jantunen (1997), 'Simulation of population exposure', Presented to Valamo Conference on Environmental Health and Risk Assessment: Health Risks of Inhaled Particles, Valamo Monastery, Heinevesi.

97. There are already significant background levels of ambient SO_2 present in the region, which must be taken into consideration while determining the cumulative effects of a development like Coega. Air quality studies and monitoring are being performed by independent contractors for the CDC. Despite repeated requests made to the CDC for access to the information, the data and reports have not been made available to the public. Data on background sulphur dioxide levels have not been released, although these are being monitored at stations in the area. Public access to this information is absolutely necessary for informed debate about the air pollution impacts of the IDZ.

98. The EIA estimates that even with high mitigation levels, PM10 levels resulting from the activities at Coega will exceed national regulatory guidelines several times: up to 60% of the time in the vicinity of the harbour.

99. Department of Environmental Affairs and Tourism (2001), *Technical Background Document for the Development of a National Ambient Air Quality Standard (NAAQS) for Sulphur Dioxide*, Environmental Quality and Protection Office, Pretoria.

100 Olszyk, D.M., G.Kats, C.L.Morrison, p. J.Dawson, I.Gocka, J.Wolf, C.R.Thompson (1990), 'Valencia Orange Fruit Yield with Ambient Oxidant or Sulphur Dioxide Exposures', Journal of the American Society for Horticultural Science, 115, 6.

101. Personal communication, Connie Muller, Managing Director of Marine Growers, 29 July, 1997.

102. Kerley, G., and A. Boshoff (1997), 'A Proposal for a Greater Addo National Park', Terrestrial Ecology Research Unit, University of Port Elizabeth, Submission to the public participation process on behalf of the South African National Parks, Port Elizabeth.

103. Council for Scientific and Industrial Research (1997), *Strategic Environmental Assessment for the Proposed IDZ and Harbour*, Pretoria.

104. Coastal and Environmental Services (2000), 'Coega Industrial Development Zone Integrated Environmental Summary Report', Report prepared for the Coega Development Corporation, Port Elizabeth, August.

105. Portnet (2000), 'Submissions to the Public Participation Process', Port Elizabeth.

106. http://www.coega.org

107. Arthur D. Little, 'Review of Environmental Impact and Strategic Environmental Assessments of Coega Harbour and Industrial Development Zone'.

108. World Bank (1998), *Summary of Air Emission and Effluent Discharge Requirements Presented in the Industry Guidelines*, Washington, July.

109. *Daily Mail & Guardian*, 28 August 2001.

110. *Business Day*, 15 February 2002.

111. The consumption was expected to peak at 135 MW, which assuming a power factor of 0.9, converts to a 150 MVA requirement. Electricity pricing is made up of several components: basic charge, maximum demand charge, active energy charge,

reactive energy charge, and transmission percentage surcharge. The actual rates depend upon the spread of energy consumption over peak, standard and off-peak times. (Interview, Jonathon Probert, April 1998.) *See also African Environmental Solutions (1997) Proposed Eastern Cape Zinc Refinery and Associated Phosphoric Acid Plant: Final Environmental Impact Report*, Report for the Coega Authority, Cape Town.

112. The anticipated electricity deal would involve the 'Megaflex' tariff structure together with a commodity-linked pricing arrangement and an 'interruptable' power discount option (about 5-10%, in return for a potential interruption of service of up to about 100 hours). In 2001, the Megaflex active energy charge for off-peak (10pm-6am weekdays, plus most of Saturday and all of Sunday) during the low-demand season (September-May) was as low as R0.0766/kWh. For peak consumption during the high demand season, the rate rises to R0.354/kWh, plus additional 'demand charges' that would lead to a maximum of R0.492/kWh at peak periods. Discounts of 12.75% are given for consumption above 132kV but a 2% surcharge is levied on consumption in the Mandela Metropole due to the nearly 900 km distance from Johannesburg.

113. Department of Public Enterprises (2002), 'Budget Vote Speech delivered by Minister Radebe', National Assembly, 16 May.

114. *Business Day*, 15 February 2002.

115. *Business Day*, 29 April 2002.

116. Fuggle, R. (1997), 'Review of Documentation Pertaining to Coega IDZ Initiative', Unpublished paper, July.

117. In Port Elizabeth, there has been a small degree of electricity cross-subsidisation with respect to the other services. To take one year as an example, the Port Elizabeth Municipal Operating Budget in 1996/97 included electricity spending of just over R405 million, while income was R477 million, leaving a R72 million surplus. Other major services ran at a loss that year, including water (R97 million expenditure, R87 million income), sewerage (R70 million expenditure, R57 million income) and refuse (R30 million expenditure, R29 million income). The entire city budget was R987 million in 1996/97, and income amounted to R1.017 billion, allowing a R30 million surplus.

118. African National Congress (1994), *The Reconstruction and Development Programme*, Johannesburg, Umanyano Publications, s.1.3.6.

119. African National Congress, *The Reconstruction and Development Programme*, s.1.4.3, 2.3.5, 4.2.2.

120. Stofile, M.A. (2000), 'Premier's Address', Rural Development Summit, Umtata, 5 October, pp. 1-2.

121. Province of the Eastern Cape Ministry of Finance and Economic Affairs (2000), *Towards Coordinated and Sustainable Infrastructure Investment in the Eastern Cape: Interim Capital Expenditure and Maintenance Plan for the Period 2000/1 to 2005/6*, Bisho, November, p. 4.

122. Funding for recurrent investment is also needed in rural municipalities. The 'Equitable Share' grant from central government would be one logical place to expand, but the Department of Water Affairs and Forestry, and Eskom should also provide much greater national-local cross-subsidies to pay for the operating and maintenance costs of, at the very least, 50 litres of water and one kiloWatt hour of electricity per person each day.

123. Stofile, 'Premier's Address', p. 1.

124. Ibid.

125. Eastern Cape Socio-Economic Consultative Council (2000), 'Advancing Democracy,

Growth and Development – The Imperative of Integrated Rural Development in the Province of the Eastern Cape', A Report on the Rural Development Summit, Umtata, 5-6 October, p. 3.

126. In July 2001, *Business Day* newspaper reported, 'It is now believed that the cost of the first phase has risen to more than R2bn, from the budgeted cost of R1.65bn. A further R3bn has now been budgeted for extra infrastructure, depending on tenant demand'. (*Business Day*, 26 July 2001)

127. Province of the Eastern Cape Ministry of Finance and Economic Affairs, *Towards Coordinated and Sustainable Infrastructure Investment in the Eastern Cape*, pp. 10-11.

128. Province of the Eastern Cape Ministry of Finance and Economic Affairs, *Towards Coordinated and Sustainable Infrastructure Investment in the Eastern Cape*, p. 13.

129. Provincial Priority Areas include: Integrated rural development, with specific consideration accorded to infrastructure development, food production and food security, and local government capacity building; Social Security, particularly with respect to improving the pension payout procedure, which constitutes a crucial support system for the poor, especially in rural areas; Transformation and Development of the Public Service in order to ensure that budgetary allocations for development are efficiently and effectively administered and managed; and HIV/Aids, which constitutes a fundamental threat to future livelihoods in the Province and will impact significantly on the Province's labour force if not appropriately addressed. In particular, it is imperative to ensure that resources allocated towards this end are actually utilised to address the issue. (Province of the Eastern Cape Ministry of Finance and Economic Affairs, *Towards Coordinated and Sustainable Infrastructure Investment in the Eastern Cape*, pp. 14-15.)

130. Province of the Eastern Cape Ministry of Finance and Economic Affairs, *Towards Coordinated and Sustainable Infrastructure Investment in the Eastern Cape*, p. 20.

131. Ibid, p. 21.

132. Ibid, p. 24.

133. Ibid, pp. 24-34.

134. The vast majority of these are concentrated in the Mandela Metropole where road traffic is considerably more intensive.

135. Province of the Eastern Cape Ministry of Finance and Economic Affairs, *Towards Coordinated and Sustainable Infrastructure Investment in the Eastern Cape*, p. 34.

136. Ibid, pp. 36-37.

137. Ibid, p. 41.

138. Ibid, p. 43.

139. Ibid, p. 44.

140. Ibid, pp. 36-37.

141. Ibid, pp. 57-59.

142. Ibid, pp. 47-51.

143. Ibid, pp. 51-57.

144. A report on these options has been developed with local stakeholders, and is available at http://www.coega.org

145. Kerley, and Boshoff, 'A Proposal for a Greater Addo National Park'.

146. As noted, piecemeal expansion is occurring anyway, and some farmworker jobs would be lost with the full-fledged development of the Greater Addo Park. The analysis is available at http://www.coega.org

147. These include Moss Ngoasheng of the CDC Board; Paul Jourdan, Jayendra Naidoo and Vanan Pillay of government's arms deal (and offsets) negotiating team; and Saki Macozoma and Mafika Mkwanazi of Transnet. Most subsequently moved on from work on Coega.

148. Allan, C. (2001), 'Coega, Conflicts of Interest and the Arms Deal', Public Service Accountability Monitor, Rhodes University.

149. Ibid.

150. *Eastern Province Herald*, 15 June 2002.

151. Fine, B. and Z.Rustomjee (1996), *The Political Economy of South Africa*, Johannesburg, Wits University Press, p. 252.

CHAPTER THREE

Lesotho's water, Johannesburg's thirst:

Communities, consumers, and mega-dams

1. Introduction

Sampling the taste of Johannesburg water allows us to pose several problems that are typically beyond the realm of public debate: the maldistribution of wealth, regional geopolitics, the plight of Basotho highlands peasants, irredeemable World Bank loan-pushing and technical incompetence, corrupting multinational corporate behaviour, and the contested merits of mega-dams. These aspects of Johannesburg's hydro-political-economic cycle are typically veiled, hidden from sight by the underground networks of piping, the transfers of loan finance from – and interest back to – Washington and Johannesburg banks, and flows of profits to the headquarters of construction companies, minus the set-asides in at least one Maseru ex-official's Swiss bank accounts.

Thanks to Pretoria's wash of pro-dam propaganda, when most suburban residents and visitors drink, bathe and flush their toilets, they do not see or feel the problems we consider in this chapter. They also generally retain confidence that Johannesburg Water, now managed by Paris-based Suez, maintains the system to the first-world standards of quality and pressure set long ago in wealthy Johannesburg.

Certainly, Sandton's sewage system, built for a low-density residential area, has recently suffered periodic ruptures due to overuse. However, hundreds of millions of rands are being invested in infrastructure because the Sandton ratepayers' federation – with huge business partners like Liberty Life's property division – successfully used the media and its own lobbying contacts in City Hall. After fighting the redistribution of city resources to the townships in 1995–96 and losing a Constitutional Court case, they rebounded to ensure an end to the periodic overflows of shit on emerald-green Sandton lawns.

Matters are very different once one journeys beyond the leafy suburbs and peri-urban 'mink and manure' belt with their multimillion rand mansions, to Johannesburg's inner-city squalor of Hillbrow, Berea, Joubert Park and the Central Business District, whose high-rise blocks regularly experience water cutoffs and leaks which steadily erode 40–80 year old cement structures. For literally millions of people living in Gauteng's informal settlements, the low quality and pressure of water, geographic distance to taps and toilets, and low standards of services are endured – and occasionally spur social protest.

Because of the mix of high quality and inadequate water services throughout Gauteng province, it is revealing first to excavate the Johannesburg water system and locate a primary source of the raw water far up in the mountains of Lesotho, at the Katse Dam that blocks the uppermost reaches of the Senqu River. Later chapters pose more durable problems about the state's municipal infrastructure policy.

Such an analysis begins with a brief survey of the most obvious costs and benefits of the LHWP (Section 2), itself a highly political exercise (Section 3). The two main critical discourses are from green environmentalists and indigenous people's advocates (Section 4), and from urban community activists (Section 5). In posing their arguments, both sources of anti-dam advocacy run up against the limits of the sustainable-development discourse (Section 7).

Pro-dam rhetorics

If we simply ask the question, who pays and who benefits disproportionately from the continent's largest dam scheme, we are confronted quickly by several confusing combinations of environmental discourses. Most importantly, the discourse of sustainable development is captured in the following sentences by Nelson Mandela, then water minister Kader Asmal, World Bank official John Roome and Pretoria's water department director-general Mike Muller:

> We in South Africa need the water from the Lesotho Highlands Water Project to meet the increase in our demand, and, in particular, to meet the needs of previously neglected communities.
>
> – President Nelson Mandela,
> 1995 letter to World Bank President James Wolfensohn[1]

The debt related to the water transfer part of this project will be redeemed by South Africa through income generated by the project. In other words, the end users will pay for the project, at tariffs well within the capabilities of the beneficiaries, making it economically viable.

> – Minister of Water Affairs and Forestry, Kader Asmal,
> Speech to an NGO workshop on the LHWP, August 1996[2]

The argument against large dams contends that they: are not economically viable; are not socially acceptable; are environmentally disastrous; can be a major cause of impoverishment, and can result in unacceptably high international debt. For this project however, the economics show that this is lowest cost supply, has a good Economic Rate of Return and demand management is being put in place; Socially the numbers involved are low, there has been 'good planning' but implementation key; Environmentally the impact is limited and has been well managed; Poverty-wise the project supports poverty reduction activities and does not squeeze out other activities; and fiscally SA bears the debt, not Lesotho and users pay – not tax payers.

The Project provides an opportunity to advance the debate that not all big dams are necessarily bad.

> – World Bank Lesotho dams task manager John Roome
> *Project Appraisal Document* for $45 million dam loan, April 1998[3]

Each society must make its own decisions about the balance between environmental protection and justifiable economic and social development ... [The second dam in the Lesotho Highlands Water Project] stands up well to scrutiny.[4]

> – Director-general of water Mike Muller
> writing in the *Mail & Guardian*, March 2001.

In contrast, a more honest pro-growth approach can be discerned in a comment by Thabo Mbeki about the South African National Defence Force's September 1998 defence of the Lesotho dam, as reported in the *Cape Times*:

The recent military intervention by South Africa and Botswana in Lesotho had demonstrated the Southern African Development Community's commitment to creating a climate conducive to foreign investment, Deputy President Thabo Mbeki told a high-powered investment conference in the city yesterday.[5]

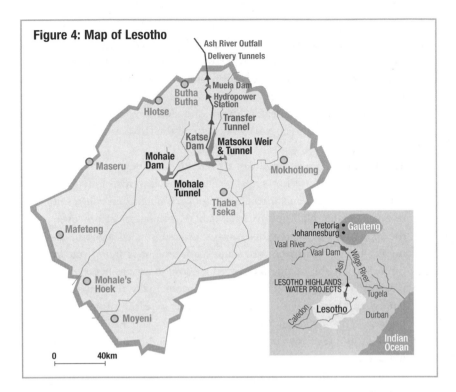

Figure 4: Map of Lesotho

Dam parameters

What motivated the extravagant, generally false claims of Mandela, Asmal, Roome and Muller? The LHWP is, in its entirety, an $8 billion, multi-phase water supply infrastructure project designed to divert rain water and runoff from the Senqu/Orange River through a series of five dams and tunnels, across the mountains of Lesotho to the urban and industrial heartland of South Africa hundreds of kilometres to the north.

In addition to provision of water, the LHWP also generates a small amount of hydropower and is anticipated ultimately to provide $50 million in annual revenues to the government of Lesotho. Katse Dam is Africa's highest dam at 185 metres. Both the dam and 70 km of diversion tunnels (together, termed Phase 1A) were completed in January 1998 at a cost of $2.5 billion (in rand prices at the time, R9.5 billion). Construction of the Mohale Dam, Mohale Tunnel and Matsoku Weir (Phase 1B) proceeded nearly immediately, at an estimated cost of R6.5 billion, with completion scheduled for 2004.

After considering the bulk of evidence associated with debates over the dam, this chapter concludes that the LHWP is a costly, corrupt, poorly-designed, badly-implemented, economically-damaging, ecologically-disastrous and distributionally-regressive megaproject. Yet the project is still advertised as critical to South Africa's future economic growth, and even as a symbol of a new-and-improved mode of regional cooperation.

A military interlude

To illustrate Pretoria's official posture, the Katse Dam's distorted importance to the South African government was reflected, in September 1998, in the route the South African National Defence Force (SANDF) took during the controversial invasion aimed at restoring power to an unpopular government which had been overthrown a few days before. Rather than deploy troops to patrol the capital city, Maseru, a platoon from Bloemfontein-based 44 Parachute Brigade quickly advanced into the mountains.[6] Much of Maseru's central business district was soon burned to the ground by looters, apparently because Botswana-based troops dawdled on their way to protect the city.

But there was no loitering in the Maluti Mountains. Once SANDF flew in and attempted to secure the Katse Dam, two troops were shot at by the Lesotho soldiers. The SANDF reacted with extreme force and took no prisoners. A *Sunday Independent* journalist later reported from Maseru:

> The common perception here is that two South African helicopters flew to the site of the dam which was being guarded by Lesotho Defence Force (LDF) troops. From the air, they opened fire on the sleeping soldiers. South African special forces troops were then landed and massacred any LDF man they could find alive.
>
> The only dispute, especially in the highland villages near the dam, is the numbers killed. Some say 16, which is the official figure; others say 27.
>
> A serving South African officer, on condition of anonymity, maintained that 'a certain captain' had perhaps been 'rather overzealous' in securing the Katse dam. But he insisted that the context should be understood. When the South African troops entered Lesotho, they were aware that some opposition politicians had threatened to blow up the dam and there was a real fear that troops at the dam might damage the installation ...
>
> The anger apparently triggered the rioting, directed initially at the many South African businesses in Maseru, but which soon spread to all foreign businesses. Once the rioting started, indiscriminate looting began and spread rapidly.

'Nobody stopped them. South African soldiers just laughed and Basotho soldiers were looting too', said an Indian shopkeeper whose store was burned to the ground and who now works as a casual shop assistant. 'They brought trucks and took away furniture on the top of cars'.

In the aftermath, Lesotho has had to deal with the loss of as many as 20,000 jobs in central Maseru and a massive dent in already badly battered investor confidence. It also faces ongoing bickering among the three major and nine minor political parties, widespread disillusionment with the entire political process and considerable anger and resentment about the events of recent months.

All in all, an extremely volatile mix. But the water has begun to flow to South Africa from the multi-billion rand investment in the mountains and millions in royalties have begun to flow into the coffers of Lesotho.

Given that the financial stakes are so high and the local political fabric so fragile, *Pax South Africanus* seems here to stay.[7]

The costs of intervention

For South Africa, damage included not only the two troops plus two medics killed in the Katse firefight, but the souring of longer-term bilateral relations. Until that point, the idea of Lesotho's unification with South Africa, potentially as an additional province, was contemplated by progressives on both sides of the border, but this prospect was snuffed out for the foreseeable future.

Moreover, according to a March 2000 report by *Mail & Guardian* journalists, no matter whether the LDF or SANDF fired first, the impression that Pretoria left was of subimperial arrogance:

> Some Basotho are crying 'cover-up' after Lesotho authorities – who invited the SA National Defence Force in the first place – moved to keep the matter out of the courts. And a senior Lesotho royal charges that the South African government and Nelson Mandela, president at the time, have ignored repeated requests for an explanation ...
>
> Meanwhile Prince Seeiso, brother of King Letsie III, this week said relations with South Africa remained strained by the Katse incident.
>
> The Lesotho royal family is known to have opposed the SADC intervention and is seen as loosely allied to the democratic opposition.

Seeiso, emphasising he spoke not on behalf of Letsie but as an individual and a principal chief, said he has been asking South African ministers to explain the Katse killings, but without success. His understanding was that LDF soldiers did not provoke the attack.

'The helicopters came and circled the area. As soon as people came out to see what was happening, they were done for'.[8]

2. Costs, benefits, and politics

How sensible was South Africa's military prioritisation of Katse, not to mention the billions of rands pumped into the LHWP, plus many billions more in future? For critics, after all, the LHWP represents the worst traditions of Western development 'solutions' to what in reality are problems associated with irrational apartheid-capitalist resource utilisation, particularly South Africa's extraordinarily unequal distribution of water.

The LHWP worsens these underlying problems by the way it merely 'bandaids' a symptom: future water shortages in the Johannesburg metropolis. At the same time, the LHWP's cost aggravates the durable development crisis of unavailability of water, by encouraging national and local officials to increase prices for impoverished urban users, without reference to their needs and ability to pay.

Alternatives to mega-dams

This chapter reflects arguments and advocacy in favour of a wholly different approach termed 'demand-side management', and in doing so, unveils divergent discursive approaches to environmental justice. In short, insist activists from Alexandra township, Lesotho's water should flow along its natural course through the Free State and Northern Cape to the Atlantic Ocean, rather than flowing through Johannesburg townships' water and sewerage pipes – which are riddled with apartheid-era leaks that drain some 40% of the incoming water – at a retail price that the World Bank recommended be set *five* times higher than existing water sources.[9]

Township pipes and taps should be repaired forthwith and Johannesburg's hedonistic corporate and high-income residential water consumers, as well as inefficient Vaal River catchment area farmers, should pay much more for water in the interests of both conservation and social justice. Lesotho's own development options should be dramatically widened in the process, with the aim of ending the bizarre residues of neo-colonial dependency associated with migrant labour bondage to South Africa, foreign debt-peonage, and the legacy of myriad misguided development projects.

This was the essence of the argument made by civic leaders in Alexandra and Soweto in late 1997 and early 1998. It was endorsed by even the neoliberal *Business Day* newspaper's environmental reporter,[10] as well as by a variety of environmental pressure groups. The critique was then taken to the World Bank's Inspection Panel, a kind of auditor-general, in April 1998 by three Alexandra residents.[11]

Backlash

But even at the level of discourse, such disputes with powerful vested interests incur costs, and the Alexandra residents suddenly encountered intense resistance:

- A subset of key civic movement leaders changed position in the wake of intense political intimidation, which took the dual form of a threatening letter from water affairs minister Kader Asmal, and ANC branch-level pressure on the civics.
- Likewise, water-sector professionals associated with the National Water Conservation Campaign and Rand Water Board reversed what were previously public opposed positions to LHWP expansion.
- An important Lesotho church group retreated from what appeared to be a certain legal confrontation with the Bank over compensation for displaced residents.
- The argument against LHWP was publicly, vociferously, rejected by Bank staff and by Asmal, who had just been named chair of the World Commission on Dams (WCD), and director-general Muller, largely on grounds of the threat of drought, but also, as they wrote in a *Mail & Guardian* article, because of the Alexandra residents' utilisation of 'the line, indeed the phrasing, of international groups opposed to the World Bank, its policies in general, its policies in the water-resource sector and its funding of dams. To be effective, and to gain formal audience, they must have local allies'.[12]
- In July 1998, the US executive director to the World Bank, Jan Piercy, refused even to meet the Alexandra residents, though they were a five-minute drive away from her five-star Sandton hotel.
- The following month, the Inspection Panel also rejected the critique, following a visit and questionable analysis by its respected, internationally known inspector, James MacNeill, who a decade earlier had served as secretary-general of the Brundtland World Commission on Environment and Development.

Defeat?

Matters seemed to subside, with *Business Day* Washington columnist Simon Barber gloating over the defeat of the Alexandra residents' argument.[13] Over the next two years, the protesters' proposed alternative strategy – demand-side management partly through higher tariffs for luxury consumption and partly through fixing water system leaks – took a back seat to supply enhancements.

The vast majority of national water project financing was directed towards major dams in the Tugela and Mkzomazi basins, the Mzimvubu basin, the Orange River, the Western Cape and the Oliphants River in Limpopo Province. This was despite the fact that such new sources of water would be physically exhausted within three decades.[14] When a major new aquifer was discovered in the Western Cape in late 2000, water bureaucrats had even less reason to impose conservation measures on the most hedonistic households, such as those in Constantia, Cape Town, whose consumption was measured at 1800 litres each day.

But at that point, other factors began to emerge that warranted a fresh look at the debate over dams and water access. Further government studies of downstream flow reduction in the Orange River confirmed the potential for an LHWP-initiated ecological catastrophe, as long predicted by environmentalists.[15] Moreover, the overriding logic of the LHWP critique based on socio-economic justice issues was quite sound, as recognised, ironically, throughout the World Commission on Dams final report in November 2000. Residents of both the Lesotho highlands and Alexandra township celebrated the report by calling jointly for a moratorium on further dam construction.

Simultaneously, the need for dramatic expansion of clean water access was amplified by a cholera outbreak due to cutoffs of free water supplies, affecting low-income rural households in KwaZulu–Natal province. Of thousands of people infected in late 2000, several dozen died. Just after the outbreak, a Constitutional Court case brought by shack-settlement leader Irene Grootboom finally guaranteed socio-economic rights, such as water, to low-income citizens.

Free water?

All this occurred during the run-up to a crucial round of municipal elections in December 2000. President Thabo Mbeki then conceded demands being made by trade unionists and NGOs for a 'lifeline' supply of water and electricity, incorporating 'free services' into prime position amongst ANC electoral campaign promises.

It is important to recall that Mbeki had earlier backed himself into a hugely embarrassing corner by questioning whether HIV caused Aids, claiming instead that expensive anti-retroviral pharmaceutical treatment was untested and dangerous, and instead that poverty was the root cause of Aids. Saving face also helps explain Mbeki's new commitment to free lifeline services, in the wake of six years of systematic water and power cutoffs to low-income residential areas.

But no one really anticipated that the election promises, already made in the 1994 RDP programme, would be kept. Instead, unaffordable retail tariffs associated with water supply in Johannesburg – indeed in all of Gauteng province – would continue to hamper water access well into the twenty-first century. Moreover, the planned Igoli 2002 corporatisation of metro Johannesburg's water supply via a consortium led by a French firm involved in LHWP construction and corruption implied yet further upward pricing pressure regardless of ANC promises.

These water-related complications have generated challenges for decades to come to the so-called 'brown' agenda – *urban ecology*, particularly as it relates to black residents with low incomes. The problems were particularly poignant and indeed ironic in January 1998, when a predicted El Nino drought failed to materialise and hence the first flow of LHWP water to Gauteng was turned back from the already overflowing Vaal River. But the price increases applied to low-income consumer bills were not similarly redirected.

Reforming Pretoria and the World Bank

In all these respects, the LHWP has become an important symbol of the extent to which the post-apartheid South African government is willing to listen and respond to socio-environmental-justice critiques of its policies and pet projects. The LHWP story provides, too, a measure of whether argumentation involving both technical and moral claims can be taken seriously within the World Bank.

Throughout, the Bank was the central organiser of technical, financial, social and ecological information about the LHWP, and will continue in this vein in future. Hence its involvement raises interesting questions about the professional competence and participatory orientation of the world's single-largest institutional investor in infrastructure, questions that Alexandra township residents put to the Inspection Panel and that deserve further consideration below.

After a review of the political context for the LHWP, the social, environmental and economic critiques can be considered. These critiques are appropriate for all bulk infrastructure projects. They pose doubts about the Bank's commitment to distributional justice and accountability – doubts also reflected in other settings across the world.

Anti-dam rhetoric

Ultimately, this chapter also considers the merits of different ecological discourses emerging from particular social struggles, or as Raymond Williams termed them, 'militant particularisms'. Contrasting discourses are intrinsic to the diverse politics of localities, but some political-ecological themes may have more universal discursive undertones.

As leading US anti-toxics activist Lois Gibbs has argued, the growing environmental justice movement asks the question 'What is morally correct?' instead of 'What is legally, scientifically, and pragmatically possible?' This, according to David Harvey, 'permits, through the medium of social protest, the articulation of ideas about a moral economy of collective provision and collective responsibility as opposed to a set of distributive relations within the political economy of profit'.[16]

The difference between environmental justice rhetoric and a sustainable-development discourse aiming to advance 'the political economy of profit' – or as Mbeki put it, 'creating a climate conducive to foreign investment' – is important to bear in mind, as we track debates over the LHWP. The clearest statement of ecological modernisation objectives is found in the United Nations *Declaration on Environment and Development* signed in Rio in June 1992 (Principle 16): 'to promote the internalisation of environmental costs and the use of economic instruments, taking into account the approach that the polluter should, in principle, bear the cost of pollution, with due regard to the public interest and without distorting international trade and investment'.

What the LHWP's green and brown critics accomplished in 1998 was to argue on legal, scientific and economic grounds that environmental and human damage in Lesotho had *not* been internalised (and often not even recognised). Their demand was that the Mohale Dam should not be built for at least another couple of decades so that more attention could be paid to improving water delivery systems from the demand side.

As we shall see, this argument was not successful, at least initially in its consideration within the World Bank Inspection Panel, although it won the blessing of the World Commission Dams final report. But nevertheless the critiques of the LHWP are worthy of close consideration, for they point to core factors underlying Johannesburg water controversies which are responsible for growing public anger: as tariffs increased, as water supplies were cut off despite extraordinary public health risks, and as the logic of water commodification and even privatisation crowded out the public interest. Then, as has happened in Johannesburg and elsewhere so many times before, social movements mobilised around the unmet demand, codified even in South Africa's 1996 Constitutional Bill of Rights, that water is a human right.

3. The political context

The political background to the five-stage LHWP is long and convoluted. The boundaries of Lesotho go back to the mid-nineteenth century, when invading European settlers of Dutch and British ancestry forced the Basotho people off the rich farming area now known as South Africa's Free State province, into the neighbouring mountains. Under subsequent British colonial rule, the LHWP was first conceived in 1954, twelve years before Lesotho's independence.

Formal government planning began in the mid-1970s. By the early 1980s, with protest in South Africa re-emerging and international sanctions beginning to gather momentum, violence broke out within Lesotho over the spoils of potential water sales to the apartheid government. Lesotho's Prime Minister, Leabua Jonathan, reacted by agreeing to the LHWP only on condition that he would control the outflow of water to South Africa. A coup soon followed in 1985, backed by South Africa, and Lesotho's new military regime pressed ahead with the alliance.[17]

Bailing out apartheid

The mid-1980s South African government was at the nadir of its pariah status. It welcomed the international legitimacy that a cross-border project, catalysed by the World Bank, would bring foreign minister Pik Botha, the architect of regional co-option, and the strongman premier, P.W. Botha. By October 1986, harsh repression, several states of emergency, and the foreign debt repayment 'standstill' of September 1985 foreclosed any chances of South African access to foreign funds.

At this crucial moment, the LHWP Treaty was announced and given controversial financial support by the Bank. The Bank's loan is worth considering in some detail in view of the ongoing campaign for cancellation of apartheid-era debts and reparation of lending profits associated with apartheid debt.[18]

Although the Bank's sister organisation, the International Monetary Fund, had granted South Africa a $1.1 billion loan as late as 1982, the Bank's last lending relations with Pretoria were during the late 1960s. But the Bank lent Lesotho $110 million for the LHWP because of South Africa's ability to stand surety. Indeed, the only financial risk analysis in the Bank's initial report concerned whether Pretoria would default.

At a conference on the LHWP sponsored by the Johannesburg NGO Group for Environmental Monitoring in August 1996, Michael Potts of the Development Bank of Southern Africa, also an LHWP funder, conceded, 'Given the limited access to foreign funds by the South African government and the limitations on contractors' funding proposals – export credit was not available to South Africa – a very complex treaty was negotiated to bypass [anti-apartheid financial] sanctions'.[19]

Merely so as to arrange the financing package, the Bank also lent Lesotho $8 million at concessionary rates through its International Development Association, in order to disguise what Asmal himself has referred to as 'sanctions busting'.[20] As environmental activist Korinna Horta recounts,

> According to the Bank's project report, preparations for project financing were so complex that it required 'the amount of staff work that would normally go into about 10 projects'. That was because Lesotho did not have the creditworthiness needed to obtain the major international funding required for Phase 1A, and giving the money directly to apartheid South Africa was politically unacceptable. World Bank documents show that the Bank was concerned about 'the project being perceived as being in the Republic of South Africa's interest' and about other possible co-financiers' 'political sensitivities' about aiding the apartheid regime. To assuage the other lenders' 'sensitivities', the World Bank helped set up a trust fund in Britain through which South Africa could service its debt.[21]

Apartheid power

In August 1996, Asmal told the NGO conference of his own later reversal on support for the LHWP: 'Ten years ago I was opposing the LHWP Treaty on political grounds and now I am called on to ensure its implementation. In the intervening years many things have changed, including, crucially, the relationship between Lesotho and South Africa, from a relationship of client-state and pariah Big Broeder to that of democratic equals'.[22]

This assessment of power relations was thrown into question a couple of weeks later, when a construction subsidiary of Anglo American Corporation, South Africa's largest firm, experienced labour problems at the Buthe Buthe construction site and called on the local police to intervene. At least five workers were killed before labour peace was restored. Pretoria's controversial invasion came just over two years after Asmal expressed his sense that South Africa and Lesotho were 'democratic equals'.

Indeed, throughout the 1990s, Maseru was rocked by popular protests and violent infighting between military factions. Conflict between three nationalist political parties intensified in the late 1990s over the spoils of a shrinking state, in part because the steady demise of South African mining jobs during the 1990s left Lesotho's economy with even fewer resources to share amongst a desperately poor population. Opposition party complaints aside, the June 2002 general election returned the ruling party to power. But without solving the underlying problem of Lesotho's perpetual underdevelopment, elites in Maseru and Pretoria could expect ongoing turmoil.

Corruption

Under such stressful economic conditions, Lesotho politics were profoundly affected by transnational construction corporations angling for a share of the enormous project. In August 1999, a court case alleging 13 counts of bribery began against the chief executive officer of the Lesotho Highlands Development Authority (LHDA), Masupha Sole. Prosecutors with access to Sole's Swiss and South African bank accounts argued that over the course of a decade, from 1988–98, he successfully induced at least $2 million from some of the largest construction and engineering consultancy firms in the world, including ABB of Sweden/Switzerland, Acres of Canada, Impregilo of Italy, and Dumez of France.[23]

Denials initially followed, but even the World Bank found itself implicated.[24] Evidence emerged that in 1994, a top Bank official, Praful Patel had sent a formal letter to the Lesotho government, demanding that Sole *not* be fired. Such an act would 'seriously jeopardise the progress of the project', according to the official. He went on to demand that the Maseru government 'consult with the Bank prior to making changes to its senior staff appointments' and even threatened 'legal action'. Later, when the letter leaked, the author dubiously claimed he drafted the command without knowledge that Sole was corrupt.

In a letter to the International Rivers Network, the Bank subsequently stated that its officials learned of the bribery only in June 1999. But the institution undermined itself again in 2002 when it refused to help finance Sole's prosecution (after initially getting good press for offering). Then, instead of debarring all the companies implicated, the Bank took action against only three middlemen intermediaries of the companies, in part because, according to a lame line of argument, the construction firms did not abuse the Bank's loan share of the project. The Lesotho affair, possibly the highest-profile case of its type in Third World history, again reminded the world of the Bretton Woods Institutions' reputation for molly-coddling corruption.

Bank president James Wolfensohn had stuck his neck out on the issue of corruption repeatedly. In October 1999 at Transparency International's International Anti-Corruption Conference in Durban, he postured, 'As far as our institution is concerned, there is nothing more important than the issue of corruption ... Corruption [is] not just political, but it [is] the single-most significant factor in the issue of development, of equity and of social justice'. Of course, there was quite a self-interested component within his message, which helps explain why Wolfensohn might have condoned the repeated sweeping of LHWP bribery under the rug: 'Corruption is now affecting the sources of funding and international balance on development assistance. At this very moment, in parliaments in developed countries, the voters of those countries are saying: We do not want to give money to any form of development assistance if it finishes up in an offshore bank account'.[25]

Finally in June 2002, based largely on evidence from the offshore account, the case against Sole was closed and he was sentenced to 18 years in jail. Charges against the major firms began to be investigated. Judge Brendon Cullinan was satisfied 'beyond a responsible doubt' that 'the accused was thus involved, over a period of nine years, in 48 corrupt or fraudulent transactions including the acceptance of 46 bribes'. Sole was paid by the multinational corporations for agreeing to 'further their private interests'.

Sole, incidentally, was not bashful. 'Bribery happens elsewhere. A bigger picture view should have been taken', he testified to Cullinan in his defence. 'The scale of the bribery is related to the scale of the Project'.[26]

There was even talk in South Africa that the multinational corporations which bribed Sole could be barred from future projects. The logical place to start was the R7 billion luxury Gautrain project connecting Pretoria, the airport, Sandton and central Johannesburg, whose contracts would be on offer at around the time the Lesotho government began prosecuting the main corporations.

At the time, Canada's Acres International drew a great deal of attention, because the same month it was implicated in Sole's bribery, the G8 Summit occurred in the luxury resort of Kananaskis. There Mbeki attempted to recruit *more* transnational corporate 'partnerships' with African states.

Paying back Lesotho – and South Africa

Is this a case for reparations? Was the LHWP yet another Third World white elephant eco-disaster, initiated by dictatorial regimes (in both South Africa and Lesotho), inappropriately financed by the World Bank, insensitive to the resulting environmental and social problems, and replete with documented evidence of corruption and winks and nods from the Bank? If so, should the people of Lesotho and South Africa be responsible for repayment of the loans associated with the LHWP?

The Jubilee network of social movements emerged by the late 1990s with the explicit objective of questioning the legitimacy of Third World debt, including 'ecological debt'.[27] A campaign was promoted by Jubilee South Africa to repudiate – and demand reimbursement for earlier payments of – what was termed 'apartheid-caused debt' as a component of more general 'Odious Debt'. By international precedent, Odious Debt did not have to be repaid if it was shown to be based upon original-debtor illegitimacy.[28]

As for potential claims against repayment of LHWP loans, the apartheid-era creditors for the Katse Dam included the World Bank ($110 million), European export credit agencies ($304 million), South Africa's export credit agency ($107 million), the Commonwealth Development Corporation ($36 million), Banque Nationale de Paris ($19.7 million), Credit Lyonnais ($17 million), Dresdner Bank ($15.8 million), Hill Samuel ($14.5 million), the European Investment Bank, the African Development Bank, and Pretoria's Development Bank of Southern Africa.

In view of the prevailing balance of forces, the post-apartheid South African government adopted a posture of active hostility to, and misinformation about, the apartheid debt campaign.[29] In turn, that led a New York lawyer to file suit on behalf of black South Africans in June 2002 against many of the major European and US banks and corporations that financed apartheid. Although the LHWP was not specifically mentioned at this stage, the potential for making similar demands based upon obvious apartheid collusion and ecological debt, not to mention corruption, remains great.

The immediate political challenge, however, is the strengthening of links between abstract campaigning for economic justice on the one hand, and on the other, concrete campaigns that unveil for ordinary people the nature of the problems, the causes, the institutions responsible, and the logical remedies. Such campaigning has already been established by 'green' advocates of social and environmental justice in Lesotho, and, simultaneously, by 'brown' advocates of socio-environmental justice in Johannesburg townships.

4. The green critique

Green criticisms of the LHWP were based on both ecological factors and the interests of indigenous people. In the Highlands, socio-economic and environmental problems associated with the LHWP were meant to have been ameliorated by World Bank staff and allied planners, particularly through the Lesotho government's Rural Development Programme and fund. However, the fund was soon embroiled in corruption scandals, along with the Muela hydropower scheme. Royalty through-flows to the Rural Development Programme were scaled back to better match 'absorptive capacity'.

Dam displacement

But even had the fund been properly allocated, resolving the LHWP's socio-ecological problems was never as straightforward as planners expected. The Katse Dam directly displaced 2,000 people – approximately 300 households – but indirectly affected at least 20,000 more who lost the use of common resources or income through the submersion of 925 hectares of arable and 3,000 ha of grazing land. Ancestral burial grounds were also flooded.

Likewise, the Mohale Dam would inundate 550 ha of extremely good cropland and forced the resettlement of 400 families. Following erosion of much of Lesotho's arable land over the past three decades, less than 9% of the country's soil is available for cultivation.

In the relatively barren Maluti Mountains, tiny woodlots and fields for cultivation and grazing are guarded carefully by local peasants. But once the water began rising, sufficient numbers and quality of replacement trees were not provided. For those peasants who lost their fuelwood, cash compensation – as little as R1 per square metre, even for thickets of full-grown poplar – was insufficient to pay for alternative fuels.

LHWP authorities initially provided the peasants with inadequate replacement fodder for cattle, and failed in some cases to give local people access to construction jobs. Moreover, valuable topsoil inundated by Katse water either was never recovered or was diverted to the gardens of European and South African consultants living in the area rather than to those forced to move by the rising waters.

Many of those displaced were given low-quality replacement housing that amounted to little more than uninsulated storage shedding. Women, children and the elderly were particularly hard hit; according to Mathato Khitsane of the Highlands Church Action Group, 'The project shows no sensitivity to the impact on gender issues and roles of women'.[30] In 1997, church surveys indicating widespread dissatisfaction on the part of many residents with resettlement schemes and provisions for reimbursement.

Notwithstanding Asmal's periodic commitments to increase levels of compensation to displacees,[31] the disputes continued during his period as water minister.[32] According to Ryan Hoover of the International Rivers Network (IRN), studies showed that 'Household income figures for the LHWP northeastern mountain region fell 65% faster than the national average during the LHWP's initial years'.[33]

In November 1999, people from Makotoko, Matala and Ha Nkokana communities displaced by the Katse and Mohale dams testified about their experiences to the World Commission on Dams:

Malisemelo Tau: The LHDA project told us ... if we move away there, and the project builds a dam there, that water can save many people's lives. We agreed to move away to save many people's lives with our water and we hoped that the project will be trusted to satisfy us with all that it promised to do for us because we save many people's lives ... When we research at our destination, we found that there is no water until now. We have a great problem of water at the new village. We get water from the river by wheelbarrows. We drink water from the river and the river is very far from us ... the owners of that place resettled by LHDA have tears running on down their cheeks every day.

Anna Moepi: Ladies and Gentlemen, our lives before the Lesotho Highlands Water Project was a nice one. We were living in peace and harmony ... Our lives in the new location leave a lot to be desired ... You see our lives as deteriorating day by day. We are worse off ... The project had initially promised that we would be trained on self-reliant projects that would include income-generating activities. Nothing is happening.

Benedict Leuta: The roads that they have built are the only good thing I can think of about the Lesotho Highlands Water Project ... But the roads also destroyed a lot. The road culverts cause erosion in our fields. And in my village we had some wells that were covered by the road ... After the road covered them, we received no compensation. We had to pay the government to come help us bring water down from high in the mountains ... We are less healthy after the dam has been built ... Also the chiefs gained because they were sub-contracted to LHDA and also received bribes from many people ... The affected people were the losers. Some people lost their land and received no compensation or employment.[34]

Pros and cons

Compensation for lost land, social goods and livelihoods was not the only social challenge. In addition, the LHWP's role in socio-economic modernisation of Lesotho villages also brought with it a dramatic increase in HIV/Aids. Already by 1992, 5% of construction workers were testing HIV-positive, and high rates of transmission to local villagers were observed in one major study.[35]

As Asmal conceded, 'Social problems such as increased alcohol abuse, increased sexually-transmitted disease and increased stock theft have all been reported in villages along the new Katse Road'.[36] However, he continued,

> These negative impacts must be weighted against the benefits arising from the project, including access to improved health and educational facilities, water supply to communities, sanitation at schools, and, at villages close to the sites, the construction of community halls, community offices, creches, open markets and road access. One must also weigh in the benefit of employment opportunities for local people, both in the construction phase and in the considerable long-term maintenance tasks.

Indeed, 157 latrines were installed in eight schools, and in seven villages, trenches were dug for water supplies, with nearly 90 km of unrelated feeder roads to be constructed by 1999. But this was relatively small consolation when considered in the context of the $2.5 billion cost of the Katse Dam. And while the introduction of tarred roads into the area brought increased trade, it also resulted in the closure of the major local store. The effect of more than a decade of road-building in the Lesotho Highlands, anthropologist James Ferguson has shown in his pathbreaking Foucauldian analysis, *The Anti-Politics Machine*, was to impoverish peasants further, as markets undermined local food production and officials milked more taxes and fees from the now accessible peasants.[37]

Eco-damage

The Katse and Mohale Dams not only aggravated land hunger, but destroyed crucial habitats of the Maluti Minnow (an endangered species), bearded vulture and four other species considered 'globally threatened'.[38]

Other potential ecological problems associated with the LHWP have also emerged. The early feasibility studies conducted by a British-German consortium failed to include an Environmental Impact Assessment, which resulted in cost overruns of 15% due to an unanticipated need to line the Katse tunnels with cement.

Soil erosion and sedimentation – which typically lowers dam capacity by 1% per year and silts intake areas – were not initially accounted for. When sedimentation was finally factored into India's infamous Sardar Sarovar Dam, it tipped the balance towards cancellation of the Bank's involvement. And reservoir-induced earthquakes in the Highlands village of Mapeleng generated a crack 1.5 km long, damaging nearly 70 houses and diverting an important water spring from the surface.

There is also a chance that the LHWP's environmental flaws will backlash against South Africa itself. According to a 1996 study by Snaddon, Wishart and Davies,

> The LHWP will eventually divert 2.2. H10^{9}m^{3}y-1 from the Headwaters of the Orange River in Lesotho, into the Ash/Liebenbergsvlei tributary of the Vaal River in the Free State. This will be the largest Inter-Basin Transfer in southern Africa, and it will result in considerable alterations of the rivers concerned. These systems will remain unstable for a very long time. The overall environmental effects of the LHWP have not adequately been assessed, and assessments of the instream flow requirements of the rivers involved in the scheme have focused only on the donor systems.[39]

In Pretoria, the original *Orange River Project Replanning Study* commissioned by Dwaf made very superficial estimates for downstream irrigation needs, ignoring, for instance, any new requirements for emergent black farmers. Dwaf admitted that even by 1996, as Katse was being completed, it could not 'yet claim that it has conclusively determined the present and future irrigation water requirements in the study area'.[40] Warned Free State University Zoology Professor Maitland Seaman, 'The [Orange] river might even dry up in exceptional years' due to the LHWP.[41]

A 1999 *Orange River Development Project Replanning Study* by consultants BKS and Ninham Shand evaded most of the thorny issues, continuing, for example, to assume that there would be no increase in water available for irrigation.[42] The study suggested that further LHWP dams beyond Mohale would be inefficient for diversion, compared to the potential for pumping more than four times as much water from the Orange River into the Vaal River from a large new proposed dam further downstream from Lesotho, at Boskraai.

Indeed, Lesotho's own access to water is also a matter of great concern, notwithstanding that the BKS/Ninham Shand study incorrectly assumed that 'formal water use along the Senqu River and its tributaries is very small and was taken to be accounted for by the compensation and environmental releases for the dams' and hence 'no further allowance was made' for Lesotho's water needs.[43]

In reality, virtually all other experts and commentators argue that there is insufficient water in the country to share with South Africa beyond the Mohale Dam. According to a rigorous 1999 official Instream Flow Requirement study of the Senqu within Lesotho, 'critically severe' biophysical and social impacts of water diversion should be anticipated.[44] At $51m^3s^{-1}$, the extraction of water along the lines anticipated in the LHWP Treaty would have mitigation and compensation implications of R20 million per year, with still 'moderate to severe' impacts under the lowest-extraction scenario of $44m^3s^{-1}$.[45] As things stood, senior SADC water official Lengolo Monyake predicted, within 10-30 years Lesotho would face severe water scarcity.[46]

Green solidarity

The social and ecological problems associated with the LHWP within Lesotho led not only to local criticism, but gained the attention of international activist/advocacy NGOs like Christian Aid, the Environmental Defence Fund (EDF) and the International Rivers Network. LHWP opponents began badgering the World Bank to provide more compensation to displacees and address the ecological damage. The activists represented, according to Addison,

> a loose coalition of environmental lobbyists, NGOs and churches. Leadership essentially comes from the California-based International Rivers Network, whose Africa coordinator, Lori Pottinger, has visited Lesotho to collect the views of villagers and has been tireless in her criticisms of the scheme, over the Internet and at conferences. The coalition also includes South African bodies such as the Group for Environmental Monitoring and the Southern African Rivers Association. Increasingly, the media in South Africa and Lesotho are carrying letters and articles questioning the high social and environmental costs and the political ramifications of the scheme.[47]

In light of these concerns, it is revealing to consider Bank LHWP Taskmanager John Roome's own assessment of 'possible controversial aspects' of the LHWP:

> The project has been in the spotlight from international NGOs. Although a detailed study of meetings and consultations have been

147

undertaken, some International NGOs (e.g. EDF, IRN) may not support the Bank's decision to proceed with the funding of Phase 1B at this time – partly related to the issues set out below (basically judgment calls on whether progress in Phase 1A has been satisfactory and whether the economics of delays to Phase 1B are acceptable), but partly on principle as part of the larger 'big dams' debate. This has taken further importance with the appointment of Prof. Asmal (the SA minister concerned) as Chair of the recently established World Commission on Dams ...

Local NGOs have been critical of the Lesotho Highlands Development Authority's level of performance on the social aspects of the project. The Lesotho Council of NGOs has however recently signed a declaration endorsing the implementation of the project. They agree that LHDA's performance has improved in recent years, but they argue that there is still room for further improvement. One local NGO (Highlands Church Solidarity and Action Centre) has from time to time taken a more aggressive stance against the project – supporting calls for Phase 1B to be delayed. As of mid-March 1998 they seemed to support the Lesotho Council of NGOs' position and have no objection to the project proceeding to Phase 1B.[48]

On the one hand, a senior bank official acknowledged that Christian Aid, IRN and EDF 'created space for greater Bank and government attention to mitigation measures'. In turn, concluded researchers Jonathan Fox and Larry Brown, such attention 'reflects a broader pattern in which public pressure from Northern NGOs encourages World Bank officials to grant more legitimacy to local NGOs as alternative interlocutors'.[49]

But on the other hand, this was also a recipe for cooption, even temporarily, and not only of Lesotho's NGOs, as Roome recorded above. As discussed below, there also arose an urgent need for the Bank and South African government to coopt – or failing that, intimidate – local organisations on the other side of the border, once the green critics were joined by activists from Soweto and Alexandra. For in 1998, the stakes suddenly rose when Johannesburg township organisations began arguing for a long postponement of the Mohale Dam.

5. The brown critique

The LHWP is, in the discourse of the South African state, a developmental project. Quotes above by Mandela and Asmal are emblematic of the marketing job. The reality, in fact, appears to be the opposite: the LHWP makes water provision to low-income, black Johannesburg residents more, not less, difficult.

Who consumes Vaal water?

The benefits of the LHWP will primarily flow to wealthy farmers, corporations and white consumers.[50] In addition, foreign investors who receive regular invitations from Thabo Mbeki – in the spirit of the quotation above, justifying armed intervention to secure Lesotho's water – would be potential beneficiaries.

Of water sold in Gauteng in 1995 by Rand Water – comprising 41% of the Vaal River System's supply – only 25% was bought by low-income consumers (i.e., 10% of the total outflow from the Vaal). In contrast, 36% went to middle- and upper-income consumers, 24% to industry, and 15% to large mines.

As for those without water due to apartheid and unaffordability, in 1995 there were an estimated 1.5 million residents who still did not have direct access to water. To supply these people with 50 litres per person per day would have required only 27 million m^3 of additional supply annually, representing a small fraction of the water that middle- and upper-income Gauteng consumers use to water their gardens and fill swimming pools[51] The LHWP's Katse Dam provides 580 million litres a year and Mohale will add another 350 million litres of water that can be delivered to Gauteng at full capacity, for a total of 930 million litres.

The World Bank had already overestimated the demand for LHWP water in Gauteng by 40% when Katse was being constructed, by Roome's own admission. Rand Water Board's own demand curves for Vaal River water during the half-century from 1998–2048 varied enormously, from 4 billion litres a year in 2048 according to a 'low demand' scenario, 4.4 billion according to a 'most probable' scenario, and up to 13 billion litres for the 'high' option.[52]

The irony of the LHWP was that regardless of such small amounts required for consumption by low-income people, an enormous additional water cost burden was already, by 1998, being borne by impoverished township dwellers. As noted above, Asmal insisted that 'the end users will pay for the project, at tariffs well within the capabilities of the beneficiaries, making it economically viable'.[53] Yet the data below throw this assessment into question.

Who pays the bill?

From the mid-1990s, Christian Aid in London, EDF in Washington and the

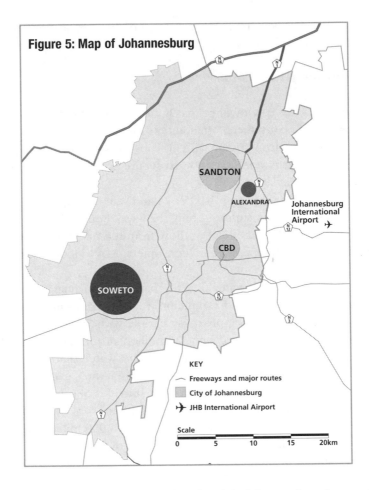

Figure 5: Map of Johannesburg

Group for Environmental Monitoring (GEM) in Johannesburg began draw-ing attention to the LHWP's demand-side issues, especially consumption and conservation. But it was only when thousands of Soweto residents marched to the Johannesburg city council in July 1996, protesting against a 30% increase in their water tariffs, that the Soweto Civic Association learned of the LHWP's cost implications from municipal officials.

The rising cost of both bulk and retail water was soon to become an important debating point, as two joint workshops with the Alexandra Civic Organisation in 1997 established that because of rising bulk water costs, the LHWP would make it harder for Gauteng municipalities to a) keep water prices down; b) desist from water cutoffs; and c) repair leak-ing pipes in the townships.

This realisation catalysed a temporary brown-green, cross-border alliance and ultimately, as explored in more detail below, an April 1998 challenge to the World Bank Inspection Panel by three of the civic leaders. By delaying the Mohale Dam for an estimated 17 years, the Alexandra residents insisted, resources could be spent on conservation and maintenance, as well as on redistributing water to township households. The residents cited a Rand Water official who argued the annual savings of a Mohale Dam delay at current interest rates was R800 million, which in a single year would have easily been sufficient to repair existing systems.[54]

If instead, the LHWP went ahead and the R800 million per annum was to be spent on servicing the Mohale Dam debt, on top of the debt servicing associated with the Katse Dam, then the bulk supply cost of Vaal River water would have to increase by a factor of at least five, to R1.50/Kl in 1995 prices, as shown in Figure 6. At that stage, according to Roome, existing bulk water supply costs in the Vaal catchment reflected present-value real costs of R0.05/Kl for a billion Kls per year supplied through the Vaal Dam; R0.10 for another 450 million Kl through Bloemhof; and R0.20 for the next 800 million Kl through Tugela Vaal. The Katse and Mohale Dams were expected to add another 800–1,000 million Kl at a cost of R1.50 for each Kl.[55]

The huge cost of Katse began accruing to Dwaf and then to Rand Water, and was quickly translated into price increases to municipalities of 35% between July 1995 and July 1998. In turn, Johannesburg passed these costs on to consumers, of whom the poor paid a higher proportion: a 55% price increase for the first block of the Johannesburg block tariff.[56] Other municipalities in Gauteng also imposed a higher increase during the late 1990s for the first block of water, than for higher volumes of consumption.

As should have been anticipated, as water prices rose, the ability of municipalities to collect services payments from low-income residents fell. That led to intensified municipal water cutoffs. In short, the poor would pay disproportionately for mega-dams which mainly benefited

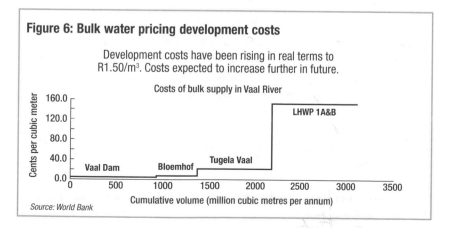

Figure 6: Bulk water pricing development costs

Development costs have been rising in real terms to R1.50/m³. Costs expected to increase further in future.

Costs of bulk supply in Vaal River

Cents per cubic meter

160.0

120.0

80.0

40.0

0.0

Vaal Dam   Bloemhof   Tugela Vaal   LHWP 1A&B

0   500   1000   1500   2000   2500   3000   3500

Cumulative volume (million cubic metres per annum)

Source: World Bank

wealthy people and big mines and industry, and would suffer cutoffs when their bills became unaffordable.

Alexandra's thirst

The injustice was even more acute because household environmental conditions faced by Johannesburg township residents during the late 1990s and today, reflect systemic apartheid-capitalist underdevelopment. Historically, these townships were primarily sites of labour reproduction, with virtually no commerce allowed and very little in the way of education and community amenities provided. Alexandra was a classical example of how townships maintained and reproduced South Africa's very poorly paid proletariat, because the southern hemisphere's wealthiest neighbourhood – Sandton – is just 5 km to the west, over a hill and across a valley and highway.[57]

Would water from Lesotho salve the wounds of apartheid-capitalism? Inadequate municipal services were integral to the development of township underdevelopment. The system ignored the oft-documented net benefits that giving low-income people adequate supplies of water and electricity yield for public health, the urban environment, gender equality, productivity, local economic development and the like.[58]

Little of that mattered in a setting that at its core was designed to squeeze as much unskilled, poorly remunerated labour time out of working-age black men as possible. Women were typically forced to remain behind in rural areas, providing an enormous 'social wage' subsidy to urban capital in the form of free child-rearing for workers too young to go to the mines and factories, health care for sick workers, and old-age care for retired workers. As expressed in the community leaders' complaint to the World Bank Inspection Panel,

> By consuming less than 2% of all South Africa's water, the country's black township residents together use less than a third of the amount used in middle- and upper-income swimming pools and gardens, not to mention white domestic (in-house) consumption or massive water wastage by white farmers who have had enormous irrigation subsidies over the years and who use 50% of South Africa's water.[59]

Reflections of the miserable state of apartheid-era infrastructure include the following:

> Out of every 100 drops that flow through Gauteng pipes, 24 quickly leak into the ground through faulty bulk infrastructure. Still more

waste occurs in leaky communal, yard and house taps. In the higher elevations of Alexandra township, these problems are witnessed in the perpetual lack of water pressure. Hundreds of thousands of low-income people in Alexandra and other townships have no immediate house or yard access to reticulated water supplied by our Johannesburg municipality, and instead receive at best only communal access, with all the public health problems that this implies. Indeed, the lack of available water on a universal basis means that public health conditions are worse; geographical segregation of low-income Gauteng residents (from wealthier residents) is more extreme; women are particularly inconvenienced, and their income-generation and caregiving capacities are reduced; and the environment is threatened (in part because of the shortage of water-borne sanitation).[60]

Rising prices

Most importantly from an economic standpoint, a large proportion of the LHWP costs were being passed from the TransCaledon Tunnel Authority (TCTA) to Dwaf, and then on to municipalities and in turn, to retail consumers. But, as noted above, those customers who had been historically oppressed by lack of access to water paid a relatively greater unit share of the bill. The LHWP costs began to be reflected as the primary basis for retail water price increases beginning in 1994. As the Inspection Panel admitted,

> Since April 1994, the bulk water tariff that TCTA charges Dwaf has slightly more than tripled, rising from R0.242/Kl to R0.751/Kl. During the same period, April 1994 to April 1998, the tariff that Dwaf charges its large consumers, including Rand Water, has slightly more than doubled, rising from R0.457/Kl to R0.945/Kl. This of course includes the amount that Dwaf pays to TCTA for LHWP water ... Rand Water's charges to the municipalities have also increased during this period. From April 1994 to April 1998, the bulk water tariff that Rand Water charges the municipalities increased ... from R1.201/Kl to R1.685/Kl.[61]

So while bulk water charges to municipalities rose by 35% in large part due to the LHWP between mid-1995 and mid-1998, the levy for the first (lowest) block of the Johannesburg block tariff increased by 55%. In sum, relatively speaking, first-block consumers paid a higher proportion of the increase than did consumers who used more water.[62]

Nevertheless, such reverse Robin Hood price increases were insufficient evidence for MacNeill, whose inspection led the Panel to ask and answer the following question about the LHWP-related price increases:

> How have the municipalities responded? At this point the linkages back to LHWP become very tenuous. At the municipal retail level in Gauteng, a host of factors impact on water charges, and on their collection, and it is simply not possible to isolate one factor against the others.[63]

This kind of analytical trepidation represents, one might argue, an *incomplete* (or even incompetent) sustainable-development discourse, because indeed factor analysis of the component costs of municipal water should have been feasible. Because 'the Panel is not satisfied that there is *prima facie* evidence linking this situation to the [LHWP], nor to the Bank's decision to proceed with financing 1B', MacNeill recommended that a full investigation not be carried out.[64]

Had such an investigation been mandated, it would have confronted the Alexandra residents' allegation that:

> Municipalities have borne the costs of rising water prices and limited retail affordability in recent months, and are passing them on to workers, who are increasingly suffering wage and retrenchment pressure, and to communities, in the form of increased levels of water cutoffs. This reflects both overall municipal fiscal stress (as central to local grants declined by 85% in real terms from 1991/92 to 1997/98) as well as higher priced bulk water costs. Debts by Gauteng municipalities for bulk sewerage and bulk water supplies that are more than 60 days overdue amounted to R69,000,000 at the end of 1997, and another R20,000,000 in water-related debts were between 30 and 60 days overdue. The 24 Gauteng municipalities raised total income of R968,000,000 from water bills to all classes of consumers in 1997 and spent R1,019,000,000 on water services (a deficit of R51,000,000). In contrast, of the 236 municipalities that report across South Africa, water bills raised R2,414,000,000 in 1997, and expenditures were just R2,388,000,000 (a surplus of R26,000,000). This is surprising given that Gauteng is South Africa's wealthiest province. The fiscal stress caused by deficits on the water account are part of the reason that the following Gauteng municipalities were declared, in December 1997, to be in default of government 'viability' criteria (sufficient cash and investments to meet one month's personnel bill): Johannesburg, Pretoria, Alberton, Brak-

pan, Randfontein, Bronkhorstpruit, Walkerville and Vereeniging Koponong.[65]

Inability to pay

In turn, the Alexandra residents continued, this fiscal crisis was being transferred to communities:

> The direct consequence of rising indebtedness has been intensified municipal 'credit control' against those households who can not afford to pay for increasingly costly water. Rand Water price increases announced in February 1998 – which were more than 50% above the inflation rate, because 75% of the increase is from the LHWP – will affect the claimants at a time that unemployment is increasing, overall municipal bills are being increased and some wealthy ratepayers are offering stiff resistance to paying their fair share. The implications of rising water prices and the lack of a 'lifeline tariff' – a basic water service available to even to the very poor – include not only switching of funds in household budgets away from other necessities, but also a dramatic increase in residential water cutoffs in Gauteng since early 1997. According to the Department of Constitutional Development's 'Project Viability', 24 out of the 30 Gauteng local authorities (representing a population of more than 12 million people) that replied to an official questionnaire, engaged in water cutoffs. These cutoffs affected 512 households in the first quarter of 1997, 932 households in the second quarter, 1,210 households in the third quarter and 5,472 households in the fourth quarter. The ability of many of these households to afford their bills was limited, as witnessed by the fact that only 252, 449, 613 and 1,064 Gauteng households were reconnected in those four quarters of 1997, respectively. There are many other potential indicators of the costs of increasing water tariffs associated with the LHWP, including public health costs and ecological problems (as excessive water-borne sanitation costs lead to informal sanitation arrangements), most of which generate a bias against low-income women, which should also be researched and factored into the water pricing and access policies. However, these are at present not being adequately considered, due to the intensive pressure municipalities face to balance their books in the very short term.[66]

The cutoffs intensified during 1998. Unfortunately, no detailed statistics about municipal 'credit control' were released from 1998 to 2001, because the Project Viability reports were so depressing that publication of the series was discontinued by Pretoria. But to illustrate the scale of the epidemic, in the black township of Leandra in neighbouring Mpumalanga province, 70,000 residents had nearly three-quarters of their water supplies cut by Rand Water for several months. The victims included *residents who paid their bills*, by virtue of being victimised by official mains cuts.[67]

MacNeill and the Inspection Panel appeared entirely unsympathetic, and by muddying the problem of affordability constraints – the main reason people don't pay their municipal bills – with an alleged culture of nonpayment, the Panel concluded that punishment was in order:

> Non-payment for services began as a strategy in the struggle against apartheid. It has continued as a habit of non-payment if not a culture of entitlement ...The Inspector was informed that the Government of South Africa, Dwaf, Rand Water and the municipalities have taken a firm position on payment for services, including water and sanitation services. Failure to pay is resulting in cutoffs. Given the many factors at play, however, it is clearly difficult, perhaps impossible, to determine the extent to which non-payment and hence cutoffs stem from this habit of non-payment or from a simple inability to pay.[68]

At issue here was whether LHWP expansion would aggravate rather than ameliorate the affordability problems. The matter was urgent, for Gauteng municipalities would continue reacting to extremely serious financial difficulties by dramatically increasing the pace of water cutoffs to low-income consumers as well as the retail price of water. The Inspection Panel did not *deny* the possibility of a direct link, but its tools of sustainable-development and environmental-impact analysis were not sophisticated enough for it to measure that link. And MacNeill appeared to mix in, for further effect, an anti-popular political bias.

The demand-side and redistributive alternative

An even larger innovation associated with the sustainable-development thesis now came into play: the strategy of demand-side management. The need for South Africa to adopt a conservation strategy was not disputed in any of the discourses, although the Bank would not accept claims (e.g. by a Rand Water official) that as great as 40% water savings could be achieved through conservation strategies.[69] Roome rebutted, 'It is not clear what the scope is for further demand management ... Demand management capabilities and their impact in South Africa are theoretical and have not yet been tried and tested'.[70]

More important than the absolute amount of water savings, was whether the additional costs associated with the LHWP would act as a disincentive to conservation. The terrifying logic here, was that in order to pay for the extremely expensive LHWP construction, its downstream buyers, especially Rand Water, would have to sell (not conserve) the LHWP water. Conservation would make the full cost-recovery of the LHWP construction costs that much harder. The Bank claimed not, and the Inspection Panel was neutral but placed its faith in Dwaf's stated commitment to conservation.

There was, however, an additional problem that very directly related to the Alexandra residents' redistributive agenda. Demand-side management entails a variety of reforms, according to the Alexandra residents:

> repairing our townships' leaky connector pipes and leaky water taps, modernising and fixing metres, changing water usage patterns through progressive block tariffs, promoting water-sensitive gardening and food production, intensifying water conservation education, regulating or prohibiting excessive watering of suburban gardens, implementing other water use regulation, clearing invasive alien trees, promoting school water audits, billing consumer with more informative material, and installing low-flow showerheads, dual-flush toilets and similar mechanical interventions.[71]

The most important and readily available demand-side strategy is the progressive block tariff, through which a free lifeline is available for all lowest-tier consumption but increasing prices are charged for subsequent consumption. The combined objectives of conservation and distributive justice via block tariffs are taken up again in Chapters Four and Five.

Interestingly, even the World Bank itself, in its 1994 *World Development Report* on infrastructure, endorsed a lifeline supply and progressive block tariffs:

> Subsidized provision of infrastructure is often proposed as a means of redistributing resources from higher-income households to the poor. Yet its effectiveness depends on whether subsidies actually reach the poor ...
>
> There are, however, ways in which infrastructure subsidies can be structured to improve their effectiveness in reaching the poor. For example, for water, increasing-block tariffs can be used – charging a particularly low 'lifeline' rate for the first part of consumption (for

example, 25 to 50 litres per person per day) and higher rates for additional 'blocks' of water. This block tariff links price to volume, and it is more efficient at reaching the poor than a general subsidy because it limits subsidized consumption. Increasing-block tariffs also encourage water conservation and efficient use by increasing charges at higher use.[72]

The Bank and Pretoria v. cross-subsidisation

This 1994 advice from head office was ignored, indeed rejected, by both Roome and MacNeill. As the Alexandra residents complained, 'The possibility for changing water usage patterns through progressive block tariffs was never factored in to LHWP demand calculations, in part because key Bank staff (though not the Bank's Washington headquarters) explicitly opposed differential pricing of water'.[73] The residents referred to Roome's October 1995 presentation to Asmal, which argued against sliding tariffs, citing in particular the case of Johannesburg.

At the time, Johannesburg (the 'Central Wits' region) had a four-block tariff structure which rose gradually from R1.20/Kl for 0–10 Kls per month, up to R3/Kl for more than 45 Kl/month consumption, as shown in Figure 7. Roome's only valid criticism of Johannesburg's water pricing model was that the rising block tariffs 'may limit options with respect to tertiary providers – in particular private concessions much harder to establish'.[74]

This criticism is understandable, although not forgiveable, in view of the World Bank goal to privatise municipal water. As we discuss in more detail in Chapter Four, private bidders would indeed be deterred if they encountered an obligation to consider redistribution – in the form of a life-

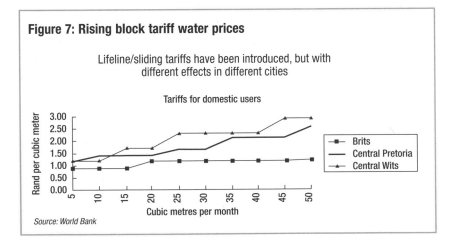

Figure 7: Rising block tariff water prices

Lifeline/sliding tariffs have been introduced, but with different effects in different cities

Tariffs for domestic users

Source: World Bank

line water supply and sharply rising tariff for hedonistic users – when pricing water to maximise profit. The reason for this is that the firm's curves for marginal cost (each additional unit) and marginal revenue (ideally running parallel, so as to 'get the prices right') necessarily depart from a redistributive water pricing structure. This is a topic we return to later.

Most South African cities moved in Roome's favoured direction, i.e., away from cross-subsidisation, prior to the ANC's September 2000 promise of a free lifeline water supply and rising block tariff. Tellingly, instead of raising the slope of Johannesburg's near-flat block tariff to levels that would have achieved social justice and conservation, the city managers hired World Bank consultants as part of the Igoli 2002 corporatisation programme. The city's strategy, until July 2001, was to provide only a small grant – R30 per month for water and a bit more for other services – to 'indigent' households whose poverty status could be confirmed through stigma-inducing 'means-testing'. Instead of finding several hundred thousand qualified households, the city signed up only a meagre 24,000 recipients.[75]

Across Gauteng, prior to the implementation of the free water policy, the Palmer Development Group found in its survey of Rand Water Board users that low-volume users had systematically been charged more than higher-volume users since 1996: 'It is evident that there is a continuing increase in tariffs in real terms, of the order of 7% per year for all blocks. Some of this increase may be related to increasing bulk supply costs and some may relate to improved service. But there is a concern that a part of the increase relates to decreasing efficiency. A further concern is that the lowest block is the one which is increasing fastest'.[76]

Indeed, amongst the municipalities served by Rand Water during the late 1990s, those at the first block of consumption paid 39% more, *after inflation*, than they had in 1996. The more hedonistic consumers' rate went up only 24% (Table 4).

Table 4: Residential water tariff increases imposed by Rand Water-supplied municipalities, 1996–2000

(Rands per thousand litres, real 2000 currency)[77]

Tariff:	1996	1997	1998	1999	2000	% rise, '96–00
Block 1	1.86	1.97	2.33	2.41	2.58	39%
Block 2	2.52	2.64	3.26	3.22	3.36	33%
Block 3	2.91	3.01	3.66	3.71	3.79	30%
Block 4	3.49	3.41	4.20	4.20	4.32	24%

The reverse Robin Hood policy ended finally, after July 2001, when the free services policy was partially adopted in Gauteng cities. At that point, Johannesburg adjusted its tariff curve in a slightly more progressive direction. Beyond the free 6 kl/household/month, a R2.30/kl price was applied up to 10 kl/h/m. From 10–15 kl/h/m, the tariff was for R4.10/kl; from 15–20 kl/h/m, R4.60; from 25–40 kl/h/m, R5.50/kl; and above 40 kl/h/m, R6.50.[78]

What would that mean, price-wise, for a grandmother in a township looking after a dozen dependents on a measly monthly pension? Even after July 2000 when the new free water policy allegedly came into effect, if she and the others consumed the 50 litres recommended for human health and hygiene each day, the roughly 20 kl per month would cost R53 in Johannesburg, nearly a tenth of her monthly income. In some towns served by Rand Water, the cost would be yet higher: R90 in Randfontein, and more than R75 in Emfuleni, Lesedi, Midvaal and Highveld East.

As for industrial tariffs, they have been kept on a regressive schedule, so that extremely high volume users (in excess of a million litres per month) pay declining rates in many towns supplied by Rand Water. In Johannesburg, the tariff was set at R4.60 in July 2001.

Asmal's agenda

Asmal, meanwhile, finally endorsed progressive block tariffs in principle before he moved to the education ministry. But as shown in Part Three, he explicitly opposed the provision of free water as the lowest-block lifeline price. Moreover, Asmal never overrode a *White Paper on Water and Sanitation* which as early as 1994 had insisted that water should be charged at full marginal cost. Inexplicably, Asmal's neoliberal bureaucrats and advisers had convinced the new minister to define lifeline price as the equivalent of 'operating and maintenance' expenses.[79] The World Bank Inspection Panel also endorsed a definition of lifeline that fell far short of being free of charge.[80]

Although his 1998 National Water Pricing Policy contained a provision for a bulk 'free' lifeline reserve of 25 litres per person per day for all South Africans, Asmal made no effort to assure that once water was provided to the water boards and municipalities, it would then be purified and supplied to residents free, or for less than operating and maintenance costs. Given the vast increases in the overall recurrent costs of bulk water supply because of the LHWP, Asmal's abstract commitment to a lifeline human reserve in the water pricing structure would offer no relief.

As chair of the World Commission on Dams, however, Asmal did benefit from a more critical group of researchers and commissioners. In November 2000, the WCD report explicitly recommended that a 'priority should be to improve existing systems before building new supply, [and] that demand-side options should be given the same significance as supply options'.[81] On a variety of other brown and green issues, the Commission backed the LHWP critics' perspectives.

Indeed, it would soon became clear that the massive contradictions between the WCD report and Dwaf's desire to expand the Lesotho dams would require yet more political obfuscation. Asmal requested that ex-president Nelson Mandela introduce the report at its London launch in November 2000, and Mandela's speech denied the obvious:

> We knew the controversy and complexities of such an undertaking [the LHWP] and had to carefully negotiate the political minefields and legal challenges, taking into consideration environmental, financial, social and economic impacts. A dam – a means to an end – which was one option among others, emerged as our best option under the circumstances.[82]

This statement, without reflection or justification, suggests some of the limits to the sustainable-development discourse. Politically, it shows that Asmal's agenda remained one of self-promotion, and demonstrates why recourse to technical arguments alone was not sufficient to serve the interests of Johannesburg's low-income township residents.

6. The limits of sustainable-development discourse

The disappointing official reactions to the brown critique of the LHWP raise the question of whether the sustainable-development argument was the appropriate discursive tactic for the Alexandra critics. The argument, as Harvey describes it, is based on the use of rational scientific (including socio-economic) enquiry in order 'to configure what would be a good strategy for sustainable economic growth and economic development in the long run. The key word in this formulation is sustainability'.[83]

The idea of sustainable development is, without question, an improvement over a purely economic approach to environmental management. A deeper consideration of costs and benefits that incorporate ecological values was welcome in the otherwise barren – if 'impeccable' – context of 1990s neoliberal hegemony. Scientific studies in the spirit of sustainable development, Harvey points out, generated a better understanding of acid rain, global warming and ozone holes demanding wide-ranging collective action beyond nation-state borders, thereby posing a challenge (legal, institutional, and cultural) to the closed bureaucratic rationality of the nation state ...

This kind of science provided crucial support to many environmental pressure groups, many of whom initially viewed scientific rationality with skepticism and distrust. The thesis of ecological modernisation [sustainable development] has now become deeply entrenched within many segments of the environmental movement. The effects, as we shall see, have been somewhat contradictory. On the one hand, ecological modernisation provides a common discursive basis for a contested rapprochement between them and dominant forms of political-economic power. But on the other, it presumes a certain kind of rationality that lessens the force of more purely moral arguments (cf. the comments of Lois Gibbs cited above) and exposes much of the environmental movement to the dangers of political cooptation.[84]

Technicism and power politics

Here controversy over the Mohale Dam reflects a broader phenomenon, not least because the World Bank and its Inspection Panel have moved onto turf traditionally associated with the 'bureaucratic rationality' – and especially the social control functions – of the nation-state. Thus if in reality the LHWP was initially in part a sanctions-busting, prestige project with crucial geopolitical overtones, and later a scheme to assure water access to some of the least deserving companies and upper-class households anywhere in the world, nevertheless, its socio-ecological critics had to be treated by project sponsors with extreme ideological care. At stake, after all, were the reputations of the World Bank, of big dam projects in general (as Roome's opening quote suggests), and of the ecologically-modernised WCD and its chairperson, Kader Asmal.

Such a challenge perpetually looms for sustainable-development technicists, as Harvey remarks: 'Some sort of configuration has to be envisaged in which ecological modernisation contributes both to growth and global distributive justice simultaneously. This was a central proposition in the Brundtland Report for example'.[85] The reality, however, is that such goals are sometimes so contradictory, as in the LHWP case, that even Brundtland Report author MacNeill was incapable of reconciling them, and resorted instead to propping up the unsustainable *status quo*.

In this context, it is therefore easy to understand the significant attention that skilled Bank technocrats paid to the LHWP's social implications –

poverty, displacement, livelihood, and downstream consumption – as well as its ecological damage. In early 1998, while formally welcoming the Katse Dam water to South Africa, Asmal himself eloquently articulated the sustainable-development thesis:

> As we move into the new millennium, as we move forward into the twenty-first century, there is ever less and less money available for building dams; there are ever fewer and fewer rivers left undammed; there is ever more and more resistance to the enormous social and environmental impacts of large dams. In the international field this tension has been recognised both by environmental groups and by those who fund major water infrastructure development.
>
> The World Commission on Dams has been established by the World Bank and the International Union for the Conservation of Nature to investigate a way to preserve the balance between the need for the development of water infrastructure, the protection of the environment and the recognition of the rights of rural populations, especially in developing countries, those people, as in Lesotho, who may lose their land, livelihoods and way of life as a result of the building of a dam.[86]

But was the brand of sustainable-development discourse claimed by Asmal, the Bank, the Inspection Panel and the WCD up to the political challenge posed by the green-brown critique?

Participation or repression?

We take up this issue in detail below, in considering the formal WCD recommendations of November 2000. But one in particular, favouring negotiations 'in which stakeholders have an equal opportunity to influence decisions from the outset of the planning process',[87] immediately came into stark conflict with the reality of Southern African politics. According to Hoover's IRN review of the LHWP against WCD recommendations,

> Participation by affected communities has been minimal at best. Affected people have had no forum to effectively negotiate how the project's dams would impact them, let alone influence the decision to build them.
>
> In late 1999 agents of Lesotho's National Security Service confiscated materials about the WCD from a man affected by the LHWP after he returned from NGO-sponsored regional hearings for the

WCD. In Lesotho, security agents routinely attend community meetings on the LHWP, inhibiting meaningful participation.[88]

Lesotho's heavy-handed state reminds us of Asmal's own intimidation of the Alexandra and Soweto civic leaders. The minister's first, behind-the-scenes, reply to the LHWP community critique was revealing, for he complained about a procedural problem: that the draft Inspection Panel claim filed by Alexandra and Soweto activists took him by surprise.[89]

But at a much more politicised level, Asmal's letter to Alexandra civic leaders on 19 March 1998 bristled with intimidation: 'In the circumstances, I cannot see any purpose in continuing the dialogue and have accordingly instructed my Department not to proceed with arrangements for the proposed workshop at which your concerns could have been systematically reviewed'.[90] Asmal wrote, 'I do not raise this as a threat', but that was certainly the implication felt in the townships, where ANC branches also began harassing the civics to lay off the LHWP. Repressive politics thus intervened where sustainable-development discourses didn't do the trick.

Bureaucratic rationality or irrationality?

Setting aside the political browbeating, there remain extensive technical questions about the Bank's and Panel's justification of the Mohale Dam.

For example, in relation to Gauteng municipalities' comprehensive failure to implement demand-side management measures, 'The Panel did not consider this because it does not relate to Bank Management acts or omissions in compliance or non-compliance with the OD'.[91] In fact a reasonable interpretation of Bank Operational Directive 4.00 – 'Design of investment programs for supplying water or energy should consider demand management' – would lead to an investigation of the ultimate municipal end-users of Bank-financed water, particularly given the well-documented bias in consumption patterns.

Or as another example, MacNeill found that there are graduations in Johannesburg's block tariffs, which did 'not appear to bear out the assertions made by the [Alexandra residents] concerning block rates'.[92] But citing the very small gradations does not contradict the Alexandra residents' argument that if *far greater* progressivity in block rates were imposed, there would be far greater success in water conservation and redistribution.

MacNeill's concern over non-payment for services[93] could be easily addressed by applying a universal (free) lifeline policy that would allow trickle flow after consumption of the first block. Such a policy would be entirely consistent with the 'culture of entitlement', disparaged by the Panel, that in turn is entirely consistent with the South African Constitution's granting of rights to water in its Bill of Rights.

It is, therefore, entirely within the spirit of sustainable-development discourse, and also consistent with environmental justice arguments, to criticise the Panel for bureaucratic *irrationality*. Specifically, its report failed to give credence to the following quite reasonable questions:

- given the bias of access – and wastefulness – in water use towards wealthier, predominantly white, consumers, *should redistributive measures become a much higher priority than at present?*
- given the perennial shortages of water in South Africa and the threat of drought, *should demand-side management be given much higher priority than at present by Dwaf, water boards and municipalities – both on redistributive and conservation grounds?*
- given not only that township infrastructure is continually plagued by systemic physical failure – and given, too, the fact that of three million (mainly rural) households who have benefited from taps installed within 0.5 km of their residence since 1994 an estimated 90% now no longer have access to water due to systemic breakdown based often on lack of affordability – *should Dwaf, water boards and municipalities use their resources to improve installation and maintenance on a more generously subsidised basis?*
- given that from 1994 to 1998, LHWP bulk water prices trebled due to dam construction costs, Dwaf bulk prices to Rand Water likewise doubled, and Rand Water prices to Gauteng municipalities soared, in a context of ongoing municipal fiscal crisis, *should urgent steps be taken to ensure that bulk water prices are frozen (as was promised by the TCTA and Dwaf) and, most importantly, that Rand Water desists from cutting off water services to entire towns and that municipalities desist from engaging in mass water cutoffs to large sections of townships (as often happens even when individual households pay their bills)?*

Alexandra's brown critics of the LHWP answered these questions firmly in the affirmative. In contrast, various defenders of the LHWP endorsed the existing pricing system, on grounds of sustainable development.

7. Conclusion

In the pages above, we have gathered sufficient evidence to conclude that a hydro-political power struggle over the costs and benefits of the mega-dams has tainted the taste of Lesotho's water. Using the LHWP case study, David Harvey's perspective on the politics of environmentalism can now be considered in more depth:

> At this conjuncture, therefore, all of those militant particularist movements around the world that loosely come together under the umbrella of environmental justice and the environmentalism of the poor are faced with a critical choice. They can either ignore the contradictions, remain with the confines of their own particularist militancies – fighting an incinerator here, a toxic waste dump there, a World Bank dam project somewhere else, and commercial logging in yet another place – or they can treat the contradictions as a fecund nexus to create a more transcendent and universal politics.
>
> If they take the latter path, they have to find a discourse of universality and generality that unites the emancipatory quest for social justice with a strong recognition that social justice is impossible without environmental justice (and vice versa). But any such discourse has to transcend the narrow solidarities and particular affinities shaped in particular places – the preferred milieu of most grassroots environmental activism – and adopt a politics of abstraction capable of reaching out across space, across the multiple environmental and social conditions that constitute the geography of difference in a contemporary world that capitalism has intensely shaped to its own purposes. And it has to do this without abandoning its militant particularist base.[94]

Green-brown fusions and fractures

When the green and brown critiques of the LHWP met, was there, in the process, the possibility of generating a more substantial anti-capitalist environmentalism? Could the Johannesburg township and Basotho peasant activists transcend 'the confines of their own particularist militancies' and generate 'a more transcendent and universal politics'?

Providing grounds for answering in the affirmative, a joint press statement in late January 1998 – signed by the Group for Environmental Monitoring, the Alexandra and Soweto civics, Earthlife Africa, the Environmental Justice Networking Forum, the Lesotho Highlands Church Action Group and the IRN – was critical of the Mohale Dam.[95] In early February, Moshe Tsehlo, acting coordinator of the Highlands Church Solidarity and Action Centre wrote to Roome that 'We will now support steps being taken by sister NGOs in South Africa to bring a case to the World Bank's Inspection Panel, claiming that the Bank has not followed its own policies'.

But the critiques were not synthesised. This was due partly to the great geographical distance between the grassroots bases, partly to the extremely effective divide-and-conquer strategies deployed by government officials in both Maseru and Pretoria to counter the growing opposition, and partly to differing conceptions of self-interest.

In the course of a February meeting between Lesotho and South African NGOs facilitated by Lesotho government officials, solidarity eroded and tensions arose between the more conservative Lesotho NGOs and their South African visitors. Even the Church Solidarity and Action Centre was forced to retreat, and withdrew its intention to support the township activists' Inspection Panel claim. The South African community leaders remained fully set against the dam and its high costs, while Basotho activists decided they mainly wanted a better deal on compensation and resettlement.

This was telling, not because it suggests that militant particularisms in two different contexts – rural and urban, green and brown – cannot be fused, but rather the opposite: militancy can too easily wane under conditions of official pressure in countries that have recent experience of deep repression, so that short-term interests prevail over longer-term solidarity. The same waning of militancy was evident when, in the wake of a funded trip to the dam for a few Soweto and Alexandra leaders and under pressure from Asmal's letter and ANC branch persecution, the two civics' top leaders withdrew their 6 March draft claim to the Inspection Panel on 20 April.

Still, enough militancy remained that three residents, David Letsie, Johny Mphou and Sam Moiloa, carried on independently a few days later, although under conditions of anonymity because of the intimidation. They were assisted by their less-vulnerable NGO supporters.

After Roome filed a rebuttal to the Alexandra residents in May, several World Bank Executive Directors visited the site in June. Despite invitations and their presence in a hotel a few kilometres from Alexandra they did not make time to meet the three residents. They subsequently approved the $45 million Mohale Dam loan. In July, the Panel's MacNeill visited and conducted a preliminary investigation of the residents' case. When in late August the Inspection Panel rejected the brown critique, and when a green critique did not immediately emerge, it appeared that community opposition to the LHWP had been crushed.

A renewed grassroots alliance, a disdainful state

But just over two years later, an explosion of LHWP criticism emerged anew, and the elusive green-brown coalition was suddenly reconfigured.

The occasion was the launch of the WCD final report, which Asmal presided over in several regions of the world during November 2000. After considering the overlap between their own socio-environmental concerns and the Commission's analysis, a Southern African Preparatory Meeting of environment NGOs and community organisations (including Alexandra and Lesotho activist groups) convened and issued a statement.

The groups called on the World Bank, other development banks, export credit agencies, bilateral agencies, governments and authorities to

immediately establish independent, transparent and participatory reviews of all their planned and ongoing dam projects. Whilst such reviews are taking place, project preparation and construction should be halted. Such reviews should establish whether the respective dams comply, as a minimum, with the recommendations of the WCD. If they do not, projects should be modified accordingly or be stopped altogether. All institutions which share in the responsibility for unresolved negative impacts of dams should immediately initiate a process to establish and fund mechanisms to provide reparations to affected communities that have suffered social, cultural and economic harm as a result of dam projects. All public financial institutions should place a moratorium on funding the planning or construction of new dams until they can demonstrate that they have complied with the above measures.[96]

The Alexandra leaders were joined by groups from Lesotho, amongst which were some that had earlier endorsed the Mohale Dam.[97] In a taped television interview, Alexandra leader Mphou was ecstatic that the previous dispute about the merits of the Mohale Dam was past: 'This is very very wonderful. Our colleagues from Lesotho agree with our problem about what is happening in our poor community in Alexandra'.[98]

But the World Bank, Kasrils and Muller ignored the request, and did not even reply to the communique from the social movements. Moiloa also criticised Asmal's uncaring attitude at the Commission report launch:

I am not satisfied with the answer from Kader Asmal. In the first place, the Inspection Panel which he claims answers us, did not answer us, because they said there is no link between the Lesotho problems and the South Africa problems. So I'm wondering, because the link I know, is water. What do these well-educated people think, that there is no link, what do they mean?

We are going to go on with the battle to make sure that the poorest of the poor are catered for. The World Bank and the South African government must stop this LHWP and concentrate on uplifting the standard of living of the people. So we are going to network more with the NGOs and community organisations of Lesotho and Gauteng, and we are going to proceed with this battle, and we are going to win it.

We are not going to stop the engagement with the World Bank. We are going to pursue the battle together with the people of Lesotho, as we have gathered from them that they do not benefit. They say it point blank to us that they do not have access to water, which is the same thing as with us. Together with them we're going to forge ahead.[99]

Renewed critiques

Whether such an informal popular alliance can hold and strengthen over time, depends upon the character of the fight being waged. After Letsie died in November 2000, Moiloa and Mphou were joined by well-known Soweto activist Trevor Ngwane, in arguing that

The WCD report made sound recommendations that, when applied to the LHWP, makes a mockery of Muller's claim to balance the needs of environment, displaced people and water consumers ...

Lesotho's poor people have been the very last to benefit from the money that Gauteng consumers pay to Maseru ... The Lesotho Highlands Water Development Fund has been unveiled as corrupt, with officials allegedly channelling funds meant for resettlement only to supporters of the ruling party.

The WCD argued that 'special attention is necessary to ensure that compensation and development measures are in place well in advance' of resettlement, and that 'a clear agreement on the sequence and stages of resettlement will be required before construction on any project preparatory work begins.

In reality, a large proportion of the rural Basotho who were displaced by the dams received no compensation, and many still have no access to safe drinking water because the cliffs are too steep to go down to the dam.

In addition, the WCD calls for 'an environmental flow release to meet specific downstream ecosystem and livelihood objectives', and insists that 'a basin-wide understanding of the ecosystem's functions, values and requirements, and how community livelihoods depend on and influence them, is required before decisions on development options are made'. There were never such studies for the Lesotho dams prior to construction.

Last year, an Instream Flow Requirement study of downstream communities and ecosystems concluded that the entire Lesotho dam project will reduce Lesotho's river systems to 'something akin to wastewater drains'.

Phase Two of the Lesotho dams project will reduce the flow of water into South Africa by 57%.

Instead of building more dams, we should have more conservation by those rich people, big companies and commercial farmers who waste the vast bulk of society's water ...

In Alexandra and Soweto, we are still suffering from apartheid-era systems that leak out roughly half the water that goes into the pipes, before they dribble from our communal taps.[100]

Moreover, Basotho peasants also continued suffering, to the point that on 19 November 2001, an extraordinary protest occurred in several Highlands sites. More than 2300 people demonstrated against the authorities. Their petition complained, 'We have tried by all possible means to get a fair and reasonable compensation for our property ... but this was all a fiasco. We were promised development ... but this has not materialised to date'.

One of the peasants' main advocacy organisations, the Transformation Resource Centre (TRC), had also planned a protest of resettled people in Maseru, but the police refused to grant permission. According to an IRN report,

> Crowds of 1000 affected people gathered at both Katse and Mohale Dams on Monday, while 300 more marched at Muela Dam. They marched and sang protest songs before delivering the petitions containing their grievances. At Mohale Dam, they rolled large stones onto project access roads, briefly stopping construction at the site. Mohale police, angered that some protesters failed to gather at pre-agreed marching areas, assaulted a group of demonstrators with batons and whips. Three elderly women required medical attention after being beaten about the face and back ...
>
> 'These protests show that affected people are running out of patience', said TRC Coordinator Motseoa Senyane, 'The World Bank and other project authorities have not adequately addressed the communities' concerns in the past. It is time that they do so'.[101]

The use and abuse of the WCD

By this time, it was evident that technical critiques and responses didn't solve the problems, but instead only revealed the shallowness of commitment by the World Bank and Pretoria to sustainable development. On the one hand, the political momentum of the green-brown alliance had been halted by intimidation in March 1998. By August that year, when MacNeill snuffed the Inspection Panel claim, the militant-particularist unity between the Alexandra residents and Basotho peasants had been fragmented.

But on the other hand, the November 2000 WCD report became another organising handle for activism. That report was, ultimately, downgraded within the Bank. The institution's senior water adviser, South African John Briscoe, actively lobbied Southern governments to reject the findings during the first few months of 2001.[102] By March 2002, Briscoe had issued the final draft of the Bank's Water Resources Sector Strategy (WRSS), which claimed to 'draw heavily' on the Commission report.[103]

In reality, it did nothing of the sort, according to social movements and NGOs active on dam issues, who reported to Briscoe in May 2002 that he had neglected

> to discuss any of the WCD's recommendations for changes in water and energy planning and management. In two of the few places where the WCD is mentioned its findings are distorted to justify the WRSS's support for major dams and privatisation. This evasiveness and dissembling is unfortunately consistent with the Water Resources Management Group's overall reaction to the WCD report ...
>
> The two main thrusts of the WRSS are promoting the privatization of urban water supply and boosting Bank funding for major dams and inter-basin transfers, which it terms 'high-reward/high-risk water infrastructure'. The 'risk' in this expression refers mainly to the risk to the Bank's reputation of being involved in controversial projects, rather than the risks to communities, national economies and the environment ...
>
> The World Bank's singularly negative and non-committal response to the WCD Report means that the Bank will no longer be accepted as an honest broker in any further multi-stakeholder dialogues. Experience since the publication of the WCD Report shows that common ground exists between civil society and forward-looking private sector and government institutions. In contrast, the World Bank's response to the WCD, its role in projects like the Bujagali dam in

Uganda, and the new draft WRSS indicate that the Bank is entering a
new era of intensified controversy and conflict.[104]

Even the *Engineering News Record* (ENR), an industry journal, was
stunned by the Bank's attitude. The ordinarily pro-dams editorialists con-
fided,

> How can a co-sponsor of this groundbreaking achievement [the
> WCD Report] justify ignoring WCD's findings? What deplorable
> hypocrisy. In the WCD guidelines, *ENR* sees the best hope for bal-
> ancing what have long been seen as irreconcilable conflicts among
> stakeholders over dam construction. If the study's own sponsors
> refuse to be guided by them, all we can anticipate is continued scle-
> rosis in dambuilding.[105]

As if on cue, Klaus Toepfer, the executive director of the UN Environment Programme – which inherited the Commission's research and dis-
semination mandate – got the drift of the multilateral financial agenda. In
May 2002, he declared that to have the WCD report 'implemented word
for word' is not a 'viable strategy'.[106]

Because the Commission report gave both the green and brown critics' case more credibility, it threatened the construction of future mega-
dams in Southern Africa. Asmal's replacement as minister of water, Ronnie
Kasrils, began denouncing the report as inapplicable to regional conditions. Moreover, during his budget speech to parliament on 15 May 2001
Kasrils endorsed the single most egregious large dam under construction in the world, at the Three Gorges on the Yangtze River, where he had
recently paid a visit: 'I must state my admiration for the determination and
care with which the Chinese government is promoting this vast undertaking'.[107]

Two months later, in July, he had found sufficient anti-WCD allies in a
South African 'multistakeholder initiative' that declared itself 'broadly supportive of the strategic priorities' of the WCD – yet the key proviso was
'that the guidelines need to be contextualised to the South African situation'.[108] This would mean, in practice, business as usual.

The same month, Kasrils also sought out similar sentiment in governments across the SADC region. Using Dwaf's banal argument that the
North is overdammed, South Africa is correctly dammed and Africa is
underdammed, they pronounced,

> While it is recognised that the development of any dam will need to
> reconcile the needs and entitlements of interested parties, including

the environment, the SADC Water Sector Ministers find the suggestions that the WCD guidelines should be made compulsory are unacceptable.

There is certainly a danger that an injudicious application of the
guidelines would make the development of water resources far
more expensive or even unaffordable. The result could be to block
the development so urgently needed by the people of the region to
improve their quality of life.[109]

Also in July 2001, SADC and other African ministers met in Lusaka to
adopt Nepad (previously known as the New African Initiative) which
includes the following objective: 'To exploit and develop the hydropower
potential of river basins of Africa'. Nepad neglects to cite, much less
rebut, enormous controversies over new dams in Africa, such as the
Mohale, the Maguge in Swaziland, the Bujagali in Uganda and the Epupa
in Namibia. Criticisms raised include:

- large dams in tropical settings have been identified as the cause of
  higher global-warming gas emissions (due to decay of plant life) than
  other energy sources;[110]
- displacement and socio-economic costs of large dams are very high
  (though rarely if ever incorporated into dam construction costs);
- downstream environmental implications are often severe;
- siltation and evaporation undermine the efficiency of dams; and
- the economic benefits of large dams very rarely approach initial estimates.

Nearly all the concerns apply to Africa's existing mega-dams, e.g., on the
Nile, Upper Volta, Zambezi and Orange Rivers. The ineffective management of dams and run-off systems by Zimbabwe, Zambia and South Africa
– in the Zambezi, Save, Limpopo and Crocodile catchments – have been
cited as contributing factors to Mozambique's deadly 2000–01 floods,
even though the dams were meant to prevent flooding. In short, without
some acknowledgement that large dams have had an often devastating
impact on societies, environments and economies, Nepad encouraged
the repetition of the problems associated with reliance upon inappropriate hydropower.

Within South Africa, Kasrils moved forward with several other substantial dams, including the controversial R1.4 billion Skuifraam Dam on
the Western Cape's scenic Berg River. A Dwaf official conceded in 2002
that Skuifraam would 'only buy an estimated two more years before
demand again equals maximum capacity'.[111] Critics argued that the dam
would be unnecessary if government took seriously the possibility of
water conservation in Cape Town. Instead of increased water tariffs for

hedonistic suburban and agro-industrial consumers, Dwaf and the Cape Town Council cited only recycling and desalination as the (costly) alternatives.

Across South Africa, Dwaf continued to accept the challenge of supply-side enhancements, instead of rigorous demand-side management. In Limpopo Province, work began on two dams in the Olifants catchment estimated to cost R900 million. In the main project, raising an existing dam by five metres would 'make an additional 16-million cubic metres a year of raw water available, which has been earmarked for new [platinum] mining development', according to a Dwaf official.[112]

Anti-dam arguments vindicated?

Finally, as concern grew that Kasrils had gone dam-crazy, Dwaf announced in mid-2001 that Phase 2 of the LHWP would be indefinitely postponed, a point the minister coyly repeated in April 2002 at the Johannesburg Press Club: 'The question of further phases of the Lesotho development is still the subject of ongoing discussion and South Africa would always deal sensitively with the issue', but that it might be possible to augment the Vaal River with 'a similar project within the country's own borders'.[113]

But in addition to the decline of gold mining in the Witwatersrand, which was already projected for in 1980s-era studies, one twisted and untenable reason emerged for the lower water-demand curve that lay behind the decision: an anticipated rise in HIV/Aids mortality rates would lower water-demand projections dramatically.[114] There are at least three logical replies:

- given a policy of increasing access to anti-retroviral medicines, it is inappropriate for the main government water agency to project mass death and decrease its delivery goals accordingly;
- people living with Aids require increased access to water in any case, because of the need for much higher levels of hygiene than those who are HIV-negative; and
- where HIV/Aids is most prevalent, in low-income and working-class black townships, the amount of water consumed is, in any case, an extremely low percentage of the total water supplied by the LHWP via the Vaal catchment.

Indeed, the more sophisticated modelling at Rand Water showed that Aids was much less significant in future consumption estimates, and that the vast bulk of savings could potentially come from demand management: 'A cost of R2 billion for implementing water demand initatives saves almost R30 billion'.[115]

The battle against LHWP's expansion was, however, still not necessarily won. According to the *Engineering News* in mid-2002, 'The options being considered as a new source of water for the country's industrial heartland include the Thukela project and a second phase of the Lesotho Highlands Water Project'.[116]

Lessons for green-brown alliances, entitlements, and syntheses

In spite of all the setbacks and uncertainties, partial victories could be declared against the LHWP, vindicating the core argument of green and brown critics, namely that the mega-dams are inappropriate to the needs of Basotho peasants and township residents alike. Some of the main objectives of the green and brown activists could be scored as progress:

- corruption of the main Basotho official by construction companies was identified and punished, with the firms next up for prosecution in mid-2002;
- no new Lesotho dams would be built in the foreseeable future, thanks to a decision apparently taken in mid-2001 and codified a year later;
- more attention and mobilisation was occurring around resettlement and compensation issues, especially in the wake of the November 2001 protests at both dam sites;
- the delegitimisation of the World Bank, Pretoria and the dam-building industry continued apace in the wake of the Bank's and Kasrils' 2001 rejection of the WCD recommendations, as the three continued to work profitably together on new dams across South Africa and the region under the guise of Nepad; and
- the September 2000 free water promise by the ANC would mean that the water cutoffs and lack of access by Alexandra and Soweto residents would, theoretically, be a thing of the past.

Ultimately, however, green and brown critiques of the LHWP must come together not merely through momentary simultaneous interests, tactical convergences and demands for moratoria, but in a fully functional and durable manner, including militant protest in town and countryside, if we are to achieve a more transcendent and universal politics. Contestation over water supplies is, after all, one of the world's most crucial geopolitical processes in coming decades, and the LHWP struggle at the end of the twentieth century offers us all manner of lessons.

In the process, we have raised doubts over the integrity of both sustainable-development discourses and the institutions which use them in partial and dubious ways. We have seen the high political stakes and the extent to which these drive politicians to act like thugs. We have seen the roles of the World Bank and multinational corporations in propping up illegitimate regimes and corrupting key officials. We have seen environmental concerns, which whether in the township or countryside are of particular importance to women, ignored or downplayed. We have seen community needs and affordability problems dismissed by incompetent analysts at the World Bank Inspection Panel as a 'culture of entitlement', again with especially adverse affects upon women, people with Aids, and other vulnerable low-income township residents.

In a way, this last insult is the one that provides the most hope. For ultimately the rights-based discourses, encompassing both environmental and social justice, must re-emerge and intertwine, across the green and brown terrains, drawing together the rural and the urban in the search for genuinely 'sustainable development'. The culture of entitlement must then move across urban and rural, from water to land and environment and gender equity and public health and all the other issues that are drawn together in this case study of hydropolitics.

In the same spirit, here is how William Cronon concluded his famous study of Chicago's ecological footprint, *Nature's Metropolis*, linking that city's impact on algae-infested downstream water to its noxious air:

> To do right by nature and people in the country, one has to do right by them in the city as well for the two seem always to find in each other their mirror image. In that sense, every city is nature's metropolis, and every piece of countryside is its rural hinterland. We fool ourselves if we think we can choose between them, for the green lake and the orange cloud are creatures of the same landscape. Each is our responsibility. We can only take them together and, in making the journey between them, find a way of life that does justice to them both.[117]

Notes

1. Cited in Asmal, K. (1996), 'Speech to Group for Environmental Monitoring Workshop on Lesotho Highlands Water Project', in Group for Environmental Monitoring (ed), Record of Proceedings: Lesotho Highlands Water Workshop, Johannesburg, 29–30 August, p. 2.

2. Asmal, 'Speech to GEM Workshop on Lesotho Highlands Water Project', p. 2.

3. World Bank (1998), *Lesotho: Lesotho Highlands Water Project – Phase 1B: Project Appraisal Document*, (17727-LSO), R98–106(PAD), Water and Urban 1, Africa Region, Washington, DC, April 30, p. 18.

4. Muller, M. (2001), 'Flood Criticism a One-Sided Discourse', *Mail & Guardian*, 30 March–5 April.

5. *Cape Times*, 2 December 1998.

6. Southall, R. (1998), 'Is Lesotho South Africa's Tenth Province?', *Indicator SA*, 15, 4.

7. *Sunday Independent*, 14 February 1999.

8. *Mail & Guardian*, 20-26 March 2000.

9. Roome, J. (1995), 'Water Pricing and Management: World Bank Presentation to the SA Water Conservation Conference', unpublished paper, South Africa, 2 October, p. 16.

10. Ballenger, J. (1998), 'Lesotho Water Project Falls Foul of Environmental Lobby Groups', *Business Day*, 22 January; see also *Business Day*, 19 March 1998.

11. The relevant documentation, including official reaction, can be found in Bond, P. and D.Letsie (2000), 'Debating Supply and Demand Characteristics of Bulk Infrastructure: Lesotho-Johannesburg Water Transfer', in M.Khosa (Ed), *Empowerment through Service Delivery*, Pretoria, Human Sciences Research Council.

12. Asmal, K. and M. Muller (1998), 'Watering down the Facts', *Mail & Guardian*, 8-14 May.

13. Barber, S. (1998), 'Vote Asmal's Gov't out of Power, But Please, No Whining', *Business Day*, 9 September.

14. Addison, G. (1998), 'Dam It, Let's Pour Concrete', *Saturday Star*, 3 November.

15. Hoover, R. (2000), 'Evaluating the LHWP Against WCD Guidelines', Unpublished report, International Rivers Network, San Francisco, 17 November, http://www.irn.org.

16. Harvey, D. (1996), *Justice, Nature and the Geography of Difference*, Oxford, Basil Blackwell, p. 389.

17. Southall, R. (1998), 'Is Lesotho South Africa's Tenth Province?', *Indicator SA*, 15, 4.

18. Horta, K. (1995), 'The Mountain Kingdom's White Oil: The Lesotho Highlands Water Project', *The Ecologist*, 25, 6; Bond, P. (1997), 'Lesotho Dammed', Multinational *Monitor*, January-February.

19. Potts, M. (1996), 'Presentation by the DBSA to the Lesotho Highlands Water Workshop', in Group for Environmental Monitoring (ed), *Record of Proceedings: Lesotho Highlands Water Workshop*, Johannesburg, 29-30 August, p. 1.

20. Lamont, J. (1997), 'SA Seeks More Control over Water Project', *Business Report*, 1 December.

21. Horta, K. (1996), 'Making the Earth Rumble: The Lesotho-South Africa Water Connection', *Multinational Monitor*, May.

22. Asmal, 'Speech to GEM Workshop on Lesotho Highlands Water Project', p. 2.

23. *Business Day*, 5 August 1999; *Washington Post*, 13 August 1999. According to the charge sheet, the firms allegedly paid the following into Sole's personal accounts: ABB, $40,410; Impregilo, $250,000; Sogreah, $13,578; Lahmeyer International, $8,674; Highlands Water Venture consortium (Impregilo, the German firm Hochtief, the French firm Bouygues, UK firms Keir International and Stirling International, and South African firms Concor and Group Five), $733,404; Lesotho Highlands Project Contractors consortium (Balfour Beatty, Spie Batignolles, LTA, and ED Zublin), $57,269; Acres International (Canada), $185,002; Spie Batignolles (France), $119,393; Dumez International (France), $82,422; ED Zublin (Germany), $444,466; Diwi Consulting (Germany), $2,439; and LHPC Chantiers, $63,959.

24. Information in this paragraph is cited in Environmental Defence Fund and International Rivers Network (1999), 'Groups call on World Bank to Ban Companies in African Bribery Scandal', Press release, Washington, DC and Berkeley, CA, 24 September.

25. International Rivers Network (2002), 'The World Bank and Corruption: Excerpts from Public Statements, Policies and Procedures', Berkeley, 26 June, http://www.irn.org.

26. The previous two paragraphs' quotes are taken from Adams, P. (2002), 'The Canadian Connection', *Financial Post*, 27 June.

27. http://www.jubileesouth.net

28. Ashley, B. (1997), 'Challenging Apartheid Debt: Cancellation a Real Option', debate, 3; World Development Movement and Action for Southern Africa (1998), *Paying for Apartheid Twice: The Cost of Apartheid Debt for the People of Southern Africa*, London, WDM and Actsa.

29. Marcus, G. (1998), 'Writing off Debt has Consequences', Sowetan, 24 June; *Sunday Independent Business Report*, 8 November 1998; for rebuttals see: Dor, G. (1998), 'SA's Poor Should not be Fooled', *Sowetan*, 30 June; Gabriel, N. (1998), 'Still Weighed Down by Burden of Apartheid's Debt', *Sunday Independent*, 15 November; and Ndungane, N. (1998), 'Maria Ramos's 'No Debt' Statement is Remarkable', *Sunday Independent Business Report*, 15 November.

30. Cited in Bond, 'Lesotho Dammed'.

31. See, e.g., Asmal, K. (1998), 'Lesotho Highlands Water Project: Success Story', Address to Muela press conference, 21 January; and (1998), 'Opening of the Lesotho Highlands Water Project', Speech, 22 January.

32. Rosenthal, J. (1998), 'Threat to Lesotho Dam Project', *Business Report*, 26 November.

33. Hoover, 'Evaluating the LHWP Against WCD Guidelines'.

34. Environmental Monitoring Group, International Rivers Network and Group for Environmental Monitoring (1999), 'Once There was a Community: Southern African Hearings for Communities Affected by Large Dams', Final Report, Cape Town, 11–12 November, #s6.6.1–6.6.3. The testimony was heard by Commissioners, tellingly, at a time when Asmal chose to be absent.

35. Kravitz, J.D., et al (1995), 'Human Immunodifficiency Virus Seroprevalence in an Occupational Cohort in a South African Community', *Archives of Internal Medicine*, 155, 15.

36. Asmal, 'Speech to GEM Workshop on Lesotho Highlands Water Project', p. 4.

37. Ferguson, J. (1991), *The Anti-Politics Machine*, Cambridge, Cambridge University Press.

38. Pottinger, L. (1996), 'The Environmental Impacts of Large Dams', in Group for Environmental Monitoring (ed), *Record of Proceedings: Lesotho Highlands Water Workshop*, Johannesburg, 29–30 August.

39. Snaddon, C.D., et al (1996), 'Some Implications of Inter-Basin Water Transfers for River Functioning and Water Resources Management in South Africa', in Group for Environmental Monitoring (ed), *Record of Proceedings: Lesotho Highlands Water Workshop*, Johannesburg, 29–30 August, p. 7.

40. Department of Water Affairs and Forestry (1996), *The Orange River Project Replanning Study*, Pretoria.

41. Seaman, M. (1996), 'Questions', in Group for Environmental Monitoring (ed), *Record of Proceedings: Lesotho Highlands Water Workshop*, Johannesburg, 29–30 August, p. 6.

42. Department of Water Affairs and Forestry (1999), *Orange River Development Project Replanning Study*, Pretoria.

43. Ibid, s.7–6.

44. Ben Cashdan's expose of this in the film *White Gold* included a Maseru official denying that the study had been completed, when it in fact was clearly marked 'Final Draft'.

45. Metsi Consultants (1999), 'The Establishment and Monitoring of Instream Flow Requirements for River Courses Downstream of LHWP Dams', Lesotho Highlands Development Authority Contract 648, Maseru, p. x. See also Transformation Resource Centre (2000), 'Lesotho's Rivers could become Waste Water Drains', http://www.irn.org

46. Cited in Addison, 'Dam It, Let's Pour Concrete'.

47. Ibid.

48. World Bank, *Lesotho: Lesotho Highlands Water Project – Phase 1B: Project Appraisal Document*, p. 18.

49. Fox, J. and L.D.Brown (1998), *The Struggle for Accountability: The World Bank, NGOs and Grassroots Movements*, Cambridge, MA, MIT Press, p. 511.

50. Archer, R. (1996), *Trust in Construction? The Lesotho Highlands Water Project*, London, Christian Aid and Maseru, Christian Council of Lesotho.

51. Ibid, pp. 58–59.

52. Rand Water (2001), 'Planning and Financing of New Augmentation Schemes for the Vaal River System', Unpublished overhead slides, Johannesburg, 13 June.

53. Asmal, 'Speech to GEM Workshop on Lesotho Highlands Water Project', p. 2.

54. *Business Day*, 13 March 1998.

55. Roome, 'Water Pricing and Management', p. 16.

56. World Bank Inspection Panel (1998), 'Lesotho/South Africa: Phase 1B of Lesotho Highlands Water Project: Panel Report and Recommendation', Washington, DC, 18 August, pa.81,fn. Signing off on the Panel report was the chairperson, Ernst-Guenther Groeder, but MacNeill was the primary author.

57. For details on this history, see Mayekiso, M. (1996), *Township Politics: Civic Struggles for a New South Africa*, New York, Monthly Review Press.

58. Bond, P. (2000), *Cities of Gold, Townships of Coal: Essays on South Africa's New Urban Crisis*, Trenton, Africa World Press, Chapter Three.

59. Alexandra residents (1998), 'Inspection Panel Claim regarding World Bank Involvement in the Lesotho Highlands Water Project', 23 April, Alexandra, pa.1.9.

60. Ibid.

61. World Bank Inspection Panel, 'Lesotho/South Africa: Phase 1B of Lesotho Highlands Water Project', pa.77.

62. Ibid, pa.81,fn.

63. World Bank Inspection Panel, 'Lesotho/South Africa: Phase 1B of Lesotho Highlands Water Project', pa.80.

64. Ibid, pa.99.

65. Alexandra residents, 'Inspection Panel Claim regarding World Bank Involvement in the Lesotho Highlands Water Project', pa.2.10.

66. Ibid, pa.2.11.

67. *Sunday Independent Reconstruct*, 20 December 1998.

68. World Bank Inspection Panel, 'Lesotho/South Africa: Phase 1B of Lesotho Highlands Water Project', pa.86.

69. *Business Day*, 13 March 1998.

70. World Bank (1998), 'The Economics of Phase 1B', Unpublished paper, Africa Region, March.

71. Alexandra residents, 'Inspection Panel Claim regarding World Bank Involvement in the Lesotho Highlands Water Project', pa.5.3.5.

72. World Bank (1994), *World Development Report 1994: Infrastructure for Development*, New York: Oxford University Press, pp. 80–81.

73. Alexandra residents, 'Inspection Panel Claim regarding World Bank Involvement in the Lesotho Highlands Water Project', pa.1.10.

74. Roome, 'Water Pricing and Management: World Bank Presentation to the SA Water Conservation Conference', pp. 50–51.

75. Ketso Gordhan, the main city manager promoting neoliberal utilities pricing and privatisation, turned down a World Bank job offer in late 2000. Instead, he became deputy chief executive of FirstRand, which included one of South Africa's most aggressively pro-privatisation merchant banks.

76. Palmer Development Group (2001), 'Rand Water: Tariff Database Survey 2', Johannesburg, March, p. 8.

77. Ibid, Table 14.

78. Information in this and the following paragraphs is from Mare, K. (2001), 'Free Basic Water: Actual Tariff Structures in Rand Water Area of Supply', Presentation to the Water Services Forum, Johannesburg, 18 July.

79. Department of Water Affairs and Forestry (1994), *Water Supply and Sanitation White Paper*, Cape Town. The most influential figures were director-general Mike Muller, former special advisor Len Abrams and Piers Cross, long associated with the World Bank, and one-time director of Mvula Trust.

80. World Bank Inspection Panel, 'Lesotho/South Africa: Phase 1B of Lesotho Highlands Water Project', pa.83.

81. Cited in Hoover, 'Evaluating the LHWP Against WCD Guidelines'.

82. Interpress Service, 18 November 2000.

83. Harvey, *Justice, Nature and the Geography of Difference*, p. 377.

84. Ibid, p. 378.

85. Ibid, p. 379.

86. Asmal, 'Opening of the Lesotho Highlands Water Project', p. 4.

87. Hoover, 'Evaluating the LHWP Against WCD Guidelines'.

88. Ibid.

89. The complaint was justifiable when it came to a meeting he had with Alexandra leaders in March 1998, but in a *Business Day* letter by local environmentalist Richard Sherman in January, the Panel claim option was noted as the logical way forward for the green-brown anti-LHWP alliance.

90. The letter continued:

   I am sure that you will understand that there is little point in engaging in dialogue with people who have already (without hearing the evidence) made up their minds on the issues and who seem to be guided by priorities and processes outside South Africa rather than by the impact of their actions on their fellow citizens.
   I should further add that, since this deals with a matter of national concern and indeed of the national interest, I will now take the necessary steps to establish whether you have a mandate from your national organisation or are indeed merely posturing. I do not raise this as a threat but rather as a reflection

of my concern that this kind of unmandated and opportunist action will undermine the strong role that I believe civil society must play in areas such as water management.

It is precisely this kind of action, that may demonstrably damage the interests of water consumers both rich and poor, that is used by those who allege that many of the organs of civil society are not really interested in similar problems or issues, but are simply concerned with opportunities and politically-mischievous activities.

Should you wish to proceed with any dialogue on this issue, I must therefore insist that you formally withdraw your request for an Inspection Panel investigation.

I represent a democratically-elected government and head a department which has a proved record of creative and real links with non-governmental organisations. However, there must be good faith on both sides if we are able to engage in honest dialogue.

Yours faithfully,
Prof. Kader Asmal, MP, Minister of Water Affairs and Forestry

Asmal, K. (1998), 'Letter to Alexandra Civic Organisation: Lesotho Highlands Water Project', 19 March, Pretoria.

91. World Bank Inspection Panel, 'Lesotho/South Africa: Phase 1B of Lesotho Highlands Water Project', pa.65.

92. Ibid, pa.81.

93. Ibid', pa.86.

94. Harvey, *Justice, Nature and the Geography of Difference*, p. 400.

95. Ballenger, J. (1998), 'Lesotho Water Project Falls Foul of Environmental Lobby Groups', *Business Day*, 22 January.

96. Southern African Preparatory Meeting (2000), 'Southern African Call to Action', Pretoria, 23 November.

97. These included the Council of NGOs, Federation of Women's Lawyers, Rural Self Help Development Association, Transformation Resource Centre, Lesotho Durhata Link, Red Cross Society, Blue Cross Society, Lesotho Youth Federation, Highlands Church Action Group, Community Legal Resource and Advice Centre, Young Christian Students, and the Lesotho NGO Credit Centre.

98. Cashdan, B. (2000), *White Gold*, interview tapes, November.

99. Ibid.

100. Moiloa, S., J.Mphou and T.Ngwane (2001), 'New Dams don't Benefit the People', *Mail & Guardian*, 8–14 June.

101. http://www.irn.org.

102. *Mail & Guardian*, 27 April–3 May 2001.

103. World Bank (2002), *Water Resources Sector Strategy: Strategic Directions for World Bank Engagement,* Washington, 25 March, p. 28.

104. McCully, P. (2002), 'Avoiding Solutions, Worsening Problems', San Francisco, International Rivers Network, http://www.irn.org, pp. 1,20,40.

105. *Engineering News* Record, 21 January 2002.

106. *Confluence: Newsletter of the Dams and Development Project*, Issue 1, May 2002.

107. Cited in *Mail & Guardian*, 8–14 June 2001.

108. *Confluence: Newsletter of the Dams and Development Project*, Issue 1, May 2002.

109. Kasrils, R. (2001), 'Opening Address', Symposium on the World Commission on Dams Report on Dams and Development: A New Framework for Decisionmaking, Pretoria, 23 July, p. 4.

110. See, especially, McCully, P. (2002), *Flooding the Land, Heating the Air: Greenhouse Gas Emissions from Dams*, International Rivers Network, Berkeley.

111. *Business Day*, 6 May 2002.

112. *Martin Creamer's Engineering News*, 12–18 April 2002.

113. Ibid.

114. *Martin Creamer's Engineering News* (28 June 2002) explained, 'When Dwaf started scrutinising the Thukela water project as a possible source of additional water to augment the Vaal river system in the 1990s, it was estimated that South Africa's population would have ballooned to 70 million by 2025. Given the likely impact of HIV/Aids – which afflicts a significant proportion of South Africa's population – it is now believed that the population will not grow beyond 52 million in the next 25 years'.

115. Thomson, R. and J. Tavares (2001), 'Water Demand Projections in Rand Water's Area of Supply', *Civil Engineering*, June.

116. *Martin Creamer's Engineering News*, 28 June 2002.

117. Cronon, W. (1991), *Nature's Metropolis: Chicago and the Great West*, New York, Norton, p. 385.

PART THREE

Unsustainable policies

SANDTON CHRONICLE

Voice of our town

DANGER ☠ INGOZI
GEVAAR KOTSI

DO NOT DRINK WATER
UNGA PHUZI AMANZI
O SE NWE METSI
MOET NIE DRINK NIE

CHOLERA

DO NOT TOUCH WATER
BLY WEG
O SE HLAPE KA METSI A NOKA
UNGA HLAMBI NGA LA MANZI

SOUL · Coca-Cola

SERVICE TO THE COMMUNITY

...ling February 2, 2001 Tel: 889-0812 Distribution complaints 249-7120 Classifieds 293-6058 Fax: 789-4070 (R1.

e.Coli seeping into boreholes

Homeowner lays charges against council

Jacci Babich

HIGH levels of e-coli are now seeping into boreholes... even in the most affluent suburbs.

This is raising more concern about the spread of cholera which has already sparked off a frenzy of activity to remove hundreds people squatting on the banks of the contaminated Jukskei River.

At least one borehole in up-market Illovo was tested with an e.coli count of more than 1 000 per 100ml - way over the acceptable level.

Hence, many homeowners are inundating purification companies with requests to have their water tested.

Local water purifying company H2O International confirmed there was "no doubt" there had been an increase in e-coli and faecal coleiforms found in underground water.

Chlorinators were hastily installed on three boreholes and purifiers on taps at the American International School of Johannesburg on the Knoppieslaagte Road following tests on the water.

"Where children are concerned, you have to be extra careful," said school head, Dr Leo Roberto.

Meanwhile, one Northern suburbs resident Charmaine Zambetti laid criminal charges against the Northern Metro council for failing to deal with underground water contamination in the Kya Sands area.

She claimed the council did not provide proper sewage facilities for the estimated 2 400 people living on council-owned land.

The charges were forwarded by the Douglasdale Police to the Department of Water Affairs for comment.

Residents in the Nooitgedacht area also asked the Northern Metro Council to test underground water near a church and a school in their area which they believe may have been contaminated by pit latrines.

A spokesman for Cydna Laboratory said every borehole should be tested annually.

Farmyards, human faeces from squatter camps, French drains and cross seepage were among the many ways in which ground water could become contaminated.

The spokesman said pollution levels were bound to increase if local authorities did not keep stringent health controls and standards in place.

For more information on testing, phone Cydna Laboratory at 7287373.

Most residents living on the polluted Jukskei River have shown no interest in leaving the area, but they are to be moved soon. See page 2.

184

CHAPTER FOUR

Eco-social injustice for working-class communities:

The making and unmaking of neoliberal infrastructure policy

With George Dor, Becky Himlin, and Greg Ruiters[1]

1. Introduction

The small amount of electricity flowing through the wires in the small Soweto house of Agnes Mohapi was meant to have been provided for free. But in the months immediately after the ANC famously promised universal free access to basic municipal services, including electricity, the opposite problem had emerged. During 2001, security officials and technical people from the state power company, Eskom, moved quickly through South Africa's best-known township, disconnecting power to those who hadn't paid their bills and arrears, which in many cases exceeded R10,000.

Mohapi is an ordinary elderly resident surviving on not much more than R600 per month. But because of what happened next, her story became the opening news handle in a front-page *Washington Post* article:

> When she could no longer bear the darkness or the cold that settles into her arthritic knees or the thought of sacrificing another piece of furniture for firewood, Agnes Mohapi cursed the powers that had cut off her electricity. Then she summoned a neighborhood service to illegally reconnect it.
>
> Soon, bootleg technicians from the Soweto Electricity Crisis Committee (SECC) arrived in pairs at the intersection of Maseka and

185

Moema streets. Asking for nothing in return, they used pliers, a penknife and a snip here and a splice there to return light to the dusty, treeless corner.

'We shouldn't have to resort to this', Mohapi, 58, said as she stood cross-armed and remorseless in front of her home as the repairmen hot-wired her electricity. Nothing, she said, could compare to life under apartheid, the system of racial separation that herded blacks into poor townships such as Soweto. But for all its wretchedness, apartheid never did this: It did not lay her off from her job, jack up her utility bill, then disconnect her service when she inevitably could not pay.

'Privatisation did that', she said, her cadence quickening in disgust. 'And all of this globalisation garbage our new black government has forced upon us has done nothing but make things worse ... But we will unite and we will fight this government with the same fury that we fought the whites in their day'.

This is South Africa's new revolution.[2]

The story of the SECC is worth returning to in detail, as we do in Chapter Six. But there is a complex political and policy context for understanding why the infrastructure in communities inhabited by Mohapi and literally tens of millions like her has not improved since liberation in 1994. This is the crux of South Africa's unsustainability: the difficulty that the new government has faced in simply addressing the basic socio-environmental needs of its main constituencies.

Consider another description of everyday life, from Tambo Square, a section of the Cape Town township Gugulethu. Caroline Nongauza, an unemployed single mother of two told her story to the SA Municipal Workers Union (Samwu):

> Visit Tambo Square squatter camp and see what other people are going through. I have been staying in this area for 13 years, but there is no improvement. There are about four taps of water providing the whole area. I have to walk 15 minutes from my shack to the tap. Imagine when I have to do the washing for my family or when I am not feeling well. We are still using the bucket system of toilets, which is disgusting. Our children are always sick as a result.
>
> We are a community without electricity and no hope for houses. The crime rate is very high because the area is dark. Children are being raped every day because of the closely packed shack life, darkness and drunkenness of parents. Much of this is because of the trauma of living in the circumstances we are staying in.[3]

The problem of inadequate access – or disconnection of supply once access has been provided – is not unique to the most elemental household services: water, sanitation and electricity. Take another high-profile example: telephones. The structuring of the state-owned company's privatisation contract in 1996 led to a similar phenomenon of 'cherry-picking' (i.e., denial of service to poor people) once an international conglomerate from Texas and Malaysia bought 30% of Telkom. Thanks both to legal obligations – imposed by parliament as a *quid pro quo* for maintaining Telkom's monopoly status for another five years – and to R48 billion in new taxpayer investments, the company rolled out 2.67 million lines to new customers through 2001. But because local phone call prices soared thanks to pressures by the new Texan managers, *two million* of the lines were subsequently cut once customers fell into debt.[4] 'Privatisation did that', Mohapi no doubt told her neighbours.

The commercialisation/privatisation of services and disconnection due to non-payment are two of the long-standing policies which have made a mockery of the ANC's 'lifeline' promises. In the process, environment and development have suffered, with women, children, the elderly and People With Aids bearing the brunt of the burdens.

What we must investigate in this chapter is whether their plight is so *systemic* that minor policy modifications to a fundamentally unjust system will inexorably fail. To be sure, the modification of a free 6 kilolitres of water per month and 50 kiloWatt hours of electricity, generally provided on a means-tested basis to indigent households beginning in mid-2001, did represent a step forward in many cases. However, as we will observe, creative sabotage by local and national bureaucracies means that for most South Africans desperate for services, the free water and electricity are still a mirage a year later. And we will also ask whether the free services promise is biased against large households, whether the amount provided is sufficient, and whether the subsequent rise in the tariff curve hurts those who consume more than the ungenerous lifeline which government is providing for free. Finally, we must consider the millions of people who will not benefit from free services without a concomitant increase in infrastructure roll-out, so that the subsidies will continue benefiting those who are better off. These features are the basis for ongoing pessimism about the ANC's commitment to serving its low-income constituencies.

Indeed, we make the argument that the systemic nature of household infrastructural inequality appears so durable that the minor reforms go largely unnoticed by people like Agnes Mohapi and Caroline Nongauza. After Part Two's exploration of the two mega-projects, Coega and the Lesotho dams, we should not be too surprised by the ongoing legacy of obscene power relations, the ravages of capital accumulation and enduring racial and gender discrimination. At Coega, as we observed, plans for huge state construction subsidies, electricity concessions and tax benefits are going forward, leaving much less scope for subsidising low-income women in Mandela Metropole and indeed across the impoverished Eastern Cape. The Lesotho Dams, we noted, raised prices for low-income Sowetans like Mohapi, but permitted hedonistic northern-suburban consumers to maintain bright green gardens all year long, repeatedly fill their swimming pools and enjoy massive amounts of water for domestic use.

In a functioning liberal democracy, the interconnections are where public policy should address social goals that the market cannot meet, and sort out environmental problems caused by the abuse of water and electricity. But household infrastructure policy adopted since 1994 has consistently failed Mohapi, Nongauza and millions like them, because the national parameters imposed upon municipal (and other) service providers did not cater for poor people's needs.

The point of this chapter, then, is to reveal the dynamic interplay between household/neighbourhood-scale projects, local and national water/sanitation and electricity delivery programmes, national infrastructure policies, and the underlying development philosophies that inform all of these. Discussing the evolution of household infrastructure will allow for more broad-reaching investigations of water and electricity in the two subsequent chapters.

We begin by the new government's inheritance from late apartheid (Section 2) and its 1994 election mandate (Section 3). A vigorous debate subsequently broke out which illustrates divergent environment and development discourses (Section 4). Part of the problem was the pressure to privatise municipal services (Section 5), and the failure to take seriously their environmental implications (Section 6). As a result, it was perhaps not surprising that once free lifeline services were finally promised, there emerged all manner of sabotage (Section 7).

Cementing status quo infrastructure

What we quickly discover in our policy autopsy is that during the first years of rule by the ANC, the determining factor in the provision of household infrastructure was what is generally termed *neoliberalism*. The most influential imperatives, in the mindset of ANC politicians and government bureaucrats, were the interrelated pressures of global competitiveness and privatisation through foreign investment. Those imperatives worked against expansion of the meagre existing (apartheid-era) system of cross-subsidisation that had slightly favoured poor and working-class communities.

In the context of rising corporate power, the countervailing progressive policy arguments based on premises of either sustainable development or environmental justice were unsuccessful during the first term of ANC rule, from 1994-99. This chapter tells that story. Only in September 2000, after six years of failure, would the political philosophy underlying official infrastructure standards and prices finally be reconsidered. The policy shift came in the ANC's *Municipal Election Manifesto*: 'ANC-led local government will provide all residents with a free basic amount of water, electricity and other municipal services, so as to help the poor. Those who use more than the basic amounts will pay for the extra they use'. This is a progressive formulation. Yet in the 18 months following the December 2000 elections, very few if any municipalities could claim to have kept that promise, for reasons we review below.[5]

The promise itself was prefigured in the 1994 RDP mandate for cross-subsidisation and the 1996 Constitution's Bill of Rights. But it had to be made more explicit in 2000 because fewer and fewer potential voters in townships and rural areas considered their standard of living to have risen since liberation. Post-apartheid municipal services experiences were nearly uniformly unsatisfactory, regardless of continual hype about delivery.

Recall, from this book's preface, Mbeki's statement at a Rio de Janeiro UN ceremony in late June 2002: 'Since the victory of democracy in 1994, seven million people have access to clean water, over one million homes for poor people have been built, over two million more homes now have electricity and every child has a place in school'.[6] In reality, this chapter shows, such claims cannot be sustained. Mbeki knows that a vast number of water, electricity and telephone accounts have been disconnected, affecting 10 million people in each category. Because of what Mohapi correctly terms 'this globalisation garbage', Pretoria's municipal infrastructure investments – water and sanitation systems, new electricity connections, local roads, stormwater drainage, and other services provided at municipal level – have, in reality, been one of the most troubling aspects of ANC rule.

It is all the more tragic because enormous opportunities existed in 1994, in the design and implementation of a national infrastructure programme, to reduce gender inequity, reorder the inherited apartheid geography, improve the environment, prevent public health problems and kick-start bottom-up local economic development strategies. Not only did the vast size of the infrastructural backlog, the ecological implications, and the implementation and management of new systems present a formidable challenge to the new government. They also presented compelling reasons for a radical redesign of everything from piping to pricing policies.

These challenges all proved too intimidating, given the neoliberal parameters adopted by most Pretoria departments. From the outset, in spite of rhetoric and Constitutional provisions to the contrary, government quickly retreated from its original electoral mandate, and adopted an infrastructure investment plan designed by World Bank staff. Those staff ignored both the Bank's own 1994 *World Development Report* entitled *Infrastructure for Development* and the ANC's RDP electoral mandate, which had promised lifeline services for all and rising block tariffs to assure redistribution.

But context is important, so we should first set the stage from the point at which neoliberalism was adopted by the outgoing apartheid regime. To move forward to the experiment with free basic services, requires that this chapter review:

- infrastructure policy directives in the RDP;
- the first democratic government's main infrastructure policy documents;
- frictions associated with the delivery process;
- contradictions in municipalities' growing reliance upon services privatisation;
- some of the more obvious environmental effects of the low-quality infrastructure planned for most urban and rural citizens; and
- the difficulty in implementing the ANC's free basic services promise.

What we will find is that there were far more continuities than change between the ungenerous housing and household infrastructure policies of the late-apartheid regime and those of the first-term ANC government.

Principles of neoliberal v. progressive infrastructure

The three most telling neoliberal principles widely followed from 1994–99 in relation to retail infrastructure were that:

- the user must pay the 'marginal cost'[7] of services (so as to avoid internal cross-subsidies);
- standards should be absolutely minimal for those who could not afford marginal cost; and
- commercialisation and indeed privatisation of infrastructure-related services had to be pursued, given the alleged national and municipal fiscal constraints.

It may be helpful to reflect quickly upon the neoliberals' quasi-religious commitment to 'get the prices right' – i.e., align prices with costs so as to avoid market distortions – when it comes to water and electricity tariffs.

As Figure 8 shows, the short-run marginal cost curve (Line A) for supply-ing water or electricity tends to fall, because it is cheaper to supply an additional unit of a service to a large consumer than a small consumer. Reasons for this include the large-volume consumers' economies of scale (i.e., bulk sales), their smaller per unit costs of maintenance, the lower administrative costs of billing one large-volume consumer instead of many small ones, and the ability of the larger consumers to buy the elec-tricity or water at a time when it is not in demand – e.g, during the mid-dle of the night – and store it for use during peak demand periods. The premise of neoliberalism is that pricing the service in a way that corre-sponds to the cost of the service, e.g., through a 30% profit mark-up across the board (Line B), assures the proper functioning of the market.

The progressive principle of cross subsidisation, in contrast, violates the impeccable logic of the market. By imposing a block tariff that rises for larger consumers (Line C), politicians distort the relationship of cost to price and hence send inefficient pricing signals to consumers. In turn, argue neoliberal critics of progressive block tariffs, such distortions of the market logic introduce a disincentive to supply low-volume users. The neoliberal logic concedes that sometimes subsidies are necessary, but the most important philosophical point, which we return to below, is that such subsidies should simply allow low-income people to buy the service *using a price structure that encourages a private investor*. In other words, subsidise the consumer not the service.

The progressive rebuttal is that the difference between Lines A and C allows not only for free universal lifeline services and a cross-subsidy from hedonistic users to low-volume users, but two additional benefits:

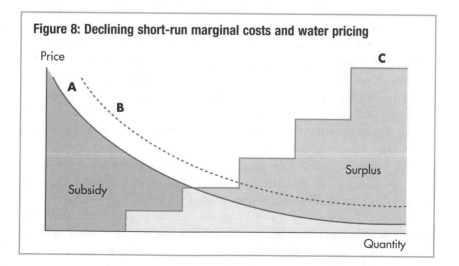

Figure 8: Declining short-run marginal costs and water pricing

- higher prices for high-volume consumption should encourage conservation which would keep the longer-run costs of supply down (i.e., by delaying the construction of new dams or power stations); and
- benefits accrue to society from the 'merit goods' and 'public goods' associated with free provision of services, such as improved public health, gender equity, environmental protection, economic spin-offs and the possibility of desegregating residential areas by class.[8]

Finally, the progressive argument for making the subsidy universal – not means-tested for only 'indigent' people – is both practical and deeply political. If the service is means-tested, it invariably leads to state coercion and stigmatisation of low-income people by bureaucrats. Further, it is an administrative nightmare to sort out who qualifies since so many people depend upon informal and erratic sources of income. More philosophically though, it is a premise of the Constitution that socio-economic rights such as water access are *universally* granted, not judged on the basis of a subjective income cut off line, especially given the differences in household size for which different low-income people are responsible. Moreover, the main international experience shows that the defence of a social welfare policy requires universality, so that the alliance of poor, working-class and middle-class people that usually win such concessions from the state can be kept intact.[9]

The contrast between the neoliberal infrastructure principles and what ANC constituents have traditionally demanded – and what was promised in the RDP and again in the 2000 municipal elections – is the core subject of this chapter. Even though the policies were subsequently adjusted, the neoliberal foundations of unsustainable household infrastructure were laid from 1994-99 and, we will see, are now extremely difficult to dig up and undergird with the values of eco-social justice.

After first considering the most crucial aspects of late-apartheid policy and socio-ecological conditions associated with infrastructure, we review the ANC government's mandate to deliver infrastructure and services to all South Africans. Next we take up the debate over standards and prices of services which broke out during the mid-1990s. Because of the victory of neoliberal arguments, we must then document the conflict over the increasingly commercialised/privatised institutional form of municipal services provision, the damaging environmental implications of infrastructure, and the failure of the free-services promise to meet adequately the needs of South Africa's poorest residents.

Later, in Chapters Four and Five, we revisit the reluctance to serve the masses by invoking a bigger problem than, merely, neoliberal policies introduced by visiting World Bank missions: the capitalist mode of production. But since policy reflects the balance of forces in any society, it is vital first to understand who is winning and who is losing, as a result of apartheid-era and post-apartheid neoliberalism applied to infrastructure.

2. Government's inheritance

When in 1994 the first democratic government was elected on the RDP platform, there was a high expectation that politicians and officials would immediately deliver improved basic services to the ANC's mass constituency.[10] Egregious late-apartheid practices had, after all, catalysed numerous 1980s social struggles associated with household infrastructure like water and electricity. These often achieved defensive successes such as preventing repossessions of houses as well as cut offs of services – but more importantly, they codified a more humane approach grounded in a rights-based discourse.

During the late-apartheid era, most of Pretoria's policies, programmes and reports introduced the 'site-and-service' approach to housing, and narrow cost-recovery principles to municipal services. The main markers of the neoliberal transition were the Independent Development Trust (IDT) housing grant (1991), the de Loor Report (1992) and the National Housing Forum accord (1994).[11]

But because of the political stalemate, it was impossible for Pretoria to conclusively lock down the desired policies. The late-apartheid regime's lack of credibility prevented even the World Bank from giving *verligte* Afrikaners like F.W. de Klerk the financial support that both desired. The infrastructure 'policy' inherited by the first democratic government was in fact merely a dubious amalgamation of highly-fragmented project-based approaches.

The context for the policy vacuum is important. After the 1980s rent and services payments boycotts became debilitating for Black Local Authorities which were nominally running the townships, virtually all the puppet-apartheid councils fell into formal bankruptcy. The apartheid government's national housing funds were redirected to municipal operating expenses. State evictions of non-payers and disconnections of vital municipal services were often unsuccessful because of social resistance. Mass action by residents and non-cooperation by municipal workers meant that only a few Conservative Party-ruled *dorpies* attempted, even temporarily, to punish black residents for rent and services payments boycotts. A few incidents of cholera caused by services cuts during the early 1990s were so widely condemned that the practice of disconnection slowed nearly to a halt.

Meanwhile, virtually no new houses for 'African' people were built by the state during the late 1980s. Instead, deregulation of racial restrictions on property ownership and the failure of banks' white client base to grow adequately led to a dramatic increase in private housing construction in the townships. Once the mid-1980s civic association protests had been snuffed by state repression,[12] the state began to endorse neoliberal presumptions about black working-class people's access to housing, fuelled by bank mortgage-bond credit on initially easy terms. For low-income unemployed black people, the state turned a blind eye to informal shack settlements – so long as they were on uncontested land – and backyard shanties within the townships.

The housing/infrastructure cul de sac

By the end of the 1980s, the contradictions and confrontations had left the following infrastructure landscape in the black residential areas:
- a series of recent township housing projects – usually poorly located, however, on cheaper land in distant locations;
- a limited number of approximately 200,000 households receiving relatively good levels of service (full electricity and fully-reticulated water and sewerage) in newly-constructed houses;
- an estimated three million households without adequate shelter;
- a slow household electrification programme run by Eskom in the main existing urban townships – though unevenly, and bedeviled by delays in implementation caused by local authority turf problems; and
- in the interstices, a dramatic increase in shack settlements without even rudimentary services.

The main component of the *de facto* late-apartheid urban policy, the private provision of bank-bonded housing, slowed to a virtual standstill from 1990-95 once interest rates on mortgage bonds had soared from their low of 12.50% in 1986 (-6% in real terms) to 20.75% (+7%) by 1989. The interest rate rise also contributed to the country's longest-ever depression, which cost many hundreds of thousands of jobs, including many held by township residents with bonds. As a result, approximately 40% of all borrowers defaulted or fell into deep arrears.

The second component, electrification, picked up slowly and then peaked at close to 400,000 new connections per year, including rural areas, in the mid-1990s. The main provider, Eskom, had reacted quickly to political pressure by increasing its high-priced but low-profit retail supply. The third component, upgrading of shack settlements and the formalisation of site-and-service programmes and projects, became the basis for 1990s infrastructure policy.

The first key statement of the late-apartheid government's intent to establish household infrastructure at inadequate levels for slightly-better formalised shack settlements was the 1991 IDT housing grant. Nelson Mandela was released and the ANC unbanned in February 1990, at the same time a trusted *verligte* ally of then-president De Klerk, Jan Steyn, was given control of the new IDT. He was instructed to dish out R2 billion to communities which cooperated with the late-apartheid regime.

Inspired by World Bank 'site-and-service' projects and policies, the R7,500 IDT capital subsidy for servicing sites was designed and largely implemented by officials associated with the Urban Foundation, a large corporate-funded think-tank and developer founded by Harry Oppenheimer and Anton Rupert in the wake of the 1976 Soweto uprising. Steyn's previous job was director of the Foundation.

However, the IDT projects were deemed mainly unsatisfactory within the black townships. Civic association critics quickly labelled them 'I Do Toilets', because the IDT financed the construction of merely a toilet. No structure, building materials or electricity connections were provided. This 'beacon of hope', as Steyn put it, was soon followed by more government 'toilets in the veld'. In very poorly located settings, they were supported by the notorious Department of Development Aid, whose mandate was to fund illegitimate 'self-governing' homelands.

There was one overriding benefit to the state from the switch in policy, away from public housing and towards site-and-service. Recognising that this new approach could help dampen the fiscal requirements associated with rapid urbanisation, Department of Housing politicians and bureaucrats drafted the 1992 *De Loor Report of the Task Group on National Housing Policy and Strategy*, which even endorsed a World Bank critique of the IDT subsidy for being 'unrealistically high'. In terms of guiding principles, as the de Loor Report put it, 'Deregulation, commercialisation and the employment of sound policies which strengthen market forces and provide access to opportunities are all strategies which need strong promotion and high priority'.[13]

An entirely different approach was adopted by civic associations and their technical colleagues in the 'urban service organisations', largely research NGOs in each of the main cities such as Planact, Development Action Group and Built Environment Support Group. In addition, criticism of the government's approach emerged from some of the grassroots activists who took part in the National Housing Forum. But the Forum's domination by Urban Foundation personnel and big business lobbyists, amplified by the ineffective ANC and civic movement delegates' uneven participation, assured that the critique would only scratch the surface.

Transition to post-apartheid site-and-service policy

In early 1994, in a controversial deal with housing minister Louis Shill following months of severe conflict, a modified site-and-service policy with a R12,500 maximum subsidy was adopted by the Forum and apartheid regime, which in turn laid the basis for post-1994 policy.[14] The key actor in the adoption of the Forum compromise as the basis for post-apartheid housing policy was the ANC representative to the Forum, and subsequently Department of Housing director-general, Billy Cobbett. According to his former colleague Mark Swilling,

> It was largely up to Cobbett as to who from the democratic movement participated in the policy process. When questioned as to why he largely kept the urban service organisations out of the national housing policy formulation process, he said that there was an emphasis from his political bosses on direct representation of political and civic leaders rather than involvement of 'experts' from the urban service organisations. This contrasted markedly from the strategy of organised business – in particular the banking institutions – who seconded large numbers of experts into the process and in so doing directly influenced the policy agenda in a way that would be impossible today, or even during the apartheid era.
>
> The democratic movement's overcommitted political and civic leaders were not equipped to deal with this army of technical expertise that were trusted with broad negotiating mandates by their principals. The consequences of this strategic (mis)calculation will be felt for many years.[15]

At the same time, in mid to late 1994, a new definition of service delivery was being proposed, and was ultimately adopted in the *White Paper on Water and Sanitation*, namely that the lifeline price of water to retail consumers should be at least equal to the 'operating and maintenance' expenses (i.e., full marginal cost), instead of being 'free'. This was, at first blush, a semantic mistake which, surely, the social-democratic water minister Kader Asmal would promptly fix. In reality, the wording represented a startling indication that neoliberal pricing principles would prevail in the crucial water sector, instead of the mandate adopted in the RDP.

3. Government's mandate

Many Democratic Movement leaders saw transitional bargaining fora like the National Housing Forum as merely stepping stones to power and policy-making. It was often remarked that all the problems caused by a weak negotiating position in the Housing Forum in 1992–93 would be swept away when a democratic government took over in 1994. So it was not obvious initially how much Cobbett's acceptance of site-and-service principles, just three months before the first democratic election, would shape future policy.

The RDP, whose far-reaching housing and infrastructure paragraphs were finalised in February 1994, was meant to change matters radically. As ANC leader Nelson Mandela remarked at the victory party on 2 May 1994, 'We have emerged as the majority party on the basis of the programme which is contained in the Reconstruction and Development book. That is going to be the cornerstone, the foundation, upon which the Government of National Unity is going to be based. I appeal to all leaders who are going to serve in this government to honour this programme'.[16]

But housing minister Joe Slovo, backed by Cobbett, dishonoured virtually all the promises when he released the first *Housing White Paper* six months later. After another four months, an infrastructure investment plan mainly drafted by the World Bank was adopted by Reconstruction and Development minister Jay Naidoo. Pulling the threads together were the Urban and Rural Development Strategies, released in October 1995. All deserve a brief review, after we first identify the mandate the ANC was given in the RDP.

Meeting housing and infrastructure needs

The RDP's chapter on 'Meeting Basic Needs' began with an ambitious statement: 'With a per capita gross national product (GNP) of more than R8,500 South Africa is classified as an upper middle income country. Given its resources, South Africa can afford to feed, house, educate and provide health care for all its citizens'.[17] The document proceeded to list a number of specific areas – many related to the International Covenant on Economic, Cultural and Social Rights – in which South Africans should consider themselves *entitled* to an adequate consumption level of goods and services.

The RDP's approach, in sum, was to ensure that essential service needs were met through vast increases in government subsidies when the market failed, and through mobilising additional resources by forcefully tapping capital markets and via off-budget methods. This was government's overarching mandate in the area of infrastructure and services. Concrete, detailed suggestions with regard to housing, land reform and services were offered to the future policy-makers.

Thus, for example, the RDP offered hope for a decent residential existence far beyond what was on offer in existing site-and-service schemes: 'As a minimum, all housing must provide protection from weather, a durable structure, and reasonable living space and privacy. A house must include sanitary facilities, storm-water drainage, a household energy supply (whether linked to grid electricity supply or derived from other sources, such as solar energy), and convenient access to clean water'.[18] The budgetary goal for housing expenditure in the RDP was 5% of the entire national budget, which at the time would have provided R10 billion each year for housing and related infrastructure investments. Indeed, this goal was repeated in the *Housing White Paper*.

But the failure of the first democratic government's housing policy to ensure such standards was due to its adoption of an 'incremental' building strategy, based upon a maximum subsidy only half of that required to build a decent house – i.e., R15,000 instead of R30,000 – and upon a bank-centred financing to 'top up' the grant with an individual home loan. The housing policy's departure from RDP provisions, and its failure on virtually all grounds save numbers of houses delivered, are beyond the scope of this chapter, but obviously have ramifications for water/sanitation and electricity because the subsidy grant was meant to pay for household infrastructure.[19]

Even where the ANC government claimed that nearly a million houses were built from 1994–99, the actual definition of a 'house', and the difference between subsidies allocated, those in the pipeline and actual titles transferred to new owners are hotly contested. Reflecting the difficulties, it is well known that without the top-up mortgage bond, the R15,000 grant only paid for a small patch of geographically marginal land, the installation of infrastructural services and a few building materials. The top-up mortgage bond was desperately needed to construct a proper house, but the proportion of subsidy recipients who got a bond fell from 17% during the late 1990s to less than 5% by the early 2000s.

It is noteworthy that the World Bank had intervened in the housing policy debate through an August 1994 mission led by deputy resident representative Juneid Ahmad. The Bank recommended to minister Slovo that the higher subsidy being discussed at the time, sufficient for a full house, be decreased in favour of 'modest site-and-service projects ... for the largest fraction of the low-income population'. Moreover, instead of prescribed assets or other means of freeing up housing credit, there should be 'well-publicised voluntary lending targets for low-income mortgage lending. It might also be possible to increase collateral security by seeking third party guarantors for low-income lenders and by making greater use of source-withholding of mortgage payments by employers'.[20] Within three months, a new policy was adopted along precisely these lines, replete with a Record of Understanding with commercial banks and a supply-side state housing guarantee scheme, which conflicted dramatically with the RDP and also failed on its own terms.

Likewise, as specified in the RDP, the rural land reform 'programme must include the provision of services to beneficiaries of land reform so that they can use their land as productively as possible' and 'must aim to redistribute 30% of agricultural land within the first five years of the programme'.[21] But as in the case of housing, a World Bank land reform team visiting in 1993 made market-oriented policy suggestions: e.g., a willing-seller, willing-buyer 'kulak' model based on small grants and unsubsidised interest rates. By mid-1994, Bank staff ultimately persuaded land affairs minister Derek Hanekom to adopt the neoliberal strategy.[22] This meant outright rejection of the recommendations of a grassroots-activist land movement which had met in Bloemfontein to make post-apartheid policy demands a few months earlier. As in the case of housing, the maximum land reform subsidy was originally set at just R15,000. Worse, the provision of rural infrastructure like water, sanitation and electricity was not considered integral to the programme. Because of its market orientation, instead of redistributing 30% of agricultural land within five years, the Department of Land Affairs redistributed less than 1%.

RDP-friendly services tariffs

According to insiders, the biggest reason for both urban (housing) and rural (land reform) retreats was the fiscal constraint: How, according to the RDP, were infrastructure and services to be paid for? The RDP specifies the need for tariff restructuring, cross-subsidies and lifeline services to the poor, in both water/sanitation and electricity:

> To ensure that every person has an adequate water supply, the national tariff structure must include the following:
> - a lifeline tariff to ensure that all South Africans are able to afford water services sufficient for health and hygiene requirements;
> - in urban areas, a progressive block tariff to ensure that the long-term costs of supplying large-volume users are met and that there is a cross-subsidy to promote affordability for the poor, and
> - in rural areas, a tariff that covers operating and maintenance costs of services, and recovery of capital costs from users on the basis

of a cross-subsidy from urban areas in cases of limited rural affordability.

The electrification programme will cost around R12 billion with
annual investments peaking at R2 billion. This must be financed
from within the industry as far as possible via cross-subsidies from
other electricity consumers. Where necessary the democratic government will provide concessionary finance for the electrification of
poor households in remote rural areas. A national Electrification
Fund, underwritten by a government guarantee, must be created to
raise bulk finance from lenders and investors for electrification.
Such a fund could potentially be linked to a Reconstruction Fund to
be utilised for other related infrastructural financing needs. A
national domestic tariff structure with low connection fees must
be established to promote affordability.[23]

There is some slight confusion embedded within the rural water mandate.[24] But by and large it should be clear that national tariff reform
should have increased cross-subsidies, using national and provincial
resources. The opposite happened. In addition, lifeline tariffs for low-
income consumers could have been supported with a more appropriate use of housing subsidies to finance deeper levels of capital
infrastructure. *Neither of these should ultimately have cost central
government anything extra beyond even the existing (planned)
urban housing and rural land reform grants.* Promises of humane
standards of infrastructure and services for all South Africans could
have been kept, and additional public health, environmental and economic benefits to all of society, particularly women and children, could
have been achieved.

There is much more to be said than there is space here, in trying to
answer in convincing detail some rudimentary questions about the con-
flict-ridden housing policy debate: why was so little state funding made
available in comparison to what was promised?; where were developers
(rather than the state and communities) deciding the form and location
of post-apartheid housing projects?; and why were so many other urban
RDP promises so explicitly violated?[25]

Briefly, the fiscal constraint argument encouraged Slovo and Cobbett to set the housing standards at pitiably low levels, and a neoliberal
ideology supportive of 'partnerships' with the private sector (especially banks) was established at the Botshabelo Housing Accord conference in October 1994. And although he had served as ANC housing
desk officer from 1992-94, Cobbett had played no role in the RDP
drafting, in view of his own responsibilities in the Transitional Execu-

tive Committee (from December 1993 when the RDP moved into final form), so there was no ownership of the ANC promises within the housing ministry when Slovo took over in May 1994. At the time, Slovo's own comment was telling: 'The only house I've ever built was a sand castle'. Dying of cancer, Slovo failed to foresee the many aspects of class apartheid and services-poverty which his new policy would introduce.

Still, no matter the problems associated with housing policy, the installation and maintenance of water, sanitation and electricity could have been accomplished in a manner consistent with the RDP. The differences between the mandate and the neoliberal approach codified just after liberation in 1994 are considered next.

4. The post-apartheid municipal services debate

In this section we find that the disjuncture between what was required and what was offered by post-apartheid neoliberal bureaucrats was no accident, though neither was it a necessary outcome. It reflected quite similar influences in the form of policy advice that flowed, during the 1980s–90s, from the World Bank and its two main South African surrogates: the Urban Foundation and the Development Bank of Southern Africa.

The main 1994–99 infrastructure policies through which we can trace the influence of neoliberal advice are:

- the *Housing White Paper* of November 1994 (Department of Housing),
- the *Water Supply and Sanitation White Paper* of November 1994 (Department of Water Affairs and Forestry, or 'Dwaf'),
- the *Urban Infrastructure Investment Framework* of March 1995 (Ministry of Reconstruction and Development, or 'RDP Ministry'),
- the *Urban and Rural Development Strategies* of October 1995 (RDP Ministry),
- the *Urban and Rural Development Frameworks* of May 1997 (Departments of Housing and Land Affairs),
- the *Municipal Infrastructure Investment Framework* of July 1997 (Department of Constitutional Development or 'DCD'),
- the *Local Government White Paper* of February 1998 (DCD),
- the April 1998 *Policy Paper on Intergovernmental Finance* (Department of Finance),
- the August 1998 *Draft Regulatory Framework for Municipal Service Partnerships* (DCD), and

- the December 1998 *White Paper on Energy Policy* (Department of Minerals and Energy Affairs).

Other papers from the Departments of Water Affairs and Forestry, and Minerals and Energy Affairs, are similar in tone and content. A variety of laws and regulations have codified these policies, even if implementation has been uneven. Notably, many of these can be read as entailing a profound conflict with the South African Constitution's socio-economic rights clauses.[26] Taken together, these core policy statements of infrastructure and municipal services policy represent the main barriers to provision of basic water, sanitation, electricity and other household and community infrastructure investments, and to the cross-subsidisation necessary to pay for the recurrent costs associated with minimally decent standards of consumption.

The neoliberal advocacy camp consistently won the debates from 1994–99 and wrote policy accordingly, not necessarily because their arguments were more coherent, but because a neoliberal outcome reflected the balance of forces in society as a whole. It is thus important to show that an alternative, progressive policy framework was (and is) feasible – providing infrastructure for all, on the basis of more dignified standards and a free lifeline bloc of water and electricity consumption. Socio–environmental injustice in poor and working-class neighbourhoods *was not inevitable*, and it took an enormous leap of logic for the policy-makers to consistently reverse their progressive mandates.

The Miif

The *Municipal Infrastructure Investment Framework (Miif)* describes the main infrastructure and services options planned by government, specifically the DCD, whose name changed in 1999 to the Department of Provincial and Local Government. The *Miif* framework, according to DCD's 'User-Friendly Guide', used 'an economic modelling exercise to estimate services backlogs, assess the capital costs that are involved in removing these backlogs, and calculate the recurrent costs of operating and maintaining the services'.[27]

Earlier, in November 1994 and March 1995, the World Bank had deployed deputy resident representative Ahmad to coordinate work on the *Urban Infrastructure Investment Framework*.[28] He persuaded Pretoria's chief infrastructure bureaucrat, Chippy Olver, that the post-apartheid government should provide only minimal standards and service levels to low-income South Africans. This became one of the prime sites of controversy, along with the issue of how to cover recurrent costs beyond low-income communities' ability to pay.

What level of services?

The first versions of *Miif* circulated amongst only a few senior policy-makers so it was only in October 1995 that anger at the ANC government's new approach first began to emerge. That month, the Ministry for Reconstruction and Development publicly issued a draft *Urban Development Strategy (UDS)* which reflected government's thinking on service provision. The UDS summary demonstrates the inadequacy of standards then contemplated for *urban* 'municipal' areas:[29]

> An average national distribution of 55:25:20 between full, intermediate and basic levels of services in municipal areas is considered a realistic target for the infrastructure investment strategy over the next ten years ...
>
> 'Basic services' means communal standpipes (water), on site sanitation, graded roads with gravel and open stormwater drains and streetlights (electricity). These services will be targeted at households with an income of less than R800 per month and charged for at between R35 and R50 per month.
>
> 'Intermediate services' entail water provision through yard taps on site, simple water-borne sanitation, narrow paved roads with no curbs and open drains and 30 amps electricity with prepaid meters for households. These should be affordable to households which earn between R800 and R1700 per month and will cost them between R100 and R130 per month.
>
> 'Full services' mean house connected water supplies, full water-borne sanitation, paved roads with curbs and piped drains and 60 amps electricity provision.
>
> It is anticipated that households in the R1700–R3500 monthly income class could afford 'low consumption' costing them between R180 and R220 per month. Households with monthly incomes of above R3500 will be assumed able to pay for 'full services at high consumption' at charges between R270 and R350 per month.[30]

The class-based services segregation quickly became controversial. Policy advocacy by the community constituency of the National Economic Development and Labour Council (Nedlac) began in early 1996, led by the SA National Civic Organisation (Sanco). Later that year, Nedlac became bogged down in corporatist politics and Sanco's spine softened.[31] A variety of other lobbying and technical interventions by the National Institute for Economic Policy[32] did have the effect of raising the infrastructure standards slightly higher than was initially proposed by the Bank's urban modelling, the draft *UDS* and early drafts of the *Miif*.

Instead of no electricity, for example, a revised *Miif* in March 1997 gave urban households the prospect of receiving an 8 Amp supply. Instead of paying R35–50 per month for these services, a subsidy of approximately R50 per low-income household was suggested by the team revising the *Miif*. Yet this was still not nearly enough to cover basic operating costs. Indeed the grant was unsustainable given Pretoria's budget constraints, and as shown below, there were substantial doubts about this method of subsidy in any event.[33]

Thus community activists could claim to have won several minor improvements over 'basic' standards of services. But there remained – as 'probably affordable to all in urban settlements' – many objectionable components of the basic *Miif* package: pit latrines, communal (not house or yard) standpipes, a weak electricity supply, gravel roads, open stormwater drains, communal waste dumps (not pavement removal), and other reflections of an extremely stingy infrastructure package. Worse, under the most realistic economic growth projections, nearly 30% of urban residents would be subject to these low standards even after the 10-year plan (1997–2006) for service provision was fully implemented.[34]

Though we do not have the space in this chapter fully to explore the rural implications of *Miif*, the standards under the low scenario were even less acceptable, with 70% of the rural population anticipated to have the 'basic' services discussed above after a decade's worth of investment. Another 20% would still have no services at all, according to the plan.[35] In both urban and rural settings, as noted below, the actual implementation progress was far slower than even the low target levels specified in *Miif*, in part because of the backward sliding associated with the government's mass disconnection policy.

Miif's mistakes

Several other criticisms of the *Miif* must also be recorded:

- The *Miif* service levels contemplated were not merely emergency services, i.e., piped water or portable toilets in slum settlements that are without water or hygienic facilities at present. The low standards represented, more fundamentally, *permanent* development policy, because the infrastructure would be cemented in at the lowest levels.
- A crucial problem in the affordability calculations was the over-optimistic projection in *Miif* that, in inflation-adjusted terms, only around 20% of urban households would still earn less than R800 per month (in 1995 rand) within ten years.

- A national tariff structure was not developed within the *Miif* consistent with the cross-subsidisation and lifeline tariff provisions mandated in the RDP.
- Environmental problems associated with the proposed standards were not adequately addressed or factored in.
- Implications of the infrastructure policy for microeconomic linkages and for macroeconomic policy were not adequately addressed or factored in as a means of overcoming affordability constraints.
- The implications of infrastructure standards for women and other vulnerable groups – e.g., People with Aids, the elderly and children – were not adequately considered and factored in.
- The spatial implications of class segregation implicit in the programme – with all the consequent economic inefficiencies – lent themselves to creation of new, post-apartheid racial ghettos where it will be physically impossible or excessively costly to upgrade from 'basic' to full services. While recognising this problem, *Miif* did nothing to counteract it; again the costs associated with neo-apartheid geography were neither calculated nor factored in.[36]
- Perhaps most importantly, public health benefits associated with increased access to services were not adequately factored in.

To take only the last revealing example, critics argued against the *Miif* Ventilated Improved Pitlatrine (VIP) sanitation standard on these health/hygiene grounds:

- There remains a need to properly drain away inflows of water used for bathing, washing and cooking (which can't be put into the dry system).
- People have great difficulty in self-constructing VIPs properly, because they require an expensive, independent external structure and complex draining and ventilation duct procedures so as to limit insect/rodent penetration.
- South Africa lacks municipal drainage/sucking capacity – and the cost of sucking to low-income residents is high when VIPs are full.
- E.coli and other bacteria from pit latrines often penetrate into the water table.
- VIPs record very low utilisation rates by young children due to fears of darkness inside VIPs. The darkness is necessary to force insects to fly to the mesh hatch atop the structure.
- People with Aids often succumb to opportunistic infections due to lack of sufficient water and electricity, and these infections require even greater amounts of water for hygiene than under normal conditions.

A literature review by leading academic public health experts at University of Western Cape suggested that a 20% additional disease abatement could be achieved by upgrading to water-borne toilets from VIPs.[37] However, Dwaf did not appear interested in factoring the benefit side into its calculations, especially if those benefits were to be realised by an entirely different ministry (Health), and if they implied that Dwaf would have substantially higher cost obligations to provide water to distant rural residents.[38] That women are the primary beneficiaries of additional state subsidies to improve standards did not matter to government, either.

Ironically, Dwaf had persistent problems in even spending its sanitation subsidy during the late 1990s mainly because it required co-payments by recipients. By 2001, Dwaf was still engaged in sanitation 'pilot projects': absolutely extraordinary, given how simple and universal is the installation of even a pit latrine. Even after cholera had become a killer threat, especially when rural migrants returned from KwaZulu–Natal to cities following the December 2000 holidays, Dwaf still did not change its policies and programmes sufficiently to allow it to spend its national budgetary allocations. Blaming municipal regulations, Dwaf director-general Mike Muller admitted that underspending in the first six months of 2001 was 75%: 'It is proving very difficult to get council resolutions formally passed to accept such grants where councils have not yet been able to get to grips with plans and budgets of their areas'.[39] It was another case of Dwaf's passing the buck for bad policy design.

The environmental costs of inadequate sanitation systems that leach into groundwater are considered in more detail below. But again it was ironic that when a June 2001 Dwaf report showed massive despoliation of South Africa's municipal water supplies, department spokesperson Themba Khumalo agreed with five-year old criticisms of the *Miif*: 'The unacceptable levels of raw sewage and bacteria in rivers, especially in Gauteng, is mainly a consequence of inadequate management of urban sanitation systems, aggravated by the appalling state of sanitation in low-income informal settlements'. According to the *Engineering News*, 'The biggest problem is experienced in densely populated areas, where sewer systems are not adequately operated and maintained'.[40]

In sum, Dwaf should have taken steps to define these eco-social costs and benefits effectively. That would have led to provision as a human right of dwelling–based piped water access – and immediate short-term emergency supplies through tanker trucks – as a human right. There would have been strongly positive overall net benefits from the standpoint of both environment and development objectives. The 'net economic return' on investments would then, logically, have incorporated not only the immediate financial return – the amount of cost recovery as a ratio of the amount invested – but also other positive 'externalities' and 'multipliers'.[41] More money could have been allocated and spent beginning in 1994, higher standards of services achieved, and more durable maintenance of systems assured.

Instead, having failed to adopt the most fundamental premises of sustainable development theory, namely the incorporation of externalities, the *Miif* and other water and electricity policy documents provided for low standards of capital investment in infrastructure, on grounds that these standards were the most that low-income South Africans could afford to pay for at the outset and to maintain over time. The option of subsidising low-income people was, in the neoliberal framework, to be avoided, a crucial point we turn to next.

Recurrent cross-subsidies?

In light of Pretoria's refusal to consider the broader economic returns to infrastructure investment, the main reason that 'basic' levels of service were imposed upon the vast majority of the poor was the allegedly high recurrent costs of water and electricity. In the absence of subsidies, these costs prohibit low-income households from paying full cost-recovery rates for even a minimal monthly amount of these services.

A subsidy should cover sufficient services – according to the RDP, for example, 'an on-site supply of 50–60 litres per capita per day of clean water' and sufficient electricity to cover the energy requirements associated with essential lighting, heating and cooking for a typical family (approximately 1 kWh per person per day) – such that all South Africans attain a minimally decent standard of living regardless of their ability to pay.

Instead, an approach emphasising cost recovery and 'limited' local-level cross-subsidies was adopted. According to the *UDS*,

> Services and infrastructure will be introduced in line with the affordability levels of communities affected. The principle that people should pay for the services to which they have access is central. This means that the level of services in each area should relate to what the consumers there can afford and are willing to pay for. Where government support is needed to ensure basic service delivery, it will be provided transparently. Deliberate steps will be taken to remove any disguised subsidies. Limited cross-subsidies to enhance household affordability and secure 'lifeline' consumption will be necessary.[42]

Two points should be made immediately. First, the *UDS* failed to mention that urban services in existing middle- and high-income areas were heavily subsidised for decades, from surpluses generated through business levies. These were ultimately based on transfers from *black* workers and consumers whose employers and retail outlets were historically, by law, located in *white* areas. Failure to recognise the historical injustice meant not only that it was not to be corrected, but that the very system of cross-subsidisation would then fall into disfavour, even though it should have been used to provide affirmative action in municipal services to black communities.

Second, the reason for the phrase 'limited cross-subsidies' in this context was because of Pretoria's explicit refusal to consider, even as an policy option exercise, restructuring the national electricity or water tariffs so that substantial cross-subsidies could be obtained. But the 'limited' cross-subsidies grudgingly conceded by the UDS would be insufficient, simply because South Africa's majority is so poor, especially in relation to the minority of luxury consumers who have never had to worry about access to full services. Municipal officials' attempts to recover *any* costs on collectively consumed services – a communal tap, for example – are often futile or too administratively expensive.

If, on the other hand, a national cross-subsidy proposal, consistent with the RDP, had been considered and adopted, it would have been relatively easy to penalise excessive use by national-scale industrial, service-sector, mining and agricultural bulk users of water and electricity, so as to fund a lifeline to residential consumers. The vast difference in use patterns would allow a small increase in tariffs for the large users and a free lifeline service to all other consumers as an entitlement. Such a progressive block tariff system would also discourage excessive usage, thereby contributing to conservation goals.

How much infrastructure can South Africa afford?

At this stage of the argument, the full cost implications of such an alternative approach should be clarified. Most importantly, how large a subsidy can South Africa afford to provide users of basic-needs infrastructural services?

Ironically, the UDS states, 'the government's aim is to increase housing's share of the budget to 5% and housing delivery to a sustained 350,000 units per annum within five years'.[43] The goal repeats not only the RDP commitment but the government's 1994 *Housing White Paper*. As noted above, the RDP envisaged that households' ongoing expenses would be offset by cross-subsidies, lifeline servicep rovision and a minimal level of support devoted tot he capital costs of housing – roughly R10 billion in public investment per annum (given a real, late 1990s budget of approximately R200 billion in 1994-currency terms). Under these reasonable assumptions, *there is no question that the supply of services at much higher levels was financially feasible for all South Africans.*

The additional capital spending required would have been roughly 10% more than was planned on state investment in infrastructure through the *Miif.*[44] Financing sources for recurrent operating and maintenance costs would have been easy to locate within existing service suppliers, but through national-scale and not merely municipal cross-subsidies. A lifeline entitlement would have been provided to all South Africans, with far greater resource conservation. And the RDP-consistent strategy also better reflected the variety of broader socio-environmental costs and benefits associated with infrastructure and services.

The multiple logics were sound. But one barrier was Olver's philosophical refusal to cross-subsidise at DCD. As noted in Chapter One, he viewed cross-subsidies by big business as a deterrent to international competitiveness: 'If we increase the price of electricity to users like Alusaf, their products will become uncompetitive and that will affect our balance of payments. I'm a socialist. But it's a fact that international capital holds sway as we come to the end of the twentieth century'.[45] As discussed in Chapter Six, Alusaf's extraordinary contribution to greenhouse gas emissions and global warming did not enter into the equation.

Another barrier was practical, which also reflected DCD's growing relationship with the World Bank, the US Agency for International Development (US Aid), and the British Department for International Development (Dfid): pressure to privatise municipal services. The pressure from these transmission belts of international capital was relentless. As a direct result, difficulties emerged in winning support for higher services standards and cross-subsidisation at the national parastatal electricity supplier, Eskom, and even from a minister, Asmal, who in principle agreed with the redistributive sentiments. Contradictions were, at least initially, overwhelming between cross-subsidisation and privatisation, commercialisation and public-private partnerships.

5. Municipal services 'partnerships'

Partly as a corollary to government's retreat from its policy mandate and its failure to deliver infrastructure of even low standards, lead bureaucrats within DCD and Dwaf also began pushing a privatisation agenda beginning in 1995.

Municipalities were encouraged to contract out infrastructure-related services to the private sector using what were initially called Public-Private Partnerships (PPPs). In 1997, the DCD issued guidelines and helped establish a Municipal Infrastructure Investment Unit based at the Development Bank of Southern Africa. This was followed by DCD's draft regulatory framework in August 1998, in which PPPs were rebaptised as Municipal Service Partnerships (MSPs) and characterised as 'a variety of risk-sharing structures within public–public, public–private and public–NGO/CBO partnerships'.[46] By December 1998, the SA Local Government Association (Salga) and DCD had negotiated a Municipal Framework Agreement with unions to regulate such partnerships.

As an aside, beginning in 1996, Dwaf's Community Water Supply and Sanitation programme commissioned several dozen extremely small-scale, rural PPPs, known as Build–Operate–Train–and–Transfer contracts, involving NGOs and some private firms. But serious problems soon emerged: unsustainability, lack of consumer affordability given cost-recovery pricing policy, poor technical design, poor community control functions, mismatched NGO/private-sector roles and expectations, systematic inconsistencies with neighbouring government-subsidised water schemes, and lack of training and transfer prospects. By 1999, the concept was in many areas evaluated as a 'failure' with respect to implementation by Dwaf and DCD. According to Masia et al, 'The gaps between practice and policy have to be addressed head on lest the policies be invalidated'.[47] The same unsatisfying project results were found to apply, as well, to Dwaf's favoured NGO implementing agency, the Mvula Trust.[48]

Class struggles over municipal services

Nevertheless, within four years of the advent of democracy, key political decision-makers had been won over to what effectively amounted to creeping privatisation of core local services: rubbish removal, water works and even municipal electricity supply. The primary advocates of privatisation were the World Bank and its private sector investment arm, the International Finance Corporation,[49] as well as local and international firms. For example, Banque Paribas, Rand Merchant Bank, Colechurch International, the Development Bank of Southern Africa, Generale des Eaux, Metsi a Sechaba Holdings, Sauer International and Suez had all met with officials of Port Elizabeth municipality by 1997, in the wake of a week-long 1996 World Bank study of the council's waterworks which suggested just one policy option: full privatisation.[50]

But there was also resistance, and not only from usual suspects like residual militant civics, Samwu and other advanced forces within Cosatu, some of the more advanced civic groups and, in places like Nelspruit, the SA Communist Party and ANC Youth League. So too was privatisation contested by some residual municipal bureaucrats – interestingly, a large fraction of 'Old Guard' (pre-1994) officials – who did not see being hired away by the incoming privatiser as attractive (or were not offered a higher-paying management position). One we interviewed in East London argued, 'PPPs are not always the best way to go. Costs creep up especially by the third year. So we don't accept that we will save money. By the time the contract expires, everything is ruined. We have lots of companies coming to do presentations, but we will not be caught. They take over your staff and you lose control over them. It is not sustainably cheaper'.[51]

Criticisms of privatisation micropractices were joined from a surprising source in early 1998, the World Bank's then chief economist and senior vice president, Joseph Stiglitz, who conceded that 'the conditions under which privatisation can achieve the public objectives of efficiency and equity are very limited' because if 'competition is lacking then creating a private, unregulated monopoly will likely result in even higher prices for consumers. And there is some evidence that, insulated from competition, private monopolies may suffer from several forms of inefficiency and may not be highly innovative'.[52]

From the conservation standpoint, privatisation is also a deterrent in many cases. Sometimes, a water concession is granted to a private company with built-in demand-side management incentives: e.g., reduce overall consumption by x% and the municipality will grant you an additional y% profit rate on each litre sold. The objective, for the municipality, is obviously to avoid the additional cost of a new supply enhancement. Even then, however, it is most likely that water conservation will occur where it is most profitable to the company, which will be poor people's access.[53]

Notwithstanding the criticisms, DCD's *White Paper* endorsed privatisation, while acknowledging several risks: 'cherry-picking' (denial of services to the poor), low quality services and unfair labour practices. Many of these lessons had emerged from the first set of pilot projects, where the French company Suez managed three small rural water systems beginning during the early 1990s.

Privatisation pilots

Many large municipalities had closed down their public housing and in some cases civil engineering departments during the 1980s as part of the first wave of local government shrinkage. Central state housing subsidies were transferred into services departments once the rates and service payments boycotts threatened many municipalities' viability.

More explicitly, white-run Eastern Cape towns were the site of several small water privatisation pilot projects: Queenstown in 1992, Stutterheim in 1994 and Fort Beaufort in 1995. Later, water privatisation in Nelspruit was promoted by the Development Bank of Southern Africa, which refused a loan to the municipality but gave one to the British firm Biwater. The contracts at Nelspruit and the Dolphin Coast were temporarily stalled in 1998 by trade union-led resistance, and even their 1999–2000 resuscitations were mired in a controversy over whether DCD Minister Valli Moosa had bargained in bad faith with Samwu. In 1999, Johannesburg's Igoli 2002 plan became the world's largest single water concession. Notably, no alternative options – such as financing strategies discussed below, were considered by the Council in spite of massive protests by Samwu workers.

Other major exploratory projects were facilitated by a R30 million US Aid grant to DCD for the development of PPP business plans in various towns. These included Cape Town, Port Elizabeth and Stellenbosch (where water and sanitation were reviewed by 1999), Benoni (fire and emergency services) and several towns where refuse removal would be privatised. In Cape Town's Khayelitsha township, the Billy Hattingh private rubbish removal scheme was so unsuccessful that by 1999, municipal workers had to be redeployed to back up the company. Samwu' attempt to gain access to a small part of the funding to promote public-public partnerships was rejected.

The early PPPs suggest a penchant for long-term management contracts, entailing 'delegation' of defined municipal functions for a 10, 25 or 30 year period. They include the operation, rehabilitation, maintenance, customer services and expansion of assets, which are, however, still owned by the municipalities. Contracts are flexible, allowing the company to extend or upgrade facilities but with municipal or non-company finances. Unlike concession contracts, they involved minimal greenfield investment, such as extension of services to townships, and hence far lower risks for the successful bidder.

Companies like Water and Sanitation South Africa (WSSA), a Suez/Group Five joint venture, promised to 'render an affordable, cost effective and optimised service, implement effective consumer management' and ensure that customers are 'willing and able to pay for services, while maximising revenue collection'.[54] Benefits also allegedly include 'a more dynamic business environment, increased productive investment, workplace democratisation, co-operation with small and micro enterprise, and more open and flexible management styles'.[55]

Sophistry is common in the water sector. In an 'open letter' in *Le Monde* in late 2001, Suez chief executive Gerard Mestrallet explicitly denied all the charges levied against his firm:

Water is a common good. We are opposed to the privatisation of water resources precisely because in our eyes water is not a commodity. We do not trade in water. We do not sell a product, but provide a service, that of making clean water continuously available to all, and returning the water to the natural habitat once it has been treated. It is the price of that service that is billed, and not water as a raw material ...

Private groups are trained to intervene quickly, to reach tangible, verifiable results, to lever financial resources in countries where public budgets are limited. They are ready to pursue their efforts in inventing technical, contractual and financial solutions suited to the reality of local conditions, under the supervision of public authorities in those countries.[56]

In practice, in the Stutterheim pilot, water services were instead characterised by WSSA's failure to serve any of the 80% of the region's township residents (classic cherry-picking), mass cut offs of water by the municipalities of township residents who could not afford payments, and the cooption of the main civic leader into WSSA's employ, thus effectively rendering silent any community protest. In the worst cases, Suez never bothered to upgrade capital, leaving many low-income black residents with the hated 'bucket system' of sanitation.[57]

Not far away, according to Lance Veotte of Samwu,

In Queenstown's townships of Mlungisi and Ezibhalene, where a Suez-Lyonnaise subsidiary has had control of the water services for a few years, they failed to fix the leaks in the existing water infrastructure and so an exorbitant amount of water loss is taking place on site. WSSA charges the municipality for all water – whether lost or used – and the council recovers the money from the communities through increased tariffs. The company earns completely risk free profit while the community remains in perpetual conflict with their local government which cuts off their water and evicts them when they can't pay higher and higher water bills.[58]

Moreover, at least one of these pilot contracts was so flawed that it invited a court challenge in September 2001. The newly demarcated Nkonkobe Municipality in the province's ex-Ciskei (homeland) disputed a 1995 10-year contract that one of its predecessor municipalities, Fort Beaufort, had agreed to with WSSA. In mid-2001, Nkonkobe found itself in arrears to WSSA by R3.2 million, representing eight months' payment. The mayor, H.M. Mdleleni, contested the contract on grounds that the original requirement for transparency and notification – ironically, in a 1974 apartheid-era law – was not complied with by the old Fort Beaufort municipality, and the MEC for local government had failed to agree to the deal. WSSA refused to recognise the termination of the deal, and to hand back municipal property.

Whatever the outcome of the debate over transparency, the main issue was evidently financial sustainability. As labour commentator Terry Bell put it, 'The government's privatisation plans could be about to suffer a major blow ...the public/private partnership with WSSA is not financially sustainable for a poor municipality. Even if the fee can be met, it could only be at the cost of reducing other services elsewhere'. Nkonkobe simply didn't have the R400,000 required to make payments to WSSA each month, and Mdleleni claimed that this problem alone should make the contract invalid, according to the *Municipal Systems Act* of 2000. Another municipal claim was that the demarcation of new communities invalidated the old contract. Canceling the WSSA deal would save Nkonkobe at least R19.8 million over the subsequent four years. Most importantly, perhaps, Mdleleni claimed that there was 'increasing public opposition' to WSSA and 'a significant amount of antagonism toward the contract' such that 'to secure public support for the contract would be unsuccessful'.[59]

Another major contractual problem emerged on the Dolphin Coast in KwaZulu-Natal. The French firm Saur (operating in a joint venture as Siza Water) won a 30-year concession there in 1999, upon which it subsequently reneged when revenues were 37% below its expectations.[60] Weak municipal politicians and officials gave in and renegotiated, as Pretoria stood by, still failing to implement water privatisation regulations to prevent such abuse of power. Soon thereafter, Biwater won the hotly-contested contract in Nelspruit, over union and community opposition, but like Suez in Fort Beaufort it was incapable of expanding its deal profitably to the low-income rural residents in the newly demarcated Greater Nelspruit.[61] Instead of expanding public sector capacity in Nelspruit, a public institution used taxpayer funds to capitalise the privatisation of water. According to Lance Veotte of Samwu,

> Municipalities find themselves unable to borrow money to extend infrastructure. In South Africa, the state has instead set up institutions such as the Municipal Infrastructure Investment Unit and the Development Bank of Southern Africa (DBSA). These, instead of capacitating municipalities to deliver services better, are hellbent on ensuring private sector involvement in basic services delivery in water, sanitation and refuse removal. Samwu believes that the DBSA

should have lent the Nelspruit municipality $10 million directly rather than loaning it to Biwater where a cut [disconnection] is pure profit.[62]

In the country's largest city, Johannesburg, Suez joined a consortium in a contract that Samwu demanded should be canceled partly because Suez was linked to the Lesotho dam corruption through a construction subsidiary. In any event, there remained substantive questions over the merits of Igoli 2002 which are worth reviewing, because the process was driven by a financial scare, and the 'alternative' to privatisation was never given a hearing.

Corporatising Johannesburg

Lack of capital was the ubiquitous reason that Johannesburg's pro-privatisation bloc – city manager Ketso Gordhan,[63] the 'Transformation Lekgotla' of 15 councilors, and a team of World Bank advisers – gave for embarking on an asset-stripping spree during the late 1990s. 'Mismanagement' was another rationale, and indeed the city's officials were having major difficulties in simply maintaining the inherited systems, in part because they refused to enter into constructive relationships with workers who could have pointed out areas for improvement.[64] But to the extent that capital-drought was genuine, the fundamental financial problem Johannesburg faced was a triple-squeeze by powerful funders.

The first group were in the national Department of Finance, which unconscionably reduced central-local grants by 85% (after inflation) from 1991–99, leaving Johannesburg with a measly R24 million in 1999.[65] Johannesburg was not particularly creative in attracting other national funds such as housing subsidies, infrastructure grants, poverty relief funds, etc., for its vast impoverished population. Finally, when the finance department granted Johannesburg R500 million in 2000, it came with extremely tight strings attached, including the rapid implementation of Igoli 2002.

The second group of stingy financiers were in the banks and insurance companies. Before 1992, they financed *white* Johannesburg's capital expansion programmes. As Johannesburg desegregated, the capital market institutions turned off their loan funds for municipal capital bonds, preferring to send financial resources into the stock market, suburban shopping centres and office buildings.[66] Johannesburg officials failed to pass by-laws against geographical discrimination ('redlining') as a first step towards compelling financial institutions to fund city bonds. The financiers' sabotage of transformation went unchallenged.[67]

The third group who denied the city money were the wealthy households and corporations who did not pay their fare share of the city rates bill. For decades, wealthy ratepayers received an enormous subsidy from township residents. Township workers laboured in factories and offices, and township consumers bought goods in shops, that were all located in white-controlled municipalities. Those factories, offices and shops paid rates to Johannesburg, while township administrations relied mainly on beerhall revenues and, during the 1980s, some central government funding. During the mid-1990s, the Sandton Ratepayers Federation and Liberty Life insurance company, a major Sandton property investor, challenged redistributive rates that would subsidise Sowetans. Although the wealthy white residents lost their case in the highest courts in 1997, the effect was to intimidate Johannesburg politicians at a crucial moment.[68]

In short, rather than decisively address the historical legacy, the politicians largely accepted the squeeze put on them by the department of finance, the private sector financiers and the ratepayers. Other government actors – Pretoria's Department of Provincial and Local Government (formerly known as DCD) and the Midrand-based Development Bank of Southern Africa - offered no comfort. Johannesburg's elected officials and bureaucrats have, as a result, shifted the costs of financial blackmail and mismanagement to those who could least afford them: low-income residents for whom life is not improving and certainly won't under Igoli 2002.

Just to take one characteristic example noted earlier as a national policy problem, the installation of Ventilated Improved Pitlatrines was agreed upon by the Transformation Lekgotla in June 1999, without public debate, participation and announcement. But in budgeting R15 million worth of pit latrines (from privatisation revenues) instead of water-borne sewage, which would obviously save money for the soon-to-be corporatised Johannesburg Water, the city officials – guided by the World Bank – failed to factor in the environmental or public health implications.[69]

Johannesburg has highly dolomitic (porous) soils. In February 2001, the result was an outbreak of high-density e.Coli which led to panic even in Sandton.[70] Rather than treat the issue as a sustained threat to the region's water table, Sandton's wealthy households and institutions invested in their own additional borehole water purification systems, consistent with the tendency to *insulating* the upper classes from socio-environmental problems, rather than *solving* those problems.

What was the shape of Johannesburg financial resources when Igoli 2002 was introduced in 1999? According to the Council, 'If the utility is independent it can then utilise its own balance sheet and its revenue stream against which it will be able to mobilise the capital resources ... If the utility functions remain within the Council the money would need to be raised by the Council which means that the credit risk would be spread across all Council activity and therefore get a much lower credit rating than the utility would be able to'.[71]

Yet this pessimism was belied by Johannesburg's enormous tax base and extremely good opportunities to cross-subsidise between wealthy, large-volume consumers/corporations and low-income, modest-consumption households. Were capital markets better regulated and provisions made for central government guarantees, there would have been no problem in raising sufficient capital for infrastructure investment.

Johannesburg's fiscal stress at the time of Igoli 2002 included more than R500 million in budget deficits over the 1998–99 period and a consequent dramatic decline in capital spending (from R1.2 billion in 1997 to R302 million in 1999).[72] Yet there was still scope for substantial redistribution, given the enormous wealth base in South Africa's main city. Even prior to the incorporation of Midrand following the December 2000 municipal demarcation, the Johannesburg Metro area could claim a rated tax base of R33.5 billion, and annual revenues arising from property taxes, other charges and levies and Regional Service Council taxes of more than R4 billion.[73] In addition, by 2000, Johannesburg raised service revenues of approximately R2 billion from sales of electricity, and R1.5 billion from water, wastewater, solid waste disposal and gas.[74]

At the time, Gauteng Province as a whole – containing 18% (7.3 million) of South Africa's total 40.5 million population – had nearly half of South Africa's wealthiest people (approximately 100,000 households with incomes of more than R10,000 per month), and less than a fifth of the country's poorest (approximately 700,000 households with incomes of less than R1,000 per month).[75] If any South African city should have been positioned to take advantage of redistributive options to assure a better life for those in formerly oppressed racial and class positions, not to mention women for whom infrastructure and services are most beneficial, it was Johannesburg.

The three most logical means of doing so from the vantagepoint of the municipality were through redistribution of wealth, income and the responsibility to pay for municipal services consumption:

- wealth redistribution could have been achieved through rerating property, both through revaluation to reflect updated values and through higher rates on property, including buildings and other improvements to the land which were not assessed due to an outmoded taxation philosophy strongly influenced by the real estate industry;

- income redistribution could have been expanded through the Regional Services Council levy on economic activity and payrolls, a small tax that had not been increased in many years; and
- services redistribution could have occurred through repricing consumption on municipal utilities in a more progressive manner, using a steeper rise in services tariffs for high levels of consumption than was attempted.

The first two strategies for redistribution could easily have been justified based upon the illegitimate wealth and income enjoyed by many Johannesburg residents – predominantly white, upper-income and male – because black, lower-income, and women residents were, throughout the city's history, systematically oppressed. The moral case for a wealth tax on Johannesburg's rich to pay for better municipal services for the poor hardly needs restating.

In addition, however, there was a central problem in Johannesburg's management of infrastructure-related services: pricing. The cost and price of water, sanitation, electricity and other municipal services are central to three other debates, namely,

- whether such services should be corporatised and privatised (and priced accordingly);
- whether conservation of natural resources can be increased through more sensitive use of electricity and water, taking into account their merit good and public-good characteristics; and
- whether all citizens of the city can claim that their constitutional rights to live in dignity are being realised through municipal services.

In each case, a firm neoliberal position emerged in the Johannesburg Council, consistent with the problems flagged above in the national infrastructure debates. These included a reluctance to offer a genuine free lifeline supply and rising block tariff.[76] Implementation problems with the existing tariffing system were legion.[77] During the late 1990s, Johannesburg also became liable for LHWP repayments, resulting in a spectacular 69% increase from 1996–99 in the nominal cost of water purchased from the Rand Water Board.[78]

By the time Igoli 2002 was established in 1999, Johannesburg's water prices became more regressive than during apartheid (i.e., with a flatter slope in the block tariff).[79] The costs associated with providing water, factoring in an unaccounted for water rate of 35%, were higher than the revenue, and even the highest-volume domestic consumers were thereby subsidised.[80] Johannesburg was, thus, a good example of a common problem, insofar as one fifth of metropolitan residents did not receive water directly at their yard or house (many thus resorting to purchasing water from extremely expensive vendors), while municipal services subsidies were often redirected from where they were intended, and captured by higher-income groups.

The main point, however, is that the neoliberal position was unsound even on simple economic grounds, because of its failure to cost in eco-factors. Johannesburg's narrow financial-rate-of-return policy would, in turn, fragment city services, thus disengaging civil servants in the water or electricity or waste-removal sectors from those in the health sector, for instance. The destruction of the holism of services provision reflected Johannesburg officials' refusal to identify and recognise major benefits that would follow from restructured tariffs and lifeline services:

- direct benefits that accrue from infrastructure provision to Johannesburg in the form of new employment;
- direct benefits that accrue to Johannesburg in the form of Small, Micro and Medium Enterprise development catalysed by infrastructure provision;
- indirect benefits that accrue to Johannesburg from infrastructure provision in the forms of private/public health improvements, ecological benefits (net against costs) associated with different degrees of infrastructure servicing, and residential desegregation; and
- indirect infrastructure benefits that accrue, particularly, to women, children, the elderly and especially People With Aids.

Recognition of all these benefits would in turn have allowed Johannesburg to redistribute wealth, income and services so as to raise capital investments and subsidies in low-income communities. Moreover, worker and community participation could have been established as integral to services and infrastructure investment so as to maximise the merit–good and public–good effects of service provision.

But without these kinds of provisions, Johannesburg's extreme and debilitating forms of inequality and uneven development could never be reversed. Instead, they would be amplified in coming years, in part because the agency doing the main strategic work was the World Bank[81] and the main company that Johannesburg Council invited to manage the corporatisation of Johannesburg Water (Proprietary) Limited was Suez, whose record of aggressive water privatisation across the Third World has been the subject of extensive criticism.[82]

Suez' business plan calls for (after-tax) profits to increase from R3.5 million in 2000–2001 to R419 million in 2008–2009, which will require excessively high water tariffs to be paid by low-income people, according to civil society critics. As noted in the previous chapter, just at the point that water privatisation was being debated, Suez subsidiary Dumez was alleged by state prosecutors to have bribed the Lesotho Highlands Water Authority's manager Masupha Sole. The latter allegedly received $20,000 at a Paris meeting in 1991 to engineer a contract renegotiation providing Dumez with an additional R2 million profit, at the expense of Johannes-burg water consumers.[83] Johannesburg officials were asked by Samwu to bar Suez from tendering, but they refused.

The continuities from apartheid to post-apartheid municipal manage-ment in Johannesburg were amplified when forced removals began in Alexandra township in February 2001, continuing to mid-2002. Other major controversies also arose when municipal and provincial authorities responsible for metropolitan housing allowed, and promoted:

- the establishment of new settlements at distances vastly removed from employment opportunities, far further away than during the apartheid era;
- the construction of small and poorly built houses – objectively worse than the apartheid-era matchboxes – in gender-unfriendly settlements often without community amenities; and
- the provision of either no or inadequate municipal water/sanitation, electricity, roads, stormwater and rubbish-removal services to low-income people, far lower than during apartheid.

The overriding objective of Johannesburg managers and politicians, endorsed repeatedly by the World Bank, was to commercialise, outsource, corporatise and privatise the bulk of Johannesburg municipal assets. The objectives of the metropolitan housing policy and Alexandra renewal plans were apparently to channel low-income people to far-away informal shantytown ghettoes and extremely low-cost housing settlements with virtually no community amenities (e.g., Diepsloot), and to forcibly remove low-income Alexandra residents as part of the gentrification of Alexandra township.

A variety of civil society organisations – especially trade unions, com-munity groups and human-rights organisations – used a myriad of oppor-tunities to firmly oppose the process:

- tens of thousands of workers, mainly affiliated to Samwu and the Inde-pendent Municipal and Allied Trade Union, regularly went on strike and demonstrated against Igoli 2002;
- tens of thousands of low-income residents, especially those aligned to the mass-based community and political groups associated with the Johannesburg Anti-Privatisation Forum, regularly protested against the main features of Igoli 2002; and
- human-rights advocates[84] and virtually all the media, especially news-papers, objected strenuously to the city's low-quality services stan-dards and to the Alexandra renewal process.

The latter process generated international condemnation of Johannes-burg municipal and Gauteng provincial housing authorities. A typical anti-

Johannesburg editorial during 2001 – this, in the country's leading elite (and generally pro-government) paper, the *Sunday Independent* – correctly protested 'bureaucratic know-it-allism and disregard for individuals and indeed communities. Sadly the events in Alex have all the elements of the worst of apartheid-style thinking and action'.[85]

As of mid-2002, it appears that only slight progress resulted from the Johannesburg protests. Igoli 2002 remains in place. There was no halt to services cut offs except electricity, due to the intimidation of Eskom by Soweto activists in October 2001. Indeed the first four months of 2002 witnessed more than 90,000 cut offs of electricity and water in Johannesburg. The problem of illegal reconnections – an estimated 19,000 – moved inexorably to the inner city. Predictably, the city's official Democratic Alliance (DA) opposition leader Mike Moriarty applauded: 'The cut offs are good but council has to be ruthless and unforgiving against people who don't pay their bills, or those who reconnect their electricity illegally'.[86]

The efficacy of resistance

As one of the most important sites of struggle for free water and electricity, and against cut offs, there is no question that the late 1990s protests in the Johannesburg area and the rise of the Anti-Privatisation Forum decisively affected the national debate. Demonstrations against municipal services grievances began occurring across South Africa.

From the national and international media perspective, the protests began in earnest in 1997. Matters sparked in February in Eldorado Park, the low-income coloured township of Johannesburg, where local political leaders had regularly engaged in populist, ethnicist campaigns against the ANC. During a day-long protest, four people were killed by police while demanding lower municipal rates. In August, protests over service payments shook East Rand and Pretoria townships and the Mpumalanga town of Secunda. In Butterworth in the distant ex-Transkei, three consecutive days of protest against municipal officials required the death by shooting of one resident before crowds finally dispersed. In KwaThema, east of Johannesburg, the houses of three ANC councillors were burned down by angry residents. The following year, in the sprawling Katorus townships, an ANC mayor was assassinated by crowds allegedly because of his proclivity to cut off services.

The protests were sometimes marked by a high level of sophistication. Thousands of residents of Tembisa went on a march that left R13 million worth of electricity meters destroyed one winter afternoon in August. The protests were venting anger over the installation of a prepaid card system for buying electricity that, in the words of local Communist Party leader Tebogo Phadu, was 'being pushed by transnational corporations – Siemens and Sony in particular ... [and that] would have a profound impact on our tradition of community organisation and mobilisation as it promotes everyone for him/herself (i.e. individualising payment), further marginalising the working class, particularly the unwaged'.[87]

By mid–1998, the conflicts had reached even deeper into East Rand townships and smaller rural towns. In the townships of Witbank and Tsakane, municipal offices and a post office were burned after evictions and summonses stripped residents of their personal property. In Amersfoort, community residents kidnapped a leading councillor in anger over mass cut offs of water which led directly to the death of an infant. Tembisa saw more strife over evictions from houses where commercial banks declared foreclosure.

The upsurge in high-profile protest continued, in places like Durban's Indian–African suburb of Chatsworth, the rural Durban township Mpumalanga, the Cape Town coloured and African townships of Tafelsig and Mandela Park, East London's townships, the Free State town of Potchefstroom, most of the Vaal-area townships, Kimberley and Upington in the Northern Cape, and Mpumalanga province's eMbalenhle. Beginning in 2000, Soweto was the most important site of protests against electricity cut offs, as we review in Chapter Six.

Meanwhile, government officials claimed to be developing regulatory capacity to look after consumer interests during the era of commercialisation and privatisation. In this regard, though, the record thus far is not encouraging.

Captive regulation

In its 1997 *Miif*, DCD argued that some of the pilots were too conservative, if anything, for failing to promote sufficient concessions to assure increased capital investments. DCD officials identified constraints in the forms of legal obstacles and uncertainties with respect to contractual issues, tendering procedures, contract monitoring requirements and dispute resolution procedures. Management contracts were said to be 'only advisable when more ambitious forms of private participation are considered undesirable'. The suspicion was, simply, that 'contractors with international linkages might engage in management contracts in order to secure a privileged position in subsequent initiatives' rather than for the sake of providing optimum services, with the effect of 'sabotaging open competition'.[88]

Having raised these concerns, DCD then proceeded to diminish the role of municipal workers as allies. The department's 1998 *Draft Regulatory Framework for MSPs* insisted that 'a municipality must consult, but is not obligated to negotiate and reach agreement regarding the labour aspects of the transfer with employees or unions as a condition for being authorised to proceed with the transfer'.[89] Rising to the challenge, Samwu became increasingly effective in generating public opposition to DCD's plans and subverting them. As Samwu's Anna Weekes described it,

> In December 1998, Cosatu and Samwu signed a framework agreement with the local government employer body, SA Local Government Association, around municipal service partnerships. The agreement was the product of months of negotiations. It concurs with national legislation that the public sector is the preferred deliverer of services and specifies that involvement of the private sector in service delivery should only be a very last resort – if there is no public sector provider willing or able to provide the service.[90]

Here emerges the classical problem associated with 'natural monopoly', namely the ability of a state institution to pass along implementation responsibilities while still controlling basic services policy on coverage, quality, access, cost, labour conditions, etc. If regulatory control is weak, it is in the private supplier's self-interest to skimp on services to the public's detriment. The propensity of a private firm, for example, to provide cross-subsidies and lifeline tariffs, is extremely low, as the World Bank explicitly warned Asmal in 1995. That 'advice' formed part of a lobbying campaign to dissuade him from invoking cross-subsidies and arose frm the belief – which we noted earlier – that sliding-scale tariffs favouring low-volume users 'may limit options with respect to tertiary providers ... in particular private concessions [would be] much harder to establish'.[91]

The extent to which a public monopoly is simply replaced by a private one gives rise to yet more concern. In late 1998, Suez announced plans to establish multi-purpose utility monopolies covering water, sanitation, refuse, roads, cable TV and telephones, to be payable through a single bill, with Casablanca already witnessing the firm's pilot linkage of several privatised municipal services. Vivendi had enormous problems in the European media and telecommunications sectors, which were cross-subsidised by its water contracts. Those problems drove the firm to the edge of bankruptcy in 2002.

Aware of this possibility, DCD acknowledged that 'The Competition Bill [of mid-1998] could create opportunities for consumers of municipal services to challenge various aspects of an MSP including tariff structures, tariff setting mechanisms and grants of monopoly rights to a service provider in both administrative and judicial forums'. Yet the document quickly reassures firms that 'the power of the Competition Tribunal to award costs to a respondent against whom a finding has been made may act to restrain consumers from initiating complaints'.[92]

In Paris, in contrast, the privatisation of water was at the very least done in a manner that deliberately distinguished retail provision from distribution, and also established geographical divides: the Left Bank going to Suez and the Right Bank to General des Eaux. These allowed 'for a compromise where there is still outside competition and larger markets beckon'.[93]

Indeed, this raises the question of whether water and energy should be managed at a local or regional level – i.e., along politico–administrative boundaries – or indeed based on geological, watershed/basin, or functional divides. Moreover, if water supply is separated from sewerage and roads, there is bound to be confusion, dislocation and diminished accountability. By fragmenting responsibility for road works, refuse removal and sanitation, residents will have to visit different company offices to register complaints, increasing the bureaucratic hurdles for consumers.

The thorniest questions are associated with 'captive regulation': the problem of private sector firms wielding effective power over a state to which it is contractually obligated. Such issues were the least transparently considered in DCD and other official work. Many of the transnational services firms have dubious track records, and not just in the notorious kickbacks and bribes associated with privatisation in Eastern Europe, Indonesia and the like. Even in France, the mayor of the city of Grenoble was imprisoned for taking bribes from Suez.

Likewise in apartheid-era South Africa, WSSA, then called Aqua-Gold, had a previous close association with repressive bantustan regimes beginning as early as 1987. This does not prove corruption in a commercial sense, but does show that unlike many other companies which disinvested, the French chose not only to stay but to accelerate their dealings with the most discredited elements of the apartheid regime. In several towns, WSSA signed agreements with unrepresentative white politicians and municipal administrations prior to democratic elections, and without going through a tender process.

Finally, if the 'basic rationale' for privatisation was that 'MSP projects can save or avoid municipal expenditures',[94] it should also be considered that a municipality has enormous burdens once a contract is signed: monitoring the concessionaire or contractor; undertaking expensive litigation in the event of disputes; establishing reliable, independent sources of information; and bearing the political and financial costs of failure.

Typically, the municipality is prevented from taking direct action on complaints.

The main dangers of municipal partnerships are associated with excessive corporate control. We have already observed that such control mitigates against both adequate service levels and cross-subsidisation. Environmental issues are just as worrisome, because DCD, Dwaf and the electricity sector all failed to adopt even a rudimentary 'polluter pays' approach in the initial round of infrastructure planning and investment.

6. Environmental implications of household infrastructure

A variety of themes have emerged in infrastructure research related to South Africa's fragile natural ecology. In most cases, there are obvious environmental benefits from improved access to infrastructure, although nuances are important, since they may lead us ultimately to question the imposition of western-style norms and standards associated with urban development. Water-related issues are considered first, including optimal sewage service levels, the negative environmental consequences associated with increased water supply, the importance of water drainage systems, and issues surrounding water quality treatment. Environmental issues related to electrification follow.

Water/sanitation and urban-ecological sustainability

In examining water supply, sewage, drainage, and treatment, it must first be noted that there are negative environmental consequences of increased water supply and indeed of the relatively high infrastructure and service levels associated with the RDP. This is true particularly with respect to dam construction, the most prevalent method for supplying water in South Africa.

Nevertheless, according to one study, even in the absence of conservation measures, in 1990 the total water supply would have had to increase by just 1.5% to provide water-borne sanitation to those not supplied with it. Furthermore, the additional households that were expected to be provided with new direct water supply would increase household water demand – which itself is responsible for less than 15% of all water use – by just 12%.[95] Providing water to under-served households would not, in short, place a substantial burden on South Africa's water supply, in comparison to ongoing wasteful users.[96]

There exist strong possibilities for reducing water demand in society, through a tough water pricing policy aimed at hedonistic users (whether corporate or high-volume retail consumers), catchment area management, fixing leaky supplies, and other demand-side management measures. Other conservation techniques include more efficient appliances, such as toilets that flush with 4.5 litres as opposed to the 9–13 litres common in South Africa, which would reduce household water consumption by 18–23%. Another example would be the installation of internal household water meters, rather than solely outside, disguised near the mains, so as to raise consume and company consciousness and reduce water demand. As shown in Chapters Three and Five, conservation makes more sense than constantly building more dams to increase the supply of water, particularly considering limits to the viability of further dam construction, and it is especially sound for the water-scarce Johannesburg metropolis.

There are situations in which water-saving short-cuts have costly environmental implications. As discussed above, government's intention to deny water access by offering pit latrines instead of water-borne sanitation to low-income urban residents is short-sighted. There is no conclusive analysis of the environmental costs and benefits associated with particular sewerage and water service levels in South Africa. But while there remain conceptual problems and data limitations that prohibit an exhaustive analysis, it is possible to explore the major environmental hazards associated with low service standards and the benefits associated with improved standards.

Both major sewerage systems, VIPs and water-borne sewage, produce pollutants. Latrines rely on soil under the VIP to filter out contaminants from the water system, and on treatment works for dealing with sludge off-site. A water-borne system controls sewage treatment at a central location off-site. Pollutants can usually be better controlled using a centralised treatment system, except in cases of sewer breakage. Groundwater and/or surface water contamination from pit latrines is virtually guaranteed, and treatment is non-existent.[97] Algae blooms in South African rivers and dams downstream of urban areas testified to the growing problem, partly caused by sewage system leaks but also due to the government's sanitation programme failure. Kasrils admitted to parliament in 2001 that 'Unacceptable sanitation services resulting in severe water pollution, especially bacteriological pollution, is a grave concern in Gauteng' and that 'a lack of funds has been identified as the hindering factor in the upgrading and maintenance of sewerage networks'.[98]

Advocates of VIPs, such as the influential consultancy Palmer Development Group, argue that excrement leaks are generally contained on-site, whereas leakage due to sewer-system failure is more concentrated and therefore poses more of a threat to the environment.[99] Sewage sys-

tem failure was so severe by 2001, due to the 85% real decline in central–local operating and maintenance subsidies during the 1990s, that a
third of all municipalities suffered major spills from sewage into their
water supplies. According to the *Engineering News*, a typical municipality's 'complement of personnel looking after the maintenance [of sewers]
has dropped to between a fifth and a quarter of pre-1990 figures'. The
notoriously neoliberal periodical conceded that in addition to 'a massive
training and education drive to inform the general public ... spending
more money on personnel and infrastructure seems to be another solution'.[100]

However, the failures of apartheid-era, resource-deprived, badly-man-
aged township sewer systems should not now be assumed as characteristic of future urban or rural developments. The lack of serious water
pollution monitoring underway in Kasrils' water department, witnessed in
the Iscor pollution discussed in the Introduction to this book,[101] is disturbing. However, given strong activist initiatives, the premise for policy
must be that water and water-borne sewage systems will in future be adequately maintained, and that leaks will be rapidly identified and patched.
In contrast, pit latrine pollutants could in fact be relatively concentrated
due to high density levels in low-income urban settlements, with no controlled treatment possible.

There is also a high variability of pollutant release by VIPs, depending
upon soil conditions and methods of sludge treatment, and the practice
of households adding sullage (washing water waste) into the VIP system.
Where the water table is high, such as in Cape Town, groundwater pollution due to pit latrines can be severe. In Winterveld, near Pretoria, the
high water table allows boreholes to serve as a reliable source of drinking
water, yet the use of pit latrines by most residents has resulted in dangerous groundwater exposure to biological contaminants such as faecal
coliform bacteria and salmonella, in turn causing a typhoid epidemic in
1991. Of 59 wells and boreholes tested in Winterveld during the early
1990s, only 12 were free of faecal coliform bacteria.[102] Where soil is non-
absorbent, the pits may overflow, exposing populations to direct sewage
and polluting surface water. In Botshabelo, where pit overflowing was
described as 'continuous' during heavy rains, high bacterial counts were
found in the river system.[103]

Low-lying land in floodplains presents another problem, for again in
the case of Botshabelo, flooding caused sewage from the pits in the
floodplain to flow directly into the river. Where there is rocky ground
and/or fissures, such as fractured bedrock or dolomite (as in much of
Gauteng), swift lateral and vertical movement of pollutants from VIPs can
be expected, which means that even short-lived pollutants like viruses

can leach into drinking water supplies or onto the surface, and will also leach quickly into the groundwater.[104] Such soil conditions pose problems for all VIP-related contaminants. Finally, on steep inclines, as in many residential areas of Natal, leakage to the surface can be expected, where people are directly exposed to the VIP sewage waste.[105] Where the soil is excessively granular in character, even most of the bacterial contaminants that are filtered out well by most soils, along with the other contaminants, escape into groundwater.

In all such cases, water-borne sanitation is especially important for protecting the surrounding environment. It should be noted that many negative results observed in cases of pit latrines were not associated with VIPs, but rather with poorly constructed, conventional pit latrines. Yet notwithstanding the improved nature of VIPs thanks to fly control and ventilation, there are no logical differences between an improved and unimproved latrine regarding flooding, overflow, and groundwater leakage.

Briefly, on-site sanitation systems do pose significant risks in the spread of disease, if conditions are less than ideal, in cases noted above. Regrettably, the South African government's elevation of short-term system affordability above other considerations risks ignoring the high costs of pit latrine pollution in inappropriate geological conditions. The overriding issue is that the poor are often forced to locate on inferior and precarious land which makes for difficult provision of services and the risk of extreme environmental pollution.

Regarding other aspects of water-related infrastructure, good water drainage systems are an important protection against flooding in crowded urban developments, where much of the land's natural drainage capacity has been inhibited by being covered with concrete and as surface vegetation is lost (due to its use as firewood as well as by land development). Flood disasters, experienced periodically in South Africa, result in billions of rands in property damage and a substantial death toll. The impervious surfaces of urban areas not only increase flood peaks during storms, but also decrease low flows between storms. Less rainwater seeps into underground aquifers and the area becomes drier when the rains stop.[106]

In addition, the soil conditions and topography of urban and rural areas makes a major difference in drainage. Drier, uncovered sections of the urban areas, often found in low-income black townships, contribute sediment to stormwater flows. This can smother aquatic life and clog dams. High pollutant loads – particularly nutrients, salts and chemicals – are products of urban run-off.[107]

Environmental destruction can be reduced by moving from open drains and gravel roads to tarred roads and closed drains beneath roads (the *Miif*'s affordability guidelines dictate that low-income communities receive the former). In both open and closed drainage, water is rapidly channelled to downstream areas, which results in heavy downstream flooding. Open drains are much less desirable in heavily settled areas due to their high potential for being blocked by solid waste (this is somewhat less of a problem with closed drains, but improved solid waste collection is required in either case). Open drains may also carry excessive amounts of sediment into the receiving water body, and have proven to be dangerous for young children who can be swept into rivers. Open drains may also facilitate erosion in the vicinity of the channels, and result in property damage to nearby homes.

It is true that tarred roads also involve environmental costs, decreasing the surface area for absorption of water, speeding up the rate of stormwater runoff, and increasing the contamination from oil and other automotive by-products to receiving water bodies. But while closed drains speed the water flow, increasing the risk of flash flooding, innovations in closed stormwater drainage systems have a huge potential for savings in construction costs and in costs to the environment.[108]

Regarding water treatment, most local water researchers stress the importance of carefully managing South Africa's limited water resources, warning that water pollution is already a serious problem. Poor water quality not only affects the country's ability to continue providing clean drinking water to a growing population, but the ecosystem as a whole suffers from a lack of biodiversity. Enormous environmental destruction is occurring, disrupting the delicate balance of interdependence among species.[109] Some of the foreseen consequences include a reduction in the water body's natural purification systems, and increasing levels of flooding and erosion as the vegetation mediating these processes is depleted.

In the case of surface water, point and non-point source pollution from dense urban settlement and industrial sources has created a serious water quality problem. Many urban streams and rivers do not meet the general effluent standards established by Dwaf. Problems like bacterial contaminants, organic silt, and nutrients, along with toxins and oil have killed off aquatic life in urban streams and polluted the major raw water supply reservoirs which now must be treated to high standards for human consumption. Most conventional water treatment plants are ill-equipped to adequately purify increasingly polluted water.[110]

The costs of pollution control are justified by the often greater costs of environmental damage and pollution clean-up. Systems that clean up water pollution or ameliorate its effects are becoming available. One temporary measure to preserve aquatic life in the wake of a pollution event is an aeration system that costs more than R25,000 per week to operate, and other even more elaborate systems have been designed to filter pollution from urban water courses.

However, a great deal of effort is required to deal with the after-effects of the pollutants in reservoirs. Control is even more difficult for the non-point sources in agricultural run-off and informal settlements (i.e., VIPs) whose effluent is not centralised through a water-borne sanitation system.

In the case of groundwater resources, prevention of pollution should receive high priority in water management. Such resources are already used to supply water to towns throughout the country, and offer enormous potential to further supplement surface water supply, especially during periods of drought. Groundwater remains three to five times cheaper to develop than surface water sources. However, pollution to aquifers is difficult to clean up. Groundwater moves much more slowly than surface water, and thus the self-cleansing properties evident in surface water are weak. The damages from groundwater pollution to ecosystems are often long term, and often lead to the abandonment of aquifers.

Other elements that could be included in a more comprehensive environmental cost-benefit analysis that in turn would justify, on economic grounds, higher infrastructural service standards, include

- purification of sewage effluent to required standards, which would generate an increased quality water supply;
- purification of drinking water reservoirs, which would have commercial fishing potential;
- removal of silt from dams, which has potential recreational benefits; restoring surface water to required standards, which would generate health care savings;
- cleaning of groundwater aquifers, which would add to property values; and
- restoration of estuaries, replacing river vegetation and rehabilitation of aquatic life/fish, which would add to the intrinsic value of the ecosystem.[111]

Electricity and environment

As with water, it is true that increased electricity service levels may cause additional social and ecological costs due to the generation of electricity to meet additional demand. However, as in the case of water, this demand would represent a tiny fraction of existing consumption: quite likely, no more than 3% additional demand, if all South African households received a lifeline electricity supply of 1kWh/person/day.

The most important point for our purposes is that environmental benefits associated with increased access to electricity occur with an increased supply beyond that envisaged in the *Miif* (5 Amps). At least 20 Amps are required to run several small appliances, especially those that substitute for dirtier energy like coal and fuelwood. (A 60 Amp supply is usually available in middle- and upper-income white households.)

Some of the environmental costs of lack of access to electricity, such as indoor air pollution, are limited to households. Others such as deforestation and pollution caused by burning coal in urban neighbourhoods are externalities that society as a whole pays for.

Based on the experience since Soweto was electrified in the 1980s, and in the first five years of the accelerated electrification programme, *under conditions that did not include RDP-style lifeline tariffs*, it has been observed that electricity generates a substitution effect for higher-value services such as powering lights, radios, televisions and small appliances. However, without a lifeline tariff, energy-intensive applications such as cooking, space heating and water heating are more expensive if electricity is used rather than coal, wood and paraffin.[112] In short, the mere availability of electricity does not change behaviour if the price is not sufficiently low to create a substitution effect.

The incremental effects of moving from one service level to the next depend substantially upon the levels of standards and whether a free lifeline tariff exists, as well as whether the retail price of small, domestically produced appliances can be subsidised. At the low infrastructure levels envisaged in the *Miif*, access to small volumes of electricity may replace the use of candles and paraffin for lighting, and batteries for small appliances, but a 5 Amp supply and a price per kiloWatt hour of around R0.30 together prevent electricity from being used for cooking or space heating.

It is possible only to make some monetary estimates of the incremental benefits of improving service levels beyond *Miif* standards, based on mid-1990s research by Clive van Horen about the positive and negative externalities associated with retail electricity provision[113] and on a range of studies undertaken of newly-electrified households around South Africa.[114]

Partly on grounds of public health, the cost of air pollution due to coal can be estimated at R307 per household per year, 25% of which would be abated if higher supplies than those envisaged through the *Miif* are provided, even in the absence of a lifeline tariff. The respective estimates for air pollution due to wood usage are R944 per household per year, of which an estimated 5% is abated at higher levels of electricity than *Miif* envisages, but again in the absence of a lifeline tariff. The cost of fuelwood collection is presently estimated at R291 per household per year, and again 5% of these costs are abated with higher electricity standards (also without a lifeline tariff). The time spent by women and children in rural households who collect wood for fires fall within the range of 5.2 to 18.6 hours per week (average 11.9). In aggregate each year, 1.2 million hours of travel time could be saved, along with 12 million tonnes of firewood.[115]

We can only guess the levels of abatement achievable by offering both higher standards and the free lifeline supply – to provide sufficient electricity to ensure cooking, a limited supply of refrigeration, water heating and space heating. The use of coal and wood for fires would then be largely limited to social purposes.

The main benefits of electrification are with respect to health, as noted below, but there are additional beneficial effects of moving to electricity from coal and wood for the sake of biodiversity, aesthetics and visibility. Adding health benefits of electrification – i.e., abatement of morbidity costs including medication, lost production, transport costs, and costs of treating in- and out-patients, and mortality costs based on a range of international studies (and adjusted to take account of South African income levels) – van Horen found large net benefits from increasing electrification standards so as to reduce some of the pollution associated with inefficient energy use.[116]

Environment and infrastructure

Summing up, improvement of infrastructure and service standards should be undertaken in part because of the negative environmental externalities associated with lower standards. It is the environment that pays when pit latrines leak pollutants into groundwater, when sewage systems fail, when improper drainage leads to flooding, erosion and the washing of human waste into surface water, and when coal and wood are used by households instead of cleaner, healthier electricity. Environmental pollution results in actual costs to health, property, and quality of life. The environment is a public good, and the public as a whole must take responsibility for it.

The only way to test the arguments for upgrading both water/sanitation and electricity access for low-income households, is to make these available in sufficient quantities on a lifeline basis. Because of several pressure points that built up during the mid-late 1990s, this suddenly appeared feasible. But how genuine was Pretoria's commitment to free household infrastructural services?

7. Sabotaging free services

Until September 2000, South Africans were becoming increasingly famil-
iar with the interrelated policies of low infrastructure standards, higher
services prices than could be afforded, mass cut offs of water and electricity, evictions and sheriff sales, privatisation and commercialisation,
captive regulation, and so many other manifestations of infrastructure
apartheid. In February 2000, water minister Ronnie Kasrils hinted that a
change of policy was feasible.[117] But it was only in September, when president Thabo Mbeki addressed a trade union conference, that suddenly
'free basic services' offered hope precisely where neoliberal policy had
failed: in pricing water, sanitation, electricity, solid waste and other municipal functions.

What caused the reversal of ANC policy? Several factors converged:
- growing alienation and apathy in townships, along with declining
  activity in ANC branches, leading to fears that substantial voter absten-
  tion would lower the ruling party's overall vote and cost it control in
  key municipalities;
- the massive outbreak of cholera, which attracted international attention and undermined popular faith in the water system (even in the
  cities, where fears of contagion soon emerged);
- Mbeki's bizarre public allegation, at the time of the July 2000 International Aids Conference in Durban, that 'HIV doesn't cause Aids, poverty
  causes' Aids', which required a rapid, face-saving backtrack, i.e.,
  addressing poverty by giving away a few drops of free water;
- the imminent September 2000 Grootboom decision in the Constitutional Court, which signalled that the Court was finally going to get
  serious about enforcing the Bill of Rights provisions on socio-economic rights in the Constitution;[118] and finally,
- a dawning realisation that the neoliberal water pricing policy was
  causing more costs than benefits for the society as a whole, and certainly for Dwaf's reputation.

To illustrate the latter point, in early 2001, Dwaf director-general Mike
Muller conceded to presenter Vuyo Mbuli, 'Perhaps we were being a little
too market-oriented' [in supplying water/sanitation services].[119]

An even more refreshing (potential) break with the past appeared in
the ANC promise in the run-up to the December 2000 municipal elections: 'The ANC-led local government will provide all residents with a free
basic amount of water, electricity and other municipal services so as to
help the poor. Those who use more than the basic amounts, will pay for
the extra they use'. Note the use of phrases like 'all residents' and 'free',
and the explicit endorsement of what is known as a 'rising block tariff' so

that those who consume more pay a higher cost per unit, in order that they cross-subsidise the poor.

Would the poor, and indeed all residents of South Africa, at least be guaranteed a 'basic' amount of water and other services? The principle is excellent, and indeed reflects the mandate from the *RDP* to implement a free lifeline plus redistributive approach to pricing services, instead of the marginal-cost based strategy that had become the conventional wisdom in Dwaf, Eskom and many municipalities.

Subversive discourses and practices

Hostile bureaucrats, whether in the state or even quasi-NGOs, have many tools at their disposal to subvert political processes.[120] Many arguments were brought into play for this purpose, requiring a brief consideration of the neoliberal discourses and progressive rebuttals. These apply to water in particular, because free lifeline electricity and other services were delayed for many months, but the principles are more general.

One allegation was that people suffering a 'culture of non-payment' spent their money on the Lotto, casinos, or cellphones. An old-guard official of the Mhlathuze Water Board, who cut off low-income people's supply at the scene of the cholera epidemic epicentre, told the *Sunday Times* in October 2000, 'People will gladly pay R7 for a two-litre Coke, but complain bitterly when they must pay the same price for more than 1,000 litres of water'.[121] In reality, studies that include highly detailed household-income analysis have shown that in virtually all of the cases of non-payment, affordability has been the universal problem.[122]

Likewise, another 'blame the victim' gambit was to accuse rural people of wanting unreasonably high standards of sanitation. This was important to explain their unwillingness to pay the R150 deposit that Dwaf required so as to access a larger subsidy that would pay for installation of a pit latrine. Once this line of argument began, it was hard to stop. There soon emerged in Pretoria a more general distaste for black rural people's primitive levels of sanitation. 'They' need much more hygienic education, and by 2002 a public education campaign was launched with Kasrils attempting to teach young rural children to wash their hands, 'the way our mothers used to teach us'.

Mvula Trust and similar NGOs delivering services to poor communities initially opposed the free water strategy and continued to promote the full cost-recovery strategy, because they argued that the free water promise would lead to the destruction of their rural-water projects.[123] Water committees had been set up to compel people to pay full cost-recovery for operating/maintenance expenses.[124] But in reality, most such projects were failing, again because ability to pay in rural areas was very limited, and receded consequent with the country's worsening unemployment and inequality.

The Trust, set up by Piers Cross – who came from the World Bank, and then returned to a Bank job coordinating African water policy – imposed the generic full-cost recovery strategy, based upon community payment of 100% operating/maintenance costs with no recurrent subsidies. Taps were typically several hundred metres from residents instead of within yards/houses, and by Mvula's own admission contributed to the spread of infectious disease. The boreholes, pumps and pipes are typically too thin or low-capacity to carry more than a maximum of 25 litres per person per day. Because of Mvula's niggardly design, people attempting to get more water closer to their houses often broke hose connections into the pipes, thus leaving merely a trickle behind at the tap. Water-borne sanitation was typically not on the agenda of Mvula projects, and most tap installations didn't even include pit latrine sanitation. A huge proportion of Mvula's rural schemes failed as a result.

Diverting attention from the failures already underway, an Mvula staffperson wrote in a widely circulated electronic newsletter in mid-2002 that 'The free basic water policy, however praiseworthy in its intentions, may be seen as a genuine threat to the success and sustainability of community-managed projects'. As for the prize-winning Nhlungwane project in Southern KwaZulu Natal, which claimed a R11,000 bank balance, 'Neither the Village Water Committee nor the community had any knowledge of the free basic water policy launched in November 2001'.[125]

Keeping partner communities ignorant of the possibilities for advocacy and redistribution was the sort of strategy that sociologists James Petras and Henry Veltmeyer pointed out in a study called 'NGOs in the service of imperialism':

> That is where the NGO's play an important function. They deflect popular discontent away from the powerful institutions towards local micro-projects, apolitical 'grassroots' self-exploitation and 'popular education' that avoids class analysis of imperialism and capitalism. On the one hand they criticise dictatorships and human rights violations but on the other they compete with radical socio-political movements in an attempt to channel popular movements into collaborative relations with dominant neoliberal elites.
>
> Contrary to the public image of themselves as innovative grassroots leaders, they are in reality grassroots reactionaries who complement the work of the IMF and other institutions by pushing

privatisation from below and demobilising popular movements, thus undermining resistance.[126]

Another sabotage strategy emerged in the form of the 'means test', by which municipalities aimed to work out who the genuinely poor are by estimating their monthly income. The extreme complexity of this strategy was illustrated by the situation in Johannesburg where 'indigent grants' reached fewer than 40,000 households, although in reality there were hundreds of thousands who should be qualifying. Johannesburg's experience was not atypical, because as demonstrated in virtually all international cases, means tests are mainly a stigmatising device, serving as a barrier to prevent state resources from getting to people who need them.

Notably, the failure of the late 1990s means tests in Johannesburg did not prevent another round in 2002 for pensioners, disabled people, Aids patients/orphans and households with below R1500 per month income. Leading metro politician Kenny Fihla bragged that 'Every resident living in Johannesburg will have basic services free of charge if they cannot afford them' beginning on July 1. Yet at the same time, the Council continued with its draconian services cut offs often based on incompetent billing: 92,400 water and electricity cuts were made from January–April 2002.[127]

Conversely, a crucial pro-business form of sabotage came from bureaucrats, especially in the DTI, backed by minister Alec Erwin, who opposed any form of cross-subsidisation in which business paid higher prices for services. Even Dwaf's 2001 'Free Basic Services' policy document also explicitly vetoed such cross-subsidies, notwithstanding the fact that the National Water Act had recently permitted the state to charge large bulk users and raw-water extraction by farmers, often for the first time.[128] Other users had been charged through Dwaf's 'Trading Account' for many years, and such accounts could have been augmented by the few hundred million rand required to assure municipalities served all existing serviced residents, and acquired capital investment funds for those without water services.

But the argument in Cabinet in October 2000 by DTI, Dwaf and the Department of Finance was that higher services bills for corporations represented a hidden tax which would impair economic growth. The cliche often evoked was that by raising water tariff rates on large corporations, you 'kill the goose that lays the golden egg'. Business South Africa had successfully won this case amongst the 'social partners' at the Nedlac Development Chamber in 1996–97, and by the time of the alleged free water policy, had trained state bureaucrats to serve their interests effectively.

Still another important technique to sabotage free services was the use of the word 'flexibility', by which a national minister was discouraged from applying pressure to a local municipality. The excuse was that each municipality had unique local circumstances, so that no overarching tariff policy with a minimum lifeline plus rising block tariff would be appropriate. Even more than flexibility, the favoured jargon of sabotage-minded bureaucrats includes abuse of the word 'sustainability' to describe entirely *self-financing* water schemes, thereby implicitly rejecting any kind of subsidy to low-income people. (Refer to the alleged merits of cost-recovery, above.)

A classic bureaucratic trick to foil the provision of free services for people was to limit it to those who had cleared their arrears with the local municipality.[129] Of course, officials rarely considered why people were already in arrears, namely the massive unemployment in townships and the relatively higher prices township and rural residents pay for electricity, compared with high-income consumers and large corporations. In Johannesburg, arrears of R1.2 billion in 1995 had soared to R4.5 billion by 2002. Instead of blaming the culture of entitlement, as has been common, a surprisingly frank consultant to the city admitted that 'Due to the country's economic position, thousands of ratepayers lost their jobs and are now unable to pay their accounts. The council was also unable to enforce credit control because it lacked efficient staff and an effective strategy'.[130]

Likewise, another trick deployed in Durban by the metro water director was to provide 6000 litres free to low-income households, but charges were levied for the full amount once consumption exceeded the free amount. In other words, the first litre after 6000 were consumed would cost the same as 6001 litres. The same metro government, often praised for being the country's most advanced in supplying water serices to the poor, also cut off water supplies to township schools in 2001.

Ironically, one concept deployed to sabotage free services delivery was 'equity'. Because the government had not invested enough capital in infrastructure by 2000, the argument was advanced that to give a free lifeline supply of water or electricity would only reward those who already had the service. Given the vast number of broken taps and electricity supply cuts, the argument was compelling at first blush. But on second glance, it is easy to see how equity was deployed as a deterrent to immediately supply free services.[131]

The related complaint many municipal officials made was of severe fiscal constraints. It was true that the Department of Finance's 'equitable share' remained vastly insufficient. But by way of rebuttal, in addition to restoring the central-municipal grants that had eroded by 85% in real terms during the 1990s, national-scale cross-subsidies in electricity and water should have been expanded to help smaller, impoverished munic- ipalities pay for the recurrent costs of free services. National–local elec- tricity cross-subsidies already existed, and were reportedly in excess of a R1 billion transfer from corporations to consumers. Likewise, Dwaf had the ability in its 1998 legislation to price water from its national office so as to cross-subsidise to poor consumers via their municipalities.

Within six weeks of the December 2000 election, sabotage of the free services promise, which the white/coloured-dominated DA also advanced to win several important municipal elections in the Western Cape, had become widespread. Samwu released a statement explaining the situation in the Western Cape town of Hermanus.

> Despite the promises of free services bandied around during the local government elections campaigns, the Democratic Alliance Council will evict the second batch of families since the elections this Saturday.
>
> Hermanus has also been lauded as having a progressive block tar- iff for water which supposedly allows the indigent to pay an afford- able amount. This has been exposed as a lie now that families are being evicted for not being able to pay their entire water bills. The DA has been proceeding quietly with evictions, hoping that media attention would not be drawn to their deceitful actions ...
>
> The union believes that these evictions are happening merely as an act of intimidation. There is no way that the families who already cannot pay for a basic human right will be able to fork out the thousands now demanded of them from private lawyers who have added on massive interest amounts. According to information received by the union, the decision to evict the families was taken by the Treasury Department of Council and a few DA Councillors – not a full sitting of newly elected councillors.[132]

Flaws in the promise

A certain amount of sabotage was built into the very nature of the ANC's promise, since even if the effort was genuine, the redistributive principle was not backed up by thoughtful, detailed provisions. To illustrate, first, the ANC's use of the word 'household' – as in a Western-style nuclear fam- ily - meant that the free services were automatically biased against large families, in favour of single-person or 'double-income, no-kids' (dinky) households. Second, the absolute amount of services to be supplied was inadequate for large families, particularly those in which People With

Aids required more water and electricity for ensuring hygienic treatment of opportunistic diseases.

In the case of water, the promise of 6000 litres per family each month was not more than a couple of toilet flushes per day for each member of a large family of eight people. Families in which Aids struck down a middle layer of adults often had as many double that number of dependents on a single property. In contrast, the RDP called for a medium-term lifeline supply of at least 50–60 litres for *each person in a household* per day, available *on-site*, not at a communal tap. The late-1990s campaign for free water by Samwu and the Rural Development Services Network endorsed the 50 litres minimum goal.

It was inexplicable that after so many years in government, Kasrils and his staff still worked on an RDP 'short-term' target closer to 25 litres per capita per day for large families. Moreover, in late 1998, Dwaf bureaucrats had attempted to revise the target figure for low-density areas *downwards* to 7 litres.[133]

In contrast, it would have been a relatively simple and cost-effective annual exercise for municipal officials to add a single additional record to each billing address. That record would allow the number of people with identification to be noted, with provisions to prevent the possibility of double-claiming the free water entitlement. Similar systems could have been established in the electricity sector. But some cities like Cape Town went ahead with an extremely inadequate 20 kiloWatt hours per household per month, amplifying all the same problems but with such a miserly lifeline amount that after a few days, the monthly free lifeline would be used up.

If courageous politicians and officials wanted to overrule the sabotage-minded colleague, what could they have done, in the wake of the cholera outbreak and growing national attention to the life-threatening state of rural water supply? A partial list applied to Dwaf would have included:

- take the bull by the horns and admit culpability for the cholera fiasco;
- start integrating benefit analysis alongside costs (comparing benefits of cholera/diarrhoea/etc.-abatement with costs of a modicum of free basic water);
- begin telling society that large water users will have to pay more, so as to start introducing water-saving technologies; and
- establish a forceful case that the users of nearly 90% of South Africa's (non-household) water – commercial farmers, forestry companies, mines, industries, commercial enterprises, and electricity generators – will pay a bit more so that the millions who have none will get a basic amount free.

The opposite strategy seems to have been chosen by Dwaf officials:

- slide around the problem, repudiate liability for cholera and other water-related diseases;
- claim that if people haven't got sanitation systems, it's their fault;
- provide a bit of Jik bleach, shovels and community-development ideology instead of proper systems;
- deny that millions of people suffer from water schemes that have broken;
- cut still further Dwaf's operating and maintenance funds for those schemes (by more than R100 million from 2001 to 2002 even before inflation, notwithstanding increases in new capital spending of R400 million, which would in turn require additional operating subsidies);
- protect big business, including commercial farmers and Eskom, from paying a fair share for water; and
- continue to maintain many of the neoliberal premises within slightly-rewritten policy documents.

Policy reversions

While the concrete struggles over municipal infrastructure were unfolding, policy redrafting was also in motion. Because the revised *Miif* and a forthcoming water white paper were in rough draft form at press time, full critiques will await another opportunity. Nevertheless, it may be useful to remind ourselves that the next stage of sabotaging free services would be in the sphere of policy discourses.

Throughout the period under review, the policy debates typically boiled down to two competing perspectives. We will also observe these differences emerging in other of the water and energy terrains in the next chapter. In a variety of areas of policy, legislation and implementation, the mainstream approach is ameliorative, and works with, rather than against, market imperatives. The critical approach relies upon a rights-based philosophy, and considers ways to sustain the alliances of poor and working people required to implement progressive policies.

All of these sabotage gimmicks are comprehensible if one takes the experience of free basic services in South Africa back to the global scale, to venues like the World Water Forum, the African Utilities Partnership or the World Bank itself, as we do in the next chapter. There, such an anti-neoliberal, pro-entitlement position simply cannot hold, in a context of thorough commodification of water.

Finally, however, as a linkage between the two chapters, consider the World Bank's *Sourcebook on Community Driven Development in the Africa Region*, produced and circulated in March 2000, a month after

Table 5: Competing perspectives on household infrastructure policy

Mainstream	Critical
a) existing policies are basically fine (although some, like the overly-generous housing policy, need tweaking to assure better alignment);	a) notwithstanding some progress associated with the free services promise, virtually all current state policies are excessively market-oriented (too stingy, insensitive to poverty, incapable of integrating gender and environmental concerns, unsympathetic to problems associated with public health and worsening geographical segregation, and even inefficient in terms of untapped economic multipliers);
b) post-apartheid laws, planning frameworks and regulations are sometimes onerous and usually unhelpful;	b) post-apartheid laws, planning frameworks and regulations are essentially technicist and disempowering, and are generally an inadequate substitute for a transformation in the balance of forces and in residual apartheid-era economic processes;
c) resources allocated for infrastructure and services are sufficient (large capital grants, plus ongoing central-local subsidies, plus limited local-level cross-subsidies from wealthy and corporate customers to the poor, plus other programmatic funds);	c) resources allocated are inadequate (by a factor of roughly five from central government, and with regard to inadequate local and national cross-subsidisation);
d) institutional arrangements for infrastructure projects are flawed (due to an excessive emphasis on greenfield developments and housing 'top-structures');	d) institutional arrangements are inappropriate (newly demarcated municipalities will struggle to meet small-town and rural needs, and the drive to corporatisation and even privatisation will worsen services inequality);
e) implementation of infrastructure projects is flawed, and because of inefficiencies in municipal delivery, there is a need for more rapid private-sector provision of services (public-private partnerships, outsourcing, and other forms of municipal services partnerships, which are generally enhanced by larger markets associated with newly demarcated municipalities);	e) implementation is flawed (municipal management remains rooted in apartheid practices, and developer-driven, bank-centred housing policy drives most funds into new, faraway projects instead of empowering municipalities and communities);
f) communities and workers remain part of the problem (the former have a culture of non-payment, the latter too dogmatically oppose privatisation and act as a labour-aristocracy);	f) communities and workers are potentially part of the solution (if community- and worker-control are enhanced);
g) while expanded infrastructure and services may have positive spin-off benefits, these are not worth calculating and incorporating into decisions regarding the levels of municipal services, capital expenditure or subsidies.	g) infrastructure and services have extremely important positive spin-off benefits – improved public health, gender equity, environmental improvement, economic multipliers, increased productivity, better educational prospects, desegregation potentials – which are absolutely vital to calculate and incorporate into decisions regarding the levels of services, capital expenditure or subsidies.

Kasrils first hinted at the free lifeline policy. Reacting to Kasrils – because there was no other major free water drive in Africa at the time – the Bank staff authoring the *Sourcebook* put their position very explicitly: 'Work is still needed with political leaders in some national governments to move away from the concept of free water for all'.[134]

8. Conclusion

The struggle against apartheid was both a struggle against the politico-juridical system of racism *and* for improved quality of life. Improved residential infrastructure and service delivery are amongst the most crucial objectives of public policy, by all accounts. Many of the aspirations and concrete demands of South Africa's oppressed peoples are reflected in the 1994 RDP and the 1996 Constitution, in particular the *entitlement* to decent standards of services. Here, in relation to the demand for higher levels of infrastructure investments and for subsidies that cover ongoing service provision, we find both the eco-social justice discourses and arguments based on the principles of sustainable development.

Despite the mandate to govern and the rise of popular movements, there was a clear continuity of policy between the late-apartheid era and democracy. Common features included an often untransformed bureaucracy, white consultants at the nerve centre of policy-making, influence by the World Bank or its proxies, and the ascendance of a new breed of conservative bureaucrats (once termed 'econocrats'). Unlike the chaotic and uncoordinated positions across most of government, there emerged a disturbing level of consensus in infrastructure-related departments and agencies during the first ANC government, that a) users should pay full cost-recovery, b) standards should be relatively low, and c) privatisation should be regularised.

In contrast, the RDP-friendly alternative was always feasible, and it is a great tragedy that to arrive at even a weak version of the original 1994 mandate only in 2000 required so many environmental and human sacrifices: the tens of thousands of cholera cases and 43,000 children who die from diarrhoea each year, communities whose shacks were ravaged by preventable fires, People With Aids whose opportunistic infections were catalysed by poor infrastructure and services, deforested landscapes, ecologies damaged by bacteriological and air pollution, and many others. But resistance was apparent through advocacy and protest, and ultimately made some difference.

During the late 1990s, the main proposal advocated by social change activists from Samwu, community organisations and associated NGOs, compatible with the Constitution and RDP, was a universal *free* lifeline to all South African consumers for the first block of water (50 litres of water per person each day) and electricity (approximately 1 kiloWatt hour per day) with steeply rising prices for subsequent consumption blocks. This was not merely a matter of human rights, although it was certainly a prime example of the eco-social justice discourse. In addition, the technical aspects of sustainable development were very powerfully conceptualised by labour and community advocates. There would be no need, in this policy framework, for means-testing or a complex administrative apparatus, nor would complete service cut offs feature. Recurrent consumption expenses would be paid for entirely from within each sector, although an additional 10% expenditure would be needed, beyond what the *Miif* budgeted, to finance the added capital costs.

Where the advocacy, sustainable-development discourses and technical arguments failed to make a dent, an extensive series of riots began over municipal services, including the assassination of an ANC East Rand mayor known for willingness to cut off power and water, as well as the burning of several ANC councillors' houses. Would this disastrous trajectory transform itself into more sustained, constructive pressure?

At first, it appeared not, in part because of the demobilisation of the national civic association movement Sanco. In contrast to the alliance between DCD and the big business lobby within Nedlac, the progressive forces failed, especially in 1996–97, to successfully challenge the intensification of services commodification. Notwithstanding firm opposition by Samwu, central government continued to advocate the privatisation of municipal services.

Also at stake in all of this was, as ever, the degree to which a capitalist state in league with big business could construct a 'social wage' policy framework that had, as a central objective, maintaining relatively low upward pressure on the private-sector wage floor. In other words, by keeping monthly operating costs of services low through denying workers access to flush toilets, hot plates and heating elements, the *Miif* also reduced the pressures that workers would otherwise have to impose upon their employers for wages sufficient for the reproduction of labour power.

In very practical ways, the social and labour movements were too weak to successfully contest the broader neoliberal trajectory, and not even the strongest rhetorical and technical critiques could have made up for lack of political clout. Indeed it was only the combination of devastating public health embarrassments, from cholera to the poverty-Aids connection, that tipped the intra-ANC debating balance back to the progressive arguments. Moreover, the neoliberal forces did not take their partial defeat on household infrastructure lying down. As we will see in the next two chapters, new terrains of local, national, regional, continental and global struggle emerged upon which the contenders fought over water and energy.

Notes

1. Extremely important background research was conducted with other colleagues on these issues during the mid-late 1990s: Pam Groenewald, Darrell Moellendorf, Thomas Mogale and David Sanders.

2. Jeter, J. (2001), 'For South Africa's Poor, a New Power Struggle', *Washington Post*, 6 November.

3. Cited in Veotte, L. (2001), 'Restructuring, Human Rights and Water Access to Vulnerable Groups', South African Municipal Workers Union presentation to the International Conference on Fresh Water, Bonn, 7 December.

4. *Business Day*, 4 July 2002.

5. The average South African may not have realised that given the barrage of advertising by Dwaf in 2001–02. Seeking credit where it was not necessarily due, Dwaf advertised repeatedly that 'As part of our Free Basic Water Programme 26 million people now receive 6000 litres of water free every month'. After the Concerned Citizens Forum of Durban complained to the Advertising Standards Authority that the marketing firm mistook individuals for households, Dwaf replied 'that it regrets this error and confirms that the advertisement will not be used again'. But how the advertisement stayed on air for so long without Dwaf itself making a correction suggests, at best, sloppiness, at worst systematic sophistry. ASA Directorate (2002), 'Ruling of the ASA Directorate,' Johannesburg, 16 May.

6. Mbeki, T. (2002), 'Address by the President of the Republic of South Africa, Thabo Mbeki, on the Occasion of the Torch Handing over Ceremony, From Rio to Johannesburg', Rio de Janeiro, 25 June.

7. As noted earlier, the word comes from neo-classical economic theory, and means simply, the cost of the next additional unit, which approximates the term 'operating and maintenance costs'.
   More generally, the costs of supplying water include the following components: abstraction (gathering water from its natural state, whether below ground in the water table, or in groundwater supplies), storage (whether in dams or in piping closer to the end-user), transport (often requiring pumping stations and long pipe systems which both require extensive ongoing maintenance), cleansing and purification, distribution (mainly the administrative costs associated with billing), and waste-water treatment. Capital and operating/maintenance costs are included to some extent in each category. Typically, the capital costs of an addition to the water system are paid for in an urban context by all existing users, as their tariffs are increased.
   In contrast, in many smaller rural projects, capital costs are included in the price of water only for those additional users, so that it becomes far more expensive for consumers to pay for water schemes, especially if they have practically no income. This is one justification for the subsidy of capital costs, which wealthier SADC governments and donor agencies often agree is their responsibility. However, until the cholera outbreak of 2000–01, even the wealthy South African government refused to subsidise the operating and maintenance costs of many of the rural water schemes that had been established since 1994.

8. By way of definition, public goods can be observed and measured, for underlying their existence are two characteristics: 'nonrival consumption' and 'nonexclusion' from consumption. Nonrival consumption means that the consumption of a public good/service by one person need not diminish the quantity consumed by anyone else. Typical examples are a lighthouse or a national defence system, which are 'consumed' by all citizens in a quantity which is not affected by the consumption of defence benefits by fellow citizens. Likewise, the benefits of a clean environment and hygienic public water system – reflecting a strong municipal water system and lifeline access to all – are enjoyed by all municipal consumers, regardless of how much water is consumed by a particular individual, although a minimum consumption level is required for all citizens, so as to prevent the spread of infectious diseases. Similar public good characteristics of state services include social benefits that come from flood control, weather forecasting, pollution abatement and other public health initiatives. The principle of nonexclusion simply means that it is impossible to prevent other citizens from enjoying the benefits of public goods, regardless of whether they are paid for. This is important, as a state determines the detailed character of social policy, and distinguishes between necessities guaranteed by the state, versus luxuries that people must pay for. Television broadcasting, for example, has benefits that relate to 'nonrivalry', in that once someone has a set they can enjoy broadcasts without regard to whatever fellow citizens are enjoying. But because television entertainment is a luxury good, even a state supplier has rights to exclude people, for instance those who do not pay licence fees or those who simply cannot afford a set of their own.

    A simpler way of putting it is that where the net benefits to society outweigh the costs associated with consumption of a good/service, the result is a 'merit good'. When the merit good benefits apply universally, so that no one can be excluded from their positive effects, the result is a 'public good'.

9. Esping-Andersen, G. (1990), *The Three Worlds of Welfare Capitalism*, Princeton, Princeton University Press.

10. For information about the RDP and its implementation, see Bond, P. and M.Khosa (Eds)(1999), *An RDP Policy Audit*, Pretoria, HSRC Press; and Bond, P. (2000), *Elite Transition: From Apartheid to Neoliberalism in South Africa*, London, Pluto Press, Chapter Three.

11. For critiques, see Bond, P. (2000), *Cities of Gold, Townships of Coal*, Trenton, Africa World Press, Part Three.

12. Mayekiso, M. (1996), *Township Politics: Civic Struggles for a New South Africa*, New York, Monthly Review Press.

13. Bond, P. (1992), 'De Loor Report is Off the Mark', *Reconstruct, Work in Progress*, August.

14. Bond, P. (1993), 'Housing Crisis Reveals Transitional Tension', *Financial Gazette*, 11 November.

15. Swilling, M. (1999), 'Rival Futures: Struggle Visions, Post-Apartheid Choices', Unpublished paper, Stellenbosch.

16. *Business Day*, 3 May 1994.

17. African National Congress/Alliance (1994), *Reconstruction and Development Programme*, Johannesburg, Umanyano Publications, s.2.1.3.

18. Ibid, s.2.5.7.

19. For a full critique, see Bond, *Cities of Gold, Townships of Coal*, Chapter Eight.

20. World Bank (1994), 'South Africa: Observations on the Direction of Housing Policy: Aide Memoire', Housing Mission, Washington, DC, August, pp. 9–13.

21. African National Congress/Alliance, *Reconstruction and Development Programme*, s.2.4.12, 2.4.14.

22. The main Bank mission leader, Robert Christiansen, had been recommending much the same in Zimbabwe. Within a few years, the failure of willing-seller, willing-buyer policy there became grounds for peasant, farmworker and war-veteran protests, and ultimately for Zimbabwe's degeneration into rural chaos. See Bond, P. and M. Manyanya (2002), *Zimbabwe's Plunge: Exhausted Nationalism, Neoliberalism and the Search for Social Justice*, Pietermaritzburg, University of Natal Press, London, Merlin Press and Trenton, Africa World Press.

23. African National Congress/Alliance, *Reconstruction and Development Programme,* s.2.6.10, 2.7.8.

24. As not only an official of the Development Bank of Southern Africa, but a long-time ANC stalwart, Mike Muller intervened in the RDP drafting process in early 1994 to assure that rural people would be disadvantaged by being forced to pay full cost-recovery, prefiguring the later *White Paper* provision. The quotes below are from DCD (1997), *User-Friendly Guide to the Miif*, Pretoria, p. 2. Although the document cited is the 1997 version of the *Miif*, the basic principles discussed were those established in 1994–95.

25. Provisional answers are offered in Bond, *Elite Transition,* Chapter Four; Bond, *Cities of Gold, Townships of Coal*, Part Three.

26. Republic of South Africa (1996), *The Constitution of the Republic of South Africa*, Act 108 of 1996, Cape Town, s.27.1.

27. Department of Constitutional Development (1997), *Municipal Infrastructure Investment Framework*, Pretoria. The quotes below are from DCD (1997), *User-Friendly Guide to the Miif*, Pretoria, p. 2. Although the document cited is the 1997 version of the *Miif*, the basic principles discussed were those established in 1994–95.

28. Ministry of Reconstruction and Development (1994–95), *Urban Infrastructure Investment Framework*, Pretoria.

29. Rural infrastructure plans had not been developed at that stage.

30. Ministry of Reconstruction and Development (1995), *Draft Urban Development Strategy*, Pretoria.

31. Sanco was, for all effective purposes, financially and politically bankrupt. By 1996, the ANC had to channel large amounts of funding to the organisation to keep it alive. A major dispute broke out in the national headquarters about the direction of Sanco's politics, with respected leaders Mzwanele Mayekiso from Alexandra, Ali Tleane from Tembisa and Maynard Menu from Soweto ultimately leading a walk-out due to Sanco's status as an ANC 'lapdog' not watchdog.

32. See, e.g., *Mail & Guardian*, 22–28 November 1996.

33. Bond, P. (1997), 'Infrastructure Plan Still a Disappointment', *South African Labour Bulletin*, 21, 2.

34. DCD, *User-Friendly Guide to the Miif*, p. 18.

35. Ibid, p. 19.

36. For details, see Bond, *Cities of Gold, Townships of Coal*, Part Two. Essentially, the resegregation of geographical areas based upon a class-apartheid model worked in the following way: when a resident of an area fitted out with pit latrines gains sufficient additional income to want a water-borne system, she will have only once choice, namely to leave her community and move to a higher-income area served by a sewage line, since incremental upgrading from pit latrines to sewage is impossible.

37. Sanders, D. and P. Groenewald (1996), 'Public Health and Infrastructure', Unpublished report to the National Institute for Economic Policy, Johannesburg.

38. Efforts to persuade government to incorporate positive benefits were made by teams from the National Institute for Economic Policy in 1996–97 and by the University of the Witwatersrand Graduate School of Public and Development Management in 1997–98. These were rebuffed, as were efforts made by two of the authors, Bond and Dor, in 1997 as minister Asmal's budget advisers, as well as periodically in subsequent years through the media and in conjunction with advocacy groups. Hostile bureaucrats and consultants proved immensely more powerful. As water affairs director-general Mike Muller summarised the latter's position:

> Why do we not calculate the ecological, public health and gender benefits of water supply to reinforce our budget requests? Such exercises have often been done and will doubtless keep economists busy for years but their calculations are open to endless challenge. Is there really any doubt about the need for services?

As for the cost side of the equation, Muller refused to mitigate against cholera and diarrhoea by providing emergency services to low-income rural residents using tanker trucks with water, because 'trucking 25 litres per person per day costs on average perhaps 30 times more than supplying water through pipes'. In the final chapter, we return to a review of how cost-benefit analysis of this sort has deadly implications. (See Muller, M. (2001), 'Media Release: Reply to Bond', Department of Water Affairs and Forestry, Pretoria, 18 April, pp. 1,2.)

39. *Business Day*, 18 September 2001.

40. *Engineering News*, 13–19 July 2001.

41. The phrase 'externality' is used to signify some (positive or negative) outcome of a market transaction *that is not included in the pricing* because its effects are directly or indirectly felt by people or the environment not associated with the transaction. Standard environmental economics acknowledges the need to incorporate externalities back into the transaction, usually by means of a tax or a market-based system (such as trading rights to pollute) which mitigates against the damage. 'Multipliers' occur when a market transaction has indirect spin-off effects.

42. Ministry of Reconstruction and Development, *Draft Urban Development Strategy*, p. 2.

43. Ibid, p. 28.

44. The full argument, which includes capital cost estimates for universal installation of what are termed 'intermediate' levels of infrastructure, can be found in Bond, P. T. Mogale and D. Moellendorf (1998), 'Infrastructure Investment and the Integration of Low-Income People into the Economy', published in Development Bank of Southern Africa Discussion Paper #4, T*he Impact of Infrastructure Investment on Poverty Reduction and Human Development*, Midrand, pp. 57–142.

45. *Mail & Guardian*, 22 November 1996. The 'I'm a socialist' bit is unsupported by any other evidence but makes for a good rhetorical ploy. 'My friends call me a mean, neoliberal bastard' was another confession in the interview.

46. Department of Constitutional Development (1998), *Draft Regulatory Framework for Municipal Service Partnerships*, Pretoria, August, p. v.

47. Masia, Walker, Mkaza, Harmond, Walters, Gray and Doyen, 'External BoTT Review', p. 11.

48. Bakker, K. (1998), 'An Evaluation of Some Aspects of Mvula's Participation in BoTT', Unpublished paper, Oxford University Department of Geography, Oxford, September.

49. In 1997, the International Finance Corporation announced a $25 million investment in Standard Bank's South Africa Infrastructure Fund, an explicit privatisation financing vehicle, although it didn't immediately follow through with the investment. The strategy is discussed in Bond, *Cities of Gold, Townships of Coal*, Chapter Four.

50. Port Elizabeth Municipality (1997), 'Public Private Partnerships for Municipal Services', Report by Director: Administration to the Executive Committee, 4 February.

51. Interview with Ruiters, December 1998.

52. Stiglitz, J. (1998), 'More Instruments and Broader Goals: Moving Toward the Post-Washington Consensus', WIDER Annual Lecture, Helsinki, Finland, 7 January, pp. 17–18. See also Stiglitz, J. (2002), *Globalization and its Discontents*, London, Allen Lane.

53. Hall, D. (2001), 'The Public Sector Water Undertaking: A Necessary Option', Public Services International Research Unit, University of Greenwich.

54. Water and Sanitation South Africa (1995), 'Standard Contract', Johannesburg, p. 1.

55. Water and Sanitation South Africa (1995), 'The Delegated Management Concept', Johannesburg, p. 1.

56. Mestrallet, G. (2001), 'The War for Water', *Le Monde*, 1 November 2001.

57. Ruiters, G. and P. Bond (1999), 'Contradictions in Municipal Transformation from Apartheid to Democracy: The Battle over Local Water Privatization in South Africa', *Working Papers in Local Governance and Democracy*, 99, 1; Bond, P. and L. Mcwabeni (1998), 'Local Economic Development in Stutterheim', in E. Pieterse (Ed), *Case Studies in LED and Poverty*, Pretoria, Department of Constitutional Development.

58. Veotte, 'Restructuring, Human Rights and Water Access to Vulnerable Groups'.

59. *Business Report*, 26 October 2001, and court documents.

60. According to a report by water researcher David Hemson,

> In the townships separated from the coastal strip by the N2 freeway and railways there is deep poverty. Two-thirds of the population earn less than R800 a month and there is opposition to the high level of monthly fixed charges imposed by Siza Water.
>
> Residents pay R36 and R24 respectively for sewerage and water connections, a cause of discontent. The charges make the 6-kilolitre free water quota an academic benefit, as a monthly bill at 10kl consumption now costs R79.
>
> Half the residents with household connections have been unable to keep up these charges; their services have been ended. The others queue with buckets for electronic water dispensers. They complain that these are often broken down.

Hemson, D. (2001), 'Dolphin Honeymoon Over', *Business Day*, 14 June.

61. Interview, Barry Jackson, Municipal Infrastructure Investment Unit, September 2001.

62. Veotte, 'Restructuring, Human Rights and Water Access to Vulnerable Groups'.

63. Gordhan was given a contract that provided him the highest salary of any civil servant in South Africa – far higher than the president's – plus an additional large performance-contract bonus if he succeeded in outsourcing, corporatising and privatising the vast bulk of city assets over a two-year period. Additional pressure was levied by the national Treasury, which provided more than R500 million in grant funds to Johannesburg, on condition of rapid implementation of Igoli 2002, overriding citizen objections. As a result of a rush-to-perform orientation, Gordhan was severely compromised. Because of rising political unacceptability, both within the ANC-dominated city council and between the manager and union/community opponents, he was not in a position to seek reappointment.

64. To consider an example, the main Igoli 2002 report noted, 'No one is responsible for R176 million of unaccounted for water [annually], substantial non-collection, inaccurate or non-reading of meters'. In addition, correlation of supply and demand

was wildly inaccurate, with mid-1999 electricity purchases amounting to 18% more than was required (including 37% more supply than demand in May 1999 alone). The inadequacy of controls on water and electricity was witnessed in the inability of Johannesburg authorities even to report to central government about infrastructure service management. Thus the June 1999 'Project Viability' questionnaire on the Johannesburg debtors book, requesting a detailed breakdown, was simply answered 'Not Available'. No records were provided on debtors who had not paid for more than three months, although many companies and large institutions continue to run arrears which vastly outstrip low-income township residents' arrears.

In addressing these problems through Igoli 2002, the assumption was that the private sector could do a more effective job than the public sector. This is not necessarily true, however, as shown in Cape Town where after pressure by Samwu, council officials utilised internal worker know-how to repair leaks. Johannesburg leak repairs worth R5 million in 1999/2000 were outsourced.

65. Financial and Fiscal Commission (1997), 'Local Government in a System of Intergovernmental Fiscal Relations in South Africa: A Discussion Document', Midrand.

66. Bond, P. (1992), 'Redlining Cuts off Jo'burg's Lifeblood', *Weekly Mail*, 17–23 April.

67. An earlier 1996 effort by an old-guard treasurer to raise money from Sumitomo Bank of Japan had failed, when finance minister Manuel (sensibly) prohibited South African municipalities from borrowing in hard-currency funds abroad.

Finally in 2000, two major loan agreements were reached. One was from the Development Bank of Southern Africa, but the other from the Rand Merchant Bank is indicative of Johannesburg's fealty to the financiers. The RMB loan was secured for repayment by the city's inflow of commercial property receipts from RMB's affiliated corporate property rates. This arrangement permitted Johannesburg to borrow at a 14% interest rate – approximately 1% below the city's average cost of funds – but was seen as extremely favourable to the lender since it entailed 120% collateral coverage. The importance of the agreement is in its contradiction of the need to establish an arm's-length (ring-fenced) relationship with a utility to secure the arrangement.

68. Reflecting the hidden victory of the Sandton property owners, the rise in rates revenues from approximately R500 million in 1995 to nearly R1.5 billion in 1997 then slowed to a halt.

69. As noted above, the Bank has been advocating this method of sanitation in South Africa for 20% of all citizens since its late 1994 Urban Infrastructure Investment Framework, on grounds that if people are too poor to pay cost-recovery tariffs for water, they should be denied the opportunity to flush. The 1999/2000 metropolitan budget included R15 million in allocations for construction of VIPs, which was 70% of all spending on wastewater projects. If supplied at R700 per unit, as estimated in the *Miif*, there was sufficient funding for more than 20,000 VIPs in the 1999/2000 budget. The R15 million was allocated from the sale of R76 million worth of fixed property, according to the Greater Johannesburg Metropolitan Council Budget Estimates.

70. *Sandton Chronicle*, February 2001.

71. Greater Johannesburg Metropolitan Council (1999), 'Igoli 2002 Conceptual Framework', Johannesburg, p. 9.

72. To illustrate, with more than 20% of Johannesburg residents lacking individual access to water taps, plans were shelved to spend R200 million in 1999/2000 through extending the water pipe grid and upgrading bulk systems (as well as installing individual meters). Only R6 million was spent on capital upgrading (Greater Johannesburg Metropolitan Council 'Igoli 2002 Conceptual Framework', p. 6.).

73. Theoretically, with an assessment rate of R0.0745, this should generate R2.5 billion in property revenue each year, but in fact in 1999/2000 the anticipated rates rev-

enue was 33% lower, at R1.66 billion. The other crucial point is that property undervaluations on the Johannesburg roll reflected a typical 15-year 'Kuznets cycle' of real estate speculation. Johannesburg, like most cities in the world, witnessed a huge upsurge of property prices during the late 1980s followed by a slump that in most neighbourhoods was in excess of 20% during the early 1990s. Had a property revalution occurred in 1999, as the real estate market in Johannesburg recovered and the next speculative bubble began, a far greater source of rates revenues could have been tapped. But to have done so would have alienated wealthy and corporate residents of the metro, at a time when Igoli 2002 aimed to persuade them that they would soon be living in a 'world class' city.

74. Main anticipated revenue and expenditure items, Greater Johannesburg Metropolitan Council, Fiscal Year 2000:

Revenue	(R million)	Expenditure	(R million)
Electricity sales	(R2,060)	General	(R3,394)
Property taxes	(R1,661)	Salaries/allowances	(R1,965)
Other charges/levies	(R1,390)	Purchases of goods	(R1,855)
Water sales	(R903)	Interest/debt redemption	(R1,010)
Wastewater charges	(R756)	Provision for bad debts	(R400)
RSC taxes	(R696)	Repairs/maintenance	(R314)
Solid waste disposal	(R277)	Capital development fund	(R106)
Gas sales	(R65)	Other	(R21)
TOTAL	**(R7,915)**	**TOTAL**	**(R7,772)**

Cited in Fitch IBCA (1999), 'City of Johannesburg', Johannesburg, June, p. 11.

75. Ibid, p. 5.

76. For example, until the September 2000 policy shift from the ANC to free basic services, Igoli 2002 adopted a ineffective 'indigency' policy – serving fewer than 40,000 households – and otherwise did not disturb the status quo. The Igoli 2002 tariff recommendations were to retain the same categories of users (with four blocks instead of the desired 8–10); to provide the first 6 kl of water free to informal settlements where meters were not installed; to lower the volume allowed in the first block from 10 kl to 6 kl for households with meters, but to only 'simulate' a lifeline tariff price (rather than offering the first block free); to raise tariffs for the second block from the then average monthly price of R50 to between R70–R80 so as to break even; and to have two subsequent tariff steps that would be profitable.

77. Johannesburg was charging a flat rate on unmetered houses in Greater Soweto and Alexandra, based on the assumption that consumption was 20 kl per household each month. (Average consumption of bulk water was in fact closer to 50 kl per household per month, with an estimated 50% being lost through leaks.) The cost of installing meters in Soweto and Alexandra was estimated at R100–120 million. Those households consuming relatively smaller amounts were paying a disproportionate share.

78. At R404 million in 1996, the cost of raw water was only beginning to reflect the surcharge the Rand Water Board added to pay for the first two dams. The following year, the cost of Johannesburg raw water purchased from Rand Water rose by 39% (with inflation below 10% and consumption up by less than 5%) to R566 million. By 1998/99 the raw water cost component of the Johannesburg water accounts increased to R643 million. And by 1999/2000 the anticipated bulk water cost was R686 million. As noted in Chapter Three, these bulk water cost increases were passed on to ordinary Johannesburg consumers in a manner that even the World Bank Inspection Panel determined was price-discriminatory against the poor, in its mid-1998 investigation of the costs and benefits of the second LHWP dam.

79. Domestic users paid R2.04 per kl for the first 10 kl per month; the next step up to 20 kl was R3.08; up to 40 kl was R4.24; and in excess of R40 kl was R5,28. Unmetered households paid R20.35 per month, even though the average usage

was estimated at 20 kl per month. The average annual unit cost of water per person in Johannesburg was R175. With an average unit cost of sanitation per person of R113, the total cost of water and sanitation per person comes to R288 each year. Meanwhile, Johannesburg's non-household tariff was R4.24 per kl, and the commercial/industrial price was R5.50 per kl, in each case as a flat tariff (the unit price is the same no matter how high the consumption level, and Johannesburg officials have never seriously considered introducing a block tariff to promote conservation).

80. However, for commercial/industrial sales, a profit of R1.30/kl was realised.

81. World Bank (2000), 'Johannesburg City Development Strategy: World Bank Grant Facility/Habitat City Assistance Strategy Programme', Washington.

82. The controversial French company has been found guilty of inducing corruption involving municipal officials in France and East Asia. It has been accused of cutting off water to the 30% of residents who could not afford bills in its main Third World pilot project, Buenos Aires (http://www.queensu.ca/msp Occasional Paper #2). And the firm was involved in such extreme corruption on the Itaipu Dam (Brazil/Paraguay) that the cost escalated from $3.4 billion to $20 billion.

83. *Business Day*, 5 August 1999; *Washington Post*, 13 September 1999.

84. The most visible were the Legal Resources Centre and high-profile liberal-rights campaigner Helen Suzman.

85. *Sunday Independent*, 18 February 2001.

86. *Sunday Times Gauteng Metro*, 19 May 2002.

87. *debate*, 3.

88. Department of Constitutional Development, *Municipal Infrastructure Investment Framework*.

89. Department of Constitutional Development (1998), *Draft Regulatory Framework for Municipal Service Partnerships*, Pretoria, August, p. 48.

90. Weekes, A. (1999), 'Letters of protest needed against the unilateral and bad faith privatisation of water in Dolphin Coast, South Africa to French transnational', Email communication, 6 February, p. 1.

91. Roome, J. (1995), 'Water Pricing and Management: World Bank Presentation to the SA Water Conservation Conference', unpublished paper, South Africa, 2 October, pp. 50–51.

92. Department of Constitutional Development, *Draft Regulatory Framework for Municipal Service Partnerships*, p. 56.

93. Lorrain, D. (1997), 'France: The Silent Change', in D. Lorrain and M. Stoker (Eds), *The Privatization of Urban Services in Europe*, p. 117.

94. Department of Constitutional Development, *Draft Regulatory Framework for Municipal Service Partnerships*, p. 74.

95. Palmer Development Group (1993), 'Urban Sanitation Evaluation', Report 385 1/93, Water Research Commission, Pretoria.

96. Palmer, I. and R. Eberhard (1994), 'Evaluation of Water Supply to Developing Urban Communities in South Africa: Phase I – Overview', Report KV 49/94, Water Research Commission, Pretoria.

97. Contaminants from sewage are of two general types, biological and chemical. Biological contaminants include pathogens in the form of bacteria and viruses, with consequent risks to human health. Chemical contaminants (or nutrients) include nitrates and phosphates, which damage ecosystems through eutrophication, which is the excessive growth of algae and other plants at the expense of other aquatic life. There are also health risks to humans and especially infants consuming nitrified

251

water. Additionally, other organic material present in waste contaminates water supplies by encouraging the growth of bacteria, which depletes the oxygen in the water (chemical oxygen demand), thereby killing aquatic life. See Palmer Development Group, 'Urban Sanitation Evaluation'.

98. *The Star*, 14 May 2001.

99. Palmer Development Group (1993), 'Sanitation and the Environment', Urban Sanitation Evaluation Working Paper B5, Water Research Commission, Pretoria.

100. *Engineering News*, 13–19 July 2001.

101. See excellent coverage in the *Sunday Times*, 18 November 2001; *Sunday Independent*, 18 November 2001; and *Beeld*, 30 November 2001, 1 December 2001.

102. Palmer Development Group (1995), 'Winterveld: Case Study of Informal Water Supply Arrangements', Water Research Commission, Pretoria.

103. Ibid.

104. Fourie, A. and M. van Ryneveld (1995), 'The Fate in the Subsurface of Contaminants associated with On-site Sanitation: A Review', *Water SA* 21, 2.

105. Palmer Development Group (1993), 'Evaluation of 2 VIP Latrine Programmes in Natal', Urban Sanitation Evaluation Working Paper B2, Water Research Commission, Pretoria.

106. Stephenson, D. (1993), 'Analysis of Effects of Urbanisation on Runoff', Report 183 1/93, Water Research Commission, Pretoria.

107. Allanson, B. (1995), 'An Introduction to the Management of Inland Water Ecosystems in South Africa', Report TT 72/95, Water Research Commission, Pretoria.

108. The main principle of a better-integrated system is to slow down the movement of urban run-off. This involves containment areas for stormwater near the site of impact, which would also allow for water treatment of the polluted urban run-off. Household rain catchment could be introduced to remove a portion of rain water from the sewer system, which could then be used by individual households to water yards or use for general washing. A third component of integrated management is the strategic planning of green areas that would absorb stormwater runoff. See Andoh, R. (1994), 'Urban Drainage: The Alternative Approach', Paper presented at WEDC Conference, Colombo, Sri Lanka.

109. Allanson, 'An Introduction to the Management of Inland Water Ecosystems in South Africa'.

110. Rencken, G.E. and D.A. Kerdachi (1991), 'The Inadequacy of Conventional Water Treatment Processes to cope with Future Poor Raw Water Quality', *Municipal Engineer*, July.

111. While it is impossible to put a price tag on a clean environment, the most direct environmental cost of pollution to water systems is the cost of the clean-up of contamination. Preliminary calculations by the Development Research Institute in Johannesburg confirm that if only a 10% reduction in water purification costs were achieved by moving all under-served households to water-borne sanitation instead of providing pit latrines, these savings would outweigh the costs for sewage treatment and greater water demand from the additional households served, by roughly R117 million per annum. Himlin, B. (1997), 'Some Environmental Cost Calculations Relating to Infrastructure', Unpublished report prepared by the Development Research Institute for the National Institute for Economic Policy, Johannesburg.

112. Thorne, S. (1996), 'Financial Costs of Energy Services in Four South African Cities', Unpublished report by the Energy and Development Research Centre, University of Cape Town, Cape Town.

113. van Horen, C. (1996), 'The Cost of Power: Externalities in South Africa's Energy Sector', PhD thesis, School of Economics, University of Cape Town, Cape Town. Note that van Horen's work did not include estimations based on a free lifeline supply, an unfortunate problem characteristic of the UCT Energy for Development Research Centre.

114. Simmonds, G. and N. Mammon (1996), 'Energy Services in Low-Income Urban South Africa: A Quantitative Assessment', Unpublished report by the Energy and Development Research Centre, University of Cape Town, Cape Town.

115. Bond, Mogale and Moellendorf, 'Infrastructure Investment and the Integration of Low-Income People into the Economy'.

116. The net effects include not only avoided environmental costs from household consumption, but also an estimate of the additional environmental costs of electricity generation by Eskom – including the effects of coal-fired power plants and ozone depletion – to supply these customers. If electrification occurs at much higher standards in urban areas, the net benefits begin at roughly R100 million in year one and rise (in present value terms) to R200 million in year two, R400 million in year four and R800 million in year eight. In rural areas, the net environmental benefits of electrification rise more gradually, to R50 million by year eight. van Horen, C. (1996), 'Eskom, its Finances and the National Electrification Programme', *Development Southern Africa*, 13, 2.

117. *Business Day*, 11 February 2001.

118. Irene Grootboom and her community in Wallacedene, in the Western Cape, were granted access to emergency shelter and services, which still had to be defined and implemented (and by June 2002 had not improved her status). The *Grootboom* decision defined, in an excessively vague manner, what is required with regard to the progressive realisation of a right, as follows: 'The requirement of progressive realisation means the State has to take steps to achieve this goal. It means that accessibility should be progressively facilitated: legal, administrative, operational and financial hurdles should be examined and where possible lowered over time'.

119. Interview, SABC tv show 'Newsmakers', 14 January 2001. Sadly, however, in subsequent letters to papers like the *Cape Times* and *Sunday Independent*, Muller fell back on defensiveness, denying his policy and his officials had done anything in the least wrong.

120. One important site where these were on display was the Development Bank of Southern Africa, where on 23 January 2001 a consultative conference with water-sector stakeholders was held. Impressively, one civil servant boldly reported back to the plenary session on the consensus within his breakaway group: things would be 'business as usual'. As for the ANC politicians, remarked the same man, 'the people who made unrealistic promises must now go and explain to the people why government won't give them their water free'.

Ironically, opposition to this attitude came from a surprising source. An official from the National Treasury, David Savage, urgently intervened with obvious anger near the very end of the event: 'If you continue to raise problems, if you put up bureaucratic obstacles, we will have to deal with you, from the top'. (Of course, in reality, the Treasury has the opposite reputation – of defunding social initiatives, not supporting them – so this puts into perspective how remarkably resistant the water bureaucrats are to change.) But this drama led virtually all the audience to sneer, as they pointed out in their objections to Savage, not unreasonably, that there wasn't enough money from Treasury.

Summing up the session, the lead consultant, Ian Palmer, said, simply, 'Let's be honest with ourselves, there is no magical new subsidy here. If a new subsidy mechanism is needed [to make available the free water], it's not possible'. (Palmer had been a consistent opponent of the RDP free water promise, so it was telling that he had been chosen by Muller for the job of designing the system.)

It thus appeared, as the brainstorm workshop drew to a close, that the bureaucrats left in a slightly more jaunty mood, for notwithstanding the threat from the National Treasury representative, they knew that they would triumph. On the way out, one man muttered, in a disgusted tone, 'Kasrils has been saying there'll be free water since last February [2000], and they still don't have a plan?' He then smiled.

121. *Sunday Times*, 9 October 2001.

122. See, e.g, the Municipal Services Project 2001 survey of Soweto household electricity bills (discussed in detail in Chapter Six), the HSRC/MSP national household survey in 2001 (http://www.queensu.ca/msp), or the University of the Free State Centre for Development Support's national study of household affordability in 2000 sponsored by the US Agency for International Development. The latter found that 'nine out of 10 lowpaying households gave unemployment, no income or too low an income as the main reasons for nonpayment' (*Business Day*, 14 March 2001).

123. Mvula chief executive Martin Rall phoned Kasrils to complain, and as late as June 2001 he was calling the free water promise 'premature'. (*Business Day*, 28 June 2001.)

124. In this, officials and NGOs hinted darkly that their overseas funders – the Dutch government was reliably mentioned by name – were not happy about the ANC's free-water promise, given how much time and effort had been spent on getting impoverished people to pay their bills.

125. van der Voorden, C. (2002), 'South Africa: Free Water still a Dream', *Water and Sanitation Weekly: Special Features Edition*, August.

126. Petras, J. and H. Veltmeyer (2001), *Globalization Unmasked*, London, Zed Press.

127. Poverty was a genuine factor in Johannesburg residents' inability to pay for services. Discounting the estimated 19,000 illegal reconnections over that period, 53,100 of the 73,400 other households (i.e., 70%) remained disconnected, according to Johannesburg revenue official Keith Sendwa. (*Pretoria News*, 6 May 2002; *Sunday Times Gauteng Metro*, 19 May 2002.)

128. In a stunning paragraph entitled 'Cross subsidise from businesses?', the Dwaf document revealed that 'the current view of national government is that municipalities should keep tariffs to commercial and industrial consumers as cost reflective as possible (no cross subsidies)'.

129. *Sunday Independent*, 20 May 2001.

130. *Sunday Times Gauteng Metro*, 19 May 2002.

131. Progressives argued, in rebuttal, that in addition to immediate supply of services, including provision of state water tankers to those without taps, Pretoria should have been spending much more on infrastructure – estimates were in the order of R150 billion over a decade – so as to connect all South Africans to at least intermediate services standards. This scale of programme was and is affordable and reasonable.

132. SA Municipal Workers Union (2001), 'Press Statement', Cape Town, 31 January.

133. Dwaf (1998), 'Compulsory National Standards Relating to the Provision of Water Services in Terms of Section 9(1)(a)', Memo CWSO 2161, Pretoria, 30 December, p. 2.

134. World Bank (2000), *Sourcebook on Community Driven Development in the Africa Region: Community Action Programs*, Africa Region, Washington, DC, 17 March, Annex 2. One of the authors, notably, was Roome.

CHAPTER FIVE

Droughts and floods:

Water prices and values in the time of cholera

With Greg Ruiters and Robyn Stein

1. Introduction

What was going on at Ngwelezane, not far from the massive Richards Bay port and industrial complex, in mid-2000? More than 130,000 people, nearly all low-income Africans, came down with cholera over the subsequent two years and more than 300 died, many as far off as Johannesburg, Limpopo Province and the Eastern Cape.[1] The outbreak hit hardest and longest in rural KwaZulu–Natal villages where water supplies were infected with the cholera bug during the 2000 winter season. The *Sunday Times* investigated the epicentre two months later and reported,

> This week, a startling picture emerged of the sequence of events that led up to the outbreak around Ngwelezane. Authorities discovered that some areas were still receiving free water in terms of a 17-year initiative of the former KwaZulu government to deal with the 1983/4 drought.
>
> 'It was eventually noticed, and it was decided to switch off the supply', said the chief executive of the Uthungulu Regional Council, B.B. Biyela. 'The people were given sufficient warning and the supply was cut off at the beginning of August'.
>
> The first cases indicating cholera were noticed in Matshana and Nqutshini in the second week of August. The first case confirmed was on August 19. At this point, health officials asked the Mhlathuze Water Board to reconnect the free water supplied by the former homeland government to the Nqutshini area.[2]

The connection fee of R51 (then US$7) imposed by Biyela was unaffordable for thousands of people. He cut off their water supply using a 'pre-paid meter' self-disconnection strategy, thus saving a few tens of thousands of rands but costing the provincial KwaZulu–Natal health authorities and the sick people tens of millions.

The incident represented yet another example of the 'soaking [of] the rich and poor, right and left alike', as two of this chapter's authors prophesised the denial of water to low-income people in *Business Day* a month earlier.[3] But ours was a 'mix of lies, halftruths and shoddy, out-of-date research', according to a robust denial from the director-general of water, Mike Muller: 'Apart from capital programmes to provide basic infrastructure for the rural poor, we are supporting local government in planning and financing its services'.[4] That support, we must remind ourselves, was premised at the time upon a 100% cost-recovery policy, a reflection of the most profound neoliberal principle, which in this case was fatal to hundreds.

The metaphor and reality of cholera

Likewise, more than a century earlier in northern Germany, the ruling class of the city of Hamburg was particularly short-termist in outlook. Evidence was abundant, in the city's terribly inadequate sanitation system, its unfiltered water, its stale air in the working-class ghettoes, its lack of good food for lower-income people, the pathetic character of the public health facilities, and the manner in which the Elbe River was reduced to a sewer by firms along its banks and run-off from domestic latrines. Underlying the structural shortcomings was a *laissez-faire* ideology championed by those bourgeois 'notables' who oversaw the Hamburg government. According to Cambridge historian Richard Evans, the significance of the cholera epidemic which killed 10,000 people in 1892 lay mainly 'in the realm of politics' because

> It demonstrated, with a graphic and shocking immediacy, the inadequacy of classical liberal political and administrative practice in the face of urban growth and social change ... In the crucible of cholera, the fusion of class interests held together since the 1860s by the liberal ideology of free trade, the primacy of merchant enterprise, and the reconciliation of divergent interests by qualified parliamentary government, came unstuck.[5]

And the political implications of 'liberalism's' (today, 'neoliberalism's') failure to prevent cholera? The backlash against Hamburg's ruling elite included the replacement of the 'helplessness of the politics of notables' with, at the very least, the 'administrative professionalism' that was in evidence in Prussia and that Hamburg necessarily sought soon thereafter. The point, Evans continues, is that cholera became a lens through which a variety of eco-social problems were focused:

> It was one of those events that, as Lenin once put it, may perhaps be ultimately insignificant in themselves, but nevertheless, as in a flash of lightning, illuminate a whole historical landscape, throwing even the obscurest features into sharp and dramatic relief ... The structures of social inequality, the operations of political power, the attitudes and habits of mind of different classes and groups in the population, come to light with a clarity of profile unimaginable in more normal times.

Back in Ngwelezane, Biyela's failure to fully cost-in the social and environmental benefits of state services was typical of the post-apartheid commodification process. As a result, water and sanitation services had broken down badly, despite the increasing prices charged by the municipalities and water boards in their effort to raise funds. According to Lance Veotte, water coordinator for Samwu,

> The working class residents of the Ngwelezane Township pay much more for water than the white middle and upper class area of Richards Bay, even though both are part of Empangeni municipality. Businesses in Empangeni pay $16 service charge and 30c per thousand litres. Rural communities who were affected by the cholera have to pay a flat [monthly consumption] rate of $2, which means that the rural poor are paying the highest price for water in the newly formed uMhlatuze municipality. Black people continue to subsidise whites ...
>
> Samwu members who work in health services went to the area for three months in an attempt to curb the epidemic. They reported that not even the clinics had water – clinics and schools must also pay or face disconnection. This is an extract from the report of the members: 'People are forced to use muddy water also used by cattle and goats. 93% of the rural schools here only get water from boreholes but 70% of these boreholes are out of service. Many schools run out of water regularly and have to resort to using dams, pools and rivers: Unsafe Water! Only three percent of the area has flush toilets! The remaining community members have pit latrines which were found to be not properly ventilated which attracts the breed-

ing of flies and other insects. In any case, 90% of the toilets are not properly built'.[6]

Problems had been flagged by the Department of Health more than a year earlier:

> It is common knowledge that lack of water and sanitation is a common cause of cholera, diarrhoeal or other illnesses that afflict so many in our country and that there is a relationship between various communicable diseases, including TB, and conditions of squalor. Yet we often have not structured our institutions and service delivery systems in ways that can easily respond to these realities.[7]

The Department of Health wasn't sufficiently in touch with catchment-area water officials until it was too late because, as services undergo commercialisation, the state becomes fragmented. The state typically skimps on functions required for integration, such as local-level Environmental Health Officers, who are particularly scarce in cholera-prone KwaZulu–Natal and Eastern Cape.[8] Water, electricity, health and other agencies adopt corporatised organisational forms, and in the process fail to pursue logical, constructive linkages and spillovers.

This happens across the spheres of government, as well, because water boards like Umgeni Water have been notoriously quick to commercialise, so as to pass on unprofitable customers in rural water schemes to nearby municipalities. Because those towns or even cities are also in the process of water privatisation, their officials claim they cannot afford to continue subsidising low-income people. Once the state has surrendered its responsibility to provide water, a company that takes a privatisation or outsourcing contract has no qualms about cutting off the service to those who cannot afford to pay the full cost-recovery market price plus a profit mark-up.

Another incident from KwaZulu–Natal demonstrates institutional and incentive problems that have emerged in rural water projects. According to *Sunday Times* reporter Mawande Jubasi, cut offs were still occurring in cholera zones fully 18 months after the epidemic began:

> David Shezi stole water for his eight children after he could no longer take the humiliation of seeing them begging for water from neighbours. But while he sat in a cell at a police station on

KwaZulu-Natal's South Coast, the man who went to the police about the theft continued to sell water to desperate people.

Samson Nqayi, chairman of the Dangaye Water Authority, a subsidiary of Umgeni Water, said he complained to police about Shezi and five co-accused to make an example of them. Nqayi, who owns a water truck, sells 25 litres of water for R1 to those who have no piped water. He also charges them R500 to install pipes to their mud huts ...

Shezi is poor, earning only R500 a month by selling fruit and vegetables to motorists near his home in Umgababa. Five years ago he saved R500 to get water connected to his hut. But then school fees, transport and food costs drove him into debt.

When his water was cut off three months ago he became dejected. He used a pipe to bypass his water meter. Then he was arrested with five other men in his village. 'I did not want to do it but I had no option', he said. 'I should be getting free water. I tried to do it the right way and I failed. Now I am sure I will go to jail because my wife and children were thirsty'.

Shezi is among one million poor people in KwaZulu-Natal who are forced into drastic measures to get water. On Friday, 300 members of an informal settlement near Queensburgh, Durban, were collecting water from the cholera-infested Umhlatuzana River. Their supply had been cut by the [Durban] unicity.

These people are the losers in a water war between the national Department of Water Affairs and Forestry, Umgeni Water and the municipalities of Durban, Pietermaritzburg, Ugu and Umgungundlovu. The municipalities and Umgeni Water say they do not have the money to provide free water. They asked Water Affairs and Forestry for R400 million and got only R120 million.[9]

Below, we explore Dwaf's ideological resistance to subsidising the operating cost of water systems. But what is most important here is that privatisers – whether water seller Samson Nqayi, multinational corporation Suez or even corporatising KwaZulu-Natal municipalities and water boards which are moving to full cost-recovery systems – are simply taking no responsibility for the social and personal costs of cholera, diarrhoea, dysentery, TB or other Aids-opportunistic infections incurred by health clinics and the patients.

A company making profits out of water sales feels no guilt when women and children suffer most. It does not repair environmental damage when women are forced to cut down trees to heat their families' food. It pays none of the local economic costs when electricity cut offs prevent small businesses from operating, or when workers are less productive because they have lost access to even their water and sanitation.

The ability to avoid the social implications of public goods associated with water and electricity allows huge multinational corporations to make enormous profits by expanding infrastructure systems just to the point where low-income people live. Usually this is a geographic decision, so that areas served by privatised services are noticeably 'cherry-picked': wealthy consumers get the services but poor people are denied access. Even before the logic of privatisation sets in, the necessary preliminary work by the neoliberal state – commercialising, delinking water from other state functions, raising tariffs, cutting off people who cannot pay their bills – all have the same effect, as Biyela proved in Ngwelezane. The theme of this chapter, therefore, is how the commodification of water causes droughts for poor people and floods for rich people and companies.

As a result, the key determinant is not whether water is privately or publicly managed, but rather whether it is in the process of being commodified. At that point, men like Biyela are just as lethal in the public sector as they would be if acting as chief executive officers of a privatised water company.

Ironically, just as the cholera epidemic began, the lead government water official, Mike Muller, wrote in *Business Day* newspaper to endorse the Mozambique government's private-sector water regulation: 'We could learn from their recent experience, which saw them dismiss the managers of newly privatised water services in Maputo for allegedly contributing to a cholera outbreak by failing to maintain services during the recent floods'.[10] Tellingly, Muller did not dismiss Biyela, Nqayi or the many others implicated – or resign, himself – once it became clear that his department's failure to maintain water services was contributing to the continuing spread of cholera in South Africa.

Nor did Muller mention that the decision to privatise Maputo's water was forced upon national authorities as part of the World Bank's strategy known as the Highly Indebted Poor Countries (HIPC) conditional debt relief initiative. That strategy reached its nadir in a letter from Bank president James Wolfensohn to Mozambican president Joaqim Chissano in March 1998, celebrating 'sharp' increases in water tariffs and calling for even higher prices prior to privatisation of the five largest cities' water systems.[11] The interconnections between all these aspects and agents of neoliberalism become clear when we examine water, for this is the most elemental of life-giving forms, and hence the most controversial when subjected to the laws of motion of capitalism.

The search for water

Water tells us much about life and death. As society emerged over the course of several hundred years, water became the stuff that cleansed, rid the town and the human body of waste, purified, cooled, quenched thirst, irrigated, offered recreation and enhanced urban aesthetics. At the same time it was also a subject of struggle between farmers, industrialists, social movements, government agencies, town planners, hygienists, gardeners, bankers and commercial water firms. At a more general level, water has had a 'civilisational' role, for tapped water and flush toilets inside homes have long been regarded as essential preconditions for modern, advanced society.

The first democratic government of South Africa well understood the deep social relationships associated with water. In its first post-apartheid *White Paper*, Dwaf recognised that 'The history of water in South Africa cannot be separated from the history of the country as a whole and all of the many factors which went to create both one of the darkest and one of the most triumphal chapters of human experience. The history of water is a mirror of the history of housing, migration, land, social engineering and development'.[12]

But by mid-2002, after eight years of ANC rule, could that history be reconciled with liberation, democracy, redistribution, reconstruction and development? What social forces could claim their water interests were being met? Success or failure in delivering water and sanitation services may, after all, become a key litmus test of progress towards social justice and meaningful citizenship, given the often grandiose claims associated with water supply. If the promises of ANC government to liberate water from the iniquitous social relations of the past are broken, the integrity of the transition process is clearly jeopardised, given the massive inherited distributional inequity and the relatively low cost of enhancing domestic water supply.

We have argued, thus far, that South Africa has witnessed two competing perspectives about how infrastructure-related services – especially water/sanitation and electricity – should be supplied, distributed and priced. In the drafting of state policy, neoliberals consistently trumped progressives committed to eco-social justice – while both continue to contest the discourse of sustainable development.

So we return, inevitably, to the technicist terrain. Our concerns here relate mainly to the regulation of markets, which are said to require adjustments so as to reduce imperfections and achieve socio-ecological efficiency. Neoliberals call for less, progressives for more. In between, it is alleged, is a balance. The balance is worked out through a series of trials and errors, approximating a cost-benefit analysis. Meanwhile, the vibrant competition between the three types of arguments – neoliberalism, sustainable development and eco-social justice – about measuring costs and benefits, is really about who should get water and under what conditions.

And these discursive exercises should not disguise a central reality about the outcome: the people in most need are often simply left out, cut off, and given no inputs aside from rioting. The reason for that, stated bluntly, is that the approach adopted so far during the era of post-apartheid government has emphasised water as a 'scarce' good, hence requiring payment based upon marginal-cost pricing, even for those who objectively *cannot afford it.*

Yet water is scarce for one main socially-constructed reason: the lack of political will to fundamentally transform inherited patterns of use. South Africa's first post-apartheid government was compelled to retain the apartheid-era hydrological bias towards supply enhancement, hence generating embarrassing surpluses through unnecessary dams, while failing to charge a sufficient price for those both who drive up the marginal cost over the longer term through their high levels of water demand and waste, and who are also those most *able* to pay.

From the standpoint of public policy, the merit good and public good characteristics associated with water in turn motivate bigger and cheaper supplies to those previously denied access. But these characteristics were by and large ignored – and even explicitly denied – in Pretoria. As noted in the previous chapter, the updated policy of 'free water', and the backlash against water privatisation in key settings, has not altered matters substantially.

Post-apartheid dehydration

Rhetoric from government, water-supply NGOs and for-profit water companies naturally differs from these realities. Moreover, although South Africa's basic patterns of water supply and demand appear to be relatively stable at the start of the twenty-first century, it is not impossible that this outcome will be altered by new policies stemming from renewed social struggle, which in turn follow logically from the medium-term unsustainability of the present trajectory. Rhetorically and in minor material ways, a small, almost insignificant, amount of progress did begin in 2000, when free lifeline water was announced as policy. Sabotage included not only the traditional tricks of bureaucrats but the very wording of the ANC's campaign promises, as we observed in the last chapter.

What is evident from the review of the first period of ANC rule, is that water and especially sanitation services to the majority of South African consumers deteriorated in relative terms. Notwithstanding publicity to the contrary, the last chapter showed that it is quite possible, maybe even quite likely, that a *lower* percentage of South Africans enjoyed access to affordable water in their homes or yards in 1999 than in 1994, given population growth in excess of 2% and low water-system installation rates. Moreover, although the figure of three million people newly supplied through government's rural *communal* taps between 1994 and 1999 was cited often enough, by mid-1999 it was semi-officially acknowledged that a vast proportion of those taps no longer worked, in the wake of systemic design flaws and affordability constraints (Section 2).

After describing an added dimension of the problem, the World Bank's insistence on applying neoliberal pricing principles to water supplies across Africa (Section 3), we can move to a potential – but debatable – antidote: the determination of water as a human right and the use of the legal apparatus to that end (Section 4).

2. The water delivery crisis

By 1998, according to Dwaf, 18 million South Africans were without basic water supply and 27 million had no basic sanitation. And yet by year-end 1998, water minister Kader Asmal was hailed for having served three million people, mainly in rural areas, with new water connections. Figures are unreliable, and in a best-case account, Nelson Mandela told parliament that 'in 1994, when the ANC was elected, some 30% of South Africans lacked access to safe supply of water near their homes. Today, after three million people have benefitted from the government's water supply programme, the percentage has been reduced to 20'.[13]

Rarely mentioned is the notorious unsustainability of the water projects, which were said by Dwaf insiders to have rendered a vast number of the new taps inoperative. Also rarely mentioned was the extraordinary upsurge in water cut offs, which included, as an example, 70,000 black township residents of Leandra, Mpumalanga, who suffered 70% water pressure cut off for several months in late 1998 at the hands of Rand Water, due to a non-payment rate of nearly 70%.[14] But amongst those suffering cuts were households which had paid their bills. This had become a general problem by the late 1990s, with a 2001 survey recording some 10 million people affected by water cuts.[15]

Water cut offs continued long after the free-water promise made by the ANC for the December 2000 municipal elections. Intense rioting against disconnections continued in major centres during 2001–02.[16] Municipal officials may have felt, on the one hand, fear that cutting people's water might evoke the Grootboom Constitutional Court precedent, in the event low-income people contested the failure of emergency services. Water minister Ronnie Kasrils was quoted by the *Sunday Times* in mid–May 2002 as accusing municipalities of 'unconstitutional' water disconnections in the event they were not offering a lifeline first. On the other hand, Kasrils quickly, conveniently – but incorrectly – clarified to readers that he could not intervene against water cut offs because the Constitution also protected local government autonomy.[17]

The ban on operating subsidies

As noted in the previous chapter, the development of water and sanitation policy reflected and in some important respects preceded the overarching urban, rural and municipal infrastructure policy processes. A mere six months after the 1994 election, Asmal's first white paper announced that 'where poor communities are not able to afford basic services, government may subsidise the cost of construction of basic minimum services but not the operating, maintenance or replacement costs'.[18] The insistence on charging the full operating and maintenance costs – and thus the refusal to keep to the mandate in the RDP that all are entitled to access to sufficient lifeline water for their reasonable needs – was based on two assertions.

First, the *Water and Sanitation White Paper* stated that if government covers operating and maintenance costs, there will be a 'reduction in finances available for the development of basic services for those citizens who have nothing. It is therefore not equitable for any community to expect not to have to pay for the recurring costs of their services. It is not the Government who is paying for their free services but the unserved'.[19] The *White Paper* thus argued for a 'some for all, not all for some' approach. But the false dichotomy between 'width' and 'depth' is presented as fact, without any reference to available sources of finance or to the potential of cross-subsidisation, as recommended in the RDP, in generating the finances available to meet everyone's entitlement to water.

Second, the *White Paper* repeated the widely held but unsubstantiated assertion that payment for services is the single defining feature that determines whether people and communities behave responsibly: 'The other reason why operating and maintenance costs should be borne by the communities is the principle of Community-Based Development. If the community expects some outside agency to be responsible for keeping their supplies going, they will have no control over the processes and lose leverage and ownership. Responsibility for keeping the service going is placed with a remote authority and accountability is lost. This will have an impact on the reliability of supplies'.[20]

The *National Sanitation Policy White Paper*, released in 1996, reiterated the 'some for all, not all for some' approach and included as a principle that the user pays: 'Sanitation systems must be sustainable. This means they must be affordable to the service provider, and payment by the user is essential to ensure this'.[21] Shortly thereafter, however, Asmal came out strongly against the misleading supply-side definition of lifeline. At the launch of the 1996 Annual Report of the Working for Water Programme, he said: 'We feel that we should not employ workers who refuse to pay for their water – provided (and this is most important) that the local authority has in place a lifeline tariff for the first five kilolitres of water per month. And note that by lifeline I mean a life-giving tariff, and not some engineering solution like the operating and maintenance costs'.[22]

In a talk on water conservation in Cape Town the same year, Asmal put it even more strongly: 'I see that the term lifeline has been hijacked: it is being taken to refer to the *operational and maintenance costs*, as a reflection of engineering elegance rather than social needs'.[23] Asmal thus repeatedly repudiated the central approach of his *White Papers*, yet still kept to the short-term aim of the RDP to provide 25 litres of water per person per day, short of the medium-term aim of 50–60 litres.

The 1997 *White Paper on a National Water Policy for South Africa* reflected an uneasy compromise between the cost recovery and life-line approaches. It conceded the right of all to have access to basic water services and included the following key proposals for incorporation into the Water Law:

- To promote the efficient use of water, the policy will be to charge users for the full financial costs of providing access to water, including infrastructure development and catchment management activities.
- To promote equitable access to water for basic needs, provision will also be made for some or all of these charges to be waived.[24]

The document also defined a 'reserve' for basic human needs: 'This will be provided free of charge in support of the current policy of Government which is to encourage the adoption of lifeline tariffs for water services to ensure that all South Africans can achieve access to basic services'.

But the 1997 *White Paper* only dealt with the first tier level, that of water in catchments under central government control. It excluded the second and third tier levels, i.e., water as distributed and delivered by agencies including water boards and local governments. In practice, the approach to basic needs thus amounted to an acceptance of the position that communities fetching water from natural sources do not need to pay for the first 25 litres per person per day. For communities that received water from built water systems, the policy did not go beyond the principle of access to basic water services and did not describe how this entitlement was to be achieved.

Clarity was continually sought, especially by leaders of the Rural Development Services Network and Samwu, who campaigned vigorously for the 50 litre per day free lifeline supply promised in the RDP. Tragically, it finally came from the water minister in 1998, as the upsurge in water cut offs was reaching epidemic proportions. Notwithstanding ambivalence about water officials' semantic twisting of 'lifeline' in his own 1994 *White Paper*, Asmal formally adopted the neoliberal interpretation of the word: 'The RDP makes no reference to free water to the citizens of South Africa. The provision of such free water has financial implications for local government that I as a national minister must be extremely careful enforcing on local government'. He obviously felt sufficiently guilty, knowing that his department could indeed raise subsidies to support impoverished municipalities through central-local transfers, to deny that his position was a 'sell out'.[25]

Project failure

With the victory of neoliberalism, Dwaf instructed its staff and all agencies carrying out community water supply and sanitation activities on its behalf to implement the *White Paper* standards and tariffs to the letter. Community water supply projects include communal standpipes at 200 metres. Despite the array of problems associated with collecting payment for water from communal standpipes, the principle of full payment for the operating, maintenance and replacement costs was insisted upon. Once projects were built, especially by Mvula Trust and other non-governmental suppliers, communities didn't receive further support.

Inexorably, extremely serious problems arose in the community water supply projects. There are varying estimates about project sustainability, with even the pro-government Mvula Trust acknowledging that roughly half of the projects it established would fail because of inability to maintain the system. The official Dwaf line by the early 2000s was that more than 80% of the taps were still working, but there were *no* national monitoring and evaluation reviews, merely tortured extrapolations of dubious small-scale reviews. One oral report by Dwaf official Helgard Muller in 1999 put the government's own cost-recovery on these projects at just 1%.

Reasons for unsustainability invariably include very real affordability constraints and an unwillingness to pay for communal standpipes. Communal standpipes are often not viewed as a significant improvement on existing sources of water. Other important reasons for failure include poor quality of construction, areas within communities without service and intermittent supply.

Moreover, the community water supply systems have led to numerous instances of inequity. Adjacent communities pay different amounts depending on the systems installed. Rural households pay for water from standpipes, whereas households in Durban getting water on site were getting the first 6 kilolitres per month for free, i.e., the amount of the breakeven point between the cost of collecting payment and the amount collected. Communities with new water systems were paying for the ongoing functioning of their systems whereas communities supplied by the former Bantustan governments often received their water for free. The notorious case of the cut off of a 17-year old free supply was noted above. Such inequities led to significant levels of community tension within and between villages. And, despite the claim to provide 'some to all', vast areas did not receive water services of any sort.

The 1994 *White Paper* considered the inequity between the new systems and those of the former Bantustans:

> This will require a substantial revision of present policy since Government grants or 'subsidies' have been given in the water sector for many years. These have generally been targeted at specific sectors of the population to promote policy objectives such as agricultural production in the commercial sector and the stabilisation of 'separate development' structures.[26]

The removal of the subsidies and replacement of inequity with equity at the lowest common denominator – *nonfunctioning* water systems where they exist at all – was the preferred strategy.

Dwaf's response to the high level of project failure was initially to move yet further from the entitlement to water as spelt out in the Constitution, partly egged on by advisers from international agencies such as the World Bank.[27] Dwaf continued to insist upon construction of communal standpipes in rural areas, but in future they were to be built with prepaid meters, whereby people must buy electronic cards to access even communally-piped water, a system declared illegal in Britain.[28]

As an aside, the use of prepaid meters can be justified by officials only by resort to inhuman logic. As the town clerk of the Ladysmith municipality, Francois Human, told the press in 2001,

> We are highly impressed with this low-cost metering system, which
> creates an invaluable mechanism for municipalities to manage and
> control resources over a vast area. Our experience is that the poor
> do want to pay for their services. Especially for those who do not
> have a regular income, it provides the opportunity to pay for water
> when they have money.[29]

And when they don't?

Instead of moving towards the medium-term aim of the RDP and providing taps on site, the Department proved willing to relax the 200 metre
criterion and allow for standpipes further apart so as to limit the number
and thereby cost of prepaid meters. Indeed, as noted in the previous
chapter, one Dwaf document circulating widely in early 1999 recommended that water supply to rural people be dropped from 25 to 7 litres
per person per day.[30]

One of the central problems, Dwaf officials continued to insist, was
financing the expansion of water supplies to low-income people. As the
free-services promise was unpacked, Muller issued several statements
confirming that no additional national subsidy funds were available to
make good on the water promise.[31]

But this was untenable, and a debate in *Business Day* ensued about
the financing of water operations.[32] To the suggestion that Dwaf tax the
abuse of water by commercial agriculture and, as short term measure, use
defence force tanker supplies to those with no access, Muller responded
that 'no case for new money can be made until it is clear that existing
funds are being properly used'.[33]

Yet because of the neoliberal policy parameters, the existing funding
for rural projects was not being properly used. Failure to spend Dwaf's
budget had been an embarrasment dating to the mid-1990s, when the
majority of water project funds were rolled over, back to the finance
ministry. Yet Dwaf's 100% cost-recovery strategy was based upon the
alleged lack of sufficient funding. Moreover, Muller was still ducking the
possibility of taxing large-volume water consumers.[34]

Water denialism

The final word on water delivery failure from Muller included a variety of
refutations: 'Why do we not truck water to the seven million who currently do not have access to basic services? The answer is that, even if
there were roads to the communities in need, trucking 25 litres per person per day costs on average perhaps 30 times more than supplying
water through pipes'.[35]

The answer hints at a cost analysis but not a benefit analysis, and in so doing shows how very little indeed Dwaf values rural people's lives. At that point, indeed, the costs of diarrhoea were being made public amidst appeals for urgent improvements in water provision. But Muller continued along the same refusenik path: 'Why do we not calculate the ecological, public health and gender benefits of water supply to reinforce our budget requests? Such exercises have often been done and will doubtless keep economists busy for years but their calculations are open to endless challenge'.

According to Ibinibini Mara of the Anti-Diarrhoeal Core Advocacy Group,

> Recent research has estimated that 43,000 people, mostly poor black children, aged between 0–5 years die from diarrhoeal diseases in South Africa each year, making it one of the leading causes of death. There are about 24 million cases of diarrhoea each year, of which three million require medical treatment. The costs of diarrhoeal disease treatments are estimated to R3.4 billion in direct medical costs, aside from the indirect costs and pain, sufferings and social dislocation caused. A Cost-Benefit Analysis on the impact of diarrhoeal diseases in South Africa by the Group for Environmental Monitoring in 2001 estimated the economic production losses around R26 billion a year.[36]

Not only was Muller blind to the vast benefits of water for the poor, but when requested to assure that, consistent with the Constitution, Dwaf ban water disconnections, he replied that 'simply passing regulations cannot force local or central governments to spend money they do not have'. As noted above, within a year Kasrils would declare that water cut offs were probably unconstitutional, but that too would apparently not bother the equivalent of the national water regulator, Muller, sufficiently to investigate declaring the disconnections a water emergency under the National Water Act.

As to the idea that the financing problem could be solved through redistributive tariffs, including national to local subsidies through Dwaf's own national 'trading account', Muller responded that this was a 'whacky distraction'. Yet his own department's studies had shown that half the water used by commercial farmers for irrigation purposes was wasted.

Likewise, the threat of E.Coli in Johannesburg's water table, thanks to the city's refusal to cross-subsidise sufficiently for improved sanitation was dismissed as 'largely meaningless'. In contrast, within a month, Kasrils admitted in parliament that a third of South African municipalities suffered spillage of sewage into water systems over a 15-month period of study, that Gauteng province was particularly hard-hit, and that Dwaf was having only 'limited success' in forcing municipalities to take remedial action.[37]

Given Muller's approach, it is no wonder that Dwaf became a leading light on the neoliberal water management circuit, winning international accolades for policy and delivery while cholera and diarrhoea were claiming thousands of lives at home. In 1999, the World Bank was proud to claim in its main strategy paper on South Africa to have been 'instrumental in facilitating a radical revision in South Africa's approach to bulk water management'.[38] Simultaneously, the Bank was using the same neoliberal approach to water across the continent.

3. World Bank water commodification

In the mid-1990s, at the same time South Africa was undergoing some of its first post-apartheid water stresses, the World Bank began issuing documents confirming the standardisation of similar policies across the world. Some of these statements, such as the book *African Water Resources*, are sufficiently vague as to disguise the commodification process: 'The strategy developed in this document is based on the principle that water is a scarce good with dimensions of economic efficiency, social equity, and environmental sustainability'.[39]

By then, it was already trite to argue that water had become a source of conflict, and that water wars would dominate in the coming century. Water scarcity levels were increasing across the world.[40] Citing the United Nations Development Programme, the BBC reported that 'the main conflict in Africa during the next 25 years could be over that most precious of commodities, water, as countries fight for access to scarce resources'. The United Nations Development Programme (UNDP) believed that 'potential water wars are likely in areas where rivers and lakes are shared by more than one country', with possible flash points around the Nile, Niger, Volta and Zambezi basins.[41]

Indeed, the semi-arid region of Southern Africa has specific problems not only with natural cycles of droughts and floods, which have been exacerbated by global warming. Moreover, the region's skewed settler-colonial mining and agricultural systems and economic development patterns make future conflict over water a certainty. Water has already served as an important lubricant of sustained geopolitical strife in Lesotho (1998), as we saw in Chapter Three, and on the Namibia/ Botswana border (ongoing). Problems also arose in relation to flood control on South African sourced rivers that flow into Mozambique during 2000–01. Historically, the conflict over water was the source of sustained colonial and apartheid oppression: for example, large dams displaced tens of thousands of people on the Zambezi River (Kariba and Cahora Bassa dams) and Orange River (Garieb Dam).

To address such conflicts, the Swedish International Development Agency advocates a more *efficient* use of water:

> The potentially greatest future cause of conflicts in the SADC region is water scarcity. Competition over natural resources may lead to serious conflicts. Hence, means to eliminate or diminish these are important to find ... As the realisation increases that fresh water of satisfactory quality is a scarce and limited resource, matters related to management of the water resources have become more into focus ...
>
> At least four conditions need to be fulfilled to carry through efficient water allocation: (1) well defined user rights, (2) pricing at its marginal cost, (3) information related to availability, value, quality, delivery times, and (4) flexibility in allocation responding to technologic, economic and institutional changes.[42]

The leap in logic that takes us from potential violent conflict to user-pay cost-recovery fees is most strongly and universally promoted by the World Bank across Africa, so it is to both the Bank's urban water utility reforms and rural project principles that we turn for more evidence of droughts for the poor and floods for the rich.

Water, power and poverty

Recovery from a major conflict, whether civil or liberation in nature, ideally entails major investments in water infrastructure, in part so as to bring about the return of displaced rural people to their traditional homes. Donors have often played a central role in providing water to impoverished people whose own resources would not sustain either capital investments or recurrent costs (operating and maintenance costs of water services ranging from bulk supply to household reticulation and smallholder irrigation). The importance of managing water extends up from micro-project level to national, regional and international policy, and donor agencies have played crucial roles at all levels.

The Bretton Woods Institutions' central coordinating and strategising role in South and Southern Africa water management deserves more consideration. The International Monetary Fund has drawn many water-related issues into its own structural adjustment programmes, whether the Enhanced Structural Adjustment Facility, Poverty Reduction and Growth Facility or Poverty Reduction Strategy Programme.[43] According to one recent report, 'A review of IMF loan policies in 40 random countries reveals that, during 2000, IMF loan agreements in 12 countries included conditions imposing water privatisation or full cost recovery. In general, it is African countries, and the smallest, poorest and most debt-ridden countries that are being subjected to IMF conditions on water privatisation and full cost recovery'.[44]

Yet it is the IMF's fraternal organisation, the World Bank, that has had primary intellectual, water policy, and project promotion roles consistent with water commodification, so the Bank is the main focus of our immediate interests. Moreover, by the late 1990s, the Bank had become involved in a wide variety of SADC water-related projects with other donors.[45] The Bank maintains a broadly dominant role in proffering advice – and sometimes giving orders – in the SADC water sector.[46] Internationally, the Bank website lists the following key international relationships – several of which were catalysed by the Bank – in advancing its water agenda:

- Global Water Partnership, which has the mandate of developing networks and knowledge for water resources management, and is based in Stockholm;
- the World Commission on Dams, which was launched by IUCN/World Conservation Union and the World Bank, together with many other partners, which is defining standards for when, where, and how dams should be designed, constructed, and operated;
- the Water and Sanitation Program, a 20-year-old partnership hosted by the Bank, to improve the access of poor people to water and sanitation services;
- the Business Partnership for Development, hosted by the NGO Wateraid in London, to develop innovative mechanisms for ensuring that private water contracts serve the needs of the poor; and
- the International Program for Technological Research in Irrigation and Drainage, hosted by the Food and Agricultural Organisation in Rome, which has the objective of developing innovative technologies for irrigation and drainage.

The Bank is a regular coordinator of, and leverage-point for, donor resources. It is a catalyst for several large dam projects, a project and water sector lender, a 'Knowledge Bank' source of information, a facilitator of civil-society involvement and promoter of a limited version of 'community participation' in water projects. The Bank is also a government policy adviser, an investor in privatised water infrastructure (through the

International Finance Corporation), a host to numerous African water agencies' Water Utilities Partnership, and the main agency imposing stipulations upon water sector management via structural adjustment and debt relief conditionality. The Bank can, therefore, claim not only to have a coherent perspective and wide-ranging market-oriented framework, but also to have applied these to water projects and policy across Africa. The African Development Bank has generally followed the same patterns.[47]

True, there are occasional disagreements amongst Bank staff. A mid-1990s debate occurred over whether retail water prices should follow a rising block tariff or instead more closely approximate the cost of production ('full cost recovery').[48] The victory of the latter argument within the Bank during the late 1990s seemed to herald an era of full-fledged water commodification, at the same time the Bretton Woods Institutions were most dogmatically insistent upon similar principles in relation to macroeconomic policy: in a phrase, 'get the prices right'.

Bank experience is drawn upon from across the world, and in conjunction with the UNDP, the Bank's World Water Forum has become the leading international forum for applying market solutions to water-related problems. The Bank also sponsored the World Commission on Dams, which included studies and submissions concerning two Southern African megadams: Kariba and Garieb. The region's two largest dams, Kariba and the Lesotho Highlands Water Project, were both catalysed and funded by the Bank.

Also of critical importance is the role of Bank water management in grassroots-level conflict resolution – via development projects such as water supply enhancement that can resolve longstanding disputes, or via restructuring Riparian water law so as to end centralised administrative allocation of water, to be replaced by water trading in specially-designed markets. In virtually all such cases, *the Bank has developed policies and projects that further the commodification of water*.

Commodifying water entails highlighting its role mainly as an 'economic good', attempting to reduce cross-subsidisation that distorts the end-user price of water (tariff), promoting a limited form of means-tested subsidisation, establishing shadow prices for water as an environmental good, solving problems associated with state control of water (inefficiencies, excessive administrative centralisation, lack of competition, unaccounted-for-water, weak billing and political interference), and in the process, fostering the conditions for water privatisation. Concrete manifestations are obvious once we consider two recent Africa-wide Bank statements on water resources management, urban and rural, that provide the conceptual underpinning for water projects and policies.

Urban utility reform

The 'Kampala Statement' of February 2001, drafted by the Bank in association with the Water Utilities Partnership, is an important review and aspirational vision of broader water policy issues in Africa, because of buy-in from African water officials.[49] In addition, the March 2000 *Sourcebook on Community Driven Development in the Africa Region* is a major internal Bank document dealing, in an appendix, with rural village water systems.

The Kampala Statement is a misleading document, for it certainly makes a strong case that poor people, and women in particular, deserve primary consideration in water policy. However, the actual content of the Statement – and all the follow-up work planned – is very much towards market-oriented reforms and what can be termed 'privatisation', a word that encompasses various types of management, outsourcing and ownership relations by which for-profit firms come to operate what were once state water services. A typical premise is the notion that 'the poor are willing and have the capacity to pay for services that are adapted to their needs'. And dealing with the semantics of privatisation, the Kampala Statement suggests that

> Reforms should not be considered synonymous with privatisation, but as a co-ordinated series of structural changes to provide better water and sanitation services to more and more people. However an increased role of the private sector in WSS delivery has been a dominant feature of the reform processes of African countries as it has been recognized as a viable alternative to public service delivery and financial autonomy.

Indeed, the premise of water privatisation had already been cemented. Not surprisingly, omitted from the Kampala Statement is any substantive information that would assist African policymakers understand and address – even via 'regulation' – four crucial drawbacks to such private parterships:

- the high profit rate extractions, in hard currency, typically demanded by transnational corporations;[50]
- the issue of whether hard-currency Bank loans are required to promote water privatisation;[51]
- the change in the incentive structure of water supply once private suppliers begin operating (especially in relation to pricing);[52] and
- the difficulty of a private supplier recognising and internalising positive socio-environmental externalities.[53]

Aside from private-sector involvement, another feature of the Kampala Statement is the strong orientation towards water-system cost recovery. As a result, the Statement denies the most fundamental reality faced by water services providers:

> The objectives of addressing the needs of the poor and ensuring cost recovery for utility companies are not in contradiction; well thought-out mechanisms for cross-subsidies, alternative service provision, and easing the cash flow demands upon the poor can allow the utility to survive whilst attending to their needs.

There is an enormous contradiction, in reality, between the drive to cost-recovery and the needs of the poor (as well as other vulnerable groups, and the environment), as discussed below.

The incentive to reform in a neoliberal mode is the universally-acknowledged fact that African water systems don't work well, especially when associated with public utilities that enjoy a relaxed budget constraint (i.e., ongoing subsidies from general revenues). Progressive critics of the African state, dating at least as far back as Frantz Fanon in *The Wretched of the Earth*, typically point to a variety of features of neo-colonialism, compradorism, neoliberal economic pressures, petit-bourgeois bureaucratic class formation, and simple power relations whereby elites can garner far more resources from local states than can the masses.

In contrast, the Kampala Statement derives the problems from one fundamental cause, namely, Africans get the prices 'wrong': 'The poor performance of a number of public utilities is rooted in a policy of repressed tariffs which leads to lack of investment, poor maintenance lagging coverage, and subsidised services reserved for the privileged who are connected to the network'. The mandate for full cost-recovery and an end to cross-subsidies – with meagre subsidies allegedly to be available for poor people at some future date – follow logically. As a result, one of the most important issues associated with water resource management, abuse of water by large-scale agro-corporate irrigation and wealthy consumers, is barely remarked upon, and the word 'conservation' is only used once, in passing.

Politically, the Kampala Statement is extremely naive – or disingenuous: 'Labour can also be a powerful ally in explaining the benefits of the reform to the general public. It is essential therefore that the utility workers themselves understand and appreciate the need for the reform'. But political resistance is probably the most interesting contradiction embedded within the Bank's water strategy.

Water for rural villages

Moving to the countryside, the Bank strategy is also articulated in the *Sourcebook on Community Driven Development in the Africa Region – Community Action Programs.*[54] According to the sourcebook, the Bank has played a key role in moving African water projects out of their previous unsustainable, failure-riven mode:

> Twenty-five years ago handpumps designed for North American farmsteads were installed in villages across Africa. They all broke down shortly after being installed. Twenty years ago robust handpumps and centralized maintenance was introduced. All the pumps broke down within one year and took months to repair. Donors were spending more and more money to maintain what was installed and less and less on new facilities.
>
> Fifteen years ago, community based management and user friendly handpumps were introduced, together with VIP latrines. Communities had to manage and pay for the maintenance of their handpumps. The approach was received with great skepticism by sector ministries: 'Villagers can't possibly maintain a pump'. Today community based management is accepted by all sector professionals across Africa as the only sustainable approach to village water supply and sanitation (with construction of low cost latrines) and increasingly to town water supply. Demand responsiveness where communities choose the facilities they want, decide how to manage and finance them, and pay part of the capital cost is also widely accepted as fundamental to sustainability.[55]

Yet the neoliberal, state-shrinking, project-level strategy is not yet complete, until two other philosophies associated with water policy are adopted, according to the *Sourcebook*. First, ' ... work is still needed with political leaders in some national governments to move away from the concept of free water for all'. Second, financial mechanisms still need fine-tuning:

> Promote increased capital cost recovery from users. An upfront cash contribution based on their willingness-to-pay is required from users to demonstrate demand and develop community capacity to administer funds and tariffs. Ensure 100% recovery of operation and maintenance costs ...[56]

In contradistinction from the urban and rural water commodification strategies, which have had such a devastating impact in South Africa and across the continent, is there any basis for *decommodifying* water by declaring it a human right, and demanding access and management systems that make the right real, not just rhetorical?

4. Water decommodification through the law?

There are two major laws that are worth examining, because they both illustrate the discursive turn to rights and justice, as well as the limitations imposed by neoliberalism in the form of reasonable fiscal resources to be spent on providing people with the water they require to live.

The National Environmental Management Act

In January 1998, the National Environmental Management Act (Nema) came into effect. It called for 'co-operative environmental governance' – a phrase derived from the constitutional mandate[57] that all spheres and organs of government are obliged to coordinate their actions – by establishing principles to be taken into account in all decision–making processes affecting the environment. Apartheid-era South African environmental law, in contrast, was fragmented and disbursed amongst a wide variety of statutes and subordinate legislation and was administered by a multitude of regulatory authorities.[58]

Nema represents law-making in the sustainable-development mode, for while insisting that 'environmental management must place people and their needs at the forefront of its concern, and serve their physical, psychological, developmental, cultural and social interest equitably', it immediately switches to Brundtland-style sustainable-development discourse, with a call for 'socially, environmentally and economically sustainable' development.[59] The idea of sustainability entails 'the integration of social, economic and environmental factors into planning, implementation and decision-making so as to ensure that development serves present and future generations',[60] which in turn follows from the Constitution's approach to 'justifiable economic and social development'.[61]

Thus Nema stipulates avoidance – or where that is impossible, minimisation and remedy – of 'the disturbance of ecosystems and loss of biological diversity ...; pollution and degradation of the environment ...; disturbance of landscapes and sites that constitute the nation's cultural heritage ...; [and] waste ...' It continues by insisting

> that the use and exploitation of non-renewable natural resources is
> responsible and equitable, and takes into account the consequences

of the depletion of the resource; that the development, use and exploitation of renewable resources and the ecosystems of which they are part do not exceed the level beyond which their integrity is jeopardised; that a risk-adverse and cautious approach is applied, which takes into account the limits of current knowledge about the consequences of decisions and actions; and that the negative impacts on the environment and people's environmental rights be anticipated and prevented, and where they cannot altogether be prevented, are minimised and remedied.[62]

Hence prevention is better than cure, but qualifications are made consistently so that sources of environmental harm and damage located in the existing mode of production are ultimately not challenged.

But here too an environmental justice thread is woven into the legal rhetoric. Nema's founding principles recognised that 'environmental justice must be pursued so that adverse environmental impacts shall not be distributed in such a manner as to unfairly discriminate against any person, particularly vulnerable and disadvantaged persons'.[63]

Yet 'adverse environmental impact' is not defined, and although capable of wide interpretation, there is the danger that a narrow reading of Nema's definition of 'environment' will nullify the broader social intent of the principle. For that foundational definition – 'the surroundings within which humans exist and that are made up of – the land, water and atmosphere of the earth; micro-organisms, plant and animal life; ... the interrelationships among and between them; and the physical, chemical, aesthetic and cultural properties and conditions of the foregoing that influence human health and wellbeing'[64] – is, after all, an eco-centric approach which explicitly avoids clarifying in plain language *social, living and working environments.*

Clear legislative language is vital in a context where a relatively untransformed judicial bench retains strong class, race, gender and other relations to the privileged of society. Nema's implicit distinction between human health and well-being, and environmental health and well-being, leaves the law more amenable to an ecotourist's conception of environmental sustainability than to someone from poor or working-class roots.

To illustrate, while Nema safeguards the right to refuse environmentally hazardous work,[65] this section of the law is curiously silent on potential, threatened or actual health threats associated with particular work practices. The balance of convenience is clearly in the hands of employers, for workers are required to comply with technical and complex administrative requirements.

There is, thus, access to environmental information in Nema – including, under certain circumstances, privately held information – and added protection for whistle blowers.[66] Yet the extent of employer disclosure will ultimately depend both upon Open Democracy Act interpretations, where considerable pressure will be exerted by corporate interests, and regulations promulgated by the Minister of Environmental Affairs and Tourism. Such ministerial regulations must be 'reasonable'[67] – i.e., objectively justifiable in the circumstances – which leaves significant room for manoeuvre, particularly in an age of commercially-protected information. As noted below, the regulations are subject to Parliamentary approval but nonetheless constitute 'subordinate legislation'.

In sum, Nema's principles are internally qualified or simply do not go far enough to address distributional issues, the root causes of environmental damage and harm, and practical power relationships on the legal battlefield.

As for compliance and enforcement provisions, Nema contains relatively far-reaching provisions which, at first glimpse, resonate with social and environmental justice values. But these provisions contain substantial terminological loopholes following compromises with key corporate-industrial interests. The 'polluter-pays' principle is fundamental, requiring 'every person, who causes, has caused or may cause significant pollution or degradation of the environment must take reasonable measures to prevent such pollution or degradation from occurring, continuing or recurring, or, insofar as such harm to the environment is authorised by law or cannot reasonably be avoided or stopped, to minimise and rectify such pollution or degradation'.[68]

However, again the qualifier 'reasonable' can be invoked when there is any alleged economic hardship or job loss associated with pollution-control measures. Moreover, those who are obliged to take 'reasonable measures' include the 'owner of land and or premises, a person in control of land or premises or a person who has the right to use the land or premises on which or in which any activity is or was performed or undertaken; or any other situation exists, which causes, has caused or is likely to cause significant pollution or degradation of the environment'.[69]

South Africa's legacy of brutal land dispossession and land tenancy should have suggested the need for sensitivity in the relative priority of *which* polluter must pay, and there is very little prospect for prosecution of predecessors-in-title. While Nema boldly declares an intention to consider any person who 'is or was responsible for, or directly or indirectly contributed to, the pollution or degradation or the potential pollution or degradation', there is no specification of whether, for example, lenders, technical specialists or predecessors-in-title can be brought into the liability net. As for costs that may be recovered, again these must be 'reasonable', and no mention is made of indirect social costs.

The provisions of the Constitution dealing with the enforcement of rights[70] are replicated and given effect in Nema,[71] including the reintroduction of class action into the South African court process and cost protections for group-plaintiffs. However, these are premised on access to justice being available to all – but given fiscal constraints and residual class privilege, these options are simply not realistic. Court procedures continue to be alienating and extremely costly. Alternative means of private party dispute resolution are vaguely provided for in Nema, but are not likely to make a substantial difference to the problem of access. In short, possibilities for integrating compliance and enforcement provisions given the existing system of civil and criminal justice do not appear to be in the least bit realistic.

The Constitution[72] sanctions national government to set minimum uniform norms and standards regarding provincial and municipal legislation, with space given for specific and technical issues pertinent to regional and local settings. But again, in the interstices of practical legislative implementation in a context of a severely compromised transition process, semi-federalism has been repeatedly entrenched, and is evident in the supreme law of the land.

Activists' concerns around uneven legislation and regulatory control in respect of the environment seemed to have been ignored in the Constitution. Environment and pollution control are 'concurrent' national and provincial government legislative responsibilities, and even more worrying, exclusive legislative competence has been granted to the provinces and indeed to municipalities in regard to monitoring and regulating waste disposal. Whether this includes hazardous waste disposal is left unclear.

As a result, Nema's chapter on integrated environmental management facilitates asymmetry in an already terribly uneven regulatory and administrative environment.[73] Nema's weak conception of integrated environmental management also surrenders socio-ecological regulatory power to other (non-environmental) national and provincial departments, with the result that the most significant polluters – the mines – will continue to enjoy protection from, for instance, the rigours of far-reaching impact assessments prior to commencement of prospecting or mining operations.

Finally, despite the philosophical devolution of regulation to the lowest most appropriate level, environmental 'co-regulation' and 'self-regulation' find their way into Nema.[74] Although paying lip service to control and also to community-based participation, Nema leaves all meaningful powers to the prerogatives of the Environment Minister's executive law-making through regulation.[75]

The National Water Act

The National Water Act (NWA) came into operation in October 1998, replacing a 1956 Water Act. Its core objectives are:
(a) meeting the basic human needs of present and future generations;
(b) promoting equitable access to water;
(c) redressing the results of past racial and gender discrimination;
(d) promoting the efficient, sustainable and beneficial use of water in the public interest;
(e) facilitating social and economic development;
(f) providing for growing demand for water use;
(g) protecting aquatic and associated ecosystems and their biological diversity;
(h) reducing and preventing pollution and degradation of water resources;
(i) meeting international obligations;
(j) promoting dam safety; and
(k) managing floods and droughts.[76]

As with Nema, the sustainable development discourse underpins the NWA, particularly the calls for sufficiency and sustainability (undefined) in the public interest and the facilitation of social and economic development. In the Brundtland mode, intergenerational equity and the meeting of basic human needs are fundamental provisions. Yet the extent to which the NWA legislates the protection, use, development, conservation, management and control of water resources, in relation to the country's vast unmet human needs, is nevertheless questionable.

Here the NWA's concept of an abstract 'Reserve' of water resources to meet both basic needs and the integrity of aquatic ecosystems is a key international legal innovation. But the basic needs provision is itself reliant upon interpretations of a 1997 Water Services Act, the constitutionally enshrined rights of access to sufficient water and environmental rights as discussed above.[77] Those interpretations are, unfortunately, subject to the vagaries of administrative decision-making and regulatory prescription by the Minister of Water Affairs and Forestry.

The lack of clarity on meeting basic needs is carried through to the pricing strategy provided for in the NWA,[78] which obliges the Water Minister to 'consider measures necessary to support the establishment of tariffs by water service authorities', and in particular to 'make allowance' for lifeline and progressive block tariffs. Yet neither the NWA nor the Water Services Act provide clues as to what is meant by a lifeline tariff, which gives rise to somewhat arbitrary determinations of the 'minimum' amount of water per day required to sustain human life and hygiene.

As we have seen, the RDP *short-term* objective of 25 litres per person per day is used, and has become not a minimum in actual water projects, but the effective *maximum* for which small pipes are installed. Nor is this amount guaranteed as a free entitlement: as noted above, official policy was generally that marginal cost should be met by consumers. Thus though laudable for including the recognition of sufficient water for basic human needs, the NWA suddenly stops short of granting the full ambit of this notion.

Interpretation of these issues will again be left to the courts, which remain a highly inadequate forum for the environmental and social justice values mandated by the Constitution. Moreover, the NWA's administration will ultimately take place by delegation – although the NWA makes it clear that this does not mean devolution – at the level of an anticipated 13 'water management areas' such as catchments or regions.

Still, administrative discretion is again fundamental to the management of these areas. To replace apartheid-era irrigation boards in rural areas, which represented pockets of white agrarian power, the NWA provides for 'water user associations', i.e., representative 'co-operative associations of individual water users who wish to undertake water related activities for their mutual benefit'.[79] Given the existing power and distributional imbalances as well as South Africa's failed land redistribution programme, the NWA is remarkably silent on ensuring the desired transformation.

Despite its 'localised', 'most appropriate level' approach to water resource management, the NWA contradicts itself by providing for ultimate national government responsibility as 'public trustee' of South Africa's water resources.[80] The Minister has responsibility for ensuring that water is allocated 'equitably' and used 'beneficially' in the public interest, while promoting environmental values.[81] The practical effect is the juxtaposition of central power, regulation and control with delegated or localised power and control, yet insufficient national-local subsidies, which throws into question effective participatory democracy at the water management area level.

The NWA proceeds to introduce a wide definition of 'water use',[82] including abstraction of water from a water resource, storing water, impeding or diverting the flow of water as well as the discharging or disposing of water found underground if this is necessary for the efficient continuation of an activity or for the safety of people (i.e., in underground mining operations). The NWA constitutes a legislative shift from a system which facilitated acquisition of private-use rights in water to a public system where allocation of water-use rights is administratively determined on a licensing basis, which in turn will be influenced by an abstract water market as set out in the pricing policy. Riperianism, the

282

doctrine developed in the South African Common Law, English law and apartheid law, is also abolished in the NWA.

Yet here, too, where the opportunity arises for social and environmental justice, the NWA gives protections to 'existing lawful water uses',[83] i.e., 'during a period of two years immediately before the date of commencement of this Act; or which has been declared an existing lawful water use'. It is only through the compulsory licensing process[84] that existing lawful water uses are ultimately challenged, but this is constrained by the spirit of the neoliberal approach, namely residual (and sacrosanct) property relations under the Riparian system.

The point was to avoid challenge to the NWA on grounds of the Constitution's protection of private property. But as a result, payment of compensation can be claimed where 'severe prejudice to the economic viability of an undertaking' has resulted in 'financial loss suffered in consequence' of a lesser water use being authorised or a substantial reduction in water use imposed through the compulsory licensing process.[85] The Dwaf budget does not, however, contain provision for major compensations. Indeed, the water services budget came under fierce attack, at one point, during the mid-1998 period of foreign financial turmoil, suffering mid-year cuts of 67% by the Department of State Expenditure, which in turn catalysed intensified fiscal discipline.

Regarding pollution, economic principles associated with sustainable-development – particularly the 'internalisation of externalities' – impinge upon social and environmental justice, for while the NWA contains a relatively more stringent polluter-pays provision that its predecessor, once again the 'measures' provided for are qualified by the test of 'reasonableness'. Clean-up or mitigation costs may be recovered from persons 'jointly and severally', and the NWA creates an offence of criminal negligence in regard to water pollution – but this is ultimately dependent upon prosecution through the courts.

Though written in apparently more plain and accessible language than the Nema, ultimately the fulfillment of the rights guaranteed in the NWA are dependent upon the say-so of a water tribunal established under the NWA, and of the courts. Considering South Africa's untransformed justice system, there are serious concerns about how fully the NWA will deliver meaningful social and environmental justice. And given South Africa's extraordinary maldistribution of water resources, the NWA's light treatment of redistribution and its somewhat fickle provisions for implementation raise significant doubts about whether any progress towards 'equity', repeated so often in the NWA, will occur in reality.

In relation to implementation, logical avenues for legal struggle abound, including Constitutional challenges such as Irene Grootboom's and trade union efforts to enforce public-public partnerships. As Lance Veotte of Samwu argues,

> Solutions can also be found in the *Water Services Act* of 1998, which stipulates that before any private provider can be brought in to deliver water, all known public alternatives must have been investigated and found to be incapable or unwilling. Samwu attempted to use this law to wipe out apartheid inequalities.
>
> For example, in 1997 Samwu fixed leaking pipes in Cape Town's townships that were allowed to decay by the apartheid government in line with their policy of providing black people with inferior services. Fixing leaks saves the municipality over R10 million per year. Budgets of the former white and black local authorities still have not been combined and apportioned equitably despite the amalgamation. In Cape Town over 300 water workers serviced white areas while only nine serviced the black majority. With these inequalities continuing, a poor level of service will be delivered that will not be appreciated or sustainable.[86]

However, the failure of authorities to take seriously public sector options is indicative of the limits of legal strategies. In short, aside from some occasional exceptions, the major water-related laws and their implementation will very likely amplify the core political dynamics stressed throughout this book.

On the one hand, we witness the tendency for government to talk eloquently about environmental justice, albeit without any intention of carrying forward the necessary radical transformation of economy, society and environment. On the other, the tools of sustainable-development analysis are often invoked, yet are applied in a manner that never truly challenges the power of capital, thanks to diverse but effective loopholes. Finally, the overriding logic of accumulation offers big business the assurance that if an economic growth discourse is invoked, capital's privilege to destroy the environment will ultimately be defended.

5. Conclusion

What does South Africa's first period of democratic transition tell us about social and ecological aspects of water? We have in previous pages considered a variety of aspects of water rhetorics, demand and supply considerations, and the politics associated with these. But what has only been hinted at, thus far, is the overdetermination of this particular debate about differential water use – and indeed much other South African socio-economic policy – by the global process known as neoliberalism.

Ultimately, Graham Thompson is correct to argue that 'a crisis in Keynesian forms of state regulation and planning in the context of a *wider crisis of global accumulation*' is at the centre of the global public policy shift to neoliberalism, including the commodification of water in many parts of the world economy. Informed by this insight, debate should logically refocus away from the pros and cons of commodification to understanding it as a symptomatic *outcome* of crisis – specifically what Thompson calls 'monetarisation ... in which the decisions about service allocation and provision are depoliticised and increasingly subordinated to the abstract and indifferent power of money'.[87]

But what are the implications for this kind of subordination of water to money, as we have witnessed it across issues of both demand and supply? Historically, after all, the conquest of water has signalled epochal shifts in entire civilisations. Most early societies were based on agriculture, requiring ever more sophisticated irrigation systems which in turn were buttressed by specific forms of political and social organisation. As Wittvogel famously argued, striking similarities in social and cultural institutions in ancient India, Egypt and China were underpinned by vast irrigation infrastructures whose maintenance needed legions of workers, artisans, and bureaucrats. These 'hydraulic civilisations' oversaw a vast system of agricultural production and environmental and social management, underscoring how the conquest of nature inevitably required the conquest/domination of people, long before formal commodification of daily life began.[88]

In the modern era, the conquest of water and the control and elimination in some parts of the globe of urban epidemics and disease together stand as a defining aspect of post-enlightenment social history and technological development. Yet these conquests were neither rationally pursued or automatic. Immense social struggles led to gradual social improvements and changed society's construction of risk, danger and good life.

To be precise, in modern South Africa amongst other sites, water was first formally supplied by private firms and water carriers, but with growing demands and an understanding of natural monopoly economies-of-scale, municipalities later took over private concessions, in the process mobilising loans and capital that were formerly off limits. The building of South African and many other cities over the past two centuries required an invisible metabolic system and exchange with natural elements which had to flow in and out of the city. Water supply and sanitation pipelines replaced the myriad of individualised labours of armies of domestic servants and water carriers.

However, the specific social mix in which social services were delivered and produced varied. In France the private sector was dominant. In Britain, the public sector – and specifically, a municipal socialist ideology – triumphed in the early part of the twentieth century. In Germany, Bismarck inaugurated a period of massive social interventions as part of state-building initiated from above. The variation is significant, with different policy rhetorics and styles emerging in each of these states, depending largely upon the balance of forces in each context.

To assess the possibilities for transcending the monetarisation of water in South Africa, we first must recognise the phases in which different realms and goods were commodified. Historically, commodity exchange first applied to prestige goods, then food, then labour, then land. That process in turn forced people into cities to work, via the enclosure movement or colonial hut taxes and similar modes of coercion. As Karl Polanyi observed, however, these latter were never perfect commodities, land because it is finite and labour because, notwithstanding an early slave-based mode of production, the modern labourer cannot be bought or sold.

The organisation of a collective water system – and other public services with public good characteristics – cannot be separated from the production of governable populations and docile but capable labouring bodies. The provision of working-class housing and infrastructural services, the consumption of water-related appliances and goods, and the teaching of hygienic habits may be likened to what Gramsci called Americanism–Fordism.[89] Thus a century ago across most of the industrialising world, water and sanitation became a trope for citizenship and urban order. In South Africa, by contrast, privatisation and ability-to-pay have threatened to drive water developments, thus stripping the meaning of wider concerns such as social citizenship, public health, gender equity, ecological integrity, and personal/social dignity.

Modern history may be written as the increasing encroachment of the commodity form on independent production for personal use. Consider such diverse commodities as clothes (originally made in the home), childcare, and now even the commodification of grief via the psychology profession. Capitalism, driven as it is by competition, externalises costs. In South Africa, the commodification of housing, elecricity, water and so on is simultaneously a political process. At the same time, water and sanitation became an active realm for new biopolitics and exercise of power, but in a proto-apartheid form which, of course, diverged from water consumption and reduced its status as a norm of universal citizenship.

Thus the commodification of water is not merely a political-economic phenomenon to be contested with interesting combinations of public-goods sustainable-development arguments and radical socio-environmental justice activism. It is about social control and the very way in which power is ordered in society.

It is in this sense that the potential backlash against the commodification of water by Kader Asmal's successor, Ronnie Kasrils, is so fragile. The fluke of a committed communist military leader being made Water Minister in June 1999, and his recognising that the extraordinarily good publicity earned by his predecessor was as unsustainable as the broken taps themselves, did not initially generate a sufficient consciousness about these power relations. By this stage, advocacy against Asmal's water policies, programmes and projects had intensified amongst progressive rural NGOs. Yet in motivating a free supply of (just) 25 litres per person each day – a great leap forward towards socio-environmental justice, to be sure – Kasrils couched his justification in the narrowest of sustainable-development terms: 'It would save money because local authorities would not be saddled with the problem of administering large numbers of small accounts', he told a media briefing in early 2000.[90]

Subsequent events showed that Kasrils was unable to identify and correct any of the sabotage tricks discussed in the previous chapter. He maintained the bias within the policy against large families. His incorrect constitutional interpretation that he had no legal power to stop municipal water cut offs was another indication that the *status quo* practices would be acceptable.[91] Indeed, although he spent most of early 2002 valiantly promoting the Palestinian cause, Kasrils' justification that a tiny free water supply 'would save money' on purely *administrative* grounds, not even mentioning the other public good provisions, suggests how easy it is to slide from an historic commitment to social justice right across the spectrum to neoliberalism.

A far different, far more expansive approach is required on the part of society and forward-looking state officials if South Africa is ever to become truly modernised with respect to water. As shown above, the lesson about differential social power comes through clearly from post-apartheid South African debates over water supply, distribution, consumption and payment, as well as constitutional rights, water law and delivery systems.

As a commodity, water requires especially large outlays of fixed capital for its production, and hence comes under the sway of the credit system since large loans have to be secured. Water therefore circulates not only in the physical form of pipes but also in the world of money, for water generates a revenue stream to pay interest on loans, amortisation and future investment. Private water firms active in South Africa include huge concerns listed on stock markets across the globe, and hence water-related revenues circulate in a very definite financial form.

Thus the basic condition for the commodification of water is the separation of the mass of the population from ownership of the means of production – including land and the 'free gifts of nature' such as water. The generalisation of private property as a social principle includes 'public' or state property. Water industry components – capture, storage, harvesting, treatment, transport, monitoring and measurement – add value at each stage and must be examined separately to judge the degree of commodification. To begin to address even small parts of South Africa's water problem forces us to look at the entire construct of property relations upon which oppression rests, and reproduces.

This may be an intimidating way to conclude. Our critique of current South African policy, legislation and practice has, after all, unfolded in part through describing the admittedly unfavourable balance of political-economic forces, and in part through examining the various socio-environmental discourses deployed in various settings, confusing as they are sometimes intended to be. Ultimately, though, it is to the capitalist mode of production that we would turn to place the ultimate blame for the present predicament. Prior to doing so, however, similar problems in South Africa's use of energy resources must be explored.

Notes

1. Although outbreaks were publicised in various sites through mid-2002, when this book went to press in July 2002, the Department of Water Affairs and Forestry had stopped updating their daily website records on cholera (http://www.dwaf.gov.za).

2. *Sunday Times*, 9 October 2001.

3. An initial foray into a public debate over class and water was published by Bond and Ruiters in *Business Day* (13 July 2000):

> Holding up an unexploded orange water balloon like a trophy, water and forestry director-general Mike Muller beamed with relief.
>
> He and a gathering of water privatisation advocates had survived a vigorous toyi-toyi by a few dozen workers, students and residents, which shut down the Urban Futures conference in Johannesburg for half an hour on Tuesday.
>
> The purposefully rude protesters had lobbed balloons at the suits, but missed. Muller, municipal bureaucrats Roland Hunter and Antony Stills of Johannesburg, and Archer Davis of Water and Sanitation SA, could get on with the workshop's business. Annoyed conference-goers sighed 'we respect their right to protest'.
>
> Yes, but as Gill Scott Heron said of 'free speech' in the US, you get that right 'only so long as you don't say too much'.
>
> For the balance of power in the workshop was evident: the suits winked and nodded at the interruption, but went on developing plans to trump work-

ers now facing retrenchments and pay cuts; township communities suffering unprecedented levels of water cut offs; and students under threat of exclusion when unaffordable Wits bills reach their mailbox.

The previous day's conference addresses by two gurus of the global city, Manuel Castells and Saskia Sassen, had warned us of precisely these trends.

Castells, a professor at the University of California at Berkeley, has the ear of President Thabo Mbeki, Brazilian President Fernando Cardoso and other forwardlooking politicians. He told the conference of a new class war, waged partly in the property markets over who gets access to urban space.

'The segregated city is different than the segmented city. When the elites quit the city the pattern of communication breaks down. It leads to ecological devastation such as deterioration of agricultural land and increases in epidemics. The problem is not overpopulation but intense concentration of poor people in megacities', he said.

Though urban class-apartheid is indisputably a global problem, Johannesburg is here (if nowhere else) a truly world-class city.

In addition to joking about SA's comparative advantage in export of electric fences to other fortress cities, Castells could have referenced another blight on Johannesburg's landscape: the embarrassing mass of empty upper-storey central business district space (CBD), where two-thirds of low-grade offices became vacant when white-run financial and service-sector firms fled north over the past decade. At the same time, hawkers and homeless people who simultaneously penetrated the street-level space can despair of ever achieving the buying power required to take up the slack capacity.

Under conditions of globalisation, which allegedly thwart state intervention in the markets, Johannesburg officials have apparently given up hope of ever putting the two – empty spaces and vast social needs – together.

Technical solutions investment incentives, business improvement districts, rates rebates and even closed-circuit cameras to allow maximum surveillance power are failing to restore Johannesburg's big-business glory.

Meanwhile, the incessant drive to attract foreign investors seems to be preventing the obvious oldstyle planning solution: expropriation of buildings whose landlords have fallen far behind in rates payments, and revival of public housing alongside transformation of streets into people's parks.

Worries about sending the wrong signals and a withered municipal fiscus have left instead a dangerous CBD where the middle class fears to tread.

Worse, the only force that could really push the city into action, urban social movements (the study of which made Castells' reputation in academia two decades ago), appear fragmented and confused. Tuesday's anticipated municipal strike was called off and angry workers dispersed.

Residents once capable of disciplined mass action through SA National Civics Organisation branches have been overtaken by what a *Business Day* report on July 5 (incorrectly) termed 'popcorn civics'.

Though not always in the news, politics in Johannesburg's townships do often degenerate into yet another global phenomenon, the 'IMF Riot': uprisings of angry people who take to the streets when subsidies are withdrawn, services are cut or prices soar.

SA is at the top of the world rankings in inequality.

Although our organised urban movements were probably the finest in the world during the mid-1980s, their subsequent demobilisation is one of the greatest of post-apartheid tragedies.

Witness the hounding of maverick councillor Trevor Ngwane out of his Soweto African National Congress leadership role by a dogmatic Johannesburg clique that would not countenance Ngwane's attempt to strike up a dialogue over the merits of Igoli 2002.

Thus, says Castells, we are witnessing a new 'concentration of the urban but without mechanisms of social integration', which in turn means that Johannesburg officials are 'adapting to global forces by playing a game of competitiveness rather than heeding concerns of citizens'.

Sassen, an Argentine scholar based at the University of Chicago, spelled out some political implications: 'The chaotic space of the megacity makes possible the emergence of informal players, such as squatters, the homeless, anarchists, lesbian and gay activists, defenders of the rights of immigrants and migrants, trade unionists, militant communities. These political subjects emerge from the condition of lack of power. But they gain a presence and power vis-a-vis each other'.

This is twenty-first-century class conflict: corporate capital versus fragments of protest. For, in Sassen's view, 'both seek a strategic domain for their power projects. Each actor is marked by incipient denationalisation, as their operations enter the global circuits'.

The Urban Futures conference was, in a very minor way, 'Seattled', though without the drenching rain that accompanied disruptive protest at the World Trade Organisation summit meeting seven months ago.

But the water balloon that no doubt takes pride of place as shrapnel on Muller's fireplace mantle still could one day detonate, soaking the rich and poor, right and left alike.

4. Muller's *Business Day* response came a month later (10 August 2000):

The columns of *Business Day* are not the place I would normally debate with Patrick Bond and Greg Ruiters. Unfortunately, it is perhaps necessary since, as they reported (Jo'burg gets Seattled, July 13), they walked out of the recent Urban Futures conference amid disruption and water bomb-throwing.

Ruiters used the platform to decry the current trend in the water sector to privatise and retrench workers, and extrapolated into a broader diatribe against government, reflected in the article. At the next event he and Bond attend, they should stay to engage in discussion so we can help them separate fact from fiction and address the real issues.

Academics should lead the intellectual debate rather than mislead the students, local government and labour cadres they seek to influence with a sloppy mix of lies, halftruths and shoddy, out-of-date research.

The fact is that there is no programme to privatise water supply. Rather, a decision was taken in 1997 that the use of the private sector for water service provision should be regulated within a structured framework, designed to ensure that all South Africans have access to water services. The use of private contractors for service provision has been going on for a long time, at local, provincial and national level.

There is also no proposal to retrench municipal water service workers. Johannesburg has promised no job losses.

Nor are there systematic programmes of water cuts, although we would hope to see, alongside free basic services to the poor, people with jobs and good services paying affordable charges for them.

If service cuts are required to achieve that, it is in the interest of the poor that they be properly applied.

There are obviously many issues that need to be addressed in the water services sector, some of which they highlight. The challenge is to manage our historically divided cities towards equity; and to ensure that democracy leads to empowerment, not disenfranchisement.

Within that, how best do we regulate service providers (public and private) to achieve a balance in favour of the poor, who do not have access to adequate services? This debate has been opened by government with the publication of draft regulations for comment that followed wide consultation on the underlying legislation.

If the provision of water and sanitation is to be at the heart of local government as historically it has been in many parts of the world we must systematically build the capacity of that local government. My department is helping to do this. Apart from capital programmes to provide basic infrastructure for the rural poor, we are supporting local government in planning and financing its services.

The broader challenge is as much about putting local government finances on a sound footing as it is about who provides services. Specifically, the challenge of making basic services affordable to all South Africans needs to be addressed.

So should we, as is proposed for the electricity industry, use a few regional water distributors rather than leaving the job to more than 200 local government administrations, the weakest of which will be responsible for serving the poorest communities with the greatest needs?

To do this job we need to engage in debates, to learn from the experience of others, preferably from their mistakes and from our own successes.

I witnessed ultraleft disruptions of Labour Party meetings in the UK in the 1970s. It was these (along with organised labour's defence of indefensible labour practices that took from the poor to give to the well-off) that helped Margaret Thatcher to power and contributed to the decimation of the public service sector that the ultraleft had claimed to be supporting.

Doing rather than talking obviously presents an awkward challenge, but our critics should remember the strategies of the leaders of apartheid who deliberately targeted technicians in Mozambique to destabilise that country. They knew that keeping services working was critical to the survival of progressive forces.

We know about that strategy in part because of the extremely effective 'action research' of my fellow 'suit', Roland Hunter, who spent time in prison for making available the military's damning documentation.

It would be nice to see similar commitment from Bond and Ruiters. They could usefully take a holiday in Mozambique, a much safer place now, and do some learning. Instead of talking about Buenos Aires and Paris, they could tell us about the approach of the Mozambican administration.

We could learn from their recent experience, which saw them dismiss the managers of newly privatised water services in Maputo for allegedly contributing to a cholera outbreak by failing to maintain services during the recent floods.

Conducting real research rather than recycling other peoples' internet reports will of course be more demanding and less fun than throwing water bombs. Similarly, participation in real debates will require some application. But engagement in the challenge of real world management with limited resources is a great educator. So there is an open invitation to Ruiters and Bond to join us in addressing the many real material problems that confront us. It could only help to make their critique and, with luck, their teaching, more effective.

They might even contribute to what I trust is a common goal of a better quality of life for our people. If they prefer to launch damp squibs and run away from debate, they can blame no one but themselves if they are dismissed as infantile leftists.

5.   Evans, R. (1987), *Death in Hamburg: Society and Politics in the Cholera Years*, 1830–1910, Harmondsworth, Penguin, p. 568

6.   Veotte, L. (2001), 'Restructuring, Human Rights and Water Access to Vulnerable Groups', South African Municipal Workers Union presentation to the International Conference on Fresh Water, Bonn, 7 December.

7.   Department of Health (1999), 'Health Sector Strategic Framework', 1999–2004, Pretoria.

8.   In KwaZulu-Natal, there were only 330 such officers in the civil service in 1999, a shortfall of 562; equivalent figures in the Eastern Cape were 228 officers, with a shortfall of 438. For more detail, see Stein, R. (2002), 'Environmental Rights: Government Turns on the Indicators', Unpublished paper, Wits University Law School.

9.   *Sunday Times*, 20 January 2002.

10.   *Business Day*, 10 August 2000.

11.   This point became a matter of fierce debate in *Sunday Independent Reconstruct* in early 1999. See Bond's 'Mozambican Parliament Questions Debt Management', 21 December 1998; rebuttal letters from the Bank's Mozambique officer Phyllis Pomerantz on 24 January 1999, and from Bond and Joe Hanlon on 7 February 1999.

12.   Department of Water Affairs and Forestry (1994), *Water Supply and Sanitation White Paper*, Cape Town, p. 2.

13.   PanAfrican News Agency, 6 February 1999.

14.   *Sunday Independent Reconstruct*, 20 December 1998.

15.   See the Municipal Services Project review of the survey, conducted with the HSRC, at http://www.queensu.ca/msp.

16.   Documentation is provided at http://southafrica.indymedia.org

17.   *Sunday Times*, 12 May 2002. The National Water Act gives the minister power to intervene in a water emergency; disconnection to a household would certainly qualify.

18.   Department of Water Affairs and Forestry (1994), *Water Supply and Sanitation White Paper*, Cape Town, p. 19.

19.   Ibid, p. 23.

20.   Ibid, p. 24.

21.   Ibid, p. 4.

22.   Asmal, K. (1996), 'Speech to the Launch of the 1995/6 Working for Water Programme Annual Report', Pretoria, 17 July, p. 1.

23.   Asmal, K. (1996), 'Speech to Cape Town Conservation workshop', Cape Town, p. 2.

24.   Department of Water Affairs and Forestry, *Water Supply and Sanitation White Paper*, p. 4.

25.   Asmal, K. (1998), 'Policy Directions of the Department of Water Affairs and Forestry', Letter to Patrick Bond, Pretoria, 8 May, p. 1. Indeed, Bond as a budget advisor in 1997 pointed out the many ways that such subsidies could be raised from Dwaf sources, including increasing an existing national programme that funded the water accounts of the old bantustan municipalities – which Asmal instead decided to phase out.

26.   Department of Water Affairs and Forestry, *Water Supply and Sanitation White Paper*, p. 19.

27.   Masia, S., J.Walker, N.Mkaza, I.Harmond, M.Walters, K.Gray and J.Doyen (1998), 'External BoTT Review', Joint report by the Department of Water Affairs and Forestry, World Bank, British Department for International Development and Unicef, Pretoria, November.

28.   Drakeford, M. (1998), 'Water Regulation and Pre-payment Meters', *Journal of Law and Society*, 25, 4.

29.   *Sunday Times*, 14 October 2001.

30.   Dwaf (1998), 'Compulsory National Standards Relating to the Provision of Water Services in Terms of Section 9(1)(a)', Memo CWS02161, Pretoria, 30 December, p. 2.

31.   E.g., interview, SABC tv show 'Newsmakers', 14 January 2001.

32.   The debate began with an article by Bond in *Business Day* (28 March 2001), at the point that the free water policy was being concluded, replete with all the sabotage techniques described in the previous chapter:

What kind of a commodity is water? With extreme scarcity predicted by 2020, should individuals and firms be reduced to buying and selling water on an open market?

The case for water trading, made by Roger Bate of the Institute of Economic Affairs in London in *Business Day* yesterday, is premised on accurate costing of water services from raindrop all the way to effluent treatment.

The water pricing policy adopted by the water affairs and forestry department in 1998, and the powers given the minister, Ronnie Kasrils, in the National Water Act, reflect the respect government shows for economic efficiency in water utilisation.

But a fatal flaw has emerged in government's strategy: systematically ignoring the benefits of water. Nor, surprisingly, does Bates bother to mention 'public goods' and 'merit goods' – disease abatement, gender equity, desegregation and economic multipliers – that flow from a nationally subsidised, administratively managed universal lifeline water supply.

From obscure KwaZulu–Natal rural councils to the Johannesburg offices of a consultancy firm that supplied Pretoria with its draft 'Free Basic Water Initiative' policy at a national workshop on Tuesday, the benefits of lifeline water are being ignored.

Residents of Ngwelezane, Empangeni, lost access to the free supply they had enjoyed since 1983. 'It was eventually noticed, and it was decided to switch off the supply', Uthungulu regional council CE B.B. Biyela told the media.

Thousands who could not afford the R51 connection fee were forced to the rivers, as Ngwelezane became the epicentre of a cholera outbreak that has infected nearly 80,000 people and killed at least 150.

The tens of thousands of rands that Biyela anticipated saving Uthungulu Council cost society, not just those sickened and killed, untold millions.

Questioned about the disaster on the SABC Newsmaker show in January, water affairs director-general Mike Muller conceded: 'Perhaps we were being a little too market-orientated'.

But after this understatement of the year, reports continued of municipal water cut offs due to inability to pay.

The prize-winning Western Cape municipality of Hermanus, once famous for water access and conservation, ditched its Working for Water commitments and began evictions and attachments of poor people's homes to offset their water arrears.

Johannesburg officials began cutting water services due to electricity account arrears, in a move experts say is constitutionally suspect.

Although he may be armed and dangerous with his Jik, shovel for pit latrines and selfhelp philosophy, Kasrils inexplicably refuses to fight antisocial bureaucrats, some of whom are brazen about their objectives.

The World Bank's *Sourcebook on Community Driven Development in the Africa Region* argued audaciously that 'work is still needed with political leaders in some national governments to move away from the concept of free water for all'.

The bank document appeared shortly after Kasrils first announced the free water policy in February 2000. Fourteen months later, a final policy has still not been produced.

Tellingly, the consultancy that authored the water affairs department's current draft has been the most effective lobbying force against free lifeline water.

Free lifeline water has been anathema to officials, consultants and suppliers. In 1994, government's first water white paper redefined a 'lifeline' tariff as covering operating and maintenance costs, which doomed hundreds of rural water schemes.

In a 1999 review the World Bank praised its own 1995 intervention in the water pricing debate as 'instrumental in facilitating a revision in SA's approach to bulk water management'.

The damage went even deeper, to the retail level, where the bank advised Pretoria that privatisation 'would be much harder to establish' if poor consumers had the expectation of a subsidised water supply, and hence that Pretoria needed a 'credible threat of cutting service'.

Together, the market-orientated cost-recovery philosophy and bureaucrats unable to shift from inhumane apartheid-era practices are sabotaging the politicians.

'ANC-led local government', the ruling party's manifesto for the December 2000 municipal elections promised, 'will provide all residents with a free basic amount of water, electricity and other municipal services, so as to help the poor. Those who use more than the basic amounts will pay for the extra they use'.

Such a cross-subsidy is sensible, and was endorsed by *Business Day* and copied by even Democratic Alliance politicians like Peter Marais.

But the devils in the detail have poked their horns up through the draft policy: 'the view of government is that municipalities should keep tariffs to commercial and industrial consumers as cost reflective as possible (no cross subsidies)'.

Muller has also insisted that no additional national subsidy funds are available to make good on the water promise, though conspicuously absent from the draft policy is any mention of the need to tax the abuse of water by commercial agriculture.

In addition to revising the inadequate new policy, Kasrils has the other urgent duty of halting the ongoing spread of cholera, using defence force tanker supplies to those with no access.

But maybe he misplaced Defence Force's orders for trucks in his haste to buy corvettes.

Maybe dragging a trailer loaded with water drums would be better use for a DaimlerBenz 4x4 than occupying Tony Yengeni's garage.

And maybe the poor will one day get the promised free water.

33. Muller replied as follows (*Business Day*, 9 April 2001):

Patrick Bond's vigilance (March 28) in the water sector is appreciated, although we would prefer a more structured debate to keep the facts straight.

First, of course government is aware of the benefits of providing basic water services. This is why more than R1.6bn of this department's budget is allocated to the purpose annually.

Second, we have never said that there is no additional money to make good on the water promise. However, no case for new money can be made until it is clear that existing funds are being properly used.

Finally, our 'demand-led' sanitation policy supports households and communities which request help to improve their sanitation. The cholera in KwaZulu Natal has forced us to reappraise (our current) approach.

– Mike Muller, Director-General Water Affairs and Forestry

34. Bond countered (*Business Day*, 10 April 2001):

Water director-general Mike Muller (*Business Day*, April 9) calls for a more structured debate about the various water disasters still unfolding. Right, then – many observers want to know why these simple steps cannot be taken by government:
- Deliver emergency supplies to all who are now without access, even by water tanker and trucks, especially in the cholera belt;
- Urgently calculate the benefits of better public health, ecological sustainability and gender equity, to justify dramatic new water-system maintenance subsidies;
- Likewise, raise minimum sanitation standards from current inadequate pit-latrine levels (which are responsible for E.Coli found last month in even Sandton's water table);

- Do not stand idly by while water is cut off to low-income people by heartless bureaucrats: implement long-delayed regulations under the 1997 Water Services Act that impose not just minimal standards – 50 litres a person a day was the medium-term reconstruction and development programme promise – but that gives your minister power to sort out municipalities behaving unconstitutionally (ranging from cholera epicentre Ngwelezane to Hermanus to Johannesburg);
- Immediately impose charges on hedonistic users of raw water (commercial farmers, mines and corporations), as allowed in the National Water Act of 1998, so as to make up for subsidy shortfalls when the treasury yet again underfunds smaller municipalities unable to cross-subsidise for free lifeline services;
- Follow local and international nongovernmental organisations' advice, in the wake of the World Commission on Dams study, by imposing a moratorium on construction of the exorbitant Lesotho dams, and delay the phase two dam (by decades) until adequate demand-side management measures are adopted.
- Prohibit the 'cherry-picking' that is a universal problem in water privatisation and commercialisation, including Eastern Cape pilots; and
- Redraft the free basic water policy to remove all ambiguity and redistribute more decisively, so as to finally reverse SA's worsening water apartheid.

Without radical changes, the Rio+10 World Summit on sustainable development in Sandton next September will be a showcase only for SA's shame, for Johannesburg's 'E.Coli 2002' water commercialisation, and for more unnecessary cholera deaths next door in Alexandra.

– Patrick Bond, Wits University

35. Muller's next full press release, partially published in *Business Day*, is as follows:

I am glad that Patrick Bond has taken up the call to structure the debate about water issues but his reply highlights the problem about the debate rather than taking us towards a solution. Rather than taking the systematic approach I have proposed, he continues haphazardly to string together different issues to support his unwavering view that somehow, government is doing things wrong.

Thus, his first point is a good development management question, why do we not truck water to the seven million who currently do not have access to basic services? The answer is that, even if there were roads to the communities in need, trucking 25 litres per person per day costs on average perhaps 30 times more than supplying water through pipes. It is in the public interest to sue money as effectively as possible by providing basic infrastructure whose operational costs will be financially sustainable. This is also what most communities say they want.

But he does not follow up on the issue. Instead he jumps to resource and welfare economics. Why do we not calculate the ecological, public health and gender benefits of water supply to reinforce our budget requests? Such exercises have often been done and will doubtless keep economists busy for years but their calculations are open to endless challenge. Is there really any doubt about the need for services?

Professor Bond then turns to a Constitutional issue. Why, he asks, are we not doing more to control water cut offs to poor households who do not pay. Well, what are we doing? The establishment of effective local government depends on achieving financial responsibility on the part of consumers as well as fair and ethical approaches by municipalities. An appropriate culture is emerging, as evidenced by recent court decisions in the Grootboom case in the Western Cape and the important decision in Durban which said, incidentally, that Government's intentions were both clear and Constitutional. However, simply passing regulations cannot force local or central governments to spend money they do not have. Professor Bond should read the judgements and encourage a more systematic and coherent approach to local government's credit control methods.

Then we turn to hard economics and public finance. Is Professor Bond really teaching his students that agriculture and industry are 'hedonistic' activities whose water use should be taxed to pay for domestic water services in other communities? There is a system of local government finance being developed and, if he does not like it, he should challenge it rather than bringing in these whacky distractions.

Next, we are on water resource management issues. Bond implies that the World Commission on Dams has proposed a moratorium on dam building. By now, we are getting so dizzy that we could miss the fact that calls for a moratorium are coming only from the NGO critics whose opposition to dams was the reason for the establishment of the Commission in the first place; such proposals do not reflect the Commission's Guidelines which the critics are apparently now disregarding. The real issue which Bond wants to talk about though is not dam construction but the management of water demand; he misses the fact that you cannot have management demand until you have good management of the overall water supply system. This is why we are working actively to develop local government's management capacity. It is also why we are concerned that Professor Bond's students may emerge with many bright ideas but without the practical skills needed to run such organisations.

Finally, moving to issues of pollution control, Professor Bond, a political scientist, makes great play of the fact that Johannesburg is often polluted by the E.Coli organism. This is hardly surprising since E.Coli is used as an indicator of human presence in the environment – as a political scientist, Professor Bond could be forgiven for being unaware that he himself is host to a vast seething mass of billions of E.Coli organisms. This is why human use of untreated groundwater is discouraged in built-up areas. So clever statements such as Johannesburg being E.Coli 2002 are simply silly – and largely meaningless – sloganeering.

I could go on further in this vein but hope that the point has been made. There is a vital role for academics and intellectuals in our policy debates. Whether in development management, welfare and resource economics, public finance, constitutional law and water resource management, there are many substantial issues which South Africans have to address.

Inter-disciplinary work has always been a challenge for universities seeking to be relevant to the real world and we would encourage the promotion of broad-based approaches. This will only succeed if there is the necessary intellectual rigour. The difficulty is however demonstrated by Professor Bond's random walk across the disciplines which, rather than take us forward, just leads into a bog of confusion. Perhaps we should take one step at a time, one discipline at a time. If Professor Bond is really concerned about the financial system for providing the basic water needs of the poor, he should perhaps start with a systematic understanding of the public finance and management issues and move forward from there. We will demand no less of his students and the University and broader society should demand no less from him and his unit.

– Mike Muller, Director-General, Department of Water Affairs and Forestry

Muller, M. (2001), 'Media Release: Reply to Bond', Pretoria, 18 April, pp. 1–2.

36. Mara, I. (2001), 'Between Diarrhoeal Diseases and HIV/Aids Debates in South Africa', Group for Environmental Monitoring, Johannesburg.

37. *Financial Mail*, 25 May 2001.

38. World Bank (1999), *Country Assistance Strategy: South Africa*, Washington DC, Annex C, p. 5.

39. World Bank (1996), *African Water Resources*, Technical Paper 331, Washington, DC, p. ix.

40. Gleik, P. (2001), 'Water and Conflict', http://www.thewaterpage.com/conflict.htm

41. Smith, R. (1999) 'Africa's Potential Water Wars', BBC News: UK http://news6.thdo.bbc.co.uk/hi/en °d/africa/newsid_454000/454926.stm

42. Swedish International Development Agency (1997), 'Environmental Security and Water Management in Southern Africa', Stockholm, pp. 11-13.

43. See, e.g., http://www.challengeglobalization.org and Grusky, S. (2001), 'IMF makes Water Privatisation Condition of Financial Support', PSIRU update, http://www.psiru.org

44. Hennig, R. (2001), 'IMF forces African Countries to Privatise Water', 8 February (http://www.afrol.com).

45. Soderstrom, E. (1998), 'Survey of Donor Involvement in the Water Sector in the SADC Region', USAID, Gabarone, Botswana (cited on Africa Water Page).

46. In 2001, the Bank had numerous ongoing SADC water projects underway. In Angola, Bank projects include urban water supply and sanitation, Luanda Water Supply project. The main Lesotho projects are the Highlands Water Project, Phase 1B and Water Sector Reform. The main Malawi project is National Water Development. Mauritius has a Bank Environmental Sewerage and Sanitation project. Mozambique has a National Water I and National Water II. The Bank promoted the Aguas de Mocambique 15-year lease contract for Maputo and four identical five-year management contracts for four other cities. Companies benefiting include Saur International (France), IPE-Aguas de Portugal (Portugal) and Mazi-Mozambique (Mozambican). In Namibia, the Bank is involved in bulk water commercialisation through Namibia Water Corporation (NamWater). In South Africa, private water contracts – pushed by the Bank originally in 1994 – include Johannesburg's Igoli 2002 and privatisation in three other towns (Queenstown, Fort Beaufort and Stutterheim), as well as Dolphin Coast and Nelspruit. The main companies are Suez, Northumbrian, Saur, Biwater/Nuon and Vivendi. In Tanzania, the Bank promoted privatisation through the Dar es Salaam Water Supply and Sanitation Project, and a rural water supply and sanitation project. In Zambia, the Bank promotes the Urban Restructuring and Water Project (including Lusaka Water and Sewerage Company) and the Mine Township Services project.

47. Yirga-Hall, G. (2001), 'Experiences and Challenges of Financing Water Systems in Africa', in *Volume II, Papers & Presentations, Reform of the Water Supply & Sanitation Sector in Africa Conference*, www.wsp.org, African Development Bank.

48. See Bond, P. (1998), 'Privatisation, Participation and Protest in South African Municipal Services: The Basis for Opposition to World Bank Promotion of Public-Private Partnerships', *Urban Forum*, 9, 1.

49. The Kampala Statement was drafted at the World Bank and issued in mid-March. It attempted to speak for 'a total of 270 participants drawn from government, the utilities (including the private sector), financial institutions, external support agencies, and civil society ...' All quotations below are from the final E-mail version sent from the Bank on 14 March, 2001.

50. These have often been cited in the 30% range, payable in hard currency (i.e., if the local currency falls, then the profit rate is even higher). According to the African Development Bank (ADB), the South Africa Infrastructure Fund projection for before-tax Internal Rate of Returns of 26-27% 'during SAIF's 15-year life in constant US dollar terms' assumes that '10% of all investments will fail; 50% of all investments will generate an IRR of 30%; and 40% of all investments will generate an IRR of 35%'. To earn such high rates of return on infrastructure investments that are often long-term in nature (often 40 years before full social and economic returns on investment are realised), and on top of that to compress the high earnings into the

early stages of investment (on average 7.5 years, given that the SAIF will shut down after 15 years), and to do so using a wide range of social infrastructure investments, implies an extremely high cost–recovery burden for direct infrastructure recipients, or dramatic cost reductions at the level of the enterprise. See African Development Bank (1997), 'Investment Proposal: South Africa Infrastructure Investment Fund', ADB Private Sector Unit, Abidjan, p. 13, Annex 6.

51. The Statement argues, on the contrary, that multilateral and bilateral agencies 'are keen to support' privatisation, and that 'In view of the limited budgetary resources in most African countries, external financing should be available to cover the operational deficit resulting from the lag between improved service and increased revenue during the initial years of PPP'. No mention is made of the lack of hard-currency revenue that comes from selling water services to low-income people, despite the need to repay the multilateral and bilateral financiers in hard currency.

52. The Statement's only concession along these lines is that 'Where price increases to cover costs and improve service are planned, these should be gradual and should follow service improvements to maintain public support'.

53. It is well known that there are public and merit good effects from provision of water and sanitation to the homes of low-income people. Instead of making a strong case for lifeline water provision, tellingly, the Kampala Statement offers only extremely shallow rhetoric on this point: 'While the role of the private sector should increase in most cases, the public aspects of water and sanitation services should not be compromised. The creation of an independent regulator and corresponding legislation before any major transfer of operational activity to the private sector can help to ensure the priority of the public interest through increased fairness, transparency, accountability and better monitoring of contract performance'.

54. World Bank (2000), *Sourcebook on Community Driven Development in the Africa Region: Community Action Programs*, Africa Region, Washington, DC, 17 March (signatories: Calisto Madavo, Jean-Louis Sarbib), Annex 2.

55. World Bank, *Sourcebook on Community Driven Development in the Africa Region*, Annex 2.

56. World Bank, *Sourcebook on Community Driven Development in the Africa Region*, Annex 2.

57. Republic of South Africa (1996), *The Constitution of the Republic of South Africa*, Act 108 of 1996, Cape Town, Chapter Three.

58. Fuggle, R.F. and M.A. Rabie (Eds)(1992), *Environmental Management in South Africa*, Cape Town, Juta.

59. Republic of South Africa (1998), *National Environmental Management Act* 107 of 1998, Cape Town, s.3.2, 2.3.

60. Ibid, s.1.29.

61. Republic of South Africa, *The Constitution of the Republic of South Africa*, s.24.b.

62. Republic of South Africa, *National Environmental Management Act*, s.2.4.a.

63. Ibid, s.2.4.c.

64. Ibid, s.1.11.

65. Ibid, s.29.

66. Ibid, s.30.

67. Ibid, s.30.2.

68. Ibid, s.28.1.

69. Ibid, s.28.2.

70. Republic of South Africa, *The Constitution of the Republic of South Africa*, s.38.

71. Republic of South Africa, *National Environmental Management Act*, s.32.

72. Republic of South Africa, *The Constitution of the Republic of South Africa*, s.44.2.

73. Ibid, Chapter Five.

74. Ibid, Chapter Eight.

75. Republic of South Africa, *National Environmental Management Act*, s.35.2.

76. Republic of South Africa (1998), *National Water Act* 36 of 1998, Cape Town, s.2.

77. Republic of South Africa, *The Constitution of the Republic of South Africa*, s.27.

78. Republic of South Africa, *National Water Act*, s.56.

79. Ibid, Chapter Eight.

80. Ibid, s.3.

81. Ibid, s.3.2.

82. Ibid, s.21.

83. Ibid, s.32.

84. Ibid, s.43-48.

85. Ibid, s.22.6.

86. Veotte, 'Restructuring, Human Rights and Water Access to Vulnerable Groups'.

87. Thompson, G. (1996), 'Ofwat and Water Privatisation', in D.Braddon and D.Foster (Eds), *Privatization: Social Science Themes,* Dartmouth, Aldershot, p. 184.

88. The seminal work is Wittfogel, K. (1957), *Oriental Despotism: A Comparative Study of Total Power*, New Haven, Yale University Press.

89. Gramsci, A. (1971)[1948], *The Prison Notebooks,* New York, International Publishers, pp. 304-306.

90. *Business Day*, 11 February 2000.

91. *Sunday Times*, 5 May 2002.

CHAPTER SIX

Power to the powerful:

Energy, electricity, equity, and environment

With Maj Fiil-Flynn and Stephen Greenberg[1]

1. Introduction

The brutal official practice of municipal services disconnections was in full swing yet again in March 2002, and resistance was not long in coming. This time the city was Cape Town, and hundreds of angry working-class and poor people disrupted downtown traffic, marching from the Keisersgracht down Darling Street, into Adderley Street to the Cape Town Unicity offices. Bold placards proclaimed, 'Water is a basic human right' and protesters accused the elected officials of comprising an 'apartheid council'.[2]

The memo delivered to the DA rulers of Cape Town was more explicit:

> We are citizens of Cape Town and people who live in areas which do not receive free basic services of water and electricity. Because we do not have water meters, we do not get the six kilolitres free basic water. Because we get our electricity from Eskom we do not get our 20 kWh of free basic electricity.
>
> We are the poor people of this city who need these free basic services the most. We are suffering every day because we do not receive free water or electricity. Every day we face the threat of being thrown out of our houses and our services being cut.

In response, Cape Town mayoral spokesperson Kylie Dawn Hatton insisted that the quarter of Cape Town residents who were most disadvantaged get their electricity not from the municipality but from Eskom:

> The city, when it implemented its free basic electricity policy, attempted to negotiate with Eskom that it would do the same. The response we got from Eskom was that they would not do this until a national policy on free electricity had been put in place. So the city can't move any further on that particular matter.

And indeed, one had to sympathise at least a tiny bit with both sides here. The city bureaucracy *was* foiled by Eskom's refusal to make good on the DA's promise of free electricity – although unsympathetically, mayor Gerald Morkel was so busy wining and dining German criminals, apparently doing favours for cash donations to the DA, that he neglected to intervene when low-income African and coloured constituents were tossed out of their council houses, or lost their water and electricity because of poverty.

If one sought to cynically justify Morkel's refusal to see the protesters, perhaps a label easily attaches to those demanding their rights in Cape Town: 'a criminal gang'. That was the description chosen by Jeff Radebe, the ANC minister of public enterprises, at a December 2001 press conference. Widespread defiance by Sowetan activists was on Radebe's mind at the time.[3] But he could just as well have been referring to another gang whose story was told at the outset of this book's Introduction: the 300 Western Cape Anti-Eviction Campaign activists who sat in at the office of Nomatyala Hangana, ANC provincial minister of housing, on 26 June 2002 – until 44 were dragged out and arrested. That gang's timing coincided with President Mbeki's trip to Calgary in search of a new partnership with the G8.

What might have deterred Radebe in the case of the anti-DA demonstration a few months earlier, was an embarrassing sign that political grievances and rhetoric are increasingly universalised at grassroots level. For the leader of the protest was none other than the ANC's Cape Town regional secretary, Max Ozinsky. The ANC took flak from *Business Day* for hypocrisy: i.e., laying blame on Cape Town's mayor for what was, in part, actually Radebe's fault. 'Some acts of political expediency are so breathtaking that they make any defence of politics well nigh impossible ... The government-controlled Eskom has resisted DA efforts to bring those customers into the fold. Again, a blush would be more appropriate than a march'.[4]

After considering the history and transition periods associated with the energy industry (Section 2), we explore the power relations and discourses emerging from the struggle over retail electricity in Soweto (Section 3). We can then reflect upon the specifically environmental implications of South Africa's filthy electricity sector (Section 4) before concluding with a review of the vigorous public policy debates that unfolded in 2001–02 (Section 5). These issues prepare us thoroughly for the final chapter, which takes up environment and development at the world scale, through the lens of the South African activist community.

2. Eskom power and the minerals–energy complex

South Africa's largest parastatal firm, the Electricity Supply Commission, still known by its Afrikaans acronym, Eskom, has had mixed fortunes in recent years, not least under the combined direction of minister Phumzile Mlambo-Ngcuka's Department of Minerals and Energy (DME) and Radebe's Office of Public Enterprises. Some of the problems relate to its triple role, as a) generator of virtually all of the country's electricity; b) sole transmitter; and c) distributor to many large corporations, municipalities, commercial farms, and to half South Africa's households, from sections of the largest municipalities to most rural villages. Other problems were prefigured by a history closely intertwined with apartheid oppression, and never quite untangled by Radebe's and Mlambo-Ngcuka's post-apartheid predecessors: Stella Sigcau at public enterprises (until 1999) and minerals and energy ministers Pik Botha of the old National Party (until 1996) and Penuell Maduna (1996–99).

Nor did Eskom genuinely 'transform', as we'll see: it took on new leaders like chairperson Ruell Khoza and chief executive Thulani Gcabashe, who, preparing for privatisation, began to wind down the slightly progressive efforts at township and rural electrification begun in earnest by Old Guard executive Ian McRae and his successor Alan Morgan during the 1990s. The neoliberal reversal was in stark contrast to the ambitious period of the early 1920s, when the Electricity Act established Eskom to fix an industry that the private sector couldn't run properly on its own.

Until the 1920s, electricity supply was a function of local authorities and private companies, and there was limited regulation. However, as demand grew, supply became fragmented between many suppliers each with their own tariffs and standards. The 1922 consolidation of the industry included an Electricity Control Board to regulate Eskom. Until 1948, Eskom operated in parallel with private companies and municipalities, remaining in a subordinate position in relation to the privately-owned Victoria Falls and Transvaal Power Company which served the lucrative mining contracts. The right of local government to build or extend power stations was subject to approval by Provincial Administrators, although this was usually easily granted. Most of the larger municipalities therefore constructed and operated their own power stations before 1962. Since then, expansion of their electricity capacity has come through buying bulk electricity from Eskom.

The relationship between mining and electricity was symbiotic, which helps explain many of the irrational characteristics of the contemporary energy industry. Coal mining is responsible for 80% of the country's primary energy needs, and exported coal accounts for a fifth of South African exports. After Australia, South Africa is the world's leading exporter.

At the same time, electricity is used to power the gold mines and heavy industry, and to beneficiate metallic and mineral products. An outstanding book, *The Political Economy of South Africa* by Ben Fine and Zav Rustomjee, puts the parastatal into economic perspective.[5] Here we locate electricity at the heart of the economy's Minerals-Energy Complex, a 'system of accumulation' unique to this country. Throughout the twentieth century, mining, petro-chemicals, metals and related activities which historically accounted for around a quarter of GDP typically consumed 40% of all electricity.

Eskom was centrally responsible for South Africa's rapid capital accumulation during the past century. At the same time, Fine and Rustomjee show, the company fostered a debilitating dependence on the (declining) mining industry. Economists refer to this as a 'Dutch disease', in memory of the damage done to Holland's economic balance by its cheap North Sea oil. Moreover, Eskom as the monopoly electricity supplier played a role in strengthening private mining capital by purchasing low-grade coal from mines that were tied to particular power stations on the basis of a guaranteed profit. This was one of the ways in which state capital fused with private capital under apartheid. In short, Eskom both provided a market to private mining houses, and a cheap supply of electricity to heavy industry and the mines.

But the damage and skews went far deeper, into the social and environmental realms. After World War Two, growing demand from new mines and manufacturing caused supply shortages, and resulted in a programme for the construction of new power stations. In the process, the apartheid state promoted Afrikaner-owned coal mines, with Eskom contracting these for a portion of its coal supply. The national grid – the linking of previously fragmented power station supplies via transmission lines – was initially formed in 1964, and extended supply into the Southern African region.

Eskom had become 'an integral part of the apartheid system, thereby constituting a threat to peace, not only for the region of Southern Africa, but also to the whole world', according to Gottfried Wellmer:

Because of its strategic importance, Eskom, its power stations, sub-stations and control centres were declared national key points in 1980 and therefore had to liaise with the security forces; all senior security officers and senior personnel at key points had to obtain security clearance. Because blacks failed to get the necessary security clearance, they were not eligible for appointment in senior positions.

Eskom established its own Counter Intelligence Unit, which closely worked with the security police and military intelligence. Key point guards were armed. Eskom created its own militia force and procured a substantial number of firearms and established its own armoury as well.

Evidence was presented under oath to the Truth and Reconciliation Commission that during the twilight years of the apartheid system, high ranking members of Eskom attempted to make available or sell a portion of its armoury to a political party engaged in a civil war against alleged ANC supporters. According to the evidence, this was authorised and done with the knowledge of the commissioner of police.

The Eskom deal formed only a small part of a wider practice of covert shipment of arms by state operatives to groups engaged in violent activities against opponents of the government, fuelling the civil war in South Africa up until shortly before the first democratic elections in 1994. In its statement to the TRC, Eskom management insisted that it was not aware of any facts which would support such allegations.[6]

Not only formal apartheid, but apartheid-capitalism itself was strengthened by Eskom. By the 1970s, the historical disjuncture between Afrikaans and English capital had more or less faded, in part because the Oppenheimer family's Anglo American Corporation gave up one of its mining companies, Gencor, to Afrikaner buyers so as to curry favour with Pretoria. Eskom contracts with coal mines allowed the state to consolidate and modernise the coal industry. The growing economic crisis, starting in the 1970s and worsening in the 1980s, led Pretoria not only to import-substitution and a protective energy laager that included an inefficient oil-from-coal scheme. The state also adopted a more aggressively export-oriented approach that favoured large-scale corporate activity, particularly in the mineral and energy sectors.

Until 1971, Eskom was not permitted to earn a profit, so prices were set with the purpose of covering costs and no more. As a result, Eskom did not have to pay taxes. An amendment to the Electricity Act in 1972 allowed

Eskom to generate capital for development purposes from surpluses on sales. Thanks to an expanded investment programme, Eskom became responsible for up to 15% of South Africa's foreign debt by the 1980s.

Until 1985, when sanctions made foreign borrowing more difficult, foreign loans were used to build Eskom's massive excess capacity through environmentally damaging coal-fired power stations. At peak in 1990, Eskom produced three-quarters of the African continent's electricity, and its 34,000 MW capacity was being extended to 43,000 MW with another 5,000 MW available in Tugela hydropower – at a time that the highest demand on record was just 21,800 MW.[7]

Eskom's power plants continued providing artificially cheap electricity to large, energy-intensive corporations and white households, including a new wave of subsidised white commercial farmers during the 1980s. Since the loans were guaranteed by the state it meant that all taxpayers, regardless of whether they benefited from the expansion of infrastructure or not, paid the bill.[8] The World Bank's generous $100 million in Eskom loans from 1951–67, and subsequent bond purchases by international banks, are coming under more scrutiny as victims of apartheid seek reparations in US and European courts for the Eskom interest and profits the banks earned, while black South Africans suffered.

By the mid-1980s, not even isolated South Africa was immune from international neoliberal trends. The 1986 *White Paper on Energy Policy* set the framework for the marketisation of the electricity sector. It called for the 'highest measure of freedom for the operation of market forces', the involvement of the private sector, a shift to a market-oriented system with a minimum of state control and involvement, and a rational deregulation in energy pricing, marketing and production.[9] In 1987 the government released a *White Paper on Privatisation and Deregulation*, which defined privatisation as 'a systematic transfer of appropriate functions, activities or property from the public sector where services, production and consumption can be regulated more efficiently by the market than price mechanisms'.[10]

As electricity provision became increasingly politicised during the 1980s, in part because of township payment boycotts, a joint National Energy Council/Eskom workshop held in 1990 called for deregulation of the supply industry. It also put forward proposals to adopt a market-oriented approach to distribution, including large, restructured distributors that would purchase power from a broker. The workshop also recommended the introduction of specific tariffs between generation and transmission, and between transmission and distribution functions (the seeds of ring-fencing). Notably, it called for supply to be run on business lines – all of which were carried forward in coming post-apartheid policies.[11]

The sorts of surreal energy problems South Africa faces in the twenty-first century reflect the kinds of predictable contradictions during a transition from apartheid economic history to a contemporary electricity pricing system all too often based on neoliberal market-policy for households, complicated by massive subsidies for big corporations, in one of the world's most unequal societies. There are at least three world-class development disasters here:

- the economy's skewed over-reliance on, and oversupply of, pollution-causing, coal-generated electricity (a topic we introduced at Coega in Chapter Two and take up again in Section 4);
- the lack of equitable access amongst households along class/race lines, with serious adverse gender and environmental implications; and
- periodic township protest associated with power cuts resulting from nonpayment.

We turn next to the last two problems, because we may come to see that social protest solves both the (pro-corporate) overproduction and (anti-black/worker/women/ecology) underconsumption dilemmas.

Black power at last

It is striking that by the time of South Africa's liberation, because of heavy mining and industrial usage, per capita electricity consumption soared to a level similar to Britain, even though black – African – South Africans were denied domestic electricity for decades. In accomplishing this feat, Eskom generated emissions of greenhouse gasses twice as high per capita as the rest of the world, alongside enormous surface water pollution, bucketing acid rain and dreadfully low safety and health standards for coal miners.

To what end? Today, most poor South Africans still rely for a large part of their lighting, cooking and heating energy needs upon paraffin (with its burn-related health risks), coal (with high levels of domestic and township-wide air pollution) and wood (with dire consequences for deforestation). Women, traditionally responsible for managing the home, are more affected by the high cost of electricity and spend greater time and energy searching for alternative energy. Ecologically-sensitive energy sources, such as solar, wind and tidal, have barely begun to be explored, while the main hydropower plant that supplies South Africa from neighbouring Mozambique is based on a controversial large dam that, experts argue, does more harm than developmental good.

Some of the township electricity problems stem directly from South Africa's racist, irrational history. Conventional wisdom even before 1948 was that 'temporary sojourners' came to cities merely to work: they would not consume much electricity – certainly not formal household appliances – since their wages were pitiably low. Finally, the electrification of Soweto began in 1979, as a pilot aimed at quelling the political volatility following the 1976 uprising, with the support of General Electric and appliance distributors who saw a huge untapped market. In the impoverished bantustan areas, electricity divisions were also established, but Eskom took over the distribution of electricity in some during the late 1980s because of their inability to maintain and administer the network. One of the first privatisation pilots was carried out in Kwanobuhle township outside Uitenhage in the Eastern Cape in the late 1980s.[12]

The politicisation of electricity was an issue from the outset. In Soweto, the 1986 rent boycott was triggered by the attempt by the hated Black Local Authorities – the local councils seen as Pretoria's black puppets – to recoup the capital costs of electrification by imposing an electricity levy on residents. Electricity charges quickly amounted to 60–70% of the total services bill to residents, and rents were also raised in a failed attempt to generate additional revenue. Across South Africa, the boycott was broader than just a rent boycott, and reflected grievances over poor services.[13] Although 95% of Soweto's formal dwellings received electricity by 1986, maladministration and poor maintenance meant the reticulation system was already crumbling by 1987. In 1988, meter reading effectively ended, and non-payment was partially based on people questioning the accuracy of the bills they were receiving.

Residents were organised into civic associations.[14] Although many were banned during Pretoria's mid-1980s States of Emergency, a Soweto People's Delegation (SPD) of community leaders formed in 1989 to communicate grievances to the government. SPD demands included write-off of arrears, upgrading of services, and affordable service charges.[15] Throughout this period, there was a dual system of electricity supply between Johannesburg and Soweto, with electricity being purchased separately by each. But Soweto's electricity cost its consumers 39% more, mainly because of industry's location in the white sections of the metropolitan area and hence Johannesburg's greater capacity to buy bulk from Eskom.[16]

The Greater Soweto Accord was signed in 1990 between the SPD, Pretoria's Transvaal Provincial Administration and the three Soweto councils. There was an agreement to write off electricity arrears in exchange for resumption of payment of an 'interim service charge' to prevent cut offs, with the implication that those who did not pay the interim charge would 'legitimately' be cut off. State funds were diverted from capital development projects to run the inevitable deficit on operating costs.[17]

Across South Africa, under similar political circumstances, progress electrifying black residential areas was slow. By 1992, more than 90% of households were electrified in just 6% of African townships. In only 20% of townships were more than half of the houses supplied with electricity. In contrast, less than 10% of houses were electrified in 52% of townships.[18] The situation in rural areas was far worse, with only 15% of farmworker households, 4% of households in rural dense settlements, and 1% of households in rural scattered settlements having access to electricity in 1992.[19] Meanwhile, corporate South Africa suffered the opposite problem – an embarrassment of energy riches – especially when terribly poor planning at Eskom two decades ago led to the massive overcapacity.

Eskom had proceeded with the construction of new generating capacity because it feared that financing by external sources would be unavailable if there was a delay, as a result of looming sanctions.[20] Eskom found itself caught between rising loan payments to apartheid's foreign bankers (as interest rates rose from the early 1980s) and escalating operating costs, in particular for coal, which saw a rapid increase in prices as a result of the global energy crisis in the 1970s. The crash of the gold price from 1981 didn't help the demand side. In order to recover costs, Eskom started increasing tariffs above the rate of inflation, which caused growing opposition from consumers. Mines and industry argued that price increases were undermining competitiveness precisely at the time the state was encouraging expansion into global markets.

The late-apartheid solution, inherited and amplified today, was to give the largest corporations and high-volume household consumers ever cheaper power, and penalise the poor with extremely expensive prepaid meter systems. The meagre electricity consumed by low-income households (less than 3% of the total) costs them at least four times – and often seven times – more per kiloWatt hour than is paid for electricity by well-connected corporates. Was it a coincidence, one might reasonably enquire, that during the transition, Eskom's finance officer, Mick Davis, revolved out the door to head a major division of Gencor–Billiton, and then won the same cheap pricing deal for the ill-fated Coega zinc smelter that he'd earlier given Alusaf?

Defenders of the big corporates argued, correctly, that they helped mop up the excess capacity and could do so at off-peak hours, and also that low-volume consumers, especially in townships, generate much larger administrative costs per unit. As a result, policy avoided the kinds of cross-subsidies – by which big users pay more per unit than those consuming a bare minimum – that the 1994 Reconstruction and Development Programme (RDP) mandated. Even a single kiloWatt hour free per day as a lifeline to each person could have a dramatic effect on consumption for those who need it, while higher prices would potentially teach big users to conserve. But far stronger continuities from apartheid to post-apartheid emerged through the neoliberal pricing principles and consequent policy of mass disconnections, thus preventing the widespread redistribution required to make Eskom's mass electrification genuinely sustainable.

Power cuts for the powerless

Today, Eskom proudly claims to be one of the New South Africa's success stories, having provided electricity to more than 300,000 households each year during the 1990s. Black residents were denied Eskom's services until the early 1980s due to apartheid, and even the 1950s–60s loans granted by the International Bank for Reconstruction and Development – a.k.a. the World Bank – failed to reconstruct and develop any black neighborhoods. The townships were, as a result, perpetually filthy because of coal and wood soot.

It was the very lack of electrified households during the early 1990s that accounted for Eskom's success. By the end of 2001, Eskom and the municipalities had together made nearly four million household connections, including farmworkers, at a cost to Eskom of R7.72 billion.[21] The percentage of households with access to electricity infrastructure increased to 70% at the end of 2000. In urban areas, the percentage of households with electricity infrastructure was 84%, with rural areas lagging behind at 50%.[22]

In spite of the roll-out of two million electricity connections, Eskom has continued to be a target of dissent. As discussed further below, Eskom receives sustained criticism from environmentalists who complain that coal-burning plants lack sufficient sulphur scrubbing equipment and that alternative renewable energy investments, especially in solar and wind power, have been negligible.

Workers are also concerned. Having fired more than 40,000 of its 85,000 employees during the early 1990s, thanks to mechanisation and overcapacity, the utility tried to outsource and corporatise several key operations in recent years. The metalworkers and mineworkers unions were told in 2000 that while electricity generation facilities would be privatised so as to open up new competition, Eskom's transmission and distribution would remain state-owned.[23] In 2001, Radebe announced a future 30% stake in Eskom's generation capacity would be sold to a private investor, with 10% to be held for black empowerment investment. Unions worry that further commercialisation will kill yet more employment, in an economy that has lost around a million formal sector jobs since the early 1990s.

Regulation of Eskom and the municipal distributors has not been successful, from the standpoint of mass electricity needs.[24] This is partly because government policy has increasingly imposed 'cost-reflective tariffs', as a 1995 document insisted. The 1998 *White Paper* is an improvement on previous versions, allowing for 'moderately subsidised tariffs' for poor domestic consumers. But it too makes the counterproductive argument that 'Cross-subsidies should have minimal impact on the price of electricity to consumers in the productive sectors of the economy'.[25] (After all, who is to define the term 'productive' here? Would lawyers or stockbrokers then qualify for minimal pricing impact?)

Worse, as discussed in Chapter Four, the Department of Provincial and Local Government's *Municipal Infrastructure Investment Framework* supports only the installation of 5–8 Amp connections for households with less than R800 per month income, which does not offer enough power to turn on a hotplate or a single-element heater. (In turn, without a higher Ampage, the health and environmental benefits that would flow from clean electricity instead go up in smoke.) Thanks to social movement advocacy, this level was at least better than the old Independent Development Trust site-and-service subsidies from 1991–94 and the original infrastructure investment policy, drafted largely by the World Bank in 1994–95, which both offered low-income households *no* electricity hook-up.

Moreover, in yet another indication of neoliberalism trumping environmental sustainability, the 1995 energy policy argued that 'Fuelwood is likely to remain the primary source of energy in the rural areas'. As if on cue, Eskom began to wind down its rural electrification programme. As it becomes a tax-paying, privatised corporation, Eskom does not even envisage electrifying the nation's far-flung schools, because 'It is not clear that having electricity in all schools is a first priority'.[26]

Moreover, notwithstanding Eskom's commercialisation fetish, its economists had badly miscalculated rural affordability during the late 1990s, so revenues were far lower than were considered financially sustainable. By estimating that customers would use 300 kWh per month, Eskom believed it could turn a profit. Yet because of high prices, consumption of even those with five years of access was less than 10 kWh per month, resulting in enormous losses for Eskom. Paying as much as R0.40 per hour (compared to a corporate average of R0.06 and bigger discounts for the Alusaf), rural women use up their prepaid meter cards within a week and can't afford to buy another until the next pension payout. This is the main reason demand levels are so low that Eskom's rate of new rural electrification connections ground to a standstill.[27]

As in the case of water, the state's subsidy was insufficient to make up the difference. By pricing electricity out of reach of the poor, the well-paid economists and consultants designing tariffs refused to incorporate 'multiplier effects' that would benefit broader society, were people granted a small free lifeline electricity supply. One indication of the health implications of electricity supply cuts was the recent upsurge in TB rates. Even in communities with electricity, the cost of power for cooking is so high that, for example, only a small proportion of Sowetans with access to electricity use it, favouring cheaper fuels.[28] The gender and environmental implications are obvious.

Because of the residual bias towards supplying large consumers, the post-apartheid government and Eskom simply neglected the implications of a benefit analysis for low-income people, focusing instead on holding down costs. There were many reasons that Eskom maintained extremely cheap power for corporate consumers: very low coal prices; exemption from tax and dividends; financing subsidies (including subsidised Reserve Bank forward cover); and the fact that consumers had largely amortised the loans needed to fund the massive generation capacity that South Africa has still not used.

In contrast, providing cheaper supplies in the form of a free lifeline subsidy, as mandated in the RDP, was not on the politicians' agenda, even when protests broke out in townships from Cape Town to Durban to Johannesburg. Even then, the first line of defence was disconnection and repression. To illustrate, the problem in Soweto reached epidemic levels when Eskom decided in early 2001 to disconnect those households whose arrears were in excess of R5,000 with payment more than 120 days overdue.[29] An anticipated 131,000 households in Soweto would be cut off due to non-payment, according to Eskom – even though the company has only 126,000 recorded consumers in the township.[30] In addition, Johannesburg Metro authorities decided, in an act of solidarity, to cut off water and then begin eviction proceeds through sheriff sales, in an attempt to pressure people to pay Eskom arrears.[31] All manner of gimmicks had been tried to encourage higher payment levels, including lottery tickets as gifts for bill payment, but Sowetans' arrears still rose to an estimated R1.1 billion by 2001.[32]

At stake was not merely Eskom's attempt to collect the R2.2 billion it suffered in arrears across South Africa, with Soweto representing the major challenge.[33] Even more important was the general principle of municipal credit control, by which disconnecting electricity consumers made it is easier to collect arrears on rates, water services and other charges. The Project Viability monitoring system of the Department of Provincial and Local Government (DPLG) reported that a total of R13.6 billion was owed to municipalities – not including arrears on Eskom's retail bills – at the end of 2001. Electricity debts accounted for 15% of this total (R2.0 billion), after rates (32%) and water (19%) debts. Total arrears owing to municipalities therefore stood at more than a quarter of yearly expenditure, with electricity arrears equal to 4% of total municipal spending. These are significant amounts, although much of this debt is current debt and to be expected.

No one illustrated this concern better than DPLG's Kevin Allan, special adviser to minister Sydney Mufamadi. At a time when the California electricity deregulation made a mockery of market mechanisms and virtually all of South Africa's privatisation exercises were going sour, Allan expressed worry over the inclement neoliberal restructuring of South Africa's electricity industry in early 2002. Six new Regional Electricity Distributors (REDS) will be set up to take over municipal supply, even though there are doubts that this is consistent with the Constitution and *Municipal Systems Act*.[34]

Restructuring along the neoliberal lines envisaged would, unfortunately, limit the ability of a town to cross-subsidise other services using electricity account surpluses.[35] This prospect looms as a serious threat, for notwithstanding vague promises of additional national–local transfers, it mitigates against ongoing municipal provision of many non-saleable services like fire protection and recreation. Naturally the lowest-income areas of municipalities – black townships and informal settlements – would be most adversely affected. Opposition to loss of electricity revenues would have been a powerful reason to oppose the restructuring format, and would have brought the mass of low-income constituencies into alliance, against the neoliberal restructuring.[36]

However, according to a *Business Day* interview in January 2002, the DPLG offered a completely contrary rationale:

> Allan said concerns within the local government ministry revolved around the effect that loosening ties between electricity distribution and local government would have on municipalities. 'These concerns include the impact on the ability of municipalities to develop effective credit control mechanisms'.[37]

Credit control may not have been effective, given poverty levels, but electricity cut offs were widespread by 2001. At that point, the DPLG's Project Viability reports and Eskom press statements together indicate an electricity disconnection rate of around 120,000 households per month.

These are likely to be higher since not all municipalities responded to the DPLG survey, and the Eskom statements focus on Soweto, where resistance was toughest. But even using this base, and making a conservative estimate of six people affected by every disconnection (since connections are made to households, sometimes with a backyard dwelling), we estimate that upwards of 720,000 people a month were being denied access to electricity for non-payment in 2001.

The overall connection target set by government of 350,000 connections a year translates to an average rate of 29,167 new connections a month. Even if we only recognise the number of disconnections after the number of reconnections are subtracted, it still means that in 2001, *there were several times as many households losing access to electricity every month as were gaining access.* As discussed in the next section, a survey of Soweto residents found that 61% of households had experienced electricity disconnections, of whom 45% had been cut off for more than one month. A random, stratified national survey conducted by the Municipal Services Project and Human Sciences Research Council (HSRC) found that 10 million people across South Africa had experienced electricity cut offs.[38]

Thus disconnection (credit control) as *punishment* became the preferred strategy, until 2000's cholera outbreak and 2001's Soweto uprising began to teach Pretoria politicians the damage. In contrast, this chapter stresses the provision of generous lifeline electricity as a reward that society should provide universally, to all its citizens, but especially to low-income households because of the positive multipliers noted above. However, to jump ahead to our conclusion, just as in the case of water, the moral and technical eco-social justice arguments had little or no impact upon electricity policy-makers. Instead, *social protest was the single major determinant of changes in retail energy policy*, whether in the form of Pretoria politicians' new use of lifeline language, Eskom's moratorium on Soweto disconnections or many municipalities' movement, albeit slow and halting, towards a free supply of electricity.

Unfortunately, the same logic of eco-social change could not be claimed by those intent on slowing South Africa's near-record levels of greenhouse gas emissions. Evidence is found not only in the failure of the campaign against the Coega IDZ documented in Chapter Two, but also in the weak, technicist stance taken by environmentalists against Pretoria's fossil fuel-addicted economy. As we will see again in the concluding chapter, failure to engage vigorously in protest against South Africa's indefensible contribution to global warming can probably only be corrected if the grassroots electricity gurus and activists of Soweto and other townships move to the next intersection: energy and global environment. As we see, that is indeed their trajectory as of mid-2002.

3. Soweto's Operation Khanyisa strikes a nerve

Speaking in Soweto on a hot afternoon in December 2001, an angry Jeff Radebe took hardest aim at the Electricity Crisis Committee (SECC) for the 'Operation Khanyisa!' – Reconnect the Power! – campaign. Radebe and an allied community network, Sanco, ventured to the historic Orlando Hall, in the heart of SECC territory, to persuade residents that they should put their Eskom payment boycott behind them, repay half their arrears and start making regular full payments.[39]

Despite his own recognition that accounts were inaccurate and that corrupt contractors were cutting electricity off and forcing people to pay high reconnection fees, Radebe offered residents only a one-month 'amnesty' to apply for reconnection to Eskom, threatening that any resident who had not done so after one month would be prosecuted. He also announced that 100% of pensioners' arrears and 50% of arrears of other residents would be set aside in a suspense account. Regardless of the accuracy or not of the arrears, residents would have to repay 50% of arrears in their name.[40]

While jeering was heard by those SECC members who were outside, prohibited from entering, the crowd of 200 gathered in the hall looked on glumly. Radebe, Sanco, the Human Rights Commission,[41] Eskom, the Johannesburg Metro and Johannesburg's corporatised City Power soon launched 'Operation Lungise' – Light Up – to persuade Sowetans that, as full-page advertisements put it, 'All you need to do is pay your current account. Every month. On time. And with those payments, we're able to keep improving service delivery'. Although quite a few Sowetans signed up for Radebe's deal, within a few months payments levels were back to pre-deal levels.[42]

The attraction of the SECC

Lacking the tools of persuasion and repression available to the state, the SECC offered a different package: community, trust and protection from disconnection. Over the previous months, more than 3,000 Soweto households had their electricity supplies illegally switched back on, after being cut when they couldn't afford to pay their often enormous monthly bills. SECC volunteers risked electrocution to do the work, and charged their neighbours nothing for the service. They occasionally had run-ins with Eskom officials and the police, and in 2001 two Vaal township residents were shot dead attempting to prevent disconnections.[43]

Soweto, the township with two million residents southwest of Johannesburg, will always be synonymous with 16 June 1976, the day police began massacring an estimated 1,000 students who protested against Afrikaans-language education and then apartheid more generally. The SECC includes dozens of charismatic disaffected former ANC stalwarts, who are the likely core opposition figures in a leftist political party that must one day emerge from the growing township alienation.

The SECC chairperson at the peak of the electricity struggle was Trevor Ngwane, who also served as secretary to the Anti-Privatisation Forum of Johannesburg-area groups mentioned in Chapter Five. Ngwane was formerly an ANC councillor for Soweto, until the ruling party expelled him in 1999 for opposing Johannesburg's Igoli 2002 privatisation strategy.

In spite of Radebe's demonisation of the 'criminals', Ngwane argued that Operation Khanyisa was an overwhelming success. By October 2001, Eskom became sufficiently intimidated that it gave in, announcing it would no longer disconnect those Sowetans who couldn't pay. Said Ngwane,

> People's Power was responsible for Eskom's U-turn. We mobilised tens of thousands of Sowetans in active protests over the past year. We established professional and intellectual credibility for our critique of Eskom, even collaborating on a major Wits University study. We demonstrated at the houses of the mayor, Amos Masondo, and local councillors, and in the spirit of non-violent civil disobedience, we went so far as to disconnect the electricity supplies of the mayor and councillors to give them a taste of their own medicine.[44]

When SECC leaders were targeted for arrest in mid-October after one councillor's supply was cut, according to Ngwane,

> 500 Sowetans presented themselves for mass arrest at Moroka Police Station, but the police were overwhelmed by our unity. The councillors then met Eskom, and we can guess what they had to say about the company's terribly unpopular policies, and how those policies are ruining the reputation of the ruling party and the government as a whole. Finally, someone is knocking sense into Eskom's senior management.

The SECC announced 'a temporary victory over Eskom, but our other demands remain outstanding':

- commitment to halting and reversing privatisation and commercialisation;
- the scrapping of arrears;

- the implementation of free electricity promised to us in municipal elections a year ago;
- ending the skewed rates which do not sufficiently subsidise low-income black people;
- additional special provisions for vulnerable groups – disabled people, pensioners, people who are HIV–positive; and
- expansion of electrification to all, especially impoverished people in urban slums and rural villages, the vast majority of whom do not have the power that we in Soweto celebrate.[45]

These were demands that Jeff Radebe, Eskom and Johannesburg would simply not meet. Radebe is a leading member of the SA Communist Party (SACP).[46] In May 1999, newly elected president Thabo Mbeki moved him from the public works ministry, where he was responsible for rapid, thorough outsourcing, to the ministry of public enterprises, so as privatise and commercialise Pretoria's largest parastatal companies.

The Orlando meeting was not Radebe's first brush with activists who branded him a sell-out. In August 2001, he used similar language to deride the two-million member Cosatu, which had embarked on a two-day national strike against the planned privatisation of electricity, telecommunications and transport.

The stakes were far higher at that stage, according to a report in *Business Day* newspaper on the eve of the World Conference Against Racism:

> Cabinet ministers were subsequently dispatched to influential radio and television programmes first to 'clarify' government positions, but also to 'show Cosatu members they are being urged to committing suicide', according to an official involved in the spin-doctoring offensive. Also part of the strategy – championed by trade and industry minister Alec Erwin, transport minister Dullah Omar and public enterprises minister Jeff Radebe – was to seek to caution Cosatu members against possible hijacking of their strike by outside elements such as those protesting at World Bank and International Monetary Fund meetings.[47]

Soweto learns about Washington

Ngwane was indeed one of the main South African protest leaders at Bank and IMF meetings, from Washington on 16–17 April 2000 to the 26 September 2000 protest in Johannesburg in solidarity with Prague demonstrators, to Washington again on 19 September 2001.[48] Was he correct to, if not hijack, at least highlight for Cosatu members the danger of these institutions? *Business Day* seemed to answer in the affirmative in the next day's edition:

> SA needs to cut import tariffs aggressively, privatise faster and more extensively, promote small business effectively and change labour laws to achieve far faster growth and job creation. This is according to a World Bank report that will soon be released publicly and has been circulating in government.[49]

Ngwane is perhaps the most capable and energetic grassroots militant in contemporary South Africa drawing these linkages. In April 2000, he and Dennis Brutus launched the World Bank Bonds Boycott at the global-justice protests in Washington.[50] Compared to water, the World Bank's advice to South African electricity policy-makers was much lower-key, and even stressed broader access to electricity prior to privatisation.

But privatisation was Washington's inexorable direction. The Bank offered predictable advice in its main website analysis of 'Energy in Africa's Development':

> Almost invariably [the price of electricity] is set at a rate not fully reflecting supply costs and so blocks the possibility to establish small private supply systems run on a commercial basis. It is well known that consumers' willingess-to-pay can exceed public tariffs by a considerable margin ...
>
> Restructuring, privatisation and price reform – so badly needed across much of the sector – also present both environmental opportunities and challenges. Increasing energy prices increase incentives for end-use efficiency, improve conversion efficiencies and help check emissions. Conversely, competition may lead to pressure to cut corners on environmental impact mitigation ...
>
> The Bank will focus on countries which demonstrate – through actions – a credible intent to privatise and to liberalise ... Liberalisation of power supply will be pursued through privatisations and the removal of legislative and commercial barriers to public/private partnerships (including in particular through adopting modern regulation and tariff setting mechanisms).[51]

It is worth focusing attention on the nature of 'modern tariff setting mechanisms'. The pricing of electricity follows the same logic as water: popular demands for a free lifeline supply and a progressive (redistributive) rising block tariff serve as a disincentive to privatisation, as we saw in previous chapters. It was, in turn, logical that Soweto's resistance to high prices and electricity disconnections would confront the underlying dynamic of privatisation and commercialisation of Eskom. As Ngwane explained,

> We believe that the drive to privatise – by milking more from the poor – seemed to instill in Eskom the most anti-social, anti-environmental strategies. We also believe that the tide has turned, internationally, against privatisation. Renationalisation is now a popular sentiment.

The most important deterrent to Eskom's privatisation was, by all accounts, the large (R2.2 billion) and growing 'debtor book'. Beyond that frightening wart on Eskom's otherwise healthy balance sheet, the most durable problem for any privatiser – whether generator, transmitter or even distributor – would be pressures to redistribute cheap national-scale supplies of power to municipalities, or eventually the REDS, so as to provide a free lifeline supply to ordinary South Africans.

Hence the Washington Consensus mantra of 'getting the prices right' would conflict with social expectations to 'get the prices wrong'. In 2001, domestic consumers paid the top Eskom price of an *average* 24.59 cents per kWh (Sowetans paid much higher average prices), while the manufacturing sector paid 12.83 cents per kWh and the mining sector paid 12.32 cents per kWh.

Recent Eskom tariff increases had hit Soweto especially hard, because earlier flat-rate subsidised tariffs, a consequence of earlier generations of social struggle, had faded as community organisation waned. In 1999, Soweto residents experienced three increases in a short period as Eskom brought tariffs in line with other areas. From 18.77 cents per kWh, the price of electricity rose by 47% to 27.6 cents per unit in the space of a year.[52]

Moreover, special discount pricing deals are typically negotiated with large consumers, such as mining and smelter operations. Prices differ substantially during the day depending on the excess capacity in electricity production. The lowest available price in 2001 was 3.5 cents per kWh, but was subject to special conditions such as supply at off-peak hours of the day and night. With its capacity to store electricity in bulk, aluminium producer Alusaf, for example, pays a low electricity charge that is also linked to the world price on aluminium.[53]

Recent changes in tariffs indicate a gradual move towards 'cost reflectivity' and away from regulated price increases. The aim is to reduce and eventually eliminate subsidies, so as to achieve 'market-related returns sufficient to attract new investors into the industry'.[54] Eskom is adjusting its prices so that restructuring has a limited effect on its own revenue. But the utility acknowledges that 'individual customers could experience significant changes in their price of electricity'. In particular, those who previously had subsidised tariffs will experience increases 'well above the average'.[55] The National Electricity Regulator has given explicit support to above-inflation tariff increases over the next few years in order to fund investment in new capacity.[56]

Rising electricity prices across South African townships already had a negative impact during the late 1990s, evident in declining use of electricity despite an increase in the number of connections. According to Statistics South Africa, the government's official statistical service, households using electricity for lighting increased from 63.5% in 1995 to 69.8% in 1999. However, households using electricity for cooking declined from 55.4% to 53.0% from 1995 to 1999, and households using electricity for heating dropped from 53.8% in 1995 to just 48.0% in 1999. Stats SA concedes a significant link between decreasing usage and the increasing price of electricity.[57]

Notwithstanding industry's substantially lower unit prices, large corporations do indeed cross-subsidise domestic consumers. Eskom's cost of supplying big consumers with a kiloWatt hour of electricity is dramatically lower than the cost associated with the same kiloWatt hour to low-volume domestic households. In 2001, the cross-subsidy from industry and municipalities to the domestic and agricultural sectors was reportedly R1.891 billion, a significant sum. Was it enough, though?

As discussed in Chapter Three, cross-subsidisation is made possible by the declining marginal cost of supplying large quantities of bulk electricity to a few numbers of huge consumers. Even with cross-subsidies, Eskom supplies the cheapest industrial electricity in the world. While in other countries, domestic consumers are charged twice as much as large industry, Eskom charges industry prices that are as little as one seventh the domestic price.[58]

One obvious problem with Eskom's low industrial tariffs immediately arises. As we explore in the section on environment and energy below, Eskom's pricing structure does not give industrial consumers an incentive to save electricity, and hence cut down on greenhouse gas emissions. The opposite is true, for the more a large consumer uses, the better its position with Eskom for the next price negotiation. Industrial consumers also argue to Eskom that increased electricity prices result in job losses – whereas, in reality, the limits to job creation are not set by electricity price inputs but instead lack of education, work skills and discrimination.[59] The large electricity consumers create very few jobs in their mechanised operations, in any case.

Even without structural economic changes, which would be desirable in any event, especially to create more jobs, it is widely accepted that industry could conserve energy and reduce current consumption by as much as 20%. DME officials recognise that industrial and mining consumers of electricity receive inappropriate economic signals and as a result lack energy awareness, information and skills, and efficient technologies. Industry has used its strong negotiating position to oppose increased cross-subsidisation for the 'free electricity' policy, and successfully lobbied trade and industry minister Erwin to intervene in Cabinet in October 2000, to prevent industrial price increases that would pay for a domestic lifeline supply.

Increasingly, the bottom line for Eskom is its need to price for the sake of making a profit: specifically, to improve return on assets to above the current 10.9%. International market-related returns come in closer to 18% to 20%, and management is expected to focus on improving returns to attract foreign partners.[60] Eskom is therefore incentivised to withdraw from its electrification programme in preparation for competition. In this way, the social and developmental aspects of electricity provision are being ditched in anticipation of the cut-throat world of profits and income generation. Where the private sector gets involved, rates of return required to ensure investment are likely to be higher than would be required if Eskom were to continue carrying out the programme under public ownership.

What this review of pricing means is that even if the World Bank's influence has not been as 'instrumental' in achieving a 'radical revision' of electricity bulk pricing as was the case in relation to water, the formidable power of industry and Pretoria's neoliberal ideological predilections follow Washington's lead. Sowetans began to get a hint of how larger volume consumers benefit, even within the domestic consumption sector, when SECC and the media began comparing the cost of minor appliance use. The price structure provided by Eskom most commonly in Soweto meant that electricity was less expensive in Sandton, as a point of comparison, if the household consumes more than 690 kWh per month (slightly higher than the average consumption in the survey discussed below). Because even boiling tea had become too expensive for many Sowetans by 2001, payments were missed and arrears rose to unprecedented levels. Then, to its ultimate regret, Eskom arrived to cut off tens of thousands of households' electricity.

Washington learns about Soweto

Agnes Mohapi's angst at having her electricity disconnected and her relief upon reconnection was documented at the outset of Chapter Four. The 2001 disconnection rampage by Eskom, affecting 20,000 families a month at peak, finally came to an end thanks to SECC resistance. But a few months later, as shown by the ANC Western Cape march against the DA (and by implication also against Eskom in part), spin-doctoring who was to blame for miserable township services provision would continue indefinitely.

Indeed, the Soweto power struggle echoed around the world, with SABC Special Assignment, CNN news, *Newsday*, *New Internationalist*, *Red Pepper* and many other media taking a closer look. Waking up on the morning of 6 November, neoliberal readers of the Washington Post must have been shocked by a front-page story, featuring both structural explanations and militant sentiments from Soweto:[61]

> What most provokes South Africans' defiance today are what they see as injustices unleashed on this developing nation by the free-market economic policies of the popularly elected, black-led governing party, the African National Congress.
>
> Materially, life here has only gotten worse since 1994 as the ANC has pursued a course of piecemeal privatisation of state industries, whittling of import taxes and loosening of controls on foreign exchange.
>
> The policies have expanded opportunities for foreign investors but so far have deepened the poverty inherited from apartheid's segregationist policies.
>
> With domestic industries more vulnerable to foreign competition and the restructuring of public enterprises, the most industrialised country in sub-Saharan Africa has lost nearly 500,000 jobs since 1993, leaving a third of the workforce unemployed. The poorest 15 million South Africans have had their annual incomes shrink by nearly a fifth of what they were before apartheid's collapse ...
>
> Hoping to generate revenue, streamline a bloated bureaucracy and extend service to blacks ignored by apartheid, the ANC announced six years ago that the government would sell public enterprises from the state-run airlines and the phone company to Eskom, the acronym for the public electricity commission. With encouragement from institutions such as the World Bank and International Monetary Fund, the government has so far auctioned off only small portions, while restructuring the public franchises into profit centers to showcase their attractiveness to potential investors
>
> The alienation felt by many poor blacks from this march to privatisation has bred street rallies calling for a revival of 'the spirit of '76' – a reference to the year of the Soweto riots, which gave the anti-apartheid campaign its second wind.

In addition to Agnes Mohapi, four SECC activists were quoted by the *Post*:

- James Buthelezi: No one has worked in months and the family survives on Buthelezi's mother's pension, less than $125 a month. Their unpaid bill is more than $3,000. 'When they came to cut off our electricity, we begged them not to', said Buthelezi, 58. 'We told them that we had babies and elderly people inside. They didn't even pause'.
- Virginia Setshedi: 'This culture of nonpayment that people say exists in Soweto, it's only because people don't have money to pay. We're getting about 50 calls each day from the community. We don't ask why or when the people were cut off, we just switch them back on. Everyone should have electricity'.
- Bongani Lubisi: 'There's definitely been a revival of the struggle mentality. We thought that when we got rid of the old government that our black government would take care of us. But instead the capitalists are getting richer while the working people lose their jobs and can't even meet their basic needs'.
- Shadrack Motau: 'We did not give up our lives and the lives of our children only to let this brazen capitalist system exploit us even more'.

These are emblematic statements, reflecting the rise of political consciousness and conflict from basic grievances about a failing state. More detail was provided in two of the SECC's core communities, Orlando East and Pimville, during a 2001 survey.

Soweto electricity consumption

In Soweto, Eskom provides electricity directly because of the success of the 1980s campaign against the Black Local Authority. The majority of consumers in the township were upgraded to a 60 Amp electricity supply by the early 1990s. The charges for electricity were changed concurrently, from a flat rate system to a metering (by credit) system. Soweto thereby receives a superior electricity service compared to other rural and urban townships.

In our 2001 qualitative survey of micro energy practices,[62] several findings were important:
- Electricity is used for convenience; respondents felt that it was both faster and easier to use than alternative sources of energy. Electricity is also safer, more hygienic and healthier to use than wood, paraffin,

coal. Nearly all – 93% – respondents prefer electricity to other fuels; many refused to list a second or third priority, but of those who did, the next preferences are coal and paraffin.

- Households have adapted their lifestyles to simple modern appliances, and find it hard to live without electricity.
- Because of the recent increases in electricity bills, two in five respondents said that they felt restricted to use less electricity than what was needed, especially for cooking traditional and time-consuming dishes for their families.
- Nearly three quarters of respondents state that because of high bills they have tried to lower electricity usage, by reducing leisure time at the television, reducing cooking and switching hot-water heaters (geysers) off during the summer. However, most respondents report that these savings did not translate into noticably lower bills.
- About half (48%) of respondents said that electricity was the worst municipal service, compared to refuse collection (17% report it is the worst service); water (13%); roads (11%); and sanitation (7%).

With respect to bills payments, the following are key findings:

- Sowetans made regular payments on their electricity accounts, with two-thirds paying R200 or less per month and one quarter paying less than R100 (the average bill was R150, equal to electricity consumption of approximately 500 kWh/month).[63]
- Households provided evidence of inconsistent billing often due to non-reading of meters. Nearly one in 10 reported that bills always come to the same amount, while two in five recorded that meters were read only occasionally. A further quarter of respondents said that Eskom never read their meters.
- Aside from disputed accounts, the main problems paying bills were long queues on pay-day, the lack of assistance in explaining bills, cut offs, and poor service from Eskom staff.
- It was often reported that Eskom staff have a negative attitude towards consumer problems. Consumers know that they must take their complaints to Eskom, but feel intimidated and therefore have many unresolved problems.
- Half of the households keep their electricity bills for more than 4 years.[64]

But because bills were higher than were affordable, arrears inexorably built up on the Soweto accounts:

- In winter, households that pay up to R200 per month are actually paying just half of what is being billed.
- Arrears naturally increase in winter, when the households are more vulnerable to electricity cut offs.

- Many people explained that although they cannot afford their entire bills, they pay part of them as assurance to Eskom that they are willing to pay to avert a cut off of their electricity.
- Nearly a fifth of the respondents have arrears that date more than 4 years, and 14% have arrears in excess of R15,000.[65]
- Because of the faulty billing problems and unaffordability constraints to paying large arrears, more than seven in 10 respondents argued that arrears of more than R15,000 should be written off by Eskom.

Finally, until the SECC interventions, arrears led to disconnections:

- Three out of five households experienced cut offs during the past year, of which 86% were due to non-payment. Only 14% of the cut offs were disputed, despite the widespread complaints of inconsistent billing.
- Of households experiencing cut offs, 10% had their cables removed permanently. This is a response usually taken by Eskom when the consumer has reconnected illegally, and the price of reconnection is usually prohibitive.

Disconnections, in turn, lead to all manner of health, environmental, social and economic problems:

- When electricity is cut off, consumers record numerous difficulties: the food gets spoiled (98%); we cannot cook the food properly (90%); our personal hygiene is negatively affected (88%); we spend more money on alternative fuels (84%); the kids cannot study properly (81%); it increases crime in the area (73%); it is degrading to my family to live without electricity (70%); the women have more work (65%); it is bad for our working life (62%); it disrupts home business (41%); it increases domestic violence in the neighbourhood (36%). All of these interlocking problems are felt more severely by women.
- For those disconnected, the length of time that the household was without electricity – i.e., either until a payment was made or supply was illegally reconnected – varied: up to one day, 9%; a couple of days, 12%; 1 week (14%); 1–2 weeks (10%); 3–4 weeks (11%); and more than a month (45%).

The environmental and health implications of not having access to electricity were discussed in Chapter Four. Because of climate and congestion, respiratory diseases are particularly common in Soweto. In a 1998 survey, two in five Sowetans reportedly suffered from respiratory problems, 2% from TB, 4% from allergies, 0.5% from cancer and 10% from other infections. More than a fifth of council-house dwellers described their health as bad. Lost working days resulted: 5% took 1–2 days off each year to recover; 9% took 3–5 days; 6% took 6–7 days; and 15% needed more than 8 days.[66]

Our survey respondents reported many fires in the neighbourhood, often caused by paraffin stoves, many of which were harmful to children. Eskom's disconnection procedures often resulted in electricity cables lying loose in the streets.[67] If a person steps on a live wire it is difficult to help them, as electricity first needs to be shut off. Anyone who touches the electrified person will her/himself be electrified.

Allegedly, Eskom employees in Soweto also leave sub-stations open, creating a potential hazard to residents, and some employees reportedly earn a second income from illegal connections (hence explaining why substations would be purposely left open). Residents of Pimville and Orlando East find themselves in a dilemma reporting these dangers since Eskom inspectors might also discover the illegal connections, hence leaving neighbouring families without electricity.

Residents are unhappy not only about the high reconnection fees charged but the fact that Eskom uses outsourced companies that earn R70 per household disconnection. No notification is given that supply will be cut off, and residents are not given time to rectify problems. Eskom disconnects entire blocks at a time by removing circuit breakers, penalising those who do pay their bills along with those who don't.

Lessons from Soweto

Electricity in Soweto remains highly controversial. Disconnections and non-payment provide extremely serious challenges to existing policies. Despite the success of the electrification programme in expanding the grid, problems such as inadequate supply of electricity, cost-recovery policies and insufficient incomes to pay for consumption continue to hamper the sector. Electricity infrastructure was upgraded in Soweto in 1993–94 with R56 million in capital spending, but according to customers the level of service is inferior.

In late 2000, the SECC was established. The committee's work reflects the need for increased consumer protection. Electricity consumers are not informed of their rights and feel intimidated to approach the bureaucracy with complaints. The consequence of a cut off for an individual household is often economic devastation and a real loss of basic rights, such as the right to human dignity in the Constitution. After 20 years of electricity supply, households have started relying heavily on electricity provision.

As arrears run into thousands of rands, consumers find it increasingly impossible to meet payments. As a result of the electricity crisis, low-income people – especially women-headed households and black South Africans – are becoming increasingly marginalised. Basic services, even when provided, are too expensive for low-income and working class households and deepen marginalisation. Even by limiting their consumption, consumers could not meet payments. As a last resort the marginalised turned to illegal strategies, such as bribing Eskom employees or connecting themselves illegally to electricity services.

The government and Eskom have chosen to solve the problems by disconnecting people from electricity services in an attempt to recoup service arrears. The 2000 municipal election promise of free lifeline electricity – a progressive, useful advance – was sabotaged by bureaucrats, who, in the case of Eskom, ignored it, or in municipalities decided that a lifeline of just 50 kWh (or less) per household per month would suffice. Such a meagre amount merely supplies light to a typical household, and does not provide enough electricity for basic needs of heating and cooking.

There has been debate within the SECC about what kind of lifeline system is preferable. The primary historic demand of community activists, picked up by the SECC, is the reinstatement of a flat-rate payment system, at least as a short-term measure. Ngwane explains,

> People want to be charged a fixed price each month that they can budget for. That price is R50 for each household in Soweto. We consider this flat-rate demand a return to our tradition of anti-apartheid struggle, because that was the demand that emerged during the 1980s in Soweto. With leaders in the Committee of Ten like Motlana, Ramaphosa, Chikane, Ncube, Masondo, Mogase and others, we won that short-term struggle. It is sad that Sowetans are using old demands against the apartheid regime in dealing with the democratic government. This is a short-term demand, reflecting growing alienation in the present circumstances, whilst we await a more equitable, sane system.[68]

A sane system has not been established, even with the free electricity lifeline promise. Ngwane continues: 'Many people in Soweto have little or no faith in the ANC keeping its promise of free basic electricity'. As in the case of lifeline water, Ngwane is also critical of the ANC's choice of the household as a unit of measurement, arguing that free lifeline supplies of electricity should be allocated on a 'per person' basis so as to avoid bias against large families.

The current SECC proposal, by contrast, Ngwane says, is for

> at least one kiloWatt hour per person per day [of free electricity]. For a family of 10 that would translate to 300 kWh per month, or

R86.10 at the current high price of R0.287 per kiloWatt hour. That is a fair subsidy – less than R9 per person per month – and we think a rich company like Eskom has the means to pay it.

In order to benefit poor households, electricity policies also need to focus on a wider range of issues, such as the affordability of basic appliances, the income in poor and working-class households, the health and environmental impacts of non-access and participation in essential decisions. However, the policy of free lifeline electricity appears to have very little support in the DME. The energy minister's 2001 budget speech to Parliament *failed to even mention the new policy.*

Continued cut offs of consumers might very well end up in increased disputes instead of solutions. As the September 2000 Grootboom ruling by the Constitutional Court showed, electricity is considered a basic human needs and can be included as a vital service, covered in terms of the Constitution's Bill of Rights:

> A society must seek to ensure that the basic necessities of life are provided to all if it is to be a society based on dignity, freedom and equality ...
>
> For a person to have access to adequate housing, ... there must be land, there must be services, there must be a dwelling ...
>
> The state's obligation to provide access to housing depends on context ... some may need access to services such as water, sewage, electricity and roads.[69]

Just as importantly, the obligation of social movements and trade unions is to move quickly to the intersection of energy and environment, where progressive analysts and activists are only beginning to grapple with the enormous challenges.

4. Energy and environment

Pleasing rhetoric encompassing South Africa's transitional ideals is often persuasive, at first blush:

> The shift in priorities for the energy sector in South Africa has been almost 180 degrees – moving from the apartheid–era single-minded emphasis on energy security to a broader concern about access to affordable energy, economic efficiency, and environmental sustainability.[70]

This is not government propaganda, but instead the considered opinion of an expert, Randall Spalding-Fecher of the University of Cape Town Energy for Development Research Centre. Spalding-Fecher, who argued this case in 2000, initiated a useful annual survey of international sustainable energy indicators. Closer examination, however, shows the inaccuracy of his conclusion about Pretoria's priorities, in light of the problems of oversupply revealed at the proposed Coega smelter (Chapter Two) and underconsumption revealed in infrastructure policy (Chapter Four), and in the practice experienced in disconnected urban and unconnected rural areas, as discussed in this chapter.

Celebratory stories of the post-apartheid 'shift' from the apartheid energy laager to neoliberalism typically leave out or gloss over affordability as well as sustainability. As for efficiency, the generation of cheap electricity in South Africa still relies on the extremely wasteful burning of low-grade coal, which has a worsening impact on the environment not just through emissions but also in requiring vast amounts of coolant water. Indeed, Eskom is the single largest consumer of raw water in South Africa. While industry benefits from cheap electricity as a competitive advantage, the negative social and environmental effects of electricity production have never been internalised into the cost.

In addition, the appalling nature of South African transport, which is too overwhelming a topic to be considered in this chapter, requires urgent, revolutionary change. This would also imply the need to radically change the space-economy, regionally and locally. It would entail much more decentralised and backward/forward-linked production processes, plus the relocation of people from distant townships to geographically more compact settings. In short, a dramatic restructuring of the urban spatial form is needed to reverse apartheid-era geography and the worsening neo-apartheid trends that have emerged since 1994 on the basis of market-based principles.

Spalding-Fecher is honest enough to admit, 'Transforming an energy economy based on vast, inexpensive supplies of coal, large public investments in synthetic liquid fuels and nuclear power, and highly inequitable access to clean household fuels, however, presents a major challenge'. His November 2000 study bears out a variety of profound concerns about environmental sustainability, because South Africa, Spalding-Fecher concedes:

- is 'the most vulnerable fossil fuel exporting country in the world' if the Kyoto Protocol is adopted, according to an International Energy Agency report;
- scores extremely poorly 'on the indicators for carbon emissions per capita and energy intensity';
- has a 'heavy reliance' on energy-intensive industries;

- suffers a 'high dependence on coal for primary energy',
- offers 'low energy prices' which in part is responsible for 'poor energy efficiency of individual sectors'; and
- risks developing a 'competitive disadvantage' by virtue of 'continued high energy intensity' which in the event of energy price rises 'can increase the cost of production'.

On the positive side, 'while the indicator for local pollution remains high, the significant improvement since 1990 is encouraging', largely thanks to the lowering of air particulates following the electrification of black townships. And the potential for renewable energy is vast, given that South Africa 'has one of the highest solar insolation rates in the world', with annual global solar radiation averages more than twice as high as Europe and 50% higher than the US.

Still, the existing levels of environmental degradation caused by coal mining, electricity generation, lack of access by the majority of low-income people, hydropower and nuclear energy are formidable. Not including net exports of greenhouse gas pollutants – since South Africa is the world's second largest exporter of coal after Australia – the energy sector contributed 78% to South Africa's share of global warming and more than 90% of all carbon dioxide emissions in 1994.

Amongst the world's worst greenhouse gas polluters

What happened subsequently? Data are still coming in, but the trends are disturbing. In 1998, South Africa emitted 354 million metric tonnes of carbon dioxide, equivalent to 2,291 kilograms of carbon per person (a 4% increase from 1990 levels).[71] South Africa is amongst the worst emitters of CO_2 in the world when corrected for both income and population size, far worse than even the United States, as shown in

Table 6: Energy sector carbon emissions, 1999[72]					
Area	Population (mns)	CO_2/ person	GDP ($bns)	CO_2/GDP (kg/$bn)	CO_2(kg)/ GDP*pop
S.Africa	42	8.22	$164	2.11	0.0501
Africa	775	1.49	$569	1.28	0.0016
USA	273	20.46	$8,588	0.65	0.0023
OECD	1116	10.96	$26,446	0.46	0.0004
World	5921	3.88	$32,445	0.71	0.0001

NOTE: The tonnes of carbon dioxide (CO_2) emissions are those measureable through fuel combustion.

Table 6. Only a few countries rival South Africa in a CO_2/GDP* population comparison, most of which are mainly producers of fossil fuels and which flare gas or oil, rather than competing with South Africa as inefficient energy consumers through the minerals beneficiation process. In terms of population size alone, many countries of the Organisation for Economic Cooperation and Development (OECD) have higher emissions, but when corrected again for both population and income, South Africa is far worse than nearly all the major developed countries.

Both globally and in South Africa, carbon emissions are growing, not reducing, in spite of economic stagnation and mass employment loss. In 1990, the average carbon emissions from fossil fuel production internationally was 1,130 kilograms per person. Already, experts judged this to be 70% above unsustainable levels, and set a target of reductions from 1990 levels – indexed at 100 – to 339 kilograms of carbon emissions per person. To reach the sustainable level would put the world at a '0' point on a sustainability vector. South Africa took no action to reduce emissions over the period 1990–98, and indeed allowed them to increase from 2,205 to 2,291 kilograms of carbon per person. Instead of lowering emissions on the 0–100 vector scale, the emissions/person ratio actually increased, from 226 in 1990 to 247 in 1998.

If political will existed in the global environmental regulatory establishment – which it *doesn't*, as we will observe in the final chapter – then punishment for excessive global greenhouse gas emissions would hit South Africa very hard. The UN Framework Convention on Climate Change was only ratified by South Africa in 1997. But, as Spalding-Fecher describes it, the 'no-regrets' policy articulated in the DME *Energy White Paper* has slowed the impulse to meaningful anti-greenhouse gas measures:

> Government has developed a climate change policy discussion document, and is currently working on a national response strategy. The discussion document mentions a wide range of possible energy strategies, including greater use of renewables and energy efficiency, as well as cleaner fossil fuels, but no specific measures. Moreover, this document has not been translated into policy yet.

Were the DME and Eskom not so financially impelled to promoting nuclear energy, as we see below, renewable sources could prosper in South Africa and electricity efficiency could be improved.

Renewable energy and efficiency versus nuclear and hydro-electricity

Renewable sources include solar and wind, but these are surprisingly underdeveloped. Only R30 million was spent on solar home heating and R18 million on solar water heating in 1998. Capital costs are expensive, as are repairs. And most micro-scale solar systems in households cannot generate sufficient electricity to serve cooking and heating purposes.

Other experiments continue. Notwithstanding erratic breezes, a wind farm at Darling in the Western Cape will produce 5 MW of power, and a Northern Cape solar chimney could potentially generate 200 MW.

Energy-efficient investments are being pursued by firms like South African Breweries, South African Pulp and Paper Industries (Sappi), and Anglogold, but the scale (R5 million) anticipated for payback within a year is still inconsequential. All told, Spalding-Fecher reckons, 'it appears that the share of energy sector investment going to clean energy would be no more than half of one percent'.

The contrast with state funding for orthodox energy sources and nuclear is phenomenal, according to Spalding-Fecher's accounting:

> The state Central Energy Fund owns the oil and gas exploration company, Soekor, the gas-to-liquid fuels producer, Mossgas, and was until recent years the owner of coal-to-liquid fuel supplier Sasol. State-owned Petronet runs the national liquid fuel pipeline system, while Portnet controls the ports used for import and export of fossil fuels. The nuclear industry was funded through the parastatal Atomic Energy Corporation (AEC), which still absorbs almost half of the Ministry of Minerals and Energy's budget.
>
> Many of these parastatal companies have received loans and subsidies of billions, or tens of billions, of Rands in the past several decades. The national government budget, therefore, only represents a small part of the state's involvement and financial burden of the sector.

To some extent, the investments do turn into revenue streams and even profits. But the year after South Africa's liberation provides one marker of wasted state monies. In 1995/96, energy spending through the DME was R515 million, of which R489 million went to the AEC (mainly for debt servicing), even though the AEC produced no new electricity since nuclear power generation had been purchased by Eskom. In addition, that year, the Central Energy Fund wrote down loans to Soekor by more than R110 million and included additional provisions for non-payment of loans to state companies by R7.3 billion. Another R1.5 billion was spent on subsidising synthetic fuels. Eskom's capital investments that year amounted to R5.4 billion and there were many other unaccounted investments in energy, through local electricity distributors, transport/pipeline companies, state oil companies, Eskom and National Research Foundation research and development in energy, and upgrading of port infrastructure for coal handling.

For South Africa to be investing only R50 million in renewable energy and a few million more on energy efficiency is scandalous. The problem of priorities appears to be getting worse, not better. Expenditure on renewable energy was less than 0.5% of the DME budget in 2002/03. At the same time, DME continued to fund the South African Nuclear Energy Corporation (successor to the AEC) to the tune of R135 million, and provided strategic loans of R266 million.[73]

Indeed, perhaps the greatest waste remains in the area of nuclear research and development. First considered in the 1960s, South Africa's nuclear industry began in 1974 with the construction of the Koeberg nuclear station. The plant was commissioned a decade later. Nuclear development consumed two-thirds of the DME's annual budget but only generated about 3% of South Africa's primary energy supply and 5% of electricity in 1997.

Opposition to nuclear energy on grounds of safety and long-term waste storage has come from sections of civil society, notably most of the environmental movement and the trade unions. By the end of 2001, Cosatu and four dozen other civil society organisations and networks were joined by another 23 regional and international organisations in opposition to a nuclear development path in South Africa.[74]

In addition, from an economic point of view, the cost of production of the Pebble Bed Modular Reactor (PBMR) has become unviable, given currency fluctuations and severe problems in Eskom's partners in Britain and the US. On a simple (non-environmental) financial basis, electricity generated from nuclear power in other countries costs up to 25% more than conventional fuels.[75]

Yet the nuclear programme continues and has even expanded in the post-apartheid era. Several reasons help explain the ANC government's persistence. First, significant investments have been sunk in the industry, and the state is attempting to get some return. It is a dubious proposition, however. The PBMR is also designed first and foremost for export, with targeted – but highly unrealistic – earnings of R18 billion a year, rather than for the generation of domestic electricity.[76] Yet most countries with nuclear generation capacity have either ceased building plants or have stalled plans to install additional capacity. The market for nuclear energy has stagnated, growing just 0.7% annually for the past decade. In comparison, renewable energy markets are growing at 25–45% per year albeit off a small base.[77]

Eskom has been working on the PBMR since 1993, and therefore has a strong financial interest in keeping the programme going. The utility holds 30% of the PBMR Project and soon established contracts with the IDC (25%), and two overseas companies, namely British Nuclear Fuel (22.5%) and Exelon (12.5%), an electricity utility of the United States. The latter firm, however, announced its withdrawal from the partnership even prior to a feasibility report by an international task team studying the project handed its findings to the South African government in April 2002. The team was unable to come to a conclusion on the financial and economic feasibility of the project, nor on the technical design.[78]

Nevertheless, proponents may point out current trends catalysed by the Bush Administration in conjunction with the once-dying US nuclear power industry. If Bush returns to the Kyoto Protocol, it will mean more pressure to declare nuclear energy a safe source of power. Nuclear lobbyists had hoped that the 'sinks' mechanism which allows credit for non-fossil fuel energy generation might include nuclear energy.

A second reason for continuing with the programme is an attempt to shift the base of electricity generation away from the environmentally damaging use of low-grade coal. However, at the time of writing, the Kyoto Protocol still prohibits the use of nuclear energy as justification for reducing greenhouse gases, and rejected the nuclear option from the Clean Development Mechanism (CDM).[79] Although South Africa is classified as a developing country in Kyoto, and is not subject to emissions reduction targets at this stage, nevertheless a CDM protocol is being piloted, and the spectre of carbon trading is on the horizon, a point we return to in the final chapter.

A final concern arises in the search for cleaner power: more mega-dams and natural gas. The government appears intent upon using hydro-electric power to a greater extent, especially from regional neighbours that have existing systems, such as Mozambique, Zambia and the Democratic Republic of the Congo. As Chapter Three's analysis of the Lesotho Highlands Water Project demonstrated, and as we see in the next chapter while surveying South Africa's role in the region, there are enormous environmental and social problems associated with hydro-electricity, not least of which is global warming gasses that are released in tropical dams due to vegetation decay.[80]

The search for cleaner natural gas within the region also deserves mention, because of the story of the exploitation of Mozambique's main gas field, at Pande. A public interest group, the Sustainable Energy and Economy Network (SEEN), discovered in 2002 that rights to the 131 million tonnes of gas at Pande were bought by the infamous Texas company Enron, with the help of the World Bank and the US government.

> In June 1994, the World Bank's International Development Association provided $30 million toward the privatisation of Mozambique's Pande gas fields. The World Bank began to act as a broker, encouraging government officials and private investors to develop Pande, claiming that the gas fields were expected to lead to gas exports to South Africa worth $150 million annually.[81]

South Africa's state-owned Sasol was the other major bidder, along with an Argentine firm. As a Clinton administration official conceded to the *New York Times*, Enron's leverage included US embassy lobbying and threats to an aid package: 'It was a little more nuanced than that. It is difficult to say we should give Mozambique $40 million a year, if it's going to take an opportunity for a $700 million project and not do it'.[82] According to SEEN,

> Enron wanted to build a $700 million, 900 kilometre pipeline from the Pande field to a direct reduced iron (DRI) steel plant in South Africa. The pipeline and steel plant were to possibly receive World Bank funding in the future. According to *Africa Energy and Mining* magazine, 'With the help of the Mozambican government, Enron began to negotiate with state-owned Industrial Development Corporation (IDC) to construct a R2.5 billion (then $573 million) DRI plant in South Africa's Northern Province. But AEM understands that Enron irked IDC by trying to push it into a quick decision'.[83]
>
> In 1995, with the deal apparently in jeopardy, President Clinton's National Security Adviser, Anthony Lake, reportedly held up a $13.5 million aid package, implying in a letter to Mozambican President Joaquim Chissano that it was contingent upon affirmation of the Enron deal. President Chissano acquiesced.

Enron ultimately folded and Sasol is carrying out the project. On the one hand, the gas could be a temporary fix, but on the other, to the extent that it will power yet another minerals smelter, the net environmental impact is negative. In sum, even when US imperialism intervenes on behalf of the US version of the Minerals-Energy Complex, virtually all aspects of South Africa's own hedonistic energy production and consumption nexus represent an attack on the environment. It is only through rethinking the economic growth path inherited from apartheid, as we attempted in the case of Coega in Chapter Two, that substantial change can be achieved. This realisation is now beginning to dawn amongst farsighted economists, as well.

Energy, environment and economics

In a useful critique which could well apply to the proposed Coega smelter, Spalding-Fecher's links energy consumption to economic development strategies, such as the DTI's Spatial Development Initiatives and investment incentives:

> The risk of these policies is that, while they may promote industrial development in the short run, they carry a high risk of 'locking in' the economy into energy intensive industries, when environmental, economic and social pressures may push South Africa in the opposite direction. The reason for this 'lock in' is that, once a major investment like a smelter is made, there are very limited opportunities to improve the energy efficiency or also the production process. Recent investments in steel and aluminium bear this out: while the processes may be optimised for that technology, the wholesale switch to a more efficient technology is very costly after construction.

A farther-ranging critique was advanced in 2001 by environmental economists J.N.Blignaut and R.M.Hassan, who argued that South Africa 'over-exploits' its mineral resource capital. Coal is a non-renewable resource. Environmental damage is never factored into the national accounts. Thus, following the argument by Herman Daly we flagged in Chapter One,

> The main question this study is concerned with is whether mineral resources have been developed and managed sustainably in South Africa, given their historical economic importance. Although the contribution of mining to national income is recorded in the current system of national accounts, the cost of depletion of these natural assets as a result of its commercial exploitation is not captured in the balance sheet of the assets. This is a very serious omission and of crucial importance to macroeconomic management and sustainable development planning, since minerals are non–renewable natural assets that can be completely exhausted.[84]

South Africa's dependence upon minerals for export earnings peaked in 1983, before the full implications of the gold price crash. The decline of mining's contribution to exports over the 15-year period from 1983–1998 was from 92% to 57%. At the same time, coal reserves declined at an increasingly rapid pace. With 36 billion tonnes in 1998, there is no danger of running out in the next two centuries. But extraction of coal has soared from 53 million tonnes in 1966 to 300 million tonnes in 1998, three–quarters of which is used domestically. The main consumer, Eskom, purchases 60% of all local coal. Given the average price of R41.31/ton in 1998, important natural resource utilisation questions arise. According to Blignaut and Hassan:

> Even if one assumes that the government is investing all of the royalties, the country is still overexploiting its mineral resource capital by about 10% compared to the user cost estimates ... From these discussions it is possible to deduct, albeit tentatively at this stage, that South Africa is consuming its mineral resources without making appropriate provision for doing so.

There are, from this brief review, several aspects of Daly's policy recommendations with which any serious economist committed to sustainability would have to grapple.[85] Daly insisted that we 'stop counting natural capital as income', which would reduce South African GDP dramatically but might then compel the elites to rethink unsustainable economic development strategies such as Coega. He suggested that government 'tax labour and income less, and tax resource throughput more', which would do a great deal to ensure both environmental sustainability and mop up South Africa's vast unemployment. He recommended that economic managers 'maximise the productivity of natural capital in the short run, and invest in increasing its supply in the long run', whereas South Africa's strategy appears to be the opposite: overinvestment in quick-and-dirty coal extraction (rather than awaiting a new generation of cleaner electricity production technologies), and underinvesting in renewable energy resources.

Finally, most importantly, Daly suggested that countries 'move away from the ideology of global economic integration by free trade, free capital mobility, and export-led growth – and toward a more nationalist orientation that seeks to develop domestic production for internal markets as the first option, having recourse to international trade only when clearly much more efficient'. This, of course, is the most profound critique of South African neoliberalism. We take up that challenge again in the final chapter.

The failure of environmentalist/community/labour nerve

There emerges, here, a very serious problem. Environment, development and social protest should come together in a synthetic red-green critique, as was attempted at Coega and achieved in a sporadic way against the Lesotho dams and in struggles over infrastructure policy. Consider the political-economic and environmental factors that converge:

- South Africa, already amongst the most unequal countries in the world in 1994, became more unequal during the late 1990s, as a million jobs were lost due largely to the stagnant economy, the flood of imports and capital/energy-intensive investment;
- billions of rands in state subsidies are wasted on capital–intensive energy-related investments such as new smelters, where profit and dividend outflows continue to crash the currency;
- the price of electricity charged to mining and smelter operations is the lowest in the world;
- a pittance is being spent on renewable energy research and development, especially compared to a dubious nuclear programme;
- greenhouse gas emissions per person, corrected for income, are amongst the most damaging anywhere, and grew worse during the 1990s;
- electricity coverage is uneven, and notwithstanding a significant expansion of coverage, millions of people have had their electricity supplies cut as the state provider moves towards commercialisation and privatisation;
- one of the world's strongest-ever urban social movements, the civics, gave enormous political attention to electricity campaigns during the 1980s, winning cheap supplies for townships, and beginning in 2000, the SECC reminded Eskom – and the world – of the ability of township activists to resist injustice;
- for most South Africans, the promise of free lifeline electricity either remains a chimera or is provided in such small amounts as to be meaningless;
- one of the world's strongest-ever labour movements, Cosatu, fought long and hard, and carries on fighting, against privatisation of electricity generation, and against a restructuring of distribution that would unevenly develop South Africa and put more pressure on municipal finances;
- the possibilities of improving gender equity through access to free lifeline electricity are vast;
- for people suffering from the recent upsurge in TB, and indeed for five million HIV-positive South Africans, the public and personal health benefits of replacing coal, wood or paraffin with electricity are vast; and
- there are other important environmental, segregation-related and economic benefits that flow from clean electricity as a replacement for

traditional fuels, which are at present not incorporated into social and financial decision-making, especially when it comes to pricing electricity.

What should logically follow is a recognition that in the struggle for energy justice, the material and subjective conditions for unity amongst environmentalists, communities, labour, women's groups and Aids advocacy organisations have never been more favourable. Moreover, the responsibility of progressive South Africans to knit together these crucial components is amongst the greatest, most urgent, to be found anywhere.

The most logical place to search for a red-green socio-environmental justice discourse that brings together ecology and access issues would be the 'South African NGO/Civil Society Energy Position Paper for the World Summit on Sustainable Development'.[86] The Position Paper does pose some very radical green arguments, calling for strong fossil-fuel reduction targets and major improvements in access. Nevertheless, its weaknesses show how far the linkages between issue areas and constituencies must still be pursued. The Position Paper:

- endorses the flawed electricity lifeline amount suggested by the ANC government, 50kWh/household/month, notwithstanding that such a small amount is biased towards small yuppy families and would have virtually no impact on consumption patterns (at a time that the demand for 1 kWh/person/day was being made by Soweto activists);
- neglects the need for at least a 20Amp household supply, which is necessary to achieve the replacement of electricity for coal/fuelwood in cooking and heating;
- ignores the implications of inclement Eskom privatisation (notwithstanding extensive trade union mobilisations), or Eskom's march up-continent to privatise other power projects and electricity systems in other African countries;
- fails to make links with other constituents by including the positive externalities of electricity, especially around gender equity, local environmental improvement and TB/Aids–infections mitigation; and
- does not really come to grips with South Africa's contribution to global warming, or with the unsustainable nature of minerals beneficiation.

Indeed, on the latter question, the environmentalists call only for 'full disclosure of power sector data and particularly all subsidies, cross-subsidies and other financial support to the production and/or consumption of energy, most particularly conventional energy, including subsidies in high energy consuming sectors such as transport, mining, agriculture and minerals beneficiation'. More disclosure is always fine (especially for desk-bound researchers). But sufficient information already exists to make the point: South Africa needs an entirely new economic strategy that breaks decisively from fossil-fuel dependency.

In the same spirit, the Paper's handling of international finance and development issues shows a disturbing naivety, e.g., in the call for 'market reform programmes, including IMF Structural Adjustment Programmes and privatisation/restructuring deals, [to] allow and provide for achieving targets for access and reduced adverse social and environmental impacts' – at a time when the rest of the progressive movement was calling for an *end* to neoliberalism and conditionality.

It is easy to criticise a process of idealistic analysis and demands when it comes from a group of largely white, petit-bourgeois environmental analysts – and the present authors are not in a position to object on those grounds alone. But what the NGO/Civil Society Energy Position Paper suggests is that the kinds of red-green discursive and practical analyses that are needed, are still a long way from being forged in post-apartheid South Africa. Most of the blame lies with the white petit-bourgeois environmentalists, who fail to do sufficient outreach to workers, township and rural communities, women's groups, Aids advocacy organisations and others who *are* continually making far-reaching demands upon the establishment.

But likewise, there has been a similar failure by the SECC and their allies (including your authors) to move, conceptually, further up the production chain, where it is possible to raise aspects of electricity generation and consumption. A tentative start was made in 2001, linking community and labour critiques of Eskom, as documented in the next section. Further work is being attempted in conjunction with the Jubilee movement's attempt to acquire reparations from apartheid-era financiers for Eskom's numerous sins against black South Africa.[87]

The one recent campaign where such issues were more forcefully raised, at Coega, was soundly defeated. The next chapter reviews more of the issue areas associated with the World Summit on Sustainable Development, surveying examples of social struggle and making links that in some cases are emerging from the organic wisdom of those engaged in struggle.

5. Conclusion

We have observed in the above mix of political struggle and qualitative research the mixed history of electricity, Soweto experiences and environmental problems. These have enormous implications for national-scale electricity restructuring. What, to conclude, is the state of public debate on these matters?

Once the political pressure was raised to a pitch in August 2001, the Wits University Graduate School of Public and Development Management hosted a filmed argument between the main contenders: social movements and trade unions on the one hand, and the state (and regulatory) energy establishment. The discussion began with Eskom and government representatives making four standard points:[88]

- First, Eskom claims to have electrified more than two million households since 1994. Substantial cross-subsidies exist between industry and households: approximately R1.9 billion (including subsidies to mainly white farmers). It is only these cross-subsidies which have allowed this process to expand as far as it has to date.

- Second, Eskom offers the world's cheapest electricity to industrial users. The overall real (after-inflation) price of Eskom supplied electricity fell by 15% from 1994–2001. One result was the attraction of major industries, such as aluminium, ferrochrome, and steel processing.

- Third, the present process of rationalisation and restructuring of the electricity sector will continue, Eskom and government insists, with the objectives of more streamlined administration, economies of scale in distribution, adoption of commercial operating principles, establishment of a level playing field for Eskom's potential competitors, revenue collection through taxing Eskom, and imposition of rational (economic-based) pricing systems characterised much less by the debilitating diversity of the present system.

- Fourth, as surplus generation capacity winds down, the DME will promote nuclear energy as an allegedly environmentally-friendly alternative.

The oppositional researchers and activists pointed out enormous contradictions embedded within the four accomplishments, which in turn suggest possibilities for dramatic reforms. Each is considered in turn.

Unsustainable electrification

First, Eskom's electrification of low-income households is unsustainable, because the per-unit price is too high for low-income households. The price to consumers via pre-paid meters is in excess of R0.30 per kiloWatt hour, which has had the effect of reducing demand for electricity far below what Eskom had itself anticipated. In turn, relatively high electricity prices – compared to disposable income – have led to a dramatic reduction in the speed and scope of rural electrification, and to an unprecedented campaign of electricity cut offs both by Eskom and by its municipal government clients. The vast majority of Eskom's white customers are able to pay on the basis of a metered credit-based system, while the vast majority of Eskom's black clients must pay on the basis of a pre-paid meter, which gives Eskom a generous source of credit from low-income people.

Electricity cut offs are being handled in a most incompetent manner, and blatant inaccuracies and vastly overinflated estimates characterise the bills received by Soweto customers. In addition, many higher-volume Eskom customers in Soweto are paying higher per-unit prices – by a few cents – than are households in Sandton who are on a different tariff system also operated by Eskom. Sowetans who consume more than the average have not been informed by local Eskom staff about their ability to change tariffs so as to have the lower rates enjoyed by Eskom's Sandton residents.

And while the cross-subsidy from industry to households is acknowledged, it should be clear that it remains insufficient to assure that low-income people gain access to sufficient electricity. Worse, reports discussed in labour–government meetings suggest that a cost–plus pricing strategy that may be adopted as Eskom commercialises could raise the electricity costs to households by 20–50%. In some regions, the price may be doubled per unit.

One important reason that the high prices and anticipated increases may be adopted by Eskom and the government is that the full set of benefits (positive externalities) associated with electricity access are not being factored in. These include a net improvement in the environment, many fewer respiratory disease and other public health problems, fewer hazards associated with fire, greatly increased gender equity, improved productivity on the part of workers, improved capacity to learn on the part of youth, greater chances for class desegregation, and many economic spin-offs from those who can use electricity for income-generating purposes.

'Cheap' power

Second, while Eskom offers the world's least expensive electricity to industrial users, as we saw in the case of the Coega smelters, this practice has several negative implications. For example, the cost of environmental damage associated with the extreme CO_2 emissions associated with coal-fired electricity generation is not taken into account in the pricing.

The distortions caused, in the process of generating electricity for mega-consumers – Alusaf, Columbus, Iscor, other Highveld projects, Saldanha, Mozal, etc. – have been part of the case against South Africa in international trade, aid and investment projects. Most recently, in 2000, South Africa's failure to cost-in environmental externalities arose in a threat to end further International Finance Corporation investment in the Mozal smelter complex. In addition, the environment is harmed by the increase in SO_2 and other emissions, which would not take place were it not for the excessively cheap electricity. Part of the rationale for large consumption was the overcapacity experienced during the 1980s–90s due to the ill-considered excess construction of coal-fired and nuclear plants by Eskom.

Moreover, as the Coega case study showed, the benefits of the large industrial projects are elusive. There are typically fewer than 1000 permanent jobs per mega-project. The projects typically generate very few, if any, backward and forward linkages. And a large share of the hard currency acquired through exports of electricity-intensive products – aluminium, stainless steel and other processed base metals – is typically siphoned off to the site of ownership. In many cases, majority ownership in the mega-industrial projects is held by companies domiciled for investor purposes in Britain or Australia, such as the Gencor-Billiton-BHP group and Anglo American Corporation. The 2000–01 crash of the rand was caused to some extent by outflows of profits and dividends to these firms' overseas investors.

Worst of all, if the mega-industrial users and the mining houses are consuming the vast bulk of the electricity in South Africa, then they are also driving up the long-run marginal cost of electricity. That means that as the current excess capacity runs out, much more expensive energy generation sources will have to be constructed.

'Restructuring' or class war?

Third, Eskom appears intent on conforming to international ideological trends associated with neoliberal electricity sector restructuring. These trends are widely recognised as contributing to extreme inequality and deprivations in state service provision in most countries. Aside from anticipated job losses invariably associated with market-driven parastatal commercialisation, which have sometimes dramatic social costs, there are objective consumer-related problems that can be identified with the electricity sector's restructuring.

The institutional restructuring proposed by the officials will result in three negative developments. One is that permission will be granted for private firms to engage in generation of up to 30% of the national market, which will in turn lead to those firms 'cherry-picking' the market so as to seek highest-profit large customers, hence reducing the scope for cross-subsidisation from industry to low-income consumers.

Another is that the proposed establishment of six Regional Electricity Distributors will excessively centralise electricity so as to disempower municipalities from using surplus revenues to subsidise other vital municipal services. A third factor, contradictory as it may appear, is that the six REDS are insufficiently centralised to take advantage of national usage by mega-consumers like the smelters and mines, leading to a smaller pool from which to gain cross-subsidies for local low-income users. Given the extreme inequality between regions in South Africa, the difficulty of a national-local cross-subsidy due to the boundaries of REDS will make the electricity sector's developmental mandate much harder to achieve.

No nukes, thanks

Fourth, the use of nuclear energy, especially pebble-bed reactors, as an alternative is highly dubious. The world now has decades of experience with nuclear accidents and hazards. The global industry is virtually dormant because of the residual danger of waste (which is only partially addressed in pebble-bed design) and the economic inefficiencies associated with nuclear power when such risks are factored into the national insurance system as a whole.

The billions of rands of South African taxpayer money and Eskom surpluses spent on nuclear research and development is shocking, compared to the tiny amounts of money available for vitally needed research on solar, wind, tidal, geothermal and other potential renewable sources. The bankruptcy and loss of investor interests from US and British partners, especially in the wake of 11 September 2001 when insurance premiums on high-risk facilities soared, is telling. Eskom, nevertheless, pushes on with its programme, notwithstanding potentially severe consequences, as discussed below.

Official concessions?

In discussion, the NER did concede that so-called 'cost-reflective' electricity pricing, which he is mandated by government to pursue, could potentially be interpreted beyond mere financial inputs/outputs, to incorporate the many social, economic and environmental costs (and benefits) of electricity. DME's main policy-maker confirmed that the various positive benefits of electricity are highly valued. This would appear to give some scope for technical discussions in the spirit of the sustainable development discourse. However, by mid–2002 there were no indications that such information had changed the course of debate – as had been the case in the water sector in the wake of the cholera epidemic.

It was pointed out by critics of the state electricity policy-makers and managers that if this openness to broader cost-benefit analysis was serious and not just rhetoric, the following electricity problems would not be so obvious in twenty-first century South Africa:

- the overall price of electricity to low-income people would not be beyond their means;
- cut offs of electricity supply, including cables and including entire geographical areas, would not be happening (instead, a lifeline supply would be provided;
- the practice of self-cut off of electricity, through inadequate income to afford pre-paid cards, would not be so common;
- the denial of electricity to thousands of schools and clinics would not be so common;
- the rural electrification programme would not be slowing down, given the many millions of people still unserved;
- the possibility of local-local electricity cross-subsidisation (from excessive consumers to those with basic-supply needs still unmet) would be firmly encouraged by the Regulator through mandatory implementation of progressive block tariffs;
- the national-local cross-subsidy from industry to domestic consumers would be larger, and the high levels of subsidies – hundreds of millions of rands per year – for commercial farmers would be more critically examined to determine whether farmworkers share the benefits adequately;
- officials at national level would not be tardy in implementing the free basic electricity supply to all South Africans promised by the ANC municipal election manifesto (the tardiness by Eskom, for example, was the basis for even Johannesburg refusing to provide the free basic amount to its own electricity customers through June 2002);
- the Regulator would not shy away from endorsing the key component of the ANC promise, namely 'all residents', which implies that under his and the government's interpretation, there is likely to be means-testing rather than a dramatic restructuring of the consumption tariff along progressive block-tariff lines;
- the unit of analysis in discussions about future implementation of the ANC free basic electricity promise would be an individual person, not a 'household', given that low-income families are often disproportionately large in number, especially given the impact of HIV/Aids;
- the cheap appliance strategy of Eskom would be made part of a broader industrial strategy to ensure that with some free electricity there will be a switch from use of wood/coal for cooking/heating to hotplates, stoves and geysers; and
- a sufficiently large free supply – e.g., 1 kWh per person per day as suggested by Soweto leaders (instead of, e.g., Cape Town's 20 kWh

per household per month) – would be offered to all South Africans as the 'basic' amount, to ensure that the benefits of free electricity are genuinely within reach of low-income people.

While the *bona fides* of the state electricity officials came under attack, the labour and social movements were, in turn, asked the logical question, 'If you are so critical, what is your alternative?' The short-hand reply was, simply: 'The RDP, the Bill of Rights of the Constitution, the Grootboom judgement, and the ANC Free Basic Electricity promise'. The longhand elaboration continues to be developed.

Whatever happens, it is likely that some or all of the dozen points above would be part of an alternative strategy and programme emerging from progressive organisations in South Africa. Too, the experiences that local civil society progressives have had with institutions like transnational corporate privatisers, the World Bank and IMF, the World Trade Organisation (WTO), the US government and European Union, donor agencies and other sources of neoliberal ideologies, will continue informing the movements for global justice. These all came together in a series of debates surrounding not only the WSSD, but also basic trends towards and against commodification. These are the subjects of the final chapter.

Notes

1. We are grateful to financial support from the Canadian IDRC for Fiil-Flynn's contribution (see 'Soweto's Electricity Crisis' at http://www.queensu.ca/msp), and the Alternative Information and Development Centre (http://www.aidc.org.za) for Greenberg's.

2. The next few paragraphs are from *Independent On Line* and Sapa, 28 March 2002.

3. Supported by the most compliant national civil society group representing townships, the SA National Civic Organisation, Radebe had offered the Sowetans a lame deal featuring the half reduction of arrears. It did not go down well, and by mid–2002, arrears levels were back to pre-deal levels.

4. *Business Day*, 2 April 2002.

5. Fine, B. and Z.Rustomjee (1996), T*he Political Economy of South Africa: From Minerals-Energy Complex to Industrialisation*, London, Christopher Hirst and Johannesburg, Wits Press.

6. Wellmer, G. (2001), 'The Foreign Financing of the Parastatal Eskom during the Apartheid Years', mimeo for Jubilee South Africa, Johannesburg, August.

7. Clarke, J. (1991), *Back to Earth: South Africa's Environmental Challenges*, Johannesburg, Southern Book Publishers, p. 33.

8. Eskom was able to hedge itself using forward cover, so it was able to borrow offshore at exactly the same rates as it borrowed locally. This meant it did not cost Eskom anything extra to borrow offshore. However, every time the rand depreciated, the Reserve Bank would be exposed because of the forward cover, and hence the taxpayer footed the additional costs incurred. In short, Eskom took

loans but, when the rand depreciated, the losses were covered by the public purse.

9. Charles Anderson Associates (1994), *National Electricity Policy Synthesis Study, Vol 1*. Report submitted to the Dept of Mineral and Energy Affairs, 12 August, pp. 12–13.

10. Republic of South Africa (1987), *White Paper on Privatisation and Deregulation*, Pretoria, pp.8–9.

11. Charles Anderson Associates, *National Electricity Policy Synthesis Study*, pp. 15–17.

12. A joint venture between Eskom, Volkswagen and the Development Bank of Southern Africa, called Kwanolec, was established to provide a new supply of electricity to township residents. Although the Black Local Authority was largely excluded from the project, many residents still felt the project remained too close to the apartheid system. See Heymans, C. (1991) 'Privatization and Municipal Reform', in M.Swilling, R.Humphries and K.Shubane (Eds), *Apartheid City in Transition*. Oxford University Press, Cape Town, p. 160.

13. Swilling, M., R.Humphries, and K.Shubane (Eds) (1991), *Apartheid City in Transition*. Oxford University Press, Cape Town.

14. Mayekiso, M. (1996), *Township Politics: Civic Struggles for a New South Africa*, New York, Monthly Review Press.

15. Soweto People's Delegation (1989), 'An Assessment of Eskom's Proposals for Resolving Problems Related to the Supply of Electricity to Soweto', Mimeo, Planact archives, Wits University Historical Papers Library; Planact (1990), 'Overview and Evaluation of the Soweto Project 1988/89', Mimeo, Planact archives, Wits University Historical Papers Library.

16. Eskom's tariff formula included a rate for peak demand plus an energy charge. Johannesburg's greater base load (constant demand) derived from industry using electricity during the day. The white city therefore paid a greater proportion of costs at the cheaper energy rate. This also served to reduce the differential between the base rate and the peak rate, because the base incorporated a large proportion of total consumption. Johannesburg also had its own generating capacity (Kelvin A and B, and Orlando power stations, and five gas turbine generators), which allowed the white areas to reduce the peak requirements that needed to be purchased from Eskom, thus reducing the peak rate charge levied by Eskom.

   In addition, because Soweto's electricity infrastructure was more recently installed, capital costs were incorporated into the tariffs, making them higher than tariffs in Johannesburg where infrastructure was paid off decades earlier. Finally, richer consumers usually pay for internal reticulation and connection of dwellings up-front through a cash payment. On the other hand, poorer consumers with insufficient resources of their own and no access to credit from financial institutions were unable to pay these up-front costs. The electricity distributors therefore financed the connection costs themselves and recovered the funds from consumers over time through the tariff.

   For details, see Swilling, Humphries, and Shubane, *Apartheid City in Transition*, p. 184; and Eberhard, A. and C.van Horen (1995) *Poverty and Power: Energy and the South African State*, Cape Town, UCT Press and London, Pluto Press, p. 95.

17. Swilling, Humphries, and Shubane, *Apartheid City in Transition*, pp. 190-191.

18. Macro-economic Research Group (1993), *Making Democracy Work: A Framework for Macroeconomic Policy in South Africa*, Cape Town, Centre for Development Studies, p. 138.

19. Eberhard and van Horen, *Poverty and Power*, p. 49.

20. Fanaroff, B. (1992) 'Trade Unions and Electrification', Paper presented at ANC National Meeting on Electrification, 6–7 February, p. 5.

21. Eskom reduced the average cost of connections from around R3400 in 1996 to just over R2500 in 2001. Eskom distribution unit executive Joe Matsau said that capital costs in rural areas had fallen by about 50% in the past five years (*Business Day*, 17 August 2000). This may be related to improving technology. But according to the DME, it is also partly the result of 'cherry-picking', with distributors undertaking the lowest cost installations through selecting areas that are economically viable to electrify at low cost. See Department of Minerals and Energy (1997), 'Re-appraisal of the National Electrification Programme and the Formulation of a National Electrification Strategy', www.dme.gov.za/energy/RE-APPRAISAL.htm.

22. National Electricity Regulator (2001), *Annual Report 2000/01*, Johannesburg, p. 14.

23. *Business Day*, 23 August 2000.

24. In 1995, through amendments to the Electricity Act of 1987, the National Electricity Regulator (NER) replaced the ineffectual Electricity Control Board (ECB) as the national regulator. It has far greater power than the ECB had, since its regulatory jurisdiction includes Eskom and local authorities. It regulates market access through licensing all producers, transmitters, distributors and sellers of electricity (greater than 5 GWh per annum). In addition, all tariffs have to be approved by the NER. The NER was tasked with providing strategic direction for the industry as a whole. It attempted to rationalise the distribution industry through the licensing process, but this failed to achieve its objectives. See Winkler, H. and J.Mavhungu (2001), 'Green Power, Public Benefits and Electricity Industry Restructuring', Report prepared for the Sustainable Energy and Climate Change Partnership, EDRC, Cape Town, p. 6.

25. Department of Minerals and Energy (1998), *White Paper on the Energy Policy of the Republic of South Africa*, Pretoria, Part Three.

26. Department of Minerals and Energy (1995), 'South African Energy Policy Document', Pretoria, pp. 96,66.

27. Another reason for low consumption is that people may not be able to afford the cost of appliances required to increase electricity use. A suggestion that has some support from electricity suppliers is the provision of a 'starter pack' when households are connected, providing the household with a hot plate or a kettle for free. Eskom investigated such an option in 1999. Even in situations where the consumer chose to sell or trade the appliance, it would still benefit the electricity sector because the appliance would presumably still be in use somewhere. Such an approach is financially viable, representing a fraction of a percent of annual expenditure in the supply sector, and also has long-term benefits for the sector by increasing consumption levels and thus reducing per unit costs of supply (Leslie, G. (2000), 'Social Pricing of Electricity in Johannesburg', Masters research report submitted to the Faculty of Management, University of the Witswatersrand, Johannesburg, p. 69).

28. Reaching the same conclusion, various mid- and late-1990s studies are reviewed in Beall, J. O.Crankshaw and S.Parnell (2002), *Uniting a Divided City: Governance and Social Exclusion in Johannesburg*, London, Earthscan, Chapter Nine; and White, C., O.Crankshaw, T.Mafokoane and H.Meintjes (1998), 'Social Determinants of Energy Use in Low Income Households in Gauteng', Department of Minerals and Energy Affairs, Pretoria.

29. Eskom's pledge in March 2001 to not disconnect households with less than R5,000 arrears, and to give consumers 90 days to pay off their bill, was not widely regarded by staff, according to the survey discussed below.

30. Eskom, (2001) 'Eskom Targets Defaulters', Eskom press statement, Sandton, 27 February; *Sowetan*, 1 March 2001.

31. *Saturday Star*, 10 March 2001; *The Star*, 17 May 2001.

32. As Radebe himself regularly admits, the figure is an estimate because of the atrociously inaccurate billing procedures.

33. In 1992 Eskom acquired Soweto's reticulation network, valued at R206 million, which amortised the arrears debt to that value. An additional 37 failing black councils signed over to Eskom in 1992, and 25 more followed in the first half of 1993. In Gauteng, Eskom also supplied directly to Alexandra, Vosloorus and Tsakane. Another 113 towns and villages were taken on in 1994. In 1996 Eskom took over assets and supply at other townships that owed more than R500 million in debt, including more of Soweto, Katlehong and Lekoa. For details, see Veck, G. (2000), 'The Politics of Power in an Economy in Transition: Eskom and the Electrification of South Africa, 1980–1995', Unpublished PhD thesis, Faculty of Commerce, University of the Witwatersrand, Johannesburg, pp. 243–245; Charles Anderson Associates, *National Electricity Policy Synthesis Study*, p. 31; and Radebe, T. (1996), 'Pay-back Time for Eskom Users', *Mail & Guardian*, 8 August.

34. The financial viability of REDS is based on stringent requirements. These include significant price increases for domestic and commercial users, the transfer of electrification funding to central government, the levying of small users' bills by local government to recoup lost revenues required to fund other municipal services, and significant reductions in operating and wholesale purchasing costs.

35. The battle regarding the authority that municipalities have to decide on tariffs and service providers erupted in the Cape Town unicity when the NER refused to approve a 1.6% additional increase to fund the supply of a free 20 kWh/month lifeline supply to poor households by the council. The unicity insisted that the mandate in the Constitution and the *Municipal Structures Act* should be interpreted as meaning local government had the right to set tariffs, and that the national government was only entitled to set general frameworks but not detailed prices (*Business Day*, 1 June 2001 and 28 August 2001).

36. The DME suggested that a transfer of R2.4 billion for 5 years would replace the surpluses. However, this has been considered inadequate to cover the lost value to local governments (*Business Day*, 18 June 2001). Thereafter, in order to recoup this lost revenue, local government would have to impose a levy of between 6% and 7% on electricity bills. See PriceWaterhouseCoopers (2000), 'Tariffs, Levies and Financial Transition Strategies', Electricity Distribution Restructuring Project, Working Paper 5, Pretoria, p. 12.

37. *Business Day*, 7 January 2002.

38. McDonald, D. (2002), 'The Bell Tolls for Thee: Cost Recovery, Cut offs and the Affordability of Municipal Services in South Africa', Municipal Services Project Special Report (http://qsilver.queensu.ca/~mspadmin/pages/Project_Publications/Reports/bell.htm).

39. For a written account, see Department of Public Enterprises (2001), 'Speech by Minister Radebe at Workshop on the Service Delivery Framework', Megawatt Park Conference Room, 30 November 2001.

40. The 'suspense account' also suggests that the full arrears will re-emerge at a later stage. Activists argued that Radebe would criminalise opposition to cut offs and when the opposition was destroyed, bring the arrears back.

41. Under the leadership of Barney Pityana (until late 2001), the Commission came to be disregarded as a potential progressive ally, having refused involvement in cases brought by the Nelson Mandela Sustainability Coalition against Coega and the Treatment Action Campaign on behalf of Aids medicines.

42. *Business Day*, 12 April 2002.

43. Ngwane, T. (2001) 'Electricity Cut offs Continue Relentlessly in Soweto', *debate*, 5.

44. This and the following quotes by Ngwane are from an interview, 18 October 2001.

45. Soweto Electricity Crisis Committee (2001), 'Press Release', 18 October, Soweto.

46. In July 2002, however, Radebe and minister in the office of the president, Essop Pahad, were voted off the SACP's national executive at its Rustenberg congress.

47. *Business Day*, 27 August 2001.

48. Extremely effective figures from the anti-apartheid movement who tackled global apartheid include Dennis Brutus, Archbishop Njongonkulu Ndungane, Fatima Meer, Virginia Setshedi and others. Their stories are told in Bond, P. (2001), *Against Global Apartheid: South Africa meets the World Bank, IMF and International Finance*, Cape Town, University of Cape Town Press.

49. *Business Day*, 28 August 2001.

50. http://www.worldbankboycott.org

51. World Bank (2001), 'A Brighter Future? Energy in Africa's Development', Washington, http://www.worldbank.org/html/fpd/energy/subenergy/energyinafrica.htm.

52. *The Star*, 15 July 1999.

53. The utility has entered into a number of long-term commodity-linked agreements, especially with energy-intensive producers in the aluminium and ferrochrome industries. The agreements vary from five to 20 years, and link the price of electricity to the international price of the commodity. In the last few years, these agreements constituted between 7.6% and 12.7% of Eskom's total sales. Eskom received revenue from these agreements to the value of around 92% of the amount that would have been generated from a standard tariff. Eskom considered the lower revenue to be adequately offset by the size of the sales and the interruptibility of the supply. See Eskom (2001), *Annual Report 2001*, Johannesburg, p. 112.

54. Eskom, *Annual Report 2001*, p. 56.

55. Eskom (2001), 'Eskom's Retail Pricing Plan 2002', Revision 1, July 2001, Megawatt Park, Johannesburg, pp. 4,7. The result of the shift to cost reflective pricing will be 'significant price increases (around 50%) for domestic (conventional credit) customers', according to PriceWaterhouseCoopers ('Tariffs, Levies and Financial Transition Strategies'). In some REDS, prices for domestic users are expected to rise by over 100% before inflation by 2010. Prices for the proposed RED 2 – i.e., most of the Eastern Cape and Free State, and parts of the Northern Cape – are expected to rise higher than anywhere else.

56. *Business Day*, 10 May 2001; *Eskom, Annual Report 2001*, p. 36.

57. Statistics South Africa (2001), *South Africa in Transition: Selected Findings from the October Household Survey of 1999 and Changes that have Occurred between 1995 and 1999*, Pretoria, pp. 78–90.

58. Leslie, 'Social Pricing of Electricity in Johannesburg'.

59. *Business Day*, 25 April 2001.

60. *Business Day*, 12 March 2002.

61. At least one South African in Washington was deeply shocked. It is hard to imagine, but at least for Bond, the spectre of the white-dominated corporate media (not just the *Sunday Independent*) becoming as reflexively pro-government as, say, the Harare *Herald*, was raised in a subsequent article by *Business Day*'s Washington correspondent Simon Barber. Stewing for three weeks, Barber's subsequent screed represents the kind of denialism about conditions on the ground that the newspaper has no business trying to depict, given its nearly nonexistent township development coverage. But because the *Post* article obviously touched a very raw nerve or two, it is interesting to review Barber's case, in these core paragraphs:

The piece depicted an SA on the brink of a new popular revolt, this time against 'the injustices unleashed on this developing nation by the free-market economic policies' of the African National Congress (ANC) government.

'Materially', wrote the *Post*'s Jon Jeter in what was presented as objective news reporting, not opinion, 'life here has only gotten worse since 1994'; so 'churches, labour unions, community activists and the poor in all black townships are dusting off the protest machinery that was the engine of the liberation struggle'.

The writer had plenty of space – three times the length of this column – to back this assertion with input from all the forces he averred were rising again. In the event, and as much as he tried to leave a different impression, his quoted sources were synoptic.

The story's focus was a Soweto household, said to comprise 28 people squashed into a five-room house plus garden shed, which was reportedly burning furniture to stay warm because Eskom had cut off the electricity for nonpayment of arrears.

The *Post*'s readers were asked to conclude SA was not a place to which sane outsiders should entrust their confidence, or capital.

On whose say-so? A number of individuals were brought forward to testify. All but one, an Eskom spokesman not permitted to give a full explanation, had ties to the Soweto Electrical Crisis Committee which believes Eskom is gouging the poor while coddling industrial users and the rich.

After quoting several individuals associated with the committee, the writer artfully turned to Patrick Bond, 'a business professor at the University of the Witwatersrand and co-director of the Municipal Services Project', for what the innocent reader would take as an outside assessment.

And guess what? Bond fully endorsed the committee. What the *Post* man failed to tell his readers was that Bond, a Belfast-born and US-educated political scientist, is a major-league antiglobalisation activist and media manipulator. He acts as mentor to committee chairman Trevor Ngwane, whom he accompanied to last year's street theatre against the IMF and World Bank.

The average reader was not to know, but an internet search quickly established Ngwane's and Bond's views informed the *Post* reporter's entire analysis.

Ngwane did get a mention, in passing, as 'a former ANC municipal council member', but neither his ousting by the ANC nor his rejection by the voters last December were deemed relevant.

Nor was the fact that several other committee activists Jeter quoted show up separately as researchers for Bond's Municipal Services Project, which turns out to be an effort to foment opposition to ANC policy from the left.

To work for a newspaper like the *Washington Post* in SA is to have the time and space to report with care and nuance. So it is a pity the writer in this case could not offer a range of perspectives even maybe from elected representatives of those claiming to be burning their furniture before hinting unrest was imminent.

This kind of reporting feeds ignorant stereotypes about SA and thereby contributes to the poverty the writer no doubt has witnessed. It also contributes to the antipathy many African elites feel towards the media.

How should government respond? Have the embassy make some effort to challenge the impression his work is creating. A letter to the editor.

– Barber, S. (2001), 'Narrowly Focused Story did SA's Government no Justice', *Business Day* 28 November.

For the record, Mohapi, Motau and Buthelezi were never MSP researchers (although Setshedi and Lubisi did carry out surveying for Maj Fiil-Flynn's study, as recognised on the website and hard-copy reports). Contrary to Barber's assumption, Ngwane was and is Bond's mentor, not the other way around (and although Bond is no 'business professor', nor is he a political scientist).

What made Barber angry was that, according to Jeter's story, Bond 'acknowledges that it is expensive to provide electricity to the poor, who use little electricity and are unable to buy it in bulk through their municipality, which results in duplicate costs for equipment, administration and labor. But he said Eskom could largely resolve the debt problem in Soweto by charging big industries a few cents more for each kilowatt of electricity, subsidising a cheaper flat rate for poor customers'.

And in a mild-mannered quote, 'Eskom has a rate structure that economically makes sense', Bond said. 'But socially it makes no sense. Their structure is good for the northern suburbanites, but we'd like to see a structure that is good for everyone. That means smaller profit margins in the short term but a healthier society in the long term'.

That was the full extent of the media manipulation. Barber's panic nicely reflects the culture of privilege that runs rife amongst the newspaper's readers.

In April 2002, Barber lost his job in Washington due to *Business Day*'s inability to finance oversees staff in the wake of the rand's crash – which in turn was hastened by exchange-control liberalisation, a policy Barber and *Business Day* supported vociferously, presumably unconscious of the danger posed by neoliberal blowback. He was last seen in Pretoria's pay, as US representative for the International Marketing Council of South Africa, replying to Jeter this time as a cranky, dishonest letter-writer to the *Washington Post* (3 July 2002):

> In an otherwise solid analysis of South African President Thabo Mbeki's effort to redefine the relationship between wealthy industrialised nations and Africa ['Recovery Plan a Defining Moment for Africa', news story, June 20], The *Post*'s Johannesburg correspondent noted that Mr. Mbeki remained 'widely respected' abroad 'despite his support of unorthodox views on the causes of Aids and his reluctance to publicly criticize President Robert Mugabe of Zimbabwe'.
>
> Mr. Mbeki does not support unorthodox views on the cause of AIDS. Listen to him:
>
> 'We can only win against HIV/Aids if we join hands to save our nation ... HIV spreads mainly through sex ... I appeal to the young people, who represent our country's future, to abstain from sex for as long as possible. If you decide to engage in sex, use a condom'.
>
> Mr. Mbeki spoke those words in 1998, and everything his government has done since then has been consistent with this call to action.
>
> The issues are complex, the choices agonizing. But a point Mr. Mbeki has long been making is now common cause: Poverty is fertile ground for HIV/Aids.
>
> With regard to Mr. Mbeki's supposedly misguided stance on Mr. Mugabe, it is inconceivable that a man who sacrificed so much to achieve democracy in South Africa would not be as genuinely committed to democracy in Zimbabwe, southern Africa and indeed the entire continent.
>
> Mr. Mbeki has made clear his rejection of what Mr. Mugabe, once a liberator, has become. 'The absence of democracy', he wrote in his on-line newsletter last year, 'is both a cause of instability and a catalyst encouraging the further underdevelopment of our countries. Dictatorship and autocracy serve to suppress the creative energies of the people and to divert them to activities directed against social development, including corruption'.

The average reader was not to know, thanks to Barber's artful choice of quotes, that Mbeki at that moment was preparing to appeal a July 5 Constitutional Court judgement against his denial of Nevirapine to HIV-positive pregnant mothers (on Aids-denialist grounds of toxicity), and that Mbeki and his cabinet had judged the presidential elections in Zimbabwe, widely understood to be unfree and unfair, as 'legitimate' (*Mail & Guardian*, 22–28 March 2002).

62.   The site of the 200-person survey was Pimville and Orlando East, where residents are predominantly working-class people, pensioners and unemployed. Most house-

holds in Soweto reside in previous council houses. A smaller section, comprising 25% of the Pimville population built after 1978, thereby representing a slightly different scenario. Women were more often the managers of energy consumption in the household and the gender representation was therefore almost 3 to 1. The survey was conducted by Sowetan researchers led by Fiil-Flynn with support from Patrick Bond, Greg Ruiters and David McDonald of the Municipal Services Project. The Sowetan researchers included: Sydney Bam, Boitomelo Huma, Babhekile Khumalo, Bongani Lubisi, Chuchu Lufuno, Richard Masenya, Ronnie Midaka, Dorothy Mthembu, Lerato Poele, Aubrey Setshedi, Virginia Setshedi and Nonhlanhla Vilakazi.

63. According to Eskom, the average domestic customer (excluding Soweto) consumes 700kWh per month, while the average in Soweto is slightly lower at 600kWh per month. In richer areas such as Sandton the average consumption is approximately 1000 kWh per month.

64. Many had kept their electricity bills since electrification of Soweto in 1980. Only 2% of the respondents do not keep their bills.

65. Boycotting of service payments was an anti-apartheid tactic until 1994. Eskom negotiations with civics led to an agreement in 1995 that half of all debt accumulated up to 30 June that year (and interest) would be written off consumer bills. As many as 60,000 customers signed the agreement and their bills were adjusted accordingly. As part of the agreement, these customers agreed to pay the remaining arrears. In total, R237 million was written off consumer bills in Soweto. However, consumers who signed these agreements claim that Eskom did not honour the agreements, while Eskom claims that consumers have not honoured the repayment scheduling. According to consumers, the arrears were not written off or reapplied if they got behind on payments. The whole process has been questioned, as consumers did not understand what they were signing in the first place.

66. Morris, A. B.Bozzoli, J.Cock, O.Crankshaw, L.Gilbert, L.Lehutso-Phooko, D.Posel, Z.Tshandu, and E.van Huysteen (1999), 'Change and Continuity: A Survey of Soweto in the late 1990s', Department of Sociology, University of the Witwatersrand, pp. 34,41,35.

67. In a shack settlement outside Cato Manor in Durban, this problem caused the death of 11 children in 2001 (*Mail & Guardian*, 16–22 March 2001).

68. Interview, August 19, 2001.

69. Constitutional Court (2000), 'Irene Grootboom v the Republic of South Africa', Johannesburg, 11,BCLR 1169.

70. Spalding-Fecher, A. (2000), 'The Sustainable Energy Watch Indicators 2001', Energy for Development Research Centre, University of Cape Town, Cape Town, November. www.edrc.uct.ac.za. Unless otherwise noted, all citations and data in the following paragraphs are from this report.

71. International Energy Agency (2000), 'CO_2 Emissions from Fuel Combustion, 1971–1998', Paris; International Energy Agency (2000), 'Key World Energy Statistics from the IEA,' Paris.

72. Source: International Energy Agency data, with final column calculated by Bond. Because Purchasing Power Parity estimates by the IEA are dubious (e.g., Zimbabwe's GDP is US$32.7 billion), the actual GDP figures are used. However, South Africa's is far less than $164 billion, so the ratios indicating South Africa's high carbon/GDP emissions are actually quite conservative.

73. Department of Finance (2001), '2002 Estimates of National Expenditure: Vote 30, Minerals and Energy', Pretoria, pp. 706–709.

74. Earthlife Africa (2002), 'Information Pack for Activists Training in Energy Issues', Johannesburg; (2001), 'Nuclear Energy Costs the Earth', Johannesburg; Congress of South African Trade Unions (2001), 'Cosatu Submission on the Eskom Conversion Bill', presented to Public Enterprises Portfolio Committee, 9 May.

75. Earthlife Africa (2001), 'Other Energy-Related Developments', Johannesburg, p. 2.

76. *Business Day*, 13 March 2000.

77. Earthlife Africa, 'Other Energy-Related Developments', p. 3.

78. *Business Day*, 22 April 2002.

79. Earthlife Africa, 'Other Energy-Related Developments', p. 4.

80. The World Commission on Dams found that in many cases, the greenhouse gas emissions from large dams exceeds those of conventional energy generation. See http://www.irn.org for more information.

81. Sustainable Energy and Economy Network (2002), 'Enron's Pawns: How US Officials and Public Institutions Played Enron's Globalisation Game', Washington, Institute for Policy Studies, March, pp. 18–20.

82. *New York Times*, 27 December 1995.

83. *International Gas Report*, 19 February 1993; *Africa Review World of Information*, February 1997; *Africa Energy & Mining*, 15 November 1995, 28 February 1996, 10 July 1996, and 22 January 1997; *Oil Daily*, 18 October 1994; U.S. Embassy report in *International Market Insight Reports*, 8 April 1997.

84. Blignaut, J.N. and R.M.Hassan (2000), 'A Natural Resource Accounting Analysis of the Contribution of Mineral Resources to Sustainable Development in South Africa', Unpublished paper, Department of Economics and Agricultural Economics, University of Pretoria (available at Nathan and Associates Environmental Economics website). The following data and quotes are from this paper.

85. Daly, H. (1996), *Beyond Growth: The Economics of Sustainable Development*, Boston, Beacon Press, pp. 88–93.

86. The version of the Position Paper cited below is from the Bali prepcom.

87. This advocacy – associated with Archbishop Njongonkulu's campaigning against Swiss banks which began in 2000 (and not necessarily with the individual damages lawsuits filed by New York lawyer Ed Fagan in 2002) – is based upon research work by Greenberg for the AIDC, and Wellmer for European progressive organisations.

88. Those taking part in the main panel, organised by Hands-On Productions, were: Nelisiwe Magubane, chief director: electricity, Department of Minerals and Energy; Xolani Mkhwanazi, chief executive officer, National Electricity Regulator; Jacob Maroga, executive director, Eskom Distribution; Neva Makgetla, senior researcher, Cosatu; Virginia Setshedi, activist, Soweto Electricity Crisis Committee; Weizmann Hamilton, Johannesburg Anti-Privatisation Forum; and Patrick Bond, co-director, Municipal Services Project. The following paragraphs were initially drafted, and not contested by Eskom and government officials, in a memo distributed to all participants: Bond, P. (2001), 'Summary of Discussion Forum – Electricity Restructuring', University of the Witwatersrand Graduate School of Public and Development Management, Johannesburg, 16 August.

PART FOUR

Environment, development, and social protest

Resistance to services commodification in Mpumalanga
Township, Durban, August 2001.

Soweto Electricity Crisis – committee protest at a Johannesburg police
station, April 2002.

CHAPTER SEVEN

Conclusion

Environmentalism, the wssd, and uneven political development

With Michael Dorsey and Thulani Guliwe

1. Introduction

Unsustainable South Africa has unfolded in two ways. In part, we have assessed the admittedly unfavourable balance of political-economic forces in the course of concrete battles over projects and policies. In part, we have examined the three major environmental-developmental discourses deployed in various settings: neoliberalism, sustainable development and eco-social justice. Certainly, the issue areas that have served as the main debating ground – water and electricity – cover only a small portion of the environment and development terrain. Nevertheless, the array of forces identified here and the arguments they rely upon can be applied to many other issues.

What is crucial, though, is analysis aimed not merely at interpreting the political-economic environment, but also changing it. What, for example, do the fights over environment and development tell us about the international situation, and the ideology and strategy required for broader social change at all scales of human interactions? The most radical possible conclusion, namely that neoliberal capitalist policies are to blame, is perhaps best drawn from a pamphlet issued by the Anti-Privatisation Forum of Gauteng social movements, and circulated across Johannesburg's townships in 2002.

Written by activists, the pamphlet thinks globally and talks locally about problems caused by *compradors* ranging from president Thabo Mbeki down to the city councillors representing the township on behalf of the ANC.[1]

The context is straightforward. Just prior to the protest/shooting incident at his suburban Kensington house, Johannesburg mayor Amos Masondo had met the SECC leadership just once. He repeatedly refused to receive petitions and declarations handed over at non-violent mass marches on his office.

So in April 2002 it was time once again to visit his home, the SECC decided. Nine months earlier, a similar visit resulted in Masondo's water supply being disconnected by two dozen activists. This time 100 protesters were bussed in from Soweto. The handbill takes up the story:

The Anti-Privatisation Forum
APF/SECC/KCR/UCOSA/WCCC/TRECRA
FREE THE KENSINGTON 50!

FIRE MASONDO NOW. After march upon march, memorandum after memorandum, Soweto residents finally decided that enough is enough. On Friday, 5 April, more than a thousand angry residents decided, at a public meeting, that Jo'burg Mayor, Amos Masondo and his corrupt councillors must go. A peaceful protest at Masondo's Kensington home on Saturday, 6 April, turned sour when Mr Mathebula, a security guard, fired wildly into the crowd, injuring 2 people. 37 of the 87 protestors arrested were pensioners and children. While they face charges of public violence and malicious damage to property, Masondo's hired gunman goes free after being charged with attempted murder.

MBEKI'S GOVERNMENT HAS DECLARED WAR ON THE POOR. In Soweto thousands of families go without water and electricity. The government has, over the past few years, cut off the water and electricity supply of thousands of families living in Soweto. Thousands more have been evicted from their homes. Recently about a thousand residents of Mandelaville, Soweto, were forcibly removed and dumped at an isolated mining hostel with no water, no electricity, no access to schools, no access to jobs. Throughout Gauteng and South Africa, Mbeki's capitalist policies are attacking the poor, robbing them of their right to a quality life. Privatisation and Gear have meant rampant unemployment and a rise in the cost of water and electricity. Now our government is joining hands with other corrupt African leaders to exploit the poor all over the continent in the 'New Partnership for Africa's Development' (Nepad). Gear and privatisation have brought profits for the rich and more suffering for the poor.

WHO ARE THE REAL CRIMINALS? Is it a crime to fight against evictions and water and electricity cut offs? Is it a crime to protest peacefully? Is it a crime for voters to demand answers from their Mayor?

The real criminals are Masondo and his councillors, who betrayed their voters. The real criminal is Mbeki and his Gear policy, crippling the poor. The real criminals are the rich who only want profit at the expense of billions of people worldwide.

We demand the unconditional release of the Kensington 50. We demand the dropping of all charges against our comrades. We demand free basic services for all. We demand an end to cut offs and evictions.

Stop privatisation! Stop Gear! Stop Nepad! Join us in the fight for free basic services.

INTENSIFY THE FIGHT AGAINST

CUT OFFS, GEAR AND PRIVATISATION!

FORWARD WITH OPERATION KHANYISA!

FIRE MASONDO AND HIS CRONIES!

This degree of antagonism between ordinary Sowetans and the leading ANC politicians, just eight years after liberation, could only have erupted after tensions had built to boiling point. First, social movements needed to gain sufficient experience and confidence to protest. Because the previous chapters have documented the basis for anger, it may be possible to skip ahead to a review of interrelationships between South African social movement activism and World Summit on Sustainable Development issues.

In-between stand five points which, in a study of Zimbabwe in early 2002, emerged in our reading as the logical trajectory of exhausted African nationalism:

- a liberation movement which won repeated elections against a terribly weak opposition, but under circumstances of worsening abstentionism by, and depoliticisation of, the masses;
- concomitantly, that movement's undeniable failure to deliver a better life for most of the country's low-income people, while material inequality soared;
- rising popular alienation from, and cynicism about, nationalist politicians, as the gulf between rulers and the ruled widened inexorably and as more numerous cases of corruption and malgovernance were brought to public attention;
- growing economic misery as neoliberal policies were tried and failed; and
- the sudden rise of an opposition movement based in the trade unions, quickly backed by most of civil society, the liberal petit-bourgeoisie

and the independent media - potentially leading to the election of a new, post-nationalist government.[2]

This latter stage was reached in Zambia in 1991, although obviously 'post-nationalism' did not translate into 'post-neoliberalism'. Nor would it have done so in Zimbabwe, where the nationalist denouement was only deferred temporarily by Robert Mugabe's presidential election trickery in March 2002. The South African government witlessly labeled that outcome as 'legitimate', probably because its key functionaries saw the writing on the wall at home. The future in South Africa is, no doubt, a political party challenge to the ANC from the left.

But given residual township and rural loyalty to the national liberation movement, this will still take years to mature. Politico–electoral change will probably come only after further debilitating economic crises and after the ability of ANC leaders to woo errant leftists and ordinary working-class people is itself exhausted. In January 2002, that capacity to open the left flap of the big ANC tent was still impressive, as Cosatu drew back into the Alliance in exchange for promised concessions. The momentum built up in the two-day August 2001 anti-privatisation strike, the threats of several more general strikes during 2002, the memories of class-war rhetoric from neoliberal ANC politicians, and the possibilities for using the WSSD in August 2002 as a site of more protest and leverage, were all temporarily abandoned by the corporatist faction of Cosatu's leadership.[3]

Nevertheless, when social movements, community organisations, people's NGOs and a variety of other forces to the left of Cosatu recovered from the blow and began to mobilise for the WSSD, the seeds of a South African Social Forum were sown. Many such seeds were blown off the fertile ground immediately, when Cosatu staff allied with mainstream NGOs, Sanco (by 2002 a shell of its former dignified movement), and churches in order to toss out the 'left–left' NGOs and social movements from the WSSD's main civil society secretariat in February 2002. It was both a shameful and logical setback for progress. However, since there are 'no permanent friends or enemies in politics', including civil society social-change movements, memories of lost trust and dignity experienced in the run-up to the WSSD will probably fade, as more urgent structural and political imperatives take over. The logic of a trajectory eventually generating unity amongst those advocating eco-social justice should not, though, prevent a consideration of how the debilitating splits emerged in 2002.

Resurgent eco-social activism and antagonism

A telling statement was made to the Global Civil Society Forum in July 2002, reminiscent of the Introduction to this book:

The Johannesburg Summit convenes against the backdrop of a city visibly scarred by the profound contradictions of its history. Wealth and poverty lie cheek by jowl, a stone's throw from the central venue of the intergovernmental conference. And Jo'burg's landscape is strewn with the waste of one hundred years of resource extraction; in the service of which South Africa's racial hierarchy was constructed with violent determination. The city's contemporary social and environmental panorama is an ever-present reminder of our country's painful past. This divided geography also reflects the state of the world as we enter the twenty-first century: a globalised world built on the foundation of imperial conquest and colonial domination, which continues to define the contours of privilege and underdevelopment ...

In the developed capitalist countries it is monopoly companies, particularly transnational corporations, which set the globalisation agenda. These corporations have the potential to determine economic, social and environmental policy of governments throughout the world. Already, the content and form of globalisation of trade, investment and capital flows, and the operation of some of the critical multilateral institutions reflect in large measure the wishes of these corporations. Combined with these forces, the nation states of the North have also continued to drive and shape the process of globalisation in a manner that suits their national interests.[4]

That this eloquent argument is not drawn from the ANC's leftwing opposition, but rather from *the party's own formal statement to civil society critics*, reflects how far left the South African political–ecological narrative is situated. In other societies, a proud ruling party would hardly denigrate the country's largest city, and then blame potential foreign investors for having too much power, i.e., for maintaining 'the contours of privilege and underdevelopment'. These are merely two of the paragraphs in the ANC statement that 'talk left, act right',[5] following a longstanding tradition that can be traced through rhetoric in the ANC's *Umrabulo* journal[6] and the SA Communist Party's *African Communist*.[7] In the latter, for example, even the late Peter Mokaba used Leninist phraseology and rhetoric against the SACP in late 2001.

The resort to leftist rhetoric coincides with community attacks on the ANC's management of Johannesburg, as described in Chapter Six, and a variety of concerns – mainly from the trade unions, but also the Treatment Action Campaign (TAC), Jubilee South Africa, the SA NonGovernmental Organisation Coalition (Sangoco), intellectuals and Pan Africanists – that monopolistic transnational corporations are being given too many handouts by Pretoria. A good defence against these charges obviously includes a tough offence, as a means of distraction.

From evidence of differing degrees of protest, and official reaction (including, sometimes, repression), presented in this book thus far, it should be obvious that only in exceptional cases do the social and environmental justice movements reach a sufficiently high level of irritation and relevance to worry the ANC. Politically, what kinds of one-line conclusions can be drawn from the preceding chapters, for activists interested in social and environmental change? Project-related campaigns against Coega and Lesotho dams involved official-style appeals, but no matter how creative, these proceeded to the detriment of organising and mass action. Attempts at infrastructure design and rural water delivery relied excessively on policy advocacy within a profoundly neoliberal framework. Hence even when it was promoted by mass organisations like Samwu and specialist NGOs in the Rural Development Services Network, the free water campaign failed until the point when tens of thousands of people came down with cholera. Grassroots mobilisations carried out in Soweto and many other townships across South Africa on behalf of residents disconnected from their electricity were, however, often successful, simply by force of nuisance – disconnecting the politicians themselves – grounded in strong moral righteousness.

If we scan the South African landscape of social protest in the early twenty-first century, several other prominent features come into view.8 The most impressive examples are the national 'stayaway' strikes of millions of workers, which were called annually against neoliberal policies beginning in 1995. Sometimes Cosatu rallies in major urban centres included mass marches that stretch for kilometres. Allied with Cosatu, the TAC did exceptionally powerful advocacy work to gain access to Aids medicines beginning in 1999, resulting in formidable pressure against government policies which had begun to be labeled 'genocidal' by responsible health practitioners such as the heads of the Medical Research Council and the SA Medical Association.9

Other extremely effective alliances have emerged around other issues, and although they have a lower profile than economic justice and Aids medicines, several key areas of activism deserve mention. The Jubilee movement put the apartheid debt on the agenda, and progressive church groups helped formed advocacy coalitions for reparations from apartheid profiteering,10 a Basic Income Grant,11 prohibitions on Genetically Modified food,12 and the cancellation of the R60 billion arms deal.13 The Landless People's Movement marched and occupied land periodically. The Environmental Justice Networking Forum included strong community-based campaigns, as well as national issue development ranging from leaded petrol to global warming.[14] Students regularly fought expulsions from universities on grounds of affordability, and in 2002 joined eight organisations – including NGOs and education–sector trade unions – which mobilised to demand free education for all, including expanded Adult Basic Education. Women's rights were pushed strongly by leading individuals, although without a sense of a broader feminist movement emerging.[15]

Overall, tough 'progressive movement' politics prevailed in gatherings of labour, communities, HIV-positive people and a few other sectors. In the background, however, was the threat of cooptation by government, especially as mediated by NGOs. This had become an international dilemma, particularly evident in Latin America and Asia, according to James Petras and Henry Veltmayer:

> When millions lose their jobs and poverty spreads to significant portions of the population, NGOs engage in preventative action focusing on survival strategies, not general strikes, and they organise soup kitchens not mass demonstrations against food hoarders, neoliberal regimes or US imperialism. NGOs demobilised the populace and fragmented the movements. In the 1980s and 1990s, from Chile, Philippines to South Korea, and beyond, NGOs have played an important role in rounding up votes for regimes which continued or even deepened the socio-economic status quo. In exchange, many NGOers ended up running government agencies or even becoming government ministers in portfolios with popular sounding titles (women's rights, citizen participation, popular power, etc.).[16]

Do these criticisms apply in South Africa? Some do, but there are, in addition, people's NGOs and more accountable service organisations and training/research agencies that work with and through the militant grassroots and labour movements.[17] However, those movements do not have a single voice, and the din of political contestation of the WSSD civil society organising process reached unprecedented levels during 2001–02. In the complicated positioning, the more radical groups formed a Social Movements Indaba, which was formerly known as the Civil Society Indaba until July 2002. In contrast, what became known as the Global Civil Society Forum was dominated by mass-based organisations closer to the mainstream, and serviced by a UN secretariat comprising talented technocrats.

Until we consider the huge failings of the WSSD, below, the positionality may not be obvious. However, lessons can be learned from the Durban World Conference Against Racism in August 2001. At that point, frustration had built up in the trade union movement to the point that

Cosatu's national leadership called a two-day national strike against ANC privatisation policies. More than four million workers heeded the call. The timing was important, for the strike humiliated the ANC on the eve of the Durban conference, attended by more than 10,000 delegates who wanted to believe that South Africa was genuinely liberated.

Still, demonstrating how fickle the politics of alliances remained, Cosatu agreed to hold a joint mass march against racism alongside the Durban ANC and the SACP, the day after a much more militant demonstration by anti-neoliberal movements which marched under the banner of the Durban Social Forum. The Social Forum pulled together an estimated 20,000 protesters on behalf of Palestinian freedom, land rights, debt cancellation, community housing and services, and the need for an alternative to neoliberalism. The mood was extremely hostile to the ANC, and neither president Mbeki nor UN secretary-general Kofi Annan deigned to personally accept the memoranda presented at the Durban convention centre.

As tensions simmered and then cooled within the ANC-SACP-Cosatu Alliance in the subsequent weeks, leaders of Cosatu joined Sangoco, the SA Council of Churches (SACC) and Sanco to take over the civil society secretariat in early 2002. The Civil Society Indaba was booted out unceremoniously, according to Cosatu, on the dual grounds that:

- The structures of the Indaba give disproportionate power to small and unrepresentative NGOs. This occurs by giving NGOs three-fold representation: through the so-called provincial representatives, the NGO constituency, and the votes given NGOs under the heading of 'rural and urban communities'. In contrast, key groups of civil society – notably the disabled and civics – have no seats at all.
- The financial management of the Secretariat to the Indaba remains open to question. Remuneration is extraordinarily high for non-profit civil society – initially topping out at over R40,000 a month, including car allowance, although this figure was reduced somewhat this January, following our protests. In addition, we have some evidence of alleged misappropriation of funds, which we can provide on request. The audit commissioned by the CSS has proven to be superficial and inadequate.[18]

The 'First Nations' of indigenous South Africans were repelled by the Cosatu-led purge, and resisted subsequent attempts to draw them back. Another angle also emerged, as reported in the *Mail & Guardian*: 'The New Partnership for Africa's Development appears to be key to the divisions in this sector ...The Civil Society Indaba has a leftist, anti-globalisation focus. It has claimed there is big brother interference from the government in the new, mainstream South African Civil Society Forum set up by Cosatu and its allies'.[19] While the first six months of 2002 led virtually all African civil society groups to reject the Nepad, later it became apparent that once Mbeki began to intervene, it was possible to criticise Nepad's form, content and process, yet still agree to 'engage' Mbeki and other African leaders in demanding a rewrite.

By no means, however, did the Cosatu-led takeover of the UN side of the WSSD require a *formal* ideological retreat. As noted, even the ANC as a political party spoke in the same anti-neoliberal language when drawing out support for a protest march 'against world poverty' on 31 August 2002.[20] The international landless people and the Social Movements Indaba would attempt, as at Durban the previous year, to draw larger and more militant crowds to their march (the same day), with a strongly anti-Mbeki message. The Landless People's Movement (LPM) made clear their desire to distance themselves in a July press statement:

> The March of the Landless on 31 August, 2002 will not include organisations which are part of the Tripartite Alliance whose record of governance has ensured the failure of land reform in South Africa. The March of the Landless will be led by the LPM on the same day in alliance with other civil society organisations. The march will be the culmination of an alternative Week of the Landless that will take place decisively outside of the formal UN processes of the WSSD.
>
> The purpose of the March of the Landless will not be to support the World Summit on Sustainable Development, or to make vague calls for 'sustainable development' through unsustainable policies like Nepad or Gear. Instead, the purpose of the March of the Landless will be to denounce the unsustainable policies being fortified by the world's elite in the Sandton Convention Centre; to focus world attention on the failure of South Africa's World Bank-style land reform programme; and to forward the demands of the 19-million poor and landless rural South Africans and 7-million poor and landless urban South Africans. That demand is: 'End Poverty: Land! Food! Jobs!'.[21]

The logic of fighting back against neoliberalism, partriarchy, racism, ecological degradation and many other ills could unite progressive South Africans, *one day* – even though the manoeuvres associated with long-held ANC-Alliance loyalties, and the bitter leftwing anger at multiple betrayals, would together prevent that clarity from emerging at the WSSD itself.

Having reviewed some of the activist initiatives that appear emblematic of the fight for a less unsustainable South Africa, we next move to the regional scale. It is there that most hope lies for consistent red-green syntheses, even if the networked social-change activists are still organising in embryonic ways (Section 2). The global scale then beckons, in part because internationalism between social movements has never been more important, and in part because the international elites clearly have no programme for cleaning up horrific environment and development messes through the WSSD (Section 3). Reviewing what works and what doesn't at different scales leads, finally, to an exploration of uneven political development, with some thoughts about how critical ecologies can transcend weaknesses we have identified throughout this book, and become eco-socialist in character (Section 4).

2. Top-down or bottom-up regional eco-development?

Global-scale political processes remain overwhelmingly hostile to social and environmental progress, notwithstanding the new activist networks' inspiring modes of anti-neoliberal resistance. But likewise, nation-states and subnational, local terrains are still unstable sites for radical, eco-socialist projects. If these barriers to social progress persist, might an appropriate scale ultimately be the 'region' – i.e., a coherent geographical-economic–socio–cultural collection of neighboring countries?

Some leading Third World left intellectuals are positing stronger regional political relations, including Walden Bello of Focus on the Global South in Bangkok[22] and Samir Amin of Third World Forum in Dakar, who advocates 'regionalisation aiming at the building of a polycentric world', in part grounded in 'grassroots labor-popular social hegemonies'.[23] The region is, indeed, an entirely appropriate arena for such political considerations. Southern Africa's rich, interrelated radical traditions include vibrant African nationalist insurgencies, once-avowed Marxist-Leninist governments (in Mozambique, Zimbabwe and Angola), mass movements (sometimes peasant-based, sometimes emerging from degraded urban ghettoes), and powerful unions, not to mention their regionally-conscious opponents in the British-Afrikaans-Portuguese nexus which ran Southern Africa's colonies during most of the twentieth century.

But notwithstanding the similar colonial and then anti-colonial norms, values and institutional orientations instilled in the majority of the Southern African citizenry since the mid-twentieth century, there has never been an explicitly regional project. Post-independence governments quickly demonstrated extreme territorial sensibilities, no matter that national boundaries established by coin-flipping white settlers, or geopolitical tradeoffs at the 1885 Berlin border-carving conference, or bizarre colonial-era deals for strategic strips of land, were and are intensely dysfunctional. Meagre efforts by the main interstate network, SADC, to coordinate sectoral and economic strategies have been largely ineffective, as dependency relations vis-a-vis the world system worsened over the past two decades. Among the most obvious casualties of uneven regionalism has been the Southern African environment, shaped as it is by cross-border ecological processes – particularly in relation to water and energy flows – and requiring ever more sophisticated arrangements for mediating human–nature relations.

The regional working class is a crucial social force in all of this. It matured during the twentieth century and quickly fell into the political arms of nationalists. Its own migratory patterns reflect victimisation and yet also revolutionary geopolitical potential, in relation to the dominant capitalism. The Washington-based enforcers of neoliberalism – which during the 1980s switched accumulation circuits away from internal industrialisation towards agro-mineral extraction, financial speculation and commercial deregulation – have enfeebled nation-states across Southern Africa, especially in relation to social welfare provision and environmental management, and in the process unintentionally given much greater social weight to organised labour and allied social movements.

The challenge, then, is increasingly obvious: namely to contest the intersections of class formation (and destruction) and ecological exploitation especially where this occurs at a regional scale between dominant global circuits of capital and denuded nation-states. To facilitate higher profits and larger volumes of foreign investment, those states simultaneously externalised the environmental costs of extraction and production, and, more generally, became hostile to social change.

The region's states remain individualised units contested by populist-nationalists and a new generation of post-nationalist political parties. For many activists, that makes electorally contesting those states terribly *unappealing*, even where post-nationalist parties are grounded in trade unions, such as in Zambia from 1991, Zimbabwe from 1999, and Namibia and South Africa within the next decade, more than likely. It is, after all, probably only the trade union-based office network in each Southern African city that can hold together the local progressive coalitions of forces needed to vote out the incumbents.

But if, in turn, political contestation of Southern African nation-states ultimately transcends the revitalised neoliberalism offered by Frederick Chiluba in Zambia and Morgan Tsvangirai in Zimbabwe, there must be a much stronger regional coherence to labour-backed politics. The ideas of the radical social movements and environmentalists would necessarily play a central role, perhaps overwhelming the corporatist instincts of so many regional trade unions. In turn, workers and their allies would draw for their twenty-first century consciousness upon a regional legacy of class formation and struggle that dates to the establishment of migrant labour systems for mines, plantations and manufacturing in the late nineteenth century.

In short, can a more coherent Southern Africa-wide vision of regionalism-from-below emerge to counteract uneven capitalist development, transcend nationalist ideology, extinguish deep-burning xenophobic fires (which have scorched potential working-class solidarity), and establish economies of scale sufficient, one day, for an Amin-style, deglobalised contribution to polycentrism? The main barrier is regionalism-from-above, specifically the new subimperialist project known as Nepad.

At the WSSD, Nepad is one of the main agenda items, having previously gone through official state and capitalist endorsement processes at both the June summit of the G8 leaders (the Group of Eight main industrial powers) in Alberta, Canada, immediately followed by the Southern African gathering of the World Economic Forum in Durban, and the July launch of the African Union (AU), also in Durban. Nepad was an exceptionally politicised process by mid-2002, not only because AU financier Muammar Gaddafi – not to mention the main propagandist for the Zimbabwean government, Jonathan Moyo – intervened to ridicule the pro-western nature of the document. The international progressive project rebuffed 'anti-imperialism' from such dubious, oppressive sources. More importantly, Nepad was partially endorsed by the SACC and SACP in July, following hard-sell meetings of African intellectuals and civil society sponsored by Pretoria's Africa Institute, that were not so successful.[24]

Nepad will continue underdeveloping Africa, and loyalty to the ANC and Mbeki in particular will wane, so that civil society may unite against the first homegrown, continental-scale neoliberal target. Beyond these points of unity for progressives, it may well be that radical environmentalism can provide an impetus to the bottom-up regional political project, given the need for far-reaching changes in eco-social power relations in each country. Because Nepad opens the door for infrastructure privatisation, the water and electricity issues again give us an opportunity to explore the politics of imperialism, subimperialism and resistance.

A subimperial partnership[25]

Because of its evolution under conditions of secrecy, in close contact with the G8 (in Okinawa in 2000 and Genoa in 2001), the Bretton Woods

Institutions and international capital (at Davos in 2001), the Nepad plan denies the rich contributions of African social struggles in its very genesis. Instead, it empowers Northern donor agency technocrats, Washington financial agencies, Geneva trade bureaucrats, machiavellian Pretoria geopoliticians and Johannesburg capitalists, in a coy mix of imperialism and South African subimperialism.

The first public protest against Nepad occurred at the July 2002 World Economic Forum regional meeting in Durban, where anti-apartheid poet Dennis Brutus, acting secretary of Jubilee South Africa, led more than a hundred demonstrators into horse-charging policemen. Brutus held up a sign for national television viewers: 'No Kneepad!'

Indeed, Nepad has gone by various names, including the African Renaissance (1996–2000), the Millennium Africa Recovery Plan (2000–July 2001) and the New African Initiative (July–October 2001). Aside from Mbeki, its main advocates are Abdelaziz Bouteflika of Algeria, Olusegun Obasanjo of Nigeria and Benjamin Mkapa of Tanzania. None can be considered democrats of even a bourgeois variety.

The document's core premise is that poverty in Africa can be cured, if only the world elite gives the continent a chance: 'The continued marginalisation of Africa from the globalisation process and the social exclusion of the vast majority of its peoples constitute a serious threat to global stability'. The phrasing becomes more slippery yet: 'We readily admit that globalisation is a product of scientific and technological advances, many of which have been market-driven ... The locomotive for these major advances is the highly industrialised nations'.

All of these arguments are better put by reversing the logic. Africa's continued poverty and degradation ('marginalisation') are a direct *outcome* of globalisation, not of a lack of globalisation. Technology lubricates but does not cause international economic dynamics. The advanced capitalist world has itself witnessed lower profits and growth since the 1970s, and the dot.com craze is only one indication of technology's *failure* to resolve capitalist crisis.

As a result, the African left has expressed thorough scepticism over Nepad's main strategies:

- privatisation, especially of infrastructure such as water, electricity, telecoms and transport, will fail because of insufficient buying power of African consumers;
- more insertion of Africa into the world economy will simply worsen fast-declining terms of trade, given that African countries produce so many cash crops and minerals whose global markets are glutted;
- multi-party elections are held, typically, between variants of neoliberal parties, as in most countries, and cannot act as a veil for the lack

of participatory democracy required to give legitimacy to so many failing African states;

- grand visions of information and communications technology are hopelessly unrealistic considering the lack of simple reliable electricity across the continent; and
- South Africa's self-mandate for peacekeeping gives no peace of mind, in the wake of Pretoria's ongoing purchase of US$5 billion worth of offensive weaponry and its unhappy record of regional military interventions.

Likewise in areas of economic reform, such as debt, capital financial flows and foreign investment, Mbeki offers only the *status quo*. Instead of promoting debt cancellation, as do virtually all serious reformers, the Nepad strategy is to 'support existing poverty reduction initiatives at the multilateral level, such as the Comprehensive Development Framework of the World Bank and the Poverty Reduction Strategy approach linked to the Highly Indebted Poor Country debt relief initiative'.

Only after trying such discredited strategies, replete with neoliberal conditions such as further privatisation, would African leaders 'seek recourse' through Nepad. Malawi's 2002 famine, because the country's grain stocks were sold following IMF advice to first repay commercial bankers, is telling.

As for speculative 'hot-money' inflows to emerging markets such as South Africa, these have harmed not helped development. Nepad calls for more, through further financial liberalisation. The vast majority of foreign loans granted to Third World governments over the past 30 years have not helped development, but have instead allied African state elites with foreign bankers. Nepad calls for more.

Nepad's solution to foreign investment drought is consistent with the worst international rhetoric about Public–Private Partnerships (PPPs) in privatised infrastructure: 'Establish and nurture PPPs as well as grant concessions towards the construction, development and maintenance of ports, roads, railways and maritime transportation ... With the assistance of sector-specialised agencies, put in place policy and legislative frameworks to encourage competition'. However, most infrastructure is of a 'natural monopoly' type, for which competition is unsuitable: roads and railroads, telephone landlines, water and sewage reticulation systems, electricity transmission and distribution, ports and the like.

Nepad cannot make a case for competition in these areas. There is, in contrast, an extremely strong case, based on public-good features of infrastructure discussed in previous chapters, for *state* control and non-profit operation. Most noticeably, privatisation of infrastructure usually prevents cross-subsidisation to enhance affordability for poor consumers.

Finally, Nepad is at its most self-contradictory when appealing 'to all the peoples of Africa, in all their diversity, to become aware of the seriousness of the situation and the need to mobilise themselves in order to put an end to further marginalisation of the continent and ensure its development by bridging the gap with the developed countries'. The hypocrisy is breathtaking. Africans falling further into poverty as a result of leadership *compradorism* and globalisation, particularly women, do not need to 'become aware of the seriousness of the situation', as much as do the elite rulers who generally live in luxury, at great distance from the masses. And when Africans in progressive civil society organisations express 'the need to mobilise themselves', they are nearly invariably met with repression.

Pretoria's own practice in all these regards – repaying apartheid debt, allowing speculative finance to wreck the currency, privatising basic services delivery at great social cost (especially damage to public health), and meting out repression to those who object – are reminders of the fact that Nepad is being tried at home, and *isn't working*. As for 'mobilising', Mbeki does not mention the mass civil-society protests that threw off the yokes of slavery, colonialism, apartheid and dictatorships. Those protests are increasingly turning against Pretoria's neoliberal, subimperial agenda.

For example, the most succinct critique of Nepad has come from an Accra meeting of the Council for Development and Social Science Research in Africa (Codesria) and Third World Network–Africa (TWN–Africa) in April 2002. According to the meeting's resolution:

> The most fundamental flaws of Nepad, which reproduce the central elements of the World Bank's *Can Africa Claim the Twenty-first Century?* and the ECA's *Compact for African Recovery*, include:
>
> (a) the neoliberal economic policy framework at the heart of the plan, and which repeats the structural adjustment policy packages of the preceding two decades and overlooks the disastrous effects of those policies;
>
> (b) the fact that in spite of its proclaimed recognition of the central role of the African people to the plan, the African people have not played any part in the conception, design and formulation of the Nepad;
>
> (c) notwithstanding its stated concerns for social and gender equity, it adopts the social and economic measures that have contributed to the marginalisation of women;
>
> (d) that in spite of claims of African origins, its main targets are foreign donors, particularly in the G8;

(e) its vision of democracy is defined by the needs of creating a functional market;

(f) it under-emphasises the external conditions fundamental to Africa's developmental crisis, and thereby does not promote any meaningful measure to manage and restrict the effects of this environment on Africa development efforts. On the contrary, the engagement that is seeks with institutions and processes like the World Bank, the IMF, the WTO, the United States Africa Growth and Opportunity Act, the Cotonou Agreement, will further lock Africa's economies disadvantageously into this environment;

(g) the means for mobilisation of resources will further the disintegration of African economies that we have witnessed at the hands of structural adjustment and WTO rules.

Codesria and TWN-Africa are not alone. During the first half of 2002, African social movements, the largest South African civil society organisation (Cosatu), and leading African intellectuals analysed Nepad and issued public statements that decry the document's lack of participation and consultation, its orientation to Western economic interests and its inability to make good on governance claims.

In January, dozens of African social movements met in Bamako, Mali, as the African Social Forum, in preparation for the Porto Alegre World Social Forum. It was one of the first substantial conferences since the era of liberation to combine progressive NGOs and social movements from all parts of the continent. The Bamako Declaration included the following paragraphs:

> A strong consensus emerged at the Bamako Forum that the values, practices, structures and institutions of the currently dominant neoliberal order are inimical to and incompatible with the realisation of Africa's dignity, values and aspirations.
>
> The Forum rejected neo-liberal globalisation and further integration of Africa into an unjust system as a basis for its growth and development. In this context, there was a strong consensus that initiatives such as Nepad that are inspired by the IMF-WB strategies of Structural Adjustment Programmes, trade liberalisation that continues to subject Africa to an unequal exchange, and strictures on governance borrowed from the practices of Western countries and not rooted in the culture and history of the peoples of Africa.

In April 2002, the Central Executive Committee of Cosatu added its view on the problems intrinsic to Nepad:

The CEC believe that the transformation of Africa can only happen if it is driven by its people. There was a strong feeling that the Nepad plan has been developed only through discussions between governments and business organisations, leaving the people far behind ...

The CEC raised concerns about the economic proposals in the Nepad. In particular, we need to ensure that macroeconomic governance does not stray too far towards stabilisation, at the cost of growth and employment creation. Moreover, the emphasis on privatisation in the section on infrastructure ignores the reality: that privatised services will not serve the poor on our continent.

These are just three examples of civil society and intellectual precedents for a critical perspective on Nepad. Notwithstanding the successful last-gasp attempts by Mbeki in June 2002 to win over church, African trade union and even SACP support for an 'engagement' with Nepad, there can be no doubt that Mbeki's plan will become a point of unification amongst progressives in African civil society:

- Progressive civil society organisations have traditionally demanded that all policies, programmes and projects of government be conducted in a transparent, participatory and respectful manner. Nepad's formulation failed on all accounts.
- Progressive civil society organisations have also traditionally provided rights-based advocacy that takes basic needs as human rights. At a philosophical foundational level, Nepad fails here, and instead promotes market-related strategies and privatised infrastructure even with respect to basic infrastructural services.
- Moreover, progressive civil society organisations have opposed the international neoliberal agenda of free markets, transnational corporate dominance of the South, lower government budgetary spending (under the rubric of alleged macroeconomic stability), and the lowering of standards for the sake of foreign investors. In terms of content, Nepad fails on these points.
- Finally, progressive civil society organisations have most forcefully promoted good governance and democracy. While Nepad gives lip-service to these ideals, it fails to take them sufficiently seriously such that obvious violations – e.g., of recent elections in Congo–Brazzaville, Madagascar, Zambia and Zimbabwe – are publicly criticised and punished. As one of Nepad's own co-authors, Senegalese president Wade put it, the leaders of Africa, including Nepad coauthors in South Africa and Nigeria, appear to have a 'trade union' approach that gives mutual support and solidarity to dictators and tyrants.

Nepad on the environment

A closer look at Africa's ecological problems and 'solutions' is also revealing. Nepad's environmental analysis combines bland sustainable-development rhetoric with faith in global eco-reform processes (like the WSSD) based on market mechanisms. Dangerously, the document also endorses an implicit and sometimes explicit Malthusianism, which blames the victim and hints at overpopulation as the source of environmental problems. Thus 'The expansion of industrial production and the growth in poverty contribute to environmental degradation of our oceans, atmosphere and natural vegetation'.

Several contradictory processes are conflated in this pop-environmental reading of the relationship between poverty and ecological degradation. Africa's main economic problem is not excessive pollution-intensive industrialisation, but insufficient industrialisation, which in turn leads to greater reliance for export earnings upon ecologically destructive raw material extraction (e.g., the rainforests and strip-mines, or the substitution of cash crops for food crops). Globalisation has exacerbated these processes, because the 'environmental degradation of our oceans, atmosphere and natural vegetation' is mainly a function of transnational and local corporate irresponsibility: e.g., overexploitative EU and East Asian fishing trawlers, pollution-intensive South African mines and metal companies which defile the air and water without paying the externality costs, and forestry companies whose alien-timber plantations destroy the integrity of African soils and water courses.

In some cases, obviously, the colonial/apartheid displacement of large populations from good farms to infertile areas led to worsening soil degradation, for which the solution is a thoroughgoing land reform and rural development programme – i.e., the opposite of the extremely meagre efforts the South African government is making. But more generally, to ascribe environmental destruction to 'growth in poverty' is to blame the masses whose poverty has worsened in part because of corporate-led globalisation.

Again, by way of distorting complex socio-environmental processes, Nepad announces, 'It is obvious that, unless the communities in the vicinity of the tropical forests are given alternative means of earning a living, they will co-operate in the destruction of the forests'. Here would have been an opportunity to target the transnational corporations and banks involved in rainforest destruction,[26] as well as mercenary armies from Zimbabwe, Angola, Uganda, Rwanda and other countries which are presently stripping timber and raw materials from the DRC, but Nepad fails to do so.

Another crucial example of Nepad ducking the issue is its two-sentence note on how the Environmental Initiative will tackle global warming: 'The initial focus will be on monitoring and regulating the impact of climate change. Labour-intensive work is essential and critical to integrated fire management projects'. Starting at home, if Mbeki was serious about offering strong leadership, he would address the fast-growing contribution of South Africa to greenhouse gas emissions and then demand far stronger global treaties and agreements on the need to reduce in absolute terms the production of global warming gasses by moving to genuinely sustainable development strategies.

Nepad's overarching ideology of market-led growth with sustainable development comes together in this paragraph:

> While growth rates are important, they are not by themselves suffi-
> cient to enable African countries achieve the goal of poverty reduc-
> tion. The challenge for Africa, therefore, is to develop the capacity to
> sustain growth at levels required to achieve poverty reduction and
> sustainable development. This, in turn depends on other factors
> such as infrastructure, capital accumulation, human capital, institu-
> tions, structural diversification, competitiveness, health and good
> stewardship of the environment.

There is, here, an annoying combination of progressive and neoliberal objectives: infrastructure, human capital, institutions, structural diversification, health and good stewardship of the environment in the first category, and capital accumulation and competitiveness in the second. Objectively, neoliberal policies have, during the past two decades, destroyed Africa's infrastructure, human capital, institutions, structural diversification, health and stewardship of the environment. The same threats exist in the water and energy sectors.

Cross-border water flows[27]

In relation to water, all South Africa's neighboring countries are affected by mismanaged systems of cross-border water acquisition and consumption, dam management, persistent pollution, limited downstream availability and related legal arrangements. While exacerbated by Pretoria's policies and practices, many of these are century-old historic arrangements associated with settler colonialism, as University of Botswana political scientist Larry Swatuk eloquently points out:

> Urban centres developed delivery systems based on the technolo-
> gies imported from water-rich Europe. Typically, the lion's share of
> supplied water went to irrigated agriculture, with mines and indus-
> tries also enjoying privileged access.

However, the attempt to reproduce Europe in Africa, also meant that indigenous food crops and farming methods were displaced by European ones, often resulting in the substitution of drought-resistant food crops with water-guzzling 'beverage' crops and minimum tillage systems with soil-eroding practices. Choices of settlement also created special water-related problems. Urban areas often developed in the wake of mineral-exploitation or strategic location considerations. Both Bulawayo and Harare, for example, were military sites. Johannesburg and Kimberley grew out of the mid-nineteenth century gold and diamond rushes. The site for Windhoek was chosen because of the presence of a spring, with Gaborone being so sited, among other reasons, because of the possibilities for dam construction. Both capital cities have long surpassed population projections at the time of settlement, so creating special water needs.

Contrary to pre-colonial patterns of human settlement, then, the colonial/settler impact has resulted in large populations congregating relatively far from adequate freshwater resources. In consequence, the region has a long history of large-scale water transfer and storage schemes. This supply-oriented thinking remains dominant today.[28]

We return to the issue of whether urban settlement, not to mention white-dominated commercial farming, should retain its historic form, or be transcended by an alternative reflecting values of eco-social justice and sustainable development. The problem Swatuk reminds us of, though, is that in the short-term Pretoria has become central to a profoundly neoliberal reconstruction of a regional 'water architecture' that features national commodification of water and catchment-level management based largely on the neoliberal pricing policies discussed in Chapters Three–Five:

South Africa and Zimbabwe are already 'experimenting' with this new management unit, with some other SADC states further behind. Mozambique, Zambia and Tanzania, for example, lack the necessary capital, technical and human resources to effectively institute these reforms. Botswana, with either only ephemeral or internationally-shared rivers, a small dispersed population and an arid climate does not envision such reforms. Lesotho and Swaziland, as small mountainous countries where many rivers rise, are also unlikely to pursue such a management form, preferring instead to participate in a variety of inter-state technical units created to manage their shared water course systems which are, themselves, not terribly unlike catchment councils at national level.[29]

Pretoria's market-based determination of regional water architecture is likely to foster yet more mega-dams, privatisation[30] and cross-catchment transfer schemes. As one example of the regard in which Pretoria holds the region, hapless South African flood-control proved lethally inadequate to Mozambicans in 2000–01. White South African farming capital's excess control of water rights allocations remains particularly noxious, when most local black rural people downstream – in both South Africa and its several water-border neighbours – are deprived of even a minimal basic amount required for survival.

Intense struggles over access to border rivers break out regularly between South Africa, Namibia, Botswana, Zimbabwe and Angola. Debates rage over the implications of proposed water pipeline transmissions from the Zambezi River's Victoria Falls to major industrial conurbations – Bulawayo and even Johannesburg – to the south, as well as from the DRC and desperately dry Namibian towns. Further dam building will accelerate evaporation, yet the revelation that tropical hydroelectricity generation contributes more to global warming than the region's huge coal-fired thermal plants is not likely to dampen Mozambican officials' enthusiasm for another three megadams on the Zambezi. The two other large World Bank regional dams – the ongoing LHWP and the Kariba Dam, the world's largest artificial lake when built on the Zambezi in 1956 – each displaced tens of thousands of indigenous people, and reparations are in order.[31]

As discussed earlier, oppositional environment, labour and social movements have arisen in South Africa recently to oppose water contamination, hedonistic usage of water, corporatisation and privatisation, and the extravagant cross-catchment water transfers via large dams and at the expense of the poor. In Zimbabwe, social movements have recently made similar rights-based claims to water access as exist in South Africa, in the broad-based National Constitutional Assembly's draft constitution. Consciousness has also grown over excess colonial-era irrigation arrangements for white commercial farmers, especially of tobacco, and Anti-Privatisation Forums emerged in Harare and Bulawayo in 2002, as well as in Mbabane, Swaziland.

Nation-state conflicts over water-rights allocations – such as between Zimbabwe and Zambia (on the Zambezi River's Kariba Lake) – in turn reflect class conflicts between lake/river-side peasants and industrialists dependent upon both hydropower and water for industrial use. Municipal and rural water-system privatisation, featuring sharp retail price increases as a central World Bank condition for Mozambican debt relief, has been widely attacked by progressives in civil society and parliament. Namibian indigenous people and environmentalists have nearly halted a major dam project, Epupa, strongly supported by President Sam Nujoma. A Southern African water network of environmental and community activists, Nawisa, came together in 1999, facilitated by the International Rivers Network and its local partners.

In most of these cases, there are not only local agents fouling the regional environment, but also a global network of neoliberal institutions aiming to commodify water and nature more generally: the World Bank and its various sponsored partnerships, transnational construction firms, for-profit French and British water corporations, and pro-privatisation merchant banks.[32] In this sense the possibility for increasing regional unity amongst workers and allied working-class social movements · requires a common ideology supportive of decommodified, destratified and ultimately non-capitalist forms of human–nature relations. Below, we note the introduction of an alternative world water treaty along precisely these lines. There is a similarly pressing need in the case of regional energy.

Regional power relations

Many of the same challenges of linking red and green across borders in Southern Africa arise in regional power generation and consumption. As in the case of water, there are common targets. Not only the World Bank and corporate energy firms, but a central agency in suburban Johannesburg looms as the locus of progressive resistance against the privatisation of electricity in coming years: Eskom.

The company is not a newcomer to the region. German researcher Gottfried Wellmer summarises Eskom's damage in apartheid-era Southern Africa:

> Eskom buttressed the [apartheid] state's claim to regional hegemony by controlling the development of electricity generation and distribution in occupied Namibia, propping up the tottering colonial empire of Portugal in Angola and Mozambique by supporting the building of the Cahora Bassa and the Gove and Calueque dams as well as the hydro-electric power stations at Ruacana in the Cunene river basin and at Cahora Bassa on the Zambezi.
>
> When these neighbours gained their independence, Eskom preferred not to depend on the supply of Mozambican power, but rather designed the establishment of its massive oversupply capacity, thereby giving the green light and go-ahead to the military to

destroy thousands of pylons along the transmission line from Cahora Bassa to Pretoria. And the protection of the Ruacana power station in 1975 became the pretext to invade Angola in an attempt to prevent the MPLA to come to power.[33]

Today, rather than destroy regional infrastructure, Eskom needs to build it up, for two reasons: both drawing down and contributing to the regional power grid, and extracting profits through electricity, telecommunications and even water system privatisation.

In the first instance, Eskom needs continued access to the regional grid so that Mozambique's hydropower will delay the need for new powerplant construction in South Africa. This is not necessarily logical, but instead reflects power relations prevailing when a desperate Mozambique signed a power supply deal with Eskom. That deals allows Cahora Bassa hydro-electricity to flow into South Africa, and then return for consumption to the capital of Maputo, particularly at the massive Mozal smelter which at peak will consume three-quarters of the country's electricity. The power system had broken down because Pretoria backed the Renamo rebels, who sabotaged the Cahora Bassa line. It was only in 1998 that the 900 kilometre power line from the dam was repaired.

In 2002, the Cahora Bassa dam operating company, HCB, complained that Eskom bought its electricity in rands at the very low price of R0.02 and then resold it to Mozambique at a high markup (undisclosed) in US dollars.[34] Despite a deal to increase the price to R0.037, and despite the historical injustice associated with Pretoria's support for Renamo, Eskom insisted that it not pay more for HCB electricity than it would cost to produce in South Africa. This was a crucial issue because HCB was compelled, beginning in 2002, to repay a $2.5 billion debt it owed to the Portuguese treasury, 28 years after it built Cahora Bassa with a loan from the Portuguese government. Portugal owns 82% of the 2,000 MW dam, and the Mozambican state the remaining 18%, but HCB is an independent company and must repay $14 million in 2002, accounting for more than 20% of Mozambique's entire foreign debt repayments.[35]

There are many other regional sites of electricity centralisation being eyed by Eskom, including more than 9,000 MW potential for regional imports. There is interest, as well, in a potential Grand Inga hydropower scheme in the DRC, which allegedly could supply 40,000 MW in the longer term, 20% more than South Africa's current capacity, with enough transmission strength to reach as far north as Italy if lines were constructed.

With such arrangements underway, Eskom enjoys a powerful lock on the design of the Southern African Power Pool. The company's stated strategic intention is to reposition the pool 'in line with global trends of liberalising and introducing competition into electricity markets'.[36] Chapter Six showed some of the micro-pricing characteristics that will invariably accompany liberalisation.

The implications of privatisation will become clear to citizens of the region and indeed the entire continent in coming months and years, as Eskom's Reuel Khoza wants Eskom Enterprises (EE) to 'spearhead involvement in Africa as the first phase of expansion into other parts of the globe'. EE firmly endorsed Nepad, and began active electricity privatisation of the Uganda Electricity Board. In a survey of what remains a murky terrain of expansion, Stephen Greenberg identified the following countries into which Eskom had ventured by 2000: Angola, Botswana, Cameroon, the DRC, Ghana, Mali, Mozambique, Swaziland, Tanzania and Zambia. Since then, major EE projects have included

- a R100 million agreement to supply water and electricity in Gambia;
- a 15-year operation and maintenance contract for the new Manantali hydro station in Mali and its associated high voltage transmission system;
- the formation of a consortium with the French firms EDF and Saur International to bid for 51% of Cameroon's Sonel;
- an alliance agreement with the Libyan power utility, Gecol;
- an agreement with Nigeria's National Electricity Power Authority covering generation and operations, electro-mechanical repairs, transmission, and rehabilitate, operate and transfer (ROT) schemes;
- consulting and management contracts in Malawi; and even
- a bid for power stations operated by the Zimbabwe Electricity Supply Authority (Zesa) as repayment for outstanding debt owed to Eskom.[37]

South Africa also threatened Zimbabwe with electricity cut offs if the debts were not at least reduced. If the outstanding amount started to increase, 'supply would be interruptible again, as was the case from January 27 to April 1, 2000', according to minister Jeff Radebe.[38] This was a telling case, because once Zesa managed to make payments on the debts, Eskom put the money into a special account to be used in feasibility studies in support of the privatisation of the Zimbabwean utility.[39] In 2001, Eskom signed a contract with Zesa to manage, operate and maintain the Hwange power station.[40] Zimbabwe's economic depression has dramatically lowered the demand for electricity, but if it increases, the Zimbabwean government will find itself massively squeezed by Eskom, which is already draining the country of so much scarce foreign exchange – as profit repatriations to Johannesburg – that most medicines are unavailable there. In mid-2002, Eskom began mass public advertising in Zimbabwe, showing a lit Johannesburg metropolitan area at night, to win hearts and minds in advance of a full takeover of Zesa.

Of greatest interest here, is that top-down Pretoria/Johannesburg regionalism has enormous clout, drawing on the ability of Mbeki to persuade global-scale elites of the righteousness of Nepad while the water privatisers and Eskom come in to collect the spoils. It is highly idealistic for anyone to imagine that global-scale reforms to environment and development processes can overcome this regional power configuration, given how the balance of forces were reflected in the WSSD. What we find in the murky WSSD process is an overwhelming reliance upon neoliberal premises, which will not only amplify South Africa's regional power but also amplify uneven development within Africa and the South more generally.

3. The WSSD's commodification of nature and life

The World Summit on Sustainable Development, held in Johannesburg in late August–early September 2002, was proceeded by various intergovernmental fora and civil society conferences. Its purported aim is to find common international discourses – and strategies and tactics – that allow governments, business and civil society to eradicate poverty, end unsustainable patterns of consumption and production, and combat environmental degradation.

In civil society, deep dissatisfaction emerged over the WSSD, as well as its African chapter, Nepad. Complaints about bad content and bad process threatened to completely delegitimise the event. As this book went to press, it appeared that the very name, Johannesburg, would go down in infamy as the global elites' last attempt – and failure – to address a world careening out of control.

The legacy of the Rio de Janeiro Earth Summit was part of the problem. The 1992 meeting established the Rio Declaration on Environment and Development, Agenda 21, the UN Convention on Climate Change, the Convention on Biological Diversity, the Statement of Forest Principles and the Commission on Sustainable Development for implementation. The Rio+5 Special Session of the UN General Assembly reviewed Agenda 21 in 1997. Numerous other conventions, treaties and protocols were agreed upon during the 1990s, though in part because of United States belligerence, as reviewed below, nothing substantive came from these (aside, perhaps, from reduced CFCs in the atmosphere). In December 2000, the General Assembly agreed to hold a 10-year review in Johannesburg, incorporating the variety of international deals. Regional WSSD meetings and preparatory committees (prepcoms) followed between mid-2001 and mid-2002, leading to an unsatisfactory chair's text in Bali with huge unresolved gaps.

The Johannesburg Summit was meant to produce a negotiated leader's statement, a negotiated plan of action and a (non-negotiated) list of sustainable development initiatives involving states, interstate relations, and business and civil society sectors. But going into the WSSD, there were few areas of genuine consensus on substantive change. Controversies dogged the Summit's preparatory process – particularly over the role of the profit motive and market mechanism in environment and development – and threatened to undermine the event. The WSSD's predetermined failure to come up with ambitious targets, timetables, monitoring systems and enforcement/punishment mechanisms suggests that the name Johannesburg will be remembered, at best, as just another site for UN blahblah, and at worst, as the amplification of corporate control over both nature and everyday life, as the WTO takes precedence over any other multilateral or national environmental regulation.

Reacting to the drafting work done in Bali, one of the leading environmental NGOs, Friends of the Earth International, issued a statement embodying a powerful – and very real – threat:

> We are appalled that two months before the Johannesburg Summit, basic and fundamental principles established at Rio remain bracketed. If the commitment to common but differentiated responsibilities (principle 7 of Rio) and the precautionary principle (principle 15 of Rio) do not get reaffirmed loud and clear at Johannesburg, the Summit will constitute a serious step backwards from Rio. This could seriously endanger the public's faith in the United Nations and the UN's ability to agree on meaningful action and embody global values.
>
> We also remain deeply concerned that the Johannesburg Summit could make sustainable development subservient to the WTO's trade agenda thus robbing the idea of sustainable development of any meaning. Many passages in the text currently suggest that governments have convinced themselves that the current WTO-driven trade regime will, in fact, deliver sustainable development. The evidence since Rio suggests otherwise. The spread of corporate globalisation has led to worsening environmental conditions worldwide and a further widening of the gap between rich and poor, both between North and South and within countries.[41]

Key chapters emerging from the Bali Preparatory Committee tackle the following topics: poverty eradication, changing unsustainable patterns of consumption and production, protecting and managing the natural resource base of economic and social development, health and sustainable development, sustainable development in a globalising world, sustainable development of small island developing states, sustainable development initiatives for Africa, and means of implementation. We can consider each in turn, and then turn to omissions from the text, barriers to change, and an alternative approach based not on elite deal-making but on civil society internationalism.

The chair's text[42]

To begin, eradicating poverty is one of the greatest global challenges facing the world today, and requires corresponding policies to address profligate wealth. As described in this book's Introduction, the host suburb for the WSSD, Sandton, offers abundant proof of why luxurious First World settings within an African country are unsustainable. Grievances associated with water, electricity, waste and access to land in Sandton together show that the WSSD stands accused of convening in conditions of extreme hypocrisy.

There are, however, various aspects of the chair's text that should be applauded. These include the restatement of the United Nations Millennium Declaration poverty-related goals of reducing by half 'the proportion of people whose income is below $1 per day, the number of people suffering from hunger, and proportion of people without access to safe drinking water'. There is also merit in the call, mainly articulated by China and the G77, for the establishment of a World Solidarity Fund for Poverty Eradication and the Promotion of Human Development in the poorest regions of the world. However, traditional problems of tied-aid, neoliberal conditionality and corruption have to be tackled effectively for this to convince aid-sceptics.

Likewise, 'women's participation in decision making at all levels, and mainstreaming gender perspectives in all policies and strategies' are essential – if terribly insufficient – steps in eradicating gender inequality and poverty. And the 'transfer of basic sustainable agricultural techniques and knowledge, including natural resource management, to small and medium–scale farmers, fishers and the rural poor' is progressive in theory, although naturally it is the involuntary transfer of sustainable agriculture from bottom to top that is more typical of the biopiracy problem.

The devils are in the details. The chair's text relies heavily for implementation upon Type–II Public–Private Partnerships and 'multi-stakeholder approaches' where transnational corporations (TNCs) operate outside of a regulatory environment. Because of inadequate regulation,

TNCs can oppose and prevent the release of safe, proven technologies to secure sustainable development. Indeed, according to researchers at the Corporate Europe Observatory,

> the corporate agenda dominates the political process of the WSSD to an extent unseen before. Nitin Desai, secretary-general of the Johannesburg Summit, has whole-heartedly embraced the world's most powerful corporate lobby groups such as the International Chamber of Commerce and the World Business Council on Sustainable Development. He has truly followed the lead of former secretary-general of the original Rio Summit, Maurice Strong, in making business his closest ally.[43]

The chair's text also lacks any statement or plan that would address the profligate wealth that has been amassed in the hands of a limited number of individuals and private institutions over the past three decades. Failing to articulate even minimalist plans to address extreme wealth is incongruous with calls for eradicating poverty, given that the world's three richest men own more than the annual production of all the countries eligible for World Bank debt relief combined.

On a positive note, the chair's text recognises that how and what 'societies produce and consume are indispensable for achieving global sustainable development'. The chair also notes the need 'to change unsustainable consumption and production patterns'. The proposed text focuses heavily on the Millennium Declaration goals, draws from the World Food Summit targets and the Brussels Programme of Action for the Least Developed Countries, and calls for implementation of International Labor Organisation (ILO) core labour standards.

However, the strategy of Southern elites also entails an expansion of primary product exports, and the chair's text endorses improved market access for developing country products. This strategy would not, indeed, change production/consumption patterns in the manner desired. Moreover, even when calling for better access to essential services, the text studiously avoids the rights discourses that are preferred amongst activists.

In the chapter on 'changing unsustainable patterns of consumption and production', the chair's text includes new analysis of how to incorporate environmental and social considerations into decision making. It endorses life-cycle approaches to environmental and development issues and suggests key sustainable development indicators, economic instruments and market incentives, and data and information systems. But the text does not focus enough on cleaner production technology, or on enhancing corporate regulation, over and above the apparently ineffective agenda for corporate responsibility. On the latter point, reflecting the efforts of the United States, Australia, Canada and the European Union, a voluntary Global Reporting Initiative will be pushed through, even though such corporate codes have had little or no success in the key sectors where sweatshop and environmentally-destructive production occur. A genuine effort at sustainable development would have imposed liability for firms, a commitment to ending unsustainable energy subsidies and stronger government commitments, instead of the promotion of partnerships and reliance upon economic instruments and market incentives.

Glaringly, there is no reference in the chapter of the text on 'The natural resource base for economic and social development' to the International Convention on Climate Change, the Kyoto Protocol or global warming, although the small islands section is a proxy of sorts. Conflict on these issues between the EU and US will continue. Other key environmental management problems treated inadequately in the text are the tendency towards water privatisation, the loss of biodiversity and the Genetically Modified Organisms/biosafety protocol. The chapter's language also undermines various existing treaties.

In a chapter entitled 'Sustainable development in a globalising world', the chair's text recognises that globalisation worsens income inequality. A serious chapter dedicated to these issues would have emphasised the need for the regulation of capital. Instead, the text discusses globalisation as a multifaceted process, with protracted discussions over costs/benefits and over the pros/cons of 'managing' globalisation or 'responding' to it. Its ongoing promotion of 'sound macroeconomic policies' is codephrasing for Washington-style austerity, and there is too great an emphasis on 'open' international trade which, in effect, prohibits protection for small countries' infant industries and for the socially essential state services that are under attack in the General Agreement on Trade in Services (Gats).[44]

In the chapter on 'Health and sustainable development', the text refers a great deal to challenges associated with HIV/Aids. However, South Africa's own movement for treatment access is much further advanced, with much more robust demands and concrete suggestions for rolling out HIV/Aids prevention and treatment programmes. In addition, health sector debates continue to rage, as reflected in the text, over access to, and protection of traditional knowledge; targets for reducing HIV infection; use of the ILO code of practice on HIV/Aids as the basis for tackling occupational health; and the sources of particulates that cause air pollution. The thorniest issues associated with Persistent Organic Pollutants, such as South Africa's own controversial use of DDT against malaria, have been deleted from the most recent draft. Disturbingly, the WSSD was also likely to endorse the WTO as the basis for addressing 'public health problems ... in a manner supportive of WTO member's rights to protect public health', which overemphasises Trade Related Intellectual Property Rights (Trips) patents on medicines except in cases of medical emergencies.

As noted, the chapter on 'Sustainable development of small island developing states' is a global warming proxy, meant to appease the most desperate Third World grouping. Instead of genuine climate change and reduction of greenhouse gases, the emphasis in the text is merely upon mitigating the impacts. This amounts to little more than disaster relief. The need for serious targets and timetables is ignored. The text lacks rigorous critique of the largest energy consumers in the world and also fails to mention the need to redress the legacy of environmentally unsound production practices, both in the Global North and Global South.

The next chapter, 'The sustainable development initiative for Africa', refers to Nepad. As discussed above, Nepad was deemed highly unsatisfactory by progressive civil society groups. The irony here, is that at the point South Africa hosts the most important conference on environment and development and persuades international elites to allow its agenda to become one of the seven main content chapters, Nepad fails to challenge any of the substantive areas or even add to the debate.

Finally, with respect to 'means of implementation', the text refuses to acknowledge the problem that overseas development aid remains conditional upon neoliberal policy implementation. The text also fails to advocate for the cancellation of Third World debt, even HIPC country debt. Overemphasis is given to the Bretton Woods Institutions and the WTO, to Public-Private Partnerships and to multi-stakeholder processes and dialogues involving TNCs. There is no mention of the need for binding regulation of TNCs, even though they have consistently demonstrated their propensity to environmental degradation and their lack of accountability to people, governments and the environment.

Issues off the table in the chair's text

Numerous issues are wholly absent from the chair's text: militarism, real policies to control wealth, biosafety, the ecological debt, the comprehensive regulation of TNCs, and unsustainable subsidies. The India-Pakistan hostilities underline the need to reduce military spending and curb nuclear proliferation. Too many countries, especially in the South, spend disproportionate amounts of their hard currency supporting large military budgets.

As noted above, one of the most important deficiencies in the chair's text is the failure to address excessive wealth. One antidote, not even hinted at in the text, would have been to raise the issue of ecological debt, which has accumulated through the extraction of natural resources, as well as the dumping of toxic and hazardous materials in the Global South, by Northern institutions and firms.

The text also fails to mention the Biosafety Protocol, which controls the release and continued use of Genetically Modified Organisms (GMOs) in the Global South. Further, the text fails to sufficiently address a variety of unsustainable subsidies in the fields of energy production and natural resource utilisation (i.e., forestry and mining). The text should have argued that funds used to subsidise unsustainable development should be directed to facilitate implementation.

What emerges from our considerations of the WSSD process, its mid-2002 draft chair's text and Nepad, is a distinct sense that *global elites are not doing enough* to solve environment and development problems, and that *for-profit corporations are ill-equipped to promote sustainable development*. The WSSD's main problems are its tendency to allow increasing scope for commodification of nature, its inadequate measures to address poverty and excessive wealth, and its orientation to implementation via TNCs, instead of through strengthened nation-states. From this maelstrom of Washington-centred geopolitical power relations, Northern corporate privilege and Southern leadership *compradorism*, can genuine sustainable development emerge?

'A test for multilateralism' – or imperialism-as-usual?

Kofi Annan himself judged that 'six clusters of issues hold the key to agreement' in Johannesburg, namely the Rio principles; finance; trade; good governance; time-bound targets; and technology transfers. He continued:

> Johannesburg is a test for multilateralism and for the international community. It is a test for all leaders who profess to care about the well-being of our planet and its people. Johannesburg must send a message of solidarity and concern, and must produce real change, on the ground in people's lives, where it matters most.
>
> Progress since the Earth Summit has been slower than expected and – more important – slower than what was needed. A setback now would be a tragic missed opportunity. Your work here can help avert the worst, and restore the hope for the future of all humankind.[45]

'The worst' loomed as a likely outcome. For although the European Union remained a formidably partisan promoter of corporate prerogatives, the clear and present danger to the world's prospects for improved environment, development and peace was the United States government. Simply taking George W. Bush's first year in power as indicative of the problem, and setting aside the obvious overarching phenomena of resurgent US imperialism and rising economic protectionism, an isolationist tendency runs rampant in the capital of the 'world's biggest rogue nation':[46]

- February 2001: Bush announces that organisations providing family planning and abortion services in the Third World would be defunded by US AID and related sources.
- February 2001: Bush refuses to join 123 nations pledged to ban the use and production of anti-personnel bombs and mines; and
- March 2001: Bush declares the 1997 Kyoto Protocol for controlling greenhouse gas emissions and global warming to be 'dead';
- March 2001: Bush officials begin the sabotage of Korean peace talks, and Bush nominates men with appalling human rights records to high-ranking jobs in the UN and Organisation of American States;
- April 2001: Bush announces $1.5 billion escalation of existing 'drugs war' in Colombia, which in reality is merely another failing counterinsurgency in the tradition of Indochina, Central America and Southern Africa;
- April 2001: Bush and his Office of the Trade Representative renew their attacks on Brazil's ability to produce antiretroviral generic drugs to combat HIV/Aids;
- April 2001: US not re-elected to the UN Human Rights Commission because of years of withholding dues to the UN (in 2001 outstanding dues were $244 million), and to consistent opposition to UNHRC resolutions supporting lower-cost access to HIV/Aids drugs, acknowledging a basic human right to adequate food, and calling for a moratorium on the death penalty;
- May 2001: Bush insists on massive military expenditure in the form of the dubious 'Star Wars' missile defence programme;
- May 2001: Bush refuses to participate in Organisation for Economic Co-operation and Development-sponsored talks in Paris on ways to crack down on off-shore and other tax and money-laundering havens;
- July 2001: Bush stands alone to oppose the UN Agreement to Curb the International Flow of Illicit Small Arms;
- July 2001: Bush is lone industrial-country leader opposed to G-8 International Plan for Cleaner Energy;
- July 2001: Bush authorises US walkout from London conference aiming to strengthen the 1972 Biological and Toxin Weapons Convention;

388

- August 2001: Bush disavows Clinton's promise that by 2006 the US would comply with the 1997 Land Mine Treaty ban (the US was one of a very few countries to oppose it originally);
- September 2001: Bush withdraws from World Conference Against Racism in Durban;
- October 2001: Bush continues the illegal US boycott of Cuba in spite of UN General Assembly resolution, for the tenth consecutive year (in the wake of 17 CIA assassination attempts on Fidel Castro), calling for an end to the US embargo, by a vote of 167 to 3;
- November 2001: Bush continues traditional US opposition to the Comprehensive [Nuclear] Test Ban Treaty and forced a vote in the UN Committee on Disarmament and Security to demonstrate its opposition to the Test Ban Treaty;
- November 2001: Bush shuns Marrakesh negotiations to revise the Kyoto Protocol on global greenhouse emissions;
- December 2001: US Senate legislates that US military personnel must not obey the jurisdiction of the proposed International Criminal Court (ICC) Treaty, to be set up in The Hague to try political leaders and military personnel charged with war crimes and crimes against humanity;
- December 2001: Bush withdraws from the 1972 Antiballistic Missile Treaty;

In addition, Bush continues isolationist traditions of Clinton and prior administrations, namely, not ratifying – even after formally signing – several crucial global governance treaties: the 1966 UN International Covenant on Economic, Social and Cultural Rights; the 1979 UN Convention on the Elimination of All Forms of Discrimination against Women; the 1982 UN Convention on the Law of the Sea; the 1989 UN Convention on the Rights of the Child; the 1989 optional protocol prohibiting execution of prisoners under age 18 within the UN International Covenant on Civil and Political Rights; and the 2000 Cartagena Protocol on Biosafety to the UN Convention on Biological Diversity. Against virtually the entire world's desires, Bush intensified Washington's promotion of the apartheid state of Israel, which with US financial and military support increased its already prodigious rate of killing and maiming Palestinians. US civil liberties, meanwhile, suffered an unprecedented clampdown after 11 September 2001, to the extent that even leading South African business officials like Tokyo Sexwale were denied entry because they had once belonged to a 'terrorist' organisation, namely the ANC.[47]

Meanwhile, other aspirant (non-US) global elites are hopelessly confused by this kind of unilateralism, largely because of their debilitating dependency, over the past few decades, upon the combined economic and military power wielded by Washington. A live microphone at the Bali PrepCom picked up WSSD secretary-general Desai's plaintive query (unintended for broadcast): 'What are we going to do about the United States?' The logical answer began to gel as this book was going to press, with periodic corporate scandals, stock market crashes and currency turbulence emanating from Wall Street. The Bush/Cheney regime was deeply implicated, not only through the Harken Energy and Halliburton corporate connections, but more generally because of its need to distract or repress the growing popular upsurge of hatred against chief executive officers.

The dangers of playing Washington's game have rarely been greater. One high-profile conservative commentator, John Podhoretz, wrote an open letter to Bush arguing, in all seriousness, that he quickly invade Iraq as a means of distracting attention from the worsening US crisis:

> Go on, Mr. President: Wag the dog.
>
> It would be good for the world, it would be good for America and it would be good politics as well.
>
> You've made it clear for 10 months now that you want to rid the world of Saddam Hussein's rule in Iraq ...
>
> You're in some domestic political trouble, Mr. President. You need to change the subject. You have the biggest subject-changer of all at your disposal. Use it.
>
> I can hear the screaming already from certain quarters. How would such a thing be different from what Bill Clinton did in 1998, when he used cruise missiles twice in response to Osama bin Laden at crucial moments during the Lewinsky scandals?
>
> Here's how it would be different, Mr. President: You'd get the job done ...
>
> There's a luscious double trap in starting the war as soon as possible, Mr. President. Your enemies are delirious with excitement about the corporate-greed scandals and the effect they might have on your popularity and the GOP's standing in November.
>
> If you get troops on the ground quickly, they will go berserk. Incautious Democrats and liberal pundits will shriek that you've gone to war solely to protect yourself from the corporate-greed scandal. They will forget the lesson they so quickly learned after Sept. 11, which is that at a time of war the American people want their political leaders to stand together.
>
> Your enemies will hurl ugly accusations at you, Mr. President. And at least one of them will be true – the accusation that you began the war when you did for political reasons.

> But that won't matter. It won't matter to the American people,
> and it won't matter as far as history is concerned.[48]

No doubt, Bush was preparing to follow this poisonous advice, which no doubt was being repeatedly proffered by Pentagon hawks. Attendance at the WSSD Johannesburg summit did not feature in whatever meagre coalition-building effort he had in mind. Thus the answer to Desai's question would become increasingly clear: people of good conscience should isolate, boycott, oppose and fight the United States government in all possible venues where its core values and dynamics – imperialism, neoliberalism, consumerism, patriarchy and anthropocentrism, amongst others – are on display.

From any call for non-violent war on Washington, two other questions immediately follow, however. The first is whether a counter-hegemonic force will emerge beyond anti-imperialist civil society protesters. For example, will the world's progressive forces include any democratic rulers of nation-states – especially from the Third World – who can take up the challenge of opposing Washington? Although internal US-based solidarity groups helped end Washington's 1960s–70s war on Vietnam and 1950s–80s support for the apartheid regime, they were terribly disempowered by 11 September 2001 terrorism, lending real substance to Podhoretz's hubris. The US populace had become sufficiently dumbed down, despondent and demobilised, that prospects remained dim for even reclaiming political rights taken by Bush, or national-level electoral democracy – through, at the minimum, a genuine reform of campaign financing.

By the early twenty-first century, there was a terribly urgent need for a resurgent Third World leadership with integrity. Beyond the weak Castro-Chavez-Aristide trio in the Caribbean, it would be self-defeating for progressives to count on self-described 'anti-imperialist' dictators like Mugabe, Gaddafi and Mahathir, or regimes in Beijing and New Delhi, for any substantive support. Brazil's Workers Party was, at the time of the WSSD, on the verge of winning an election, but Lula had already compromised his principles by committing to repay the country's Odious Debt and giving the vice-presidency to a conservative business elite.

Moreover, where would South Africa's leadership stand in relation to US imperialism? The answer, as demonstrated both in Pretoria's support for the Bush-Blair war against Afghanistan and in Nepad, was: with Washington/London no matter how humiliating this would come to be.[49]

Civil society movements for global justice would, as a result, have to continue building popular support for their causes without recourse to reliable, powerful nation-states in the foreseeable future.[50] On the other hand, such alliances would be dangerous in any case. British author George Monbiot described the global justice movements as beneficiaries of a reality check caused by the 2001 terrorist attacks on the US:

> To the extent we had an effective dynamic before 11 September, we've had one since. That hasn't changed. What's changed is that we're less visible in the media and we've been caused to think about both our tactics and strategy. The big set-piece protests were very effective at drawing attention to the issues but they're not a good way to precipitate change. Look, it's like the Peasants' Revolt. The peasants revolt, they meet the king, the king promises them the earth and they all go home. Whereupon their leaders are hanged and nothing happens. If we follow that model, we're doomed, so you could say that 11 September, by putting a roadblock in the way of that model, did us a favour.[51]

The second logical line of questioning is also, at first sight, debilitating: is the problem merely a very evil group of pro-corporate, fossil fuel-addicted, militarily-minded Republicans who stole the US presidential election in December 2000? Or is it, more broadly, the internal *processes* and *power politics* associated with early twenty-first-century *capitalism*, evident not only through the actions of the 'executive committee of the bourgeoisie' at 1600 Pennsylvania Avenue, but also inside the Union Buildings in Pretoria?

Notwithstanding abundant ANC rhetoric to the contrary, the South African government had failed along quite similar lines in addressing domestic environment/development problems. In the spirit and even the style of Washington, Pretoria's overall vision of regional capital accumulation had become overtly biased towards privatisation, neoliberalism, destructive mega-projects and South African subimperialism, augmented by R60 billion worth of military offensive capabilities. The problems associated with Pretoria's own unsustainable development trajectory are evident in the five areas upon which UN secretary general Kofi Annan places greatest emphasis.

The Wehab challenge (for South Africa)

Annan's five key areas of WSSD progress – Water/sanitation, Energy, Health, Agriculture and Biodiversity, or Wehab – will be highlighted in the Johannesburg Political Declaration. According to Annan, the WSSD should adopt the following objectives:

- *Water*. Provide access to at least one billion people who lack clean drinking water and two billion people who lack proper sanitation.
- *Energy*. Provide access to more than two billion people who lack modern energy services; promote renewable energy; reduce over-consumption; and ratify the Kyoto Protocol to address climate change. We need to make clean energy supplies accessible and affordable. We need to increase the use of renewable energy sources and improve energy efficiency. And we must not flinch from addressing the issue of overconsumption – the fact that peo-ple in the developed countries use far more energy per capita than those in the developing world.
- *Health*. Address the effects of toxic and hazardous materials; reduce air pollution, and lower the incidence of malaria and African guinea worm, which are linked with polluted water and poor sanitation. The links between the environment and human health are powerful. Toxic chemicals and other hazardous materi-als are basic elements of development. Yet more than one billion people breathe unhealthy air, and three million people die each year from air pollution – two-thirds of them poor people, mostly women and children, who die from indoor pollution caused by burning wood and dung. Tropical diseases are closely linked with polluted water sources and poor sanitation. Conventions and other steps aimed at reducing waste and eliminating the use of certain chemicals and substances can go a long way to creating a healthier environment.
- *Agricultural productivity*. Work to reverse land degradation, which affects about two-thirds of the world's agricultural lands. As a result, agricultural productivity is declining sharply, while the number of mouths to feed continues to grow. In Africa, especially, millions of people are threatened with starvation. We must increase agricultural productivity, and reverse human encroach-ment on forests, grasslands and wetlands.
- *Biodiversity and ecosystem management*. Reverse the processes that have destroyed about half of the world's tropical rainforest and mangroves, and are threatening 70% of the world's coral reefs and decimating the world's fisheries. About 75% of marine fish-eries have been fished to capacity, while 70% of coral reefs are endangered. We must reverse this process, preserving as many species as possible, and clamping down on illegal and unsustain-able fishing and logging practices, while helping people who cur-rently depend on such activities to make a transition to more sustainable ways of earning their living.[52]

In the Bali chair's text, however, virtually all the detailed provisions are vague, lack specific targets and timeframes, and thus demonstrate that the elites have no desire to overcome financial constraints that are the inevitable barrier to poor people's access to water, energy, healthcare, land and the preservation of species. Recognising the likelihood of failure and delegitimisation, South African government leaders unsuccessfully attempted – at Bali and in a special UN-hosted session in July under Mbeki's direction – to pull together the divergent elite approaches.[53] So it is worthwhile reminding ourselves of the unsatisfactory South African stance on these issues.

This book has shown how Pretoria has addressed environment and development with a combination of excellent constitutional guarantees and political campaign promises on the one hand, but neoliberal policy and excessively market-oriented programmes and projects on the other. We can focus on these elements of Wehab, noting the WSSD's rhetorical commitments, and then summarising South Africa's post-1994 weaknesses.

First, in relation to water, the trends in virtually all countries point towards the commodification and privatisation of water. The UN amplifies the trends by promoting PPPs (the preferred euphemism for privatisation), albeit momentarily disguised through ambitious promises of improved access to water/sanitation:

> 8. Launch an action programme, with financial and technical assistance from developed countries, to halve by 2015 the proportion of people lacking access to improved sanitation, through the development and implementation of efficient sanitation systems and infrastructure while safeguarding human health.
>
> 22. Achieve the UN Millennium Declaration goal to halve, by the year 2015, the proportion of people who are unable to reach or afford safe drinking water ...
>
> 23. Support developing countries in developing integrated water resources management and water efficiency plans by 2005 ... Facilitate the establishment of Public–Private Partnerships by providing stable and transparent regulatory frameworks, involving all concerned stakeholders, and monitoring the performance and improving accountability of public institutions and private companies.

That paragraph 23 will cancel out paragraphs 8 and 22, due to the need to realise a large profit margin in water/sanitation distribution, goes unremarked upon. Likewise, as discussed in Chapters Three–Five, Pretoria has come under sustained criticism for its water policies, with respect to:

- failure to enforce the constitutional right to water;
- failure to withdraw permission to municipal and catchment-area water managers to engage in life-threatening water cut offs to millions of people;
- failure to make good on promises of a free lifeline supply, and to define the supply so that people receive 50–60 litres of water per person per day;
- failure to provide sufficient subsidies to run rural water programmes and projects where municipal support is not yet in place;
- failure to deliver emergency water in cholera-stricken areas through emergency water tanker trucks;
- failure to monitor, regulate and repair rural water projects run on a semi-privatised basis;
- failure to deliver sanitation due to excessive emphasis on cost recovery and co-payment;
- failure to spend annual budget allocations efficiently, resulting in roll-overs;
- failure to consider the overall costs of construction of mega-dams (as an alleged supply-side solution to water scarcity in the largest cities, instead of demand-side management),
- failure to ensure dam safety, especially in relation to the flooding affecting Mozambique in 2000–01;
- failure to redistribute water resources enjoyed below cost, due to apartheid subsidies, by white farmers;
- failure to regulate and where necessary halt destructive water use by forestry plantations;
- failure to prevent water pollution by TNCs, especially in the mining/metals and agricultural sectors; and
- failure to implement regulations on municipal water privatisers, even in the wake of their nationally-publicised crises in Dolphin Coast and Nkonkobe.

The same pro-privatisation tendencies can be uncovered in the energy sector. The WSSD chair's text includes four key paragraphs, each with various detailed optional provisions for implementing programmes:

> 9. Launch an action programme to reduce by half the number of people who currently lack access to modern energy services.
>
> 14. Increase investment in cleaner production and eco-efficiency in all countries through incentives and support schemes.
>
> 17. Promote the implementation of the recommendations and conclusions of the ninth session of the Commission on Sustainable Development (CSD-9) on energy for sustainable development rele-

vant to the respective domestic situations, bearing in mind the principle of common but differentiated responsibilities, and taking into account that energy is central to achieving the goals of sustainable development ... Promote international Public–Private Partnership cooperation programmes for promoting affordable, energy efficient and advanced fossil fuel and renewable energy technologies.

18. Promote an integrated approach to policy making at national and regional levels for transport services ... with a view to providing efficient transportation, reducing energy consumption and pollution.

Amidst the innocuous chatter, the third of these provisions is dangerous. Public–Private Partnerships introduce the profit motive in a manner that, we have seen in Chapter Six in Soweto, invariably puts pressure on low-income people to drop out of the system. The South African electricity sector has provided more than two million new household electricity connections since the early 1990s and is beginning to adopt the free lifeline mandate for electricity. Nevertheless, as Chapter Six showed, Pretoria has various shortcomings:

- failure to provide a sustainable, affordable supply of electricity to low-income households, with sufficient ampage to allow substitution for traditional cooking fuels;
- failure to prevent the move (indicated in the 1998 *White Paper*) towards 'cost-reflective' tariffs imposed by both Eskom and municipalities, even though these prevent cross-subsidies and discount the incorporation of social and environmental costs of maldistributed energy;
- failure to prevent the cut offs of low-income households (with 10 million people affected, according to a 2001 national survey), and especially failure to prevent Eskom's 20,000 cut offs per month in Soweto until forced to by community pressure;
- failure to develop more creative biomass, wind and solar sources;
- failure to recognise the unsustainability of nuclear energy;
- failure to promote conservation, including more energy-efficient methods of production, transport and consumption;
- failure to wean SA industry (and other government departments) off greenhouse-gas emitting, electricity-intensive (and capital-intensive) production, such as metals smelting;
- failure to overcome the mistaken notion that cheap electricity will attract foreign direct investment;
- failure to address problems in utilisation and distribution of liquid fuels, including the lack of safe public rail and bus transport to cut emissions.

CONCLUSION

In the field of health, the chair's text includes five key paragraphs:

43. The Rio Declaration states that human beings are at the centre of concerns for sustainable development, and that they are entitled to a healthy and productive life in harmony with nature. The goals of sustainable development can only be achieved in the absence of a high prevalence of debilitating illnesses while population health requires poverty eradication. There is an urgent need to address the causes of ill health and their impact on development, with particular emphasis on women and children, as well as other vulnerable groups of society such as people with disabilities, elderly persons, and indigenous people.

44. Strengthen the capacity of healthcare systems to deliver basic health services to all in an efficient, accessible and affordable manner aimed at preventing, controlling and treating diseases and to reduce environmental health threats ...

45. Combat HIV/Aids by reducing HIV infection rates by 25% by 2005 in the most affected countries and globally by 2010, as well as combat Malaria, TB and other diseases ...

46. Reduce respiratory diseases and other health impacts resulting from air pollution, including from some traditional cooking and heating practices, with particular attention to women and children who are most exposed to indoor air pollution by: (a) Strengthening regional and national programmes, including through public/private partnerships ...

47. Implement the commitments and objectives contained in the Declaration on the Trips Agreement and Public Health adopted at Doha in a manner supportive of the protection of public health and of the promotion of access to medicines for all, while recognising the gravity of the public health problems afflicting many developing and least developed countries, especially those resulting from HIV/Aids, tuberculosis, malaria and other epidemics.

Without doubt, these would be helpful steps. There are, however, insufficient commitments to funding, while problems associated with privatisation and cost-recovery policies imposed by the World Bank and IMF are ignored. Likewise, Pretoria is castigated for several health policies:

- failure to address Aids crisis by providing clear health education on viral nature of the infection, and instead resorting to Aids-denialist arguments;
- failure to provide antiretroviral (ARV) Aids medicines, especially in the wake of the mid-April Cabinet commitment that allegedly

allows access to pregnant women and rape survivors (a position that has been considered appropriate and feasible by the state since 1994);
- failure to investigate and plan for the provision of ARVs for the five million South Africans who are HIV-positive;
- failure to take advantage of 1997 Medicines Act and international trade provisions that allow production of generic ARVs or parallel import of ARVs;
- failure to ensure sufficient funding for the rest of the public health system, including free primary healthcare for all and maintenance of some vitally-needed tertiary facilities, as promised in 1996;
- failure to sufficiently regulate the medical schemes, private (for-profit) health care providers, and managed care initiatives;
- failure to prevent the departure of health personnel;
- failure to address the health-impairing policies of other government departments (especially water, energy and housing); and
- failure to build sufficient clinics in underserved areas or provide Essential Drugs List medicines.

With regard to agriculture, the chair's text includes a key paragraph providing for the 'right to food' and other progressive language. But there are, in the text, no serious means of implementing or enforcement, aside from the dangerous 'market-based incentives ... to monitor and manage water use and quality':

> 35. Agriculture plays a crucial role in addressing the needs of a growing global population, and is inextricably linked to poverty eradication, especially in developing countries. Sustainable agriculture and rural development (SARD) is essential to the implementation of an integrated approach to increasing food production and enhancing food security and food safety in an environmentally sustainable way.

Pretoria's agriculture and land policies are regular objects of protest, regarding:
- failure to redistribute more than a tiny fraction (less than 2%) of arable land, notwithstanding a 1994 campaign promise to have distributed 30% by 1999;
- failure to restitute more than a small percentage of land stolen by the white apartheid regime in living memory;
- failure to provide emergent small black farmers with sufficient technical support – irrigation, cultivation assistance, appropriate fertilisers and pesticides, credit and marketing;

- failure to provide food security for all South Africans, including price controls and state production of basic foodstuffs during times of food-price inflation; and
- failure to penalise the unsustainable land utilisation and agricultural practices of large farmers, including corporations.

On biodiversity, the chair's text includes a key paragraph, but conspicuously fails to mention the Biosafety Protocol:

> 39. Biodiversity plays a critical role in overall sustainable development and is essential to our planet and human well being and is being lost at unprecedented rates due to human activities. Convention on Biological Diversity (CBD) is the key instrument for the conservation and sustainable use of biological diversity and to put in place by 2010 measures to halt biodiversity loss at the global, regional, sub-regional and national levels requires actions at all levels.

Pretoria is subject to criticism for its biodiversity policies, with respect to:
- failure to prohibit or even regulate Genetically Modified Organisms and Genetic Engineering in relation especially to foodstuffs;
- failure to protect South Africa from biopiracy; and
- failure to utilise the Doha WTO Summit, to support calls from many developing countries in the Like Minded Group and Development Box group.

Could a stronger chair's text have been drafted going into Johannesburg? Given the bloody-minded character of US rulers, Washington's reaction to a more rights-based, less corporate-centred strategy might have been yet another walkout. Would that have mattered? It is hard to say, because the experience since Rio is that no matter how many high-minded provisions are included in UN conference resolutions, the real test is whether national-level democracy is sufficiently advanced to make the promises stick. In turn, achieving such democracy far transcends even the obvious challenges of electoral fairplay, for which Bush's gang has already shown scant regard, as witnessed by the disenfranchisement of 100,000 African–American voters in Florida.[54] Building a more genuine movement for sustainable development requires, first, stronger impulses towards environmental, social and economic justice in each country and then the emergence of an interlinked political narrative that draws together the justice and sustainable development discourses into what, below, we will call an eco-socialist project.

Practically speaking, however, what would this amount to in international terms, such that future WSSD-type circuses can be more forcefully confronted with a progressive alternative? A cursory examination of what is at stake in the international water wars, and an alternative treaty, may be helpful prior to drawing overall political conclusions.

An alternative: A world water treaty[55]

Manifestos are never *durably* picked out of thin air. They must, like the 1955 Freedom Charter and 1994 Reconstruction and Development Programme, reflect the existing, sometimes longstanding, social struggles for justice. They must themselves codify and extend the democratic impulses in such social change movements, by incorporating text that reverberates with the vast majority of oppressed human beings. Such a manifesto is coming from the water sector. Although it is still early in the process, a vanguard of water activists are speaking in a unifying language about their diverse ecologies and societies. It is not impossible to envisage a potential future WSSD-type event characterised not by commodification of everything, but by the converse.

The *decommodifying* potential of a 'Treaty Initiative to Share and Protect the Global Water Commons' was on display at the mid-2001 'Blue Planet' conference, hosted in Vancouver by the Council of Canadians, a 100,000-member citizens' group. The aim was to advance 'a global water revolution, the first of many international civil society meetings to take back control of our water'. Several hundred representatives of indigenous peoples, Third World communities, anti-globalisation activists, radical youth, public-sector trade unions, environmentalists, anti-dam campaigners, World Bank watchers, and consumer groups together sought routes that lead from multi-faceted resistance towards alternative conceptions of water management.

The radical Blue Planet manifesto and global treaty aiming at prohibiting the privatisation of water are seminal documents in the international fightback. They stress the essential nature of water to social and eco-system life, and the cultural resonances and alternative spiritualities associated with water in aboriginal communities. The documents provide a broad-based way of arguing for water as a human right, that will have universal applicability in sites of struggle around the world. Five scales of water struggle are, in the process, being fused: local communities; national governments; world water policy fora;[56] sites of global rule such as Free Trade Agreements and the Bretton Woods Institutions; and the more general takeover of water by multinational corporations.

There is broad-based unity amongst progressive critics, against water-related damage emanating from several sources: mega-dams and cross-catchment water transfers; despoliation of groundwater and aquifers;

municipal water privatisation; price hikes and 'water poverty'; agribusiness abuse of water in the wake of the water-guzzling green revolution; global warming/drying; scarcity and wastage; and the extension of corporate bill-of-rights protections to water via the Gats. In all these respects, water is becoming a locus of worldwide protest. Water struggles tend to achieve diverse objectives: bridge traditional red/green divides; link North and South in solidarity; build upon the notion of a global Commons that mustn't be privatised; focus on the public (especially municipal government) character of service delivery; involve the expansion of the service through expanded labour and jobs; and offer a way to practice local self-management and sustainable consumption.

Thus if water becomes a public good protected from the market, it also serves a progressive political trend towards an expansive eco-social localism, unlike the establishment's faddish 'communitarianism' which leads inexorably to gated-community protections. But while locally grounded, it is only by confronting issues of more general concern to the movement against corporate globalisation that the water struggles will come to fruition. Targets emerge in the form of the World Bank/IMF, big government aid agencies, water corporations like Suez and Vivendi, Free Trade Agreements and neoliberal advocacy agencies.

The key sector-specific enemies of Blue Planet include the pro-privatisation World Water Council mainly consisting of major water firms; the World Bank-linked Global Water Partnership based in Scandinavia; Business Partners for Development; the Gats as a lever for water companies to invade Third World countries; and other promoters of the Dublin Principles and Hague Declaration which advanced the proposition that water is an economic good. In contrast, processes that have been promoting water decommodification include the P-7 Declaration on Water authored by Vandana Shiva; the Cochabamba Declaration emanating from the Coordinada struggle of low-income residents against water-privatiser Bechtel; and the Global Water Contract of the Group of Lisbon social democrats, who hope to transform the World Water Forum into a parliament.

But even if the main contradiction between North and South is that the former have water networks and the latter must still expand access to more than a billion people without potable water and decent sanitation, the process of commodification is similar. Those with the networks – including residents of most Third World cities' elite neighbourhoods – will have to begin addressing overconsumption; those without must address the need for provision of, at minimum, a free lifeline supply of water for subsistence purposes. Not just a matter for households, in which women would benefit most, this might also include irrigation in the context of radical land and agricultural reform.

Here, perhaps, the only real cleavage emerges. For most of the world, the human right to a subsistence water supply must ultimately occur on a free lifeline basis. But a free lifeline supply would not mean the right to lifestyles which, in the wealthy North, are insensitive to real – not just socially constructed – water scarcity. Such scarcity comes from poorly located urban areas such as Johannesburg, far from natural bodies of fresh water. Scarcity is also a reflection of aquifer degradation, which is becoming common in most urban areas.

Council of Canadians director Maude Barlow describes the implications for commodification: 'When we have a famine somewhere, our response is not: Oh goody, customers for life! Yet that is exactly the way the scarcity argument is playing out when it comes to water'. Or, as Shiva put it, 'Sustainable development is capitalism's way of turning the threat of ecological crisis into an opportunity'. Capitalism has colonised the world so thoroughly that the alleged ability of private companies to fix system leaks and provide more efficient services has become common sense. But such conventional wisdom can be undone. Typical red/green conflicts pit jobs against protection of resources from extraction. Water does not have this feature, and so transcends what is usually a false paradox between equity and efficiency.

Unfortunately, in part because Pretoria again plays a mediating role in these matters, the WSSD-related Waterdome in Randburg would host – and give succour to – some of the most aggressive privatisation-oriented companies and banks in the world. Indeed, more generally, the Johannesburg WSSD would promote the interests of corporations and 'third-way' market-mechanisms for environmental commodification, in the manner predetermined by the Rio Earth Summit 10 years earlier.

Corporate power and genocidal instincts

Led by billionaire businessman and UN bureaucrat Maurice Strong, Rio eliminated the UN Centre on Transnational Corporations (a critical think-tank), gave birth to the World Business Council on Sustainable Development, and mapped a role for corporations to guide (un)sustainable development. In the same spirit, the 'Global Compact' signed by Kofi Annan, initially with 44 transnational corporations, had expanded by 2002 to several hundred – although amazingly, the signatories were still secret at the time of the WSSD. The Compact contained no mandatory monitoring or enforcement mechanisms. Notorious companies with appalling human rights and environment records were beneficiaries of the UN's branding exercise: e.g., Aventis, despite irresponsible handling of transgenic crops; Nike, despite labour repression in its Asian factories; Rio

Tinto, despite Indonesian human rights abuses; and Unilever, despite dumping toxic waste in southern India.[57]

From the inauspicious corporate-driven process launched at the Rio Earth Summit, the twenty-first century's eco-social war for the heart and soul of UN-mandated global environmental governance had begun. The battleground moved to Johannesburg in 2002, as commodification took on greater urgency, the more that corporate profits came under attack from global economic turbulence. Under these conditions, as a means of illustrating how dangerous it is for Annan and the UN to risk their reputation in this fanciful manner, we can consider the most crucial, life-and-death choice that corporations are making in the WSSD's host city.

South Africa risks the imminent death of many millions of people, whose lives should be saved but won't be because of Pretoria's lethal combination of neoliberalism and *compradorism*. Deaths due to HIV/Aids in coming years will far outstrip diarrhoea's massacre of 43,000 children each year. Given the vast scale of looming depopulation, the sorts of lessons we learned from cholera outbreaks – from Hamburg in 1892 to Ngwelezane in 2000 – are profound. They relate to management of water in both urban and rural environments, but the relationship between nature and society unveiled by the spectre of such a preventable, fatal disease is of a more general nature.

The basic problem is the tendency in capitalism to commodify everything, and in turn to reduce the state apparatus to an accomplice. Writing in 1987, Richard Evans draws a telling link to South Africa's single biggest killer, Aids:

> The study of popular and official reactions to cholera in the nineteenth century reveals many similarities to public attitudes towards Aids, the epidemic that is threatening society at the end of the twentieth century. In both cases, socially stigmatised groups have been blamed, fear of contagion has produced panic reactions, and official responses have varied from the coercive to the indifferent. Medical opinion has been divided, and prevention has been more widely discussed than cure. The limits of public education have been clearly revealed when medical advice has clashed with deep-rooted lifestyles.[58]

The deep-rootedness of Aids' destructive capacities far transcends an internet-surfing president's eccentric medical ideas. However, even without distractions from Aids dissidents, the South African government would be hampered in rolling out Aids treatment – potentially transforming the disease from inexorably fatal to a manageable, chronic illness such as diabetes – by three structural factors associated with corporate power:[59]

- the pressure exerted by international and domestic financial markets to keep the budget deficit to 3% of GDP;[60]
- the residual power of pharmaceutical manufacturers to defend their rights to 'intellectual property' (monopoly patents on life-saving medicine);[61] and
- the vast size of the reserve army of labour which allows companies to replace sick workers with desperate, unemployed people instead of providing treatment.

The latter point deserves elaboration, simply because so many lives are at risk. The point is also illustrated by neoliberal discourses advanced during 2001–02 – a time when it appeared that inexpensive antiretroviral medicines would indeed be available following the retreat by pharmaceutical corporations from their lawsuit against Pretoria.

In 1997, a Medicines Act amendment had allowed for import or even local production of generic alternatives to the patented drugs. After international protests against the pharmaceutical companies' arrogance – i.e., claiming billions of dollars in profits while millions of people died – the withdrawal from the law suit sparked hope that corporations and the state would immediately begin saving the lives of their workers and citizens.

Aside, very reluctantly, from Anglo American, it was not to be, for a simple reason: a particularly narrow, privatised cost-benefit analysis. Perhaps the principle was expressed most succinctly by financier George Soros, who was asked about treating HIV-positive South Africans in an April 2002 interview with the SA Broadcasting Corporation. He answered, 'I think to provide treatment to the bulk of the people is just not feasible. I think to provide treatment for instance to qualified workers actually saves money, actually saves money for companies'. The interviewer responded, 'Aren't you uncomfortable to talk in a way that is a kind of death sentence to those who we can't afford to treat?' Replied Soros, 'I think the cost of providing actual treatment to everyone at the present. I don't think it's realistic. It's not achievable'.[62]

In a similar tone, pro-corporate commentator Ken Owen remarked:

> I am sceptical about most doomsday economic scenarios generated by the Aids epidemic. I assume that in 10 years' time medical science will have found cheaper ways of lengthening the lives of Aids patients and that in the meantime, deaths will occur overwhelmingly among people (of all races) who have less than a matric education.

For the rest of this decade, at least, the lost workers will be quite readily replaceable from the millions of unemployed, and society will adjust in a myriad of ways to labour shortages. For example, a million domestic workers constitute a reserve pool of labour that can be drawn into industry; the death of Madam and Eve society is perhaps in sight.[63]

In late July 2002, as this book was going to press, AngloGold began conceding ground on antiretroviral access, signing a deal with the National Union of Mineworkers to begin treatment regimes. Perhaps the pressure applied by a strong union leadership, especially mineworker leader Gwede Mantashe, can be repeated in other unions in future. But the analysis provided here of the structural *capitalist* barriers to treatment leads, unfortunately, to a pessimistic prediction: without labour movement intervention, the mass of low-paid and low-skilled workers will, more than ever, be treated as expendable: 'quite readily replaceable from the millions of unemployed'. Those testing HIV-positive and demanding medicines will remain most vulnerable to early dismissal.

Corporate callousness combined with state coercion had, by this time, begun depopulating South Africa by hundreds of thousands of people, with millions more to follow in coming years. The structural problems associated with rampant neoliberalism work in tandem with the two key environmental issue areas in this book: water and energy. South Africa has, in short, an Aids pandemic, periodic cholera epidemics, and ongoing degradation of health in the form of rising TB, dysentery, diarrhoea, and opportunistic infections that could easily be prevented by the supply of clean water and energy in every South African home.

As in nineteenth century Hamburg, the immediate barriers to life are not just capitalists, but those who serve them: twenty-first century Pretoria politicians and bureaucrats responsible for our contemporary household environments – in the Departments of Health, of Water Affairs and Forestry, of Provincial and Local Government, of Minerals and Energy, and of Public Enterprises – and their underlings in the water boards, Eskom and virtually all the municipalities. These state bodies remain populated by either the Old Guard bureaucrats who were responsible for the racial–apartheid legacy, or New Guard neoliberals who see nothing particularly wrong with class apartheid.

Evans ends by drawing the sorts of political conclusions that we are also confronted with in South Africa:

Cholera both revealed and reflected patterns of inequality that had a longer term impact in terms of health and sickness, life and death.

> If we are to confront these problems with any hope of reducing their power and removing their causes, then a willingness to involve the state in the shaping of society, essential though it is, is not enough. That involvement must also be based on a recognition that the fundamental issue to be tackled is social inequality, not wealth creation or moral improvement. Above all, state intervention must be subject to democratic control. Otherwise it can all too easily become an authoritarian, disciplining force which pays scant regard to the needs of the community as a whole, and ends by assaulting people's bodies and minds instead of healing them.[64]

These are universal lessons, which are being advanced through the resurgence of anti-neoliberal sentiment across the world since the 1990s, brought to the attention of global media in Seattle in December 1999. It is perhaps too early to say, but it may be that the underlying theme of these social protests will become *de*commodification, as a necessary precursor to a more thoroughgoing human liberation. But any attempt to universalise an eco-socialist politics, grounded in human-rights values and suffused with a radicalised version of sustainable development analysis, will confront the problem of uneven political development.

4. The uneven politics of environment and development

Should a book that has demonstrated how so many extreme forms of human indignity and environmental degradation become mundane, systemic processes, end in despair? When all of us who live in this region know so many people who fought for liberation from colonialism and apartheid, and remain so dissatisfied, that would be a logical conclusion.

To the contrary, though, those practitioners of neoliberalism, especially the framers of global-scale corporate environmentalism, did not count on one crucial post-Rio phenomenon: namely, where there is collusion by governments, multilateral agencies and corporations to plunder the environment and hijack humanity, the radical forces of civil society are never too far behind. In search of a synthesis, we conclude by looking at social protest with sympathy, but as critically as possible from both theoretical and practical standpoints.

Decommodification, life and liberation

As we have seen throughout this book, the demand for lifeline supplies of water and electricity is being made from the urban ghettos like Soweto where disconnections remain a problem, to the many rural areas which have still not received piped water. The need for free access to antiretroviral medicines, for five million HIV-positive South Africans, is acute. A campaign for a Basic Income Grant has also been taken up by churches and trade unions. The Landless People's Movement objects to the failure of a commodified land reform policy designed by the World Bank, and insists upon access to land as a human right. Such demands, based upon the political principle of decommodification, are central to campaigns ranging from basic survival through access to health services, to resistance to municipal services privatisation.

The verb decommodify has become popular amongst progressive strategists in part through studies of social policy conducted by Gosta Esping-Andersen, a Swedish academic. In his book *The Three Worlds of Welfare Capitalism*, Esping-Andersen points out that during the first half of the twentieth century, the Scandinavian welfare state grew because of urban–rural, worker–farmer, red–green alliances which made universalist demands on the ruling elites.

Those demands typically aimed to give the working class and small farmers social protection from the vagaries of employment, especially during periodic recessions. They therefore allowed people to escape the prison of wage labour, by weaving a thick, state-supplied safety net as a fall-back position. To decommodify their constituents' labour in this manner required, in short, that the alliance defend a level of social protection adequate to meet basic needs. Over a period of decades, this took the form of generous pensions, healthcare, education, and other free state services which, like childcare and eldercare, disproportionately support and liberate women.[65]

The electoral weight and grassroots political power of the red–green alliance was sufficient to win these demands, which were paid for through taxing wealthy households and large corporations at high rates. They were defended until recently, when corporate power and the ideology of competitiveness have forced some cutbacks across Scandinavia. A similar although much less far–reaching construction of welfare-state policies occurred elsewhere across the world, in the context of a Cold War that required western capitalism to put on a more humane face against the East Bloc and to maintain state spending, in the spirit of John Maynard Keynes, so as to boost macroeconomic growth.

In the post-war US, in contrast, corporations lobbied more effectively against state entitlements such as healthcare and pensions, preferring to hold control over workers through company health and pension plans which would then deter workers from going on strike. (The failure to decommodify labour-power helps explain the durability of the US trade union movement's pro-corporate – and often pro-imperialist – position, until it began shifting leftward in the mid-1990s.)

As the 1950s–60s virtuous cycle of economic growth and expanding social policy came to an end, it was replaced not by a strengthened socialist struggle as the limits of such reforms were reached, but rather by an era of neoliberalism, which began during the late 1970s. Because the balance of forces has been inauspicious, for a variety of reasons, this recent period of class war by ruling elites continues to be characterised by austerity-oriented economic policies, shrinkage of social programmes, privatisation, trade and financial liberalisation, corporate deregulation, and what is often termed 'the commodification of everything'.

In a setting as unequal as South Africa – with 45% unemployment and, alongside Brazil and Guatemala, the world's highest income disparities – the neoliberal policies adopted during the 1990s pushed even essential state services such as water and electricity beyond most households' ability to pay. As we have seen in previous chapters, some of these policies were adopted before political liberation from apartheid in 1994, but many were the result of influence on Nelson Mandela's ANC by the World Bank, US AID and other global and local neoliberals during the late 1990s.

We have repeatedly drawn out various problems associated with the neoliberal approach to basic services. They often relate to the dismissive regard with which positive eco-social externalities associated with water/sanitation, energy and other services are understood by neoliberals, for whom 'the economic logic of dumping a load of toxic waste in the lowest-wage country is impeccable', Lawrence Summers informed us. The failure to fully incorporate social and environmental benefits of state services is typical of commodification, because when state services undergo commercialisation, the state fragments itself as water, electricity, health and other agencies adopt arm's-length, non-integrated relationships that reduce them to mere 'profit-centres'. Service disconnections follow logically.

As we have also seen in the pages above, the first stage of resistance to the commodification of water and electricity often takes the form of a popular demand for a short-term, inexpensive flat rate applicable to all consumers. In Durban, community groups are, at the time of writing, mobilising for a R10 monthly fee for all municipal services, alongside an insistence that no one's supply be cut off.

More compellingly, for medium-range policy a redistributive demand for decommodification is advanced by groups like the SA Municipal Workers Union, Rural Development Services Network, Johannesburg Anti-Privatisation Forum and Soweto Electricity Crisis Committee: a specific minimal daily amount of water (50 litres) and electricity (1 kiloWatt hour) to be supplied to each person *free*. The free services should be financed not only by subsidies from central government, but also by a rising block tariff in which the water and electricity bills for high-volume consumers and corporations rise at a more rapid rate when their usage soars to hedonistic levels.

When charged at ever-higher rates, the consumption of services by hedonistic users should decline, which would be welcome. South Africa is a water-scarce country, especially in the Johannesburg area which depends upon socio-ecologically destructive Lesotho dams. The WSSD host is also one of the world's worst sites of greenhouse gas emissions, when corrected for population and relative income. Hence conservation through higher rates for large consumers makes eco-socio-economic sense on merely technical grounds.

These demands, grounded in decades of social struggles to make basic services a human right were originally given political credibility with the promise of lifeline services and rising block tariffs in the Reconstruction and Development Programme of 1994, the ANC's campaign platform in the first democratic election. They were partially incorporated in the 1996 Constitution, which guarantees that 'everyone has the right to an environment that is not harmful to their health or well-being ... everyone has the right to have access to healthcare services, including reproductive health care; sufficient food and water; and social security'.

As documented in several chapters, the World Bank immediately became the most effective opponent of this philosophical principle and political strategy, arguing (incorrectly) that South Africa does not have sufficient resources to make good on the RDP or Constitution. Beginning by drafting infrastructure investment policy in late 1994, Bank staff then played a self-described 'instrumental' role in 'facilitating a radical revision in South Africa's approach to bulk water management' in 1995, when the water minister, Kader Asmal, accepted advice not to supply South Africans with free water.

To reiterate a key point, the main criticism of a free lifeline and rising block tariff offered by Bank water official John Roome was that water privatisation contracts 'would be much harder to establish' if poor consumers had the expectation of getting something for nothing. If consumers didn't pay, Roome continued, Asmal needed a 'credible threat of cutting service'.[66] In short, a private supplier logically objects to serving low-income people with even a small lifeline consumption amount. Hence the demand for such a rising block tariff is indeed, as Roome pointed out, a serious deterrent to privatisation.

Demands to reverse the government's full cost-recovery policy by labour and social movements were made during the late 1990s, and Asmal's mid-1999 replacement, Kasrils, began hinting at a policy change in February 2000 after rural water projects broke down at a dramatic rate – mainly because impoverished residents could not keep the vital service maintained by themselves without a subsidy, as Asmal had demanded. When cholera broke out in August 2000, less than four months before nation-wide municipal elections, the ANC government reacted by promising a free services lifeline. It was progress, although for poor households the promise was half the amount needed, and for electricity was undefined but in practice amounted to only a tenth of essential needs.

As might have been predicted, Roome and his colleagues saw Kasrils' and the ANC's free-services promise as potentially dangerous. In March 2000, the Bank's Orwellian-inspired *Sourcebook on Community Driven Development in the Africa Region* laid out the policy on pricing water: 'Work is still needed with political leaders in some national governments to move away from the concept of free water for all ... Promote increased capital cost recovery from users. An upfront cash contribution based on their willingness-to-pay is required from users to demonstrate demand and develop community capacity to administer funds and tariffs. Ensure 100% recovery of operation and maintenance costs'.[67]

Social disasters from such rigid neoliberal policy were strewn across Africa, especially when low-income people simply could not afford any state services, or cut back on girls' schooling or healthcare when cost recovery became burdensome. In October 2000, the Bank was instructed by the US Congress never to impose these user-fee provisions on education and healthcare, and in 2002 a campaign by progressive NGOs in the US expanded to decommodify water as well.

In South Africa, since free water came into effect in July 2001 as official policy – notwithstanding widespread sabotage by municipal and national bureaucrats responsible for administering the policy – there have been no new water privatisations, in large part due to the fear that cherrypicking and supply cuts will be deemed unconstitutional. Moreover, some of the major pilot cases have resulted in disaster.

For example, Saur had to renegotiate its Dolphin Coast contract in mid-2001 due to lack of profits, with research showing that it regularly denies services to poor people. For similar reasons, Saur also pulled out of its Maputo, Mozambique contract in late 2001. Having been thrown out of Fort Beaufort (also known as Nkonkobe), Suez's subsidiary is responding with a lawsuit for millions of dollars in damages.

The Johannesburg Water Company, also managed by Suez, is controversially introducing pit latrines in spite of porous soil and the spread of the E.Coli bacteria, to prevent poor people flushing their toilets. If these are unacceptable, Johannesburg Water offers a low-flush 'shallow sewage' system to residents of 'condominium' (single-storey) houses arranged in rows, connected to each other by sanitation pipes much closer to the surface. Given the limited role of gravity in the gradient and the mere trickle of water that flows through, community residents are required to negotiate with each other, over who will physically unblock sewers every three months. With this sort of attitude, public health problems, including mass outbreaks of diarrhoea and even cholera, will continue to embarrass officials in the WSSD host city.

Electricity privatisation also remains an acute source of conflict. The SECC continues to hold protests against politicians who insist that the inclement privatisation of the state electricity utility, Eskom, requires cut offs of power to those who can't pay. At one point in 2001, when Eskom was cutting the supplies of 20,000 Soweto households each month, activists went door-to-door like Robin Hood, illegally reconnecting people for free. The SECC achieved folk-hero status as a result.

The other acute embarrassment for the South African government remains its fear of alienating international pharmaceutical companies. Hence Mbeki maintains an Aids-denialist posture, claiming that antiretroviral medicines are either too toxic or that they don't work. But the same spirit of decommodification has emerged from the TAC and its international allies like the Aids Coalition to Unleash Power (ACT UP), Medicins sans Frontieres and Oxfam. Like activists demanding free water and electricity, the Campaign has also hit the barrier of transnational (and local) corporate power.

The same conflicts were imported into the broader WSSD process, beginning at the Rio Earth Summit in 1992. Privatisation of basic services is moving ahead at great speed globally, under the rubric of Public–Private Partnerships. Nepad was drafted by a team under Mbeki's direction, and also calls for a massive dose of foreign investment in privatised infrastructure. If African leaders genuinely embrace the neoliberal plan, which would simply extend the economic policies that have ravaged the continent the past two decades, the most powerful water privatisers and Eskom would be the main beneficiaries. Mbeki won official endorsements of the plan at both the June 2002 summit of the G8 leaders in Alberta, Canada and the July launch of the Africa Union in Durban. Demonstrations by anti-capitalists from African and Canadian social movements embarrassed Mbeki at each event, leading him to brand the criticisms 'easy, routine, uninformed and cynical'.[68]

Towards green socialism?

The green and red critiques reviewed above come together in Johannesburg. What the South African experience these last few years shows, is that full cost-recovery doesn't work and will be resisted, especially if combined with cut offs of services. Those services create additional social welfare in the form of public/merit goods, but only if they are not privatised because solely the state – if it genuinely represents society – has an in-built incentive to use services like water and electricity to promote public health, gender equity, environmental protection and economic spin-offs.

Not only do privatisers ignore public goods, they are also inevitably opposed to free lifeline supplies and redistributive pricing. Hence, as so many South Africans have learned these last few years, the fight against privatisation is also a fight to decommodify the basic services we all need, simply to stay alive. And by winning that fight, there is a chance that the state can be won over to its logical role: serving the democratically determined needs and aspirations of that huge majority for whom the power of capital has become a profound threat to social and environmental well-being.

The socialist strategy has always entailed making profound demands – in some discourses, 'a transitional programme' and in others, 'non-reformist reforms' – upon the capitalist state. When invariably the *class power* of capital is challenged in the process, no matter how feasible the demands are in fiscal/administrative respects, the question of socialist revolution inexorably emerges. The demands for decommodification are popular, sane, logical and backed by solid democratic organisation.

On behalf of capital, the state must resist, and the South African state has typically done so by deploying the rhetoric of globalisation. Recall, for example, the quote by Chippy Olver, manager of the WSSD process for the Department of Environmental Affairs and Tourism. Previously, when he was the state's infrastructure policy director, Olver was confronted by the first round of demands that subsidies be used to help low-income people get free electricity, instead of helping mega-polluters like the Alusaf smelter. Rejecting the request, Olver made clear the nature of the class struggle ahead: 'If we increase the price of electricity to users like Alusaf, their products will become uncompetitive and that will affect our balance of payments'.[69]

Where does that leave those arguing for traditions of human rights, decommodification and socialism-from-below? In coming months and years, four sorts of tasks present themselves:

- link up the demands and campaigns for free services, medicines and universal-entitlement income grants;
- translate these from the spheres of consumption to production, beginning with creative renationalisation of privatised services, restructured municipal work, expansion of the nascent cooperative sector and establishment of state-driven local generic drug manufacturing;

- strengthen the basis for longer-term alliances between poor and working people, that are in the first instance rooted in civil society and that probably within the next decade will also be taken up by a mass workers' party; and

- regionalise and internationalise these principles, strategies and tactics, just as Pretoria politicians and Johannesburg capital intensify their subimperialist ambitions across Africa, using concepts of deglobalisation and the formula of internationalism plus the nation-state.

One very hopeful sign of the last is the emergence of Anti-Privatisation Forums in the three largest South African cities and, in mid-2002, in Mbabane, Swaziland and Harare and Bulawayo, Zimbabwe. In each, mass-democratic activist groups are at the core, supported by explicitly socialist activists like those grassroots ideologues who drafted the handbill at the outset of this chapter, as well as organised socialist revolutionaries. Third World debt rupidation and campaigns to kick out the World Bank and IMF, supported by the growing movement around the world to defund the Bank through the Bonds Boycott tactic, are common starting points.

Additionally, the more that South African subimperialism emerges as a key problem, the more unity these movements will find in common opponents. The Southern African People's Solidarity Network is one of the main vehicles for ideological development. The African Social Forum will also continue expanding through debt, trade, environment and other sectoral networks.[70]

The terrain is, therefore, being prepared for a deep-rooted challenge to capitalism. Aside from short-term splits over divided loyalties to exhausted political parties, which can be expected not only in South Africa but in many sites of African struggle, the prospects for unity between radical communities, labour, women, environmentalists and health activists have never been greater. The kinds of internationalist, anti-capitalist sentiments that rocked Europe during 2002 and scared so many globo-elites in their summits and conferences in prior years are becoming rooted in at least some Southern African soils. Through growing direct links to similar grassroots campaigns in places as diverse as Accra, Cochabamba, Narmada Valley and Porto Alegre, the struggle to decommodify life has enormous potential to grow from autonomous sites of struggle like Soweto into a full-fledged socialist movement. But that terrain also contains potholes which have to be recognised and filled in.

Uneven eco-socialist politics

This book has sought to document the great hope that has been sown through the seeds of some recent social justice struggles occurring at various scales:

- the living *body* of the HIV-positive individual – for example, one of millions of South African rape victims – facing a fatal disease, but through intense struggle against even president Mbeki, winning antiretroviral medicines to hold Aids at bay;
- the *household*, where a woman may celebrate preliminary victory in the campaign for free lifeline water and electricity;
- the Soweto *neighbourhood* that successfully resists service cuts through anti-disconnection activism;
- the *metropolitan-wide* campaigning that tentatively began in Nelson Mandela Metropole and that must deepen across South Africa, in favour of more progressive economic development, and against the Coegas of the world;
- policy debates that typically occur at the *nation-state* scale, which progressives can win not through technicist inputs but rather through mass mobilisation, direct action and humiliation of the neoliberal government;
- *regional* African cross-border grassroots alliances, such as those prefigured by the growing resistance to Nepad, or through the Lesotho dam struggles that bring together peasants and workers to seek joint green and brown solutions; and
- *global-scale* protests against an international elite that, faced with eco-social crises such as water scarcity and global warming, attempt to revitalise capitalism by making profits out of resource trading.

But it would be unfair to conclude without once again noting some of the philosophical and practical pitfalls of green-red consciousness. Some pitfalls fall away when we asses the limits of the eco-social justice movement and consider their relevance to particular scales, instead of invoking full-fledged universalism. That strategy gets us beyond both the constraints of localism and the utopianism of global-reformism.

Other divisions disappear when alliances form against the 'green business' approach. That philosophy was concisely articulated in 1989 by three authors associated with Anglo American Corporation, mixing neoliberal principles with sustainable development rhetoric:

> We must make the free enterprise system market mechanism work for us and use it to guide research and development and technological innovation. The last thing one wants is to have these functions micro-managed by government. The taxpayer has traditionally borne the brunt of the costs of environmental damage. This burden could now become an opportunity for profit for the imaginative investor in new technologies.[71]

Much of the counter-hegemonic challenge is to continue expanding our scientific knowledge so that glib opportunity for profit strategies – also known as 'green imperialism' – are no longer so readily adopted by policy-makers. To do that requires, in part, that we establish dialectical-strategic directions which we began identifying in Chapter One, so that the *conceptual* barriers that keep the critical ecology movements of various types apart, can in future be taken away.

Recall from Chapter One that Andrew Jamison posited four types of environmentalism: civic work on campaigns and social ecology; professional interventions based upon science and law; militant direct action; and personal environmentalism. We had little or no experience, in our studies, with the fourth. The first could be said to encompass the work of Mandela Metropole community activists, Basotho peasants, Alexandra campaigners, and the most forward-looking leaders from municipal unions and advocacy-oriented NGOs who argued for the human right to services.

The second category includes many of this book's readers: namely, technical experts and NGO-based or academic supporters of eco-social change activism, who try to provide intellectual buttressing to the popular organisations. The third is exemplified by the Soweto electricity activists, who, regrettably, are amongst the few genuinely victorious forces documented in the pages above. Militancy pays, it seems, because mild-mannered lobbying and project- or policy-wonk inputs by experts are, simply, incapable of raising the cost of business-as-usual.

That leads us, in Table 7, to Jamison's typology of how the dichotomy between green business and critical ecology, which we observed in many ways in the case studies above, can be transcended.

In the first row, Jamison concedes that green business can sometimes, perhaps often, co-opt environmentalism into the nexus of capital accu-

Table 7: Dialectics of environmentalisms and eco-socialism[72]

TERRAIN	GREEN BUSINESS	CRITICAL ECOLOGIES	ECO-SOCIALISM
type of agency	TNCs, states and global agencies	environmentalists and green NGOs	hybrid red-green networks
forms of action	commercial, brokerage	popularisation, resistance	exemplary mobilisation
ideal of 'science'	theoretical, expert	factual, lay	situated, contextual
knowledge sources	disciplines	traditions	experiences
competencies	professional	personal	synthetic

mulation, using concepts of sustainable development. The critical ecology movements resist, drawing upon concepts of environmental justice. But the battle of environmentalists and green NGOs against TNCs, states and global agencies will not succeed without a dialectical advance to the next stage: hybrid red-green networks. Examples are found in South Africa, from Mandela Metropole to Lesotho-Alexandra to Soweto, though not without limitations discussed above.

As for emblematic forms of action, the commercial, brokerage functions of green business come into direct cultural conflict with the repertoire of resistance tactics utilised by the eco-social justice activists. The eco-socialist project, in contrast, has to advance to the stage of what Jamison terms 'exemplary mobilisation', in which the ideas that 'Another World is Possible' and 'Socialism is the future, build it today' become more than the slogans of Porto Alegre and the SACP, and take on real meaning.

Intellectual buttressing remains crucial, and hence the ideal articulation of 'science' is also worth dwelling upon briefly. This book has spent inordinate time considering discourses, ranging from the 'theoretical, expert' inputs – no matter how flawed in reality – of promoters working from a green business standpoint, to the factual and lay languages of activists. What we seek is to build upon the second by defying the first, and achieving a situated, contextual science. The knowledge sources that undergird such efforts are typically divided into the technical disciplines of green business, the political traditions of eco-social justice, and the transcendental experiences of the eco-socialist project. As for the terrain of competencies, the green-business suits claim professionalism; the critical ecologists invoke personal commitment; and eco-socialists strive for a synthetic understanding of personal, professional and, above all, political.

With a similar grasp of the dialectic challenge, one of the leading contemporary historical materialists, David Harvey, insists that eco-socialist programmes must be explicitly forward-looking, and hence must

> deal in the material and institutional issues of how to organise production and distribution in general, how to confront the realities of global power politics and how to displace the hegemonic powers of capitalism not simply with dispersed, autonomous, localised, and essentially communitarian solutions (apologists for which can be found on both right and left ends of the political spectrum), but with a rather more complex politics that recognises how environmental and social justice must be sought by a rational ordering of activities at different scales.[73]

Thus it is vital to transcend both technical and political critiques of flawed cost-benefit analysis applied to Port Elizabeth's economic strategy, of Inspection Panel mandates established in the LHWP case, of infrastructure policy, and of so many other environmental and developmental challenges discussed in the pages above. Beyond that, we have to think more broadly about how society should manage its inherited environment. The rational ordering of South Africa's space economy must be considered one of the fundamental starting points for future attacks on the irrational socio-ecological utilisation – really, despoliation – of natural resources more generally.

Settlement patterns in question

A good place to start such consideration is the South African city, of which Johannesburg is surely the worst offender. Harvey remarks,

> If biocentric thinking is correct and the boundary between human activity and ecosystemic activities must be collapsed, then this means not only that ecological processes have to be incorporated into our understanding of social life: it also means that flows of money and of commodities and the transformative actions of human beings (in the building of urban systems, for example) have to be understood as fundamentally ecological processes.
>
> The environmental justice movement, with its emphasis upon marginalised and impoverished populations exposed to hazardous ecological circumstances, freely acknowledges these connections. Many of the issues with which it is confronted are specifically urban in character. Consequently, the principles it has enunciated include the mandate to address environmental justice in the city by the cleaning up and rebuilding of urban environments.[74]

This line of thinking takes us immediately to, but also far beyond, the questions raised above, over how cities are allocated their share of natural resources. Although it is vital not to assume any anti-urban sentiments (as do many ecological radicals), we have arrived at a position where it is only honest to address the ecological discourse established a century and a half ago in Marx and Engels' *Communist Manifesto*. There we find the call for a 'gradual abolition of all the distinction between town and country by a more equable distribution of the populace over the country'.

Johannesburg was born, after all, merely because of the discovery in 1886 of gold, that centuries-old relic of faithlessness in the value of money. But is Johannesburg's future golden or grim? There are now more industrial substitutes for gold. In the wake of dramatic financial market turbulence since the mid-1990s, the luxury consumption market for gold jewellery is unreliable. It is difficult to achieve profitable yields from ever-deeper mining operations. South African gold mining remains ecologically offensive, and particularly water-polluting. Add labour-related factors such as health, safety and migrancy, and there should be no geographical or locational grounds for Johannesburg continuing as South Africa's economic heartland over coming decades and centuries. Agglomerations of industry, particularly the outdated overcapacity that characterises uncompetitive Gauteng manufacturing, offer little basis for economic strength in a more flexible era based increasingly on the South African government's strategy, albeit a failure thus far, to promote export-oriented growth. It should be logical for Johannesburg gradually to decline, much like a Detroit or other rust belt towns.

If the response to Johannesburg's decline is the construction of a more humane system of production, it will require more than transcending the potent Minerals-Energy Complex that continues to prove so ecologically and economically self-destructive. At one point recently, South Africa promised a far greater degree of political capacity to shift production systems not only sectorally into more 'sustainable', redistributive systems (such as using relatively decommodified, basic-needs infrastructure as the basis for kick-starting more balanced economic development), but also geographically.

As the ANC RDP mandated in 1994, 'Macroeconomic policies must take into consideration their effect upon the geographic distribution of economic activity. Additional strategies must address the excessive growth of the largest urban centres, the skewed distribution of population within rural areas, the role of small and medium-sized towns, and the future of declining towns and regions, and the apartheid dumping grounds'.[75] Amongst many other RDP promises, this was immediately broken in government's 1995 *Draft Urban Development Strategy*:

> The country's largest cities are not excessively large by international standards, and the rates of growth of the various tiers also appear to be normal. Hence there appears to be little reason to favour policies which may artificially induce or restrain growth in a particular centre, region or tier ... The growth rate is sufficiently normal to suggest that effective urban management is possible and there is, therefore, no justification for interventionist policies which attempt to prevent urbanisation.[76]

Indeed, because 'South Africa's cities are more than ever strategic sites in a transnationalised production system' the debate has to be joined by a wider questioning of South Africa's insertion in the international division of labour.[77] The same challenge can be posed of many Southern African cities, according to Swatuk:

> All of these patterns of settlement and attendant problems are exaggerated in the context of apartheid engineering, replicated to a large degree in Zimbabwe and Namibia, and to varying degrees in Botswana, Swaziland and Zambia: alienation of fertile land and the creation of plantation agriculture; forced removals of indigenous people and their relocation to arid 'homelands'; the creation of ill- or non-serviced 'locations' which in the beginning were little more than dormitories for cheap labour.
>
> Moreover, this 'crush' of people in barren environs was made all the worse in the post-colonial and post-apartheid periods as the movement of indigenous people was no longer restricted. Families from the rural areas joined husbands and fathers in the townships and 'high-density suburbs'; many others made the trek to urban areas in search of work. At the same time, the early post-apartheid period saw a large influx of Africans from beyond the SADC region into the urban and peri-urban areas.
>
> Changing global structures of production and South African state-makers' attempts to find a neoliberal solution to them have also exacerbated settlement problems in the region. Countries which had long supplied labour to the mines and farms of South Africa in recent years have seen the return of tens of thousands of these citizens, retrenched as the South African mining industry continues to restructure. So, cities like Blantyre and Maseru are increasingly overrun with the newly unemployed and displaced.
>
> Taken together, what these facts reveal is water security for the few and insecurity for the many. As stated at the outset of this paper, this is a 'crisis' that is socially constructed. Its roots are historical, the result of deliberate actions taken in the service of settler and colonial interests. Its contemporary manifestations result from a combination of continuing elite privilege, shallow social and physical science, and the collective actions of millions of people responding 'logically' to abiding conditions of poverty and underdevelopment.[78]

A revolution is surely required to right these eco-social wrongs. Harvey concludes his analysis of environmental justice discourses by noting that 'There is a long and arduous road to travel to take the environmental justice movement beyond the phase of rhetorical flourishes, media successes, and symbolic politics, into a world of strong coherent political organising and practical revolutionary action'.[79]

That too might be the key lesson to be learnt from the most conceptually advanced of the environmental justice struggles considered above. Alexandra residents protested against the neoliberal South African state's prioritising of 'development', which in practical terms meant an awesome distributional bias towards big corporations and wealthy (mainly white) consumers. That imbalance was exacerbated by the state deploying merely token strategies to redirect water. In retrospect, the protest brought mainly a momentary conscientisation value to the water struggle.

Other approaches failed as well. Though necessary, the reformist and technicist critiques of the LHWP, advanced via the World Bank Inspection Panel, are clearly insufficient to foster real momentum for change, or to more decisively generate the alliances required for a broader – brown-green, urban-rural – critique of environmental injustice. The only alternatives left are practical but no less revolutionary: anti-capitalist analysis, demands and organising.

5. Conclusion

Since the early 1970s, the world has witnessed three broad discourses emerging around environmental management: neoliberalism, sustainable development and eco-social justice. The area between these is sometimes grey, and partisans often move fitfully – often largely rhetorically – between the camps. But the studies of existing environmental conditions in South Africa and of the emblematic policy and project case studies, give us a sense of how these discourses played out in a country characterised by a dramatic political power shift in 1994, but also by residual economic domination by corporate interests and a surprising degree of ideological adherence to the Washington Consensus world-view.

What underlies the discourses, however, is not only material interest but also political power to transform a particular discourse into a hegemonic discourse. What this means, concretely, is that South Africa is replete with radical intentions based on a highly politicised history and the obvious legacies of apartheid-capitalism on the one hand, with centrist bargaining fora and severely compromised legislative processes on the other; and in their most concrete manifestations, in actual cases of environmental management, extremely conservative policies and practices reflecting, above all, the dominance of major economic actors.

This is all widely understood, and does not go unchallenged. One expression of the implications of uneven political power relations for moral discourses about environmental management was provided by Constitutional Court judge Albie Sachs: 'People who have washing machines have no right to condemn others who dirty streams with their laundry. Those who summon up energy with the click of a switch should hesitate before denouncing persons who denude forests in search of fire-wood. It is undeniably distasteful to spend huge sums on saving the white rhino when millions of black children are starving'.[80]

And yet the privileges and prejudices of elites and of those companies which still wish society to take the overall burden of externalised environmental costs remain in place. It is in this sense that to firmly address the generation of socio-ecological inequality and the failure of South Africa to even achieve a modicum of 'sustainable development' can be traced not just to existing power relations but further, to the capitalist mode of production. The *structural* relationship between the capitalist mode of production and environmental crisis, and the need to articulate such a relationship in policy, legislation and concrete practice, is explained by Paul Burkett:

> Mainstream environmentalism bypasses the connections between capitalism's social relations of production and the system's tendency to devour, dispose of, and degrade nature to the point of threatening the basic conditions of human-material reproduction. Sustainable development, we are told, can be achieved via state policies (so-called 'green' tax/subsidy schemes and other technical fixes) and changes in individual behavior (recycling, marketing and consumption of more ecologically correct products, etc.) without changing the class relations between people and necessary conditions of their material reproduction. The assumption here is that eco-destruction is an inessential 'externality' of capitalism which does not fundamentally implicate the system's essential relations of class-exploitation and competition.[81]

Notwithstanding South Africa's rights-based rhetoric and various attempts to tinker with environmental management problems through technical, market-oriented solutions, two factors are obvious: the imperatives of ecological exploitation and the impossibility of more fundamental reversals of environmental degradation. In contrast, an eco-socialist perspective starts with the very ingredient missing from virtually all post-apartheid government initiatives: popular mobilisation. In this sense, the issues associated with the survival of society's oppressed communities can only be understood and tackled through an increasing convergence of green, brown, feminist, racial/ethnic justice, and class politics - or, militant particularisms, as Raymond Williams and David Harvey describe them.

That kind of serious environmentalism, Harvey insists, must claim the broadest appropriate terrain as its mandate, including cultural and spiritual features of ecological and social life, and seek to rationally reorder the space economy in a way that directly confronts capitalism's neoliberal discourses:

> The reinsertion of 'rational ordering' indicates that such a movement will have no option, as it broadens out from its militant particularist base, but to reclaim for itself a noncoopted and nonperverted version of the theses of ecological modernisation. On the one hand that means subsuming the highly geographically differentiated desire for cultural autonomy and dispersion, for the proliferation of tradition and difference within a more global politics, but on the other hand making the quest for environmental and social justice central rather than peripheral concerns.
>
> For that to happen, the environmental justice movement has to radicalise the ecological modernisation discourse.[82]

As neoliberal economic orthodoxy continues to prevail in so many areas of South African environment and development, and as sustainable-development discourses, policies and legislation fall far short of resolving the interlocking crises, it is to more radical confrontations with powerful forces that South Africa's eco-social justice movements inexorably will be drawn. All of us hope to track these, because the South African movements have continued to successfully call forth local citizen activism and generous international solidarity with a simple appeal: 'Another World is Possible!' – but only if you join us!

Notes

1. One such policy was Growth, Employment and Redistribution, or Gear. SECC leader Trevor Ngwane early on labelled Mbeki's New Partnership for Africa's Development a 'Gear for Africa'.

2. Bond, P. and M.Manyanya (2002), *Zimbabwe's Plunge: Exhausted Nationalism, Neoliberalism and the Search for Social Justice*, Maritzburg, University of Natal Press, London, Merlin Press and Trenton, Africa World Press.

3. As this book went to press, Cosatu's Zwelinzima Vavi announced a resumption of hostilities, exactly one month before the WSSD: 'Privatisation of basic services has continued unabated. The bloodbath of job losses has intensified despite millions protesting against this attack on the working-class living standards since 1999. It is

against this background that Cosatu decided to lift the suspension and continue its programme of mass mobilisation' (*Business Report*, 23 July 2002).

4.	African National Congress (2002), 'Statement to the Global Civil Society Forum on the World Summit on Sustainable Development', Johannesburg, July.

5.	Talk left, act right? The critique of the inhumanity of Johannesburg cannot disguise that in socio-economic terms, matters deteriorated under ANC rule as a function of municipal and national urban policies. Moreover, the rude treatment of transnational corporate capital is merely a veil for South African deference to footloose investors, including through their systematic empowerment at the World Trade Organisation.

6.	http://www.anc.org.za

7.	http://www.sacp.org.za

8.	For a rundown on the many 1994–99 anti-government protests caused by Pretoria's deviations from the RDP mandate, see Bond, P. (2000), *Elite Transition: From Apartheid to Neoliberalism in South Africa*, London, Pluto and Maritzburg, University of Natal Press, Chapter Six.

9.	Other notable allies included the other trade union federations and especially the National Education, Health and Allied Workers Union (Nehawu), Sangoco, the SACP, the SA Council of Churches (SACC), the Aids Law Project, the Aids Consortium and various orphanages and hospices.

10.	A 2002 lawsuit against US and European companies and banks was only one of the many activities underway to raise consciousness about the historical legacy of injustice. The Archbishop of Cape Town, Njongonkulu Ndungane, did particularly high-profile advocacy.

11.	A Cape Town-based coalition with strong labour backing is given support by the South African New Economics Foundation.

12.	Other local and international groups active on South African GM campaigning include Environmental Justice Networking Forum, Sangoco, BioWatch, Safe Age, Greenpeace, Friends of the Earth and Earthlife Africa.

13.	Intellectual backing from Economists Allied for Arms Reduction and the Ceasefire Campaign were important.

14.	Some of the important players here included the Sustainable Energy and Climate Change Partnership, South African Climate Action Network, the Minerals and Energy Policy Center, the Greenhouse Project, the Group for Environmental Monitoring, the Environmental and Development Agency and the Environmental Monitoring Group.

15.	The journal *Agenda* continued to provide extremely valuable analytical material about the racial and economic justice intersections with women's empowerment.

16.	Petras, J. and H. Veltmayer (2001), *Globalization Unmasked: Imperialism in the twenty-first Century*, London, Zed Press, p. 132.

17.	Three high-profile leftwing think-tanks and popular education centres are Khanya College, the International Labour Resource and Information Group and the Alternative Information and Development Centre, but there are many others that qualify as being organically connected to social movements.

18.	'Statement by Cosatu, the SA Council of Churches, South African Youth Council, Disability Sector and Sanco on Civil Society Participation in the WSSD', Johannesburg, 17 January, 2002. It should be noted that the director of the Indaba, Jacqui Brown, was cleared of charges and in a July 2002 labour arbitration hearing, won the right to reclaim her job.

19.	*Mail & Guardian*, 24 May 2002. For more on the Social Movement Indaba critique of Cosatu's action, see http://southafrica.indymedia.org

20. Likewise, even the SACP's mild-mannered ideological programme for its July 2002 congress contained a somewhat illogical critique of 'The challenge of an attempted neoliberal hegemony over Nepad' (given that the ANC leadership had imposed precisely that hegemony): 'We should not be surprised to find that powerful forces internationally, much of the media (including within our country), and the local conservative liberal opposition political parties, are working full-time to hegemonise and interpret Nepad for their own purposes ... In the view of the SACP not all of the existing Nepad document is sufficiently buttressed to deal decisively with this attempted neo-liberal hegemony of the initiative' (http://www.sacp.org.za).

21. National Land Committee and Landless People's Movement (2002), 'Joint Press Statement: SA Landless will not March with Cosatu', 23 July.

22. http://www.focusweb.net

23. Amin, S. (1999), 'Regionalisation in Response to Polarising Globalisation', in B.Hettne, A.Inotai and O.Sunkel (Eds), *Globalism and the New Regionalism*, London, Macmillan, p. 77.

24. *Business Day*, 3–5 July 2002.

25. A full critique of Nepad with the major African civil society statements from January–May 2002 and a point-by-point rebuttal of the document's provisions, can be found in Bond, P. (Ed)(2002), *Fanon's Warning: A Civil Society Reader on the New Partnership for Africa's Development*, Trenton, Africa World Press and Cape Town, Alternative Information and Development Centre. The citations below, including those of the original Nepad document, are also accessible at http://www.aidc.org.za

26. http://www.ran.org

27. Drawn from Bond, P., D.Miller and G.Ruiters (2000), 'Regionalism, Environment and the Southern African Proletariat', *Capitalism Nature Socialism*, 11, 3.

28. Swatuk, L. (2002), 'The New Water Architecture in Southern Africa: Reflections on Current Trends, Paper presented to the international workshop, 'Gold for/of the Future? Sustainable Water Management in Southern Africa and Germany and the Role of the Private Sector', organised by Coordination Southern Africa, Bonn, 3–5 May.

29. Ibid.

30. The prolific role of US AID and DFID in bringing regional water utility and municipal administrators to South Africa for fact-finding missions is just one indication of this pernicious influence.

31. A few tentative steps to internal South African reparations for displaced people are being taken, thanks to community pressure, at the sites of the Loskop and Gariep dams.

32. For details, see Bond, P., D.McDonald and G.Ruiters (2001), 'Water Privatisation in SADC Countries', commissioned by the Environmental Monitoring Group, Cape Town, 23 October; see also forthcoming papers on municipal privatisation in Maputo, Harare, Lusaka and Mbabane by Municipal Services Project researchers: http://www.queensu.ca/msp

33. Wellmer, G. (2001), 'The Foreign Financing of the Parastatal Eskom during the Apartheid Years', Unpublished paper, Frankfurt.

34. *Business Day*, 18 January 2002.

35. Agence France Press, 12 July 2002.

36. Eskom (2001), *Eskom Annual Report*, 2001, Johannesburg, p. 18.

37. Greenberg, S. (2002), 'Eskom, Electricity Sector Restructuring and Service Delivery in South Africa', Alternative Information and Development Centre, Cape Town, June. Documentation available in *Business Day* editions: 9 March 2000, 26 April 2000, 10 August 2000, 12 September 2000, 17 October 2000, 10 November 2000,

29 November 2000, 25 January 2001, 27 March 2001, 8 November 2001, 12 March 2002, 16 July 2002.

38. *Business Day*, 26 April 2000.

39. *Business Day*, 27 March 2001.

40. *Business Day*, 8 November 2001.

41. Friends of the Earth International (2002), 'Remarks on the Chair's Text', 20 June, Amsterdam.

42. The text can be accessed at http://www.johannesburgsummit.org

43. http://www.corporateeurope.org/un/desailetter.html. For more on the dangers of Type-II partnerships, see Corporate Europe Observatory (2002), 'Rio +10 and the Privatisation of Sustainable Development', Amsterdam, 6 May.

44. Several alternative texts were tabled by the end of the third PrepCom, with the US proposing a 'positive' statement, the EU suggesting a balanced text, and the G77/China insisting on a short paragraph that would avoid defining globalisation and instead focus on difficulties experienced by developing countries. The major background issue was whether the WTO would become the default organisation and set of rules governing Multilateral Environmental Agreements.

45. Annan, K. (2002), 'Remarks to the Friends of the Chair of the Preparatory Committee of the World Summit on Sustainable Development', New York, 17 July, http://www.un.org/News/Press/docs/2002/sgsm8307.doc.htm.

46. The list below and subsequent paragraph are drawn from information in duBoff, R. (2002), 'Mirror, Mirror on the Wall, Who's the Biggest Rogue of All?', ZNet Commentaries, 28 April; and Vally, S. and P.Bond (2001), 'An Appropriate Welcome for Powell at Wits', *Mail & Guardian*, 5 June.

47. Mbeki turned the other cheek. But there was nothing much new here. Washington played an extraordinarily anti-democratic role in Southern Africa during the 1960s–80s, entailing the CIA's decades-long support of the apartheid regime, including assistance in the arrest of Nelson Mandela; the encouragement by the US secretary of state Henry Kissinger of Pretoria's invasion of Angola in 1975; US patronage of Renamo's war in Mozambique; and Ronald Reagan's 'constructive engagement' policy, which prolonged apartheid's life during the 1980s. Following Reagan's lead, the US vice president 'elected' in November 2000, Dick Cheney, was a US senator, and voted in favour of keeping Mandela in prison and against anti-apartheid sanctions. As the chief executive of the oil services company Haliburton during the 1990s, Cheney sustained the Sani Abacha regime in Nigeria, when not creatively adjusting his firm's balance sheet. See Blum, W. (2000), *Rogue State: A Guide to the World's Only Superpower*, Boston, Common Courage.

48. Podhoretz, J. (2002), 'October Surprise, Please', *New York Post*, 16 July.

49. One emblematic source of humiliation was Mbeki's decision to codify the unfree, unfair Zimbabwe election of March 9-10 2002 as 'legitimate' one week in a Cabinet decision, and the next to suspend Zimbabwe from the Commonwealth because of G8 pressure. This kind of political alignment represented the worst of all possible worlds.

50. It hardly needs adding that forces demanding global change via Islamic fundamentalist terror (e.g., Al-Qaeda) did infinite more harm than good. So too would global justice movements have to start distinguishing between allegedly friendly forces – e.g., Oxfam Great Britain – which erratically moved to the right, endorsing free trade in the alleged interests of poverty reduction.

51. *The Observer*, 14 July 2002.

52. Cited in African National Congress (2002), 'World Summit on Sustainable Development: A Briefing Note for ANC Branches and Other Local Structures', Johannesburg, July.

53   Mbeki's gambit included alliance building through a 'Friends of the Chair' technique that took on a terrible force – comparable to what journalist Alexander Cockburn calls 'coerced harmony' – at the Doha WTO meeting. South Africa's friends for the WSSD were Argentina, Brazil, Canada, China, Denmark, Egypt, France, Germany, Ghana, India, Indonesia, Italy, Jamaica, Japan, Jordan, Mexico, Nigeria, Norway, Russian Federation, Senegal, Sweden, Uganda, United Kingdom, United States and Venezuela.

54.   Palast, G. (2002), *The Best Democracy Money Can Buy: An Investigative Reporter Exposes the Truth about Globalisation, Corporate Cons and High Finance Fraudsters*, London, Pluto Press.

55.   See documentation of the proposed treaty initiative at http://www.canadians.org and in Barlow, M. and T. Clarke (2002), *Blue Gold: The Battle Against Corporate Theft of the World's Water*, Toronto, Stoddart, pp. xvii-xviii. See also Petrella, R. (2001), *The Water Manifesto: Arguments for a World Water Contract*, London, Zed Press, and Shiva, V. (2002), *Water Wars: Privatisation, Pollution and Profit*, Boston, South End Press. The report in the section below originally appeared as 'Blue Planet Targets Commodification of World's Water', coauthored by Bond and Karen Bakker, in *ZNet Commentary*, 27 July 2001 and *GreenLeft Weekly*, 18 July 2001.

56.   These include the WSSD and follow-up meetings in Kyoto in 2003 and Montreal in 2006.

57.   See http://www.corpwatch.org for much more information on the Global Compact and particularly destructive TNCs. High-profile leaders of NGOs, human rights groups and think-tanks implicated in the Global Compact scam as Advisory Board members or supporters included officials of Amnesty International, Carnegie Foundation for International Peace, Conservation International, Global Sullivan Principles, Human Rights Watch, the International Institute for Environment and Development, Lawyers' Committee for Human Rights, International Save the Children Alliance World Conservation Union, World Resources Institute, Worldwide Fund for Nature. Labour participants included the International Federation of Chemical, Energy and Mineworkers' Unions, the International Confederation of Free Trade Unions, the AFL-CIO and the Union Network International.

58.   Evans, R. (1987), *Death in Hamburg: Society and Politics in the Cholera Years*, 1830-1910, Harmondsworth, Penguin, pp. 568.

59.   Bond, P. (2001), *Against Global Apartheid: South Africa meets the World Bank, IMF and International Finance*, Cape Town, University of Cape Town Press, Chapters Eight and Nine.

60.   Recall Parks Mankahlana, Mbeki's main spokesperson, who in 2000 justified to Science magazine why the SA Department of Health refused to provide a relatively inexpensive (R100 million per year) antiretroviral treatment to pregnant, HIV-positive women: 'That mother is going to die and that HIV-negative child will be an orphan. That child must be brought up. Who is going to bring the child up? It's the state, the state. That's resources, you see' (cited in The Citizen, 14 July 2000 and *Mail & Guardian*, 21 July 2000).

      Amongst others in the ANC leadership, Trevor Manuel took up the denialist cause in December 2001:

> The little I know about anti-retrovirals is that unless you maintain a very strict regime ... unless you have the facilities to deal with all of that, because you understand what is happening to your body, they can pump you full of anti-retrovirals, sadly, all that you're going to do, because you are erratic, is to develop a series of drug-resistant diseases inside your body. (BBC and Sapa reports, 3 December 2001.)

Instead of saving lives, the finance ministry's priorities were to slash corporate taxes from 48% in 1994 to 30% today; to find sufficient resources to import roughly R60 billion worth of high-tech arms; and to repay roughly $25 billion worth of apartheid-era foreign debt and a bit more in apartheid domestic debt, which could have been declared Odious in legal terms. These were just some of the reflections of fiscal laxity which local and international bankers generally approved of, in contrast to saving lives through expanding state health spending and other social budgets, which the bankers have explicitly not supported.

61. South African trade minister Alec Erwin's loyalty to Northern corporations ahead of Southern people is discussed in Keet, D. (2002), 'South Africa's Official Position and Role in Promoting the World Trade Organisation', Cape Town, Alternative Information and Development Centre and Bond and Manyanya, *Zimbabwe's Plunge*, Chapter Four.

62. Interview with Ben Cashdan, SABC TV, 27 April 2002.

63. *Business Day*, 28 May 2002.

64. Evans, *Death in Hamburg*, p. 568.

65. Esping-Andersen, G. (1990), *The Three Worlds of Welfare Capitalism*, Princeton, Princeton University Press.

66. Roome, J. (1995), 'Water Pricing and Management: World Bank Presentation to the SA Water Conservation Conference', unpublished paper, South Africa, 2 October.

67. World Bank (2000), *Sourcebook on Community Driven Development in the Africa Region: Community Action Programs*, Africa Region, Washington, DC, 17 March (signatories: Calisto Madavo, Jean-Louis Sarbib), Annex 2.

68. *Business Report*, 4 July 2002.

69. *Mail & Guardian*, 22–28 November 1996.

70. http://www.aidc.org.za

71. Huntley, B., R. Siegfried and C. Sunter (1989), *South African Environments into the Twenty-first Century*, Cape Town, Human and Rousseau Tafelburg, p. 35. For a similar techno-fix approach to environmental problems (in an otherwise extremely compelling period analysis), see Clarke, J. (1991), *Back to Earth: South Africa's Environmental Challenges*, Johannesburg, Southern Book Publishers.

72. Adapted from Jamison, A. (2001), *The Making of Green Knowledge: Environmental Politics and Cultural Transformation*, Cambridge, Cambridge University Press.

73. Harvey, D. (1996), *Justice, Nature and the Geography of Difference*, Oxford, Basil Blackwell, pp. 400–401.

74. Ibid, p. 392.

75. ANC/Alliance (1994), *Reconstruction and Development Programme*, Johannesburg, Section 4.3.4.

76. Ministry of Reconstruction and Development (1995), *Draft Urban Development Strategy*, Pretoria, p. 9.

77. Ibid, p. 41.

78. Swatuk, 'The New Water Architecture in Southern Africa'.

79. Harvey, *Justice, Nature and the Geography of Difference*, p. 402.

80. Sachs, A. (1990), *Protecting Human Rights in a New South Africa*, Cape Town, Oxford University Press.

81. Burkett, P. (1995), 'Capitalization Versus Socialization of Nature', *Capitalism, Nature, Socialism*, 6, 4, p. 92.

82. Harvey, *Justice, Nature and the Geography of Difference*, p. 401.

References

Adams, P. (2002), 'The Canadian Connection', *Financial Post*, 27 June.

Addison, G. (1998), 'Dam It, Let's Pour Concrete', *Saturday Star*, 3 November.

Adler, G. (1993), 'From the 'Liverpool of the Cape' to 'The Detroit of South Africa': The Automobile Industry and Industrial Development in the Port Elizabeth-Uitenhage Region', *Kronos: Journal of Cape History*, 20.

Advertising Standards Authority Directorate (2002), 'Ruling of the ASA Directorate', Johannesburg, 16 May.

African Development Bank (1997), 'Investment Proposal: South Africa Infrastructure Investment Fund', Abidjan, ADB Private Sector Unit.

African Environmental Solutions (1997), 'Proposed Eastern Cape Zinc Refinery and Associated Phosphoric Acid Plant: Final Environmental Impact Report', Report for the Coega Authority, Cape Town.

African National Congress (1994), *The Reconstruction and Development Programme*, Johannesburg, Umanyano Publications.

   (2002), 'Statement to the Global Civil Society Forum on the World Summit on Sustainable Development', Johannesburg, July.

   (2002), 'World Summit on Sustainable Development: A Briefing Note for ANC Branches and Other Local Structures', Johannesburg, July.

Albritton, R., M.Itoh, R.Westra and A.Zuege (Eds) (2001), *Phases of Capitalist Development*, London, Palgrave.

Alexandra residents (1998), 'Inspection Panel Claim regarding World Bank Involvement in the Lesotho Highlands Water Project', 23 April, Alexandra.

Allan, C. (2001), 'Coega, Conflicts of Interest and the Arms Deal', Public Service Accountability Monitor, Rhodes University.

Allanson, B. (1995), 'An Introduction to the Management of Inland Water Ecosystems in South Africa', Report TT 72/95, Water Research Commission, Pretoria.

Amin, S. (1999), 'Regionalisation in Response to Polarising Globalisation', in B.Hettne, A.Inotai and O.Sunkel (Eds), *Globalism and the New Regionalism*, London, Macmillan.

Andoh, R. (1994), 'Urban Drainage: The Alternative Approach', Paper presented at WEDC Conference, Colombo, Sri Lanka.

Angel, S. (1995), 'The Future Lies in a Global System of Competitive Cities', *Countdown to Istanbul, 1.*

Annan, K. (2002), 'Remarks to the Friends of the Chair of the Preparatory Committee of the World Summit on Sustainable Development', New York, 17 July, http://www.un.org/News/Press/docs/2002.

Archer, R. (1996), *Trust in Construction? The Lesotho Highlands Water Project*, London, Christian Aid and Maseru, Christian Council of Lesotho.

Arthur D. Little (1997), 'Review of Environmental Impact and Strategic Environmental Assessment of Coega Harbour and Industrial Development Zone', July.

Ashley, B. (1997), 'Challenging Apartheid Debt: Cancellation a Real Option', debate, 3.

Asmal, K. (1996), 'Speech to the Launch of the 1995/6 Working for Water Programme Annual Report', Pretoria, 17 July.

   (1996), 'Speech to Group for Environmental Monitoring Workshop on Lesotho Highlands Water Project', in Group for Environmental Monitoring (ed), Record of Proceedings: Lesotho Highlands Water Workshop, Johannesburg, 29-30 August.

   (1996), 'Speech to Cape Town Conservation workshop', Cape Town.

   (1998), 'Lesotho Highlands Water Project: Success Story', Address to Muela press conference, 21 January; and (1998), 'Opening of the Lesotho Highlands Water Project', Speech, 22 January.

   (1998), 'Policy Directions of the Department of Water Affairs and Forestry', Letter to Patrick Bond, Pretoria, 8 May.

Asmal, K. and M. Muller (1998), 'Watering down the Facts', *Mail & Guardian*, 8-14 May.

428

Bakker, K. (1998), 'An Evaluation of Some Aspects of Mvula's Participation in BoTT', Unpublished paper, Oxford University Department of Geography, Oxford, September.

Ballenger, J. (1998), 'Lesotho Water Project Falls Foul of Environmental Lobby Groups', *Business Day*, 22 January.

Barber, S. (1998), 'Vote Asmal's Gov't out of Power, But Please, No Whining', *Business Day*, 9 September.

(2001), 'Narrowly Focused Story did SA's Government no Justice', *Business Day* 28 November.

Barlow, M. and T.Clarke (2002), *Blue Gold: The Battle Against Corporate Theft of the World's Water*, Toronto, Stoddart.

Beall, J. O.Crankshaw and S.Parnell (2002), *Uniting a Divided City: Governance and Social Exclusion in Johannesburg*, London, Earthscan.

Biel, R. (2000), *The New Imperialism: Crises and Contradictions in North/South Relations*, London, Zed.

Blignaut, J.N. and R.M.Hassan (2000), 'A Natural Resource Accounting Analysis of the Contribution of Mineral Resources to Sustainable Development in South Africa', Unpublished paper, Department of Economics and Agricultural Economics, University of Pretoria.

Blum, W. (2000), *Rogue State: A Guide to the World's Only Superpower*, Boston, Common Courage.

Bond, P. (1992), 'Redlining Cuts off Jo'burg's Lifeblood', *Weekly Mail*, 17-23 April.

(1992), 'De Loor Report is Off the Mark', *Reconstruct, Work in Progress*, August.

(1993), 'Housing Crisis Reveals Transitional Tension', *Financial Gazette*, 11 November.

(1997), 'Lesotho Dammed', *Multinational Monitor*, January-February.

(1997), 'Infrastructure Plan Still a Disappointment', *South African Labour Bulletin*, 21, 2.

(1998), 'Privatisation, Participation and Protest in South African Municipal Services: The Basis for Opposition to World Bank Promotion of Public-Private Partnerships', *Urban Forum*, 9, 1.

(2000), *Elite Transition: From Apartheid to Neoliberalism in South Africa*, London, Pluto Press, and Pietermaritzburg, University of Natal Press.

(2000), *Cities of Gold, Townships of Coal: Essays on South Africa's New Urban Crisis*, Trenton NJ, Africa World Press.

(2001), *Against Global Apartheid: South Africa meets the World Bank, IMF and International Finance*, Cape Town, University of Cape Town Press.

(2001), 'Summary of Discussion Forum: Electricity Restructuring', University of the Witwatersrand Graduate School of Public and Development Management, Johannesburg, 16 August.

(2002), 'Local Economic Development Debates in South Africa', Occasional Paper, Municipal Services Project, February, http://www.queensu.ca/msp.

(Ed)(2002), *Fanon's Warning: A Civil Society Reader on the New Partnership for Africa's Development*, Cape Town, AIDC and Trenton, Africa World Press.

Bond, P., S.Hosking and J.Robinson (1998), 'Local Economic Development Choices in Port Elizabeth', paper presented to the Workshop on Local Economic Development, Department of Constitutional Development, Cape Town, April.

Bond, P. and M.Khosa (Eds) (1999), *An RDP Policy Audit*, Pretoria, Human Sciences Research Council Press.

Bond, P. and D.Letsie (2000), 'Debating Supply and Demand Characteristics of Bulk Infrastructure: Lesotho-Johannesburg Water Transfer', in M.Khosa (Ed), *Empowerment through Service Delivery*, Pretoria, Human Sciences Research Council.

Bond, P. and M.Manyanya (2002), *Zimbabwe's Plunge: Exhausted Nationalism, Neoliberalism, and the Search for Social Justice*, Pietermaritzburg, University of Natal Press, London, Merlin Press, and Trenton, Africa World Press.

Bond, P., D.McDonald and G.Ruiters (2001), 'Water Privatisation in SADC Countries', commissioned by the Environmental Monitoring Group, Cape Town, 23 October.

Bond, P. and L.Mcwabeni (1998), 'Local Economic Development in Stutterheim', in E.Pieterse (Ed), *Case Studies in LED and Poverty*, Pretoria, Department of Constitutional Development.

Bond, P., D.Miller and G.Ruiters (2000), 'Regionalism, Environment and the Southern African Proletariat', *Capitalism Nature Socialism*, 11, 3.

Bond, P.T.Mogale and D.Moellendorf (1998), 'Infrastructure Investment and the Integration of Low-Income People into the Economy', published in Development Bank of Southern Africa Discussion Paper #4, *The Impact of Infrastructure Investment on Poverty Reduction and Human Development*, Midrand.

Brenner, R. (2002), *The Boom and the Bubble*, London, Verso.

Burkett, P. (1995), 'Capitalization Versus Socialization of Nature', *Capitalism, Nature, Socialism*, 6, 4.

Cashdan, B. (2001), *White Gold*, video, Johannesburg.

Charles Anderson Associates (1994), *National Electricity Policy Synthesis Study*, Vol 1. Report submitted to the Dept of Mineral and Energy Affairs, 12 August.

Clarke, J. (1991), *Back to Earth: South Africa's Environmental Challenges*, Johannesburg, Southern Book Publishers.

Coastal and Environmental Services (2000), 'Coega Industrial Development Zone Integrated Environmental Summary Report', Report prepared for the Coega Development Corporation, Port Elizabeth, August.

Congress of South African Trade Unions (2001), 'Cosatu Submission on the Eskom Conversion Bill', presented to Public Enterprises Portfolio Committee, 9 May.

Constitutional Court (2000), 'Irene Grootboom v the Republic of South Africa', Johannesburg.

Corporate Europe Observatory (2002), 'Rio +10 and the Privatisation of Sustainable Development', Amsterdam, 6 May.

Council for Scientific and Industrial Research (1997), *Strategic Environmental Assessment for the Proposed IDZ and Harbour*, Pretoria.

Cronon, W. (1991), *Nature's Metropolis: Chicago and the Great West,* New York, Norton.

Daly, H. (1996), Beyond Growth: The Economics of Sustainable Development, Boston, Beacon Press.

Daly, H. and J.Cobb (1994), *For the Common Good*, Boston, Beacon Press.

Department of Constitutional Development (1997), *Municipal Infrastructure Investment Framework*, Pretoria.

(1997), *User-Friendly Guide to the Miif*, Pretoria.

(1998), *Draft Regulatory Framework for Municipal Service Partnerships*, Pretoria, August.

Department of Environmental Affairs and Tourism (2001), *Technical Background Document for the Development of a National Ambient Air Quality Standard (NAAQS) for Sulphur Dioxide*, Environmental Quality and Protection Office, Pretoria.

Department of Finance (2001), '2002 Estimates of National Expenditure: Vote 30, Minerals and Energy', Pretoria.

Department of Health (1999), 'Health Sector Strategic Framework', 1999-2004, Pretoria.

Department of Minerals and Energy (1995), 'South African Energy Policy Document', Pretoria.

(1997), 'Re-appraisal of the National Electrification Programme and the Formulation of a National Electrification Strategy', www.dme.gov.za/energy/RE-APPRAISAL.htm.

(1998), *White Paper on the Energy Policy of the Republic of South Africa*, Pretoria.

Department of Public Enterprises (2001), 'Speech by Minister Radebe at Workshop on the Service Delivery Framework', Megawatt Park Conference Room, 30 November 2001.

(2002), 'Budget Vote Speech delivered by Minister Radebe', National Assembly, 16 May.

Department of Water Affairs and Forestry (1994), *Water Supply and Sanitation White Paper*, Cape Town.

(1996), *The Orange River Project Replanning Study*, Pretoria.

(1997), 'Overview of Water Resources Availability and Utilisation in South Africa', Pretoria.

(1998), 'Compulsory National Standards Relating to the Provision of Water Services in Terms of Section 9(1)(a)', Memo CWS02161, Pretoria, 30 December.

(1999), *Orange River Development Project Replanning Study*, Pretoria.

Dor, G. (1998), 'SA's Poor Should not be Fooled', Sowetan, 30 June.

Drakeford, M. (1998), 'Water Regulation and Pre-payment Meters', *Journal of Law and Society*, 25, 4.

duBoff, R. (2002), 'Mirror, Mirror on the Wall, Who's the Biggest Rogue of All?', ZNet Commentaries, 28 April.

Earthlife Africa (2001), 'Other Energy-Related Developments', Johannesburg.

(2001), 'Nuclear Energy Costs the Earth', Johannesburg.

(2002), 'Information Pack for Activists Training in Energy Issues', Johannesburg.

Eastern Cape Socio-Economic Consultative Council (2000), 'Advancing Democracy, Growth and Development – The Imperative of Integrated Rural Development in the Province of the Eastern Cape', A Report on the Rural Development Summit, Umtata, 5-6 October.

Environmental Defence Fund and International Rivers Network (1999), 'Groups call on World Bank to Ban Companies in African Bribery Scandal', Press release, Washington, DC and Berkeley, CA, 24 September.

Environmental Monitoring Group, International Rivers Network and Group for Environmental Monitoring (1999), 'Once There was a Community: Southern African Hearings for Communities Affected by Large Dams', Final Report, Cape Town, 11-12 November.

Eskom (2001), *Annual Report 2001*, Johannesburg.

(2001), 'Eskom's Retail Pricing Plan 2002', Revision 1, July 2001, Megawatt Park, Johannesburg.

Esping-Andersen, G. (1990), *The Three Worlds of Welfare Capitalism*, Princeton, Princeton University Press.

Evans, R. (1987), *Death in Hamburg: Society and Politics in the Cholera Years*, 1830–1910, Harmondsworth, Penguin.

Fanon, F. (1963)[1961], *The Wretched of the Earth*, New York, Grove Press.

Ferguson, J. (1991), *The Anti-Politics* Machine, Cambridge, Cambridge University Press.

Financial and Fiscal Commission (1997), 'Local Government in a System of Intergovernmental Fiscal Relations in South Africa: A Discussion Document', Midrand.

Fine, B. and Z.Rustomjee (1996), *The Political Economy of South Africa: From Minerals-Energy Complex to Industrialisation*, London, Christopher Hirst and Johannesburg, Wits University Press.

Fitch IBCA (1999), 'City of Johannesburg', Johannesburg, June.

Foster, J. (2002), *Ecology against Capitalism*, New York, Monthly Review Press.

Fourie, A. and M. van Ryneveld (1995), 'The Fate in the Subsurface of Contaminants associated with On-site Sanitation: A Review', Water SA 21, 2.

Fox, J. and L.D.Brown (1998), *The Struggle for Accountability: The World Bank, NGOs and Grassroots Movements*, Cambridge, MA, MIT Press.

Friends of the Earth International (2002), 'Remarks on the Chair's Text', 20 June, Amsterdam.

Fuggle, R. (1997), 'Review of Documentation Pertaining to Coega IDZ Initiative', Unpublished paper, July.

Fuggle, R.F. and M.A. Rabie (Eds)(1992), *Environmental Management in South Africa*, Cape Town, Juta.

Gabriel, N. (1998), 'Still Weighed Down by Burden of Apartheid's Debt', Sunday Independent, 15 November.

Gleik, P. (2001), 'Water and Conflict', http://www.thewaterpage.com/conflict.htm.

Greater Johannesburg Metropolitan Council (1999), 'Igoli 2002 Conceptual Framework', Johannesburg.

Greenberg, S. (2002), 'Eskom, Electricity Sector Restructuring and Service Delivery in South Africa', Alternative Information and Development Centre, Cape Town, June.

Grobicki, A. (1997), 'Proposed Coega IDZ Water Demands, and Constraints on Supply', Abbott Grobicki Consulting, Port Elizabeth, July.

Grossmann, H. (1992)[1929], *The Law of Accumulation and Breakdown of the Capitalist System*, London, Pluto.

Grusky, S. (2001), 'IMF makes Water Privatisation Condition of Financial Support', PSIRU update, http://www.psiru.org.

Hall, D. (2001), 'The Public Sector Water Undertaking: A Necessary Option', Public Services International Research Unit, University of Greenwich.

Hardt, M. and A.Negri (2000), *Empire*, Cambridge, Harvard University Press.

Harvey, D. (1985), *Consciousness and the Urban Experience*, Oxford, Basil Blackwell.
(1996), *Justice, Nature and the Geography of Difference*, Oxford, Basil Blackwell.
(2001) Spaces of Capital: Towards a Critical Geography, New York, Routledge.

Hemson, D. (2001), 'Dolphin Honeymoon Over', *Business Day*, 14 June.

Hennig, R. (2001), 'IMF forces African Countries to Privatise Water', 8 February, http://www.afrol.com.

Henninen, O., H. Kruize, O. Breugelmans, E. Lebret, E. Samoli, L. Georgoulis, K. Katsouyanni, M. J. Jantunen (1997), 'Simulation of population exposure', Presented to Valamo Conference on Environmental Health and Risk Assessment: Health Risks of Inhaled Particles, Valamo Monastery, Heinevesi.

Henwood, D. (1998), *Wall Street*, London, Verso.

Heymans, C. (1991), 'Privatization and Municipal Reform', in M.Swilling, R.Humphries and K.Shubane (Eds), *Apartheid City in Transition*. Oxford University Press, Cape Town.

Hilferding, R. (1981)[1910], *Finance Capital*, London, Routledge & Kegan Paul.

Himlin, B. (1997), 'Some Environmental Cost Calculations Relating to Infrastructure', Unpublished report prepared by the Development Research Institute for the National Institute for Economic Policy, Johannesburg.

Hoover, R. (2000), 'Evaluating the LHWP Against WCD Guidelines', Unpublished report, International Rivers Network, San Francisco, 17 November, http://www.irn.org.
(2002), 'Mozal Smelter Threatens Quality of Life in Mozambique', *groundWork*, 4, 2, June.

Horta, K. (1995), 'The Mountain Kingdom's White Oil: The Lesotho Highlands Water Project', *The Ecologist*, 25, 6.
(1996), 'Making the Earth Rumble: The Lesotho-South Africa Water Connection', *Multinational Monitor*, May.

Hosking, S. (1999), 'Comparing Heavy Industry and Agro-aquaculture Options in the Coega River Mouth Area', *South African Journal of Agricultural Economics*, 38, 1.

Hosking, S. and P.Bond (2000), 'Infrastructure for Spatial Development Initiatives or for Basic Needs? Port Elizabeth's Prioritisation of the Coega Port/IDZ over Municipal Services,' in M.Khosa (Ed), *Empowerment through Service Delivery*, Pretoria, Human Sciences Research Council.

Huntley, B., R.Siegfried and C.Sunter (1989), *South African Environments into the Twenty-first Century*, Cape Town, Human and Rousseau Tafelburg.

Institute for Development Planning and Research (1997), 'The Port Elizabeth and Uitenhage Socio-Economic Development Monitor 1997', University of Port Elizabeth, Port Elizabeth.

International Congress of Free Trade Unions (1995), *EPZs in Asia: Who Profits?*, Brussels.

International Energy Agency (2000), 'CO2 Emissions from Fuel Combustion, 1971-1998', Paris.
(2000), 'Key World Energy Statistics from the IEA,' Paris.

International Rivers Network (2002), 'The World Bank and Corruption: Excerpts from

REFERENCES

Public Statements, Policies and Procedures', Berkeley, 26 June, http://www.irn.org.

Jamison, A. (2001), *The Making of Green Knowledge: Environmental Politics and Cultural Transformation*, Cambridge, Cambridge University Press.

Jauch, H. and D.Keet (1996), *A SATUCC Study on Export Processing Zones in Southern Africa: Economic, Social and Political Implications*, Cape Town, International Labour Resource and Information Group.

Jean-Paul, M. and M. Szymanski (1996), *Behind the Wire: Anti-Union Repression in the Economic Processing Zones,* International Confederation of Free Trade Unions, Brussels, April.

Jeter, J. (2001), 'For South Africa's Poor, a New Power Struggle', *Washington Post*, 6 November.

Jourdan, p., K.Gordhan, D.Arkwright, and G.de Beer (1996), 'Spatial Development Initiatives (Development Corridors): Their Potential Contribution to Investment and Employment Creation', Working Paper, Development Bank of Southern Africa, Midrand, October.

Kagarlitsky, B. (2000), *The Twilight of Globalization: Property, State and Capitalism*, London, Pluto.

Kasrils, R. (2001), 'Opening Address', Symposium on the World Commission on Dams Report on Dams and Development: A New Framework for Decisionmaking, Pretoria, 23 July.

Keet, D. (2002), 'South Africa's Official Position and Role in Promoting the World Trade Organisation', Cape Town, Alternative Information and Development Centre.

Kerley, G., and A. Boshoff (1997), 'A Proposal for a Greater Addo National Park', Terrestrial Ecology Research Unit, University of Port Elizabeth, Submission to the public participation process on behalf of the South African National Parks, Port Elizabeth.

Kravitz, J.D., et al (1995), 'Human Immunodifficiency Virus Seroprevalence in an Occupational Cohort in a South African Community', *Archives of Internal Medicine*, 155, 15.

Lamont, J. (1997), 'SA Seeks More Control over Water Project', *Business Report,* 1 December.

Leslie, G. (2000), 'Social Pricing of Electricity in Johannesburg', Masters research report submitted to the Faculty of Management, University of the Witswatersrand, Johannesburg.

Lorrain, D. (1997), 'France: The Silent Change', in D.Lorrain and M.Stoker (Eds), *The Privatization of Urban Services in Europe*.

Macey, D. (2000), *Frantz Fanon: A Life*, London, Granta.

Macro-economic Research Group (1993), *Making Democracy Work: A Framework for Macroeconomic Policy in South Africa*, Cape Town, Centre for Development Studies.

Mandela Metropole Sustainability Coalition (2001), *Sustainable Development at Coega? Problems and an Alternative*, September, http://www.coega.org.

Mara, I. (2001), 'Between Diarrhoeal Diseases and HIV/Aids Debates in South Africa', Group for Environmental Monitoring, Johannesburg.

Mare, K. (2001), 'Free Basic Water: Actual Tariff Structures in Rand Water Area of Supply', Presentation to the Water Services Forum, Johannesburg, 18 July.

Maritime Education and Research Information Technology (2001), *Report on the Economic Evaluation of the Proposed Port of Ngqura and Development of a Container Terminal*, Stellenbosch.

Masia, S., J.Walker, N.Mkaza, I.Harmond, M.Walters, K.Gray and J.Doyen (1998), 'External BoTT Review', Joint report by the Department of Water Affairs and Forestry, World Bank, British Department for International Development and Unicef, Pretoria, November.

Mayekiso, M. (1996) *Township Politics: Civic Struggles for a New South Africa*, New York, Monthly Review Press.

Mbeki, T. (2002), 'Address by the President of the Republic of South Africa, Thabo Mbeki, on the Occasion of the Torch Handing over Ceremony, From Rio to Johannesburg',

Rio De Janeiro, 25 June.

McCully, P. (2002), 'Avoiding Solutions, Worsening Problems', San Francisco, International Rivers Network, http://www.irn.org.

(2002), *Flooding the Land, Heating the Air: Greenhouse Gas Emissions from Dams*, International Rivers Network, Berkeley.

McDonald, D. (Ed) (2002), *Environmental Justice in South Africa*, Columbus, Ohio University Press and Cape Town, University of Cape Town Press.

(2002), 'The Bell Tolls for Thee: Cost Recovery, Cut offs and the Affordability of Municipal Services in South Africa', Municipal Services Project Special Report (http://qsilver.queensu.ca/~mspadmin/pages/Project_Publications/Reports/bell.htm).

Mestrallet, G. (2001), 'The War for Water', *Le Monde*, 1 November 2001.

Metsi Consultants (1999), 'The Establishment and Monitoring of Instream Flow Requirements for River Courses Downstream of LHWP Dams', Lesotho Highlands Development Authority Contract 648, Maseru.

Ministry of Reconstruction and Development (1994-95), *Urban Infrastructure Investment Framework*, Pretoria.

(1995), *Draft Urban Development Strategy*, Pretoria.

Morris, A. B.Bozzoli, J.Cock, O.Crankshaw, L.Gilbert, L.Lehutso-Phooko, D.Posel, Z.Tshandu, and E.van Huysteen (1999), 'Change and Continuity: A Survey of Soweto in the late 1990s', Department of Sociology, University of the Witwatersrand.

Muller, M. (2001), 'Flood Criticism a One-Sided Discourse', *Mail & Guardian*, 30 March-5 April.

(2001), 'Media Release: Reply to Bond', Department of Water Affairs and Forestry, Pretoria, 18 April.

Murray, J., R.Everist, and J.Williams (1996), *Lonely Planet: South Africa, Lesotho and Swaziland*, Hawthorn, Australia, Lonely Planet.

Nababsing V. (1997), 'Gender issues in EPZ industrialisation', in SATUCC/ILO, *Report of the Follow Up Regional Trade Union Workshop on Export Processing Zones, Environment and Sustainable Development*, Pretoria, 3-5 May.

National Electricity Regulator (2001), *Annual Report 2000/01*, Johannesburg.

National Land Committee and Landless People's Movement (2002), 'Joint Press Statement: SA Landless will not March with Cosatu', 23 July.

Ndungane, N. (1998), 'Maria Ramos's 'No Debt' Statement is Remarkable', *Sunday Independent Business Report*, 15 November.

Nelson Mandela Metropolitan Municipality (2001), 'Workshop: Free Basic Services', 10 May.

Olszyk, D.M., G.Kats, C.L.Morrison, p. J.Dawson, I.Gocka, J.Wolf, C.R.Thompson (1990), 'Valencia Orange Fruit Yield with Ambient Oxidant or Sulphur Dioxide Exposures', *Journal of the American Society for Horticultural Science*, 115, 6.

Pakes, T. and Nel, H. (1997), 'Proposed Coega Industrial Development Zone (IDZ): Preliminary Economic Assessment', Report commissioned by the Coega IDZ Section 21 Company, Port Elizabeth.

Palast, G. (2002), *The Best Democracy Money Can Buy: An Investigative Reporter Exposes the Truth about Globalisation, Corporate Cons and High Finance Fraudsters*, London, Pluto Press.

Palmer Development Group (1993), 'Urban Sanitation Evaluation', Report 385 1/93, Water Research Commission, Pretoria.

(1993), 'Evaluation of 2 VIP Latrine Programmes in Natal', Urban Sanitation Evaluation Working Paper B2, Water Research Commission, Pretoria.

(1993), 'Sanitation and the Environment', Urban Sanitation Evaluation Working Paper B5, Water Research Commission, Pretoria.

(1994), 'Botshabelo: Case Study of Water Supply and Sanitation Arrangements', Water Research Commission, Pretoria.

(1995), 'Winterveld: Case Study of Informal Water Supply Arrangements', Water Research Commission, Pretoria.

REFERENCES

(2001), 'Rand Water: Tariff Database Survey 2', Johannesburg, March.

Palmer, I. and R. Eberhard (1994), 'Evaluation of Water Supply to Developing Urban Communities in South Africa: Phase I—Overview', Report KV 49/94, Water Research Commission, Pretoria.

Pape, J. *et al* (2001), 'Spatial Development Initiatives and Industrial Development Zones: Part of the solution or part of the problem?', International Labour Information and Research Group, University of Cape Town.

Petras, J. and H. Veltmayer (2001), *Globalization Unmasked: Imperialism in the Twenty-first Century*, London, Zed.

Petrella, R. (2001), *The Water Manifesto: Arguments for a World Water Contract*, London, Zed Press.

Planact (1990), 'Overview and Evaluation of the Soweto Project 1988/89', Mimeo, Planact archives, Wits University Historical Papers Library.

Podhoretz, J. (2002), 'October Surprise, Please', *New York Post*, 16 July.

Potts, M. (1996), 'Presentation by the DBSA to the Lesotho Highlands Water Workshop', in Group for Environmental Monitoring (ed), *Record of Proceedings: Lesotho Highlands Water Workshop*, Johannesburg, 29-30 August.

Port Elizabeth Municipality (1997), 'Public Private Partnerships for Municipal Services', Report by Director: Administration to the Executive Committee, 4 February.

(2001), 'Indigent Management Report,' March.

Port Elizabeth City Engineer's Department (1998), 'Memorandum', 22 January.

Portnet (2000), 'Submissions to the Public Participation Process', Port Elizabeth.

Pottinger, L. (1996), 'The Environmental Impacts of Large Dams', in Group for Environmental Monitoring (ed), *Record of Proceedings: Lesotho Highlands Water Workshop*, Johannesburg, 29-30 August.

Pretorius, L. (2001), 'Industrial Free Zones in Mozambique: A Case Study of Mozambique', International Labour Resource and Information Group, Cape Town, Occasional Paper #6.

PriceWaterhouseCoopers (2000), 'Tariffs, Levies and Financial Transition Strategies', Electricity Distribution Restructuring Project, Working Paper 5, Pretoria, p. 12.

Province of the Eastern Cape Ministry of Finance and Economic Affairs (2000), *Towards Coordinated and Sustainable Infrastructure Investment in the Eastern Cape: Interim Capital Expenditure and Maintenance Plan for the Period 2000/1 to 2005/6*, Bisho, November.

Radebe, T. (1996), 'Pay-back Time for Eskom Users', *Mail & Guardian*, 8 August.

Rand Water (2001), 'Planning and Financing of New Augmentation Schemes for the Vaal River System', Unpublished overhead slides, Johannesburg, 13 June.

Reid, R. (1998), 'Developments in the Structure and Ownership of Ports Worldwide', Presented to Intermodal Africa 98 Conference, Mercer Management Consulting, Inc, 11 March.

Rencken, G.E. and D.A. Kerdachi (1991), 'The Inadequacy of Conventional Water Treatment Processes to cope with Future Poor Raw Water Quality', Municipal Engineer, July.

Republic of South Africa (1987), *White Paper on Privatisation and Deregulation*, Pretoria.

(1996), *The Constitution of the Republic of South Africa*, Act 108 of 1996, Cape Town.

(1998), *National Environmental Management Act* 107 of 1998, Cape Town.

(1998), National Water Act 36 of 1998, Cape Town.

Richardson, Ed (1997), 'Coega: Now or never', *Eastern Province Herald*, 4 July.

(1997), 'Who'll bankroll the R1,5bn harbour project?', *Financial Mail*, 10 July.

(2001), 'Making the Leap', *Leadership*, April.

Robinson, J. (1996), *The Power of Apartheid: State Power and Space in South African Cities*, Oxford, Butterworth-Heinemann.

Roome, J. (1995), 'Water Pricing and Management: World Bank Presentation to the SA

Water Conservation Conference', unpublished paper, South Africa, 2 October.

Rosenthal, J. (1998), 'Threat to Lesotho Dam Project', *Business Report*, 26 November.

Ruiters, G. (2002), 'The Economics and Mechanics of Public Private Partnerships', forthcoming Municipal Services Project *Occasional Paper*, Johannesburg, http://www.queensu.ca/msp.

Ruiters, G. and P.Bond (1999), 'Contradictions in Municipal Transformation from Apartheid to Democracy: The Battle over Local Water Privatization in South Africa', *Working Papers in Local Governance and Democracy*, 99, 1.

SA Municipal Workers Union (2001), 'Press Statement', Cape Town, 31 January.

Sachs, A. (1990), *Protecting Human Rights in a New South Africa*, Cape Town, Oxford University Press.

Sachs, J. and D.Bloom (1998), 'Geography, Demography, and Economic Growth in Africa', presented at the Brookings Panel on Economic Activity, Washington, September.

Sachs, W. (Ed)(2002), *The Jo'burg Memorandum for the World Summit on Sustainable Development: Fairness in a Fragile World*, Berlin, http://www.boell.de.

Sanders, D. and P.Groenewald (1996), 'Public Health and Infrastructure', Unpublished report to the National Institute for Economic Policy, Johannesburg.

Sauer, W. and A.Booth (1998), 'Impact Assessment of the Coega Harbour on the Fishing Activities, Estuaries and Phytoplankton Production in Algoa Bay', Port Elizabeth, January.

Seaman, M. (1996), 'Questions', in Group for Environmental Monitoring (ed), *Record of Proceedings: Lesotho Highlands Water Workshop*, Johannesburg, 29-30 August.

Shiva, V. (2002), *Water Wars: Privatisation, Pollution and Profit*, Boston, South End Press.

Silva McGillivray and Port Elizabeth Municipality (1997), 'Coega Industrial Development Zone Bulk water supply infrastructure requirements', Report commisioned by the Coega IDZ Section 21 Company.

Simmonds, G. and N. Mammon (1996), 'Energy Services in Low-Income Urban South Africa: A Quantitative Assessment', Unpublished report by the Energy and Development Research Centre, University of Cape Town, Cape Town.

Snaddon, C.D., et al (1996), 'Some Implications of Inter-Basin Water Transfers for River Functioning and Water Resources Management in South Africa', in Group for Environmental Monitoring (ed), *Record of Proceedings: Lesotho Highlands Water Workshop*, Johannesburg, 29-30 August.

Soderstrom, E. (1998), 'Survey of Donor Involvement in the Water Sector in the SADC Region', USAID, Gabarone, Botswana.

South African Government Communications and Information Services (1999), 'Defence Summary, September 1999', http://www.gov.za/projects/procurement/nip.htm. (2002), 'Statement on Cabinet Meeting', Pretoria, 26 June.

Southall, R. (1998), 'Is Lesotho South Africa's Tenth Province?', *Indicator* SA, 15, 4.

Southern African Preparatory Meeting (2000), 'Southern African Call to Action', Pretoria, 23 November.

Southern African Trade Union Coordinating Council (1996), 'Export Processing Zones in Southern Africa: Social, political and economic implications', International Labour Resource and Information Group, Centre for Southern African Studies, and Labour Law Unit, University of Cape Town, Cape Town.

Soweto Electricity Crisis Committee (2001), 'Press Release', 18 October, Soweto.

Soweto People's Delegation (1989), 'An Assessment of Eskom's Proposals for Resolving Problems Related to the Supply of Electricity to Soweto', Mimeo, Planact archives, Wits University Historical Papers Library.

Spalding-Fecher, A. (2000), 'The Sustainable Energy Watch Indicators 2001', Energy for Development Research Centre, University of Cape Town, Cape Town, November. www.edrc.uct.ac.za.

Statistics South Africa (2001), *South Africa in Transition: Selected Findings from the October Household Survey of 1999 and Changes that have Occurred between*

1995 and 1999, Pretoria.

Stein, R. (2002), 'Environmental Rights: Government Turns on the Indicators', Unpublished paper, Wits University Law School.

Stephenson, D. (1993), 'Analysis of Effects of Urbanisation on Runoff', Report 183 1/93, Water Research Commission, Pretoria.

Stiglitz, J. (1998), 'More Instruments and Broader Goals: Moving Toward the Post-Washington Consensus', WIDER Annual Lecture, Helsinki, Finland, 7 January.
(2002), *Globalization and its Discontents*, London, Allen Lane.

Stofile, M.A. (2000), 'Premier's Address', Rural Development Summit, Umtata, 5 October.

Summers, L. (1991), 'Memo', Office of the World Bank Chief Economist, Washington, December 12, http://www.whirledbank.org.

Sustainable Energy and Economy Network (2002), 'Enron's Pawns: How US Officials and Public Institutions Played Enron's Globalisation Game', Washington, Institute for Policy Studies, March.

Swatuk, L. (2002), 'The New Water Architecture in Southern Africa: Reflections on Current Trends, Paper presented to the international workshop, 'Gold for/of the Future? Sustainable Water Management in Southern Africa and Germany and the Role of the Private Sector', organised by Coordination Southern Africa, Bonn, 3-5 May.

Swedish International Development Agency (1997), 'Environmental Security and Water Management in Southern Africa', Stockholm.

Swilling, M. (1999), 'Rival Futures: Struggle Visions, Post-Apartheid Choices', Unpublished paper, Stellenbosch.

Swilling, M., R.Humphries, and K.Shubane (Eds) (1991), *Apartheid City in Transition*. Oxford University Press, Cape Town.

Thompson, G. (1996), 'Ofwat and Water Privatisation', in D.Braddon and D.Foster (Eds), *Privatization: Social Science Themes*, Dartmouth, Aldershot.

Toennies, F. (1955)[1887], *Community and Society*, London, Routledge and Kegan Paul.

Thomson, R. and J.Tavares (2001), 'Water Demand Projections in Rand Water's Area of Supply', *Civil Engineering*, June.

Thorne, S. (1996), 'Financial Costs of Energy Services in Four South African Cities', Unpublished report by the Energy and Development Research Centre, University of Cape Town, Cape Town.

Transformation Resource Centre (2000), 'Lesotho's Rivers could become Waste Water Drains', http://www.irn.org.

Vally, S. and P.Bond (2001), 'An Appropriate Welcome for Powell at Wits', *Mail & Guardian*, 5 June.

van der Voorden, C. (2002), 'South Africa: Free Water still a Dream', W*ater and Sanitation Weekly: Special Features Edition*, August.

van Horen, C. (1996), 'Eskom, its Finances and the National Electrification Programme', *Development Southern Africa*, 13, 2.
(1996), 'The Cost of Power: Externalities in South Africa's Energy Sector', PhD thesis, School of Economics, University of Cape Town, Cape Town.

Veck, G. (2000), 'The Politics of Power in an Economy in Transition: Eskom and the Electrification of South Africa, 1980-1995', Unpublished PhD thesis, Faculty of Commerce, University of the Witwatersrand, Johannesburg.

Veotte, L. (2001), 'Restructuring, Human Rights and Water Access to Vulnerable Groups', South African Municipal Workers Union presentation to the International Conference on Fresh Water, Bonn, 7 December.

Water and Sanitation South Africa (1995), 'Standard Contract', Johannesburg.
(1995), 'The Delegated Management Concept', Johannesburg.

Wellmer, G. (2001), 'The Foreign Financing of the Parastatal Eskom during the Apartheid Years', mimeo for Jubilee South Africa, Johannesburg, August.

Weekes, A. (1999), 'Letters of protest needed against the unilateral and bad faith privatisation of water in Dolphin Coast, South Africa to French transnational', Email communication, 6 February.

Western Cape Anti-Eviction Committee (2002),'Jailed: Mandela Park and Tafelsig Anti-Eviction Campaign', Cape Town, 26 June.

(2002), 'Press Statement', Cape Town, 28 June.

White, C., O.Crankshaw, T.Mafokoane and H.Meintjes (1998), 'Social Determinants of Energy Use in Low Income Households in Gauteng', Department of Minerals and Energy Affairs, Pretoria.

Winkler, H. and J.Mavhungu (2001), 'Green Power, Public Benefits and Electricity Industry Restructuring', Report prepared for the Sustainable Energy and Climate Change Partnership, EDRC, Cape Town.

Wittfogel, K. (1957), *Oriental Despotism: A Comparative Study of Total Power*, New Haven, Yale University Press.

Wooldridge, T., N.Klages, and M.Smale (1997), 'Proposed Harbour Development at Coega (Feasibility Phase): Specialist Report on the Near-shore Environment', Report commissioned by the Coega IDZ Section 21 Company, Port Elizabeth.

World Bank (1994), *World Development Report 1994: Infrastructure for Development*, New York, Oxford University Press.

(1994), 'South Africa: Observations on the Direction of Housing Policy: Aide Memoire', Housing Mission, August.

(1996), *African Water Resources*, Technical Paper 331, Washington, DC.

(1998), *Summary of Air Emission and Effluent Discharge Requirements Presented in the Industry Guidelines*, Washington, July.

(1998), 'The Economics of Phase 1B', Unpublished paper, Africa Region, March.

(1998), *Lesotho: Lesotho Highlands Water Project—Phase 1B: Project Appraisal Document,* (17727-LSO), R98-106(PAD), Water and Urban 1, Africa Region, Washington, DC, April 30.

(1999), *Country Assistance Strategy: South Africa*, Washington DC.

(2000), 'Johannesburg City Development Strategy: World Bank Grant Facility/Habitat City Assistance Strategy Programme', Washington.

(2000), *Sourcebook on Community Driven Development in the Africa Region: Community Action Programs*, Africa Region, Washington, DC, 17 March.

(2001), 'A Brighter Future? Energy in Africa's Development', Washington, http://www.worldbank.org/html/fpd/energy/subenergy/energyinafrica.htm.

(2002), *Water Resources Sector Strategy: Strategic Directions for World Bank Engagement* Washington, 25 March.

World Bank Inspection Panel (1998), 'Lesotho/South Africa: Phase 1B of Lesotho Highlands Water Project: Panel Report and Recommendation', Washington, DC, 18 August.

World Development Movement and Action for Southern Africa (1998), *Paying for Apartheid Twice: The Cost of Apartheid Debt for the People of Southern Africa*, London, WDM and Actsa.

Yirga-Hall, G. (2001), 'Experiences and Challenges of Financing Water Systems in Africa', in *Volume II, Papers & Presentations, Reform of the Water Supply & Sanitation Sector in Africa Conference*, Abidjan, African Development Bank.

Zimbabwe Congress of Trade Unions (1999), 'Industrial Relations and Sustainable Development in Export Processing Zones', Harare.

Index

439